13 x 71

PØ

HANDBOOK OF WIRELESS NETWORKS AND MOBILE COMPUTING

WILEY SERIES ON PARALLEL AND DISTRIBUTED COMPUTING
Series Editor: Albert Y. Zomaya

Parallel and Distributed Simulation Systems / Richard Fujimoto

Surviving the Design of Microprocessor and Multimicroprocessor Systems: Lessons Learned / Veljko Milutinović

Mobile Processing in Distributed and Open Environments / Peter Sapaty

Introduction to Parallel Algorithms / C. Xavier and S. S. Iyengar

Solutions to Parallel and Distributed Computing Problems: Lessons from Biological Sciences / Albert Y. Zomaya, Fikret Ercal, and Stephan Olariu (*Editors*)

New Parallel Algorithms for Direct Solution of Linear Equations / C. Siva Ram Murthy, K. N. Balasubramanya Murthy, and Srinivas Aluru

Practical PRAM Programming / Joerg Keller, Christoph Kessler, and Jesper Larsson Traeff

Computational Collective Intelligence / Tadeusz M. Szuba

Parallel and Distributed Computing: A Survey of Models, Paradigms, and Approaches / Claudia Leopold

Fundamentals of Distributed Object Systems: A CORBA Perspective / Zahir Tari and Omran Bukhres

Pipelined Processor Farms: Structured Design for Embedded Parallel Systems / Martin Fleury and Andrew Downton

Handbook of Wireless Networks and Mobile Computing / Ivan Stojmenović (*Editor*)

HANDBOOK OF WIRELESS NETWORKS AND MOBILE COMPUTING

Edited by

Ivan Stojmenović
University of Ottawa
Universidad Nacional Autonoma de México

A WILEY-INTERSCIENCE PUBLICATION
JOHN WILEY & SONS, INC.

For ordering and customer service, call 1-800-CALL-WILEY

Library of Congress Cataloging-in-Publication Data Is Available.

ISBN 0-471-41902-8

Printed in the United States of America

10 9 8 7 6 5 4 3 2 1

Contents

16 Broadcast Scheduling for TDMA in Wireless Multihop Networks   347

Errol L. Lloyd

17 Mobile Ad Hoc Networks and Routing Protocols   371

Yu-Chee Tseng, Wen-Hua Liao, and Shih-Lin Wu

18 Routing with Guaranteed Delivery in Geometric and   393
Wireless Networks

Jorge Urrutia

Contributors

Dharma P. Agrawal, University of Cincinnati, Department of Electrical Engineering and Computer Science, Cincinnati, Ohio 45221

Michel Barbeau, Carleton University, School of Computer Science, Ottawa, Ontario KIS 5B6, Canada

Stefano Basagni, University of Texas at Dallas, Department of Computer Science, Richardson, Texas 75083

Azzedine Boukerche, University of North Texas, Department of Computer Science, Denton, Texas 762034

Raffaele Bruno, Consiglio Nazionale delle Ricerche (CNR), Istituto CNUCE, 56010 Ghezzano, Pisa, Italy

Marco Conti, Consiglio Nazionale delle Ricerche (CNR), Istituto CNUCE, 56010 Ghezzano, Pisa, Italy

Christos Douligeris, Institute of Computer Science, FORTH, Heraklion, Crete, Greece

Afonso Ferreira, CNRS Mascotte, 13S INRIA Sophia Antipolis, BP 93, F-06902 Sophia Antipolis Cedex, France

Jérôme Galtier, France Telecom R&D and CNRS Mascotte, 13S INRIA Sophia Antipolis, BP 93, F-06902 Sophia Antipolis Cedex, France

Xia Gao, University of Illinois at Urbana-Champaign, Coordinated Science Laboratory, Urbana, Illinois 61801

Silvia Giordano, Swiss Federal Institute of Technology, Institute of Computer Communications and Applications, CH-1015 Lausanne, Switzerland

Albert Gräf, Johannes Gutenberg University, Department of Music Informatics, 55099 Mainz, Germany

Enrico Gregori, Consiglio Nazionale delle Ricerche (CNR), Istituto CNUCE, 56010 Ghezzano, Pisa, Italy

Sandeep K. S. Gupta, Arizona State University, Department of Computer Science and Engineering, Tempe, Arizona 85287

Hung-Yun Hsieh, Georgia Institute of Technology, School of Electrical and Computer Engineering, Atlanta, Georgia 30332

Qinglong Hu, IBM Almaden Research Center, San Jose, California

Jeannette C. M. Janssen, Dalhousie University, Department of Mathematics and Statistics, Halifax, Nova Scotia B3H 3J5, Canada

Thomas Kunz, Carleton University, Systems and Computer Engineering, Ottawa, Ontario K1S 5B6, Canada

Dik-Lun Lee, Hong Kong University of Science and Technology, Department of Computer Science, Clear Water Bay, Hong Kong

Wang-Chien Lee, Verizon Laboratories, Waltham, Massachusetts

Wen-Hua Liao, National Central University, Department of Computer Science and Information Engineering, Tao-Yuan, Taiwan

Stephanie Lindsey, Washington State University, School of Electrical Engineering and Computer Science, Pullman, Washington 99164

Errol L. Lloyd, University of Delaware, Department of Computer Science and Information Sciences, Newark, Delaware 19716

Andrew D. Myers, University of Texas at Dallas, Department of Computer Science, Richardson, Texas 75083

Thomas McKenney, Johannes Gutenberg University, Department of Music Informatics, 55099 Mainz, Germany

Koji Nakano, Japan Advanced Institute for Science and Technology

Thyagarajan Nandagopal, University of Illinois at Urbana-Champaign, Coordinated Science Laboratory, Urbana, Illinois 61801

Lata Narayanan, Concordia University, Department of Computer Science, Montreal, Quebec H3G 1M8, Canada

Stephan Olariu, Old Dominion University, Department of Computer Science, Norfolk, Virginia 23529

Andrzej Pelc, Unversité du Québec à Hull, Departement d'Informatique, Hull, Québec J8X 3X7, Canada

Paolo Penna, CNRS Mascotte, 13S INRIA Sophia Antipolis, BP 93, F-06902 Sophia Antipolis Cedex, France

Cauligi S. Raghavendra, University of Southern California, Department of Electrical Engineering, Los Angeles, California 90089

Lakshmi Ramachandran, Trillium Digital Systems, International Tech Park, Bangalore 560 066, India

Harilaos G. Sandalidis, Telecommunications Systems Institute, 37 Iroon Polytechniou Str., Crete, Greece

Raghupathy Sivakumar, Georgia Institute of Technology, School of Electrical and Computer Engineering, Atlanta, Georgia 30332

Krishna M. Sivalingam, Washington State University, School of Electrical Engineering and Computer Science, Pullman, Washington 99164

Pradip K. Srimani, Clemson University, Department of Computer Science, Clemson, South Carolina 29634

Peter Stavroulakis, Telecommunications Systems Institute, 37 Iroon Polytechniou Str., Crete, Greece

Ivan Stojmenović, DISCA, IIMAS, Universidad Nacional Autonoma de Mexico, Mexico D.F., Mexico

Yu-Chee Tseng, National Chiao-Tung University, Department of Computer Science and Information Engineering, Hsin-Chu 300, Taiwan

Jorge Urrutia, Universidad Nacional Autonoma de Mexico, Instituto de Matematicas, Mexico D.F., Mexico

Thanos Vasilakos, FORTH, Institute of Computer Science, Heraklion, Crete, Greece

Jie Wu, Florida Atlantic University, Department of Computer Science and Engineering, Boca Raton, Florida 33431

Shih-Lin Wu, Chang Gung University, Department of Electrical Engineering, Tao-Yuan, Taiwan

Jianliang Xu, Hong Kong University of Science and Technology, Department of Computer Science, Clear Water Bay, Hong Kong

Qing-An Zeng, University of Cincinnati, Department of Electrical Engineering and Computer Science, Cincinnati, Ohio 45221

Jingyuan Zhang, University of Alabama, Department of Computer Science, Tuscaloosa, Alabama 35487

Preface

The past five decades have witnessed startling advances in computing and communication technologies that were stimulated by the availability of faster, more reliable, and cheaper electronic components. The design of smaller and more powerful devices enabled their mobility, which is rapidly changing the way we compute and communicate. For instance, the worldwide number of cellular phone subscribers has quadrupled in the last five years and has grown to over half a billion (see www.gsmdata.com). Wireless and mobile networks are emerging as networks of choice, due to the flexibility and freedom they offer. The use of satellite, cellular, radio, sensor, and ad hoc wireless networks, wireless local area networks (LAN), small portable computers, and personal communication systems (PCS) is increasing. These networks and devices support a trend toward computing on the move, known as mobile computing, nomadic computing, or computing anywhere anytime. The applications of mobile computing and wireless networks include e-commerce, personal communications, telecommunications, monitoring remote or dangerous environments, national defense (monitoring troop movements), emergency and disaster operations, remote operations of appliances, and wireless Internet access.

This handbook is based on a number of self-contained chapters and provides an opportunity for practitioners and researchers to explore the connection between various computer science techniques and develop solutions to problems that arise in the rapidly emerging field of wireless networks. The mobile computing area deals with computing and communication problems that arise in packet radio networks, mobile cellular systems, personal communication systems, and wireless local area networks. The main direction of the book is to review various algorithms and protocols that have been developed in this area, with emphasis on the most recent ones.

This book is intended for researchers and graduate students in computer science and electrical engineering, and researchers and developers in the telecommunications industry. Although much has been written, especially recently, in this rapidly growing field, no other book treats problems in wireless networks from a computer science perspective, although a number of books that follow the engineering approach exist. The editor taught a computer science graduate course with the same title and contents as this handbook, but was not able to find any book that covered even half of the topics covered here (the course outline and transparencies for lectures given by me in the course can be found at www.site.uottawa.ca/~ivan). This handbook can be used as a textbook and a reference for use by students, researchers, and developers.

MOBILE AND WIRELESS NETWORKING ISSUES

Mobile users do not necessarily use wireless interfaces. Instead, they can simply connect to fixed networks with a wired interface while away from their home or office. On the other hand, a fixed-location user may use a wireless interface (via a LAN) in an office environment. Other examples include wireless local loops, which provide fixed wireless access for voice and data transfer and high-speed Internet access. Wireless networks may use a fixed infrastructure as a backbone. For instance, cellular networks connect a mobile phone to the nearest base station (BS). A BS serves hundreds of mobile users in a given area (cell) by allocating frequencies and providing hand-off support. BSs are linked (by wireline, fiberline, or wireless microwave links) to base station controllers that provide switching support to several neighboring BSs and serve thousands of users. Controllers are in turn connected to a mobile switching center that is capable of serving more than 100,000 users. Mobile switching centers are finally connected directly to the public service telephone network (PSTN). Therefore only the first and perhaps the last connection (if the other user is also using a mobile phone) are normally wireless. However, the wireless link poses design challenges. The main difference between wired and wireless links is in the type of communication. Wired links normally provide one-to-one communication without interference, whereas wireless links use one-to-many communication that has a considerable noise and interference level and bandwidth limitations. Simultaneous wireless communications require channel separation, where channel may refer to time, frequency, or code. The channel capacity typically available in wireless systems is much lower than what is available in wired networks. The regulated frequency spectrum further limits the number of users that can be served concurrently. Mobile devices use battery power, and limited power resources pose further design challenges. High noise levels cause larger bit-error rates. Forward error correction algorithms or error detection schemes (such as cyclic redundancy control) followed by buffering and selective retransmission must be used. One-to-many free space communication is also insecure, since a third party may easily receive the same messages. Encryption and decryption procedures that provide security require, at the same time, significant power and bandwidth resources.

Some wireless networks do not have a fixed infrastructure as a backbone. Examples are ad hoc networks, sensor networks, and wireless LANs. Wireless networks of sensors are likely to be widely deployed in the near future because they greatly extend our ability to monitor and control the physical environment from remote locations and improve the accuracy of information obtained via collaboration among sensor nodes and online information processing at those nodes. Networking these sensors (empowering them with the ability to coordinate among themselves on a larger sensing task) will revolutionize information gathering and processing in many situations. Sensors are normally small, cheap devices with limited computing power. The typical size of a sensor is about one cubic centimeter. However, the SmartDust project is attempting to determine whether an autonomous sensing, computing, and communication system can be packed into a cubic millimeter mote to form the basis of integrated, massively distributed sensor networks. Sensors can be placed in an indoor environment at convenient locations. Alternatively, hundreds or thousands of them can be placed in a field. For example, sensor nodes can be air-dropped from a helicopter to cover an open field and report on vehicular activity or troop movement. Each node contains one or more of the following sensor types: acoustic, seismic, magnetic, infrared, and visual imaging. Once the sensors are in place, each of them can detect neighboring sensors and decide about their transmission radius so that the number of sensors receiving signals is within some limit. This is a nontrivial problem in itself. For instance, a recently published algorithm, in which each node transmits hello messages using radius kr, where r is a fixed small radius and k is modified until the number of responses is within limits, is not deterministic, has collision problems, and does not guaranty the process convergence or connectivity of the obtained network.

Sensors should alternate between sleeping and active periods so that the life of each sensor, and overall network life, is maximized. They could be divided into clusters for further power savings.

The detection and reporting of target movements is also a nontrivial problem. If every sensor that detects movement reports it to a center, too many messages are generated, causing collision problems and reducing sensor energy too quickly. A recently proposed algorithm (which assumes that each sensor knows its own geographic location and is able to detect the direction of an object that is "visible") suggests that all nodes whose neighboring nodes lie on the same side of a straight line from the node to the detected object should report the object's presence. It was expected that there would be exactly two such nodes (located at tangents from the object to the convex hull of the sensors). This solution, however, may activate more sensors (the criteria can be satisfied for more nodes) or may not activate any sensor at all (for example, when the object is located inside the convex hull of the sensors). Even when exactly two such sensors are selected, the sensors could be too close to the line segment between them, causing computational errors in object location based on two object directions. An alternative solution is to select only locally extreme sensors in four directions (N, S, E, and W) or possibly eight directions (including NW, NE, SW, and SE), and to combine the data obtained along the paths from them to a center that collects the data. Sensors that combine data will only forward "significant" improvements in the object's location. We can envision similar applications for monitoring environmental pollutants and their source and direction of movement. Several computer science projects along these lines (e.g., sensor information technology, diffusion-based networking, mobile scripts for target tracking, queries for collaborative signal processing), are currently ongoing (www.darpa.mil/ito/research/sensit, http://netweb.usc.edu/scadds, http://strange.arl.psu.edu/RSN, www.cs.columbia.edu/dcc/asn, etc.).

A similar wireless network technology that has received significant attention in recent years is the ad hoc network. Mobile ad hoc networks consist of wireless hosts that communicate with each other in the absence of a fixed infrastructure. They are used in disaster relief, conferences, and battlefield environments. Wireless LANs are designed to operate in a small area such as a building or office complex. The communication between two hosts in wireless LANs, sensor, and ad hoc networks is not always direct. Hosts in wireless LANs, sensor, and ad hoc networks use the same frequency for communication. Direct (or single-hop) transmission between any two hosts may require significant power (power normally decreases with the square or higher degree of distance between hosts) and is prone to collisions with other such transmissions. Thus, two hosts normally communicate via other hosts in the network (multihop communication). The solution to this involves solving routing problems. Collisions are difficult to detect because of the hidden station problem. Two hosts that do not communicate directly may simultaneously transmit messages to a common neighbor, causing collision. Mobile networks should provide support for routing by maintaining communication during mobility. In order to maintain an ongoing routing task (e.g., ongoing phone call) or to facilitate route establishment or paging, mobile networks must also provide support for location management, that is, keeping track of the host location.

The performance of wireless networks greatly depends on the choice of the medium access control (MAC) scheme. For instance, MAC protocols used in cellular networks in the United States and Europe differ. The IS-95 standard used in the United States uses code division multiple access (CDMA), whereas the GSM standard used in Europe uses TDMA (time division multiple access) on the top of FDMA (frequency DMA). CDMA provides more channels but at the expense of more noise and interference. These differences prevent interoperability and global mobility, and also create obstacles to standardization of the third generation (3G) of cellular systems.

Ad hoc, sensor, and wireless local area networks may use the IEEE 802.11 standard for medium access, in which hosts wait for a randomly selected number of transmission-free slots (back-off counter) before transmitting a message. Other standards (e.g., HIPERLAN) are also available. One emerging MAC layer technology is Bluetooth (www.bluetooth.net). It provides short-range (about 10 meters), low-cost wireless connectivity among hosts such as computers, printers, scanners, PCs, or sensors. In Bluetooth environments, hosts are organized into piconets, with one host in each piconet serving as master and a limited number (up to seven) of slave hosts directly linked to the master.

Satellites are in wide use for broadcast services and long distance and international phone services to stationary users. Low-earth orbit (LEO) satellite systems, such as Teledesic (expected to be operational in 2003 and consisting of 288 satellites), will provide mobile communications to every point on earth. Satellites are organized in concentric orbits and maintain links with several satellites in neighboring orbits and nearest satellites in the same orbit.

Wireless ATM (asynchronous transfer mode) is an emerging technology for support of voice and data transmission. ATM connections rely partly on wireless networks. New challenges in the design of wireless ATM include varying channel characteristics, quality of service support, and support of end-to-end ATM connection as the user moves from one location to the other. ATM is a connection-oriented technology, so after a mobile user's move to a new location, connection rerouting has to be performed. In a cellular network or ATM connections, location management schemes are needed in order to provide updated location information when a connection to a mobile user needs to be set up (routed) or rerouted.

The Wireless Application Protocol (WAP, www.wapforum.org) allows the development of applications that are independent of the underlying wireless access technology, and adapts existing website contents for transmission over wireless links and display on mobile devices. WAP architecture consists of a mobile client that sends an encoded request to a gateway and receives an encoded response from the gateway via a wireless network. The gateway, in turn, sends a request to a server and receives a response (content) from it over a wired network. WAP consist of application, session, transaction, security, transport, and wireless layers. Mobile devices require mobile operating systems (OSs) that are small in size and memory (e.g., 300 KB) and are able to operate with little processing power and satisfy real-time requirements, such as voice traffic.

BRIEF OUTLINE OF THIS HANDBOOK

The wide range of topics in this handbook makes it an excellent reference on wireless networks and mobile computing. Because each chapter is fully self-contained, readers can focus on the topics that most interest them. Most of the chapters (if not all) in this handbook have great practical utility. The handbook emphasizes computer science aspects, including implementation. Mathematical and engineering aspects are also represented in some chapters, since it is difficult to separate clearly all the issues among the three areas. Even when other aspects are clearly dominant, they are a good supplement to the rest of the handbook.

A short outline of the material presented in each of the chapters of this volume follows. The purpose is to identify the contents and also to aid diverse readers in assessing just what chapters are pertinent to their pursuits and desires. Each chapter should provide the reader with the equivalent of consulting an expert in a given discipline by summarizing the state of the art, interpreting trends, and providing pointers to further reading.

It is a challenging task to clearly divide chapters into discrete areas because of overlaps. One such classification that will be attempted here is to divide the chapters into five main research areas: multiple access schemes, cellular networks, data communication, multihop networks, and mobile computing. Many chapters deal with more than one of these areas, so clear separation is difficult. As a quick guide through the chapter topics, the first half of the chapters deal with multiple access schemes, data communication, and cellular networks; and other half deal with multihop networks and mobile computing. We shall now elaborate in more detail on each chapter, and try to group chapters into the five listed areas.

Cellular networks were certainly the first and so far most successful commercial application of wireless networks. The research in this area is hence more advanced than in the others. Nevertheless, it remains a hot research topic because of emerging technologies such as the third generation (3G) of mobile phone systems. Chapters 1–5 deal primarily with cellular networks.

Chapter 1 discusses handoff, which is the mechanism for transferring an ongoing call from one base station to another as a user moves through the coverage area of a cellular system. It must be fast and efficient to prevent the quality of service from degenerating to an unacceptable level. Admission control is a related problem, in which the radio resource management system has to decide if a new call arrival or a request for service or handoff may be allowed into the system. Handoffs are normally prioritized with respect to new calls. Four conventional handoff schemes in a voice-based, single traffic system (nonpriority schemes, priority schemes, handoff call queuing schemes, and originating and handoff calls queuing schemes) are summarized in this chapter. In addition, two handoff schemes with and without preemptive priority procedures for integrated voice and data wireless mobile networks are also covered in detail.

Mobile phone users move among base stations but do not always register with the current base station, to avoid communication overhead and excessive battery use. There exists a trade-off between the frequency of location update by the mobile phone user and the delay in locating a user when a phone call is made. Chapter 2 reviews existing solutions to the location management problem.

Chapters 3, 4, and 5 discuss the media access control problem in cellular networks. They are therefore at the intersection of the first two research areas of this handbook—multiple access schemes and cellular networks. Media access control in cellular networks is achieved primarily by assigning different frequencies to users that are connected to the same or neighboring base stations, and repeating the same frequencies when the corresponding base stations are sufficiently far apart to avoid or minimize the interference.

Chapter 3 describes fixed-channel assignment schemes in cellular networks, with the emphasis on recent heuristic algorithms that apply genetic algorithms, tabu search, neural networks, fuzzy logic, and other heuristics in solving problems. Channel assignment is generally classified into fixed and dynamic. In fixed channel assignment (FCA), channels are nominally assigned in advance according to the predetermined estimated traffic intensity at various base stations. In dynamic channel assignment (DCA), channels are assigned dynamically as calls arrive. It is more efficient in terms of channel usage, but requires more complex and time-consuming control. Hybrid channel assignment (HCA) combines the two approaches by dividing the frequencies into two separate ranges, one for FCA and other for DCA. In borrowing channel assignment (BCA), the channel assignment is initially fixed. If there are incoming calls for a cell whose channels are all occupied, the cell borrows channels from its neighboring cells and thus call blocking is prevented.

Cochannel interference is the most critical of all interference that occurs in cellular radio. The same channel cannot be assigned to two users that are connected to the same or two "close" base stations since such cochannel interference is likely to cause an unacceptable signal-to-noise ratio. The minimal distance between two base stations that can use the same channel is called the reuse distance. If this is the only type of interference considered, the channel assignment problem reduces to a multicoloring problem. In a multicoloring problem defined on a graph, each base station is demanding a certain number of colors (that is, frequencies), so that any two neighboring nodes get a disjoint set of colors (and, of course, colors assigned to each node are all distinct). When translated to cellular systems, nodes are base stations, and two base stations are "neighbors" in graph terms if the distance between then is less than the reuse distance. Chapter 4 studies this simplified version of the famous graph coloring problem that is known to be computationally difficult. Algorithms and lower bounds for this problem (including FCA, DCA, BCA, and HCA problem statements) are surveyed.

The secondary source of interference in cellular systems is adjacent channel interference. The filters for each channel at base stations are not ideal, and allow the signals from neighboring channels, with reduced strength, to generate noise. In a general problem statement, two base stations (i.e., cells) that are at a distance i (where i is the minimal number of cell crossings between two cells) cannot be assigned two frequencies that differ by less than c_i. The cosite constraint c_0 indicates the channel separation at the same base station, which is normally high compared to other constraints. The intersite constraints c_i ($i > 0$) most often take smaller values, especially one or two. An intersite constraint of one indicates that the two base stations must use distinct frequencies, whereas zero constraint indicates that the two cells may reuse frequencies. More precisely, in a good channel assignment, they actually should reuse the frequencies. Chapter 5 gives an overview of algorithms and lower bounds for this problem. It also discusses relevant results on graph labeling, which form the basis of many of the algorithms.

Several chapters deal with multiple access schemes. Since the wireless medium is inherently a shared resource, controlling channel access becomes a central theme that determines the system capacity, complexity, and cost. Chapter 6 focuses on the design and implementation of media access control (MAC) protocols for cellular telephony, wireless ATM, and ad hoc networks. Fundamental MAC protocols include frequency division multiple access (FDMA), time division multiple access (TDMA), code division multiple access (CDMA), and random access schemes such as ALOHA and carrier sense multiple access (CSMA).

Chapter 7 discusses the integration of voice and data traffic in wireless networks. It concentrates on Bluetooth technology (the de facto standard for wireless personal area networks), IEEE 802.11 technology (the main standard for wireless local area networks), and the UMTS technology for third generation cellular systems.

Fairness among mobile or wireless users implies that the allocated channel bandwidth is in proportion to the "weights" of the users. Fair queuing in the wireless domain poses significant challenges due to unique issues in the wireless channel such as location-dependent and bursty channel error. Hence, it is imperative to provide fair channel access among multiple contending hosts. Chapter 8 identifies key issues in wireless fair queuing, defines a wireless fair service model, and surveys algorithms from contemporary literature.

Chapters 9 and 10 deal with organization issues for medium access in radio networks, which are distributed systems with no central arbiter, consisting of n radio transceivers, also called stations. The wireless environment is single-hop one, meaning that each station is able to hear a transmission from any other station. The time is slotted, and all transmissions occur at slot boundaries. Chapter 9 describes how each station can assign to itself a unique identifier in the range $[1, n]$ so that the i-th user is able to transmit the message in the i-th slot. This provides collision-free TDMA transmission in a round robin fashion. The algorithms are distributed, and their analysis is based on combinatorial facts of binomial distribution, tree partitions, and graphs. Initialization protocols with and without collision detection capabilities, and using one of several channels for communication, are presented. The leader election problem designates one of the stations as leader. Chapter 10 surveys recent protocols on the leader election problem in single-hop, single-channel radio networks.

Chapters 10–14 deal primarily with data communication issues in wireless networks, with considerable overlap with all other listed areas.

Mobile wireless environments are characterized by asymmetric communication. The downlink communication from base station, satellite, or other server is much greater than the uplink communication capacity. In broadcast, data are sent simultaneously to all users residing in the broadcast area. Each user in a data broadcast problem has a list of desired files or data it wants to receive from the server. The order and frequency for each file or datum that is broadcast should take access efficiency and power conservation into account. Access efficiency concerns how fast a request is satisfied, whereas power conservation concerns how to reduce a mobile client's power consumption when it is accessing the data it wants. Chapter 11 surveys various techniques and problem formulations for wireless data broadcast, sometimes also refereed to as broadcast scheduling.

Digital broadcasting systems are expected to replace current FM radio and television technology. Chapter 12 considers the design of DAB (digital audio broadcasting) networks. The DAB system transmits whole ensembles consisting of multiple radio programs and other data services, and allows an ensemble to be transmitted on a single channel even if the corresponding transmitters may interfere. The task is to arrange services into a collection of ensembles for each request area, and to assign channels to the resulting ensembles. The problem can be formulated as the combined bin packing and graph coloring problem. Several basic heuristics, lower bounding algorithms, and the tabu search solution are described.

With the increasing number of wireless and mobile devices using the Internet, researchers have been studying the impact of wireless networking technologies on the different layers of the network protocol stack. Chapter 13 focuses on the transport layer in microcell and macrocell wireless networks. The task in the transport layer is to organize the speed of transmissions, acknowledgment, and possible retransmissions of every packet of a data transfer. It deals primarily with the network congestion problem. The unique characteristics of wireless networks that result in poor performance for existing protocol standards are identified (such as reduced bandwidth, which needs to be distinguished from congestion), and approaches that have been proposed to address these characteristics are surveyed.

Chapter 14 focuses on security and fraud detection problems in mobile and wireless networks, and presents some solutions to several aspects of the security problem, such as authentication of mobile users and fraud detection in mobile phone operations. Further increases in network security are necessary before the promise of mobile telecommunication can be fulfilled.

Chapters 14–24 deal with multihop wireless networks. Their primary characteristic is that mobile or wireless stations, phones, users, sensors, or other devices (let us call them nodes) cannot communicate directly with any other node in the network. Thus, they communicate with each other via other nodes, through several hops. The network is then modeled by a graph where two nodes are linked if and only if they can directly communicate. If that graph is a complete graph (where each node can directly communicate to any other node), the network is called a single-hop one. Cellular networks and transport protocols also deal with multihop networks, but the problems studied and solution presented are not significantly based on the underlying graph model.

Ad hoc networks are a key to the evolution of wireless networks. They are typically composed of equal nodes that communicate over wireless links without any central control. Ad hoc wireless networks inherit the traditional problems of wireless and mobile communications, such as bandwidth optimization, power control, and transmission quality enhancement. In addition, the multihop nature and the lack of fixed infrastructure bring new research problems such as configuration advertising, discovery and maintenance, as well as ad hoc addressing and self-routing. Many different approaches and protocols have been proposed and there are even multiple standardization efforts within the Internet Engineering Task Force, as well as academic and industrial projects. Chapter 15 focuses on the state of the art in mobile ad hoc networks. It highlights some of the emerging technologies, protocols, and approaches (at different layers) for realizing network services for users on the move in areas with possibly no preexisting communications infrastructure. People-based networks, where information is transmitted using "people" (i.e., personal devices such as personal digital assistants), are also discussed.

To avoid interference of signals arriving from several neighbors to a single host, or simultaneous transmissions from two neighboring hosts, each host should create its own transmission schedule. That is, each host should decide which time slots are available for collision-free transmissions. Chapter 16 explores the computational and algorithmic complexity of broadcast scheduling, which, in general form, is an NP-complete problem. The chapter reviews existing broadcast scheduling approximation, off-line and on-line, and centralized and distributed algorithms, and discusses their effect on the quality of the schedules produced.

In a wireless network, routing the message (finding a path between a source and a destination node) is a basic data communication protocol. A mobile ad hoc network consists of a set of mobile hosts capable of communicating with each other without the assistance of base stations. Chapter 17 reviews the existing routing algorithms for networks consisting of nodes that do not have information about their geographic position.

Recently, the location of a sensor or station was made feasible by adding a GPS low-power, small-size receiver that is able of determining its location (latitude, longitude, and height) within a few millimeters by cooperating with existing satellite and auxiliary earth networks. GPS also provides global timing to stations. Position information enables development of localized routing methods (greedy routing decisions are made at each node, based solely on the knowledge of positions of neighbors and the destination, with considerable savings in communication overhead and with guaranteed delivery provided location update schemes are efficient for a given movement pattern). When GPS is not available, the relative position of neighboring nodes may be determined based on strength of signals from neigboring nodes, or some other alternative means. Chapter 18 surveys routing algorithms in communication networks, where nodes are aware of their geographic position and those of their neigboring nodes. The algorithms take advantage of geometric properties of planar networks, constructing a planar subgraph of a given wireless network. Guaranteed delivery is a salient property of the algorithms, assuming destination location is accurate and the network is modeled by unit graphs. In a unit graph, all nodes have the same transmission radius, and two nodes can directly communicate if and only if their distance is less than that radius.

Chapter 19 surveys energy-efficient routing protocols for wireless ad hoc networks. It includes evaluation of energy consumption in ad hoc routing protocols, localized routing algorithms that optimize based on power and other metrics, network topology generation designed to optimize power consumption, routing algorithms that balance power consumption among all network nodes, and algorithms that maximize nodes' lifetimes.

A set of nodes in a network is dominating if all the nodes in the system are either in the set or neighbors of nodes in the set. Chapter 20 reviews simple and efficient distributed algorithms for calculating a connected dominating set in ad hoc wireless networks, where connections of nodes are determined by their geographic distances. Applications of dominating sets in reducing the cost of routing, multicasting, and broadcasting are also discussed.

Chapter 21 reviews research on routing in ad hoc and sensor wireless networks in the light of node mobility, changes in node activity, and availability of methods to determine the absolute or relative coordinates of each node. Various approaches in the literature are classified according to some criteria. Mobility is apparently a very difficult problem to handle in ad hoc networks, and all proposed solutions have significant drawbacks. Additional problems arise with "sleep" period operation, that is, changes in a node's activity status with or without mobility. Although significant progress has been made on routing with a known destination location, issuing location updates to enable efficient routing requires further investigation.

Chapter 22 surveys communication-related issues arising in the context of low earth orbit (LEO) satellite constellations. In particular, it studies the impact of the predictable movement of the satellites on the techniques used in topological design, routing, and handover strategies.

In a multicasting problem, a message is to be sent from a node to several other nodes in the network. Chapter 23 briefly reviews multicasting methods that were proposed in the literature for wired networks, and then gradually relaxes the requirement that all nodes be stationary, discussing multicast protocols for cellular networks (characterized by a fixed infrastructure with mobile end nodes) and ad hoc networks (infrastructureless mobile networks).

Broadcasting is the task of forwarding a message from a source (or central facility) to all the nodes in the network. Chapter 24 reviews broadcasting algorithms in radio networks, under different communication scenarios and different amounts of knowledge of the network. The chapter primarily deals with the worst-case analysis of algorithms.

Chapters 25–28 deal primarily with mobile computing or computing and communication protocol issues in the presence of node mobility.

Chapter 25 presents the basic characteristics of mobile IP, which is a protocol that allows transparent routing of IP datagrams to mobile nodes on the Internet. Each mobile node is always identified by its home address, regardless of its current point of attachment to the Internet. When away from its home, information about its current point of attachment to the Internet is provided through a care-of address associated with the node. The home agent sends datagrams destined for the mobile node through a tunnel to the care-of address. After arriving at the end of the tunnel, each datagram is then delivered to the mobile node. Routing, security, and management issues are discussed based on the most recent activities of the relevant standardization bodies.

Chapter 26 surveys data management schemes in wireless mobile environments. Mobile computing can possibly be viewed as a variation of traditional distributed computing from the data management point of view. In general, there are two possible scenarios. In the first, the entire database is distributed only among the wired components, e.g., the mobile switching stations (MSS), each base station managing its own share of the database with the additional capability of locating the components of the databases that are not locally available. In the second approach, the entire database is distributed over both the wired and wireless components of the system. The functionality of a database management system depends on the design of database and replication of data schemes. These issues are handled, in some form or other, via caching data in the mobile units and periodically validating this data using different techniques. The protocols and frequency of validation of the data have a profound influence on the performance of data management in mobile environments.

The advent of distributed computing has had a major influence in the computing industry in recent years, witnessed by the growth of mobile computers and networked computing systems. The desire to share resources, to parcel out computing tasks among several different hosts, and place applications on machines most suitable to their needs, has led to distributed programming systems such as CORBA and DCOM, which predominate in the marketplace. Pervasive computing can be defined as access to information and software applications anytime and anywhere. Users are mobile and services are provided by collections of distributed components collaborating together. Recent advances in mobile computing, service discovery, and distributed computing are key technologies to support pervasive computing. Chapter 27 is about software technologies used to address problems in mobile, distributed, and pervasive computing. It reviews characteristics, software architecture, and key open communication technologies (service discovery and distributed computing) to support pervasive computing.

Recent advances in wireless and mobile computing, and inexpensive, portable devices have resulted in the emergence of indoor wireless networks. Chapter 28 focuses on challenges specific to this environment. It discusses design issues and options for the physical layer, and dwells at length on a few media access control (MAC) layer protocols that have been proposed for the indoor environment. It is shown how these problems have been dealt with in some popular and well-accepted technologies, namely, Wireless LAN (IEEE 802.11), HomeRF and Bluetooth. Network topology and self-organization of such networks, with special reference to Bluetooth, which has very interesting topology construction problems, is also discussed.

RECOMMENDED READING

Each chapter in the handbook is accompanied by its own reference section. However, it is necessary for the reader to refer to journals and conference proceedings to keep up with the recent developments in the field.

Some of the important journals that publish articles in the area of wireless networks and mobile computing in the field are:

- *ACM Computer Communication Review* (www.acm.org)
- *ACM Mobile Computing and Communications Review* (http://www.acm.org/sigmobile/MC2R)
- *Communications of the ACM* (www.acm.org)
- *IEEE/ACM Transactions on Networking* (www.ton.cc.gatech.edu)
- *IEEE Communications Magazine* (www.computer.org)
- *IEEE Pervasive Computing* (www.computer.org/pervasive)
- *IEEE Transactions on Mobile Communications* (www.computer.org/tmc)
- *IEEE Transactions on Parallel and Distributed Systems* (www.computer.org)

- *IEEE Transactions on Selected Areas in Communication* (www.computer.org)
- *IEEE Transactions on Vehicular Technology* (www.computer.org)
- *IEEE Transactions on Wireless Communications* (www.ee.ust.hk/~eekhaled)
- *International Journal of Wireless Information Networks* (www.baltzer.nl)
- *IEEE Communication Letters* (www.computer.org)
- *International Journal of Communication Systems*
- *International Journal of Satellite Communications*
- *Journal of Parallel and Distributed Computing*
- *Mobile Networks and Applications* (www.baltzer.nl/monet)
- *Wireless Communications and Mobile Computing* (www.wiley.com)
- *Wireless Networks* (www.acm.org/journals/125.html)
- *Wireless Personal Communication* (www.baltzer.nl)

The reader is also encouraged to refer to the proceedings of some of the main events and conferences that cover the topics, for example:

- ACM International Conference on Mobile Computing and Networking MOBICOM (www.acm.org/sigmobile)
- International Workshop on Discrete Algorithms and Methods for Mobile Computing and Communications (DIAL M for Mobility)
- International Workshop on Wireless Mobile Multimedia, WoW MoM
- International Workshop on Modeling, Analysis and Simulation of Wireless and Mobile Systems, MSWiM
- ACM Symposium on Mobile Ad Hoc Networking and Computing, MobiHoc
- ACM Wireless Mobile Internet Workshop
- IEEE INFOCOM (www.ieee-infocom.org)
- IEEE International Parallel and Distributed Processing Symposium, IPDPS (www.ipdps.org)
- IEEE Vehicular Technology Conference, VTC
- IEEE Hawaii International Conference on System Sciences, Software Technology Track (www.hicss.org)
- International Conference on Parallel Processing
- IEEE International Conference on Distributed Computing and Systems
- IASTED International Conference on Parallel and Distributed Computing and Systems (www.iasted.com/confrences)
- IEEE International Conference on Computer Communications and Networks, ICC-CN (www.icccn.cstp.umkc.edu)
- International Conference on Communications in Computing, CIC (www.cs.utep.edu/~cic)
- IEEE GLOBECOM

- IEEE Symposium on Computers and Communications (www.comsoc.org/iscc)
- IEEE International Conference on Universal Personal Communications

The Internet is becoming the major source of information in this area, since the majority of researchers put their own papers on their web pages. From my own experience, the primary source of information is the research index that can be found at http://citeseer.nj.nec.com/cs. This is a citation database that links papers according to their subject and mutual citations, and provides the web and e-mail addresses for many of the authors (and, of course, Internet search engines can locate most of the remaining ones).

ACKNOWLEDGMENTS

The editor is grateful to all the authors for their contributions to the quality of this handbook. The assistance of reviewers for all chapters is also greatly appreciated. The University of Ottawa and Universidad National Autonoma de Mexico provided an ideal working environment for the preparation of this handbook, including computer facilities for efficient Internet search, communication by electronic mail, and writing my own contributions.

The editor is thankful to Dr. Albert Zomaya, editor of the Parallel and Distributed Computing book series at Wiley, for his support and encouragement in publishing this handbook. The editor also appreciates the support of Dr. Stephan Olariu for encouraging publication of this handbook by Wiley instead of other publishers that also offered contracts. Dr. Philip Meyler, editor at Wiley, also deserves special mention for his timely and professional cooperation, and for his decisive support of this project.

Finally, I thank my children Milos and Milica and my wife Natasa for making this effort worthwhile and for their patience during the numerous hours at home that I spent in front of the computer.

I hope that the readers will find this handbook informative and worth reading. Comments from readers will be greatly appreciated.

SITE, University of Ottawa, Ottawa, Ontario, Canada   Ivan Stojmenović
  Ivan@site.uottawa.ca
  ivan@leibniz.iimas.unam.mx; www.site.uottawa.ca/~ivan
DISCA, IIMAS, UNAM, Mexico D.F., Mexico

April 2001

HANDBOOK OF
WIRELESS NETWORKS
AND MOBILE COMPUTING

CHAPTER 1

Handoff in Wireless Mobile Networks

QING-AN ZENG and DHARMA P. AGRAWAL
*Department of Electrical Engineering and Computer Science,
University of Cincinnati*

1.1 INTRODUCTION

Mobility is the most important feature of a wireless cellular communication system. Usually, continuous service is achieved by supporting handoff (or handover) from one cell to another. Handoff is the process of changing the channel (frequency, time slot, spreading code, or combination of them) associated with the current connection while a call is in progress. It is often initiated either by crossing a cell boundary or by a deterioration in quality of the signal in the current channel. Handoff is divided into two broad categories—hard and soft handoffs. They are also characterized by "break before make" and "make before break." In hard handoffs, current resources are released before new resources are used; in soft handoffs, both existing and new resources are used during the handoff process. Poorly designed handoff schemes tend to generate very heavy signaling traffic and, thereby, a dramatic decrease in quality of service (QoS). (In this chapter, a handoff is assumed to occur only at the cell boundary.) The reason why handoffs are critical in cellular communication systems is that neighboring cells are always using a disjoint subset of frequency bands, so negotiations must take place between the mobile station (MS), the current serving base station (BS), and the next potential BS. Other related issues, such as decision making and priority strategies during overloading, might influence the overall performance.

In the next section, we introduce different types of possible handoffs. In Section 1.3, we describe different handoff initiation processes. The types of handoff decisions are briefly described in Section 1.4 and some selected representative handoff schemes are presented in Section 1.5. Finally, Section 1.6 summarizes the chapter.

1.2 TYPES OF HANDOFFS

Handoffs are broadly classified into two categories—hard and soft handoffs. Usually, the hard handoff can be further divided into two different types—intra- and intercell handoffs. The soft handoff can also be divided into two different types—multiway soft handoffs and softer handoffs. In this chapter, we focus primarily on the hard handoff.

Handbook of Wireless Networks and Mobile Computing, Edited by Ivan Stojmenović.
ISBN 0-471-41902-8   © 2002 John Wiley & Sons, Inc.

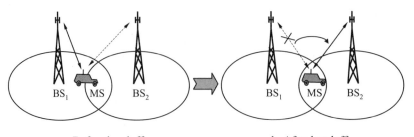

a. Before handoff   b. After handoff

Figure 1.1   Hard handoff between the MS and BSs.

A hard handoff is essentially a "break before make" connection. Under the control of the MSC, the BS hands off the MS's call to another cell and then drops the call. In a hard hand-off, the link to the prior BS is terminated before or as the user is transferred to the new cell's BS; the MS is linked to no more than one BS at any given time. Hard handoff is primarily used in FDMA (frequency division multiple access) and TDMA (time division multiple access), where different frequency ranges are used in adjacent channels in order to minimize channel interference. So when the MS moves from one BS to another BS, it becomes impossible for it to communicate with both BSs (since different frequencies are used). Figure 1.1 illustrates hard handoff between the MS and the BSs.

1.3   HANDOFF INITIATION

A hard handoff occurs when the old connection is broken before a new connection is activated. The performance evaluation of a hard handoff is based on various initiation criteria [1, 3, 13]. It is assumed that the signal is averaged over time, so that rapid fluctuations due to the multipath nature of the radio environment can be eliminated. Numerous studies have been done to determine the shape as well as the length of the averaging window and the older measurements may be unreliable. Figure 1.2 shows a MS moving from one BS (BS_1) to another (BS_2). The mean signal strength of BS_1 decreases as the MS moves away from it. Similarly, the mean signal strength of BS_2 increases as the MS approaches it. This figure is used to explain various approaches described in the following subsection.

1.3.1   Relative Signal Strength

This method selects the strongest received BS at all times. The decision is based on a mean measurement of the received signal. In Figure 1.2, the handoff would occur at position A. This method is observed to provoke too many unnecessary handoffs, even when the signal of the current BS is still at an acceptable level.

1.3.2   Relative Signal Strength with Threshold

This method allows a MS to hand off only if the current signal is sufficiently weak (less than threshold) and the other is the stronger of the two. The effect of the threshold depends

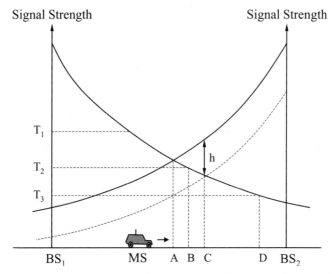

Figure 1.2 Signal strength and hysteresis between two adjacent BSs for potential handoff.

on its relative value as compared to the signal strengths of the two BSs at the point at which they are equal. If the threshold is higher than this value, say T_1 in Figure 1.2, this scheme performs exactly like the relative signal strength scheme, so the handoff occurs at position A. If the threshold is lower than this value, say T_2 in Figure 1.2, the MS would delay handoff until the current signal level crosses the threshold at position B. In the case of T_3, the delay may be so long that the MS drifts too far into the new cell. This reduces the quality of the communication link from BS_1 and may result in a dropped call. In addition, this results in additional interference to cochannel users. Thus, this scheme may create overlapping cell coverage areas. A threshold is not used alone in actual practice because its effectiveness depends on prior knowledge of the crossover signal strength between the current and candidate BSs.

1.3.3 Relative Signal Strength with Hysteresis

This scheme allows a user to hand off only if the new BS is sufficiently stronger (by a hysteresis margin, h in Figure 1.2) than the current one. In this case, the handoff would occur at point C. This technique prevents the so-called ping-pong effect, the repeated handoff between two BSs caused by rapid fluctuations in the received signal strengths from both BSs. The first handoff, however, may be unnecessary if the serving BS is sufficiently strong.

1.3.4 Relative Signal Strength with Hysteresis and Threshold

This scheme hands a MS over to a new BS only if the current signal level drops below a threshold and the target BS is stronger than the current one by a given hysteresis margin. In Figure 1.2, the handoff would occur at point D if the threshold is T_3.

1.3.5 Prediction Techniques

Prediction techniques base the handoff decision on the expected future value of the received signal strength. A technique has been proposed and simulated to indicate better results, in terms of reduction in the number of unnecessary handoffs, than the relative signal strength, both without and with hysteresis, and threshold methods.

1.4 HANDOFF DECISION

There are numerous methods for performing handoff, at least as many as the kinds of state information that have been defined for MSs, as well as the kinds of network entities that maintain the state information [4]. The decision-making process of handoff may be centralized or decentralized (i.e., the handoff decision may be made at the MS or network). From the decision process point of view, one can find at least three different kinds of handoff decisions.

1.4.1 Network-Controlled Handoff

In a network-controlled handoff protocol, the network makes a handoff decision based on the measurements of the MSs at a number of BSs. In general, the handoff process (including data transmission, channel switching, and network switching) takes 100–200 ms. Information about the signal quality for all users is available at a single point in the network that facilitates appropriate resource allocation. Network-controlled handoff is used in first-generation analog systems such as AMPS (advanced mobile phone system), TACS (total access communication system), and NMT (advanced mobile phone system).

1.4.2 Mobile-Assisted Handoff

In a mobile-assisted handoff process, the MS makes measurements and the network makes the decision. In the circuit-switched GSM (global system mobile), the BS controller (BSC) is in charge of the radio interface management. This mainly means allocation and release of radio channels and handoff management. The handoff time between handoff decision and execution in such a circuit-switched GSM is approximately 1 second.

1.4.3 Mobile-Controlled Handoff

In mobile-controlled handoff, each MS is completely in control of the handoff process. This type of handoff has a short reaction time (on the order of 0.1 second). MS measures the signal strengths from surrounding BSs and interference levels on all channels. A handoff can be initiated if the signal strength of the serving BS is lower than that of another BS by a certain threshold.

1.5 HANDOFF SCHEMES

In urban mobile cellular radio systems, especially when the cell size becomes relatively small, the handoff procedure has a significant impact on system performance. Blocking probability of originating calls and the forced termination probability of ongoing calls are the primary criteria for indicating performance. In this section, we describe several existing traffic models and handoff schemes.

1.5.1 Traffic Model

For a mobile cellular radio system, it is important to establish a traffic model before analyzing the performance of the system. Several traffic models have been established based on different assumptions about user mobility. In the following subsection, we briefly introduce these traffic models.

1.5.1.1 *Hong and Rappaport's Traffic Model (Two-Dimensional)*

Hong and Rappaport propose a traffic model for a hexagonal cell (approximated by a circle) [5]. They assume that the vehicles are spread evenly over the service area; thus, the location of a vehicle when a call is initiated by the user is uniformly distributed in the cell. They also assume that a vehicle initiating a call moves from the current location in any direction with equal probability and that this direction does not change while the vehicle remains in the cell.

From these assumptions they showed that the arrival rate of handoff calls is

$$\lambda_H = \frac{P_h(1 - B_O)}{1 - P_{hh}(1 - P_f')} \lambda_O \qquad (1.1)$$

where

P_h = the probability that a new call that is not blocked would require at least one handoff

P_{hh} = the probability that a call that has already been handed off successfully would require another handoff

B_O = the blocking probability of originating calls

P_f' = the probability of handoff failure

λ_O = the arrival rate of originating calls in a cell

The probability density function (pdf) of channel holding time T in a cell is derived as

$$f_T(t) = \mu_C e^{-\mu_C t} + \frac{e^{-\mu_C t}}{1 + \gamma_C}[f_{T_n}(t) + \gamma_C f_{T_h}(t)] - \frac{\mu_C e^{-\mu_C t}}{1 + \gamma_C}[F_{T_n}(t) + \gamma_C F_{T_h}(t)] \qquad (1.2)$$

where

$f_{T_n}(t)$ = the pdf of the random variable T_n as the dwell time in the cell for an originated call

$f_{T_h}(t)$ = the pdf of the random variable T_h as the dwell time in the cell for a handed-off call

$F_{T_n}(t)$ = the cumulative distribution function (cdf) of the time T_n

$F_{T_h}(t)$ = the cdf of the time T_h

$1/\mu_C$ = the average call duration

$\gamma_C = P_h(1 - B_O)/[1 - P_{hh}(1 - P_f')]$

1.5.1.2   El-Dolil et al.'s Traffic Model (One-Dimensional)

An extension of Hong and Rappaport's traffic model to the case of highway microcellular radio network has been done by El-Dolil et al. [6]. The highway is segmented into micro-cells with small BSs radiating cigar-shaped mobile radio signals along the highway. With these assumptions, they showed that the arrival rate of handoff calls is

$$\lambda_H = (R_{cj} - R_{sh})P_{hi} + R_{sh}P_{hh} \tag{1.3}$$

where

P_{hi} = the probability that a MS needs a handoff in cell i

R_{cj} = the average rate of total calls carried in cell j

R_{sh} = the rate of successful handoffs

The pdf of channel holding time T in a cell is derived as

$$f_T(t) = \left(\frac{\mu_C + \mu_{ni}}{1 + G} \right) e^{-(\mu_C + \mu_{ni})t} + \left(\frac{\mu_C + \mu_h}{1 + G} \right) e^{-(\mu_C + \mu_h)t} \tag{1.4}$$

where

$1/\mu_{ni}$ = the average channel holding time in cell i for a originating call

$1/\mu_h$ = the average channel holding time for a handoff call

G = the ratio of the offered rate of handoff requests to that of originating calls

1.5.1.3   Steele and Nofal's Traffic Model (Two-Dimensional)

Steele and Nofal [7] studied a traffic model based on city street microcells, catering to pedestrians making calls while walking along a street. From their assumptions, they showed that the arrival rate of handoff calls is

$$\lambda_H = \sum_{m=1}^{6} [\lambda_O(1 - B_O) P_h\beta + \lambda_h(1 - P_f') P_{hh}\beta] \tag{1.5}$$

where

β = the fraction of handoff calls to the current cell from the adjacent cells

$\lambda_h = 3\lambda_O(1 - B_O) P_I\beta$

P_I = the probability that a new call that is not blocked will require at least one handoff

The average channel holding time T in a cell is

$$\overline{T} = \frac{(1 + \alpha_1)(1 - \gamma)}{\mu_w + \mu_C} + \frac{\gamma(1 + \alpha_2)}{\mu_o + \mu_C} + \frac{\alpha_1(1 - \gamma) + \gamma\alpha_2}{\mu_d + \mu_C} \tag{1.6}$$

where

$1/\mu_w$ = the average walking time of a pedestrian from the onset of the call until he reaches the boundary of the cell

$1/\mu_d$ = the average delay time a pedestrian spends waiting at the intersection to cross the road

$1/\mu_o$ = the average walking time of a pedestrian in the new cell

$\alpha_1 = \mu_w P_{delay}/(\mu_d - \mu_w)$

$\alpha_2 = \mu_o P_{delay}/(\mu_d - \mu_o)$

$P_{delay} = P_{cross}P_d$, the proportion of pedestrians leaving the cell by crossing the road

P_d = the probability that a pedestrian would be delayed when he crosses the road

$\gamma = \lambda_H(1 - P_f')/[\lambda_H(1 - P_f') + \lambda_O(1 - B_O)]$

1.5.1.4   *Xie and Kuek's Traffic Model (One- and Two-Dimensional)*

This model assumes a uniform density of mobile users throughout an area and that a user is equally likely to move in any direction with respect to the cell border. From this assumption, Xie and Kuek [8] showed that the arrival rate of handoff calls is

$$\lambda_H = E[C]\,\mu_{c-dwell} \tag{1.7}$$

where

$E[C]$ = the average number of calls in a cell

$\mu_{c-dwell}$ = the outgoing rate of mobile users.

The average channel holding time T in a cell is

$$\overline{T} = \frac{1}{\mu_C + \mu_{c-dwell}} \tag{1.8}$$

1.5.1.5   *Zeng et al.'s Approximated Traffic Model (Any Dimensional)*

Zeng et al.'s model is based on Xie and Kuek's traffic model [9]. Using Little's formula, when the blocking probability of originating calls and the forced termination probability of handoff calls are small, the average numbers of occupied channels $E[C]$ is approximated by

$$E[C] \approx \frac{\lambda_O + \lambda_H}{\mu} \tag{1.9}$$

where $1/\mu$ is the average channel holding time in a cell.

Therefore, the arrival rate of handoff calls is

$$\lambda_H \approx \frac{\mu_{c-dwell}}{\mu_C}\lambda_O \tag{1.10}$$

Xie and Kuek focused on the pdf of the speed of cell-crossing mobiles and refined previous results by making use of biased sampling. The distribution of mobile speeds of handoff calls used in Hong and Rappaport's traffic model has been adjusted by using

$$f^*(v) = \frac{vf(v)}{E[V]} \tag{1.11}$$

where $f(v)$ is the pdf of the random variable V (speed of mobile users), and $E[V]$ is the average of the random variable V.

$f^*(v)$ leads to the conclusion that the probability of handoff in Hong and Rappaport's traffic model is a pessimistic one, because the speed distribution of handoff calls are not the same as the overall speed distribution of all mobile users.

Steele's traffic model is not adaptive for an irregular cell and vehicular users. In Zeng et al.'s approximated traffic model, actual deviation from Xie and Kuek's traffic model is relatively small when the blocking probability of originating calls and the forced termination probability of handoff calls are small.

1.5.2 Handoff Schemes in Single Traffic Systems

In this section, we introduce nonpriority, priority, and queuing handoff schemes for a single traffic system such as either a voice or a data system [6–14]. Before introducing these schemes, we assume that a system has many cells, with each having S channels. The channel holding time has an exponential distribution with mean rate μ. Both originating and handoff calls are generated in a cell according to Poisson processes, with mean rates λ_O and λ_H, respectively. We assume the system with a homogeneous cell. We focus our attention on a single cell (called the marked cell). Newly generated calls in the marked cell are labeled originating calls (or new calls). A handoff request is generated in the marked cell when a channel holding MS approaches the marked cell from a neighboring cell with a signal strength below the handoff threshold.

1.5.2.1 Nonpriority Scheme
In this scheme, all S channels are shared by both originating and handoff request calls. The BS handles a handoff request exactly in the same way as an originating call. Both kinds of requests are blocked if no free channel is available. The system model is shown in Figure 1.3.

With the blocking call cleared (BCC) policy, we can describe the behavior of a cell as a $(S + 1)$ states Markov process. Each state is labeled by an integer i ($i = 0, 1, \cdots, S$), repre-

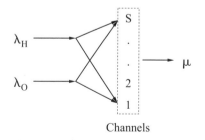

Figure 1.3   A generic system model for handoff.

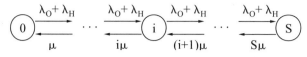

Figure 1.4 State transition diagram for Figure 1.3.

senting the number of channels in use. The state transition diagram is shown in Figure 1.4. The system model is modeled by a typical $M/M/S/S$ queueing model.

Let $P(i)$ be the probability that the system is in state i. The probabilities $P(i)$ can be determined in the usual way for birth–death processes. From Figure 1.4, the state equilibrium equation is

$$P(i) = \frac{\lambda_O + \lambda_H}{i\mu} P(i-1), \qquad 0 \le i \le S \tag{1.12}$$

Using the above equation recursively, along with the normalization condition

$$\sum_{i=0}^{S} P(i) = 1 \tag{1.13}$$

the steady-state probability $P(i)$ is easily found as follows:

$$P(i) = \frac{(\lambda_O + \lambda_H)^i}{i!\,\mu^i} P(0), \qquad 0 \le i \le S \tag{1.14}$$

where

$$P(0) = \frac{1}{\displaystyle\sum_{i=0}^{S} \frac{(\lambda_O + \lambda_H)^i}{i!\,\mu^i}} \tag{1.15}$$

The blocking probability B_O for an originating call is

$$B_O = P(S) = \frac{\dfrac{(\lambda_O + \lambda_H)^S}{S!\,\mu^S}}{\displaystyle\sum_{i=0}^{S} \frac{(\lambda_O + \lambda_H)^i}{i!\,\mu^i}} \tag{1.16}$$

The blocking probability B_H of a handoff request is

$$B_H = B_O \tag{1.17}$$

Equation (1.16) is known as the Erlang-B formula.

A blocked handoff request call can still maintain the communication via current BS until the received signal strength goes below the receiver threshold or until the conversation is completed before the received signal strength goes below the receiver threshold.

1.5.2.2 *Priority Scheme*

In this scheme, priority is given to handoff requests by assigning S_R channels exclusively for handoff calls among the S channels in a cell. The remaining $S_C (= S - S_R)$ channels are shared by both originating calls and handoff requests. An originating call is blocked if the number of available channels in the cell is less than or equal to $S_R (= S - S_C)$. A handoff request is blocked if no channel is available in the target cell. The system model is shown in Figure 1.5.

We define the state i ($i = 0, 1, \cdots, S$) of a cell as the number of calls in progress for the BS of that cell. Let $P(i)$ represent the steady-state probability that the BS is in state i. The probabilities $P(i)$ can be determined in the usual way for birth–death processes. The pertinent state transition diagram is shown in Figure 1.6. From the figure, the state balance equations are

$$\begin{cases} i\mu P(i) = (\lambda_O + \lambda_H)\, P(i-1) & 0 \le i \le S_C \\ i\mu P(i) = \lambda_H\, P(i-1) & S_C < i \le S \end{cases} \tag{1.18}$$

Using this equation recursively, along with the normalization condition

$$\sum_{i=0}^{S} P(i) = 1 \tag{1.19}$$

the steady-state probability $P(i)$ is easily found as follows:

$$P(i) = \begin{cases} \dfrac{(\lambda_O + \lambda_H)^i}{i!\,\mu^i}\, P(0) & 0 \le i \le S_C \\[3mm] \dfrac{(\lambda_O + \lambda_H)^{S_C} \lambda_H^{i-S_C}}{i!\,\mu^i}\, P(0) & S_C \le i \le S \end{cases} \tag{1.20}$$

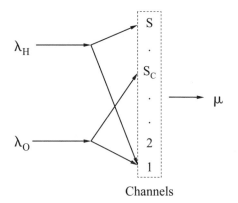

Figure 1.5   System model with priority for handoff call.

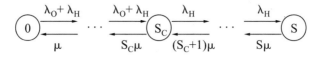

Figure 1.6 State transition diagram for Figure 1.5.

where

$$P(0) = \left[\sum_{i=0}^{S_C} \frac{(\lambda_O + \lambda_H)^i}{i! \mu^i} + \sum_{i=S_C+1}^{S} \frac{(\lambda_O + \lambda_H)^{S_C} \lambda_H^{i-S_C}}{i! \mu^i} \right]^{-1} \tag{1.21}$$

The blocking probability B_O for an originating call is given by

$$B_O = \sum_{i=S_C}^{S} P(i) \tag{1.22}$$

The blocking probability B_H of a handoff request is

$$B_H = P(S) = \frac{(\lambda_O + \lambda_H)^{S_C} \lambda_H^{S-S_C}}{S! \mu^S} P(0) \tag{1.23}$$

Here again, a blocked handoff request call can still maintain the communication via current BS until the received signal strength goes below the receiver threshold or the conversation is completed before the received signal strength goes below the receiver threshold.

1.5.2.3 *Handoff Call Queuing Scheme*

This scheme is based on the fact that adjacent cells in a mobile cellular radio system are overlayed. Thus, there is a considerable area (i.e., handoff area) where a call can be handled by BSs in adjacent cells. The time a mobile user spent moving across the handoff area is referred as the degradation interval. In this scheme, we assume that the same channel sharing scheme is used as that of a priority scheme, except that queueing of handoff requests is allowed. The system model is shown in Figure 1.7.

To analyze this scheme, it is necessary to consider the handoff procedure in more detail. When a MS moves away from the BS, the received signal strength decreases, and when it gets lower than a threshold level, the handoff procedure is initiated. The handoff area is defined as the area in which the average received signal strength of a MS receiver from the BS is between the handoff threshold level and the receiver threshold level.

If the BS finds all channels in the target cell occupied, a handoff request is put in the queue. If a channel is released when the queue for handoff requests is not empty, the channel is assigned to request on the top of the queue. If the received signal strength from the current BS falls below the receiver threshold level prior to the mobile being assigned a channel in the target cell, the call is forced to termination. The first-in-first-out

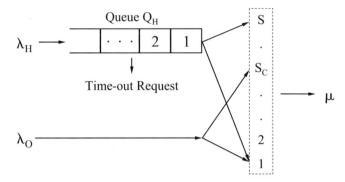

Figure 1.7   System model with priority and queue for handoff call.

(FIFO) queueing strategy is used and infinite queue size at the BS is assumed. For a finite queue size, see the discussion in the next secton. The duration of a MS in the handoff area depends on system parameters such as the moving speed, the direction of the MS, and the cell size. We define this as the dwell time of a mobile in the handoff area and denote it by random variable $T_{h-\text{dwell}}$. For simplicity of analysis, we assume that this dwell time is exponentially distributed with mean $E[T_{h-\text{dwell}}]$ $(= 1/\mu_{h-\text{dwell}})$.

Let us define the state i $(i = 0, 1, \cdots, \infty)$ of a cell as the sum of channels being used in the cell and the number of handoff requests in the queue. It is apparent from the above assumptions that i is a one-dimensional Markov chain. The state transition diagram of the cell is given in Figure 1.8. The equilibrium probabilities $P(i)$ are related to each other through the following state balance equations:

$$
\begin{cases}
i\mu P(i) = (\lambda_O + \lambda_H)P(i-1) & 0 \le i \le S_C \\
i\mu P(i) = \lambda_H P(i-1) & S_C < i \le S \\
[S\mu + (i-S)(\mu_C + \mu_{h-\text{dwell}})]\, P(i) = \lambda_H P(i-1) & S < i \le \infty
\end{cases}
\tag{1.24}
$$

Using the above equation recursively, along with the normalization condition of equation (1.13), the steady-state probability $P(i)$ is easily found as follows:

$$
P(i) =
\begin{cases}
\dfrac{(\lambda_O + \lambda_H)^i}{i!\,\mu^i}P(0) & 0 \le i \le S_C \\[3ex]
\dfrac{(\lambda_O + \lambda_H)^{S_C}\lambda_H^{i-S_C}}{i!\,\mu^i}P(0) & S_C < i \le S \\[3ex]
\dfrac{(\lambda_O + \lambda_H)^{S_C}}{S!\,\mu^S}\dfrac{\lambda_H^{i-S_C}}{\displaystyle\prod_{j=1}^{i-S}[S\mu + j(\mu_C + \mu_{h-\text{dwell}})]}P(0) & S < i \le \infty
\end{cases}
\tag{1.25}
$$

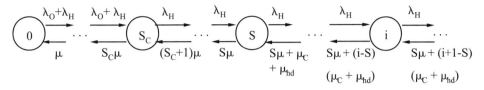

Figure 1.8 State transition diagram for Figure 1.7.

where

$$P(0) = \left\{ \sum_{i=0}^{S_C} \frac{(\lambda_O + \lambda_H)^i}{i!\,\mu^i} + \sum_{i=S_C+1}^{S} \frac{(\lambda_O + \lambda_H)^{S_C}\lambda_H^{i-S_C}}{i!\,\mu^i} \right.$$

$$\left. + \sum_{i=S+1}^{\infty} \frac{(\lambda_O + \lambda_H)^{S_C}}{S!\,\mu^S} \frac{\lambda_H^{i-S_C}}{\prod_{j=1}^{i-S}[S\mu + j(\mu_C + \mu_{h-\text{dwell}})]} \right\}^{-1} \qquad (1.26)$$

The blocking probability B_O for an originating call is

$$B_O = \sum_{i=S_C}^{S} P(i) \qquad (1.27)$$

The forced termination probability B_H of handoff requests is

$$P_f' = \sum_{k=0}^{\infty} P(S + k)P_{fh|k} \qquad (1.28)$$

where $P_{fh|k}$ is a probability that a handoff request fails after joining the queue in position $k + 1$ and it is given by

$$P_{fh|k} = 1 - \left(\frac{\mu_C + \mu_{h-\text{dwell}}}{\mu S + \mu_C + \mu_{h-\text{dwell}}} \right)^k \prod_{i=1}^{k} \left\{ 1 - \left(\frac{\mu_C + \mu_{h-\text{dwell}}}{\mu S + \mu_C + \mu_{h-\text{dwell}}} \right)\left(\frac{1}{2} \right)^i \right\} \qquad (1.29)$$

This scheme can be said to be equivalent to the $S_C = S$.

1.5.2.4 *Originating and Handoff Calls Queuing Scheme*

We consider a system with many cells, each having S channels. In the BS, there are two queues Q_H and Q_O for handoff requests and originating calls, respectively (Figure 1.9). The capacities of Q_H and Q_O are M_H and M_O, respectively. A handoff request is queued in Q_H if it finds no free channels on arrival. On the other hand, an originating call is queued in Q_O when on arrival it finds available channels less than or equal to $(S - S_C)$. A request call is blocked if on arrival its own queue is full.

An originating call in the queue is deleted from the queue when it moves out of the cell before getting a channel. Also, a handoff request is deleted from the queue when it passes

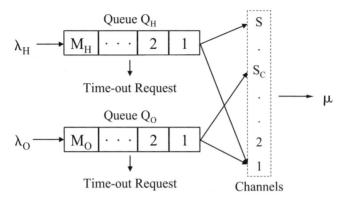

Figure 1.9   System model.

through the handoff area before getting a new channel (i.e., forced termination) or the conversation is completed before passing through the handoff area. A blocked handoff request call can still maintain the communication via the current BS until the received signal strength goes below the receiver threshold or the conversation is completed before passing through the handoff area. A blocked handoff call can repeat trial handoffs until the received signal strength goes below the receiver threshold. However, the capacity of M_H of queue Q_H is usually large enough so that the blocking probability of handoff request calls can be neglected. Thus, repeated handoff requests are excluded from any discussion.

In this method, the state of the marked cell is defined by a two-tuple of nonnegative integers (i, j), where i is the sum of s_b busy channels and j is the number of originating calls in Q_O. Note that if $s_b < S$, then $i = s_b$, and $i = q_h + S$ when $s_b = S$, where q_h is the number of handoff requests in Q_H. It is apparent from the above assumptions that (i, j) is a two-dimensional Markov chain. The state transition diagram of the cell is given in Figure 1.10.

Since the sum of all state probabilities $P(i, j)$ is equal to 1, we have

$$\sum_{i=0}^{S_C-1} P(i, 0) + \sum_{i=S_C}^{S+M_H} \sum_{j=0}^{M_O} P(i, j) = 1 \tag{1.30}$$

In the state transition diagram there are $N_T = (S + M_H + 1)(M_O + 1) - S_C M_O$ states. Therefore, there are N_T balance equations. However, note that any one of these balance equations can be obtained from other $N_T - 1$ equations. Adding the normalizing equation (1.30), we can obtain N_T independent equations. Though N_T is usually rather large, we can obtain all the probabilities $P(i, j)$ (for $i = 0, 1, 2, \cdots, S + M_H$ and $j = 0, 1, 2, \cdots, M_O$) using the following iterative method.

Step 1: Select an arbitrary initial (positive) value for λ_H. [If we use λ_H given by (1.10), we can improve the speed of the convergence.]

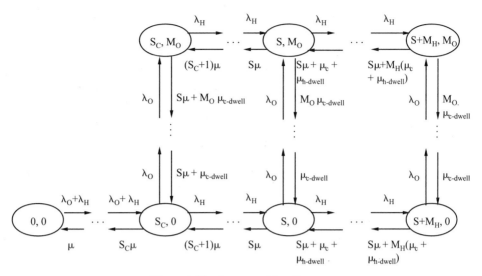

Figure 1.10 State transition diagram.

Step 2: Compute all the probabilities $P(i, j)$ (for $i = 0, 1, 2, \cdots, S + M_H$ and $j = 0, 1, 2, \cdots, M_O$) using SOR (successive over-relation) method.

Step 3: Compute the average number of calls holding channels using the following formula:

$$E[C] = \sum_{i=1}^{S_C-1} iP(i, 0) + \sum_{i=S_C}^{S} i \sum_{j=0}^{M_O} P(i, j) \qquad (1.31)$$

Step 4: Compute new λ_H substituting (1.31) into (1.7). If $|new\ \lambda_H - old\ \lambda_H| \leq \varepsilon$, stop execution. Otherwise, go to Step 2. Here ε is a small positive number to check the convergence.

Based on the above $P(i, j)$s, we can obtain the following performance measures of the system.

The blocking probability B_O of an originating call is

$$B_O = \sum_{i=S_C}^{S+M_H} P(i, M_O) \qquad (1.32)$$

The blocking probability B_H of a handoff request is equal to the probability of its own queue being filled up. Thus,

$$B_H = \sum_{j=0}^{M_O} P(S + M_H, j) \qquad (1.33)$$

The average L_O length of queue Q_O is:

$$L_O = \sum_{j=1}^{M_O} j \sum_{i=S_C}^{S+M_H} P(i, j) \tag{1.34}$$

and the average length L_N of queue Q_H is:

$$L_H = \sum_{i=S+1}^{S+M_H} (i - S) \sum_{j=0}^{M_O} P(i, j) \tag{1.35}$$

Since the average number of originating calls arrived and deleted from the queue in unit time are $(1 - B_O)\lambda_O$ and $\mu_{c\text{—dwell}}L_O$, respectively, the time-out probability of originating calls is given by

$$P_{O\text{—out}} = \frac{\mu_{c\text{—dwell}}L_O}{(1 - B_O)\lambda_O} \tag{1.36}$$

Similarly, the time-out probability of handoff request calls in the queue Q_H is given by

$$P_{H\text{—out}} = \frac{\mu_{h\text{—dwell}}L_H}{(1 - B_H)\lambda_H} \tag{1.37}$$

Therefore, the probability of an originating call not being assigned a channel and the forced termination probability of a handoff request are given by

$$P_O = B_O + (1 - B_O)F_{O\text{—out}} \tag{1.38}$$

and

$$P_f' = B_H + (1 - B_H)P_{H\text{—out}} \tag{1.39}$$

Once a MS is assigned to a channel and if a call is in progress, any subsequent cell boundary crossings necessitates further handoffs. The handoff probability P_h of a call is the probability that the call holding time T_C (random variable) exceeds the dwell time $T_{c\text{—dwell}}$ (random variable) of the user in a cell, i.e.,

$$P_h = \Pr\{T_C > T_{c\text{—dwell}}\} \tag{1.40}$$

Assuming that T_C and $T_{c\text{—dwell}}$ are independent, we can easily get

$$P_h = \frac{\mu_{c\text{—dwell}}}{\mu_C + \mu_{c\text{—dwell}}} \tag{1.41}$$

The forced termination probability P_f that a call accepted by the system is forced to terminate during its lifetime is a true measure of the system performance. It is important to distinguish between this probability and the failure probability P_f' of a single handoff attempt. The forced termination probability P_f of handoff calls can be expressed as

$$P_f = \sum_{l=1}^{\infty} P_h P_f' [(1 - P_f') P_h]^{l-1} = \frac{P_h P_f'}{1 - P_h(1 - P_f')} \tag{1.42}$$

For special situations, solutions are already known for the case of $M_H = \infty$ and $M_H = 0$ when $M_O = 0$. In the system with $M_H =$ finite, an originating call is blocked if the number of available channels in the cell is less than or equal to $S - S_C$. A handoff request is blocked if on arrival it finds that Q_H is filled.

In this case, we consider the case for $M_O = 0$. The two-dimensional state-transition diagram becomes one-dimensional ($j = 0$). Therefore, the state probabilities can easily be obtained as follows:

$$P(i,0) = \begin{cases} \dfrac{a^i}{i!} P(0,0) & 0 \le i \le S_C \\[3mm] \left(\dfrac{a}{b}\right)^{S_C} \dfrac{b^i}{i!} P(0,0) & S_C \le i \le S \\[3mm] \dfrac{\left(\dfrac{a}{b}\right)^{S_C}}{S!} \dfrac{b^i P(0,0)}{\prod\limits_{j=1}^{i-S}(S+jh)} & S+1 \le i \le S+M_H \end{cases} \tag{1.43}$$

where $a = \dfrac{\lambda_O + \lambda_H}{\mu}$, $b = \dfrac{\lambda_H}{\mu}$, and $h = \dfrac{\mu_C + \mu_{h-\text{dwell}}}{\mu}$,

$$P(0,0) = \left\{ \sum_{i=0}^{S_C} \frac{a^i}{i!} + \left(\frac{a}{b}\right)^{S_C} \sum_{i=S_C+1}^{S} \frac{b^i}{i!} + \frac{\left(\dfrac{a}{b}\right)^{S_C}}{S!} \sum_{i=S+1}^{S+M_H} \frac{b^i}{\prod\limits_{j=1}^{i-S}(S+jh)} \right\}^{-1} \tag{1.44}$$

and

$$\lambda_H = E[C]\,\mu_{c-\text{dwell}} = \mu_{c-\text{dwell}} \sum_{i=1}^{S} i P(i,0) \tag{1.45}$$

Therefore, the blocking probability B_O of an originating call is

$$B_O = \sum_{i=S_C}^{S+M_H} P(i,0)$$

$$= \left[\frac{a^{S_C}}{S_C!} + \left(\frac{a}{b}\right)^{S_C} \sum_{i=S_C+1}^{S} \frac{b^i}{i!} + \frac{\left(\dfrac{a}{b}\right)^{S_C}}{S!} \sum_{i=S+1}^{S+M_H} \frac{b^i}{\prod\limits_{j=1}^{i-S}(S+jh)} \right] P(0,0). \tag{1.46}$$

The average length L_H of queue Q_H is

$$L_H = \sum_{i=S+1}^{S+M_H} (i-S)P(i,0). \tag{1.47}$$

1.5.3 Handoff Schemes in Multiple Traffic Systems

In this section, we discuss nonpreemptive and preemptive priority handoff schemes for a multiple traffic system, such as an integrated voice and data system or integrated real-time and nonreal-time system. Although we focus our attention just on integrated voice and data systems, the results can be extended to other similar systems. Before introducing these schemes, we make the following assumptions for our discussion. The call holding time T_{CV} of voice calls is assumed to have an exponential distribution with mean $E[T_{CV}]$ ($= 1/\mu_{CV}$). The data length T_{CD} is also assumed to have an exponential distribution with mean $E[T_{CD}]$ ($= 1/\mu_{CD}$). The dwell time $T_{c\text{--dwell}}$ (the random variable) of mobile users in a cell is assumed to have an exponential distribution with mean $E[T_{c\text{--dwell}}]$ ($= 1/\mu_{c\text{--dwell}}$). The random variable $T_{h\text{--dwell}}$ is defined as the time spent in the handoff area by voice handoff request calls and is assumed to have an exponential distribution with mean $E[T_{c\text{--dwell}}]$ ($= 1/\mu_{c\text{--dwell}}$). The channel holding time of a voice (or data) call is equal to the smaller one between $T_{c\text{--dwell}}$ and T_{CV} (or T_{CD}). Using the memoryless property of the exponential pdf, we see that the random variables T_V and T_D (the channel holding time of voice and data calls) are both exponentially distributed, with means $E[T_V]$ [$= 1/\mu_V = 1/(\mu_{CV} + \mu_{c\text{--dwell}})$] and $E[T_D]$ [$= 1/\mu_D = 1/(\mu_{CD} + \mu_{c\text{--dwell}})$], respectively. We assume that the arrival processes of originating voice and data calls and voice and data handoff calls in a cell are Poisson. The arrival rates of originating voice and data calls are designated as λ_{OV} and λ_{OD}, respectively. We denote the arrival rates of voice and data handoff requests by λ_{HV} and λ_{HD}, respectively. A data handoff request in the queue of the current cell is transferred to the queue of target cell when it moves out of the cell before getting a channel. The transfer rate is given by

$$\lambda_{\text{time--out}} = L_{qd}\mu_{c\text{--dwell}} \tag{1.48}$$

where L_{qd} is the average length of data queue.

We define a new variable λ_{HT} by

$$\lambda_{HT} = \lambda_{HD} + \lambda_{\text{time--out}} = N_D\mu_{c\text{--dwell}} \tag{1.49}$$

where N_D is the average number of data handoff requests in a cell.

1.5.3.1 Nonpreemptive Priority Handoff Scheme

We consider a system with many cells each having S channels. As the system is assumed to have homogeneous cells, we focus our attention on a single cell called the marked cell. A system model is shown in Figure 1.11. In each BS, there are two queues, Q_V and Q_D, with capacities M_V and M_D for voice and data handoff requests, respectively.

Newly generated calls in the marked cell are called originating calls. For voice users, there is a handoff area. For data users, the boundary is defined as the locus of points where

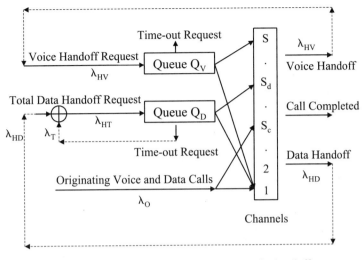

Figure 1.11 System model with two queues for handoffs.

the average received signal strength of the two neighboring cells are equal. The process of generation for handoff request is same as in previous schemes.

A voice handoff request is queued in Q_V on arrival if it finds no idle channels. On the other hand, a data handoff request is queued in Q_D on arrival when it finds $(S - S_d)$ or fewer available channels, where S_d is the number of usable channels for data handoff users. An originating voice or an originating data call is blocked on arrival if it finds $(S - S_c)$ or fewer available channels, where S_c is the number of channels for both originating calls. No queue is assumed here for originating calls. A handoff request is blocked if its own queue is full on its arrival.

If there are channels available, the voice handoff request calls in Q_V are served based on the FIFO rule. If more than $(S - S_d)$ channels are free, the data handoff request calls in Q_D are served by the FIFO rule. A voice handoff request in the queue is deleted from the queue when it passes through the handoff area before getting a new channel (i.e., forced termination) or its communication is completed before passing through the handoff area. A data handoff request can be transferred from the queue of the current cell to the one of the target cells when it moves out of the current cell before getting a channel.

A blocked voice handoff request maintains communication via the current BS until the received signal strength falls below the receiver threshold or the conversation is completed before passing through the handoff area. However, the probability of a blocked voice handoff request call completing the communication before passing through the handoff area is neglected. A blocked voice handoff request can repeat trial handoffs until the received signal strength goes below the receiver threshold. However, the capacities of M_V and M_D of queues are usually large enough so that the blocking probability of handoff request calls can be neglected. Thus, repeated trials of blocked handoff requests are excluded from any discussion.

The state of the marked cell is defined by a three-tuple of nonnegative integers (i, j, k), where i is the sum of the number of channels used by voice calls (including originating calls and handoff requests) and the number of voice handoff requests in the queue Q_V, j is the number of channels used by data handoff requests, and k is the number of data handoff requests in the queue Q_D. It is apparent from the above assumptions that (i, j, k) is a three-dimensional Markov chain.

In the state transition diagram, there are $N_T = (S + M_V - S_d + 1)(S_d + 1)(M_D + 1) + S_d(S_d + 1)/2$ states. Therefore, the state transition diagram leads to N_T balance equations. Equilibrium probabilities $P(i, j, k)$ are related to each other through the state balance equations. However, note that any one of these balance equations can be obtained from other $N_T - 1$ equations. Since the sum of all state probabilities is equal to 1, we have

$$\sum_{j=0}^{S_d} \sum_{i=0}^{S+M_V-j} P(i, j, 0) + \sum_{j=0}^{S_d} \sum_{i=S_d-j}^{S+M_V-j} \sum_{k=1}^{M_D} P(i, j, k) = 1 \tag{1.50}$$

Adding the normalizing equation (1.50), we can obtain N_T independent equations in which λ_{HV} and λ_{HT} are two unknown variables. Using equation (1.7), we can get

$$\lambda_{HV} = E[C_V]\, \mu_{c-\text{dwell}} \tag{1.51}$$

Adding equations (1.49) and (1.51) leads to $N_T + 2$ nonlinear independent simultaneous equations. Though N_T is usually rather large, all the probabilities $P(j, j, k)$ (for $i = 0, 1, 2, \ldots, S + M_V; j = 0, 1, 2, \ldots, S_d$, and $k = 0, 1, 2, \ldots, M_D$) can be obtained by solving $N_T + 2$ nonlinear independent simultaneous equations, as illustrated in the next section.

Step 1: Select arbitrary initial (positive) values for λ_{HV} and λ_{HT}.

Step 2: Compute all the probabilities $P(i, j, k)$ (for $i = 0, 1, 2, \ldots, S + M_V, j = 0, 1, 2, \ldots, S_d$, and $k = 0, 1, 2, \ldots, M_D$) using the SOR method.

Step 3: Compute the average numbers $E[C_V]$ of voice calls holding channels, and compute the average numbers N_D of data channel requests in a cell using the following relations:

$$E[C_V] = \sum_{i=0}^{S-S_d} i \sum_{j=0}^{S_d} \sum_{k=0}^{M_D} P(i, j, k) + \sum_{i=S-S_d+1}^{S} i \sum_{j=0}^{S-i} \sum_{k=0}^{M_D} P(i, j, k)$$
$$+ \sum_{j=0}^{S_d} (S-j) \sum_{i=S-j+1}^{S+M_V-j} \sum_{k=0}^{M_D} P(i, j, k) \tag{1.52}$$

and

$$N_D = \sum_{j=1}^{S_d} j \sum_{i=0}^{S+M_V-j} \sum_{k=0}^{M_D} P(i, j, k) + \sum_{k=1}^{M_D} k \sum_{j=0}^{S_d} \sum_{i=S_d-j}^{S+M_V-j} P(i, j, k) \tag{1.53}$$

Step 4: Compute new λ_{HV} by substituting (1.52) into (1.51). Compute new λ_{HT} by substituting (1.53) into (1.49). If $|new\ \lambda_{HV} - old\ \lambda_{HV}| \leq \varepsilon$ and $|new\ \lambda_{HT} - old\ \lambda_{HT}| \leq \varepsilon$, stop execution. Otherwise, go to Step 2. Here ε is a small positive number to check the convergence.

Based on the above $P(i, j, k)s$, we can obtain the following performance measures of the system.

The blocking probability of an originating voice call or originating data call is

$$B_O = B_{OV} = B_{OD} = \sum_{j=0}^{S_d} \sum_{i=S_V-j}^{S+M_V-j} \sum_{k=0}^{M_D} P(i, j, k) \tag{1.54}$$

The blocking probability B_{HV} of a voice handoff request is

$$B_{HV} = \sum_{j=0}^{S_d} \sum_{k=0}^{M_D} P(S + M_V - j, j, k) \tag{1.55}$$

The blocking probability B_{HD} of a data handoff request is

$$B_{HD} = \sum_{j=0}^{S_d} \sum_{i=S_d-j}^{S+M_V-j} P(i, j, M_D) \tag{1.56}$$

The average length L_{qv} of queue Q_V is

$$L_{qv} = \sum_{i=S+1}^{S+M_V} (i - S) \sum_{j=0}^{S_d} \sum_{k=0}^{M_D} P(i - j, j, k) \tag{1.57}$$

The average length L_{qd} of queue Q_D is

$$L_{qd} = \sum_{k=1}^{M_D} k \sum_{j=0}^{S_d} \sum_{i=S_d-j}^{S+M_V-j} P(i, j, k) \tag{1.58}$$

Since the average number of voice handoff requests arrived and deleted in unit time are $(1 - B_{HV})\lambda_{HV}$ and $\mu_{h-\text{dwell}}L_{qv}$, respectively, the time-out probability of a voice handoff requests in the queue Q_V is given by

$$P_{V-\text{out}} = \frac{\mu_{h-\text{dwell}}L_{qv}}{(1 - B_{HV})\lambda_{HV}} \tag{1.59}$$

Therefore, failure probability of a voice handoff request for single handoff attempt is

$$P'_{fV} = B_{HV} + (1 - B_{HV}) P_{V-\text{out}} \tag{1.60}$$

The voice user in a cell is given by

$$P_h = \Pr\{T_{CV} > T_{c-\text{dwell}}\} \tag{1.61}$$

Assuming that T_{CV} and $T_{c-\text{dwell}}$ are independent, we can easily get

$$P_h = \frac{\mu_{c-\text{dwell}}}{\mu_{CV} + \mu_{c-\text{dwell}}} \tag{1.62}$$

The forced termination probability P_{fV} of voice calls can be expressed as

$$P_{fV} = \sum_{l=1}^{\infty} P_h P_{fV}'[(1 - P_{fV}') P_h]^{l-1} = \frac{P_h P_{fV}'}{1 - P_h(1 - P_{fV}')} \tag{1.63}$$

Using Little's formula, the average value of waiting time T_W of data handoff requests in the queue is given by

$$T_W = \frac{L_{qd}}{(1 - B_{OD})\lambda_{OD} + (1 - B_{HD})\lambda_{HT}} \tag{1.64}$$

Average value of time T_S (random variable) of a call in a cell is

$$T_S = \frac{N_D}{(1 - B_{OD})\lambda_{OD} + (1 - B_{HD})\lambda_{HT}} \tag{1.65}$$

Let us define N_h as the average number of handoffs per data handoff request during its lifetime. Thus, we have

$$N_h = \frac{N_h T_W + E[T_{CD}]}{T_S} \tag{1.66}$$

Then,

$$N_h = \frac{(1 - B_{OD})\lambda_{OD} + (1 - B_{HD})\lambda_{HT}}{E[C_D]\,\mu_{CD}} \tag{1.67}$$

where

$$E[C_D] = \sum_{j=1}^{S_d} j \sum_{i=0}^{S+M_V-j} \sum_{k=0}^{M_D} P(i,j,k) \tag{1.68}$$

Therefore, the average transmission delay (except average data length) T_{delay} of data is

$$T_{\text{delay}} = N_h T_W = \frac{L_{qd}}{E[C_D]\,\mu_{CD}} \tag{1.69}$$

1.5.3.2 Preemptive Priority Handoff Scheme

This scheme is a modification of a nonpreemptive priority handoff scheme, with higher priorities for voice handoff request calls. In this scheme, a handoff request call is served if there are channels available when such a voice handoff request call arrives. Otherwise, the voice handoff request can preempt the data call, when we assume there is an ongoing data call, if on arrival it finds no idle channel. The interrupted data call is returned to the data queue Q_D and waits for a channel to be available based on the FIFO rule. A voice handoff request is queued in Q_V by the system if all the channels are occupied by prior calls and the data queue Q_D is full (i.e., data calls cannot be preempted by voice handoff calls when the data queue Q_D is full). It is possible to think of another scheme where data calls in service can be preempted by voice handoff calls irrespective of whether the queue Q_D is full or not. However, the same effect can be observed if the queue capacity is increased to a relatively large value.

The same state of the marked cell is assumed and represented by a three-tuple of nonnegative integers (i, j, k) as defined in the nonpreemptive priority handoff scheme. In the state transition diagram for the three-dimensional Markov chain model there are $N_T = (S - S_d + 1)(S_d + 1)(M_D + 1) + (S_d + M_D + 1)M_V + S_d(S_d + 1)/2$ states. Therefore, as in the nonpreemptive priority handoff scheme, we can get N_T balance equations through the state transition diagram. Equilibrium probabilities $P(i, j, k)$ are related to each other through the state balance equations. However, note that any one of these balance equations can be obtained from other $N_T - 1$ equations. Since the sum of all state probabilities is equal to 1, we have

$$
\sum_{j=0}^{S_d} \sum_{i=0}^{S-j} P(i, j, 0) + \sum_{j=0}^{S_d} \sum_{i=S_d-j}^{S-j} \sum_{k=1}^{M_D} P(i, j, k) + \sum_{i=S+1}^{S+M_V} \sum_{k=0}^{M_D} P(i, 0, k)
$$
$$
+ \sum_{j=1}^{S_d} \sum_{i=S-j+1}^{S+M_V-j} P(i, j, M_D) = 1 \tag{1.70}
$$

The probabilities $P(j, j, k)$ (for $i = 0, 1, 2, \ldots, S + M_V; j = 0, 1, 2, \ldots, S_d$, and $k = 0, 1, 2, \ldots, M_D$) can be obtained by using the same method of computation in the nonpreemptive priority handoff scheme. The differences are:

$$
E[C_V] = \sum_{i=0}^{S-S_d} i \sum_{j=0}^{S_d} \sum_{k=0}^{M_D} P(i, j, k) + \sum_{i=S-S_d+1}^{S} i \sum_{j=0}^{S-i} \sum_{k=0}^{M_D} P(i, j, k)\backslash
$$
$$
+ \sum_{j=0}^{S_d} (S-j) \sum_{i=S-j+1}^{S+M_V-j} P(i, j, M_D) \tag{1.71}
$$

$$
N_D = \sum_{j=1}^{S_d} j \sum_{i=0}^{S-j} \sum_{k=0}^{M_D} P(i, j, k) + \sum_{j=1}^{S_d} j \sum_{i=S-j+1}^{S+M_V-j} P(i, j, M_D) + \sum_{k=1}^{M_D} k \sum_{j=0}^{S_d} \sum_{i=S_d-j}^{S-j} P(i, j, k)
$$
$$
+ \sum_{k=1}^{M_D-1} k \sum_{i=S+1}^{S+M_V} P(i, 0, k) + M_D \sum_{j=0}^{S_d} \sum_{i=S-j+1}^{S+M_V-j} P(i, j, M_D) \tag{1.72}
$$

and

$$E[C_D] = \sum_{j=1}^{S_d} j \sum_{i=0}^{S-j} \sum_{k=0}^{M_D} P(i, j, k) + \sum_{j=1}^{S_d} j \sum_{i=S-j+1}^{S+M_V-j} P(i, j, M_D) \tag{1.73}$$

Therefore, the performance measurements can be obtained by equations (1.54)–(1.69).

1.6 SUMMARY

The basic concept of handoff in mobile cellular radio systems has been introduced. Several different traffic models have been described and briefly discussed. Four conventional handoff schemes in single traffic systems—i.e., nonpriority scheme, priority scheme, handoff call queueing scheme, and originating and handoff call queuing schemes—have been summarized in this chapter. The two handoff schemes with and without preemptive priority procedures for integrated voice and data wireless mobile networks have also been covered in detail.

REFERENCES

1. M. Gudmundson, Analysis of handover algorithms, *Proc. IEEE VTC '91,* pp. 537–542, May 1991.

2. V. Kapoor, G. Edwards, and R. Snkar, Handoff criteria for personal communication networks, *Proc. IEEE ICC '94,* pp. 1297–1301, May 1994.

3. G. P. Pollini, Trends in handover design, *IEEE Commun. Magazine,* pp. 82–90, March 1996.

4. N. D. Tripathi, J. H. Reed, and H. F. Vanlandingham, Handoff in Cellular Systems, *IEEE Personal Commun.,* December 1998.

5. D. Hong and S. S. Rappaport, Traffic model and performance analysis for cellular mobile radio telephone systems with prioritized and nonprioritized handoff procedures, *IEEE Trans. Veh. Technol.,* Vol. VT-35, No. 3, pp. 448–461, August 1986.

6. S. A. El-Dolil, W. C. Wong, and R. Steele, Teletraffic performance of highway microcells with overlay macrocell, *IEEE J. Select. Areas in Commun.,* Vol. 7, No. 1, pp. 71–78, January 1989.

7. R. Steele and M. Nofal, Teletraffic performance of microcellular personal communication networks, *IEE PROCEEDINGS-I,* Vol. 139, No. 4, August 1992.

8. H. Xie and S. Kuek Priority handoff analysis, *Proc. IEEE VTC '93,* pp. 855–858, 1993.

9. Q-A. Zeng, K. Mukumoto, and A. Fukuda, Performance analysis of mobile cellular radio systems with two-level priority reservation handoff procedure, *IEICE Trans. Commun.,* Vol. E80-B, No. 4, pp. 598–604, April 1997.

10. S. Tekinay and B. Jabbari, A measurement-based prioritization scheme for handovers in mobile cellular networks, *IEEE J. Select. Areas in Commun.,* Vol. 10, No. 8, Oct. 1992.

11. Q-A. Zeng, K. Mukumoto, and A. Fukuda, Performance analysis of mobile cellular radio systems with priority reservation handoff procedures, *Proc. IEEE VTC '94,* Vol. 3, pp. 1829–1833, June 1994.

12. R. B. Cooper, *Introduction to Queueing Theory,* 2nd ed. New York: Elsevier North Holland, 1981.

13. J. D. Wells, Cellular system design using the expansion cell layout method, *IEEE Trans. Veh. Technol.,* Vol. VT-33, May 1984.

14. H. Akimaru and R. B. Cooper, *Teletraffic Engineering.* Ohm, 1985.

15. Q-A. Zeng and D. P. Agrawal, Performance analysis of a handoff scheme in integrated voice/data wireless networks, *Proc. IEEE VTC 2000 Fall*, Vol. 4, pp. 1986–1992, September 2000.

16. Q-A. Zeng and D. P. Agrawal, An analytical modeling of handoff for integrated voice/data wireless networks with priority reservation and preemptive priority procedures, *Proc. ICPP 2000 Workshop on Wireless Networks and Mobile Computing*, pp. 523–529, August 2000.

CHAPTER 2

Location Management in Cellular Networks

JINGYUAN ZHANG

Department of Computer Science, University of Alabama

2.1 INTRODUCTION

It has been known for over one hundred years that radio can be used to keep in touch with people on the move. However, wireless communications using radio were not popular until Bell Laboratories developed the cellular concept to reuse the radio frequency in the 1960s and 1970s [31]. In the past decade, cellular communications have experienced an explosive growth due to recent technological advances in cellular networks and cellular telephone manufacturing. It is anticipated that they will experience even more growth in the next decade. In order to accommodate more subscribers, the size of cells must be reduced to make more efficient use of the limited frequency spectrum allocation. This will add to the challenge of some fundamental issues in cellular networks. Location management is one of the fundamental issues in cellular networks. It deals with how to track subscribers on the move. The purpose of this chapter is to survey recent research on location management in cellular networks. The rest of this chapter is organized as follows. Section 2.2 introduces cellular networks and Section 2.3 describes basic concepts of location management. Section 2.4 presents some assumptions that are commonly used to evaluate a location management scheme in terms of network topology, call arrival probability, and mobility. Section 2.5 surveys popular location management schemes. Finally, Section 2.6 summarizes the chapter.

2.2 CELLULAR NETWORKS

In a cellular network, a service coverage area is divided into smaller hexagonal areas referred to as cells. Each cell is served by a base station. The base station is fixed. It is able to communicate with mobile stations such as cellular telephones using its radio transceiver. The base station is connected to the mobile switching center (MSC) which is, in turn, connected to the public switched telephone network (PSTN). Figure 2.1 illustrates a typical cellular network. The triangles represent base stations.

The frequency spectrum allocated to wireless communications is very limited, so the

Handbook of Wireless Networks and Mobile Computing, Edited by Ivan Stojmenović. **27**
ISBN 0-471-41902-8   © 2002 John Wiley & Sons, Inc.

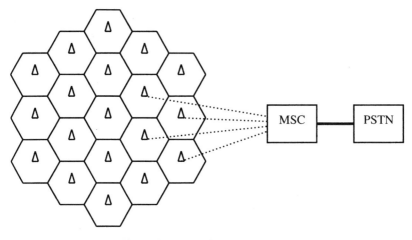

Figure 2.1   A typical cellular network.

cellular concept was introduced to reuse the frequency. Each cell is assigned a certain number of channels. To avoid radio interference, the channels assigned to one cell must be different from the channels assigned to its neighboring cells. However, the same channels can be reused by two cells that are far apart such that the radio interference between them is tolerable. By reducing the size of cells, the cellular network is able to increase its capacity, and therefore to serve more subscribers.

For the channels assigned to a cell, some are forward (or downlink) channels that are used to carry traffic from the base station to mobile stations, and the others are reverse (or uplink) channels that are used to carry traffic from mobile stations to the base station. Both forward and reverse channels are further divided into control and voice (or data) channels. The voice channels are for actual conversations, whereas the control channels are used to help set up conversations.

A mobile station communicates with another station, either mobile or land, via a base station. A mobile station cannot communicate with another mobile station directly. To make a call from a mobile station, the mobile station first needs to make a request using a reverse control channel of the current cell. If the request is granted by the MSC, a pair of voice channels will be assigned for the call. To route a call to a mobile station is more complicated. The network first needs to know the MSC and the cell in which the mobile station is currently located. How to find out the current residing cell of a mobile station is an issue of location management. Once the MSC knows the cell of the mobile station, it can assign a pair of voice channels in that cell for the call. If a call is in progress when the mobile station moves into a neighboring cell, the mobile station needs to get a new pair of voice channels in the neighboring cell from the MSC so the call can continue. This process is called handoff (or handover). The MSC usually adopts a channel assignment strategy that prioritizes handoff calls over new calls.

This section has briefly described some fundamental concepts about cellular networks such as frequency reuse, channel assignment, handoff, and location management. For detailed information, please refer to [6, 7, 20, 31, 35]. This chapter will address recent research on location management.

2.3 LOCATION MANAGEMENT

Location management deals with how to keep track of an active mobile station within the cellular network. A mobile station is active if it is powered on. Since the exact location of a mobile station must be known to the network during a call, location management usually means how to track an active mobile station between two consecutive phone calls.

There are two basic operations involved in location management: location update and paging. The paging operation is performed by the cellular network. When an incoming call arrives for a mobile station, the cellular network will page the mobile station in all possible cells to find out the cell in which the mobile station is located so the incoming call can be routed to the corresponding base station. The number of all possible cells to be paged is dependent on how the location update operation is performed. The location update operation is performed by an active mobile station.

A location update scheme can be classified as either global or local [11]. A location update scheme is global if all subscribers update their locations at the same set of cells, and a scheme is local if an individual subscriber is allowed to decide when and where to perform the location update. A local scheme is also called individualized or per-user-based. From another point of view, a location update scheme can be classified as either static or dynamic [11, 33]. A location update scheme is static if there is a predetermined set of cells at which location updates must be generated by a mobile station regardless of its mobility. A scheme is dynamic if a location update can be generated by a mobile station in any cell depending on its mobility. A global scheme is based on aggregate statistics and traffic patterns, and it is usually static too. Location areas described in [30] and reporting centers described in [9, 18] are two examples of global static schemes. A global scheme can be dynamic. For example, the time-varying location areas scheme described in [25] is both global and dynamic. A per-user-based scheme is based on the statistics and/or mobility patterns of an individual subscriber, and it is usually dynamic. The time-based, movement-based and distance-based schemes described in [11] are three excellent examples of individualized dynamic schemes. An individualized scheme is not necessarily dynamic. For example, the individualized location areas scheme in [43] is both individualized and static.

Location management involves signaling in both the wireline portion and the wireless portion of the cellular network. However, most researchers only consider signaling in the wireless portion due to the fact that the radio frequency bandwidth is limited, whereas the bandwidth of the wireline network is always expandable. This chapter will only discuss signaling in the wireless portion of the network. Location update involves reverse control channels whereas paging involves forward control channels. The total location management cost is the sum of the location update cost and the paging cost. There is a trade-off between the location update cost and the paging cost. If a mobile station updates its location more frequently (incurring higher location update costs), the network knows the location of the mobile station better. Then the paging cost will be lower when an incoming call arrives for the mobile station. Therefore, both location update and paging costs cannot be minimized at the same time. However, the total cost can be minimized or one cost can be minimized by putting a bound on the other cost. For example, many researchers try to minimize the location update cost subject to a constraint on the paging cost.

The cost of paging a mobile station over a set of cells or location areas has been studied against the paging delay [34]. There is a trade-off between the paging cost and the paging delay. If there is no delay constraint, the cells can be paged sequentially in order of decreasing probability, which will result in the minimal paging cost. If all cells are paged simultaneously, the paging cost reaches the maximum while the paging delay is the minimum. Many researchers try to minimize the paging cost under delay constraints [2, 4, 17].

2.4 COMMON ASSUMPTIONS FOR PERFORMANCE EVALUATION

2.4.1 Network Topology

The network topology can be either one-dimensional or two-dimensional. As demonstrated in Figure 2.2, in one-dimensional topology, each cell has two neighboring cells if they exist [17]. Some researchers use a ring topology in which the first and the last cells are considered as neighboring cells [11]. The one-dimensional topology is used to model the service area in which the mobility of mobile stations is restricted to either forward or backward direction. Examples include highways and railroads.

The two-dimensional network topology is used to model a more general service area in which mobile stations can move in any direction. There are two possible cell configurations to cover the service area—hexagonal configuration and mesh configuration. The hexagonal cell configuration is shown in Figure 2.1, where each cell has six neighboring cells. Figure 2.3 illustrates a mesh cell configuration. Although eight neighbors can be assumed for each cell in the mesh configuration, most researchers assume four neighbors (horizontal and vertical ones only) [2, 3, 5, 22]. Although the mesh configuration has been assumed for simplicity, it is not known whether the mesh configuration, especially the one with four neighbors, is a practical model.

2.4.2 Call Arrival Probability

The call arrival probability plays a very important role when evaluating the performance of a location management scheme. If the call arrival time is known to the called mobile station in advance, the mobile station can update its location just before the call arrival time. In this way, costs of both locate update and paging are kept to the minimum. However, the reality is not like this. Many researchers assume that the incoming call arrivals to a mobile station follow a Poisson process. Therefore, the interarrival times have indepen-

Figure 2.2   One-dimensional network topology.

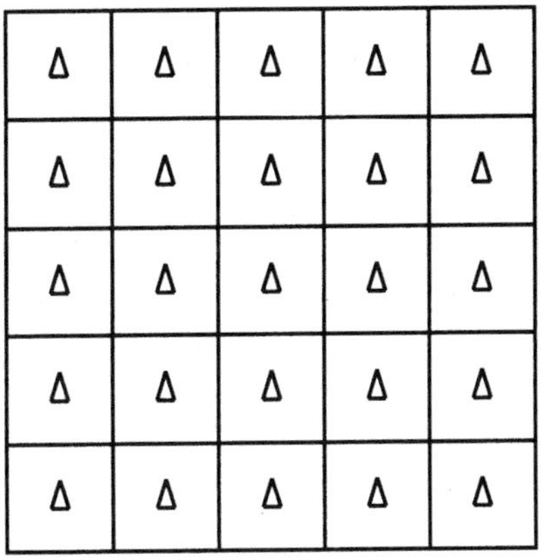

Figure 2.3 Two-dimensional network topology with the mesh configuration.

dent exponential distributions with the density function $f(t) = \lambda e^{-\lambda t}$ [2, 19, 22]. Here λ represents the call arrival rate. Some researchers assume the discrete case. Therefore, the call interarrival times have geometric distributions with the probability distribution function $F(t) = 1 - (1 - \lambda)^t$ [1, 17, 24]. Here λ is the call arrival probability.

2.4.3 Mobility Models

The mobility pattern also plays an important role when evaluating the performance of a location management scheme. A mobility model is usually used to describe the mobility of an individual subscriber. Sometimes it is used to describe the aggregate pattern of all subscribers. The following are several commonly used mobility models.

Fluid Flow Model
The fluid flow model has been used in [43] to model the mobility of vehicular mobile stations. It requires a continuous movement with infrequent speed and direction changes. The fluid flow model is suitable for vehicle traffic on highways, but not suitable for pedestrian movements with stop-and-go interruption.

Random Walk Model
Many researchers have used the discrete random walk as the mobility model. In this model, it is assumed that time is slotted, and a subscriber can make at most one move during a time slot. Assume that a subscriber is in cell i at the beginning of time slot t. For the one-dimensional network topology, at the beginning of time slot $t + 1$, the probability that the subscriber remains in cell i is p, and the probability that the subscriber moves to cell $i + 1$ or cell $i - 1$ is equally $(1 - p)/2$ [11, 24].

The discrete random walk model has also been used in the two-dimensional network topology [2, 17]. For the hexagonal configuration, the probability that the subscriber remains in the same cell is p, and the probability that the subscriber moves to each neighboring cell is equally $(1 - p)/6$. The concept of *ring* has been introduced to convert the two-dimensional random walk to the one-dimensional one. A simplified two-dimensional random walk model has been proposed in [5].

Markov Walk Model

Although the random walk model is memoryless, the current move is dependent on the previous move in the Markov walk model. In [11], the Markov walk has been used to model mobility in the one-dimensional ring topology. Three states have been assumed for a subscriber at the beginning of time slot t: the stationary state (S), the left-move state (L), and the right-move state (R). For the S state, the probability that the subscriber remains in S is p, and the probability that the subscriber moves to either L or R is equally $(1 - p)/2$. For the L (or R) state, the probability that the subscriber remains in the same state is q, the probability that the subscriber moves to the opposite state is v, and the probability that the subscriber moves to S is $1 - q - v$. Figure 2.4 illustrates the state transitions.

In [12], the authors split the S state into SL and SR—a total of four states. Both SL and SR are stationary, but they memorize the most recent move, either leftward (for SL) or rightward (for SR). The probability of resuming motion in the same direction has been distinguished from that in the opposite direction.

Cell-Residence-Time-Based Model

While one group of researchers uses the probability that a mobile station may remain in the same cell after each time slot to determine the cell residence time implicitly, another group considers the cell residence time as a random variable [2, 19, 22]. Most studies use the exponential distribution to model the cell residence time because of its simplicity. The Gamma distribution is selected by some researchers for the following reasons. First, some important distributions such as the exponential, Erlang, and Chi-square distributions are special cases of the Gamma distribution. Second, the Gamma distribution has a simple Laplace–Stieltjes transform.

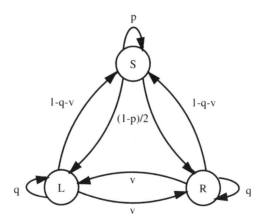

Figure 2.4   The state transitions of the Markov walk model.

Gauss–Markov Model

In [21], the authors have used the Gauss–Markov mobility model, which captures the velocity correlation of a mobile station in time. Specifically the velocity at the time slot n, v_n, is represented as follows:

$$v_n = \alpha v_{n-1} + (1 - \alpha)\mu + \sqrt{1 - \alpha^2} x_{n-1}$$

Here $0 \leq \alpha \leq 1$, μ is the asymptotic mean of v_n when n approaches infinity, and x_n is an independent, uncorrelated, and stationary Gaussian process with zero mean. The Gauss–Markov model represents a wide range of mobility patterns, including the constant velocity fluid flow models (when $\alpha = 1$) and the random walk model (when $\alpha = 0$ and $\mu = 0$).

Normal Walk Model

In [41], the authors have proposed a multiscale, straight-oriented mobility model referred to as *normal walk*. They assume that a mobile station moves in unit steps on a Euclidean plane. The ith move, Y_i, is obtained by rotating the $(i-1)$th move, Y_{i-1}, counterclockwise for θ_i degrees:

$$Y_i = R(\theta_i)Y_{i-1}$$

Here θ_i is normally distributed with zero mean. Since the normal distribution with zero mean is chosen, the probability density increases as the rotation angle approaches zero. Therefore, a mobile station has a very high probability of preserving the previous direction.

Shortest Path Model

In [3], the authors have introduced the shortest path model for the mobility of a vehicular mobile station. The network topology used to illustrate the model is of the mesh configuration. They assume that, within the location area, a mobile station will follow the shortest path measured in the number of cells traversed, from source to destination. At each intersection, the mobile station makes a decision to proceed to any of the neighboring cells such that the shortest distance assumption is maintained. That means that a mobile station can only go straight or make a left or right turn at an intersection. Furthermore, a mobile station cannot make two consecutive left turns or right turns.

Activity-Based Model

Instead of using a set of random variables to model the mobility pattern, an actual activity-based mobility model has been developed at the University of Waterloo [38, 39]. The model is based on the trip survey conducted by the Regional Municipality of Waterloo in 1987. It is assumed that a trip is undertaken for taking part in an activity such as shopping at the destination. Once the location for the next activity is selected, the route from the current location to the activity location will be determined in terms of cells crossed. The activity-based mobility model has been used to test the performance of several popular lo-cation management schemes [39]. It has shown that the scheme that performs well in a random mobility model may not perform as well when deployed in actual systems.

2.5 LOCATION MANAGEMENT SCHEMES

2.5.1 Location Areas

The location areas approach has been used for location management in some first-genera-tion cellular systems and in many second-generation cellular systems such as GSM [30]. In the location areas approach, the service coverage area is partitioned into location areas, each consisting of several contiguous cells. The base station of each cell broadcasts the identification (ID) of location area to which the cell belongs. Therefore, a mobile station knows which location area it is in. Figure 2.5 illustrates a service area with three location areas.

A mobile station will update its location (i.e., location area) whenever it moves into a cell that belongs to a new location area. For example, when a mobile station moves from cell B to cell D in Figure 2.5, it will report its new location area because cell B and cell D are in different location areas. When an incoming call arrives for a mobile station, the cel-lular system will page all cells of the location area that was last reported by the mobile sta-tion.

The location areas approach is global in the sense that all mobile stations transmit their location updates in the same set of cells, and it is static in the sense that location areas are fixed [11, 33]. Furthermore, a mobile station located close to a location area boundary will perform more location updates because it moves back and forth between two location areas more often. In principle, a service area should be partitioned in such a way that both the location update cost and the paging cost are minimized. However, this is not possible

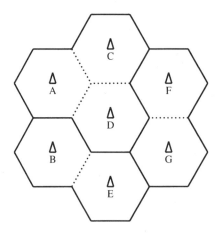

Figure 2.5 A service area with three location areas.

because there is trade-off between them. Let us consider two extreme cases. One is known as "always-update," in which each cell is a location area. Under always-update, a mobile station needs to update its location whenever it enters a new cell. Obviously, the cost of location update is very high, but there is no paging cost because the cellular system can just route an incoming call to the last reported cell without paging. The other is known as "never-update," in which the whole service area is a location area. Therefore there is no cost of location update. However, the paging cost is very high because the cellular system needs to page every cell in the service area to find out the cell in which the mobile is currently located so an incoming call can be routed to the base station of that cell.

Various approaches for location area planning in a city environment, the worst-case environment, are discussed in [25]. The simplest approach is the use of heuristic algorithms for approximating the optimal location area configuration. The approach collects a high number of location area configurations and picks up the best one. Although the approach does not guarantee the optimal location area configuration, the optimal solution can be approximated when the number of experiments is high. A more complex approach is based on area zones and highway topology. A city can have area zones such as the city center, suburbs, etc. Moreover, population movements between area zones are usually routed through main highways that connect the area zones. Naturally, the size of a location area is determined by the density of mobile subscribers, and the shape is determined by the highway topology. Location updates due to zig-zag movement can be avoided if location areas with overlapping borders are defined. The most complex approach is to create dynamic location area configurations based on the time-varying mobility and traffic conditions. For example, when the network detects a high-mobility and low-traffic time zone, it decides to reduce the number of location areas to reduce location updates. When the network detects an ordinary mobility and high-traffic time zone, it decides to increase the number of location areas to reduce paging. The above approaches are based on the mobility characteristics of the subscriber population.

The authors in [25] also discussed location area planning based on the mobility characteristics of each individual mobile subscriber or a group of mobile subscribers. Another per-user dynamic location area strategy has been proposed in [43]. Their strategy uses the subscriber incoming call arrival rate and mobility to dynamically determine the size of a subscriber's location area, and their analytical results show their strategy is better than static ones when call arrival rates are subscriber- or time-dependent.

In the classical location area strategy, the most recently visited location area ID is stored in a mobile station. Whenever the mobile station receives a new location area ID, it initiates a location update. In [19], the author has proposed a two location algorithm (TLA). The two location algorithm allows a mobile station to store the IDs of two most recently visited location areas. When a mobile station moves into a new location area, it checks to see if the new location is in the memory. If the new location is not found, the most recently visited location is kept and the other location is replaced by the new location. In this case, a location update is required to notify the cellular system of the change that has been made. If the new location is already in the memory, no location update is performed. When an incoming call arrives for a mobile station, two location areas are used to find the cell in which the mobile station is located. The order of the locations selected to locate the mobile station affects the performance of the algorithm. The possible strategies include random selection and the most recently visited location area first. This study shows that TLA significantly outperforms the classical location area strategy when the call-to-mobility ratio is low (i.e., the subscriber moves more frequently than calls are received) or when the location update cost is high. When the location update cost is low, the performance of TLA degrades if the variance of the residence times is small. It has been mentioned that TLA can be easily implemented by modifying the existing IS-41 system [14].

In [37], the authors have proposed a selective location update strategy. Their proposal is based on the location areas approach. The idea behind their proposal is that it is a waste of scarce wireless bandwidth to do a location update at a location in which a mobile station stays for a very short interval of time and has an extremely low probability of receiving a call. In their proposal, each subscriber updates only in certain preselected location areas, called update areas, based on his/her own mobility pattern. To determine update areas, a genetic algorithm is used to optimize the total location management cost, which is the weighted average of the location management costs in the individual location areas, which are functions of the subscriber's update strategy. The corresponding paging cost will be higher because the cellular system needs to track a mobile station down to the current location area from the last known location area. The tracking-down can be based on the location area interconnection graph in which the node set represents the location areas and the edge set represents the access paths (roads, highways, etc.) between pairs of location areas. Their experiments have shown that for low user location probability, low to moderate call arrival rate, and/or comparatively high update cost, skipping updating in several location areas leads to a minimization of the location management cost.

In [3], the authors have proposed a dynamic location area strategy that minimizes the cost of location update subject to a constraint on the number of cells in the location area. They have proposed and used the shortest distance mobility model for vehicular subscribers, instead of the independent and identically distributed model. They have proved the location update optimal problem is NP-complete [16], and have provided a heuristic greedy algorithm to generate an approximate solution, which consists of location areas of irregular shape. They have also shown that the optimal rectangular location update areas are very close approximations to the irregular areas generated by the greedy algorithm. To page a subscriber within a location area, the authors have considered the trade-off between the paging cost and the paging delay. They have proposed a dynamic selective paging strategy, which is to minimize the paging cost subject to a constraint on the paging delay [4]. They use the subscriber's mobility pattern and incoming call rate to partition the location area, then page the partition sequentially until the subscriber is found.

2.5.2 Reporting Cells

Another location management strategy is to use reporting cells or reporting centers [9, 18]. In the reporting cells approach, a subset of cells have been selected from all cells. Those selected cells are called reporting cells, and the other cells are called nonreporting cells. The base station of each cell broadcasts a signal to indicate whether the cell is a reporting cell or not. Therefore, a mobile station knows whether it is in a reporting cell or not. Figure 2.6 illustrates a service area with four reporting cells, marked by solid black triangles. For each reporting cell i, its vicinity is defined as the collection of all nonreporting cells that are reachable from cell i without crossing another reporting cell. The reporting cell belongs to its own vicinity. For example, the vicinity of cell C includes cells A, C, and F in Figure 2.6.

A mobile station will update its location (i.e., cell ID) whenever it moves into a new reporting cell. For example, when a mobile station moves from cell B to cell A then to cell C in Figure 2.6, it will report its new location because cell B and cell C are two different reporting cells. However, if a mobile station moves from cell B to cell A then move back into cell B, no location update is necessary. When an incoming call arrives for a mobile station, the cellular system will page all cells within the vicinity of the reporting cell that was last reported by the mobile station.

The reporting cells approach is also global in the sense that all mobile stations transmit their location updates in the same set of reporting cells, and it is static in the sense that reporting cells are fixed [11, 33]. The reporting cells approach also has two extreme cases, always-update and never-update. In the always-update case, every cell is selected as reporting. Therefore, a mobile station needs to update its location whenever it enters a new cell. As before, the cost of location update is very high, but there is no paging cost. In the never-update case, every cell is nonreporting. Therefore, there is no cost of location update. However, the paging cost is very high because the cellular system needs to page every cell in the service area to find out the cell in which the mobile station is currently located. The goal here is how to select a subset of reporting cells to minimize the total location management cost, which is the sum of the location update cost and the paging cost.

The idea of reporting centers/cells has been first proposed in [9]. In [9], the authors define the cost of paging based on the largest vicinity in the network because the cost of paging increases with the size of the vicinity in which the paging is performed. Associating with each reporting cell a weight that reflects the frequency that mobile subscribers enter into that cell, they define the cost of location update as the sum of the weights of all the reporting cells. The problem is to select a set of reporting centers to minimize both the size

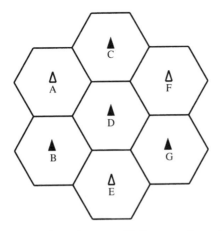

Figure 2.6   A service area with four reporting cells.

of the largest vicinity and the total weight of the reporting centers. Considering those two contradicting goals, they try to bound the size of the largest vicinity and to minimize the total weight of the reporting centers, which is reflected in their formal definition of the reporting centers problem. The reporting centers problem is defined on a mobility graph in which the vertex corresponds to a cell, and two vertices are connected by an edge if and only if the corresponding cells overlap. In addition, each vertex is assigned a weight to reflect the frequency that mobile subscribers update their locations at that cell. They have shown that for an arbitrary topology of the cellular network, finding the optimal set of reporting centers is an NP-complete problem [16]. For the case of unweighted vertices, they have presented an optimal solution for ring graphs and near optimal solutions for various types of grid graphs, including the topology of the hexagonal cellular network. For the case of weighted vertices, they have presented an optimal solution for tree graphs and a simple approximation algorithm for arbitrary graphs.

Although the results in [9] are excellent but theoretical, the results in [18] are more practical. In [18], the authors use the topology of a hexagonal cellular network with weighted vertices. They redefine the reporting centers problem, which is to select a subset of reporting cells to minimize the total signaling cost, which is the sum of both the location update and paging costs. A procedure has been given to find an approximate solution to the reporting centers problem. Simulations have shown that their scheme performs better than the always-update scheme and the never-update scheme.

A per-user dynamic reporting cell strategy has been proposed in [12]. Their strategy uses the direction information at the time of location update to derive optimal "asymmetric" reporting boundaries. In addition, they have used the elapsed time since the last update to choose the cell order in which a mobile station is paged in the event of an incoming call. Their ideas have been evaluated using a Markovian model over a linear topology. Although it is listed here as a variant of the reporting cells approach, it also can be considered as a variant of the distance-based approach.

2.5.3 Time-Based Location Update Strategies

The simplest time-based location update strategy is described in [11]. Given a time threshold T, a mobile station updates its location every T units of time. The corresponding paging strategy is also simple. Whenever there is an incoming call for a mobile station, the system will first search the cell the mobile station last reported, say i. If it is not found there, the system will search in cells $i + j$ and $i - j$, starting with $j = 1$ and continuing until the mobile station is found. Here a ring cellular topology is assumed. The time-based strategy is dynamic in the sense that the cells for reporting are not predefined. The time threshold T can be determined on a per-user basis. The advantage of this strategy is its simplicity. The disadvantage is its worst overall performance compared to the other dynamic location update strategies. This is mainly because a mobile station will keep updating its location regardless of its incoming call arrival probability and its mobility pattern.

In [1], the authors have proposed a time-based strategy in which a mobile station dynamically determines when to update its location based on its mobility pattern and the incoming call arrival probability. Whenever a mobile station enters a new cell, the mobile station needs to find out the number of cells that will be paged if an incoming call arrives and the resulting cost for the network to page the mobile station. The weighted paging cost at a given time slot is the paging cost multiplied by the call arrival probability during that time slot. A location update will be performed when the weighted paging cost exceeds the location update cost.

Another time-based strategy has been proposed in [32]. The strategy is to find the maximum amount of time to wait before the next location update such that the average cost of paging and location update is minimized. The author has shown that the timer-based strategy performs substantially better than a fixed location area-based strategy.

The location update scheme proposed in [44] is modified from the time-based approach. The time-based location update starts with setting the timer to a given time threshold t. When the timer expires, the mobile station reports its current location. It is hard to know the distance covered by a mobile station during the time period t, which makes the paging job hard. In order to make the paging job easier, the location update scheme in [44] keeps track of the maximal distance traveled since the last update. When it is time for location update, the mobile station reports both its current cell and the traveled maximal distance R. The location update occurs either when the timer expires or when the traveled maximal distance exceeds the last reported maximal distance. The paging operation is based on the last reported cell and the maximal distance R. The system will search all R rings surrounding the last reported cell. In order to keep the paging operation under the delay constraint, a distance threshold is imposed on the possible R a mobile station can report. The scheme is speed-adaptive. When the mobile station is decelerating, the reported maximal distance will become smaller and smaller. The distance becomes 0 when it stops at the destination, such as home. In this case, there is absolutely no location update or paging costs.

2.5.4 Movement-Based Location Update Strategies

In the movement-based location update strategy [11], each mobile station keeps a count that is initialized to zero after each location update. Whenever it crosses the boundary between two cells, it increases the count by one. The boundary crossing can be detected by comparing the IDs of those two cells. When the count reaches a predefined threshold, say M, the mobile station updates its location (i.e., cell ID), and resets the count to zero. The movement-based strategy guarantees that the mobile station is located in an area that is within a distance M from the last reported cell. This area is called the residing area of the mobile station. When an incoming call arrives for a mobile station, the cellular system will page all the cells within a distance M from the last reported cell. The movement-based strategy is dynamic, and the movement threshold M can be determined on a per-user basis, depending on his/her mobility pattern. The advantage of this strategy is its simplicity. The mobile station needs to keep a simple count of the number of cell boundaries crossed, and the boundary crossing can be checked easily.

Due to its simplicity, the movement-based location update strategy has been used to study the optimization of the total location update and paging cost. In [2], the authors have proposed selective paging combined with the movement-based location update. In the movement-based strategy, when an incoming call arrives, the cellular system will page all the cells within a distance of M, the movement threshold, from the last reported cell of the called mobile station. Here the paging is done within one polling cycle. However, if the system is allowed to have more than one polling cycle to find the called mobile station, the authors propose to apply a selective paging scheme in which the system partitions the residing area of the called mobile station into a number of subareas, and then polls each subarea one after the other until the called mobile station is found. Their result shows that if the paging delay is increased from one to three polling cycles, the total location update and paging cost is reduced to halfway between the maximum (when the paging delay is one) and the minimum (when the paging delay is not constrained). They also show that although increasing the allowable paging delay reduces the total cost, a large paging delay does not necessarily translate into a significant total cost reduction. The authors also introduce an analytical model for the proposed location tracking mechanism that captures the mobility and the incoming call arrival pattern of each mobile station. The analytical model can be used to study the effects of various parameters on the total location update and paging costs. It can also be used to determine the optimal location update movement threshold.

In [22], the authors have proposed a similar analytical model that formulates the costs of location update and paging in the movement-based location update scheme. Paging is assumed to be done in one polling cycle. The authors prove that the location update cost is a decreasing and convex function with respect to the movement threshold, and the paging cost is an increasing and convex function with respect to the threshold. Therefore, the total costs of location update and paging is a convex function. An efficient algorithm has been proposed to obtain the optimal threshold directly. It has been shown that the optimal threshold decreases as the call-to-mobility ratio increases, an increase in update cost (or a decrease in polling cost) may cause an increase in the optimal threshold, and the residence time variance has no significant effect on the optimal threshold.

An enhanced version of the movement-based location update with selective paging strategy has been proposed in [13]. The difference is that when a subscriber moves back to the last reported cell, the movement count will be reset to zero. The effect is that the total location update and paging cost will be reduced by about 10–15%, with a slightly increased paging cost.

In [42], the authors have proposed two velocity paging schemes that utilize semireal-time velocity information of individual mobile stations to dynamically compute a paging zone for an incoming call. The schemes can be used with either the movement- (or distance-) based location update. The basic velocity paging scheme uses the speed without the direction information at the time of last update, and the resulting paging zone is a smaller circular area. The advanced velocity paging scheme uses both speed and direction information at the time of last update, and the resulting paging zone is an even smaller sector. Their analysis and simulation have shown that their schemes lead to a significant cost reduction over the standard location area scheme.

2.5.5 Distance-Based Location Update Strategies

In the distance-based location update strategy [11], each mobile station keeps track of the distance between the current cell and the last reported cell. The distance here is defined in terms of cells. When the distance reaches a predefined threshold, say D, the mobile station updates its location (i.e., cell ID). The distance-based strategy guarantees that the mobile station is located in an area that is within a distance D from the last reported cell. This area is called the residing area of the mobile station. When an incoming call arrives for a mobile station, the cellular system will page all the cells within a distance of D from the last reported cell. The distance-based strategy is dynamic, and the distance threshold D can be determined on a per-user basis depending on his/her mobility pattern. In [11], the authors have shown that the distance-based strategy performs significantly better than the time-based and movement-based strategies in both memoryless and Markovian movement patterns. However, it has been claimed that it is hard to compute the distance between two cells or that it requires a lot of storage to maintain the distance information among all cells [2, 22]. In [28, 44], the authors have shown that if the cell IDs can be assigned properly, the distance between two cells can be computed very easily.

In [17], the authors have introduced a location management mechanism that incorporates the distance-based location update scheme with the selective paging mechanism that satisfies predefined delay requirements. In the distance-based strategy, when an incoming call arrives, the cellular system will page all the cells within a distance of D, the distance threshold, from the last reported cell of the called mobile station within one polling cycle. If the system is allowed to have more than one polling cycle to find the called mobile station, the authors propose to apply a selective paging scheme in which the system partitions the residing area of the called mobile station into a number of subareas, and then polls each subarea one after the other until the called mobile station is found. Their result shows that the reduction in the total cost of location update and paging is significant even for a maximum paging delay of two polling cycles. They also show that in most cases, the average total costs are very close to the minimum (when there is no paging delay bound) when a maximum paging delay of three polling cycles is used. The authors also have derived the average total location update and paging cost under given distance threshold and maximum delay constraint. Given this average total cost function, they are able to determine the optimal distance threshold using an iterative algorithm.

A similar distance-based location update strategy has been independently developed in [24]. In [24], the authors have derived the formula for the average total cost, which captures the trade-off between location update and paging costs. They have shown that the optimal choice can be determined by dynamic programming equations that have a unique solution. Solution of the dynamic programming equations for the one-dimensional Markov mobility model can be found using two approaches. One approach is to solve the equations explicitly; the other uses an iterative algorithm. It has been shown the iterative algorithm will converge geometrically to the unique solution.

In [21], the authors have introduced a predicative distance-based mobility management scheme that uses the Gauss–Markov mobility model to predict a mobile station's position at a future time from its last report of location and velocity. When a mobile station reaches some threshold distance d from the predicated location, it updates its location. That guarantees that the mobile station is located in an area that is within a distance d from the predicated location. When an incoming call arrives for the mobile station, the system is able to find the mobile station at and around its predicated location in descending probability until the mobile station is found. Their simulation results show that the predictive distance-based scheme performs as much as ten times better than the regular one.

In [41], the authors have introduced the look-ahead strategy for distance-based location tracking. In the regular distance-based strategy, the mobile station reports its current cell at location update. The look-ahead strategy uses the mobility model to find the optimal future cell and report that cell at location update. In this way, the rate of location update can be reduced without incurring extra paging cost. Their strategy is based on a multiscale, straight-oriented mobility model, referred to as "normal walk." Their analysis shows that the tracking cost for mobile subscribers with large mobility scales can be effectively reduced.

Recall that the distance information is not available in the current cellular network. However, in [28] the authors have pointed out that the distance between two cells can be computed easily if the cell address can be assigned systematically using the coordinate system proposed for the honeycomb network in [36]. The coordinate system has three axes, x, y, and z at a mutual angle of 120° between any two of them, as indicated in Figure 2.7. These three axes are, obviously, not independent. However, this redundancy greatly simplifies cell addressing. The origin is assigned $(0, 0, 0)$ as its address. A node will be assigned an address (a, b, c) if the node can be reached from the origin via cumulative a movements along the x axis, b movements along the y axis, and c movements along the z axis.

In [28], the authors first show that if (a, b, c) is an address for cell A, all possible addresses for cell A are of form $(a + d, b + d, c + d)$ for any integer d. Starting from the nonunique addressing, they propose two forms of unique cell addressing schemes, referred to as the shortest path form and the zero-positive form.

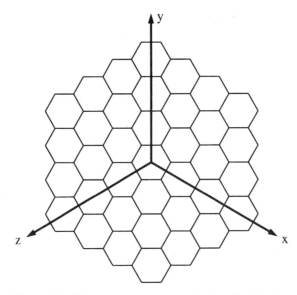

Figure 2.7 The x-y-z coordinate system for cell addressing.

A node address (a, b, c) is of the shortest path form if and only if the following conditions are satisfied:

1. At least one component is zero (that is, $abc = 0$)
2. Any two components cannot have the same sign (that is, $ab \leq 0$, $ac \leq 0$, and $bc \leq 0$)

A node address (a, b, c) is of the zero-positive form if and only if the following conditions are satisfied:

1. At least one component is zero (that is, $abc = 0$)
2. All components are nonnegative (that is, $a \geq 0$, $b \geq 0$, and $c \geq 0$)

If node A has (a, b, c) as the address of the shortest path form, the distance between node A and the origin is $|a| + |b| + |c|$. If node A has (a, b, c) as the address of the zero-positive form, the distance between node A and the origin is $\max(a, b, c)$. To compute the distance, i.e., the length of the shortest path, between two cells S and D, first compute the address difference between S and D. Assume that $D - S = (a, b, c)$, then distance $|D - S| = \min(|a - c| + |b - c|, |a - b| + |c - b|, |b - a| + |c - a|)$.

To compute the distance between two cells in a cellular network with nonuniformly distributed base stations, the authors in [15] have shown how to design an optimal virtual hexagonal networkwith a uniform virtual cell size such that each virtual cell will contain at most one base station. An address can be assigned to a base station based on the position of the base station in the virtual hexagonal network. Therefore the distance between two cells can also be computed as shown in the above paragraph.

2.5.6 Profile-Based Location Management Strategies

In the profile-based location management strategy, the cellular system keeps the individual subscriber's mobility pattern in his/her profile. The information will be used to save the costs of location update and paging. A profile-based strategy has been proposed in [40] to save the cost of location update. The idea behind his strategy is that the mobility pattern of a majority of subscribers can be foretold. In [40], the author has proposed two versions of the alternative strategy (alternative to the classic location area strategy). The first version uses only long-term statistics, whereas the second version uses short or medium events as well as the long-term statistics with increased memory. In the first version, a profile for each individual subscriber is created as follows. For each time period $[t_i, t_j)$, the system maintains a list of location areas, $(A_1, p_1), (A_2, p_2), \ldots, (A_k, p_k)$. Here A_f is the location area and p_f is the probability that the subscriber is located in A_f. It is assumed that the location areas are ordered by the probability from the highest to the lowest, that is, $p_1 > p_2 > \ldots > p_k$. If the subscriber moves within the recorded location areas, $A_1, A_2, \ldots, A_k$ during the corresponding period $[t_i, t_j)$, the subscriber does not need to perform location update. Otherwise, the subscriber reports its current location, and the system will track the subscriber as in the classical location area strategy. Therefore, location updates can be significantly reduced. When an incoming call arrives for the subscriber at time t_g (with $t_i \leq t_g < t_j$), the system will first page the subscriber over the location area A_1. If not found there, the system will page A_2. The process will repeat until the location area A_k. In order to save the paging cost, the author has introduced a second version. The second version takes advantage of the short or medium events and requires more memory. One is paging around the last connection point if the time difference is short enough. The other is reordering the set of location areas based on the short or medium events. Both analytical and simulation results show that the alternative strategy has better performance than the classical strategy in radio bandwidth utilization when the subscribers have high or medium predictable mobility patterns.

In [29], the authors have adopted a similar profile based location strategy and studied its performance more thoroughly. Specifically, they have studied the performance in terms of radio bandwidth, fixed network SS7 traffic, and the call set-up delay. After investigating the conditions under which the profile-based strategy performs better than the classical one, they have concluded that the profile-based strategy has the potential to simultaneously reduce the radio link bandwidth usage and fixed network SS7 load at the expense of a modest increase in paging delay.

Another profile-based location management algorithm has been proposed in [38]. The profile used in their algorithm contains the number of transitions a subscriber has made from cell to cell and the average duration of visits to each cell. The profile can be represented as a directed graph, where the nodes represent visited cells and the links represent transition between cells. The weight of link (a, b), $N_{a,b}$, is the number of transitions from cell a to cell b, and the weight of node b, T_b, is the average time of visits in cell b. The profile is built and stored in the mobile station. Their algorithm uses individual subscriber profiles to dynamically create location areas for individual subscribers and to determine the most probable paging area. A location update is triggered when a subscriber enters a cell that is not part of the previous location area. The mobile station first looks up the new cell in the subscriber profile. If it is not found, a classical location update is performed. If the subscriber profile contains the new cell, the list of its neighbors previously visited is read together with the number of times the subscriber has moved to those cells from the new cell. The average weight W of the links to neighboring cells is calculated. The cells corresponding to the links whose weight is greater than or equal to the average weight W are added to the new location area in decreasing link weight order. Once selected cells from the first ring of neighboring cells have been added to the personal location area, the above steps are repeated using the newly selected cells by decreasing link weight order. Those steps are repeated until the personal location area size has reached its limit or until no other cells are left for inclusion. During a location update, all T_n values for the cells of the new location area are transmitted to the network to be used for subsequent paging attempts. When an incoming call arrives for the subscriber, the average value of T_n among all cells in the current location area is calculated, and cells whose T_n value is greater or equal to the average form the paging area to be used in the first round of paging. If the first attempt is not successful, all cells in the location area are paged in the second round. They have built an activity based mobility model to test the proposed algorithm. Their test results show that their algorithm significantly outperforms the fixed location area algorithms in terms of total location management cost at a small cost of additional logic and memory in the mobile station and network.

2.5.7 Other Tracking Strategies

Topology-Based Strategies

Topology-based tracking strategies have been defined in [10]. A topology-based strategy is a strategy in which the current location area is dependent on the following: the current cell, the previous cell, and the location area that the subscriber belonged to while being in the previous cell. Here location areas can be overlapped. Whenever the current location area is different from the previous location area, a location update is needed. In fact, topology-based strategies are very general. Location areas, overlapping location areas, reporting cells (or centers), and distance-based strategies belong to the topology-based group. However, the time-based and movement-based strategies are not topology-based strategies.

LeZi-Update Strategy

In [8], the authors have proposed the LeZi-update strategy, in which the path of location areas a mobile station has visited will be reported instead of the location area. For every mobile station, the system and the mobile station will maintain an identical dictionary of paths, which is initially empty. A path can be reported if and only if there is no such path in the dictionary. This guarantees that every proper prefix of the reported path is in the dictionary. The path to be reported can be encoded as the index of the maximal proper prefix plus the last location area. This will dramatically reduce the location update cost. The dictionary is stored as a "trie," which can be considered as the profile. When an incoming call arrives, the system will look up the trie of the called mobile station and compute the blended probability of every possible location area based on the history. Those location areas can be paged based on the blended probability from the highest to the lowest.

Load-Sensitive Approaches

Recently, load-sensitive approaches have been proposed. The idea behind these approaches is that nonutilized system resources can be used to improve the system knowledge about the subscriber location. In [23], the authors have proposed an active tracking strategy in which nonutilized system resources are used for queries. A query is applied to each cell by the system when the system detects that the load on the local control channel drops below a predefined threshold. A query is similar to paging. However, paging is conducted when a call arrives to the subscriber and its objective is to set up a call while a query is initiated when there are nonutilized system resources; its objective is only to increase the knowledge about the subscriber location. Queries are initiated to complement location updates, not to replace them. Queries are virtually cost-free, yet have the benefit of reducing the cost of future paging.

In [27], the authors have proposed a load adaptive threshold scheme (LATS for short) in which nonutilized system resources are used to increase the location update activity. The system determines a location update threshold level based on the load for each cell and announces it to the subscribers. Each subscriber computes its own location update priority and performs a location update when its priority exceeds the announced threshold level. Therefore, whenever the local cell load on the cell is low, the location update activity will increase. That will reduce the cost of future paging. The authors' analysis shows that the LATS strategy offers a significant improvement not only at lightly loaded cells, but also at heavily loaded cells. Both active tracking and LATS can be used in addition to any other dynamic tracking strategy.

In [26], the author has proposed an interactive tracking strategy in which the rate of location update is based on the dynamic activity of an individual subscriber as well as the local system activity. Both the system and the mobile station will keep a look-up table $(T_1, d_1), (T_2, d_2), \ldots, (T_k, d_k)$. Here T_i is a time threshold and d_i is a distance threshold. In addition, $T_1 \geq T_2 \geq \ldots \geq T_k$ and $d_1 \leq d_2 \leq \ldots \leq d_k$. The look-up table specifies that a mobile station that travels within a smaller area should report its position less frequently. Starting from the last location update, the mobile station will track the traveled distance d, in cells, and the elapsed time t. Whenever the traveled distance d reaches d_i and the elapsed time t reaches T_i, the mobile station performs its location update. If an incoming call arrives at time t for the subscriber, the system checks the look-up table, and performs the following calculations. If $t \geq T_1$, the area to be searched has a radius of d_1, and if $T_{i-1} > t > T_i$, the area to be searched has a radius of d_i. A mobile station may maintain several look-up tables for different locations and load conditions. The network determines and announces which look-up table is to be used. It has been shown that the interactive tracking strategy is superior to the existing tracking methods used in the current system, and performs better than the distance-based strategy, which is considered the most efficient tracking strategy.

2.6 SUMMARY

Radio can be used to keep in touch with people on the move. The cellular network was introduced to reuse the radio frequency such that more people can take advantage of wireless communications. Location management is one of the most important issues in cellular networks. It deals with how to track subscribers on the move. This chapter has surveyed recent research on location management in cellular networks.

Location management involves two operations: location update and paging. Paging is performed by the network to find the cell in which a mobile station is located so the incoming call for the mobile station can be routed to the corresponding base station. Location update is done by the mobile station to let the network know its current location. There are three metrics involved with location management: location update cost, paging cost, and paging delay.

Network topology, call arrival probability, and mobility patterns have a great impact on the performance of a location management scheme. This chapter has presented some assumptions that are commonly used to evaluate a location management scheme. Finally, this chapter has surveyed a number of papers on location management in cellular networks that have been published recently in major journals and conference proceedings.

ACKNOWLEDGMENTS

The author would like to thank Guangbin Fan for drawing the figures in this chapter. The author would also like to thank Paul Schwartz of Ampersand Grapics Ltd. and Susan Vrbsky of the University of Alabama for suggesting changes that improved the presentation.

REFERENCES

1. I. F. Akyildiz and J. S. M. Ho, Dynamic mobile user location update for wireless PCS networks, *Wireless Networks, 1,* 187–196, 1995.
2. I. F. Akyildiz, J. S. M. Ho, and Y.-B. Lin, Movement-based location update and selective paging for PCS networks, *IEEE/ACM Transactions on Networking, 4,* 4, 629–638, 1996.
3. A. Abutaleb and V. O. K. Li, Location update optimization in personal communication systems, *Wireless Networks, 3,* 205–216, 1997.
4. A. Abutaleb and V. O. K. Li, Paging strategy optimization in personal communication systems, *Wireless Networks, 3,* 195–204, 1997.
5. I. F. Akyildiz, Y.-B. Lin, W.-R. Lai, and R.-J. Chen, A new random walk model for PCS networks, *IEEE Journal on Selected Areas in Communications, 18,* 7, 1254–1260, 2000.
6. U. Black, *Mobile and Wireless Networks,* Upper Saddle River, NJ: Prentice Hall, 1996.
7. U. Black, *Second Generation Mobile and Wireless Networks,* Upper Saddle River, NJ: Prentice Hall, 1999.
8. A. Bhattacharya and S. K. Das, *LeZi-Update: An Information-Theoretic Approach to Track Mobile Users in PCS Networks,* MOBICOM, Seattle, 1999, pp. 1–12.
9. A. Bar-Noy and I. Kessler, Tracking mobile users in wireless communications networks, *IEEE Transactions on Information Theory, 39,* 6, 1877–1886, 1993.
10. A. Bar-Noy, I. Kessler, and M. Naghshineh, Topology-based tracking strategies for personal communication networks, *Mobile Networks and Applications, 1,* 49–56, 1996.
11. A. Bar-Noy, I. Kessler, and M. Sidi, Mobile users: To update or not to update? *Wireless Networks, 1,* 175–185, 1995.
12. Y. Birk and Y. Nachman, Using direction and elapsed-time information to reduce the wireless cost of locating mobile units in cellular networks, *Wireless Networks, 1,* 403–412, 1995.
13. V. Casares-Giner and J. Mataix-Oltra, On movement-based mobility tracking strategy—An enhanced version, *IEEE Communications Letters, 2,* 2, 45–47, 1998.
14. EIA/TIA, *Cellular Radio-Telecommunications Intersystems Operations* (Revision C), Technical Report IS–41, EIA/TIA, 1995.
15. G. Fan and J. Zhang, Virtual cellular networks for non-uniformly distributed base stations, in *Proceedings of the 30th Annual International Conference on Parallel Processing,* Valencia, Spain, September 2001.

16. M. R. Garey and D. S. Johnson, *Computers and Intractability: A Guide to the Theory of NP-Completeness,* San Francisco: W. H. Freeman, 1979.

17. J. S. M. Ho and I. F. Akyildiz, Mobile user location update and paging under delay constraints, *Wireless Networks, 1,* 413–425, 1995.

18. A. Hac and X. Zhou, Locating strategies for personal communication networks: A novel tracking strategy, *IEEE Journal on Selected Areas in Communications, 15,* 8, 1425–1436, 1997.

19. Y.-B. Lin, Reducing location update cost in a PCS network, *IEEE/ACM Transactions on Networking, 5,* 1, 25–33, 1997.

20. Y.-B. Lin and I. Chlamtac, *Wireless and Mobile Network Architectures,* New York: Wiley, 2001.

21. B. Liang and Z. J. Haas, *Predictive Distance-Based Mobility Management for PCS Networks,* INFOCOM, New York, 1999.

22. J. Li, H. Kameda and K. Li, Optimal dynamic mobility management for PCS networks, *IEEE/ACM Transactions on Networking, 8,* 3, 319–327, 2000.

23. H. Levy and Z. Naor, Active tracking: Locating mobile users in personal communication service networks, *Wireless Networks, 5,* 467–477, 1999.

24. U. Madhow, M. L. M. Honig, and K. Steiglitz, Optimization of wireless resources for personal communications mobility tracking *IEEE/ACM Transactions on Networking, 3,* 6, 698–707, 1995.

25. J. G. Markoulidakis, G. L. Lyberopoulos, D. F. Tsirkas, and E. D. Sykas, Evaluation of location area planning scenarios in future mobile telecommunication systems, *Wireless Networks, 1,* 17–25, 1995.

26. Z. Naor, *Tracking Mobile Users with Uncertain Parameters,* MOBICOM, Boston, 2000.

27. Z. Naor and H. Levy, LATS: A load-adaptive threshold scheme for tracking mobile users, *IEEE/ACM Transactions on Networking, 7,* 6, 808–817, 1999.

28. F. G. Nocetti, I. Stojmenovic, and J. Zhang, Addressing and routing in hexagonal networks with applications for location update and connection rerouting in cellular networks, submitted for publication.

29. G. P. Pollini and C.-L. I, A profile-based location strategy and its performance, *IEEE Journal on Selected Areas in Communications, 15,* 8, 1415–1424, 1997.

30. M. Rahnema, Overview of the GSM systems and protocol architecture, *IEEE Communications Magazine, 43,* 92–100, 1993.

31. T. S. Rappaport, *Wireless Communications—Principles and Practice,* Upper Saddle River, NJ: Prentice Hall, 1996.

32. C. Rose, Minimizing the average cost of paging and registration: A timer-based method, *Wireless Networks, 2,* 109–116, 1996.

33. S. Ramanathan and M. Steenstrup, A survey of routing techniques for mobile communication networks, *Mobile Networks and Applications, 1,* 89–104, 1996.

34. C. Rose and R. Yates, Minimizing the average cost of paging under delay constraints, *Wireless Networks, 1,* 211–219, 1995.

35. J. Schiller, *Wireless Communications,* Boston: Addison-Wesley, 2000.

36. I. Stojmenovic, Honeycomb networks: Topological properties and communication algorithms, *IEEE Transactions on Parallel and Distributed Systems, 8,* 10, 1036–1042, 1997.

37. S. K. Sen, A. Bhattacharya, and S. K. Das, A selective location update strategy for PCS users, *Wireless Networks, 5,* 313–326, 1999.

38. J. Scourias and T. Knuz, A Dynamic individualized location management algorithm, in *Pro-*

ceedings 8th IEEE International Symposium on Personal, Indoor, and Mobile Radio Communications, Helsinki, Finland, September 1997, pp. 1004–1008.

39. A. A. Siddiqi and T. Kunz, *The Peril of Evaluating Location Management Proposals through Simulations,* Dial M, Seattle, 1999, pp. 78–85.

40. S. Tabbane, An alternative strategy for location tracking, *IEEE Journal on Selected Areas in Communications, 13,* 5, 880–892, 1995.

41. I-F. Tsai and R.-H. Jan, The look ahead strategy for distance-based location tracking in wireless cellular networks, *ACM Mobile Computing and Communications Review, 3,* 4, 27–38, 1999.

42. G. Wan and E. Lin, Cost reduction in location management using semi-realtime movement information, *Wireless Networks, 5,* 245–256, 1999.

43. H. Xie, S. Tabbane, and D. J. Goodman, Dynamic location area management and performance analysis, in *Proceedings 43rd IEEE Vehicular Technology Conference,* Secaucus, NJ, May 1993, pp. 536–539.

44. J. Zhang, A Cell ID Assignment scheme and its applications, in *Proceedings ICPP Workshop on Wireless Networks and Mobile Computing,* Toronto, Canada, August 2000, pp. 507–512.

CHAPTER 3

Heuristics for Solving Fixed-Channel Assignment Problems

HARILAOS G. SANDALIDIS and PETER STAVROULAKIS

Telecommunication Systems Institute, Chania, Crete, Greece

3.1 INTRODUCTION

The tremendous growth of the mobile users' population coupled with the bandwidth requirements of new cellular services is in contrast to the limited spectrum resources that have been allocated for mobile communications. The objective of channel allocation is to assign a required number of channels to each cell such that efficient frequency spectrum utilization is provided and interference effects are minimized. A fixed-channel assignment problem models the task of assigning radio spectrum to a set of transmitters on a permanent basis. The formulation of this problem as a combinatorial one in the beginning of the 1980s led a number of computer scientists and operations research scientists to try and find optimal solutions. Heuristic techniques can give near-optimal solutions at a reasonable computational cost for algorithmically complex or time-consuming problems such as channel assignment. An overview of the most basic heuristic fixed-channel assignment schemes in the literature is the subject of this study.

3.2 RESOURCE MANAGEMENT TASKS

Cellular radio systems rely on a subsequent allocation and reuse of channels throughout a coverage region. Each cell is allocated a group of radio channels. Neighboring cells are given channel groups that contain completely different channels. By limiting the coverage area within the boundaries of a cell, the same group of channels may be used to cover different cells that are separated from one another by some distance.

Cellular mobile communication systems are characterized by their high degree of capacity. Consequently they have to serve the maximum possible number of calls, though the number of channels per cell is limited. On the other hand, cells in the same cluster must not use the same channel because of the increased possibility of various kinds of interference that appear mainly during the busy hours of the system. Hence the use of techniques that are capable of ensuring that the spectrum assigned for use in mobile communications will be optimally utilized is gaining ever-increasing importance. This makes the

Handbook of Wireless Networks and Mobile Computing, Edited by Ivan Stojmenović.

ISBN 0-471-41902-8 © 2002 John Wiley & Sons, Inc.

tasks of resource management more and more crucial [44]. Some of the important objectives of resource management are the minimization of the interference level and handoffs as well as the adaptation to varying traffic and interference scenarios. Due to the time- and space-varying nature of the cellular system, the radio resource management tasks need to adapt to factors such as interference, traffic, and propagation environment. Some of the radio resource management tasks performed by cellular systems include admission control, power control, handoff, and channel assignment [58]:

- *Frequency management and channel assignment.* The proper management of frequencies is very important in the development of a good communications plan because the available electromagnetic spectrum is highly congested. During the planning stage, if proper care is not taken in selecting frequencies, the frequencies chosen may interfere with each other. Channel assignment is the process that allocates calls to the channels of a cellular system. The main focus on research concerning channel assignment is to find strategies that give maximal channel reuse without violating the interference constraints so that blocking is minimal.

- *Handoff.* Handoff is the mechanism that transfers an ongoing call from one base station (BS) to another as a user moves through the coverage area of a cellular system. Therefore, it must be fast and efficient to prevent the quality of service from degenerating to an unacceptable level. This is probably the most sensitive aspect of the mobility provision and is an essential element of cellular communications, since the process chosen for handoff management will affect other mobility issues.

- *Admission control.* Whenever a new call arrives (or a request for service or a handoff), the radio resource management system has to decide if this particular call may be allowed into the system. An algorithm making these decisions is called an admission control algorithm and prevents the system from being overloaded. New and continuing calls can be treated differently. For example, handoffs may be prioritized, new calls may be queued, etc.

- *Power control.* In cellular networks, it is desirable to maintain bit error rates above a chosen minimum. This would require the carrier to interference ratio of the radio links be maintained above a corresponding minimum value for the network. Power control is a specific resource management process that performs this task.

It is evident that an integrated radio resource management scheme can make necessary trade-offs between the individual goals of these tasks to obtain better performance and increase system capacity within specified quality constraints. However, a combination of individual radio resource management tasks is also possible. For example, handoff and channel assignment tasks, or power control assisted admission schemes can be combined to provide interesting results [55].

3.3 INTERFERENCE IN CELLULAR SYSTEMS

The major factor that determines the number of channels with a predetermined quality is the level of received signal quality that can be achieved in each channel. This level strongly depends on the interference effects. Some possible sources of interference may be another carrier in the same cell, a call in progress in a neighboring cell, other base stations operating in the same frequency band, or any noncellular system that radiates in the same frequency band. Interference on voice channels causes crosstalk—the subscriber hears interference in the background due to another call. On control channels, interference leads to missed calls and blocked calls. Interference is more severe in urban areas, due to industrial interference and a large number of base stations and mobiles in the proximity. It has been recognized as a major bottleneck in increasing capacity. Interference to a channel that serves a particular call occurs mainly when a user in an adjacent cell uses the same channel (cochannel interference), a user in the same region uses an adjacent channel (cosite interference), or a user in an adjacent region uses an adjacent channel (adjacent channel interference) [28].

3.3.1 Cochannel Interference

Frequency reuse increases the system's spectrum efficiency, but interference due to the common use of the same channel may occur if the system is not properly planned. This kind of interference is called cochannel interference. Cochannel interference is the most critical of all interferences that occur in cellular radio; it depends on cellular traffic. The possibility of cochannel interference appearing is greater in the busy hours of a cellular system. The total suppression of cochannel interference is achieved by not using the frequency reuse concept, which is contradictory to the whole idea of the cellular radio. Thus, in order to obtain a tolerable value of cochannel interference, the system planner has to take into account the reuse distance D.

When the size of each cell in a cellular system is roughly the same, cochannel interference is independent of the transmitted power and becomes a function of the radius of the cell R and the reuse distance D. The factor

$$Q = \frac{D}{R} = \sqrt{3 \cdot K} \tag{3.1}$$

is called the cochannel interference reduction factor or reuse factor and is the measure of cochannel interference. The Q factor determines spectral efficiency within a cell and is related to the number of cells in the cluster K.

Assuming that all the cells transmit the same power, the frequency reuse distance D can be increased by increasing K. One could expect that by making K as large as possible, all problems concerning cochannel interference could be solved. An advantage of large clusters is the fact that the interference from cochannel cells decreases because the distance between the cochannel cells also increases with the increase in cluster size. On the other hand, the available bandwidth and therefore the available number of channels is fixed. When K is large, the number of channels per cell is small. That causes spectrum inefficiency.

3.3.2 Cosite and Adjacent Channel Interference

In addition to cochannel interference, a second source of noise is the interference between two adjacent channels of the same (cosite interference) or adjacent cells (adjacent channel interference). It should be noted that the adjacent channel here is not the close neighboring channel in a strict communication sense, but rather the nearest assigned channel in the same cell and can be several channels apart.

Cosite and adjacent channel interference result from equipment limitations, mainly from imperfect receiver filters that allow nearby frequencies to leak into the passband. The problem can be particularly serious if one adjacent channel user is transmitting in close range to a receiver that is attempting to receive a weaker signal using a neighboring channel. Several techniques can be used in order to solve this problem. The total frequency spectrum is usually split into two halves so that the reverse channels that compose the up-link (mobile to base station) and the forward channels that compose the down-link (base station to mobile) can be separated by half of the spectrum. If other services can be inserted between the two halves, then a greater frequency separation can be attained [19].

Cosite and adjacent channel interference can also be minimized through careful channel assignments. By keeping the frequency separation between each channel in a given cell as large as possible, these types of interference may be reduced considerably. Some designers also prevent a source of adjacent channel interference by avoiding the use of adjacent channels in geographically adjacent cell sites. This strategy, however, is dependent on the cellular pattern. For instance, if a seven-cell cluster is chosen, adjacent channels are inevitably assigned to adjacent cells.

3.3.3   Intermodulation

Intermodulation distortion (IMD) is a nonlinear phenomenon that occurs when some multiplexed frequency channels go through a nonlinear device such as a power amplifier. The nonlinear characteristic of such a device generates several undesired cross-modulation terms, mainly at frequencies $2f_i - f_j$, $3f_i - 2f_j$, $f_i + f_j - f_k$ and $2f_i + f_j - 2f_k$ where i, j, and k range over N, the total number of frequencies present. These terms may fall inside the desired band of interest and therefore may affect the carrier-to-noise ratio performance links used in cellular systems. Equal channel spacing may create problems in the sense that it increases the number of intermodulation distortion terms that fall on the desired frequency channels. Therefore the number of intermodulation distortion terms are affected by the channel assignment scheme used [26].

3.4   FREQUENCY MANAGEMENT AND CHANNEL ASSIGNMENT ISSUES

Efficient spectrum resource management is of paramount importance due to increasing demands of new services, rapid and unbalanced growth of radio traffic, and other factors. A given radio spectrum (bandwidth) dedicated for cellular communications can be divided into a set of disjoint and noninterfering radio channels. Techniques such as frequency, time, and code division can be used in order to divide the radio spectrum. In frequency division, the spectrum is divided into frequency bands. In time division, the usage of the channel is divided into time slots that are disjoint time periods. Finally, in code division, the channel separation is achieved by using different modulation codes.

Moreover, other techniques based on the combination of the above methods can be used [28].

Since the radio spectrum is finite in mobile radio systems, the most significant challenge is to use the radio-frequency spectrum as efficiently as possible. Geographic location is an important factor in the application of the frequency reuse concept in mobile cellular technology to increase spectrum efficiency. The techniques for increasing the frequency spectrum can be classified as [37]:

- Increase the number of radio channels
- Improve spatial frequency spectrum reuse
- Use proper frequency management and channel assignment techniques
- Improve spectrum efficiency in time
- Reduce the load of invalid calls (call forwarding, queuing, etc.)

The function of frequency management is to divide the total number of available channels into subsets that can be assigned to each cell either in a fixed fashion or dynamically. The terms frequency management and channel assignment are often confused. Frequency management refers to designating set-up channels and voice channels, numbering the channels, and grouping the voice channels into subsets (done by each system according to its preference). Channel assignment has to do with the allocation of specific channels to cell sites and mobile units. A fixed channel set that consists of one or more subsets is assigned to a cell site on a long-term basis. During a call, a specific channel is assigned to a mobile unit on a short-term basis [37].

Frequency planning is therefore one of the most challenging tasks in designing a cellular mobile network. An accurate radio planning tool is essential for calculating predicted signal strength coverage and interference levels and satisfying the overall grade of service. The allocation of frequency channels to cells in a cellular network is a critical element of the design process since it affects the two major metrics of any cellular network: capacity and quality of service. The basic input data of a good frequency planning algorithm are the numbers of required channels for each cell and interference probabilities between each pair of cells using the same (cochannel interference) or adjacent channels (adjacent channel interference) of a certain band. This data is usually provided by measurements or by simulation of radio wave propagation in the areas of interest.

Different benefit criteria should be taken into account when allocating channels to base stations. First of all, the interference between each pair of cells must not exceed a certain maximum threshold. This can be expressed using a proper compatibility matrix, which is a squared matrix that has as many rows or columns as cells in the system. The element values of the matrix represent the minimum allowable distance between channels in two cells. Channels should be allocated as to satisfy all traffic requirements per cell while observing the compatibility constraints.

The assumptions regarding interference require the use of a large margin in the minimum acceptable signal-to-interference ratio in order to cope with the variations in the desired received and interference signals on both links. These signal variations are basically due to:

- *Propagation conditions,* due to path loss and fading appearance.
- *User mobility*—when the mobile approaches the cell boundary, the cochannel interference at the mobile increases.
- *Traffic load*—if more users share the same channel, cochannel interference in the system increases.

Moreover, it is important to spread channels within individual cells as far as possible. Careful design in order to avoid the appearance of intermodulation effects should also take place. Frequencies should be established such that no significant intermodulation products from any combination of cosited transmitter frequencies fall on any other channel in use in that vicinity. This usually implies third- and fifth-order compatibility. In densely populated areas, this strategy is difficult to implement completely, but in order to avoid unwanted mobile receiver outputs resulting from interference, implementation of at least third-order compatible frequency plans is highly desirable.

3.5 CHANNEL ASSIGNMENT

Channel assignment is a fundamental task of resource management that increases the fidelity, capacity, and quality of service of cellular systems by assigning the required number of channels to each cellular region in such a way that both efficient frequency spectrum utilization is provided and interference effects are eliminated. The channel allocation strategy can be seen as a method of assigning available channels to calls originating in the cells. If the strategy is unable to assign a channel, the call is blocked. The basic goal to be achieved by channel allocation techniques under the prism of the rapidly growing demand for cellular mobile services is to efficiently utilize the available spectrum so as to achieve optimum system performance.

The main focus on research concerning channel assignment is to find strategies that give maximal channel reuse without violating the constraints so that blocking is minimal. Constraints can be classified into three categories [14]:

1. The frequency constraint specifies the number of available frequencies (channels) in the radio spectrum. This constraint is imposed by national and international regulations.
2. The traffic constraints specify the minimum number of frequencies required by each station to serve a geographic area. These constraints are empirically determined by the telecommunications operators.
3. The interference constraints are further classified as:
   - *The cochannel constraint*—the same channel cannot be assigned to certain pairs of radio cells simultaneously.
   - *The adjacent channel constraint*—frequencies adjacent in the frequency domain cannot be assigned to adjacent radio cells simultaneously.
   - *The cosite constraint*—any pair of channels assigned to a radio cell must occupy a certain distance in the frequency domain.

Constraints in the frequency assignment problem are therefore multiple and some of them are conflicting. The most severe limitation is the frequency constraint. This constraint imposes a high degree of frequency reuse by the stations and consequently increases the difficulty of satisfying the interference constraints.

Most channel assignment schemes are quite detailed and founded largely on ad-hoc principles. Moreover the channel assignment schemes are evaluated using different benchmarks following extended simulations with a variety of assumptions regarding the mobile radio environment. Some of these assumptions might be the cellular topology, the different choice of reuse factors, the use of different traffic patterns, the incorporation of propagation factors, the use of mobility, etc. The combination of these factors makes a systematic comparison of the various channel allocation methods quite infeasible and a true decision of the best scheme is difficult to attain.

Roughly speaking, channel assignment is generally classified into fixed and dynamic assignment. In fixed channel assignment (FCA), channels are nominally assigned to cells in advance according to the predetermined estimated traffic intensity. In dynamic channel assignment (DCA), channels are assigned dynamically as calls arrive. The latter method makes cellular systems more efficient, particularly if the traffic distribution is unknown or changes with time, but has the disadvantage of requiring more complex control and is generally time consuming. Various extensions or combinations of the above two schemes have been discussed in the literature. The most basic ones are hybrid channel assignment (HCA) and borrowing channel assignment (BCA). In HCA, the set of the channels of the cellular system is divided into two subsets; one uses FCA and the other DCA. In the BCA scheme, the channel assignment is initially fixed. If there are incoming calls for a cell whose channels are all occupied, the cell borrows channels from its neighboring cells and thus call blocking is prevented.

FCA is the simplest off-line allocation scheme. It has been used as the primary allocation technique for first- and second-generation cellular systems and outperforms DCA and other schemes under uniform and heavy traffic loads. Moreover FCA problems can serve as bounds for the performance of HCA and DCA schemes. For these reasons, FCA constitutes a significant research subject for the operations research, artificial intelligence, and mobile communication fields [34].

3.6 FIXED-CHANNEL ASSIGNMENT PROBLEM

A lot of existing systems are operating with fixed-channel assignment, in which channels are permanently assigned to cells for exclusive use. Cells that have the same reuse distance can use the same channels. This uniform channel distribution is efficient if the traffic distribution of the system is also uniform. However, for nonuniform traffic environments, a uniform channel distribution results in poor channel utilization. Cells in which traffic load is high may not have enough channels to serve calls, whereas spare channels may exist in some other cells with low traffic conditions. It is, therefore, appropriate to use nonuniform channel distribution. In this case, the number of nominal channels assigned to each cell depends on the expected traffic profile in that cell. Hence, heavily loaded cells are assigned more channels than lightly loaded ones.

FCA is also shown to be sensitive to temporal and spatial traffic variations and hence is not able to attain a high degree of channel efficiency. However, this scheme is very simple in design and is very efficient for stationary, heavy traffic loads. In fact, the greatest advantage of FCA is the low call service time. Due to the already assigned channels among cells, the process of finding a channel to serve a call does not require elaborate control. Hence, calls do not have to wait and are either served or blocked.

In order to achieve better performance in mobile networks operating with the FCA, proper frequency planning is required. The available frequency band is usually partitioned into a set of channels having the same bandwidth of frequencies, and channels are numbered from 1 to a given maximum N. In fact, a mobile user needs two channels—the first one for the mobile-to-base station link and the second for the base-to-mobile station link. However, as these two channels are assigned together, a lot of studies consider a channel to contain only one link.

A cellular network can be described by a weighted graph in which the nodes correspond to the cells or the transmitters and the edges join nodes that correspond to adjacent cells or transmitters in the network. The weight of the edges (0, 1, 2) represents the separation that the frequencies corresponding to the cells or transmitters should have between each other in order to prevent interference. Hence, the frequency assignment problem (FAP) can be treated as a graph coloring problem in which the main task is to assign colors (frequencies) to the nodes so that the absolute difference between the colors of any pair of nodes is at least the weight of the edge joining them.

The interference constraints in a cell network are usually described by an $N \times N$ symmetric matrix called compatibility matrix C. The compatibility matrix is a matrix whose elements give the separation that should exist between the channels corresponding to the cell row and the cell column. This separation is represented by a natural number with values 0, 1, 2, etc. An element equal to 0 means that the two cells do not interfere and therefore the same channel may be reused. In this case, mobile stations located in each cell can share the same channel. An element equal to 1 means that the transmitters located in these cells must use channels that maintain a minimum separation of one unit. That is, cochannel interference between the two transmitters is unacceptable but interference of adjacent channels is allowed. This situation corresponds to neighboring cells . An element equal to 2 or higher means that these cells must use channels separated by at least two units. This is usually required for channels in the same cell, depending on the base station equipment [1].

Based on the previous comments, a general formulation of a $N \times N$ compatibility matrix C is:

$$C = \begin{bmatrix} c_{11} & c_{12} & \cdots & c_{1N} \\ c_{21} & c_{22} & \cdots & c_{2N} \\ \vdots & \vdots & \ddots & \vdots \\ c_{N1} & c_{N2} & \cdots & c_{NN} \end{bmatrix} \tag{3.2}$$

where if $c_{ij} = c_{jj}$ there is cosite constraint
$\qquad c_{ij} = 0$ there is no constraint in channel reuse
$\qquad c_{ij} = 1$ there is cochannel constraint
$\qquad c_{ij} \geq 2$ there is adjacent channel constraint

When planning real radio networks, the channel assignment problem may involve a large number of cells. This implies a large compatibility matrix. However, in general, the elements of the compatibility matrix can take only a very limited number of values, depending on the compatibility constraints considered in the specific problem. The criteria used to obtain the compatibility matrix may vary according to the use of certain features of the system such as dynamic power control, discontinuous transmission, and frequency hopping, which are characteristic of GSM networks. The compatibility matrix has to be constructed with extreme precision so that it reflects the real network as closely as possible. A badly estimated constraint (0 instead of 1) may cause interference if the solution involves the reuse of the same channel in affected cells, causing an obvious degradation of service. The compatibility matrix is therefore the most critical parameter for solving the FAP problem. When only the cochannel constraint is considered, the compatibility matrix is a binary matrix [1, 20].

The channel requirements for each cell in an N-cell radio network are described by a N-element requirement vector with nonnegative integer elements. A requirement vector indicates the number of frequencies to be used in each cell. This variable depends on the population index, the total number of subscribers, the average traffic generated at peak time, and the grade of service of the network. Usually, the network statistics kept by the base stations and the network management system are used to estimate the requirement vector. When there is no existing cellular network in an area, the expected traffic is estimated using proper predictions. The value of this requirement in a real system is generally a function of time due to the new calls, call termination, and transfer of existing calls between adjacent cells (handoffs). However, in fixed-channel assignment problems, the requirement vector is assumed to be constant with time [1].

By taking the above formulation into account, various combinatorial optimization problems for various criteria occur. Combinatorial problems are optimization problems that minimize a cost or energy function whose variables have two possible values (usually 0 and 1). As previously mentioned, channel assignment is equivalent to the graph coloring problem, which belongs to the class of NP-complete problems. For this kind of problem, there is no known algorithm that can generate a guaranteed optimal solution in an execution time that may be expressed as a finite polynomial of the problem dimension. Different optimization versions of the FAP could be developed such as maximizing all the traffic, minimizing the number of frequencies used, and minimizing the interference over the network. The most basic combinatorial formulations discussed in the literature are the following [34]:

- *Minimum order FAP (MO-FAP)*. Assign channels so that no interference occurs and minimize the number of different frequencies used.

- *Minimum span FAP (MS-FAP)*. Assign channels so that no interference occurs and minimize the span (difference between the maximum and minimum frequency used).

- *Minimum (total) interference FAP (MI-FAP)*. Assign channels from a limited channel set and minimize the total sum of weighted interference.

- *Minimum blocking FAP (MB-FAP)*. Assign channels so that no interference occurs and minimize the overall blocking probability of the cellular network.

An unsophisticated approach to solving an instance of a combinatorial NP-complete problem is simply to find all the feasible solutions of a given problem, evaluate their objective functions, and pick the best. However, it is obvious that this approach of complete enumeration is rather inefficient. Although it is possible, in principle, to solve any problem in this way, in practice it is not, because of the huge number of possible solutions to any problem of reasonable size. In case of NP-complete problems, it has been shown that the time required to find exact solutions increases exponentially with the size of the problem [47]. Heuristic methods have been suggested in the literature as an alternative approach to handling such problems.

3.7 HEURISTIC TECHNIQUES FOR COMBINATORIAL OPTIMIZATION

According to Reeves [47], a heuristic is a technique that gives near-optimal solutions at reasonable computational cost without being able to guarantee either feasibility or optimality or to state how close to optimality a particular feasible solution is. Heuristic techniques are hence nonalgorithmic methods that are applied to algorithmically complex or time-consuming problems in which there is not a predetermined method to generate efficient solutions. In general, there is no analytic methodology to explain the way the heuristic converges to a solution; this is achieved with the partial control of some external factors and hence heuristics are often said to be guided random search methods. Heuristics have been suggested to solve a wide range of problems in various fields including artificial intelligence, and continuous and discrete combinatorial optimization [47].

A lot of heuristics are problem-specific, so that a method that works for one problem cannot be used to solve a different one. However, there is an increasing interest in techniques that have a broader application area. Over the last few decades, several general-purpose heuristics have been developed and have proved to be very powerful when applied to a large number of problems.

Various measures of performance can be considered, such as the quality of the best solution found, the time to get there, the algorithm's time to reach an acceptable solution, the robustness of the method, etc. Briefly speaking, a new heuristic is acceptable if it can satisfy one of the following requirements [45]:

- It can produce high-quality solutions more quickly than other methods.
- It identifies higher-quality solutions better than other approaches.
- It is easy to implement.
- It is less sensitive to differences in problem characteristics, data quality, or tuning parameters than other approaches.
- It has applications to a broad range of problems.

Computational intelligence is an important category of heuristic methods. This field contains the main general-purpose heuristic strategies that have developed during the last decades: neural networks, evolutionary algorithms, and fuzzy logic.

Neural networks (NNs) were inspired by the structure of biological neural systems and their way of encoding and solving problems. They can be characterized as parallel architecture information processing systems, usually possessing many, say, n inputs and one or more outputs. A NN can be viewed as a set of simple, interconnected processing elements, called neurons, acting in parallel. Neurons are organized in layers and are linked together using unidirectional connections (or synapses), each connection having a weight associated with it. The function of a neuron is to sum up all its weighted input values and then generate an output via a transfer (or activation) function. In the specific Hopfield model, the combinatorial optimization problem consists of minimizing a discrete objective function that is a weighted sum of constraints. By translating the cost function into a set of weights and bias values, the neural network becomes a parallel optimizer. It can be shown that given the initial values of the problem, the network yields a stable solution.

Evolutionary algorithms (EAs) were developed from studies of the processes of natural selection and evolutionary genetics and their study as well as their application to various problems is a subject of the field known as evolutionary computation. There are a variety of evolutionary models that have been proposed but the three fundamental ones are genetic algorithms (GAs), evolution strategies (ESs), and evolutionary programming (EP). All these approaches maintain a population of structures or individuals, each of which is assigned a fitness value that measures how close the individual is to the optimum solution of the problem. The individual that best corresponds to the optimum solution arises after a number of generation processes. In each generation, individuals undergo operations such as selection of the fitter ones and other transformations that modify existing structures and generate new ones. GAs and ESs are two representative EAs created to solve numerical optimization problems, whereas EP applies to problems related to artificial intelligence and machine learning.

Finally, fuzzy logic is a methodology that captures the uncertainties associated with human cognitive processes such as thinking and reasoning. The knowledge that relates inputs and outputs is expressed as rules in the form "if A, then B," where A and B are linguistic labels of fuzzy sets determined by appropriate membership functions. Fuzzy systems were developed to face real problems that cannot be expressed by mathematically rigorous models and hence they are rarely applied to combinatorial optimization.

Two other famous heuristics for combinatorial optimization are simulated annealing and tabu search. Simulated annealing is based on thermodynamic considerations, with annealing interpreted as an optimization procedure. The method generates a sequence of states based on a cooling schedule for convergence. However the main drawback of simulated annealing is that the convergence behavior strongly depends on the appropriate choice of various parameters, leading to poor performance. Tabu search performs an aggressive exploration of solution space and directs the search in a desirable direction by avoiding inefficient paths. This enables computation times to be reduced in comparison to techniques such as simulated annealing. The method, however, requires large memory capacity, where a historical set of individuals is kept, which becomes insufficient for large-scale problems.

The above two heuristic techniques belong to the category of local search combinatorial methods. In local search methods, the optimization process starts with a suboptimal solution to a particular problem and searches a defined neighborhood of this solution for a better one. Having found one, the process restarts from the new solution and continues to iterate in this way until no improvement can be found on the current solution. This final solution is unlikely to be the global optimum, though, with respect to its neighborhood, it is locally optimal [47].

Swarm intelligence is a new challenging branch of artificial intelligence that takes advantage of the collective behavior of animals with limited intellectual faculties (insects, flocks of birds, schools of fish) to solve algorithmically complex problems. In a seminal work by Dorigo et al. [12], intelligent "artificial ants" were used to find the shortest path on constrained graphs. Ant systems can be applied to combinatorial and quadratic optimization problems.

Simulated annealing, tabu search, NNs, EAs, and swarm intelligence are alternative heuristic techniques that can be used as combinatorial optimizers. There are no strict criteria to determine the applicability of these methods to combinatorial problems and hence the choice of a heuristic depends mainly on the specifics of each case study. In the case of combinatorial problems, various empirical studies showed that [38, 47]:

- Simulated annealing and tabu search are better in local searches but have the drawbacks mentioned above.

- Swarm intelligence and particularly ant systems are distributed techniques and can be used primarily in adaptive environments.

- Neural networks are efficient in local searches in which they have been shown to have the fastest time convergence. Another benefit of using the neural network approach is that, after sufficient training by some representative input data, the neural networks can make use of the essential characteristics learned. Nevertheless, neural networks very often have local minima. Moreover, they are very sensitive to parameter variations, a matter of great importance for real-time operation.

- EAs are very effective in solving optimization problems that require global search of their parameters, due to the variety of individuals generated recursively by a specified population. Their greatest problem is, however, their poor time performance, which is compensated for either by using hybrid methods or by implementing them in parallel machines.

3.8 HEURISTIC FCA SCHEMES

Based on the FCA formulations discussed previously, heuristic methods have been proposed with varying success. The majority of these heuristics have been tested using some well-known benchmark instances. The most basic of them are [34]:

1. The Philadelphia instances, characterized by 21 hexagons denoting the cells of a cellular system around Philadelphia and used extensively by researchers mainly for MS-FAP formulation (Figure 3.1). The Philadelphia problems are among the most studied FAP instances. The problems consist of cells located in a hexagonal grid, and have only soft constraints. A vector of requirements is used to describe the demand for channels in each cell. Transmitters are considered to be located at cell centers and the distance between transmitters in adjacent cells is taken to be 1. Separa-

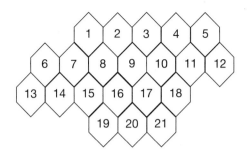

Figure 3.1 Philadelphia network structure.

tion distances are specified. For each cell, a demand is given [3]. There are nine instances. Figure 3.2 shows the demand for the original Philadelphia instance.

2. The instances available via the EUCLID (European Cooperation for the Long-term in Defence) CALMA (Combinatorial Algorithms for Military Applications) project. The CALMA instances differ from other frequency assignment problems by their specific distance/separation constraints. The instances also contain equality constraints, to model that two frequencies at a fixed distance have to be assigned to their corresponding vertices. The set of instances contains MO-FAPs, MS-FAPs, and MI-FAPs. Eleven instances were provided by CELAR (Centre d'Electronique de l'Armement France), whereas a second set of 14 GRAPH (Generating Radio Link Frequency Assignment Problems Heuristically) instances was made available by the research group of Delft University of Technology.

Other benchmark instances have been introduced by the COST 259 Project on Wireless Flexible Personalized Communications [34], by Castelino et al. [7], Hao et al. [24], and Crisan and Mühlenbein [9, 10]. The most representative heuristics for each FCA combinatorial formulation are discussed in this section. It must be noted that only the FCA schemes based on the general-purpose heuristics referred to in the previous section are discussed. For further information regarding the application of other heuristics, the reader is referred to [34].

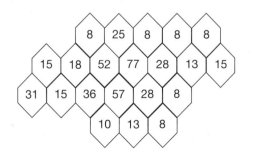

Figure 3.2 Original instance.

3.8.1 MO-FAP

The MO-FAP problem can be solved quite efficiently by considering exact and heuristic techniques. The majority of the heuristic methods proposed derive from the CALMA project. Kapsalis et al. [27] examined the performance of a genetic algorithm. The results are less than satisfactory since an optimal solution was derived for only two instances. Several local search techniques such as tabu search and simulated annealing are discussed in Tiourine et al. [54]. The heuristics were optimal, combining the lower and upper bounds for 6 of a total of 10 number of instances. Tabu search with a different neighborhood function is also examined in Bouju et al. [4]. For the same project, a different evolutionary approach, called evolutionary search, was proposed by Crisan and Mühlenbein [9]. This heuristic variant consists of the repeated mutation of a solution based on a certain mutation operator. The computational results are comparable with the results of the tabu search, simulated annealing, or variable depth search in Tiurine et al. [54]. Another genetic algorithm approach was developed by Cuppini [11]. However, computational results are only reported for a small example.

3.8.2 MS-FAP

MS-FAP is the most studied FCA problem. For this problem, analytic techniques have been provided by many researchers and lower bounds have been tested extensively on the Philadelphia distances. Heuristic methods also have been developed but they seem to be less accurate in providing optimal solutions in all cases; more difficult benchmark instances are necessary to distinguish among the heuristics.

The first heuristics were proposed in the 1970s and 1980s [5, 50, 59]. Box [5] proposed a simple iterative technique based on a ranking of the channel requirements of various cells in descending order of assignment difficulty. This is a measure of how hard it is to find a compatible frequency to satisfy a given channel requirement. The order is changed when a denial occurs, and channels are assigned to each cell based on the assignment difficulty during each iteration. Zoellner and Beall [59] proposed a technique examining cochannel interference that assigns channels using a frequency-exhaustive or requirement-exhaustive strategy. Moreover, Siravajan et al. [50] developed a collection of techniques based on the previous approaches and examined their performance on 13 Philadelphia instances.

Hurley et. al. [25] described a software system called FASoft that operates as a planning tool for frequency assignment and proposed possible heuristics like tabu search, simulated annealing, and genetic algorithms based on Philadelphia instances. Valenzuela et. al. [56] applied also a GA and tested their model on eight Philadelphia instances. In three cases, the optimal solution was found.

In the framework of the CALMA project, all heuristics performed equally and found the optimal solution. An application of the tabu search is discussed in Tiourine et al. [54].

Kim and Kim [29] proposed an efficient two-phase optimization procedure for the MS-FAP based on the notion of frequency reuse patterns. Their heuristic was tested on randomly generated instances. Finally, Wang and Rushforth [57], described several channel assignment algorithms based on local search techniques. Experiments showed that in many cases the best of these techniques outperform existing heuristic approaches in the quality of the solution obtained with very reasonable execution times.

3.8.3 MI-FAP

For the case of MI-FAP, a lot of heuristics have been proposed by many different research groups. Genetic algorithms and tabu search seem to be especially popular for this channel assignment formulation. In the framework of the CALMA project, Tiourine et. al. [54] applied simulated annealing and variable depth search. A genetic algorithm was proposed by Kapsalis et al. [27]. Kolen [33] proposed a genetic algorithm with optimized crossover that generated the best child of two parents. Its performance was examined on the CALMA benchmark instances. It outperformed other heuristics but was applied only to small networks. Therefore, for very large networks, less sophisticated heuristics should be applied [34]. Maniezo and Carbonaro [42] applied a heuristic named ANTS based on the ant colony optimization. The heuristic scheme tested on CALMA and Philadelphia instances and outperformed other schemes based on simulated annealing approaches.

Besides research on the CALMA instances, several other researches have appeared. The Hopfield model is the most typical neural network used in solving combinatorial problems. In 1991 Kunz [35] proposed the first Hopfield model to find adequate solutions for the FCA problem, including cochannel and cosite interference constraints. Kunz's neural-network model, however, required a large number of iterations in order to reach the final solution. Funabiki and Takefuji [17] suggested another neural network composed of hysteresis McCulloch–Pitts neurons. Four heuristics were used to improve the convergence rate of channel assignment. The results were favorable in some cases, but not in others. Unfortunately, the minimization of the described cost function is quite a difficult problem due to the danger of getting stuck in local minima. A more improved Hopfield model that accelerates the time performance of the generated solutions and reduces the number of iterations appeared in Kim et al. [31]. Another Hopfield NN model with the addition of adjacent channel constraints was examined by Lochtie [39]. Lochtie and Mehler [40] also examined MI-FAP using a neural network for 58 cells of a real cellular network. They extended the results to incorporate adjacent channel interference as well [41]. Smith and Palaniswami [53] formulated the MI-FAP as a nonlinear integer programming and applied a Hopfield and a self-organized neural network to the problem. In this formulation, the weight of the interference depends on the distance between the frequencies and the penalty is inversely proportional to the difference between the assigned frequencies. Smith et al. [52] applied a simulated annealing approach to a real point-to-point wireless network.

Genetic algorithms are applied by Kim et al. [30] to obtain interference-free assignments. They tested several crossover and mutation operators for a couple of Philadelphia instances in which the span of available frequencies is fixed to the best lower bound of Gamst [18]. Lai and Coghill [36] also discuss a genetic algorithm approach. However, their model is examined on two instances. Crisan and Muhlenbein [10] applied a genetic algorithm using advanced crossover and mutation operators to real instances with 670 and 5500 transmitters. Ngo and Li [46] succesfully applied a genetic algorithm with a special binary encoding for the demand cosite constraints. Smith et al. [52] presented a genetic algorithm in which the crossover is used to reduce the adjacent and cochannel interference, whereas the mutation operator is used to reduce the cosite interference.

Dorne and Hao [13, 14] applied evolutionary search to a number of instances for real networks with up to 300 vertices. An assignment is represented in such a way that all cosite constraints are satisfied. In [13], a mutation operator that concentrates on the change of conflicting frequencies was used, whereas in [14] several ways of dealing with the cosite constraints were discussed. In [23] the same authors investigate the performance of the crossover operator in a genetic algorithm/evolutionary search. Hao et al. [24] applied tabu search to solve instances of a real network with at most 600 transmitters. In their formulation, they tried to minimize the span of the assignment by repeatedly solving MI-FAPs. The length of the tabu list was not constant, but varied during the search.

Tabu search was applied by Castelino et al. [7] to find an assignment with minimal unweighted interference for instances with up to 726 vertices and compare the performance with a genetic algorithm and a steepest descent heuristic. In Castelino et al. [8], a heuristic called tabu thresholding introduced by Glover [21] was applied on the same instances. Finally, Abril et al. [1] applied a multiagent system based on an ANTS algorithm using data from GSM networks in operation in Spain and compared it with a simulated annealing approach.

3.8.4 MB-FAP

MB-FAP has been a topic of research in a lot of studies and is usually solved using exact analytic solutions like integer programming techniques. One heuristic using simulated annealing was reported by Mathar and Mattfeldt [43]. The authors investigated the use of several algorithms based on the simulated annealing approach by using a proper model. In a set of computational experiments, all variants were shown to give acceptable solutions when compared to optimal solutions obtained by analytic approaches.

3.8.5 Other Formulations

Several other models have been proposed. An attractive approach is the combination of characteristics of the MO-FAP, MS-FAP, MB-FAP, and MI-FAP models. For example, Duque-Antón et al. [15] and Al-Khaled [2] provided a simulated annealing model to solve a FAP with a cost function that is a linear combination of interference, blocking probability, and span terms. Knälmann and Quellmalz [32] applied simulated annealing with a cost function that is a convex combination of the mean interference and the maximum interference obtained by the assignment.

Capone and Trubian [6] applied tabu search to a FAP model that considers all interferers by evaluating the carrier-to-interference ratio in the whole service area. The objective is to maximize the sum of traffic loads offered by regions in which the ratio between the received power and the sum of powers received from interfering transmissions is above a threshold value.

Sandalidis et al. [48, 49] compared a Hopfield neural network and a special evolutionary algorithm called combinatorial evolutionary strategy in order to find the proper channels that have to be borrowed for a borrowing channel assignment (BCA) scheme.

3.9 CONCLUSIONS

The fixed-channel assignment problem is one of the most difficult problems in mobile computing. Because of its complexity, a lot of heuristics have been developed to give adequate solutions. This survey has focused on the use of general purpose heuristic approaches mainly from the field of computational intelligence and local search methods. The majority of these heuristics treat the FAP as a combinatorial optimization problem and try to minimize a cost function that is based on the assumptions set by the designer. Of course, the problem has generated a lot of interest and a variety of heuristic methods are being proposed by several researchers. However, due to the fact that the heuristic schemes are evaluated using different benchmarks and have different optimization criteria, the best heuristic FAP is not easy to estimate accurately.

As the use of heuristic methods in mobile communications and particularly in resource management has been growing rapidly over recent years, there is a lot more work to be done as these methods are applied to the area of channel resource management. Further research should be based on:

- The development of a reliable benchmark to serve as a unique platform for the validation of the existing and forthcoming heuristic schemes.
- The incorporation of other constraints beyond the existing ones (interference, traffic, etc.) in order for the problem to correspond to more realistic scenarios.
- The examination of cellular network design (channel assignment, optimal base station location, power control, etc.) as a unified problem.

REFERENCES

1. Abril J., Comellas F., Cortes A., Ozon J., and Vaquer M., A Multiagent system for frequency assignment in cellular radio networks, *IEEE Transactions on Vehicular Technology, 49,* 5, 1558–1565, 2000.
2. Al-Khaled F. S., Optimal radio channel assignment through the new binary dynamic simulated annealing algorithm, *International Journal of Communication Systems, 11,* 327–336, 1998.
3. Anderson L. G., A Simulation study of some dynamic channel assignment algorithms in a high capacity mobile telecommunications system, *IEEE Transactions on Communications, 21,* 1294–1301, 1973.
4. Bouju A., Boyce J. F., Dimitropoulos C. H. D., Vom Scheidt G., Taylor J. G., Likas A., Papageorgiou G., and Stafylopatis A., Intelligent search for the radio links frequency assignment problem, *International Conference for Digital Signal Processing (DSP'95),* Limassol, Cyprus, 1995.
5. Box F., A Heuristic technique for assigning frequencies to mobile radio nets, *IEEE Transactions on Vehicular Technology, 27,* 57–74, 1978.
6. Capone A. and Trubian M., Channel Assignment problem in cellular systems: A new model and a tabu search algorithm, *IEEE Transactions on Vehicular Technology, 48,* 4, July 1999.

7. Castelino D. J., Hurley S., and Stephens N. M., A tabu search algorithm for frequency assignment, *Annals of Operations Research, 63,* 301–319, 1996.

8. Castelino D. J., Hurley S., and Stephens N. M., A surrogate constraint tabu thresholding implementation for the frequency assignment problem, *Annals of Operations Research, 86,* 259–270, 1999.

9. Crisan C. and Mühlenbein H., The frequency assignment problem: A look at the performance of evolutionary search, *Lecture Notes in Computer Science, 1363,* 263–274, 1998.

10. Crisan C. and Mühlenbein H., The breeder genetic algorithm for frequency assignment, *Lecture Notes in Computer Science, 1498,* 897–906, 1998.

11. Cuppini M., A Genetic Algorithm for channel assignment problems, *European Transactions on Telecommunications and Related Technologies, 5,* 285–294, 1994.

12. Dorigo M., Maniezzo V., and Colorni A., The ant system: Optimization by a colony of cooperating agents, *IEEE Transactions on Systems, Man, and Cybernetics—Part B, 26,* 1, 29–41, 1996.

13. Dorne R. and Hao J.-K., An evolutionary approach for frequency assignment in cellular radio networks, *IEEE International Conference on Evolutionary Computing,* Perth, Australia, 1995.

14. Dorne R. and Hao J.-K., Constraint handling in evolutionary search: A case study of the frequency assignment, *Lecture Notes in Computer Science, 1141,* 801–810, 1996.

15. Duque-Antón M., Kunz D., and Rüber B., Channel assignment for cellular radio using simulated annealing, *IEEE Transactions on Vehicular Technology, 42,* 14–21, 1993.

16. EUCLID CALMA Project, ftp.win.tue.nl, Directory/pub/techreports/CALMA, 1995.

17. Funabiki N. and Takefuji Y., A neural network parallel algorithm for channel assignment problems in cellular radio networks, *IEEE Transactions on Vehicular Technology, 41,* 430–437, 1992.

18. Gamst A., Some lower bounds for a class of frequency assignment problems, *IEEE Transactions on Vehicular Technology, 35,* 8–14, 1986.

19. Gibson, J. D., *The Communications Handbook,* Boca Raton, FL: CRC Press, 1997.

20. Giortzis A. I. and Turner L. F., Application of mathematical programming to the fixed channel assignment problem in mobile radio networks, *IEEE Proceedings on Communications, 144,* 257–264, 1997.

21. Glover F., Tabu thresholding: Improved search by nonmonotonic trajectories, *ORSA Journal on Computing, 7,* 426–442, 1995.

22. Hale W. K, Frequency assignment: Theory and applications, *Proceedings of IEEE, 68,* 1497–1514, 1980.

23. Hao J.-K and Dorne R., Study of genetic search for the frequency assignment problem, *Lecture Notes in Computer Science, 1063,* 333–344, 1996.

24. Hao J.-K., Dorne R., and Galinier P., Tabu search for frequency assignment in mobile radio networks, *Journal of Heuristics, 4,* 47–62, 1998.

25. Hurley S., Smith D. H., and Thiel S. U., FASoft: A system for discrete channel frequency assignment, *Radio Science, 32,* 1921–1939, 1997.

26. Jung H. and Tonguz O. K., Random spacing channel assignment to reduce the nonlinear intermodulation distortion in cellular mobile communications, *IEEE Transactions on Vehicular Technology, 48,* 5, 1666–1675, 1999.

27. Kapsalis A., Rayward-Smith V. J, and Smith G. D., Using genetic algorithms to solve the radio link frequency assignment problem, in D. W. Pearson, N. C. Steele, and R. F. Albrecht (Eds.), *Proceedings of the Second International Conference on Artificial Neural Networks and Genetic Algorithms,* New York: Springer Verlag, 1995.

28. Katzela I., and Nagshineh M., Channel assignment schemes for cellular mobile telecommunication systems, a comprehensive survey, *IEEE Personal Communications,* 10–31, 1996.

29. Kim S. and Kim S.-L., A Two-phase algorithm for frequency assignment in cellular mobile systems, *IEEE Transactions on Vehicular Technology, 43,* 542–548, 1994.

30. Kim J.-S., Park S. H., Dowd P. W., and Nasrabadi N. M., Channel assignment in cellular radio using genetic algorithms, *Wireless Personal Communications, 3,* 273–286, 1996.

31. Kim J.-S., Park S. H, Dowd P. W., and Nasrabadi N. M., Cellular radio channel assignment using a modified hopfield network, *IEEE Transactions on Vehicular Technology, 46,* 4, 957–967, 1997.

32. Knälmann A. and Quellmalz A., Solving the frequency assignment problem with simulated annealing, *IEEE Conference Publication, 396,* 233–240, 1994.

33. Kolen A. W. J., *A Genetic Algorithm for Frequency Assignment,* Technical report, Maastricht University, 1999.

34. Koster, A. M. C. A., *Frequency Assignment—Models and Algorithms,* PhD thesis, Maastricht University, 1999.

35. Kunz D., Channel Assignment for cellular radio using neural networks, *IEEE Transactions on Vehicular Technology, 40,* 188–193, 1991.

36. Lai W. K. and Coghill G. G., Channel assignment through evolutionary optimization, *IEEE Transactions on Vehicular Technology, 45,* 91–95, 1996.

37. Lee, W. C. Y., *Mobile Cellular Telecommunications Systems,* New York: McGraw Hill, 1989.

38. Lin C. T. and Lee C. S. G., *Neural Fuzzy Systems: A Neuro-Fuzzy Synergism to Intelligent Systems,* Upper Saddle River, NJ: Prentice-Hall, 1996.

39. Lochtie G. D., Frequency channel assignment using artificial neural networks, *IEEE International Conference on Antennas and Propagation,* 948–951, 1993.

40. Lochtie G. D. and Mehler M. J., Subspace approach to channel assignment in mobile communication networks, *IEEE Proceedings, 142,* 179–185, 1995.

41. Lochtie G. D. and Mehler M. J., Channel assignment using a subspace approach to neural networks, *IEEE Conference Publication, 407,* 296–300, 1995.

42. Maniezzo V. and Carbonaro A., An ANTS heuristic for the frequency assignment problem, Special Issue on Ant Algorithms, *Future Generation Computer Systems, 16,* 8, 927–935, 2000.

43. Mathar R. and Mattfeldt J., Channel assignment in cellular radio networks, *IEEE Transactions on Vehicular Technology, 42,* 647–656, 1993.

44. Mehrotra, A., *Cellular Radio: Analog and Digital Systems,* Norwood, MA: Artech House, 1994.

45. Michalewicz Z., *Genetic Algorithms + Data Structures = Evolution Programs,* New York: Springer-Verlag, 3rd edition, 1996.

46. Ngo C. Y. and Li, V. O. K., Fixed channel assignment in cellular radio networks using a modified genetic algorithm, *IEEE Transactions on Vehicular Technology, 47,* 163–171, 1998.

47. Reeves C. R, *Modern Heuristic Techniques for Combinatorial Problems,* New York: McGraw Hill, 1995.

48. Sandalidis H. G., Stavroulakis P. P, and Rodriguez-Tellez J., Borrowing channel assignment strategy using computational intelligence methods, *IEEE 48th Annual Vehicular Technology Conference (VTC '98),* Ottawa, Ontario Canada, pp. 1685–1689, 1998.

49. Sandalidis H. G., Stavroulakis P. P., and Rodriguez-Tellez J., Borrowing channel assignment strategies based on heuristic techniques for cellular systems, *IEEE Transactions on Neural Networks, 10,* 1, 176–181, 1999.

50. Sivarajan K. N., McEliece R. J., and Ketchum J. W., Channel assignment in cellular radio, *Proceedings of the 39th IEEE Vehicular Technology Conference,* 846–850, 1989.

51. Smith K. A., A Genetic Algorithm for the channel assignment problem, *IEEE Global Communications Conference,* 2013–2017, 1998.

52. Smith K. A., Kim B. K., and Sargent G. F., Minimizing channel interference in real cellular radio networks, *IEEE Global Communications Conference,* pp. 2192–2197, 1998.

53. Smith K. A. and Palaniswami M., Static and dynamic channel assignment using neural networks, *IEEE Journal on Selected Areas in Communications, 15,* 238– 249, 1997.

54. Tiourine S. R., Hurkens C. A. J., and Lenstra J. K., Local search algorithms for the radio link frequency assignment problem, *Telecommunication Systems, 13,* 293–314, 2000.

55. Tripathi N. D, Reed J. H., and Vanlandingham H. F, Handoff in cellular systems, *IEEE Personal Communications,* 26–39, 1998.

56. Valenzuela C., Hurley S., and Smith D. H., A Permutation based genetic algorithm for minimum span frequency assignment, *Lecture Notes in Computer Science, 1498,* 907–916, 1998.

57. Wang W. and Rushforth C. K., An adaptive local-search algorithm for the channel assignment problem (CAP), *IEEE Transactions on Vehicular Technology, 45,* 459–466, 1996.

58. Zander J., Radio resource management in future wireless networks: Requirements and limitations, *IEEE Communications Magazine,* 30–36, 1997.

59. Zoellner J. A. and Beall C. L., A breakthrough in spectrum conserving frequency assignment technology, *IEEE Transactions on Electromagnetic Compatibility, 19,* 313–319, 1977.

CHAPTER 4

Channel Assignment and Graph Multicoloring

LATA NARAYANAN

Department of Computer Science, Concordia University, Montreal, Quebec, Canada

4.1 INTRODUCTION

In a cellular network, there are ongoing requests for communication links from mobiles in each cell to the base stations responsible for the cell. In FDMA or TDMA networks, the available spectrum is divided into narrow frequency channels, and each communication request is served by the assignment of a frequency channel. Spectrum is a scarce resource, and careful assignment of channels to calls is critical to being able to maximize the number of users in the network. Cellular networks employ a low-power transmitter in every cell, which makes it possible to reuse the same frequency channel in different cells. Frequency reuse, however, is limited by two kinds of radio interference. Cochannel interference is caused by two simultaneous transmissions on the same channel. To avoid this, once a channel is assigned to a certain call, it should not be reused by another call in an area where it may cause significant interference. Adjacent channel interference is the result of signal energy from an adjacent channel spilling over into the current channel.

In this chapter, we model cellular data and communication networks as graphs with each node representing a base station in a cell in the network and edges representing geographical adjacency of cells. Associated with each node v in the graph at any time is a set $C(v)$, which is the set of calls or active mobiles in the cell served by v. The size of the set $C(v)$ is denoted $w(v)$ and called the weight of the node v. Cochannel interference constraints are modeled in terms of reuse distance; it is assumed that the same channel can be assigned to two different nodes in the graph if and only if their graph distance is at least r. We do not deal with adjacent channel interference in this chapter; see Chapter 20 for models and solutions for this problem. For our purposes, the objective of an algorithm for the channel assignment problem is, at time instant t, to assign $w_t(v)$ channels to each node v in the network, where $w_t(v)$ is the weight of the node v at time t, in such a way that cochannel interference constraints are respected, and the total number of channels used over all nodes in the network is minimized. The problem can thus be seen as a graph multicoloring problem.

The channel assignment problem has been studied extensively in the past two decades. A look at an online research index turns up hundreds of papers on the subject. The researchers involved include radio and electrical engineers, operations researchers, graph theorists, and computer scientists of all stripes. In this chapter, we limit ourselves to papers taking a graph-theoretic approach to the problem and, furthermore, to results that prove some bounds on the performance of the proposed algorithms. A comprehensive survey of channel assignment strategies proposed in the engineering literature is given in [26] and techniques used in operations research can be found in [21]. The relationship to graph coloring and multicoloring was set out in detail in [13]. We use the competitive analysis framework to analyze algorithms. Basic definitions are given in Section 4.2; see [3] for more details on competitive analysis and [2] for graph theory. A large part of our focus will be on the so-called hexagon graphs (see Figure 4.1). It is well known that these are a very imperfect approximation of real-life cells; nevertheless, they provide a convenient idealization that continues to be useful in practice. We will look at different values of the reuse distance parameter; this amounts to multicoloring powers of hexagon graphs. We will also look at the results on unit disk graphs. These are the intersection graphs of equal-sized disks in a plane, where a disk represents a transceiver and its transmission area. Finally, we will mention a few results on graphs where adjacent cells have some overlapping areas.

Since the processing of calls and assignment of frequencies is an ongoing process and present decisions can influence future ones, the channel assignment problem is best modeled in an online fashion. The graph to be multicolored changes over time. These changes can be modeled as an ordered sequence of graph–call vector pairs $\{(G, C_t) : t \geq 0\}$ where C_t is the set of new and ongoing calls to be serviced at time t. Clearly, $C_t \cap C_{t+1}$ may not be empty. This brings us to an important issue—whether or not a node, when allocating channels for the next time step, can change the channels it has already assigned to its ongoing local calls on previous steps. An algorithm said to be nonrecoloring if once having assigned a channel in response to a particular new call, it never changes that assignment (i.e., recolors the call).

The available technology, however, allows for a limited rearrangement of frequency channels. It is interesting, therefore, to also consider algorithms that allow recoloring of calls. In this case, the actual set of calls at any given time step is no longer relevant; just

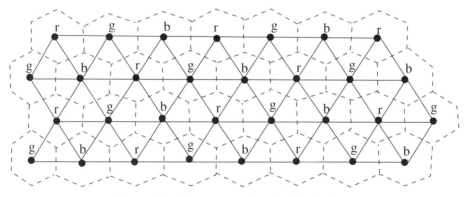

Figure 4.1   A hexagon graph with a 3-coloring.

the number of calls at any step suffices to specify the problem. Thus, the problem can now be modeled as multicoloring a sequence of weighted graphs given by $\{(G, w_t): t \geq 0\}$ If arbitrary recoloring is allowed, it is not difficult to see that the competitive ratio of any algorithm for this online problem is no better than the performance ratio of an algorithm for the static version of the problem. Essentially, at every time step, run the algorithm for the static version of the problem, with no concern for how many calls get recolored. Another motivation for studying the static problem is that the weight of a node can be considered to represent the expected traffic in the corresponding cell, and an offline solution then gives a nonuniform, precomputed fixed assignment to be used in the online setting.

It is intuitively clear that recoloring is a very powerful tool, and algorithms that are allowed to recolor are more powerful than those that are not. Upper and lower bounds that confirm this are reported in the later sections. An interesting challenge would be to develop algorithms that do allow recoloring but only a limited amount. Alternatively, there could be a cost associated with recoloring, and the algorithm would have to minimize this cost along with other objectives, or keep the cost below a specified allowable limit. As far as the author is aware, there has not been significant work in this area.

Another important issue concerns whether the algorithm uses centralized or distributed control. Some algorithms are inherently centralized: they require knowledge of all nodes and their current assignments before being able to make an assignment. The strategy in [35] for reuse distance 2, and the algorithm with competitive ratio 2 for reuse distance 3 given in [9] are centralized strategies. A commonly used strategy precomputes channels to be assigned to different cells; new calls are assigned channels from these precomputed sets. This strategy is completely distributed and requires no online communication with neighbors. There are still other algorithms that can be implemented in a distributed manner, but they require a limited amount of communication with nearby base stations to ensure that no conflict occurs. To limit the amount of information about other nodes that needs to be collected to aid in decision making, the concept of the locality of an algorithm was introduced in [19]. An algorithm is said to be k-local if the only information available to a node, apart from its own history, is the current weights of nodes that are within graph distance k from it. A certain amount of precomputed information independent of the weight sequence, such as a base coloring of the graph, is also allowable. This model makes sense for recoloring algorithms; indeed knowing the weight of a neighbor also gives some knowledge about the decisions the neighbor would make in the current time step. However, for nonrecoloring algorithms, it would make more sense to allow a k-local algorithm to also collect information about the current color assignments of nodes in its k-locality. The distributed algorithms described in this chapter are for the most part synchronous. They proceed in rounds, and a mechanism to synchronize the rounds is assumed. In [41], however, the algorithm is asynchronous, and is proved to be free of deadlock and starvation. No bounds are proved on performance, as in the number of channels used in the average case or worst case.

There are very few lower bounds known for this problem, for either recoloring or nonrecoloring algorithms. Janssen and Kilakos [17] show that for general k-colorable graphs, the competitive ratio of any 1-local recoloring algorithm is at least $k/2$ and that of any nonrecoloring algorithm is at least k. These bounds are tight. However, for hexagon graphs or their powers, tight lower bounds are not known. A straightforward lower bound is the clique bound [10]: clearly all nodes in any clique in the graph need disjoint sets of channels. Thus the maximum over all cliques in the graph over the total weight of the clique is a lower bound for the number of channels needed. Another lower bound is given by odd cycles [37]: an odd cycle with n nodes needs at least $2W/(n-1)$ colors, where W is the sum of weights of all nodes in the cycle. Most of the known algorithms are deterministic, and the lower bounds are for deterministic algorithms as well. Randomized algorithms are given in [27, 48]; the simulation results are promising but no performance bounds are proved.

A related problem to the channel assignment problem is that of online call control. Suppose the size of the available spectrum is fixed to be C. Then given a sequence of weighted graphs, the call control problem is to assign channels to the nodes so as to maximize the total number of calls admitted. In this case, some calls may actually be rejected, so the number of channels assigned to a node in a time step may be less than its weight. An algorithm for channel assignment can generally be converted to one for online call control. Moreover, the performance bound for channel assignment also translates to a condition for blocking in the case of online control. Suppose an algorithm always produces a channel assignment with at most kD channels when given a weighted graph, where D is the clique bound mentioned above. Then it is easy to see that given a spectrum with C channels, the algorithm will not block unless there is a weighted clique in the graph with total weight more than C/k. A few recent papers study the call control problem [4, 28, 39] in both static and online versions. The static version is very similar to the maximum independent set problem. For the online version, Caragiannis et al. [4] give a randomized algorithm with competitive ratio 2.934 in hexagon graphs, and also give a lower bound of 1.857 on the competitive ratio of any randomized algorithm for the problem on such graphs. It is assumed that a single frequency channel is available.

Another related problem is the problem of list coloring [8]. In this problem, every node of the graph has associated with it a list of colors, which in our case is the list of available frequency channels. The problem is to find a proper coloring of nodes such that each node is colored with a color from its list. A number of sequential solutions are known [1, 22, 44]. The relationship to channel assignment was noticed in [11, 31], and a distributed protocol was given in [11].

The rest of this chapter is organized as follows. Section 4.2 defines the terms we use. Section 4.3 outlines the basic types of algorithms proposed in the literature, and Section 4.4 summarizes the known lower bound results. Section 4.5 discusses the static version of the problem, and Section 4.6 the online version. We conclude with a discussion of open problems in Section 4.7.

4.2 PRELIMINARIES

4.2.1 Graph-Theoretic Preliminaries

Let $G = (V, E)$ denote an interference graph, where the node set V denotes cells or base stations that require call service, and the edge set E represents geographical proximity of cells and therefore the possibility of cochannel interference. A weighted graph is a pair

(G, w) where G is an interference graph, w is a weight vector indexed by the nodes of G, and $w(v)$ represents the number of calls to be served at node v. A static snapshot of the network at a fixed instant of time is given by a weighted graph (G, w). The goal of an algorithm for the static channel assignment problem, at that instant in time, is to be able to allocate $w(v) \geq 0$ distinct channels to each node $v \in V$ such that no two adjacent nodes have channels in common. In graph-theoretic parlance, what is required is a proper multicoloring of G with distinct colors representing distinct channels.

Formally, a proper multicoloring of the weighted graph (G, w) where $G = (V, E)$ consists of a set of colors C and a function f that assigns to each $v \in V$ a subset $f(v)$ of C such that

- $\forall v, |f(v)| = w(v)$: each node gets $w(v)$ distinct colors
- $\forall (u, v) \in E, f(u) \cap f(v) = \phi$: two neighboring nodes get disjoint sets of colors.

Thus, a proper multicoloring is equivalent to a valid channel assignment and vice versa. We use the terms "colors" and "channels" interchangeably in the sequel. Many of the algorithms use a base coloring of the underlying unweighted graph G; it should be clear from the context when the base color of a node is being referred to, rather than the channels it is assigned. It is convenient to treat the set of available channels to be a set of natural numbers. We further assume without loss of generality that any such set can be suitably reordered or partitioned. The span of a channel assignment is the cardinality of the set C.

For the online channel assignment problem, the set of calls to be served changes with time. Furthermore, calls cannot always be considered interchangeable and, therefore, the identities of individual calls may be relevant. We define a call graph to be a pair (G, C), where G is an interference graph and C is a call vector indexed by the nodes of the graph. $C(v)$ represents the set of ongoing and new calls requiring service at a node at a particular instant of time. A call graph has a one-to-one correspondence with a weighted graph, where $w(v) = |C(v)|$. We model the changes in the set of calls over time as an ordered sequence of call graphs $\{(G, C_t) : t \geq 0\}$, where C_t represents the set of calls to be serviced at time t. At time instant t, an online algorithm must arrange to perform an assignment for the call graph (G, C_t) before moving on to the call graph (G, C_{t+1}) at the next time instant $t + 1$. It must perform this assignment with no knowledge of the later graphs in the sequence. As mentioned in the introduction, an algorithm for the online problem may be recoloring or nonrecoloring. A recoloring algorithm can change the channels assigned to a call while the call is in progress, whereas in a nonrecoloring algorithm, a call keeps the channel it is initially assigned for its entire duration.

If unlimited recoloring is allowed, the online problem becomes equivalent to the static problem, as an algorithm for the static problem can be used at every time step of the online algorithm. In this case, since the calls *can* be considered interchangeable, it is the number of calls at a node that is the relevant parameter. Thus, it is enough to consider the sequence of weighted graphs $\{(G, w_t) : t \geq 0\}$ corresponding to the sequence of call graphs, and in fact, it suffices to consider each element of this sequence completely independently of the others. In practice, though, it is generally desirable to reassign channels to calls as little as possible.

We refer to finite induced subgraphs of the infinite triangular lattice as hexagon graphs (see Figure 4.1). A unit disk graph is the intersection graph of disks of equal diameter in the plane. They can also be described in terms of distance or proximity models, which consist of a value $d \geq 0$ and an embedding of nodes in the plane such that (u, v) is an edge if and only if the Euclidean distance between u and v in the specified embedding is at most d. For each fixed pair or real values $r, s > 0$ a graph G can be drawn in $\mathcal{R}^d$ in an (r, s)-civilized manner if its nodes can be mapped to points in $\mathcal{R}^d$ so that the length of each edge is at most r and the distance between any two points is at least s.

An independent (or, stable) set in G is a set $V' \subseteq V$ such that for any $u, v \in V'$, $(u, v) \notin E$. Note that a proper multicoloring of G is essentially a covering of G with stable sets; each stable set of nodes corresponds to a color and a node v appears in exactly $w(v)$ such sets. The weighted chromatic number of a weighted graph (G, w), denoted $\chi(G, w)$, is the smallest number m such that there exists a multicoloring of G of span m, i.e., $\chi(G, w)$ is the optimal number of colors required to properly multicolor G. Let the weight of a maximal clique in (G, w) be defined as the sum of the weights of the nodes belonging to the clique; note that when G is a hexagon graph, the only maximal cliques are isolated nodes, edges, or triangles. The weighted clique number, denoted $\omega(G, w)$ is the maximum weight of any maximal clique in the graph. The weighted chromatic number and clique number of a call graph are defined in an analogous fashion. For integers $k \geq 1$, we define the k-locality of a node v to be the induced subgraph consisting of those nodes in G whose graph distance from v is less than or equal to k.

Given $G = (V, E)$, the graph $G' = (V, E')$ is defined by $E' = E \cup E^2 \cup \ldots \cup E^{r-1}$. Thus any pair of nodes at distance $i < r$ in G is connected by an edge in G'. The problem of channel assignment in a weighted graph (G, w) with reuse distance r is thus the same as multicoloring the graph G'. The unweighted clique number of G' is the maximum size of any clique in G', and is denoted $\omega(G')$. Similarly, the chromatic number of G', the minimum number of colors needed to color G', is denoted by $\chi(G')$. It is known that when G is a hexagon graph, $\chi(G') = \omega(G')$ (see Section 4.5.3), and an optimal coloring can be computed in polynomial time. We assume that such an optimal coloring of the graph G' is available; thus, every node in G' is assigned a color from the set $\{1, 2, \ldots, \chi(G')\}$. If G is a hexagon graph, we say that G^2 is a square graph. Figure 4.1 shows a base coloring with red, blue, and green (r, b, and g) colors for a hexagon graph. It is easy to see that a square graph can be base colored with seven colors; Figure 4.8 shows such a coloring. We define $N_r(v)$ to be all neighbors of v in G', and $H_r(v)$ to be $w(v) + \Sigma_{u \in N_r(v)} w(u)$. Finally, given a assignment of channels to $N_r(v)$, $RC_r(v)$ is defined to be the number of channels assigned to more than one node in $N_r(v)$. Thus $RC_r(v)$ is a measure of the reuse of channels within $N_r(v)$.

4.2.2 Performance Measures

An approximation algorithm for the static channel assignment problem is said to have performance ratio r if on any weighted graph (G, w), the algorithm uses at most $r\chi(G, w) + O(1)$ channels. We use a standard yardstick for measuring the efficacy of online algorithms: that of competitive ratios [25, 3]. Given an online algorithm P that processes a sequence of N call graphs (G, C_t), $t = 0, \ldots, N$, let $S(P_t)$ denote the span of the channel assignment (multicoloring) computed by P after step t, i.e., after graph (G, C_t) has been processed. Let $S_N(P) = \max_t \{S(P_t)\}$ and $\chi_N(G) = \max_t \{\chi(G, C_t)\}$. We say that P is a c-competitive algorithm if and only if there is a constant b independent of N such that for any input sequence

$$S_N(P) \leq c \cdot \chi_N(G) + b$$

In other words, a c-competitive algorithm uses at most c times as many channels (colors) overall as the optimal offline algorithm would. We note that all of the algorithms discussed in this chapter in fact satisfy the stricter requirement

$$S(P_t) \leq c \cdot \chi(G, C_t) + b$$

for all $t \geq 0$, i.e., they approximate the optimal span within a factor of c at all times while still processing the input sequence online. All of the lower bounds mentioned in this chapter hold for the above definition of c-competitive (and therefore imply lower bounds on algorithms satisfying the stricter requirement).

4.3 BASIC TYPES OF ALGORITHMS

In this section, we describe the basic types of algorithms developed for channel assignment seen as a graph multicoloring problem.

4.3.1 Fixed Assignment

Fixed assignment (FA) is a very simple, nonrecoloring strategy for channel assignment. In this strategy, the nodes are partitioned into independent sets, and each such set is assigned a separate set of channels [30]. It is easy to see that this works very well when the traffic is described by a uniform distribution. However, it behaves quite poorly in the worst case. In particular, the algorithm is k-competitive where k is the chromatic number of the underlying graph. In [17], it is shown that this is the best possible for arbitrary k-colorable graphs.

4.3.2 Borrowing Algorithms

To improve the performance of FA, one idea has been to assign nominal sets of channels as with FA, but allow borrowing of available channels [7, 18, 37, 35]. A simple method is to have a two-phase algorithm. In the first phase, every node uses as many channels as it needs from its own nominal set of channels. In the second phase, a node borrows channels if necessary from its neighbors' sets of channels. Some mechanism to avoid conflicts caused by two neighbors trying to borrow the same channel from a mutual neighbor in the second phase is usually needed. One such mechanism might be to restrict the borrowing in some way. For example, red nodes can only borrow green channels, green nodes can only borrow blue channels, and blue nodes can only borrow red channels.

4.3.3 Hybrid Channel Assignment

Another variation of FA is to assign nominal sets of channels to nodes, but divide these sets into reserved and channels. The node may use all the channels from its own set, both reserved and borrowable ones, but may only use the borrowable channels from its neighbors, provided they are not being used by any of the neighbors. Many hybrid strategies have been studied in the literature [24, 47], but performance bounds are not generally given. Jordan and Schwabe [23] analyze a simple hybrid channel assignment strategy; the results for small values of reuse distance are not as good as the borrowing strategies.

4.3.4 Dynamic Channel Assignment

The main characteristic common to all dynamic channel assignment (DCA) schemes is that all channels are kept in a central pool and are assigned dynamically to radio cells as new calls arrive in the system. A channel is eligible for use in any cell, provided interference constraints are met. DCA strategies vary in the criterion used to select the channel to be assigned from the set of all eligible channels. They also vary in whether they are centralized or distributed, and in the synchronization mechanism used in the latter case. A wide variety of selection criteria to choose the assigned channel can be found in the literature. For example, in [49], the algorithm tries to maximize the amount of reuse: roughly, the channel that has been used the most often at distance r but least often at distances $r + 1$ and $r + 2$ is used. A number of recently proposed DCA schemes are based on measurement of signal strength from various eligible channels and aim to increase the reusability of channels (see, for example, [43]). A commonly used strategy [5, 15, 41], is the purely greedy strategy of using the minimum numbered channel among those eligible. This is the only DCA strategy for which bounds on the competitive ratio are known.

4.4 LOWER BOUNDS

Graph multicoloring is well known to be NP-hard for arbitrary graphs. Mcdiarmid and Reed showed that it is also NP-hard to multicolor a hexagon graph with reuse distance 2 [35]; the proof can be adapted for other values of reuse distance as well. It is also known that multicoloring unit disk graphs is NP-hard; see for example, [12]. Janssen and Kilakos [17] showed that for a k-colorable graph, any nonrecoloring algorithm has competitive ratio at least k, and any 1-local recoloring algorithm has competitive ratio at least $k/2$.

As mentioned earlier, the clique bound $\omega(G, w)$ is always a lower bound on the minimum number of channels needed to multicolor (G, w) [10]. Another lower bound is provided by odd cycles. Since the maximum size of an independent set in an n-node odd cycle is $(n - 1)/2$, any color can be assigned to at most $(n - 1)/2$ nodes. Therefore, the minimum number of channels needed for an odd cycle with n nodes and reuse distance 2 is at least $2W/(n - 1)$ colors, where W is the sum of weights of all nodes in the cycle. Thus, a 9-cycle with equal weight on all nodes requires at least $9\omega(G, w)/8$ channels, and in fact this number suffices. Since the smallest odd cycle that is a hexagon graph is of length 9, no algorithm for channel assignment with reuse distance 2 can guarantee using less than

$9\omega(G, w)/8$ channels on all weighted hexagon graphs. For higher values of reuse distance, there are hexagon graphs G such that G^r is an induced 5-cycle (see Figure 4.2). Therefore for reuse distance 3 or higher, no algorithm for channel assignment can guarantee using less than $5\omega(G, w)/4$ channels on all weighted hexagon graphs.

In [19], a lower bound for the competitive ratio of any recoloring algorithm was shown. The constraint that recoloring can only occur in response to a change in demand within a node's immediate neighborhood is added. A recoloring algorithm is said to have recoloring distance k if a node recolors its calls during a time step only if a change of weight has occurred within its k-locality.

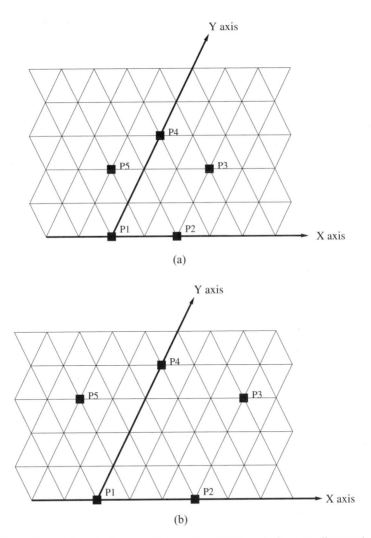

Figure 4.2   (a) 5-cycle for reuse distance 3 and (b) 5-cycle for reuse distance 4.

The following technical lemma aids the proof of the lower bound.

Lemma 1.4.1 [19] Let P be a path of length ℓ, with weight n on each of its $\ell + 1$ nodes. Then the minimal number of colors required to color P such that the end nodes have exactly α colors in common, is at least $2n + 2\alpha/(\ell - 1)$ when ℓ is odd, and at least $2n + 2(n - \alpha)/\ell$ when ℓ is even.

Let P, n, and ℓ be as in the statement of the lemma. Let u and v be the end nodes of P, and let u' and v' be the neighbors of u and v, respectively [See Figure 4.3(a)]. Then P' is constructed from P as follows. Node u is split into two connected nodes, u_1 and u_2, which are assigned weight α and $n - \alpha$, respectively. Similarly, node v is split into the connected nodes v_1 and v_2, with weight α and $n - \alpha$, respectively [Figure 4.3(b)]. Obviously, coloring P such that u and v have exactly α colors in common is equivalent to coloring P' such that u_1 and v_1 receive the same colors, and u_2 and v_2 receive completely different colors. Next, the graph P'' is constructed from P' as follows. Nodes u_1 and v_1 are identified into one node uv_1, and nodes u_2 and v_2 are joined by an edge [Figure 4.3(c)]. It is easy to see that any coloring of P'' is equivalent to a coloring of P' in which u_1 and u_2 receive the same colors, and u_2 and v_2 receive different colors, which in turn is equivalent to a coloring of P as required by the lemma.

To determine a lower bound on the minimal number of colors needed to color P'', observe the following. If ℓ is odd, then the subgraph of P'' induced by all nodes except u_2

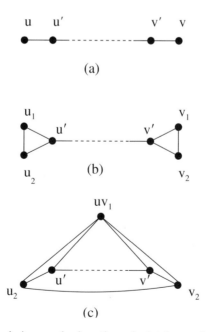

Figure 4.3 Multicoloring a path where the endpoints have colors in common.

and v_2 is an odd cycle of length ℓ. The sum of the weights on this cycle is $(\ell - 1)n + \alpha$, and the maximum size of an independent set in this cycle is $\frac{1}{2}(\ell - 1)$. Hence the minimum number of colors needed to color P'' is at least

$$\frac{(\ell - 1)n + \alpha}{\frac{1}{2}(\ell - 1)} = 2n + \frac{2\alpha}{\ell - 1}$$

If ℓ is even, then P'' consists of an odd cycle of length $\ell + 1$, plus a node (uv_1) that is joined to four consecutive nodes of this cycle. So the maximal size of an independent set in P'' is $\frac{1}{2}\ell$. The sum of the weights on the nodes of P'' is $(\ell - 1)n + \alpha + 2(n - \alpha) = (\ell + 1)n - \alpha$. Hence, the minimum number of colors needed to color P'' is at least

$$\frac{(\ell + 1)n - \alpha}{\frac{1}{2}\ell} = 2n + \frac{2(n - \alpha)}{\ell}$$

as claimed in the lemma.

The above lemma can be used to prove a lower bound on any online algorithm with re-coloring distance k, using an adversary argument. The adversary chooses a hexagon graph, and at any step can raise or increase the weight at any node. The algorithm must respond by assigning colors corresponding to the increased weight.

The following argument is from [19]. Fix an online algorithm with recoloring distance $k \geq 0$. There is a strategy for the adversary that forces the algorithm to use at least $2n + n/2(k + 1)$ colors, whereas the offline algorithm never needs more than $2n$ colors. The graph used by the adversary is shown in Figure 4.4. Let u and v be two nodes at distance 3

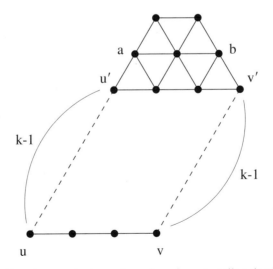

Figure 4.4 Graph used by adversary to show a lower bound on any online algorithm with recoloring distance k.

of each other along one axis of the grid. The adversary starts by raising the weight on u and v to n. If $k > 0$, the adversary continues to raise the weight to n on all nodes along two parallel axes of length $k - 1$, which make an angle of $\pi/3$ with the axis uv, and which start at u and v, respectively. The algorithm may color and recolor as desired.

Let u' and v' be the last nodes of the axis growing out of u and v, respectively, on which the weight has been raised. Nodes u' and v' have distance $k - 1$ from u and v, respectively. Next, the adversary raises the weight to n on two nodes, a and b, situated as follows. Node a is a neighbor of u', situated along the axis uu', at distance k from u. Node b is a neighbor of v' and lies at distance k from v, but is situated at an angle $\pi/3$ from the axis vv', and thus lies at distance 2 from node a (see Figure 4.4).

The next moves of the adversary will only involve nodes at distances greater than k from u and v, so the colors on u and v are now fixed. Let α be the number of colors that u and v have in common. The strategy of the adversary now depends on α. If $\alpha \geq n/2$, then the adversary raises the weight to n on the nodes c and d, which can be observed to have distance greater than k to both u and v. The nodes of positive weight now lie on a path of length $2k + 3$. By Lemma 4.4.1, the algorithm must now use at least $2n + n/(2k + 2)$ colors. If $\alpha < n/2$, the adversary raises the weight of node e, the common neighbor of a and b to n. By Lemma 4.4.1, the algorithm will have to use at least $2n + n/2(k + 1)$ colors. The number of colors needed by the off-line algorithm is $2n$. The above construction can be repeated as many times as desired, proving that there are infinitely long sequences on which the ratio bound of $1 + 1/4(k + 1)$ is achieved.

For the special case $k = 0$, a better bound can be proved [19]. Janssen et al. [19] also show a lower bound on the competitive ratio for any nonrecoloring online algorithm. For such algorithms, the adversary can specify which colors the algorithm should drop, by which it can force the remaining colors to stay. Thus, stronger lower bounds can be obtained for nonrecoloring algorithms. A graph and a sequence of requests can be created such that the offline algorithm could always color the graph using n colors, but any nonrecoloring online algorithm is forced to use $2n$ colors. The following theorem summarizes the lower bound results in [19]:

Theorem 1.4.2

1. Any online algorithm with recoloring distance $k \geq 0$ has competitive ratio at least $1 + 1/4(k + 1)$.

2. Any online algorithm with recoloring distance 0, acting on a hexagon graph of diameter at least 3, has competitive ratio at least $1 + 2/7$.

3. Any nonrecoloring online algorithm has competitive ratio at least 2.

4.5 THE STATIC CASE

In this section we describe the results on static channel assignment. The algorithms described here can be used as recoloring algorithms in the online setting as well. Hexagon graphs, unit disk graphs, odd cycles, and outerplanar graphs are the best-known upper bounds for the various classes of graphs and are summarized in Table 4.1.

TABLE 4.1   Best-known upper bounds for recoloring algorithms

Graph	Competitive ratio of best known algorithm
Odd cycles	1 [37]
Outerplanar graphs	1 [37]
Hexagon graphs, $r = 2$	$\frac{4}{3}$ [37, 35]
Hexagon graphs, $r = 3$	$\frac{7}{3}$ [9]
Hexagon graphs, $r > 3$	4 [23]
Unit disk graphs	3 [12, 32, 40]
k-colorable graphs	$\frac{k}{2}$ [17]

4.5.1   Reuse Distance 2 in Hexagon Graphs

As stated in the introduction, for this case, FA has a competitive ratio of 3. To see that this is a tight bound, consider a network with a red node, blue node, and green node, no two of which are adjacent to each other, and each of which has a weight of w. It is easy to see that $\chi(G, w) = \omega(G, w)$, whereas FA must use different colors for each and therefore uses three times the number of colors required.

Borrowing Strategies

There is a simple borrowing strategy called fixed preference allocation (FPA) that cuts the number of channels used by FA down by a factor of two. The key idea is as follows. Divide the channels into three sets of $\lceil \omega(G, w)/2 \rceil$ channels each. A red node takes as many red channels as it needs, starting from the first, and if it still needs more channels, takes green channels starting from the end. Similarly, blue nodes borrow from red if necessary, and green nodes borrow from blue. Suppose this assignment of channels causes a conflict between a green node and a red node that are neighbors. Then their combined weight must be greater than $\omega(G, w)$, a contradiction. Thus, the assignment is conflict-free, and the algorithm is $\frac{3}{2}$-competitive.

However, the best known algorithms have a competitive ratio of $\frac{4}{3}$ [37, 35, 42], and all make use of the structure of the hexagon graph. The algorithms in [35, 42] have slightly different descriptions, but are identical and centralized. Narayanan and Shende [37] give a different algorithm that can be implemented in a distributed fashion. Furthermore, it was modified and implemented in a local manner, as shown in [19]. The general idea in all is as follows. The algorithm consists of three phases. At the end of the first phase, the resulting graph is triangle-free. At the end of the second phase, the resulting graph is bipartite. The third phase finishes up by assigning channels to the bipartite graph.

We go on to describe the algorithm in detail now. Let $D = 3 \lceil \omega(G, w)/3 \rceil$; we divide the channels into four sets of $D/3$ channels each. The four sets will be called the red, blue, green, and purple sets of channels. As stated earlier, the algorithm can be divided into three phases. In the first phase, each node takes as many channels as needed from its nominal set of channels. For example, red nodes take as many red channels as needed and decrease their weight accordingly. Consider the resulting graph induced by nodes

Figure 4.5 A noncorner node of degree 2 (left), a corner node of degree 2 (center), and a corner node of degree 3 (right).

of positive weight. Suppose there is an triangle in this graph. This means that all three nodes had weight greater than $D/3$, a contradiction. Thus the remaining graph is triangle-free. This implies, furthermore, that any node in the graph with degree 3 has all neighbors of the same color, and the only way it has two neighbors of different colors is if they are all in a straight line (see Figure 4.5 for different types of nodes of degree at least 2). We call a node a corner node if it is of degree 2 or 3 and all its neighbors are of the same color.

The second phase is a borrowing phase, in which nodes borrow from a specified color set and only borrow channels that are unused at any neighbors. In particular, red corner nodes with green neighbors borrow available blue channels, blue corner nodes with red neighbors borrow available green channels, and green corner nodes with blue neighbors borrow available red channels. It is not difficult to see that all such corner nodes receive enough channels to complete their assignment, and drop out of the next phase.

From Figure 4.6, it is obvious that the resulting graph induced by nodes of positive weight at this stage cannot have a cycle and is thus bipartite. Furthermore, any edge in this bipartite graph has weight at most $D/3$, and all nodes that are endpoints of these edges can be assigned channels from the purple set in the final phase. An isolated node with remaining weight at most $D/3$ can use purple channels, and one with remaining weight at least $D/3$ can be shown to have neighbors that are light enough so that it can finish its assignment using borrowed channels from neighbors and purple channels.

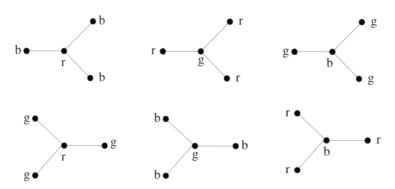

Figure 4.6 The orientations of corner nodes. After the second phase, corner nodes of the type in the second row drop out.

The Greedy Strategy

The greedy strategy is generally understood to be a nonrecoloring strategy in the online setting. However, it also makes sense for the static problem, and a distributed recoloring version of the greedy strategy was formulated and analyzed in [38]. Recall that in every step in the greedy strategy, every node is assigned the minimum numbered channels not being used by its neighbors. Some ordering of the nodes must be used in order to perform the assignment. In a distributed implementation, the ordering must take care to avoid two neighbors performing the assignment simultaneously, thereby deciding that a particular channel is available and claiming it. Prakash et al. [41] give a distributed implementation that focuses on how this mutual exclusion type of problem is solved, but do not give any bounds on the number of channels needed. In [38], the authors suggest a simple synchronization strategy based on rounds: first red nodes assign channels, followed by blue nodes, which are followed by green nodes. In this recoloring version of the greedy strategy, the red nodes do not have to consider any other nodes while performing their assignment, the blue nodes have to consider only the red nodes, and the green nodes have to consider all neighbors.

The key lemma used in [38] to analyze the maximum number of channels used by the greedy algorithm for an arbitrary graph and reuse distance is the following:

Lemma 4.5.1 Let $mc(v)$ be the highest channel used by the node v. For the greedy algorithm, and for any node v, $mc(v) \leq \min\{H_r(v) - RC_r(v), w(v) + \max_{u \in N_r(v)} mc(u)\}$.

The number of distinct channels used by nodes in $N_r(v)$ is at most $H_r(v) - w(v) - RC_r(v)$. Therefore, v will never use a channel higher than $H_r(v) - RC_r(v)$. Also, if u is a node in $N_r(v)$ that uses the highest channel in v's neighborhood, v will never use more than the next $w(v)$ channels.

For the case of reuse distance 2 in hexagon graphs, the above lemma can be used to show that the greedy algorithm can never use a channel higher than $5\omega(G, w)/3$. To see this, observe that red and blue nodes can never use a channel higher than $\omega(G, w)$. For a green node v, if $w(v) \leq 2\omega(G, w)/3$, then since no neighbor of v uses a channel higher than $\omega(G, w)$, we have $mc(v) \leq \omega(G, w) + w(v)$. If instead $w(v) > 2\omega(G, w)/3$, then $mc(v) \leq H_2(v) \leq 5\omega(G, w)/3$. Finally, this is a tight bound, as shown by Figure 4.7. The reader

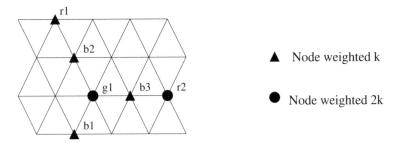

Figure 4.7 An example in which the greedy algorithm uses $5\omega(G, w)/3$ channels.

can verify that $\omega(G, w) = 3k$, and that there is an optimal assignment using $3k$ channels, but the greedy algorithm will use $5k$ channels. Thus, the greedy algorithm uses 5/3 times the optimal number of channels required.

Distributed Algorithms

Janssen et al. [19] give a framework to analyze distributed algorithms. In particular, an algorithm is said to be k-local if the only information available to a node apart from its own history is the current weights of nodes that are within graph distance k from it. However, since the nodes themselves communicate via a wireline network, it is reasonable to allow nodes to exchange other information with nodes in their k-locality. In particular, a node may send the list of channels it is using to the nodes in its k-locality. By this revised definition, the greedy algorithm and FPA can be seen to be 1-local. Although the 4/3-approximation algorithm described earlier is not distributed, two distributed implementations of the algorithm in [37] are given in [19]. Algorithms with better competitive ratios are shown for increasing values of locality. The best known results for k local algorithms for small values of k are summarized in Table 4.2. The corresponding lower bounds that follow from Theorem 4.4.2 are also given for comparison.

4.5.2   Reuse Distance 3 in Hexagon Graphs

For reuse distance 3, since there is a 7-coloring for any square graph, FA has a competitive ratio of 7. The borrowing strategy given by [17] has a competitive ratio of 3.5. The best-known algorithm was given by Feder and Shende [9]. We describe it briefly here. The graph is divided into seven independent sets, according to the base coloring, and each set is assigned a nominal set of ℓ channels. Call a node "heavy" if its weight is greater than ℓ and light otherwise. The algorithm proceeds in two phases. In the first phase, each node takes as many channels as needed from its own nominal set. All light nodes are done in this phase and drop out. In the second phase, any remaining (heavy) node borrows as many unused channels as needed from its neighbors' nominal sets.

It remains to show that the unused channels in a heavy node v's neighborhood suffice to finish v's assignment. Note that the neighborhood of any node v can be covered by four cliques (see Figure 4.8). Thus, the total weight of the neighborhood of v is at most $4\omega(G, w) - 3w(v)$ and this forms an upper bound on the number of channels needed for the algorithm to work. For $\ell = 2\omega(G, w)/5$, for example, it is clear that $4\omega(G, w) - 3w(v) \leq 7\ell$ for any heavy node v. However, this would give an algorithm with performance ratio 2.8.

TABLE 4.2   Best known k-local algorithms

Recoloring distance	Lower bound on competitive ratio	Best known
0-local	9/7	3
1-local	9/8	3/2
2-local	13/12	17/12
4-local	21/20	4/3

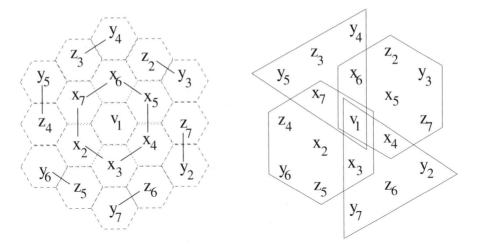

Figure 4.8 The neighborhood of a node v contains exactly three nodes of each base color different from v's, and can be covered with three cliques.

The authors of [9] perform a more careful analysis of the neighborhood of a heavy node v to show that $\ell = \omega(G, w)/3$ suffices. For instance, they observe that a node v of base color i has three neighbors of each base color $\neq i$, but many of the channels used are the same. Thus, some of the weight of the two lighter neighbors can be charged to the heaviest neighbor of that color. This means that for a heavy node v, if all three of its neighbors of a particular base color are light, then only one of them counts, and the other two can be considered to be of zero weight, since all the channels assigned to them would also be assigned to the heaviest neighbor. Another observation is that there cannot be too many heavy nodes in the neighborhood of a heavy node v. In particular, there can either be at most four heavy nodes if all are outer neighbors of v (see Figure 4.8), or at most three if one of them is an neighbor of v.

Thus, there are only four possibilities for v's neighborhood: It contains (a) at most one node of each distinct base color, except for two pairs of heavy nodes, each corresponding to a base color different from v's and from each other; (b) at most one node of each distinct base color except for a triple of heavy nodes, all of the same color; (c) at most one node of each distinct color; and (d) at most one node of each distinct color, except for a pair of heavy nodes of a color different from v's. In the first two cases, there are two nodes whose demand can effectively be reduced by $\omega(G, w)/3$ since this corresponds to reused channels. Thus, the total weight of v's neighborhood is at most $4\omega(G, w) - 3w(v) - 2\omega(G, w)/3 \leq 7\omega(G, w)/3$, which implies that there are sufficient channels for v to borrow to complete its assignment. The other cases are more complicated, but lead to the same conclusion. See [9] for details.

It is possible to construct a square graph G such that $\chi(G, 2) = \omega(G, w)$, but the algorithm needs $7\omega(G, w)/3$ channels, thus the competitive ratio of the algorithm is exactly 7/3.

We note here that Feder and Shende [9] mention a centralized strategy for this case that has competitive ratio at most 2. This uses a simple idea involving a convex hull technique. The algorithm follows from the following simple observation. Consider an embedding of a square graph on a triangular lattice. Extract a node on the convex hull of the graph. It is easy to see that its neighborhood can be covered with two cliques. Hence, if every node in v's neighborhood is already assigned channels from the set $[1, \ldots, 2\omega(G, w)]$, then v can also find channels from this set without conflicting with any neighbors. Therefore, the algorithm first constructs an ordering of nodes by computing the convex hull of the nodes, removing a hull node, and repeating this process on the remaining nodes. Finally, nodes are assigned channels in the reverse of this ordering. It is clear that $2\omega(G, w)$ channels suffice.

In [38], the authors show that the recoloring greedy strategy has a competitive ratio between 7/3 and 23/8 for reuse distance 3 in hexagon graphs and, thus, for the recoloring case, the borrowing strategy is at least as good as the greedy strategy.

4.5.3 Arbitrary Graphs

Janssen and Kilakos [17] show that for general k-colorable graphs, a generalization of the FPA strategy discussed earlier has a performance ratio of $k/2$. In what follows, we discuss some specific classes of graphs that have been studied in the context of radio channel assignment. These include odd cycles, outerplanar graphs, and graphs derived from hexagon graphs, either by considering arbitrary reuse distance in such graphs, or by considering networks that have a certain amount of overlap between adjacent cells. Other interesting classes of graphs are unit disk graphs and graphs that can be drawn in an (r, s)-civilized manner.

Odd Cycles and Outerplanar Graphs
Odd cycles and outerplanar graphs can be multicolored optimally using simple linear time sequential algorithms. The chromatic number of an odd cycle with $2m + 1$ nodes is $\max\{\omega(G, w), \lceil W/m \rceil\}$, where W is the sum of the weights of all nodes in the cycle. The centralized algorithm given in [37] first finds the minimum index k such that $\Sigma_{i=1}^{2k+1} w_i \leq k\chi(G, w)$. Such an index must exist, because m satisfies the above property. Then the algorithm uses contiguous colors in a cyclic manner from the colors $[1, \chi(G, w)]$ to color nodes 1 to $2k$. The remaining nodes are colored based on their parity, as in a bipartite graph. The optimal algorithm for odd cycles is extended in [37] to derive an optimal algorithm to multicolor outerplanar graphs.

Arbitrary Reuse Distance in Hexagon Graphs
We consider the case of arbitrary reuse distance for hexagon graphs. The problem of channel assignment in a hexagon graph (G, w) with reuse distance r is equivalent to multicoloring the graph (G^r, w). As stated in Section 4.4, there exist graphs (G^r, w) that require $5\omega(G^r, w)/4$ channels. An upper bound of 6 for the performance ratio of the greedy strategy follows from the observation that the neighborhood of any node in a graph G^r can always be covered with 6 cliques. However, a borrowing strategy similar to the one in [9] for reuse distance 3 has a better upper bound. In particular, as shown in [35] and [45], for a hexagon graph G with reuse distance r, $\omega(G^r) = \chi(G^r) = 3r^2/4$ if r is even and $(3r^2 + 1)/4$

otherwise. This was used in [38] to derive an algorithm for channel assignment with performance ratio $18r^2/(3r^2 + 20)$ if r is even, and $(18r^2 + 6)/(3r^2 + 21)$ when r is odd.

The best known performance ratio for channel assignment for reuse distance $r > 3$ is achieved by an algorithm called cluster partitioning in [23]. The key idea is to partition the graph into clusters that are maximal cliques, as with FA. However, unlike FA, where identical sets of channels are assigned to corresponding cells in different clusters, here, sets of D channels are assigned to entire clusters, in such a way that any pair of clusters containing cells that are within distance $r - 1$ are assigned different sets. Calls arising in any cluster are assigned channels from its nominal set of channels. Furthermore, it turns out that it is possible to color the clusters with four colors such that any two clusters that have nodes within distance $r - 1$ of each other get different colors. Thus, four sets of channels suffice, which implies a performance ratio of 4 for the algorithm.

Overlapping Cells

Matula et al. [34] define a model for channel assignment in cellular networks that include overlapping cell segments. In particular, instead of assuming the network to consist of disjoint hexagonal cells, each served by a single base station, they assume that adjacent cells include an overlap region that can be covered by both transceivers. Cell segments thus fall into two classes: those that can be covered by a single transceiver and those that can covered by two. (If the overlap segments are larger, then there is a third type of segment that can be covered by three transceivers.) The channel assignment problem is then modeled by a regular tripartite graph with three sets of nodes: (a) transceiver nodes with degree 7, (b) cell segment nodes with degree 1, and (c) cell segment nodes with degree 2. There is an edge between transceiver node i and cell segment j if transceiver node i covers the segment j. A channel assignment is an assignment of integers to edges such that the total weight assigned to all edges outgoing from a transceiver node is at most the number of channels it holds, and the total weight on all edges incoming to a cell segment is equal to the number of mobiles in the cell segment. Using network flow techniques, they derive a capacity–demand theorem that states that a channel assignment is always possible unless there is a connected subregion of cell segments containing more channel requests than the total capacity of all transceivers within or on the boundary of the subregion and covering any part of the subregion with an overlapping segment.

A subsequent paper [6] uses the same model as described above. The authors propose a new load balancing algorithm called the cluster algorithm and show that it has a competitive ratio of 4 when applied to the channel assignment problem.

Unit Disk Graphs

Unit disk graphs are intersection graphs of equal sized disks in the plane. It is easy to see that given the distance model, multicoloring is equivalent to coloring for unit disk graphs: a node with weight w can be replaced with w nodes of weight 1 in close proximity to each other. Such graphs can be seen as a more general model of cellular networks. Also, a hexagon graph for any reuse distance r is a unit disk graph.

Unit disk graphs can be used to model broadcast networks where the nodes are transceivers of equal power and two nodes that are within transmission range of each other are within each other's disks and are therefore neighbors. Neighboring nodes may not broadcast simultaneously; coloring a unit disk graph thus gives a broadcast schedule for the corresponding ad hoc network. The number of colors required is the number of rounds required in the broadcast schedule.

In [12], it is shown that the coloring problem for unit disk graphs is NP-complete for any fixed number of colors $k \geq 3$, even if the distance model is given. 3-approximation algorithms for the problem are given in [12, 32, 40]. The algorithm in [12] works as follows. Divide the part of the plane containing the unit disk graph into strips of width $\sqrt{3}/2$. The induced subgraph in each strip is a cocomparability graph and can therefore be colored optimally using $\omega(G, w)$ colors. Furthermore, a node in a given strip may be a neighbor of a node in its own strip, an adjacent strip, or a node that is two strips away, but no other nodes in the graph. Therefore, three disjoint sets of $\omega(G, w)$ colors can be used to color the nodes in three adjacent strips, and then the sets of colors can be reused. Marathe et al. [32] use an algorithm by Hochbaum [14] for coloring arbitrary graphs in $\delta(G) + 1$ colors [where $\delta(G)$ is the maximum δ such that G contains a subgraph in which every node has degree at least δ] and prove that it has performance ratio 3 for unit disk graphs. Peeters [40] has shown that coloring the nodes greedily and sequentially using a lexicographic ordering of the nodes also achieves a performance ratio of 3.

McDiarmid and Reed [36] study the case when the number of nodes is infinite. For V, a countable set of points in the plane, the upper density of V is defined as in $f_{x>0} f(x)$ where $f(x)$ is the supremum of the ratio $|V \cap S|/x^2$ over all open $x \times x$ squares S with sides aligned with the axes. They show that for any countable set of points V in the plane with a finite positive upper density, the ratio of chromatic number by clique number tends to $2\sqrt{3}/\pi$ which is about 1.103 as the radius of the disks tends to infinity.

Marathe et al. [33] give approximation algorithms for the coloring and distance 2 coloring problem in graphs that can be drawn in an (r, s)-civilized manner.

4.6 THE ONLINE CASE

In this section, we describe algorithms for online channel assignment that do not perform reassignment of channels. Once a call is assigned a channel, it "keeps" the channel for its entire duration. While there has been a lot of work on online graph coloring (see, for example, [16, 29, 46]), there has been very little work on online graph multicoloring. The best known upper bounds for the various classes of graphs are summarized in Table 4.3.

TABLE 4.3   Best-known upper bounds for nonrecoloring algorithms

Graph	Competitive ratio of best-known algorithm
Hexagon graphs, $r = 2$	3 [30]
Hexagon graphs, $r = 3$	4 [9]
Hexagon graphs, $r > 3$	4 [23]
Unit disk graphs	6 [32]
k-colorable graphs	k [17]

4.6.1 Reuse Distance 2 in Hexagon Graphs

FA is a nonrecoloring strategy that has a competitive ratio of 3. A lower bound of 2 for this case was derived in [19] for the competitive ratio of any nonrecoloring strategy. The only other nonrecoloring strategy to have been investigated in terms of its competitive ratio is the greedy strategy. In this algorithm, every node simply uses the lowest numbered channels that are not being used currently by any of its neighbors. The competitive ratio of this strategy is at most 3, since the neighborhood of any node can be covered with three cliques. In [4], a careful case-by-case analysis of the neighborhood of a node was used to show an upper bound of $2.5\omega(G, w)$ for the number of channels used by this algorithm, under the assumption that calls, once started, never terminate. In contrast, in [38], a graph and sequence of weight vectors was given to show that the greedy algorithm would use $2.5\omega(G, w)$ channels while the optimal offline algorithm would use only $\omega(G, w)$ channels. Thus the competitive ratio of the greedy algorithm was shown to be at least 2.5.

4.6.2 Reuse Distance 3 in Hexagon Graphs

FA has a competitive ratio of 7 for this case. The only other nonrecoloring strategy to have been studied for this case is the greedy strategy. Since the neighborhood of any node can be covered with 4 cliques (see Figure 4.8), it is easy to see that $4\omega(G, w)$ channels will suffice for the greedy strategy. In [38], a lower bound of 3 is shown on the competitive ratio of the greedy strategy: a graph and a sequence of weight vectors are given on which the greedy strategy uses at least three times the number of channels needed by an offline algorithm.

4.6.3 Arbitrary Graphs

For a k-colorable graph, FA has a competitive ratio of k. For a hexagon graph with arbitrary reuse distance, as already mentioned, the neighborhood of a node can be covered with 6 cliques. Thus, the greedy strategy has a competitive ratio of at most 6 for this case. The greedy strategy is also shown to have a competitive ratio of 6 for unit disk graphs in [32]. The cluster partitioning algorithm has a competitive ratio of 4 for hexagon graphs with arbitrary reuse distance [23].

4.7 DISCUSSION AND OPEN PROBLEMS

The problem of channel assignment has been extensively studied over the last decade. However, many key questions remain unanswered as yet. For reuse distance 2, in the static case, what is a tight bound on the number of channels required in the worst case? It is known that $4\omega(G, w)/3$ channels suffice, and that there is a graph requiring $9\omega(G, w)/8$ channels. In the online case, in which once assigned a channel, a call retains it for its duration, what is a tight bound on the competitive ratio of an online algorithm? It is known that 2 is a lower bound, while the greedy algorithm achieves a competitive ratio of 2.5. Table 4.2 demonstrates that for increasing values of k, distributed algorithms in which nodes have access to information about their k-localities can achieve better competitive ratios. At the same time, the limitations posed by restricting the locality of an algorithm are not completely understood yet.

For reuse distance 3, very little is known, and the gap between the known lower bound and best known upper bound is quite wide. Although a few authors have proposed randomized algorithms, there are no known bounds on the competitive ratios of these algorithms.

Prakash et al. [41] propose several desirable features of channel assignment algorithms. Some of these are features such as minimizing connection set-up time and energy conservation at mobile hosts, which would apply to the distributed algorithms studied here. Another quality that is considered important is minimizing the number of hand-offs. Although intercell handoffs were not taken into account by any of the algorithms described here, clearly the nonrecoloring algorithms do not create any intracell handoffs. On the other hand, the recoloring algorithms can potentially force many intracell handoffs to occur. Designing algorithms that would limit the number of such handoffs would be an interesting avenue for future research. Finally, adaptability to load distributions is a desirable feature of channel assignment algorithms. Although it is clear that dynamic channel allocation does better than fixed allocation in this regard, it would be useful to know where the borrowing strategies stand in the picture.

REFERENCES

1. N. Alon and M. Tarsi Colorings and orientations of graphs, *Combinatorica, 12*(2): 125–134, 1992.

2. J. Bondy and U. Murty, *Graph Theory with Applications,* London: Macmillan, 1976.

3. A. Borodin and R. El-Yaniv, *Online Computation and Competitive Analysis,* Cambridge: Cambridge University Press, 1998.

4. I. Caragiannis, C. Kaklamanis, and E. Papaionnou, Efficient online communication in cellular networks, in *Symposium on Parallel Algorithms and Architecture,* Bar Harbor, ME: ACM Press, 2000.

5. D. C. Cox and D. O. Reudink, Dynamic channel assignment in two dimension large-scale mobile radio systems, *Bell Sys. Tech. J., 51:* 1611–28, 1972.

6. P. Cresenzi, G. Gambosi, and P. Penna, Online algorithms for the channel assignment problem in cellular networks, in *Proceedings of Dial M for Mobility,* Boston: ACM Press, 2000.

7. S. Engel and M. M. Peritsky, Statistically-optimum dynamic server assignment in systems with interfering servers, *IEEE Transactions on Vehicular Technology, 22:* 203–209, 1973.

8. P. Erdos, A. L. Rubin, and H. Taylor, Choosability in graphs, in *Proceedings of the West Coast Conference on Combinatorics, Graph Theory, and Computing,* pp. 125–157, 1979.

9. T. Feder and S. M. Shende, Online channel allocation in FDMA networks with reuse constraints, *Inform. Process. Lett., 67*(6): 295–302, 1998.

10. A. Gamst, Some lower bounds for a class of frequency assignment problems, *IEEE Trans. Veh. Technol., 35*(1): 8–14, 1986.

11. N. Garg, M. Papatriantafilou, and T. Tsigas, Distributed list coloring: how to dynamically allocate frequencies to mobile base stations, in *Symposium on Parallel and Distributed Processing,* pp. 18–25, 1996.

12. A. Graf, M. Stumpf, and G. Weibenfels, On coloring unit disk graphs, *Algorithmica, 20:* 277–293, 1998.

13. W. K. Hale, Frequency assignment: Theory and applications, *Proceedings of the IEEE, 68*(12): 1497–1514, 1980.

14. D. S. Hochbaum, Efficient bounds for the stable set, vertex cover, and set packing problems, *Discrete Applied Mathematics, 6:*243–254, 1983.

15. C. L. I and P. H. Chao, Local packing-distributed dynamic channel allocation at cellular base station, *Proceedings of GLOBECOM,* Houston, TX: IEEE, 1993.

16. S. Irani, Coloring inductive graphs online, in *Symposium on the Foundations of Computer Science,* pp. 470–479, New York: IEEE, 1990.

17. J. Janssen and K. Kilakos, Adaptive multicolourings, *Combinatorica, 20*(1):87–102, 2000.

18. J. Janssen, K. Kilakos, and O. Marcotte, Fixed preference frequency allocation for cellular telephone systems, *IEEE Transactions on Vehicular Technology, 48*(2):533–541, March 1999.

19. J. Janssen, D. Krizanc, L. Narayanan, and S. Shende, Distributed online frequency assignment in cellular networks, *Journal of Algorithms, 36:*119–151, 2000.

20. J. M. Janssen, Channel assignment and graph labeling, in I. Stojmenovic (Ed.), *Handbook of Wireless Networks and Mobile Computing,* New York: Wiley, 2002.

21. B. Jaumard, O. Marcotte, and C. Meyer, Mathematical models and exact methods for channel assignment in cellular networks, in B. Sansó and P. Soriano, editors, *Telecommunications Network Planning,* Norwell, MA: Kluwer, 1999.

22. T. R. Jensen and B. Toft, *Graph Coloring Problems,* New York: Wiley, 1995.

23. S. Jordan and E. J. Schwabe, Worst-case performance of cellular channel assignment policies, *Wireless Networks, 2:* 265–275, 1996.

24. T. Kahwa and N. Georganas, A hybrid channel assignment scheme in large-scale cellular-structured mobile communication systems, *IEEE Transactions on Communications, 4:* 432–438, 1978.

25. A. Karlin, M. Manasse, L. Rudolph, and D. Sleator, Competitive snoopy caching, *Algorithmica, 3*(1): 70–119, 1988.

26. I. Katzela and S. Naghshineh, Channel assignment schemes for cellular mobile telecommunication systems: A comprehensive survey, *IEEE Personal Communications, 3,* 3, 10–31, 1996.

27. L. Le Bris, A simple randomized algorithm for the fixed frequency assignment problem, 1997.

28. S. Leonardi, A. Marchetti-Spaccamela, A. Prescuitti, and A. Rosen, Online randomized call control revisited, In *Symposium on Discrete Algorithms,* pp. 323–332, San Francisco: ACM Press, 1998.

29. L. Lovasz, M. Saks, and W. Trotter, An online graph coloring algorithm with sub-linear performance ratio, *Discrete Math, 75:* 319–325, 1989.

30. V. H. MacDonald, Advanced mobile phone service: The cellular concept, *Bell Systems Technical Journal, 58*(1), 1979.

31. E. Malesinsca, An optimization method for the channel assignment in mixed environments, In *Proceedings of MOBICOM,* Berkeley, CA: ACM Press, 1995.

32. M. V. Marathe, H. Breu, H. B. Hunt, S. S. Ravi, and D. J. Rosenkrantz, Simple heuristics for unit disk graphs, *Networks, 25:* 59–68, 1995.

33. M. V. Marathe, S. O. Krumke, and S. S. Ravi, Approximation algorithms for broadcast scheduling in radio networks, in *Proceedings of Dial M for Mobility,* Dallas, TX: ACM Press, 1998.

34. D. Matula, M. Iridon, C. Yang, and H. C. Cankaya, A graph-theoretic approach for channel assignment in cellular networks, in *Proceedings of Dial M for Mobility,* Dallas, TX: ACM Press, 1998.

35. C. McDiarmid and B. Reed, Channel assignment and weighted colouring. Submitted for publication, 1997.

36. C. McDiarmid and B. Reed, Colouring proximity graphs in the plane, *Discrete Mathematics, 199:* 123–137, 1999.

37. L. Narayanan and S. Shende, Static frequency assignment in cellular networks, *Algorithmica, 29:* 396–409, 2001.

38. L. Narayanan and Y. Tang, Worst-case analysis of a dynamic channel assignment strategy, in *Proceedings of Dial M for Mobility 2000,* pp. 215–227, Boston: ACM Press, 2000.

39. G. Pantizou, G. Penatris, and P. Spirakis, Competitive call control in mobile networks, in *Proceedings of ISAAC '97,* New York: Springer-Verlag, pp. 404–413, 1997.

40. R. Peeters, On coloring *j*-unit sphere graphs. Technical Report FEW 512, Department of Economics, Tilburg University, Tilburg, The Netherlands, 1991.

41. R. Prakash, N. Shivaratri, and M. Singhal, Distributed dynamic channel allocation for mobile computing, in *Principles of Distributed Computing,* Ottawa, Canada: ACM Press, pp. 47–56, 1995.

42. N. Schabanel, S. Ubeda, and Zerovnik, A note on upper bounds for the span of frequency planning in cellular networks. Submitted for publication, 1997.

43. M. Serizawa and D. Goodman, Instability and deadlock of distributed dynamic channel allocation, *Proc. 43rd IEEE VTC,* pp. 528–531, 1993.

44. C. Thomassen, Every planar graph is 5-choosable, *Journal of Combinatorial Theory, Series B, 62:* 180–181, 1994.

45. J. van den Heuvel, R. A. Leese, and M. A. Shepherd, Graph labeling and radio channel assignment, *Journal of Graph Theory, 29:* 263–283, 1999.

46. S. Vishwanathan. Randomized online graph coloring. *Journal of Algorithms, 13:* 657–669, 1992.

47. W. Yue, Analytical methods to calculate the performance of a cellular mobile radio communication system with hybrid channel assignment, *IEEE Transactions on Vehicular Technology, 40, 2,* 453–459, 1991.

48. J. Zerovnik, On a distributed randomized algorithm for frequency assignment, in *Proceedings of the High Performance Computing Symposium,* San Diego, pp. 399–404, 1999.

49. M. Zhang and T.-S. P. Yum, Comparisons of channel assignment strategies in cellular mobile telephone systems, *IEEE Transactions in Vehicular Technology, 38:* 211–215, 1989.

CHAPTER 5

Channel Assignment and Graph Labeling

JEANNETTE C. M. JANSSEN

Department of Mathematics and Statistics, Dalhousie University, Halifax, N.S., Canada

5.1 INTRODUCTION

Due to rapid growth in the use of wireless communication services and the corresponding scarcity and high cost of radio spectrum bandwidth, it has become increasingly important for cellular network operators to maximize spectrum efficiency. Such efficiency can be achieved by optimal frequency reuse, i.e., the simultaneous use of the same part of the radio spectrum by communication links in different locations of the network. Optimal frequency reuse is constrained by noise levels, resulting from interference between communication links, that must be kept at acceptable levels (see [25]).

In the previous chapter [28], the problem of assigning channels to minimize spectrum use while satisfying interference constraints was discussed in its simplest form. In this form, each pair of cells in the network can either use the same channel simultaneously or not. However, for networks based on frequency division (FDMA) or time division (TDMA), there can be a significant difference in the amount of interference between channels that are near each other in the radio spectrum and channels that are far apart. This implies that the distance between cells that use channels close together in frequency must be greater than the distance between cells that use channels that are far apart. The constraints for channel assignment resulting from this consideration are referred to as *channel separation constraints*.

As discussed in [28], a graph model can be used for the channel assignment problem. The nodes of the graph correspond to cells or their base stations and the edges represent cell adjacency. We assume that a fixed demand for channels is given for each cell, and that a channel assignment assigning exactly that many channels to the cell must be found. The algorithms reviewed here apply to the static situation. However, in many cases the same algorithms can also be used in the dynamic situation, where the demand for channels changes over time. Algorithms based on a preassigned set of channels per node (such as Algorithms A and A′, described in Section 5.3) can be directly adapted to the dynamic case. Other algorithms can be adapted if limited reassignment of the channels used to carry ongoing calls is permitted. From another viewpoint, the static demand could represent the average or maximum possible demand for channels in the cell, and the fixed channel assignment based on this demand is expected to perform well even in the dynamic situa-

Handbook of Wireless Networks and Mobile Computing, Edited by Ivan Stojmenović.
ISBN 0-471-41902-8 © 2002 John Wiley & Sons, Inc.

tion. In the graph model given here, the demand is represented by a positive integer $w(v)$, associated with each node v of the graph.

An assignment of integer values to the nodes of a graph so that certain conditions are satisfied is referred to as a *graph labeling*. A coloring of a graph can thus be seen as a special case of a graph labeling, satisfying the condition that the labels of adjacent nodes must be distinct. The framework of graph labeling gives us the possibility to incorporate the channel separation constraints. We represent these constraints by a nonincreasing sequence of positive integer parameters $c_0, c_1, \ldots, c_k$ (so that $c_0 \geq c_1 \geq \ldots \geq c_k$). Making the reasonable assumption that graph distance relates to physical distance between cells, we require that channels assigned to nodes (cells) at graph distance i from each other must have a separation of at least c_i.

The constraint c_0 represents the separation between channels assigned to the same cell and is referred to as the *cosite constraint*. The constraints between different cells are referred to as *intersite constraints*. Although the cosite constraint is often high compared to the other constraints, the intersite constraints most often take smaller values, especially one and two. In somewhat confusing terms, an intersite constraint of one, which indicates that channels assigned to the corresponding cells must be distinct, is often referred to as a *cochannel constraint*. An intersite constraint of two, which codifies the requirement that channels assigned to a pair of cells cannot be next to each other in the radio spectrum, is often called an *adjacent-channel constraint*. Note further that graph labeling usually refers to an assignment of one channel per node, so that c_0 is irrelevant. In Section 5.3, we will show how graph labelings can be useful in finding algorithms for channel assignment problems with demands greater than 1. We will now proceed with a formal definition of the model described, and a review of other relevant models.

5.1.1 Graph Models

The definitions and notations used in this chapter are consistent with those introduced in the previous chapter [28]. For a general background on graph theory, the reader is referred to [8].

A *constrained graph* $G = (V, E, c_0, \ldots, c_k)$ is a graph $G = (V, E)$ and positive integer parameters $c_0, \ldots, c_k, c_0 \geq c_1 \geq \ldots \geq c_k$ called its *constraints*. The constraints represent the prescribed channel spacing for pairs of channels assigned to the same node or to different nodes. More precisely, c_i represents the constraint between nodes at graph distance i from each other. The *reuse distance* of G equals $k + 1$, the minimum graph distance between nodes that can use the same channel. For consistency, the constraint between nodes whose distance is at least the reuse distance is defined to be zero.

A *constrained, weighted* graph is a pair (G, w) where G is a constrained graph and w is a positive integral weight vector indexed by the nodes of G. The component of w corresponding to node u is denoted by $w(u)$ and called the *weight* of node u. The weight of node u represents the number of calls to be serviced at node u. We use $w_{\max}$ to denote $\max\{w(v) \mid v \in V\}$ and $w_{\min}$ to denote the corresponding minimum weight of any node in the graph. For any set $S \subseteq V$, we use $w(S)$ to denote the sum of the weight of all nodes in S.

In the context of our graph model, a formal definition of a channel assignment can now be given. A *channel assignment* for a constrained, weighted graph (G, w) where $G = (V, E,$

$c_0, \ldots, c_k$) is an assignment f of sets of nonnegative integers (representing the channels) to the nodes of G satisfying the conditions:

$$|f(u)| = w(u) \qquad \text{for all } u \in V$$
$$i \in f(u) \text{ and } j \in f(v) \Rightarrow |i - j| \geq c_\ell \qquad \text{for all } u, v \in V \text{ so that } d_G(u, v) = \ell.$$

The bandwidth used by a channel assignment is represented by its span. The *span* $S(f)$ of a channel assignment f of a constrained weighted graph is the difference between the lowest and the highest channel assigned by f. The span of a constrained, weighted graph (G, w) denoted by $S(G, w)$, is the minimum span of any channel assignment for (G, w).

The regular layouts often used for cellular networks can be modeled as subgraphs of an infinite lattice. An n-dimensional lattice is a collection of points in $\mathbb{R}^n$ by n that are linear integer combinations of the generating vectors $e_1, \ldots, e_n$. The graph corresponding to the lattice has the points as its nodes, and two nodes are adjacent precisely when one can be obtained from the other by adding a generating vector.

The linear layout of mobile networks for car phones running along highways can be modeled as a path that is a subgraph of the line lattice. The line lattice is a one-dimensional lattice generated by $\mathbf{e} = (1)$. The line lattice is bipartite. Another bipartite graph is the square lattice, which is generated by $\mathbf{e}_2 = \binom{0}{1}$ and $\mathbf{e}_1 = \binom{1}{0}$. A subgraph of the square lattice is called a *bidimensional grid*.

The type of graph most commonly used to model cellular networks is the hexagon graph. Hexagon graphs are subgraphs of the triangular lattice, which is generated by $\mathbf{e}_1 = \binom{1}{0}$ and $\mathbf{d} = \binom{1/2}{1/2 \sqrt{3}}$. Hexagon graphs model the adjacencies between hexagonal cells in a regular cellular layout resembling a honeycomb. This layout is popular with network designers since hexagons resemble the circular area around a transmitter where its signals can be comfortably received. In urban networks, hexagonal networks cannot always be achieved because of limitations of terrain. On the other hand, networks based on satellite systems operate with almost perfect hexagon-based networks.

Channel assignment algorithms are often built on a basic assignment of one channel per node, known as a graph labeling. Formally, a graph labeling of a graph $G = (V, E)$ is any assignment $f: V \to \mathbb{N}$ of integers to the nodes. The labeling f satisfies the constraints $c_1, \ldots c_k$ if for all pairs of nodes u, v at distance $d = d_G(u, v) \leq k$ from each other, $|f(u) - f(v)| \geq c_d$. The span $S(f)$ of a labeling f is defined as $S(f) = \max f(V)$, the value of the highest label assigned by f. Note: if the lowest label used is zero, then the definition of the span of a graph labeling is consistent with that of a channel assignment.

In order to use a graph labeling to find channel assignments for weight vectors with components greater than 1, one must know the "offset" that is needed when the labeling is repeated. This notion is captured in the definition of cyclic span. The *cyclic span* of a labeling f is the smallest number M such that, for all pairs of nodes u, v at graph distance d from each other ($d \leq k$), $|f(u) - f(v)| \geq M - c_d$.

The first paper to consider graph labelings for constraints $c_1, \ldots c_k$, [15], referred to them as $L(c_1, \ldots c_k)$-labelings. The specific case of a graph labeling with $c_1 = 2, c_2 = 1$ is called a *radio coloring*, [10], or λ-coloring (see for example [4]). Labelings for graphs with constraints $c_1, c_2, \ldots, c_k = k, k - 1, \ldots, 2, 1$, where k is the diameter of the graph, are called *radio labelings*, and were studied by Chartrand et al. [6].

A related model is based on a representation of the constraints by the minimum distance that must exist between pairs of cells that are assigned channels a fixed distance apart in the radio spectrum (see [26, 37], for example). More precisely, a set of nonincreasing parameters $d_0, d_1, \ldots, d_k$ is given and a channel assignment f has to fulfill the condition that for any pair of nodes (cells) u and v

$$i \in f(u) \text{ and } j \in f(v) \text{ and } |i - j| = \ell \Rightarrow d(u, v) > d_\ell$$

The distance $d(u, v)$ can either be used to mean the physical distance between the corresponding base stations or the graph distance between the nodes. If graph distance is used, then the correspondence between this model and our model is that $d_\ell = \min\{i | c_i < \ell\}$ for $\ell > 0$, $d_0 = k + 1$, and $c_i = \min\{\ell | i > d_\ell\}$. In this model, d_0 equals the reuse distance.

Another model assumes that for each pair of adjacent nodes u, v a separation constraint $c_{u,v}$ is given (see for example [30]). A channel assignment f must satisfy the condition that, for each pair u, v

$$i \in f(u) \text{ and } j \in f(v) \Rightarrow |i - j| \geq c_{u,v}$$

This model is useful if geographical distance is not the only cause of interference, a case often seen in urban environments where additional factors like obstructing structures and antenna placement affect interference levels. In such cases, the interference information is often obtained from measurements, and is reported in the form of an interference matrix with entries for each pair u, v.

The above model is more general than the one used in this chapter. However, the latter model is consistent with the one described above .This is easily seen by setting $c_{u,v} = c_i$ for all pairs of nodes u and v at graph distance $i \leq k$ from each other, and $c_{u,v} = 0$ for all other pairs of nodes. Most of the lower bounding techniques described in Section 5.2 originally referred to this general model.

5.1.2 Algorithmic Issues

In this chapter, only channel assignment algorithms for which theoretical bounds on their performance have been established are discussed. The papers not considered here roughly fall into three categories. The first of these propose heuristics and give experimental results without theoretical analysis. The second group focuses on implementation issues arising from specific technologies and protocols, and the final group gives exact solutions to certain specific instances by using combinatorial optimization methods such as integer programming.

The term "performance ratio" refers here to the *asymptotic* performance ratio. Hence, a channel assignment f is said to be *optimal* for a weighted constrained graph G if $S(f) = S(G, w) + O(1)$. The span is assumed to be a function of the weights and the size of the graph, so the $O(1)$ term can include terms dependent on the constraints $c_0, c_1, \ldots, c_k$. An approximation algorithm for channel assignment has performance ratio k when the span of the assignment produced by the algorithm on (G, w) is at most $kS(G, w) + O(1)$.

The version of the channel assignment problem considered here is a generalization of the graph coloring problem, which is well known to be NP-complete for general graphs. A reduction to Hamiltonian paths shows that channel assignment is NP-complete even for graphs of diameter 2 with constraints $c_1 = 2$, $c_2 = 1$. This was proved in the seminal paper on graph labelings by Griggs and Yeh [15]. (The same result, with the same proof, was presented without reference to the original result six years later by Fotakis and Spirakis in [11].)

McDiarmid and Reed [27] have proved that multicoloring is NP-hard for hexagon graphs, which implies that channel assignment for hexagon graphs with general constraints is NP-hard. The proof involves a reduction of the multicoloring problem to the problem of coloring a planar graph. The proof can easily be adapted to demonstrate the NP-hardness of channel assignment for hexagon graphs under any specific choice of constraints $c_0, c_1, \ldots, c_k$.

The algorithms described in this chapter are all *static*. This means that such algorithms attempt to find the best possible channel assignment for one particular constrained graph and one particular weight vector. In realistic networks, the demand for calls changes continuously. However, as indicated in the previous chapter, there is a strong connection between on-line algorithms, which can account for changes in weights, and static algorithms.

The algorithms presented assume a global control mechanism that implements the assignment in the whole graph. In reality, it may be desirable to implement channel assignment in a distributed manner, i.e., the decision on the assignment of channels can be taken at each node independently or after limited consultation between the node and its local neighborhood. Once again, little of the research presented here targets the distributed case specifically. However, I have indicated for each algorithm what information must be present at a node and how much communication between nodes is needed. It can therefore be quickly determined which algorithms can be implemented so that each node finds its own channel assignment.

5.2   LOWER BOUNDS

In order to evaluate any algorithm and to be able to give bounds on its performance ratio, it is essential to have good lower bounds. Some lower bounds, such as those based on the maximum demand in a cell, are straightforward to obtain. Others can be derived from representations of the channel assignment problem as a graph coloring problem or a traveling salesman problem. In this section, I will give an overview of the lower bounds available for channel assignment with constraints.

An early paper by Gamst [12] presents a number of lower bounds based on sets of nodes that have a prescribed minimum constraint between them. More precisely, a *d-clique* in a constrained graph $G = (V, E, c_0, c_1, \ldots)$ is a set of nodes so that for any pair of nodes u, v, $d_G(u, v) \leq d$. Note that a d-clique corresponds to a clique in G^d, the graph obtained from G by adding edges between all pairs of nodes with distance at most d in G.

Any two nodes in a d-clique have constraint at least c_d between them, and thus any two channels assigned to nodes in the d-clique have to have separation at least c_d. This leads directly to the following bound, adapted from [12]. For any constrained, weighted graph (G, w), where $G = (V, E, c_0, c_1, \ldots, c_k)$

$$S(G, w) \geq \max\{c_d\, w(C) - c_d | C \text{ a } d\text{-clique of } G\} \tag{5.1}$$

For the special case $d = 0$, the clique consists of only one node and this bound transforms into a bound derived from the maximum weight on any node:

$$S(G, w) \geq \max\{c_0\, w(v) - c_0 | v \in V\} \tag{5.2}$$

The clique bound can be extended to a bound based on the total weight of a graph and the size of a maximum independent set. A *d-independent* set in a constrained graph G is an independent set in G^d. In other words, it is a set of nodes so that for any pair of nodes u, v, $d_G(u, v) > d$. If $\alpha_d(G)$ denotes the maximum size of a d-independent set in G, then in any channel assignment for G, at most α_d nodes can obtain channels from any interval $\{k, k + 1, \ldots, k + c_d - 1\}$. This leads to the following bound, stated slightly differently in [33]:

$$S(G, w) \geq \max\{c_d\, w(H)/\alpha_d(H) - c_d | H \text{ a subgraph of } G\} \tag{5.3}$$

5.2.1 Traveling Salesman Bounds

Several authors ([22, 15, 17, 31, 33]) have noted that the channel assignment problem can be reframed as a generalization of the traveling salesman problem (TSP). For any channel assignment of a graph with weight one on every node, an enumeration of the nodes in nondecreasing order of the assigned channels will constitute an open TSP tour (Hamiltonian path) of the nodes. The difference between the channels assigned to two consecutive nodes in the tour is at least equal to the constraint between the nodes. Hence, the span of the assignment is at least equal to the cost of the tour, with the cost of traveling between two nodes u and v being the constraint between these two nodes. Therefore, the cost of an optimal TSP tour is a lower bound on the span of the channel assignment.

If the weights are greater than one, one can derive a similar bound from a generalized TSP problem. Here, the goal is to find a minimum cost tour such that every node v is visited $w(v)$ times. Note that this corresponds to a regular TSP if every node v is expanded into a clique of size $w(v)$, where the cost between any two nodes in this clique is defined to be c_0, whereas the nodes in cliques corresponding to different nodes of the original graph inherit the cost between those original nodes. If the constraints in a graph have the property that $c_i + c_j \geq c_k$, for all i, j, k so that $i + j \geq k$, then the corresponding TSP problem is Euclidean, and the cost of the optimal tour equals the cost of the best channel assignment. Note that this property holds for nonincreasing constraints $c_0, \ldots, c_k$ precisely if $2c_k \geq c_0$.

For any constrained, weighted graph (G, w) (where $G = (V, E, c_0, \ldots, c_k)$), let $c_G \in \mathbb{Z}^{V \times V}$ be the vector that represents the constraints between pairs of nodes of G. Given a set of nodes V, a weight vector $w \in \mathbb{Z}^V$ and a cost vector $c \in \mathbb{Z}_+^{V \times V}$, let $\text{TSP}(V, w, c)$ be the cost of the minimum traveling salesman tour through V, where each node v is visited $w(v)$ times, and costs are given by c. Then the following bound, first given in [33], holds:

$$S(G, w) \geq \max\{TSP(U, w, c_G) - c_0 | U \subseteq V_G\} \qquad (5.4)$$

(Vectors w and c_G are considered to be restricted to U.)

The minimal TSP tour can be as hard to compute as the optimal channel assignment, so this bound is only of practical interest for relatively small channel assignment problems. However, the TSP approach can be used to find a lower bound that is easy to calculate. As mentioned in [33], the lower bound for the TSP given by Christofides (see for example [7]), which is derived from minimum spanning trees and is easy to compute, may be used to approximate the TSP bound.

A linear programming relaxation of the generalized TSP problem can also be used to derive lower bounds for channel assignment (see [20]). A TSP tour is seen as a collection of edges, so that each node is covered by exactly two of these edges. Not every such edge cover corresponds to a TSP tour, but the minimum edge cover will constitute a lower bound for the TSP tour. Moreover, a fractional relaxation of the edge cover problem will give lower bounds that are easy to compute.

Given a set of nodes V, a weight vector $w \in \mathbb{Z}^V$ and a cost vector $c \in \mathbb{Z}_+^{V \times V}$, a fractional edge cover is a vector $y \in \mathbb{Q}^{V \times V}$ so that $\Sigma_w y_{vw} \geq 2$ for each $v \in V$. The cost of a *fractional edge cover* y is defined as $\Sigma_{vw \in E} c(vw) y_{vw}$. Letting $EC^*(V, w, c)$ be the minimum cost of any fractional edge cover of node set V, with weight and cost vectors w and c, respectively. The following is a relaxation of the TSP bound:

$$S(G, w) \geq EC^*(V, w, c_G) - c_0 \qquad (5.5)$$

This bound can be refined by adding some of the *subtour constraints,* which explicitly forbid solutions that consist of disconnected cycles. Potentially, there are an exponential number of subtour constraints, but in practice a small number of subtour constraints, added in an iterative manner, will lead to good approximations of the value of the TSP tour. The bound obtained in this way is referred to as the Held–Karp bound. In [23] it is shown that for a wide variety of randomly generated instances, the cost of the optimal tour is on average less than 0.8% of the Held–Karp bound, and for real-world instances the gap is almost always less than 2%. A version of this approach to the TSP bound was implemented by Allen et al.; computational results are presented in [1].

The edge cover problem can also be analyzed using polyhedral methods, to yield a family of explicit lower bounds (see [16]). One specific edge cover bound was used in [19] to solve the "Philadelphia problem," a benchmark problem from the early days of the frequency assignment problem.

5.2.2 Tile Cover Bounds

Bounds derived from the TSP and its relaxations may not be very good if $c_i + c_j < c_k$ for some indices i, j, k such that $i + j \geq k$. In this case, a piece of the tour consisting of three consecutive nodes u, v, w so that $d(u, v) = i$, $d(v, w) = j$, and $d(u, w) = k$ will contribute an amount of $c_i + c_j$ to the tour, whereas the separation between channels at u and w must be at least c_k. In this case, one approach is to break a channel assignment into chunks of nodes that receive consecutive channels. Such chunks will be referred to as "tiles," and the cost of a tile will be related to the minimum bandwidth required to assign channels to its nodes. The channel assignment problem is thus reduced to a problem of covering the nodes with tiles, so that each node v is contained in at least $w(v)$ tiles. The fractional version of the tile cover problem can be easily stated and solved, and then used to bound the minimum span of a channel assignment. Since the tile cover method is not widely known, but gives promising results, we shall describe it in some detail in this section.

The tile cover approach was first described in [20]. The method can be outlined as follows. For a constrained graph G, a set T of possible tiles that may be used in a tile cover is defined. All tiles are defined as vectors indexed by the nodes of G.

A collection of tiles (multiple copies allowed) can be represented by a nonnegative integer vector $y \in \mathbb{Z}_+^T$, where $y(t)$ represents the number of copies of tile t present in the tiling. A *tile cover* of a weighted constrained graph (G, w) is such a vector y with the property that $\Sigma_{t \in T} y(t)t(v) \geq w(v)$ for each node v of G.

A cost $c(t)$ is associated with each tile $t \in T$. The cost of each tile t is derived from the minimal span of a channel assignment for (G, t) plus a "link-up" cost of connecting the assignment to a following tile. This "link-up" cost is calculated using the assumption that the same assignment will be repeated.

The *cost* of a tile cover y is defined as $c(y) = \Sigma_{t \in T} y(t)c(t)$. The minimal cost of a tile cover of a weighted, constrained graph (G, w) will be denoted by $\tau(G, w)$. In order to derive lower bounds from tile covers, it must be established that for the graphs and constraints under consideration

$$S(G, w) \geq \tau(G, w) - k$$

where k is a constant that does not depend on w.

The problem of finding a minimum cost tile cover of (G, w) can be formulated as an integer program (IP) of the following form:

Minimize $\Sigma_{t \in T} c(t)y(t)$ subject to:
$$\Sigma_{t \in T} t(v)y(t) \geq w(v) \qquad (v \in V)$$
$$y(t) \geq 0 \qquad (t \in T)$$
$$y \text{ integer}$$

The linear programming (LP) relaxation of this IP is obtained by removing the requirement that y must be integral. Any feasible solution to the resulting linear program is called a *fractional* tile cover. The minimum cost of a fractional tile cover gives a lower bound on the minimum cost of a tile cover.

By linear programming duality, the maximum cost of the dual of the above LP is equal to the minimum cost of a fractional tile cover. Thus, any vector that satisfies the inequalities of the dual program gives a lower bound on the cost of a minimum fractional tile cover, and therefore on the span of the corresponding constrained, weighted graph. The maximum is achieved by one of the vertices of the polytope $TC(G)$ representing the feasible dual solutions and defined as follows:

$$TC(G) = \left\{ x \in \mathbb{Q}_+^V : \sum_{v \in V} t(v)x(v) \leq c(t) \text{ for all } t \in \mathcal{T} \right\}$$

A classification of the vertices of this polytope will therefore lead to a comprehensive set of lower bounds that can be obtained from fractional tile covers. For any specific constrained graph, such a classification can be obtained by using vertex enumeration software, e.g., the package `lrs`, developed by Avis [2].

In [18], 1-cliques in graphs with constraints c_0, c_1 were considered. In this case the channel assignment was found to be equivalent to the tile cover problem. Moreover, the fractional tile cover problem is equivalent to the integral tile cover problem for 1-cliques, leading to a family of lower bounds that can always be attained. None of the bounds was new. Two bounds were clique bounds of the type mentioned earlier. The third bound was first given by Gamst in [12], and can be stated as follows:

$$S(G, w) \geq \max\{c_0 w(v) + (\mu c_1 - c_0)w(C - v) - c_0 | C \text{ a clique of } G, v \in C\} \quad (5.6)$$

where μ is such that $(\mu - 1)c_1 < c_0 \leq \mu c_1$.

The tile cover approach led to a number of new bounds for graphs with constraints c_0, c_1, c_2. The bounds are derived from so-called nested cliques. A *nested clique* is a d_1-clique that contains a d_2-clique as a subset ($d_2 < d_1$). It is characterized by a node partition (Q, R), where Q is the d_2-clique and R contains all remaining nodes. A triple (k, u, a) will denote the constraints $k = c_0$, $u = c_{d_2}$, and $a = c_{d_1}$ in a nested clique. Note that in a nested clique with node partition (Q, R) with constraints (k, u, a), every pair of nodes from Q has a constraint of at least u, while the constraint between any pair of nodes in the nested clique is at least a.

The following is a lower bound for a nested clique (Q, R) with parameters (k, a, u):

$$S(G, w) \geq a \sum_{v \in Q} w(v) + u \sum_{v \in R} w(v) - u \quad (5.7)$$

This bound was first derived in [12] using ad-hoc methods. The same bound can also be derived using edge covers.

Using tile covers, a number of new bounds for nested cliques with parameters $(k, u, 1)$ are obtained in [22]. The following is a generalization of bound (5.6). (The notation $w_{Q\max}$ and $w_{R\max}$ is used to denote the maximum weight of any node in Q and R, respectively.)

$$S(G, w) \geq (k - \mu\delta)w_{Q\max} + \delta \sum_{v \in Q} w(v) + \epsilon \sum_{v \in R} w(v) - k \quad (5.8)$$

where

$$\mu = \left\lfloor \frac{k}{u} \right\rfloor, \quad \delta = (\mu + 1)u - k$$

and

$$\epsilon = \min\left\{ \frac{\delta}{k - 2u + 1}, \frac{2u + \mu\delta - \mu}{k + 1} \right\}$$

Bound (1.3), obtained from the total weight on a clique, was extended, leading to

$$S(G, w) \geq u\left(\sum_{v \in Q} w(v) + w_{Rmax} \right) + \frac{k - u}{k - 1} \sum_{v \in R, v \neq v_{Rmax}} w(v) - k \tag{5.9}$$

A bound of $(2u - 1)w_{Qmax} + \Sigma_{v \in R}w(v) - \kappa$ for nested cliques where Q consists of one node was obtained in [34]. This bound is generalized in [22] to all nested cliques:

$$S(G, w) \geq (2u - 1)w_{Qmax} + \nu \sum_{v \in Q, v \neq v_{Qmax}} w(v) + \sum_{v \in R} w(v) - k \tag{5.10}$$

where

$$\nu = u - \max\left\{ \frac{u - 1}{\mu}, \frac{\delta - 1}{\mu - 1} \right\}$$

Finally, we mention the following two tile cover bounds from [22] for nested cliques with parameters (k, u, a):

$$S(G, w)) \geq (3u - k + 2\delta) \sum_{v \in Q} w(v) + (k - 2\delta)w_{Rmax} + \delta \sum_{v \in R} w(v) - k \tag{5.11}$$

where $\delta = 3a - k$, and

$$S(G, w) \geq u\left(\sum_{v \in V} w(v) + w_{Rmax} \right) + \frac{3a - u}{2} \sum_{v \in R, v \neq v_{Rmax}} w(v) - k \tag{5.12}$$

In [40], a bounding technique based on network flow is described. Since no explicit formulas are given, it is hard to compare these bounds with the ones given in this section. However, in an example the authors of [40] obtain an explicit lower bound that can be improved upon using edge covers [1] or tile cover bounds [22].

5.3 ALGORITHMS

In this section, an overview is given of algorithms for channel assignment with general constraints. Some of these algorithms are adaptations of graph multicoloring algorithms as described in the previous chapter and others are based on graph labeling. An overview of the best-known performance ratios of algorithms for different types of graphs and constraints is presented in Table 5.1.

TABLE 5.1 An overview of the performance ratios of the best known algorithms for different types of graphs. A * indicates that the performance ratio depends heavily on the constraints; see the text of Section 5.3 for details

Constraints	Performance ratio	Reference
Bipartite graphs		
$c_0, c_1 : c_0 \geq 2c_1$	1	
$c_0, c_1 : c_0 > 2c_1$	1	[14]
Paths		
c_0, c_1, c_2	$\max\{1, (2c_1 + c_2)/c_0$	[42, 13]
c_0, c_1, c_2, c_3	*	[39]
Bidimensional grid		
c_0, c_1, c_2	$\max\{1, (2c_1 + 3c_2)/c_0\}$	[13, 39]
c_0, c_1, c_2, c_3	$\max\{1, 5c_1/c_0, 10c_2/c_0\}$	[3]
Odd cycles (length n)		
$c_0, c_1 : c_0 \geq (2nc_1)/(n-1)$	1	[21]
$c_0, c_1 : 2c_1 \leq c_0 < (2nc_1)/(n-1)$	$1 + 1/(4n-3)$	[21]
$c_0, c_1 : c_1 \leq c_0 < 2c_1$	$1 + 1/(n-1)$	[21]
c_0, c_1, c_2	$\max\{1, 3c_1/c_0, 6c_2/c_0\}$	[15]
Hexagon graphs		
$c_0, c_1 : 9/4\, c_1 \leq c_0$	$\max\{1, 3c_1/c_0\}$	—
$c_0, c_1 : 2c_1 < c_0 \leq 9/4\, c_1$	$<4/3 + 1/100$	[21]
$c_0, c_1 : c_0 \leq 2c_1$	$4/3$	[21]
c_0, c_1, c_2	*	[39]
$c_0, c_1, c_2 : c_1 \geq 2c_2$	$5/3 + c_1/c_2.$	[9]

Most of the work done has been for the case where only a cosite constraint c_0 and one edge constraint c_1 are given. As with multicoloring, a base coloring of a graph G with one color per node can be used to generate a coloring for a weighted channel assignment problem having G as its underlying graph.

Algorithm A (for graphs with chromatic number k)
Let $G = (V, E, c_0, c_1)$ be a constrained graph, and w an arbitrary weight vector. Assume that a base coloring $f: V \rightarrow \{0, 1, \dots, k-1\}$ of the nodes of G is given.

ASSIGNMENT: Let $s = \max\{c_0, kc_1\}$. Each node v receives the channels $f(v) + is$, $i = 0, 1, \dots, w(v) - 1$.

Algorithm A has a performance ratio of $\max\{1, kc_1/c_0\}$, and is therefore optimal if $c_0 \geq kc_1$. It is a completely distributed algorithm, since every node can assign its own channels independently of the rest of the network. The only information needed by a node to be able to compute its assignment is its base color.

The base coloring used in Algorithm A can be seen as a graph labeling satisfying the constraint $c_1 = 1$. A modified version of Algorithm A, based on graph labelings, can be formulated as follows.

Algorithm A′ (based on graph labeling)

Let $G = (V, E, c_0, c_1, \ldots, c_k)$ be a constrained graph, and w an arbitrary weight vector. Assume that a labeling $f: V \to \mathbb{N}$ is given which satisfies the constraints $c_1, \ldots, c_k$ and has cyclic span M.

ASSIGNMENT: Let $s = \max\{c_0, M\}$. Each node v receives the channels $f(v) + is$, $i = 0, 1, \ldots$, $w(v) - 1$.

Algorithm A′ has a performance ratio of $\max\{1, M/c_0\}$ and is therefore optimal if $c_0 \geq M$. Like Algorithm A, it is a completely distributed algorithm, where the only local information needed at each node is the value of the labeling at that node.

The method of repeating a basic channel assignment of one channel per node has existed since the channel assignment problem first appeared in the literature. This method is referred to as fixed assignment (FA), as each node has a fixed set of channels available for its assignment (see for example [9, 35, 25, 28]).

A type of labeling that gives regular, periodic graph labelings for lattices was defined in [39], and called *labeling by arithmetic progression.* Such a labeling is a linear, modular function of the coordinates of each node.

Definition 5.3.1

A labeling f of a t-dimensional lattice is a labeling by arithmetic progression if there exist nonnegative integers $a_1, \ldots, a_t$ and n such that for each node v with coordinates $(m_1, \ldots, m_t)$, $f(v) = a_1 m_1 + \ldots + a_t m_t \bmod n$. The parameter n is called the cyclic span of the labeling. Given integers $c_1, c_2, \ldots$, where $c_1 \geq c_2 \geq \ldots$, such a labeling satisfies the constraints $c_1, c_2, \ldots$ if for all pairs of nodes u, v at graph distance i in the lattice, $|f(u) - f(v)| \geq \max\{c_i, n - c_i\}$. A labeling by arithmetic progression is considered optimal for a given set of constraints if its cyclic span is as small as possible.

Given f, a labeling by arithmetic progression, $f(m_1, m_2)$ denotes the value of the labeling at the node with coordinates (m_1, m_2). Labelings by arithmetic progression are easy to define and with Algorithm A′ they can be used to find channel assignment algorithms. Moreover, their regularity may be helpful in designing borrowing methods that will give better channel assignments for nonuniform weights.

5.3.1 Bipartite Graphs

For bipartite graphs with constraints c_0 and c_1, Algorithm A gives optimal channel assignments if $c_0 \geq 2c_1$. If $c_0 < 2c_1$, bipartite graphs can be colored optimally using Algorithm B, given by Gerke [14]. Like Algorithm A, this algorithm uses base coloring of the nodes, but if a node has demand greater than any of its neighbors, it initially gets some channels that are $2c_1$ apart (which allows interspersing the channels of its neighbors), while the later channels are c_0 apart.

Algorithm B (for bipartite graphs when $c_1 \leq c_0 \leq 2c_1$)

Let $G = (V, E, c_0, c_1)$ be a constrained bipartite graph of n nodes, where $c_1 \leq c_0 \leq 2c_1$, and w an arbitrary weight vector. Assume a base coloring $f: V \to \{0,1\}$ is given.

For each node v, define $p(v) = \max\{w(u) \mid uv \in E \text{ or } u = v\}$.

ASSIGNMENT: Initially, each node v receives channels $f(v)c_1 + 2ic_1$, $i = 0, 1, \ldots, p(v) - 1$. If $w(v) > p(v)$, then v receives the additional channels $f(v)c_1 + 2p(v)c_1 + ic_0$, $i = 0, \ldots, w(v) - p(v) - 1$.

The span of the assignment above is at most $\max_{(uv) \in E} \{c_0 w(u) + (2c_1 - c_0)w(v)\}$. It follows from lower bound 5.6 that the algorithm is (asymptotically) optimal. In fact, [14] gives a more detailed version of the algorithm above that is optimal in the absolute sense.

For higher constraints, the only results available are for graph labelings of specific bipartite graphs. Van den Heuvel et al. [39] give labelings by arithmetic progression for subgraphs as the line lattice (paths). Such labelings only have n (the cyclic span) and $a_1 = a$ as parameters. If f is such a labeling, then a node v defined by the vector me will have value $f(v) = ma \bmod n$. The parameters of the labelings are displayed in the table below. These labelings are optimal in almost all cases. The exception is the case where there are three constraints c_1, c_2, and c_3, and $2c_2 - c_3 \le c_1 \le (\frac{1}{2})c_2 + c_3$. For this case, a periodic labeling not based on arithmetic progressions is given in the same paper.

Constraints	n	a
c_1, c_2	$2c_1 + c_2$	c_1
$c_1, c_2, c_3 : c_1 \ge c_2 + c_3$	$2c_1 + c_2$	c_1
$c_1, c_2, c_3 : c_2 + (1/3)c_3 \le c_1 \le c_2 + c_3$	$3c_2 + 2c_3$	$c_2 + c_3$
$c_1, c_2, c_3 : c_1 \le c_2 + (1/3)c_3$	$3c_1 + c_3$	c_1

For paths of size at least five, these labelings include the optimal graph labeling satisfying constraints $c_1 = 2$, $c_2 = 1$ given by Yeh in [42], and the path labelings for general constraints c_1, c_2 by Georges and Mauro in [13]. Note that Algorithm A$'$, used with any of these labelings with cyclic span n, has a performance ratio of $\max\{1, n/c_0\}$.

The near-optimal labeling for unit interval graphs given in [32] can be applied to paths with constraints $c_1, c_2, \ldots, c_{2r}$, where $c_1 = c_2 = \ldots = c_r = 2$ and $c_{r+1} = \ldots c_{2r} = 1$, to give a labeling with cyclic span $2r + 1$. Using this labeling in Algorithm A$'$ leads to a performance ratio of $\max\{1, (2r + 1)/c_0\}$.

Van de Heuvel et al. [39] also give an optimal labeling by arithmetic progression for the square lattice and constraints c_1, c_2. The labeling given has cyclic span $n = 2c_1 + 3c_2$ and is defined by the parameters $a_1 = c_1$, $a_2 = c_1 + c_2$. The square lattice is the Cartesian product graph of two infinite paths, and similar labelings can also be derived from the results on products of paths given in [13].

Bertossi et al. [3] give a labeling for constraints $c_1 = 2$, $c_1 = c_3 = 1$ of span 8 and cyclic span 10. This labeling can be transformed into a labeling for general c_1, c_2, c_3 as follows. Let $c = \max\{c_1/2, c_2\}$, and let f be the labeling for $c_1, c_2, c_3 = 2, 1, 1$. Let $f'(u) = cf(u)$. It is easy to check that f' is a labeling for c_1, c_2, c_3 of cyclic span $10c$. Using this labeling with Algorithm A$'$ gives a performance ratio of $\max\{1, 5c_1/c_0, 10c_2/c_0\}$. The same authors give a labeling for bidimensional grids with constraints $c_1 = 2$, $c_2 = 1$, which is just a special case the labeling by arithmetic progression given above.

The same authors also give labelings for graphs they call *hexagonal grids,* with constraints $c_1, c_2 = 2, 1$ and $c_2, c_1, c_3 = 2, 1, 1$. Hexagonal grids are not to be confused with hexagon graphs, which will be discussed in Section 5.3.3. In fact, hexagonal grids are subgraphs of the planar dual of the infinite triangular lattice. Hexagonal grids form a regular arrangement of 6 cycles, and are bipartite.

Labelings for the hypercube Q_n were described and analyzed in [15, 24, 41]. Graph labelings for trees with constraints $c_1, c_2 = 2, 1$ were treated in [5] and [15]. These labelings are obtained using a greedy approach, which is described in Section 5.3.4.

5.3.2 Odd Cycles

Channel assignment on odd cycles was first studied by Griggs and Yeh in [15]. The authors give a graph labeling for constraints $c_1, c_2 = 2, 1$ of span 4 and cyclic span 6. The labeling repeats the channels 0, 2, 4 along the cycle, with a small adaptation near the end if the length of the cycle is not divisible by 3. As described in the previous section, this labeling can be used for general constraints c_1, c_2 if all values assigned by the labeling are multiplied by $\max\{c_2, c_1/2\}$. Using Algorithm A', this leads to an algorithm with performance ratio $\max\{1, 3c_1/c_0, 6c_2/c_0\}$.

In [21], three basic algorithms for odd cycles are combined in different ways to give optimal or near-optimal algorithms for all possible choices of two constraints c_0 and c_1.

The first of the three algorithms in [21] is based on a graph labeling that satisfies one constraint c_1. This labeling has cyclic span $c_R = 2nc_1/(n - 1)$. It starts by assigning zero to the first node, and then adding c_1 (modulo c_R) to the previously assigned channel and assigning this to the next node in the cycle. At a certain point, this switches to an alternating assignment. This labeling is then used repeatedly, as in Algorithm A'. Since this particular form of Algorithm A' will be used to describe the further results in this chapter, I will state it explicitly below.

Algorithm C (for odd cycles)
Let $G = (V, E, c_0, c_1)$ be a constrained cycle of n nodes, where $n > 3$ is odd, and w be an arbitrary weight vector. Fix $s = \max\{c_0, c_R\}$. Let the nodes of the cycle be numbered $\{1, \ldots, n\}$, numbered in cyclic order, where node 1 is a node of maximum weight in the cycle. Let $m > 1$ be the smallest odd integer such that $s \geq 2m/(m - 1)c_1$ (it can be shown that such an integer must exist).

ASSIGNMENT: To each node i, the algorithm assigns the channels $b(i) + js$, where $j = 0, \ldots, w(i) - 1$, and the graph labeling $b : V \to [0, s - 1]$ is defined as follows:

$$b(i) = \begin{cases} (i - 1)c_1 \bmod s & \text{when } 1 \leq i \leq m, \\ 0 & \text{when } i > m \text{ and } i \text{ is even}, \\ (m - 1)c_1 \bmod s & \text{when } i > m \text{ and } i \text{ is odd}. \end{cases}$$

Note that this algorithm can only be implemented in a centralized way, since every node must know all weights, in order to calculate m, and so determine its initial assignment value.

The second algorithm is a straightforward adaptation of the optimal algorithm for multicoloring an odd cycle, described in [29] and discussed in the previous chapter. The span used by this algorithm is $\lceil \omega/2 \rceil s$.

Algorithm D (for odd cycles)

Let $G = (V, E, c_0, c_1)$ be a constrained cycle of n nodes, where $n > 3$ is odd, and w be an arbitrary weight vector. Fix $s = \max\{c_0, 2c_1\}$, and $\omega = \max\{2\Sigma_{v \in V} w(v)/(n-1), 2w_{\max}\}$.

Let f be an optimal multicoloring of (G, w) using the colors $\{0, 1, \ldots, \omega - 1\}$. Such an f exists since $\chi(G, w) \leq \omega$.

ASSIGNMENT: For each node v, replace each color i in $f(v)$ with the channel f_i, where

$$f_i = \begin{cases} is & \text{if } i \leq \lceil \omega \backslash 2 \rceil - 1, \\ c_1 + (i - \lceil \frac{\omega}{2} \rceil)s & \text{otherwise.} \end{cases}$$

Algorithms C and D only give good assignments for weight vectors with specific properties, but they can be combined to give near-optimal algorithms for any weight vector. How they are combined will depend on the relation between the parameters. First, note that Algorithm C is optimal if $c_0 \geq c_R = 2nc_1/(n-1)$.

If $2c_1 \leq c_0 < c_R$, then Algorithms A, C, and D can be combined to give a linear time algorithm with performance ratio $1 + 1/(4n - 3)$, where n is the number of nodes in the cycle. The algorithm is described below.

Given a weight vector w, compute $\delta = \Sigma_{v \in V} w(v) - (n-1)w_{\max}$. If $\delta \leq 0$, Algorithm D is used, with spectrum $[0, c_0 w_{\max}]$. The span is at most $c_0 w_{\max}$, which is within a constant of lower bound (5.2), so the assignment is optimal.

If instead $\delta > 0$, Algorithm C is combined with either Algorithm A or D to derive an assignment. Denote by f_1 the assignment computed by Algorithm C for (G, w') where $w'(v) = \min\{w(v), \delta\}$. This assignment has span at most $c_R \delta$.

Consider the remaining weight $\overline{w}$ after this assignment. Clearly $\overline{w}_{\max} = w_{\max} - \delta$. We will denote by f_2 the assignment for $(G, \overline{w})$, and compute it in two different ways depending on a key property of $\overline{w}$. If there is a node v with $\overline{w}(v) = 0$ at this stage, we have a bipartite graph left. Then f_2 is the assignment computed by Algorithm A for $(G, \overline{w})$. This assignment has a span of at most $c_0 \overline{w}_{\max}$.

If all nodes have nonzero weight, then Algorithm D is used to compute f_2, the assignment for $(G, \overline{w})$. It can be shown that in this case, $\omega = 2\overline{w}_{\max}$, so this assignment also has a span of at most $c_0 \omega/2 = c_0 \overline{w}_{\max}$. Thus, in either case, f_2 has span at most $c_0 \overline{w}_{\max}$.

The two assignments f_1 and f_2 are then combined by adding $c_R \delta + c_0$ to every channel in f_2, and then merging the channel sets assigned by f_1 and f_2 at each node. This gives a final assignment of span at most $(c_R - c_0) \delta + c_0 \overline{w}_{\max} + c_0$. Using the lower bounds (5.2) and (5.3), it can be shown that the performance ratio of the algorithm is as claimed.

If $c_0 < 2c_1$, Algorithms B and C can be combined into a linear time approximation algorithm with performance ratio $1 + 1/(n - 1)$, where n is the number of nodes in the cycle. The combination algorithm is formed as follows.

First, find the assignment f_1 computed by Algorithm C for (G, w') where $w'(v) = w_{\min}$ for every node v. Then, find the assignment f_2 computed by Algorithm B for (G, w'') where $w''(v) = w(v) - w_{\min}$. Finally, combine the two assignments by adding $c_R w_{\min} + c_0$ to each channel of f_2 and then merging the channel sets assigned by f_1 and f_2.

Using bound 1.6, it can be shown that the algorithm has performance ratio $1 + 1/(n - 1)$ as claimed.

In [13], optimal graph labelings for odd cycles with constraints c_1, c_2 are given. If $c_1 > 2c_2$, or $c_1 \leq 2c_2$ and $n \equiv 0 \bmod 3$, the span is $2c_1$, and the cyclic span is $3c_1$. Using Algorithm A′ in combination with this labeling gives a performance ratio of $\max\{1, 3c_1/c_0\}$. For the remaining case, the span is $c_1 + 2c_2$ and the cyclic span is $c_1 + 3c_2$, leading to a performance ratio for Algorithm A′ of $\max\{1, (c_1 + 3c_2)/c_0\}$. In [3], Bertossi et al. give a graph labeling for cycles of length at least 4 with constraints c_1, c_2, $c_3 = 2, 1, 1$. The span of the labeling is 4, and its cyclic span is 6. Adapting this labeling to general parameters c_1, c_2, c_3 and using Algorithm A′ gives a performance ratio of $\max\{1, 3c_1/c_0, 6c_2/c_0\}$.

5.3.3 Hexagon Graphs

The first labelings for hexagon graphs were labelings by arithmetic progression given by van den Heuvel et al. in [39]. The labelings, as defined by their parameters a_1, a_2, and n, are given in the table below.

Parameters	n	a_1	a_2
$c_1 \geq 2c_2$	$3c_1 + 3c_2$	$2c_1 + c_2$	c_1
$(3/2)c_2 \leq c_1 \leq 2c_1$	$9c_2$	$5c_2$	$2c_2$
$c_1 \leq (3/2)c_2$	$4c_1 + 3c_2$	$2c_1 + c_2$	c_1

It can be easily seen that hexagon graphs admit a regular coloring with three colors. Hence Algorithm A will be optimal for constraints c_0, c_1 so that $c_0 \geq 3c_1$. A channel assignment algorithm for hexagon graphs with constraints c_0, $c_1 = 2, 1$ with performance ratio 4/3 was given in [36].

In [21], further approximation algorithms for hexagon graphs and all values of constraints c_0, c_1 are given. All algorithms have performance ratio not much more than 4/3, which is the performance ratio of the best known multicoloring algorithm for hexagon graphs (see [28]). The results are obtained by combining a number of basic algorithms for hexagon graphs and bipartite graphs. The algorithm described below is similar to the one in [36].

Algorithm E (for 3-colorable graphs)
Let $G = (V, E, c_0, c_1)$ be a constrained graph, and w be an arbitrary weight vector. Fix $s = \max\{c_1, c_0/2\}$ and $T \geq 3w_{max}$, T a multiple of 6. Let $f: V \to \{0, 1, 2\}$ be a base coloring of G. Denote base colors 0, 1, 2 as red, blue and green, respectively.

A set of red channels is given, consisting of a first set $R_1 = [0, 2s, \ldots, (T/3 - 2)s]$ and a second set $R_2 = [(T/3 + 1)s + c_0, (T/3 + 3)s + c_0, \ldots, (2T/3 - 1)s + c_0]$. Blue channels consist of first set $B_1 = [(T/3)s + c_0, (T/3 + 2)s + c_0, \ldots, (2T/3 - 2)s + c_0]$ and second set $B_2 = [(2T/3 + 1)s + 2c_0, (2T/3 + 3)s + 2c_0, \ldots, (T - 1)s + 2c_0]$, and green channels consist of first set $G_1 = [(2T/3)s + 2c_0, (2T/3 + 2)s + 2c_0, \ldots, (T - 2)s + 2c_0]$ and second set $G_2 = [s, 3s, \ldots, (T/3 - 1)s]$.

ASSIGNMENT: Each node v is assigned $w(v)$ channels from those of its color class, where the first set is exhausted before starting on the second set, and lowest numbered channels are always used first within each set.

Note that the spectrum is divided into three parts, each containing $T/3$ channels, with a separation of s between consecutive channels. The first part of the spectrum consists of alternating channels from R_1 and G_2, the second part has alternating channels from B_1 and R_2, and the third part has alternating channels from G_1 and B_2. The span used by Algorithm E equals $sT + 2c_0 = \max\{c_1, c_0/2\}T + 2c_0$, where T is at least $3w_{\max}$.

To obtain the optimal algorithms for hexagon graphs and different values of the parameters c_0, c_1, Algorithm E is modified and combined with Algorithms A and B.

Algorithm A for hexagon graphs has a performance ratio of $\max\{1, 3c_1/c_0\}$. As noted, when $c_0 \geq 3c_1$ the algorithm is optimal. When $c_0 \geq (9/4)c_1$, the performance ratio of equals $3c_1/c_0$, which is at most $4/3$. For the case where $2c_1 < c_0 \leq (9/4)c_1$, a combination of Algorithms A for hexagon graphs and Algorithm E followed by a borrowing phase and an application of Algorithm B results in an algorithm with performance ratio less than $4/3 + 1/100$ The algorithm is outlined below.

Let D represent the maximum weight of any maximal clique (edge or triangle) in the graph. It follows from lower bound (1.3) that $S(G, w) \geq c_1 D - c_1$. For ease of explanation, we assume that D is a multiple of 6.

Phase 1: If $D > 2w_{\max}$, use Algorithm A for hexagon graphs on (G, w') where $w'(v) = \min\{w(v), D - 2w_{\max}\}$. If $D \leq 2w_{\max}$, skip this phase, and take $w'(v) = 0$ for all v. The span needed for this phase is no more than $\max\{0, D - 2w_{\max}\}3c_1$.

Phase 2: Let $T = \min\{2w_{\max}, 6w_{\max} - 2D\}$. Use Algorithm E on (G, w''), where $w''(v) = \min\{w(v) - w'(v), T/3\}$, taking T as defined. The span of the assignment is $\min\{2w_{\max}, (6w_{\max} - 2D)\}c_0/2 + 2c_0$. It follows from the description that after this phase, in every triangle there is at least one node that has received a number of channels equal to its demand.

Phase 3: Any node that has still has unfulfilled demand tries to borrow channels assigned in Phase 2 from its neighbors according to the following rule: red nodes borrow only from blue neighbors, blue from green, and green from red. A red node v with $w(v) > w'(v) + w''(v)$, where $w_B(v)$ is the maximum number of channels used during Phase 2 by any blue neighbor of v, receives an additional $\min\{w(v) - w'(v) - w''(v), T/3 - w_B(v), T/6\}$ channels from the second blue channel set B_2, starting from the highest channels in the set. A similar strategy is followed for blue and green nodes. It can be shown that the graph induced by the nodes that still have unfulfilled demand after this phase is bipartite.

Phase 4: Let $\overline{w}$ denote the weight left on the nodes after the assignments of the first three phases. Use Algorithm A to find an assignment for $(G, \overline{w})$, which has a span of $c_0\overline{w}_{\max}$.

The assignments of all four phases are then combined without conflicts, as in the theorems for odd cycles. The final assignment has span at most $(2w_{\max})c_0/2 + c_0(w_{\max}/3) + \Theta(1) = (4/3)c_0w_{\max} + \Theta(1)$. It then follows from lower bounds (5.2) and (5.3) that the performance ratio equals $1 + 3(c_0 - 2c_1)/c_0 + (9c_1 - 4c_0)/3c_1$. When $2c_1 < c_0 \leq (9/4)c_1$, this is always less than $4/3 + 1/100$. In particular, the maximum value is reached when $c_0/c_1 = 3/\sqrt{2}$. When $c_0 = 2c_1$ or $c_0 = 9c_1/4$, the performance ratio is exactly $4/3$.

When $c_0 \leq 2c_1$, a linear time approximation algorithm with performance ratio $4/3$ is obtained from an initial assignment by Algorithm E, followed by a borrowing phase and a phase where assigned channels are rearranged in the spectrum, and finally an application of Algorithm B. The algorithm follows.

Let

$$L = \max\{c_0 w(u) + (2c_1 - c_0)(w(v) + w(r))|\{u, v, r\} \text{ a triangle}\}$$

and let T be the smallest multiple of 6 larger than $\max\{L, Dc_1\}/c_1$. It follows from lower bounds (5.6) and (5.3) that $Tc_1 - \Theta(1)$ is a lower bound for the span of any assignment.

Phase 1: Use Algorithm E on (G, w') where $w'(v) = \min\{w(v), T/3\}$ and T is defined above. In this case s, the separation between channels, equals c_1, so the span of the assignment is Tc_1.

Phase 2: Any red node v of weight greater than $T/3$ borrows $\min\{w(v) - T/3, T/3 - w_B(v), T/6\}$ channels, where $w_B(v)$ is the maximum weight of any blue neighbor of v. The channels are taken only from the second blue channel set, and start with the highest channels. Blue and green nodes borrow analogously, following the borrowing rules given earlier (red $\rightarrow$ blue $\rightarrow$ green $\rightarrow$ red).

Phase 3: Any red node v of weight more than $T/3$, whose blue neighbors have weight at most $T/6$, will squeeze their assigned channels from their second set as much as possible. More precisely, the last $T/6 - w_B(v)$ channels assigned to v from R_2 are replaced by $\min\{w(v) - T/3 - w_B(v), 2c_1/c_0(T/6 - w_B(v))\}$ channels with separation c_0 which fill the part of the spectrum occupied by the last $T/6 - w_B(v)$ channels of R_2. For example, let $T = 24$, $c_0 = 3$, and $c_1 = 2$. Suppose v is a red corner node with at least two green neighbors, where $w(v) = 13$ and let $w_B(v) = 1$. In Phase 1, v received the channels 21, 25, 29, 33 from the set R_2, whereas at least one blue neighbor of v received the channel 19 from B_1 and no other channels from B_1 or B_2 were used by any neighbor of v. Then in Phase 2, v borrows all four blue channels in B_2, and in Phase 3, squeezes the part of the spectrum [21, 33] of R_2 to get five channels. In particular, it uses the channels 21, 24, 27, 30, 33 instead of the four channels mentioned above. The reader can verify that in this example, cosite and intersite constraints are respected.

Phase 4: Let $\bar{w}$ be the weight vector remaining after Phase 3. It can be shown that the graph induced by the nodes with positive remaining weight is bipartite. We use Algorithm B to find an assignment for $(G, \bar{w})$, which has a span of $L' = \max\{c_0\bar{w}(u) + (2c_1 - c_0)\bar{w}(v)|(u, v) \in E\}$.

The assignments of different phases are then combined without causing conflicts, in the same way as described before, to give a final assignment of span at most $(4/3) Tc_1 + \Theta(1)$. From the definition of T, we have that $Tc_1 - \Theta(1)$ is a lower bound, which gives the required performance ratio of 4/3.

In [3], a labeling is given for hexagon graphs with constraints $c_1, c_2, c_3 = 2, 1, 1$. (Hexagon graphs are referred to as *cellular grids* in this paper.) The labeling has a span of 8, which is proven to be optimal, and a cyclic span of 9. Moreover, when examined it can be determined that this labeling is, in fact, a labeling by arithmetic progression, with parameters $n = 9$, $a = 2$, $b = 6$. It therefore follows from the results of van de Heuvel et al. that the labeling is optimal, since 9 is the optimal span even for constraints $c_1, c_2 = 2, 1$. This labeling can be used with Algorithm A′ to give a performance ratio of $\max\{1, 9\lceil(c_1/2)\rceil/c_0,$ $9c_2/c_0\}$.

Algorithm A′ is based on a uniform repitition of an assignment of one channel per node, and will therefore work best when the distribution of weights in the network is fairly uniform. To accommodate for nonuniform weights, Fitzpatrick et al. [9] give an algorithm for hexagon graphs with parameters c_0, c_1, c_2, where $c_0 = c_1$ and $c_1 \geq 2c_2$, which combines an assignment phase based on a labeling by arithmetic progression with two borrowing phases, in which nodes with high demand borrow unused channels from their neighbors.

The labeling f that is the basis of the algorithm is defined by the parameters $a = c_1$, $b = 3c_1 + c_2$, and $n = 5c_1 + 3c_2$. It can be verified that f indeed satisfies the constraints c_1 and c_2. It is also the case that $c_2 \leq f(i, j) \leq n - c_2$ even for nodes (i, j) at graph distance 3 of $(0, 0)$. So, any channel assignment derived from f has the property that the nodes at graph distance 3 also have separation at least c_2. (This implies that the given labeling satisfies the constraints c_1, c_2, c_3; in fact, when $c_1, c_2 = 2, 1$, the labeling is the same as the one given in [3].)

More precisely, v can calculate $T(v)$, where

$$T(v) = \max\left\{\sum_{u \in C} w(u) \mid C \text{ a clique, } d(u, v) \leq 1 \text{ for all } u \in C\right\}$$

The algorithm then proceeds in three phases, as described below.

Phase 1. Node v receives channels $f(v) + in$, $0 \leq i < \min\{w(v), T(v)/3\}$.

Phase 2. If v has weight higher than $T(v)/3$, then v will borrow any unused channels from its neighbor $x = (i + 1, j)$.

Phase 3. If v still has unfulfilled demand after the last phase, then v borrows the remaining channels from its neighbor $y = (i + 1, j - 1)$.

The algorithm can be implemented in a distributed manner. Every node $v = (i, j)$ knows its value under f, $f(i, j)$, and is able to identify its neighbors and their position with respect to itself, and receive information about their weight. Specifically, v is able to identify the neighbors $(i + 1, j)$ and $(i + 1, j - 1)$, and to calculate the maximum weight on a clique among its neighbors.

Using lower bound 5.1, applied to a 2-clique of the graph, it can be shown that the performance ratio of this algorithm equals $5/3 + c_1/c_2$.

5.3.4 Other Graphs

For general graphs, a method to obtain graph labelings is to assign channels to nodes greedily. The resulting span depends heavily on the order in which nodes are labeled, since each labeled node at graph distance i from a given node disqualifies $2c_i - 1$ possible labels for that node. Given the ordering, a greedy labeling can be found in linear time. Almost all work involving greedy labelings has been done for constraints $c_1, c_2 = 2, 1$. In this section we will assume that the constraints are these, unless otherwise noted.

Any labeling for the given constraints will have span at least $\Delta + 1$, as can be deduced from examining a node of maximum degree and its neighbors. It can be deduced from Brooks' theorem (see [8]), that each graph G with maximum degree Δ has a labeling with span at most $\Delta^2 + 2\Delta$.

Griggs and Yeh [15] observe that trees have a labeling of span at most $\Delta + 2$. Nodes are labeled so that nodes closer to the root come first. Each unlabeled node then has at most one labeled neighbor, and at most $\Delta - 1$ labeled nodes at distance 2 from it. The authors conjecture that it is NP-hard to decide whether a particular tree has minimum span $\Delta + 1$ or $\Delta + 2$. This conjecture was proven false by Chang and Kuo [5].

Sakai [32] uses a *perfect elimination ordering* to show that chordal graphs have a labeling of span at most $(\Delta + 3)^2/4$. A perfect elimination ordering $v_1, v_2, \ldots, v_n$ of the nodes has the property that for all i, $1 \leq i \leq n$, the neighbors of v_i in the subgraph induced by v_1, $v_2, \ldots, v_{i-1}$ form a clique. A similar approach was later used by Bodlaender et al. [4] to obtain upper bounds on labelings of graphs with fixed tree width.

Planar graphs are of special interest in the context of channel assignment, since a graph representing adjacency relations between cells will necessarily be planar. In [38], van den Heuvel and McGuinness use methods such as used in the proof of the four color theorem to prove that all planar graphs with constraints c_1, c_2 admit a graph labeling of span at most $(4c_1 - 2)\Delta + 10c_2 + 38c_1 - 23$.

5.4   CONCLUSIONS AND OPEN PROBLEMS

I have given an overview of channel assignment algorithms that take channel spacing constraints into consideration. I have also reviewed the lower bounds and lower bounding techniques available for this version of the channel assignment problem. Many of the algorithms described are based on graph labeling, hence an overview of relevant results on graph labeling is included in this exposition.

All the algorithms reviewed in this chapter have proven performance ratios. Very little is known about the best possible performance ratio that can be achieved. A worthwhile endeavor would be to find lower bounds on the performance ratio of any channel assignment algorithm for specific graphs and/or specific constraint parameters.

Other types of constraints may arise in cellular networks. Many cellular systems operate under *intermodulation constraints,* which forbid the use of frequency gaps that are multiples of each other. Channel assignment under intermodulation constraints is related to *graceful labeling* of graphs. Another type of constraint forbids the use of certain channels in certain cells. Such constraints may be external, resulting from interference with other systems, or internal, when an existing assignment must be updated to accomodate growing demand. This problem is related to *list coloring*.

In practice, the most commonly encountered channel separation constraints are cosite constraints and intersite constraints of value 1 or 2. This situation corresponds to a constrained graph with parameters $c_0, c_1, \ldots, c_k$, where $c_1 = \ldots = c_j = 2$ and $c_{j+1} = \ldots = c_k = 1$. Much work on graph labelings focusses on constraints 1 and 2, most specifically, constraints $c_1, c_2 = 2, 1$ and $c_1, c_2, c_3 = 2, 1, 1$. As shown above, graph labelings can be repeated to accomodate demands of more than one channel per node. It would be useful to see if there are any better ways to use these graph labelings, possibly via borrowing techniques, to accomodate high, nonuniform demand.

ACKNOWLEDGMENTS

Thanks to Nauzer Kalyaniwalla for many helpful comments.

REFERENCES

1. S. M. Allen, D. H. Smith, S. Hurley, and S. U. Thiel, *Using Lower Bounds in Minimum Span Frequency Assignment*, pp. 191–204. Kluwer, 1999.

2. D. Avis, *lrs: A Revised Implementation of the Reverse Search Vertex Enumeration Algorithm*, May 1998. ftp://mutt.cs.mcgill. ca/pub/doc/avis/Av98a.ps.gz.

3. A. A. Bertossi, C. M. Pinotti, and R. B. Tan, Efficient use of radio spectrum in wireless networks with channel separation between close stations, in *Proceedings of DialM 2000*, August 2000.

4. H. L. Bodlaender, T. Kloks, R. B. Tan, and J. van Leeuwen, Approximations for λ-coloring of graphs, in H. Reichel and S. Tison (Eds.), *STACS 2000, Proceedings 17th Annual Symposium on Theoretical Aspects of Computer Science*, volume 1770 of *Lecture Notes in Computer Science*, pp. 395–406, Berlin: Springer-Verlag, 2000.

5. G. J. Chang and D. Kuo, The $L(2, 1)$-labeling problem on graphs, *SIAM J. Discr. Math., 9*: 309–316, 1996.

6. G. Chartrand, D. Erwin, F. Harary, and P. Zang, Radio labelings of graphs, *Bulletin of the Institute of Combinatorics and its Applications*, 2000. (To appear).

7. W. J. Cook, W. H. Cunningham, W. R. Pulleyblank, and A. Schrijver, *Combinatorial Optimization*, New York: Wiley-Interscience, 1998.

8. R. Diestel, *Graph Theory*, 2nd ed. New York: Springer-Verlag, 2000.

9. S. Fitzpatrick, J. Janssen, and R. Nowakowski, Distributive online channel assignment for hexagonal cellular networks with constraints, Technical Report G-2000-14, GERAD, HEC, Montreal, March 2000.

10. D. Fotakis, G. Pantziou, G. Pentaris, and P. Spirakis, Frequency assignment in mobile and radio networks, in *Proceedings of the Workshop on Networks in Distributed Computing*, DIMACS Series. AMS, 1998.

11. D. A. Fotakis and P. G. Spirakis, A hamiltonian approach to the assignment of non-reusable frequencies, in *Foundations of Software Technology and Theoretical Computer Science—FST TCS'98*, volume LNCS 1530, pp. 18–29, 1998.

12. A. Gamst, Some lower bounds for a class of frequency assignment problems, *IEEE Trans. Veh. Technol., 35*(1): 8–14, 1986.

13. J. P. Georges and D. W. Mauro, Generalized vertex labelings with a condition at distance two, *Congressus Numerantium, 109:* 47–57, 1995.

14. S. N. T. Gerke, Colouring weighted bipartite graphs with a co-site constraint, unpublished, 1999.

15. J. R. Griggs and R. K. Yeh, Labeling graphs with a condition at distance 2, *SIAM J. Discr. Math., 5:* 586–595, 1992.

16. J. Janssen and K. Kilakos, Polyhedral analysis of channel assignment problems: (I) Tours, Technical Report CDAM-96-17, London School of Economics, LSE, London, 1996.

17. J. Janssen and K. Kilakos, A polyhedral analysis of channel assignment problems based on tours, in *Proceedings of the 1997 IEEE International Conference on Communications.* New York: IEEE. 1997. Extended abstract.

18. J. Janssen and K. Kilakos, Polyhedral analysis of channel assignment problems: (II) Tilings, Manuscript, 1997.

19. J. Janssen and K. Kilakos, An optimal solution to the "Philadelphia" channel assignment problem, *IEEE Transactions on Vehicular Technology, 48*(3): 1012–1014, May 1999.

20. J. Janssen and K. Kilakos, Tile covers, closed tours and the radio spectrum, in B. Sansó and P. Soriano (Eds.), *Telecommunications Network Planning*, Kluwer, 1999.

21. J. Janssen and L. Narayanan, Channel assignment algorithms for cellular networks with constraints, *Theoretical Comp. Sc. A,* 1999. to appear, extended abstract published in the proceedings of ISAAC'99.

22. J. C. M. Janssen and T. E. Wentzell, Lower bounds from tile covers for the channel assignment problem, Technical Report G-2000-09, GERAD, HEC, Montreal, March 2000.

23. D. S. Johnson, L. A. McGeoch, and E. E. Rothberg, Asymptotic experimental analysis for the Held-Karp traveling salesman bound, in *Proceedings of the 7th Annual ACM-SIAM Symposium on Discrete Algorithms,* 1996. To appear.

24. K. Jonas, *Graph Coloring Analogues with a Condition at Distance Two: L(2, 1)-Labelings and List λ-Labelings.* PhD thesis, Dept. of Math., University of South Carolina, Columbia, SC, 1993.

25. I. Katzela and M. Naghshineh, Channel assignment schemes for cellular mobile telecommunications: a comprehensive survey, *IEEE Personal Communications,* pp. 10–31, June 1996.

26. R. A. Leese, Tiling methods for channel assignment in radio communication networks, *Z. Angewandte Mathematik und Mechanik, 76:* 303–306, 1996.

27. Colin McDiarmid and Bruce Reed, Channel assignment and weighted colouring, *Networks,* 1997. To appear.

28. L. Narayanan. Channel assignment and graph multicoloring, in I. Stojmenovic (Ed.), *Handbook of Wireless Networks and Mobile Computing*, New York: Wiley, 2001.

29. L. Narayanan and S. Shende, Static frequency assignment in cellular networks, in *Proceedings of SIROCCO 97,* pp. 215–227. Carleton Scientific Press, 1977. To appear in *Algorithmica.*

30. M. G. C. Resende R. A. Murphey, P. M. Pardalos, Frequency assignment problems, in D.-Z Du and P. M. Pardalos (Eds.), *Handbook of Combinatorics.* Kluwer Academic Publishers, 1999.

31. A. Raychaudhuri, *Intersection assignments, T-colourings and powers of graphs*, PhD thesis, Rutgers University, 1985.

32. D. Sakai, Labeling chordal graphs: Distance two condition, *SIAM J. Discrete Math., 7:* 133–140, 1994.

33. D. Smith and S. Hurley, Bounds for the frequency assignment problem, *Discr. Math., 167/168:* 571–582, 1997.

34. C. Sung and W. Wong, Sequential packing algorithm for channel assignment under conchannel and adjacent channel interference constraint, *IEEE Trans. Veh. Techn., 46*(3), 1997.

35. S. W. Halpern, Reuse partitioning in cellular systems, in *Proc. IEEE Conf. on Veh. Techn.,* pp. 322–327. New York: IEEE, 1983.

36. S. Ubéda and J. Zerovnik, Upper bounds for the span in triangular lattice graphs: application to

frequency planning for cellular network. Technical Report 97–28, Laboratoire de l'Informatique du Parallélisme, ENS, Lyon, France, September 1997.

37. J. van den Heuvel, Radio channel assignment on 2-dimensional lattices. Technical Report LSE-CDAM-98-05, Centre for Discrete and Applicable Mathematics, LSE, 1998.

38. J. van den Heuvel and S. McGuinness, Colouring the square of a planar graph. Technical Report LSE-CDAM-99-06, Centre for Discrete and Applicable mathematics, LSE, http://www.cdam.lse.ac.uk/Reports, 1999.

39. J. van den Heuvel, Robert Leese, and Mark Shepherd, Graph labelling and radio channel assignment, *Journal of Graph Theory, 29*(4), 1998.

40. Dong wan Tcha, Yong Joo Chung, and Taek jin Choi, A new lower bound for the frequency assignment problem, *ACM/IEEE Trans. Networking, 5*(1): 34–39, 1997.

41. M. A. Whittlesey, J. P. Georges, and D. W. Mauro, On the lambda-coloring of Q_n and related graphs, *SIAM J. Discr. Math., 8:* 499–506, 1995.

42. R. K. Yeh, *Labeling graphs with a condition at distance 2*. PhD thesis, Department of Mathematics, University of South Carolina, Columbia, SC, 1990.

CHAPTER 6

Wireless Media Access Control

ANDREW D. MYERS and STEFANO BASAGNI

Department of Computer Science, University of Texas at Dallas

6.1 INTRODUCTION

The rapid technological advances and innovations of the past few decades have pushed wireless communication from concept to reality. Advances in chip design have dramatically reduced the size and energy requirements of wireless devices, increasing their portability and convenience. These advances and innovations, combined with the freedom of movement, are among the driving forces behind the vast popularity of wireless communication. This situation is unlikely to change, especially when one considers the current push toward wireless broadband access to the Internet and multimedia content.

With predictions of near exponential growth in the number of wireless subscribers in the coming decades, pressure is mounting on government regulatory agencies to free up the RF spectrum to satisfy the growing bandwidth demands. This is especially true with regard to the next generation (3G) cellular systems that integrate voice and high-speed data access services. Given the slow reaction time of government bureaucracy and the high cost of licensing, wireless operators are typically forced to make due with limited bandwidth resources.

The aim of this chapter is to provide the reader with a comprehensive view of the role and details of the protocols that define and control access to the wireless channel, i.e., wireless media access protocols (MAC) protocols. We start by highlighting the distinguishing characteristics of wireless systems and their impact on the design and implementation of MAC protocols (Section 6.2). Section 6.3 explores the impact of the physical limitations specific to MAC protocol design. Section 6.4 lists the set of MAC techniques that form the core of most MAC protocol designs. Section 6.5 overviews channel access in cellular telephony networks and other centralized networks. Section 6.6 focuses on MAC solutions for ad hoc networks, namely, network architectures with decentralized control characterized by the mobility of possibly all the nodes. A brief summary concludes the chapter.

6.2 GENERAL CONCEPTS

In the broadest terms, a wireless network consists of nodes that communicate by exchanging "packets" via radio waves. These packets can take two forms. A unicast packet con-

Handbook of Wireless Networks and Mobile Computing, Edited by Ivan Stojmenović.
ISBN 0-471-41902-8   © 2002 John Wiley & Sons, Inc.

tains information that is addressed to a specific node, whereas a multicast packet distributes the information to a group of nodes. The MAC protocol simply determines when a node is allowed to transmit its packets, and typically controls all access to the physical layer. Figure 6.1 depicts the relative position of the MAC protocol within a simplified protocol stack.

The specific functions associated with a MAC protocol vary according to the system requirements and application. For example, wireless broadband networks carry data streams with stringent quality of service (QoS) requirements. This requires a complex MAC protocol that can adaptively manage the bandwidth resources in order to meet these demands. Design and complexity are also affected by the network architecture, communication model, and duplexing mechanism employed. These three elements are examined in the rest of the section.

6.2.1   Network Architecture

The architecture determines how the structure of the network is realized and where the network intelligence resides. A centralized network architecture features a specialized node, i.e., the base station, that coordinates and controls all transmissions within its coverage area, or cell. Cell boundaries are defined by the ability of nodes to receive transmissions from the base station. To increase network coverage, several base stations are interconnected by land lines that eventually tie into an existing network, such as the public switched telephone network (PTSN) or a local area network (LAN). Thus, each base station also plays the role of an intermediary between the wired and wireless domains. Figure 6.2 illustrates a simple two-cell centralized network.

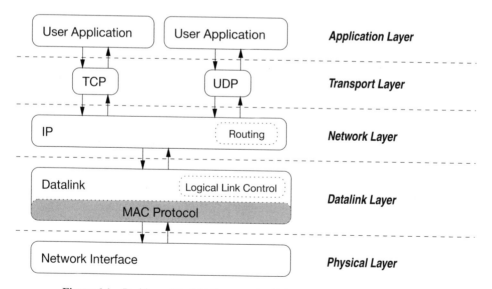

Figure 6.1   Position of the MAC protocol within a simplified protocol stack.

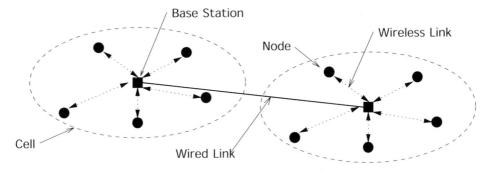

Figure 6.2 Centralized network architecture.

Communication from a base station to a node takes place on a downlink channel, and the opposite occurs on an uplink channel. Only the base station has access to a downlink channel, whereas the nodes share the uplink channels. In most cases, at least one of these uplink channels is specifically assigned to collect control information from the nodes. The base station grants access to the uplink channels in response to service requests received on the control channel. Thus, the nodes simply follow the instructions of the base station.

The concentration of intelligence at the base station leads to a greatly simplified node design that is both compact and energy efficient. The centralized control also simplifies QoS support and bandwidth management since the base station can collect the requirements and prioritize channel access accordingly. Moreover, multicast packet transmission is greatly simplified since each node maintains a single link to the base station. On the other hand, the deployment of a centralized wireless network is a difficult and slow process. The installation of new base stations requires precise placement and system configuration along with the added cost of installing new landlines to tie them into the existing system. The centralized system also presents a single point of failure, i.e., no base station equals no service.

The primary characteristic of an ad hoc network architecture is the absence of any predefined structure. Service coverage and network connectivity are defined solely by node proximity and the prevailing RF propagation characteristics. Ad hoc nodes communicate directly with one another in a peer-to-peer fashion. To facilitate communication between distant nodes, each ad hoc node also acts as a router, storing and forwarding packets on behalf of other nodes. The result is a generalized wireless network that can be rapidly deployed and dynamically reconfigured to provide on-demand networking solutions. An ad hoc architecture is also more robust in that the failure of one node is less likely to disrupt network services. Figure 6.3 illustrates a simple ad hoc network.

Although a generic architecture certainly has its advantages, it also introduces several new challenges. All network control, including channel access, must be distributed. Each ad hoc node must be aware of what is happening in its environment and cooperate with other nodes in order to realize critical network services. Considering that most ad hoc systems are fully mobile, i.e., each node moves independently, the level of protocol sophistication and node complexity is high. Moreover, each ad hoc node must maintain a signifi-

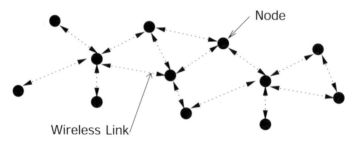

Figure 6.3   Ad hoc network architecture.

cant amount of state information to record crucial information such as the current network topology.

Given its distributed nature, channel access in an ad hoc network is achieved through the close cooperation between competing nodes. Some form of distributed negotiation is needed in order to efficiently allocate channel resources among the active nodes. The amount of overhead, both in terms of time and bandwidth resources, associated with this negotiation will be a critical factor of the overall system performance.

6.2.2   Communication Model

The communication model refers to the overall level of synchronization present in the wireless system and also determines when channel access can occur. There are different degrees of synchronization possible; however, there are only two basic communication models. The synchronous communication model features a slotted channel consisting of discrete time intervals (slots) that have the same duration. With few exceptions, these slots are then grouped into a larger time frame that is cyclically repeated. All nodes are then synchronized according to this time frame and communication occurs within the slot boundaries.

The uniformity and regularity of the synchronous model simplifies the provision of quality of service (QoS) requirements. Packet jitter, delay, and bandwidth allotment can all be controlled through careful time slot management. This characteristic establishes the synchronous communication model as an ideal choice for wireless systems that support voice and multimedia applications. However, the complexity of the synchronization process depends on the type of architecture used. In a centralized system, a base station can broadcast a beacon signal to indicate the beginning of a time frame. All nodes within the cell simply listen for these beacons to synchronize themselves with the base station. The same is not true of an ad hoc system that must rely on more sophisticated clock synchronization mechanisms, such as the timing signals present in the global positioning system (GPS).

The asynchronous communication model is much less restrictive, with communication taking place in an on-demand fashion. There are no time slots and thus no need for any global synchronization. Although this certainly reduces node complexity and simplifies communication, it also complicates QoS provisioning and bandwidth management. Thus, an asynchronous model is typically chosen for applications that have limited QoS requirements, such as file transfers and sensor networks. The reduced interdependence between nodes also makes it applicable to ad hoc network architectures.

6.2.3 Duplexing

Duplexing refers to how transmission and reception events are multiplexed together. Time division duplexing (TDD) alternates transmission and reception at different time instants on the same frequency band, whereas frequency division duplexing (FDD) separates the two into different frequency bands. TDD is simpler and requires less sophisticated hardware, but alternating between transmit and receive modes introduces additional delay overhead. With enough frequency separation, FDD allows a node to transmit and receive at the same time, which dramatically increases the rate at which feedback can be obtained. However, FDD systems require more complex hardware and frequency management.

6.3 WIRELESS ISSUES

The combination of network architecture, communication model, and duplexing mechanism define the general framework within which a MAC protocol is realized. Decisions made here will define how the entire system operates and the level of interaction between individual nodes. They will also limit what services can be offered and delineate MAC protocol design. However, the unique characteristics of wireless communication must also be taken into consideration. In this section, we explore these physical constraints and discuss their impact on protocol design and performance.

Radio waves propagate through an unguided medium that has no absolute or observable boundaries and is vulnerable to external interference. Thus, wireless links typically experience high bit error rates and exhibit asymmetric channel qualities. Techniques such as channel coding, bit interleaving, frequency/space diversity, and equalization increase the survivability of information transmitted across a wireless link. An excellent discussion on these topics can be found in Chapter 9 of [1]. However, the presence of asymmetry means that cooperation between nodes may be severely limited.

The signal strength of a radio transmission rapidly attenuates as it progresses away from the transmitter. This means that the ability to detect and receive transmissions is dependent on the distance between the transmitter and receiver. Only nodes that lie within a specific radius (the transmission range) of a transmitting node can detect the signal (carrier) on the channel. This location-dependent carrier sensing can give rise to so-called hidden and exposed nodes that can detrimentally affect channel efficiency. A hidden node is one that is within range of a receiver but not the transmitter, whereas the contrary holds true for an exposed node. Hidden nodes increase the probability of collision at a receiver, whereas exposed nodes may be denied channel access unnecessarily, thereby underutilizing the bandwidth resources.

Performance is also affected by the signal propagation delay, i.e., the amount of time needed for the transmission to reach the receiver. Protocols that rely on carrier sensing are especially sensitive to the propagation delay. With a significant propagation delay, a node may initially detect no active transmissions when, in fact, the signal has simply failed to reach it in time. Under these conditions, collisions are much more likely to occur and system performance suffers. In addition, wireless systems that use a synchronous communications model must increase the size of each time slot to accommodate propagation delay. This added overhead reduces the amount of bandwidth available for information transmission.

Even when a reliable wireless link is established, there are a number of additional hardware constraints that must also be considered. The design of most radio transceivers only allow half-duplex communication on a single frequency. When a wireless node is actively transmitting, a large fraction of the signal energy will leak into the receive path. The power level of the transmitted signal is much higher than any received signal on the same frequency, and the transmitting node will simply receive its own transmission. Thus, traditional collision detection protocols, such as Ethernet, cannot be used in a wireless environment.

This half-duplex communication model elevates the role of duplexing in a wireless system. However, protocols that utilize TDD must also consider the time needed to switch between transmission and reception modes, i.e., the hardware switching time. This switching can add significant overhead, especially for high-speed systems that operate at peak capacity [2]. Protocols that use handshaking are particularly vulnerable to this phenomenon. For example, consider the case when a source node sends a packet and then receives feedback from a destination node. In this instance, a turnaround time of 10 μs and transmission rate of 10 Mbps will result in an overhead of 100 bits of lost channel capacity. The effect is more significant for protocols that use multiple rounds of message exchanges to ensure successful packet reception, and is further amplified when traffic loads are high.

6.4 FUNDAMENTAL MAC PROTOCOLS

Despite the great diversity of wireless systems, there are a number of well-known MAC protocols whose use is universal. Some are adapted from the wired domain and others are unique to the wireless one. Most of the current MAC protocols use some subset of the following techniques.

6.4.1 Frequency Division Multiple Access (FDMA)

FDMA divides the entire channel bandwidth into M equal subchannels that are sufficiently separated (via guard bands) to prevent cochannel interference (see Figure 6.4). Ignoring the small amount of frequency lost to the guard bands, the capacity of each subchannel is C/M, where C is the capacity associated with the entire channel bandwidth. Each source node can then be assigned one (or more) of these subchannels for its own exclusive use. To receive packets from a particular source node, a destination node must be listening on the proper subchannel. The main advantage of FDMA is the ability to accommodate M simultaneous packet transmissions (one on each subchannel) without collision. However, this comes at the price of increased packet transmission times, resulting in longer packet delays. For example, the transmission time of a packet that is L bits long is $M \cdot L/C$. This is M times longer than if the packet was transmitted using the entire channel bandwidth. The

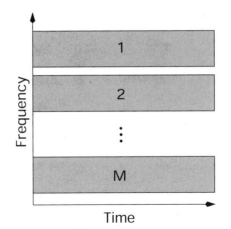

Figure 6.4 Frequency division multiple access.

exclusive nature of the channel assignment can also result in underutilized bandwidth resources when a source node momentarily lacks packets to transmit.

6.4.2 Time Division Multiple Access (TDMA)

TDMA divides the entire channel bandwidth into M equal time slots that are then organized into a synchronous frame (see Figure 6.5). Conceptually, each slot represents one channel that has a capacity equal to C/M, where C is again the capacity of the entire channel bandwidth. Each node can then be assigned one (or more) time slots for its own exclusive use. Consequently, packet transmission in a TDMA system occurs in a serial fashion,

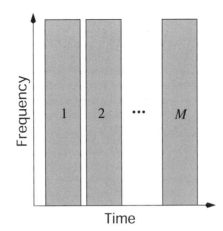

Figure 6.5 Time division multiple access.

with each node taking turns accessing the channel. Since each node has access to the entire channel bandwidth in each time slot, the time needed to transmit a L bit packet is then L/C. When we consider the case where each node is assigned only one slot per frame, however, there is a delay of $(M - 1)$ slots between successive packets from the same node. Once again, channel resources may be underutilized when a node has no packet(s) to transmit in its slot(s). On the other hand, time slots are more easily managed, allowing the possibility of dynamically adjusting the number of assigned slots and minimizing the amount of wasted resources.

6.4.3 Code Division Multiple Access (CDMA)

While FDMA and TDMA isolate transmissions into distinct frequencies or time instants, CDMA allow transmissions to occupy the channel at the same time without interference. Collisions are avoided through the use of special coding techniques that allow the information to be retrieved from the combined signal. As long as two nodes have sufficiently different (orthogonal) codes, their transmissions will not interfere with one another.

CDMA works by effectively spreading the information bits across an artificially broadened channel. This increases the frequency diversity of each transmission, making it less susceptible to fading and reducing the level of interference that might affect other systems operating in the same spectrum. It also simplifies system design and deployment since all nodes share a common frequency band. However, CDMA systems require more sophisticated and costly hardware, and are typically more difficult to manage.

There are two types of spread spectrum modulation used in CDMA systems. Direct sequence spread spectrum (DSSS) modulation modifies the original message by multiplying it with another faster rate signal, known as a pseudonoise (PN) sequence. This naturally increases the bit rate of the original signal and the amount of bandwidth that it occupies. The amount of increase is called the spreading factor. Upon reception of a DSSS modulated signal, a node multiplies the received signal by the PN sequence of the proper node. This increases the amplitude of the signal by the spreading factor relative to any interfering signals, which are diminished and treated as background noise. Thus, the spreading factor is used to raise the desired signal from the interference. This is known as the processing gain. Nevertheless, the processing gain may not be sufficient if the original information signal received is much weaker than the interfering signals. Thus, strict power control mechanisms are needed for systems with large coverage areas, such as a cellular telephony networks.

Frequency hopping spread spectrum (FHSS) modulation periodically shifts the transmission frequency according to a specified hopping sequence. The amount of time spent at each frequency is referred to as the dwell time. Thus, FHSS modulation occurs in two phases. In the first phase, the original message modulates the carrier and generates a narrowband signal. Then the frequency of the carrier is modified according to the hopping sequence and dwell time.

6.4.4 ALOHA Protocols

In contrast to the elegant solutions introduced so far, the ALOHA protocols attempt to share the channel bandwidth in a more brute force manner. The original ALOHA protocol was developed as part of the ALOHANET project at the University of Hawaii [3]. Strangely enough, the main feature of ALOHA is the lack of channel access control. When a node has a packet to transmit, it is allowed to do so immediately. Collisions are common in such a system, and some form of feedback mechanism, such as automatic re-peat request (ARQ), is needed to ensure packet delivery. When a node discovers that its packet was not delivered successfully, it simply schedules the packet for retransmission.

Naturally, the channel utilization of ALOHA is quite poor due to packet vulnerability. The results presented in [4] demonstrate that the use of a synchronous communication model can dramatically improve protocol performance. This slotted ALOHA forces each node to wait until the beginning of a slot before transmitting its packet. This reduces the period during which a packet is vulnerable to collision, and effectively doubles the chan-nel utilization of ALOHA. A variation of slotted ALOHA, known as p-persistent slotted ALOHA, uses a persistence parameter p, $0 < p < 1$, to determine the probability that a node transmits a packet in a slot. Decreasing the persistence parameter reduces the num-ber of collisions, but increases delay at the same time.

6.4.5 Carrier Sense Multiple Access (CSMA) Protocols

There are a number of MAC protocols that utilize carrier sensing to avoid collisions with ongoing transmissions. These protocols first listen to determine whether there is activity on the channel. An idle channel prompts a packet transmission and a busy channel sup-presses it. The most common CSMA protocols are presented and formally analyzed in [5].

While the channel is busy, persistent CSMA continuously listens to determine when the activity ceases. When the channel returns to an idle state, the protocol immediately transmits a packet. Collisions will occur when multiple nodes are waiting for an idle chan-nel. Nonpersistent CSMA reduces the likelihood of such collisions by introducing ran-domization. Each time a busy channel is detected, a source node simply waits a random amount of time before testing the channel again. This process is repeated with an expo-nentially increasing random interval until the channel is found idle.

The p-persistent CSMA protocol represents a compromise between persistent and non-persistent CSMA. In this case, the channel is considered to be slotted but time is not syn-chronized. The length of each slot is equal to the maximum propagation delay, and carrier sensing occurs at the beginning of each slot. If the channel is idle, the node transmits a packet with probability p, $0 < p < 1$. This procedure continues until either the packet is sent, or the channel becomes busy. A busy channel forces a source node to wait a random amount of time before starting the procedure again.

6.5 CENTRALIZED MAC PROTOCOLS

In this section, we provide an overview of two of the most prevalent centralized wireless networks. Cellular telephony is the most predominant form of wireless system in current operation. Wireless ATM is generating a lot of interest for its ability to deliver broadband multimedia services across a wireless link. Each system will be briefly highlighted and the MAC protocol will be examined.

6.5.1 Cellular Telephony

The advanced mobile phone system (AMPS) is an FDMA-based cellular system [6]. The system features 832 full-duplex channels that are grouped into control and data channels.

Each cell has a full-duplex control channel dedicated to system management, paging, and call setup. There are also 45–50 data channels that can be used for voice, fax, or data. The base station grants access to a data channel in response to a call setup request sent on the control channel. A data channel remains assigned to a specific node until it is relinquished or the node moves outside the current cell. Access to the control channel is determined using a CSMA-based MAC protocol. The base station periodically broadcasts the status of the control channel, and a node transmits its setup request (possibly in contention with other nodes) when the control channel is idle. Collisions among setup requests are resolved using randomized retransmissions.

The IS-136 cellular system is a digital version of the AMPS system [7]. As such, it operates within the same spectrum using the same frequency spacing of the original AMPS system. Each data channel is then slotted and a time frame of six slots is used. This allows the system to support multiple users within a single AMPS data channel. An assignment of one slot per frame can support a total of six users transmitting at a rate of 8.1 kb/s. Higher data rates can be achieved by successively doubling the number of assigned slots up to a maximum of 48.6 kb/s. Channel access remains relatively unchanged from the original AMPS system.

The IS-95 cellular system is a CDMA-based wireless network in which all the base stations share a common frequency band with individual transmissions being distinguished by their PN sequences [8]. Strict power control ensures that all transmitted signals reach the base station with the same power level. This allows a more equitable sharing of the system power resources while minimizing systemwide cochannel interference. However, the equalized power levels make it difficult to determine when a node is about to leave one cell and enter another. A node must communicate with multiple base stations simultaneously, allowing it to measure the relative signal quality of each base station. Handover is then made to the base station with the best signal characteristics. This type of system requires complex and costly hardware both within the base stations and nodes.

Cdma2000 is the third generation (3G) version of the IS-95 cellular system. Cdma2000 is backward compatible with the current system, allowing legacy users to be accommodated in future 3G systems. Many other proposed 3G cellular systems have also adopted a CDMA interface. This includes the 3G version of GSM known as the universal mobile telecommunications services (UMTS) [9].

6.5.2 Wireless ATM

Asynchronous transfer mode (ATM) is a high-performance connection-oriented switching and multiplexing technology that uses fixed-sized packets to transport a wide range of integrated services over a single network. These include voice, video, and multimedia services that have different QoS requirements. The ability to provide specific QoS services is one of the hallmarks of ATM. Wireless ATM is designed to extend these integrated services to the mobile user.

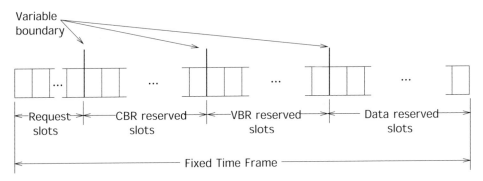

Figure 6.6 PRMA/DA protocol.

Similar to cellular systems, wireless ATM nodes send requests to the base station for service. The specific QoS requirements of an application are included in these request messages. The base station then collects these requirements and allocates the uplink and downlink channels accordingly. Thus wireless ATM MAC protocols typically follow a three-phase model. In the first phase, a request message is sent on a random access control channel, usually using a slotted ALOHA protocol. The second phase involves the base station scheduling uplink and downlink transmissions according to the QoS requirements of the current traffic mix. Preference is given to delay-sensitive data, such as voice packets, whereas datagram services must make due with any remaining capacity. The third phase involves the transmission of packets according to the schedule created in phase two.

The PRMA/DA [10] and DSA++ [11] protocols are two examples of this three-phase MAC design using FDD, whereas MASCARA [12] and DTDMA [13] use TDD. Each of these protocols are respectively illustrated in Figures 6.6 through 6.9 and Table 6.1 summarizes their relative characteristics.

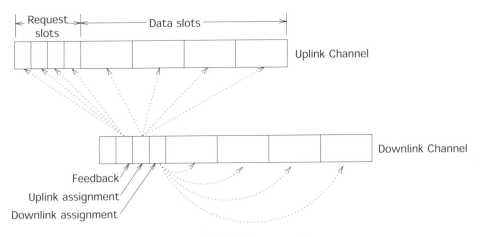

Figure 6.7 DSA++ protocol.

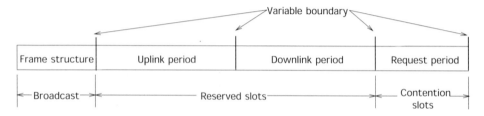

Figure 6.8 MASCARA protocol.

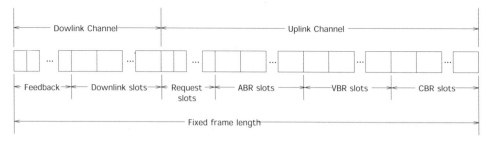

Figure 6.9 DTDMA protocol.

6.6 AD HOC MAC PROTOCOLS

Ad hoc networks do not have the benefit of predefined base stations to coordinate channel access, thus invalidating many of the assumptions held by centralized MAC designs. In this section, we focus our attention on MAC protocols that are specifically designed for ad hoc networks.

A possible taxonomy of ad hoc MAC protocols includes three broad protocol categories that differ in their channel access strategy: contention protocols, allocation protocols, and a combination of the two (hybrid protocols).

Contention protocols use direct competition to determine channel access rights, and resolve collisions through randomized retransmissions. The ALOHA and CSMA protocols

TABLE 6.1 Wireless ATM MAC protocol relative characteristics

	PRMA/DA	DSA++	MASCARA	DTDMA
Duplexing	FDD	FDD	TDD	TDD
Frame type	fixed	variable	variable	fixed
Algorithm complexity	medium	medium	high	high
Communication complexity	low	medium	high	medium
Channel utilization	medium	high	medium	high
Control overhead	medium	high	high	medium

introduced in Sections 6.4.4 and 6.4.5 are prime examples. With the exception of slotted ALOHA, most contention protocols employ an asynchronous communication model. Collision avoidance is also a key design element that is realized through some form of control signaling.

The contention protocols are simple and tend to perform well at low traffic loads, i.e., when there are few collision, leading to high channel utilization and low packet delay. However, protocol performance tends to degrade as the traffic loads are increased and the number of collisions rise. At very high traffic loads, a contention protocol can become unstable as the channel utilization drops. This can result in exponentially growing packet delay and network service breakdown since few, if any, packets can be successfully exchanged.

Allocation protocols employ a synchronous communication model and use a scheduling algorithm that generates a mapping of time slots to nodes. This mapping results in a transmission schedule that determines in which particular slots a node is allowed to access the channel. Most allocation protocols create collision-free transmission schedules, thus the schedule length (measured in slots) forms the basis of protocol performance. The time slots can either be allocated statically or dynamically, leading to a fixed and variable schedule length.

The allocation protocols tend to perform well at moderate to heavy traffic loads as all slots are likely to be utilized. These protocols also remain stable even when the traffic loads are extremely high. This is due to the fact that most allocation protocols ensure that each node has collision-free access to at least one time slot per frame. On the other hand, these protocols are disadvantaged at low traffic loads due to the artificial delay induced by the slotted channel. This results in significantly higher packet delays with respect to the contention protocols.

Hybrid protocols can be loosely described as any combination of two or more protocols. However, in this section, the definition of the term hybrid will be constrained to include only those protocols that combine elements of contention- and allocation-based channel access schemes in such a way as to maintain their individual advantages while avoiding their drawbacks. Thus, the performance of a hybrid protocol should approximate a contention protocol when traffic is light, and an allocation protocol during periods of high load.

6.6.1 Contention Protocols

Contention protocols can be further classified according to the type of collision avoidance mechanism employed. The ALOHA protocols make up the category of protocols that feature no collision avoidance mechanism, i.e., they simply react to collision via randomized retransmissions. Most contention protocols, however, use some form of collision avoidance mechanism.

The busy-tone multiple access (BTMA) protocol [14] divides the entire bandwidth into two separate channels. The main data channel is used for the transmission of packets, and occupies the majority of the bandwidth. The control channel is used for the transmission of a special busy-tone signal that indicates the presence of activity on the data channel. These signals are not bandwidth-intensive, thus the control channel is relatively small.

The BTMA protocol operates as follows. When a source node has a packet to transmit, it first listens for the busy-tone signal on the control channel. If the control channel is idle, i.e., no busy-tone is detected, then the node may begin transmitting its packet. Otherwise, the node reschedules the packet for transmission at some later time. Any node that detects activity on the data channel immediately begins transmitting the busy-tone on the control channel. This continues until the activity on the data channel ceases.

In this way, BTMA prevents all nodes that are two hops away from an active source node from accessing the data channel. This significantly lowers the level of hidden node interference, and therefore reduces the probability of collision. However, the number of exposed nodes is dramatically increased and this may result in a severely underutilized data channel.

The receiver-initiated busy-tone multiple access (RI-BTMA) protocol [15] attempts to minimize the number of exposed nodes by having only the destination(s) transmit the busy-tone. Rather than immediately transmitting the busy-tone upon detection of an active data channel, a node monitors the incoming data transmission to determine whether it is a destination. This determination takes a significant amount of time, especially in a noisy environment with corrupted information. During this time, the initial transmission remains vulnerable to collision. This can be particularly troublesome in high-speed systems where the packet transmission time may be short.

The wireless collision detect (WCD) protocol [2] essentially combines the BTMA and RI-BTMA protocols by using two distinct busy-tone signals on the control channel. WCD acts like BTMA when activity is first detected on the main channel, i.e., it transmits a collision detect (CD) signal on the BTC. RI-BTMA behavior takes over once a node determines it is a destination. In this case, a destination stops transmitting the CD signal and begins transmitting a feedback-tone (FT) signal. In this way, WCD minimizes the exposed nodes while still protecting the transmission from hidden node interference.

These busy-tone protocols feature simple designs that require only a minimal increase in hardware complexity. Because of its unique characteristics, the WCD protocol is the overall performance leader, followed by RI-BTMA and BTMA, respectively [2]. Furthermore, the performance of busy-tone protocols are less sensitive to the hardware switching time since it is assumed that a node can transmit and receive on the data and control channels simultaneously. However, wireless systems that have a limited amount of RF spectrum may not be able to realize a separate control and data channel. In such cases, collision avoidance using in-band signaling is necessary.

The multiple access with collision avoidance (MACA) protocol [16] uses a handshaking dialogue to alleviate hidden node interference and minimize the number of exposed nodes. This handshake consists of a request-to-send (RTS) control packet that is sent from a source node to its destination. The destination replies with a clear-to-send (CTS) control packet, thus completing the handshake. A CTS response allows the source node to transmit its packet. The absence of a CTS forces a node to reschedule the packet for transmission at some later time. Figure 6.10 illustrates the operation of the MACA protocol.

Consider the case where node *B* wishes to send a packet to node *A*. Node *B* first transmits an RTS, which reaches nodes *A*, *C*, and *D* (Figure 6.10a). Node *A* then responds by

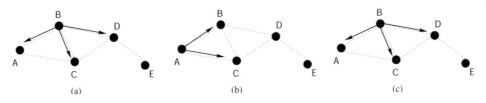

Figure 6.10   MACA protocol operation.

sending a CTS, which reaches nodes *B* and *C*, thus completing the handshake (Figure 6.10b). At this point, *B* is free to send its packet (Figure 6.10c).

Notice that a hidden node is likely to overhear the CTS packet sent by a destination node, whereas an exposed node is not. Thus, by including the time needed to receive a CTS and packet in the respective RTS and CTS packets, we reduce the likelihood of hidden node interference and the number of exposed nodes simultaneously.

The MACAW protocol [17] enhances MACA by including carrier sensing to avoid collisions among RTS packets, and a positive acknowledgement (ACK) to aid in the rapid recovery of lost packets. To protect the ACK from collision, a source node transmits a data sending (DS) control packet to alert exposed nodes of its impending arrival. Improvements are also made to the collision resolution algorithm to ensure a more equitable sharing of the channel resources.

The MACA with piggyback reservations (MACA/PR) protocol [18] enhances MACA by incorporating channel reservations. This allows the system to support QoS sensitive applications. Each node maintains a reservation table (RT) that is used to record the channel reservations made by neighboring nodes. A source node makes a reservation by first completing a RTS/CTS exchange. It then sends the first real-time packet, whose header contains the time interval specifying the interval in which the next one will be sent. The destination responds with an ACK carrying the equivalent time interval. Other nodes within range note this reservation in their RT and remain silent during the subsequent time intervals. Thus, the source node can send subsequent real-time packets without contention. To ensure proper bookkeeping, the nodes periodically exchange their RTs.

The MACA by invitation (MACA-BI) protocol [19] reverses the handshaking dialogue of MACA. In this case, the destination node initiates packet transmission by sending a request-to-receive (RTR) control packet to the source node. The source node responds to this poll with a packet transmission. Thus, each node must somehow predict when neighbors have packets for it. This means that each node must maintain a list of its neighbors along with their traffic characteristics. In order to prevent collision, the nodes must also synchronize their polling mechanisms by sharing this information with their neighbors.

These MACA-based contention protocols minimize collisions by reducing the negative effect of hidden and exposed nodes through simple handshaking dialogues. However, the exchange of multiple control packets for each data packet magnifies the impact of signal propagation delay and hardware switching time. To some extent, the MACA/PR and

MACA/BI protocols alleviate these problems by reducing the amount of handshaking, yet the amount of state information maintained at each node can be substantial.

6.6.2 Allocation Protocols

There are two distinct classes of allocation protocols that differ in the way the transmission schedules are computed. Static allocation protocols use a centralized scheduling algorithm that statically assigns a fixed transmission schedule to each node prior to its operation. This type of scheduling is similar to the assignment of MAC addresses for Ethernet interface cards. Dynamic allocation protocols uses a distributed scheduling algorithm that computes transmission schedules in an on-demand fashion.

Since the transmission schedules are assigned beforehand, the scheduling algorithm of a static allocation protocol requires global system parameters as input. The classic TDMA protocol builds its schedules according to the maximum number of nodes in the network. For a network of N nodes, the protocol uses a frame length of N slots and assigns each node one unique time slot. Since each node has exclusive access to one slot per frame, there is no threat of collision for any packet type (i.e., unicast or multicast). Moreover, the channel access delay is bounded by the frame length. Because of the equivalence between system size and frame length, classic TDMA performs poorly in large-scale networks.

The time spread multiple access (TSMA) protocol [20] relaxes some of the strict requirements of classic TDMA to achieve better performance while still providing bounded access delay. The TSMA scheduling algorithm assigns each node multiple slots in a single frame, and permits a limited amount of collisions to occur. These two relaxations allow TSMA to obtain transmission schedules whose lengths scale logarithmically with respect to the number of nodes. Furthermore, TSMA guarantees the existence of a collision-free transmission slot to each neighbor within a single frame.

The source of this "magic" is the scheduling algorithm that makes use of the mathematical properties of finite fields. An excellent introduction to finite fields can be found in [21]. The scheduling algorithm is briefly outlined as follows. For a network of N nodes, the parameters q (of the form $q = p^m$, where p is a prime and m an integer) and integer k are chosen such that $q^{k+1} \geq N$ and $q \geq kD_{max} + 1$, where D_{max} is the maximum node degree. Each node can then be assigned a unique polynomial f over the Galois field $GF(q)$. Using this polynomial, a unique TSMA transmission schedule is computed where bit $i = 1$ if $(i \bmod q) = f(\lfloor i/q \rfloor)$, otherwise $i = 0$.

As shown in [20], that this TSMA scheduling algorithm provides each node with a transmission schedule with guaranteed access in each time frame. The maximum length of this schedule is bounded by

$$L = O\left(\frac{D_{max}^2 \log^2 N}{\log^2 D_{max}} \right)$$

Notice that the frame length scales logarithmically with the number of nodes and quadratically with the maximum degree. For ad hoc networks consisting of thousands of nodes with a sparse topology (i.e., small D_{max}), TSMA can yield transmission schedules that are much shorter than TDMA. Table 6.2 compares the frame lengths of TDMA and TSMA for

TABLE 6.2   Frame lengths of classic TDMA versus TSMA

	$D_{max} = 2$	$D_{max} = 5$	$D_{max} = 10$	$D_{max} = 15$
TDMA	1000	1000	1000	1000
TSMA	49	121	529	961

a network of $N = 1000$ nodes. For TSMA protocols a $\Omega(\log n)$ lower bound has been proved for L in [22]. We notice that there is still a gap between the TSMA upper bound and the mentioned logarithmic lower bound. Therefore, there is still room for improvement (more likely on the lower-bound side). TSMA-like protocols have also been deployed as a basis for implementing broadcast (i.e., one-to-all communication) in ad hoc networks. Upper and lower bound for deterministic and distributed TSMA-based broadcast can be found in [23, 24] and [25], respectively.

With mobile ad hoc networks, nodes may be activated and deactivated without warning, and unrestricted mobility yields a variable network topology. Consequently, global parameters, such as node population and maximum degree, are typically unavailable or difficult to predict. For this reason, protocols that use only local parameters have been developed. A local parameter refers to information that is specific to a limited region of the network, such as the number of nodes within x hops of a reference node (referred to as an x-hop neighborhood). A dynamic allocation protocol then uses these local parameters to deterministically assign transmission slots to nodes. Because local parameters are likely to vary over time, the scheduling algorithm operates in a distributed fashion and is periodically executed to adapt to network variations.

Dynamic allocation protocols typically operate in two phases. Phase one consists of a set of reservation slots in which the nodes contend for access to the subsequent transmission slots. This is similar to many of the wireless ATM protocols studied in Section 6.5. Lacking a coordinating base station, contention in this phase requires the cooperation of each individual node to determine and verify the outcome. Successful contention in phase one grants a node access to one or more transmission slots of phase two, in which packets are sent.

A great number of dynamic allocation protocols have been proposed. The protocols [26–29] are just a few excellent examples of this two-phase design. They use a contention mechanism that is based on classic TDMA. Essentially, the nodes take turns contending for slot reservations, with the earliest node succeeding. This results in a high degree of unfairness that is equalized by means of a reordering policy. Although these protocols create transmission schedules that are specific to the local network topology, they still require global parameters.

In contrast, the five-phase reservation protocol (FPRP) [29] is designed to be arbitrarily scalable, i.e., independent of the global network size. FPRP uses a complex frame structure that consists of two subframe types, namely reservation frames and information frames. As illustrated in Fig. 6.11, a reservation frame precedes a sequence of k information frames. Each reservation frame consists of ℓ reservation slots that correspond to the ℓ information slots of each information frame. Thus, if a node wants to reserve a specific information slot, it contends in the corresponding reservation slot. At the end of the reserva-

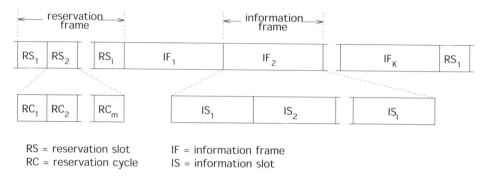

RS = reservation slot   IF = information frame
RC = reservation cycle   IS = information slot

Figure 6.11 Frame and slot structure of FPRP.

tion frame, a TDMA schedule is created and used in the following k information frames. The schedule is then recomputed in the next reservation frame.

In order to accommodate contention, each reservation slot consists of m reservation cycles that contain a five-round reservation dialogue. A reservation is made in the first four rounds, whereas the fifth round is used for performance optimization. The contention is summarized as follows. A node that wishes to make a reservation sends out a request using p-persistent slotted ALOHA (round 1), and feedback is provided by the neighboring nodes (round 2). A successful request, i.e., one that did not involve a collision, allows a node to reserve the slot (round 3). All nodes within two hops of the source node are then notified of the reservation (round 4). These nodes will honor the reservation and make no further attempts to contend for the slot. Any unsuccessful reservation attempts are resolved through a pseudo-Bayesian resolution algorithm that randomizes the next reservation attempt.

In [29], FPRP is shown to yield transmission schedules that are collision-free; however, the protocol requires a significant amount of overhead. Each reservation cycle requires a number of hardware switches between transmitting and receiving modes. Each round of contention must also be large enough to accommodate the signal, propagation delay and physical layer overhead (e.g., synchronization and guard time). Add this together and multiply the result by m reservation cycles and ℓ reservation slots, and the end result is anything but trivial. Furthermore, the system parameters k, ℓ and m are heuristically determined through simulation and then fixed in the network. This limits the ability of FPRP to dynamically adapt its operation to suit the current network conditions, which may deviate from the simulated environment.

6.6.3 Hybrid Protocols

A protocol that integrates TDMA and CSMA is introduced in [30]. The idea is to permanently assign each node a fixed TDMA transmission schedule, yet give the nodes an opportunity to reclaim and/or reuse any idle slots through CSMA-based contention. Nodes have immediate channel access in their assigned slots, and may transmit a maximum of two data packets. Nodes wishing to transmit a packet in an unassigned slot must first determine its status through carrier sensing. If the slot is idle, each competing node attempts to transmit a single packet at some randomly chosen time instant.

As illustrated in Figure 6.12, a large portion of each idle slot is sacrificed in order to accommodate randomized channel access. Hidden nodes can also interfere with the ability of a node to successfully use its assigned slot. Thus nodes are prevented from using slots that are allocated to nodes that are exactly two hops away. Although this can be achieved in a fixed wireless system, it is unclear how this can be accomplished in a mobile environment. Furthermore, the reliability of multicast transmissions can only be assured in assigned slots.

The ADAPT protocol [31] addresses the problem of hidden node interference by integrating a CSMA-based contention protocol that uses collision avoidance handshaking into a TDMA allocation protocol. As illustrated in Figure 6.13, each time slot is subdivided into three intervals. In the priority interval, nodes announce their intentions to use their assigned slots by initiating a collision avoidance handshake with the intended destination. This ensures that all hidden nodes are aware of the impending transmission. The contention interval is used by nodes wishing to compete for channel access in an unassigned time slot. A node may compete if and only if the channel remains idle during the priority interval. The transmission interval is used for the transmission of packets. Access to the transmission interval is determined as follows. All nodes have access to the transmission interval in their assigned slots. A node that successfully completes an RTS/CTS handshake in the contention interval of an unassigned slot may access the transmission interval. Any unsuccessful handshake in the contention interval is resolved using the exponential backoff algorithm presented in [32].

Extensive simulation results demonstrate that ADAPT successfully maintains priori-

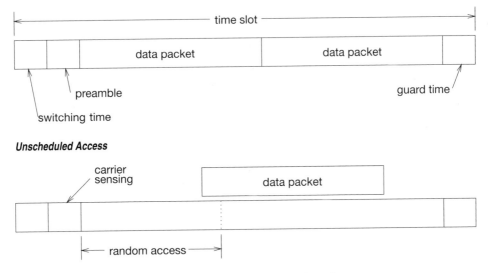

Figure 6.12   Hybrid TDMA/CSMA channel access.

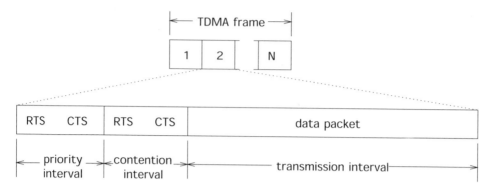

Figure 6.13   The ADAPT protocol.

tized access to assigned slots and exhibits high channel utilization in sparse network topologies [33]. However, the results do not factor in any physical constraints, such as propagation delay and hardware switch-over time, which can significantly increase overall protocol overhead. Furthermore, the handshaking mechanism employed in the contention interval does not support multicast packet transmissions.

The ABROAD protocol [34] accommodates multicast packets by altering the contention mechanism of ADAPT. The RTS/CTS signaling in the priority interval does not need to be modified since its primary purpose is to simply inform nodes of activity in an assigned slot. However, the use of a RTS/CTS dialogue fails in the contention interval due to the potential collision among the CTS responses, i.e., information implosion. ABROAD uses a form of negative feedback response to avoid this problem. Thus, a node responds with a negative CTS (NCTS) when a collision is detected in the contention interval or remains silent otherwise. There are a few cases in which this type of handshaking fails, yet simulation results and analysis demonstrate that the probability of failure is small, e.g., less than 4% in networks with low bit error rates [34].

The AGENT protocol [35] integrates the unicast capabilities of ADAPT with the multicast capabilities of ABROAD. The result is a generalized MAC protocol that is able to provide a full range of effective single-hop transmission services. AGENT uses the same frame and slot structure of ADAPT, as well as the handshaking dialogue of the priority interval. The control signaling in the contention interval is based on a combination of ADAPT and ABROAD.

Thus, to gain access to the transmission interval of a slot s, a source node i first transmits a RTS control packet. This occurs at the beginning of the priority interval in an assigned slot, or the beginning of the priority interval, otherwise. The reception of a RTS in the priority interval elicits a CTS response. On the other hand, the reception of a RTS in the contention interval generates a CTS response only when it is associated with a unicast packet. Any collision detected in the contention interval will cause a NCTS to be transmitted.

Once this initial control signaling is finished, a node can determine its eligibility to transmit its packet p in the transmission interval. If s is assigned to i, then source node i is granted permission to transmit p without restriction. Otherwise, the following rules must be applied.

1. If any CTS control signaling is detected in the priority interval, then i must withhold the transmission of p to avoid collision with the owner of s.
2. If a NCTS response is received in the contention interval, then multiple source nodes are contending for s, and i must withhold the transmission of p to avoid collision.
3. If p is a unicast packet and a corresponding CTS is received, then i may transmit p in the transmission interval.
4. If p is a multicast packet and no signaling response is received, then i may transmit p in the transmission interval.

Any failure to transmit p in this manner is resolved by the backoff algorithm of ADAPT.

For example, consider the ad hoc network of Figure 6.14. The current slot is assigned to node B, which has a multicast packet addressed to nodes A and C, and node D has a unicast packet addressed to node E. Then B sends a RTS in the priority interval [Figure 6.14(a)] to which A and C respond with a CTS [Figure 6.14(b)]. Node D sends its RTS in the contention interval [Figure 6.14(c)], and E responds with a CTS [Figure 6.14(d)]. When this signaling ends, both B and D are free to transmit their respective packets.

To eliminate unnecessary control signaling, a node that is attempting to transmit a packet in an unassigned slot refrains from sending a RTS when a CTS is detected in the priority interval. There are also a number of ambiguous cases that arise when dealing with multicast packets. To ensure proper signaling behavior, a node that transmits a RTS in the priority interval also sends a jamming RTS (JAM) in the contention interval.

The analysis and simulation presented in [35] demonstrate that the performance of AGENT closely matches that of a contention protocol under light traffic loads. As the load

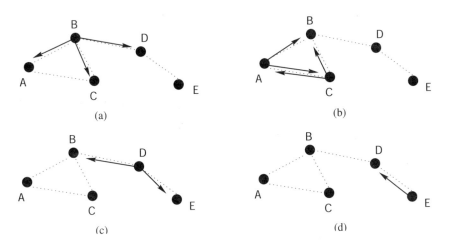

Figure 6.14 Example of AGENT signaling.

is increased, the performance of AGENT mirrors that of its underlying allocation protocol. It is further shown that AGENT is not biased toward one traffic type or another. This allows a more equitable sharing of channel resources between unicast and multicast traffic. However, the application of AGENT is somewhat limited due to the use of a TDMA scheduling algorithm. For larger networks consisting of thousands of nodes, the current AGENT protocol may no longer be a feasible alternative. Moreover, the network size is typically unknown and time-varying.

A more general framework for the integration of multiple MAC protocols is presented in [36]. This metaprotocol framework dynamically combines any set of existing MAC protocols into a single hybrid solution. This hybrid protocol essentially runs each of these component protocols in parallel. The decision of whether or not to transmit is then derived from a weighted average of the decisions made by the individual component protocols. The properties of the metaprotocol framework ensure that the hybrid protocol always matches the performance of the best component protocol without knowing in advance which protocol will match the unpredictable changes in the network conditions. This combination is entirely automatic and requires only local network feedback.

To simplify the presentation of the metaprotocol framework, we restrict our attention to slotted time and assume that immediate channel feedback is available at the end of each slot. Figure 6.15 illustrates a combination of M component protocols, $P_1, \ldots, P_M$. Each component protocol P_i is assigned a weight w_i and produces a decision $D_{i,t}$, $0 \leq D_{i,t} \leq 1$ that indicates the transmission probability in a given slot t. No assumptions are made concerning how each component protocol reaches its decision. The final decision D_t is computed as a function of the weighted average of the $D_{i,t}$ values:

$$D_t = F\left(\frac{\sum_{i=1}^{M} w_{i,t} D_{i,t}}{\sum_{i=1}^{M} w_{i,t}} \right)$$

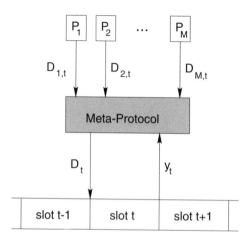

Figure 6.15   The metaprotocol framework.

The function F can be chosen in several ways, but for simplicity we will use $F(x) = x$. The value of D_t is then rounded using randomization to produce a binary decision $\tilde{D}_t$ for slot t.

At the end of each slot, the weights of the component protocols is adjusted according to the channel feedback, from which we can conclude the correctness of the final decision $\tilde{D}_t$. For example, if collision occurs, then a decision to transmit was wrong. Let y_t denote the feedback at the end of slot t, where $y_t = 1$ indicates a correct decision and $y_t = 0$ indicates the opposite. Then the correct decision z_t can be retrospectively computed as

$$z_t = \tilde{D}_t y_t + (1 - \tilde{D}_t)(1 - y_t)$$

Using z_t, the weights are updated according to the following exponential rule

$$w_{i,t+1} = w_{i,t} \cdot e^{-\eta|D_{i,t} - z_t|}$$

The term $|D_{i,t} - z_t|$ represents the deviation of protocol P_i from the correct decision z_t. If there is no deviation, then the weight remains unchanged. Otherwise, the relative weight decreases with increasing deviation. The constant $\eta > 0$ controls the magnitude of the weight change and thus greatly influences the stability and convergence of the metaprotocol. Note that the direct use of equation 6.1 will ultimately cause underflow in the weight representation since the weights decrease monotonically. This problem is easily solved in practice by renormalizing the weights when needed.

Numerous practical applications of the metaprotocol framework demonstrate its capability to dynamically optimize many of the critical parameters of MAC protocols to match the prevailing network conditions [36, 37]. Examples include the manipulation of the transmission probability of contention protocols and the transmission schedules of allocation protocols.

6.7 SUMMARY

The aim of this chapter is to provide a comprehensive view of the role of MAC protocols in wireless systems. We first described the characteristics of wireless systems that affect the design and implementation of MAC protocols. Then we presented some fundamental MAC protocols whose spirit pervades basically all the protocols used today in wireless networks. Specific protocols are then described in detail, based on the specific architecture for which they are deployed (either the centralized architecture typical of cellular systems or the distributed architecture of ad hoc networks).

Our discussion indicates that the problem of designing efficient MAC protocols is a crucial problem in the more general design, implementation, and deployment of wireless networks, in which the demand for bandwidth-greedy application is growing fast and the available RF spectrum is still very narrow.

REFERENCES

1. D. Goodman, *Wireless Personal Communications Systems,* Reading, MA: Addison-Wesley, 1998.

2. A. Gummalla and J. Limb, Wireless collision detect (WCD): Multiple access with receiver initiated feedback and carrier detect signal, *Proc. IEEE ICC'00,* vol. 1, pp. 397–401, New Orleans, LA, June 2000.

3. N. Abramsom, Development of the ALOHANET, *IEEE Trans. Inform. Theory, 31,* 2, 119–23, March 1985.

4. L. Roberts, ALOHA packet system with and without slots and capture, *Comput. Commun. Rev., 5,* 2, 28–42, April 1975.

5. L. Kleinrock and F. Tobagi, Packet switching in radio channels. I. Carrier sense multiple access models and their throughput delay characteristics, *IEEE Trans. on Commun., COM-23,* 12, 1400–1416, Dec. 1975.

6. ANSI/EIA/TIA, Mobile station–sand station compatibility specification. Technical Report 553, EIA/TIA, 1989.

7. EIA/TIA. 800MHz TDMA cellular radio interface—Mobile station–base station compatibility—Digital control channel. Technical Report IS-136, EIA/TIA, 1994.

8. EIA/TIA. Mobile station–base station compatibility standard for dual-mode wideband spread-spectrum cellular system. Technical Report IS-95, EIA/TIA, 1993.

9. M. Oliphant, Radio interfaces make the difference in 3G cellular systems, *IEEE Spectrum,* 53–58, Oct. 2000.

10. J. Kim and I. Widjaja, PRMA/DA: A new media access control protocol for wireless ATM, *Proc. IEEE ICC'96,* pp. 1–19, Dallas, TX, June 1996.

11. D. Petras and A. Krämling, MAC protocol with polling and fast collision resolution for ATM air interface, *IEEE ATM Workshop,* San Fransisco, CA, Aug. 1996.

12. N. Passas *et al.,* Quality-of-service-oriented medium access control for wireless ATM networks, *IEEE Commun. Mag.,* 43–50, Nov. 1997.

13. D. Raychaudhuri and N. Wilson, ATM-based transport architecture for multiservices wireless personal communication networks, *IEEE JSAC, 12,* 8, 1401–1414, Oct. 1992.

14. F. Tobagi and L. Kleinrock, Packet switching in radio channels. II. The hidden terminal problem in carrier sense multiple-access and the busy-tone solution, *IEEE Trans. on Commun., COM-23,* 12, 1417–1433, Dec. 1975.

15. C. Wu and V. Li, Receiver-initiated busy tone multiple access in packet radio networks, *Comput. Commun. Rev., 17,* 5, 336–342, Aug. 1987.

16. P. Karn, MACA—A new channel access protocol for packet radio, *Proc. ARRL/CRRL Amateur Radio 9th Comput. Networking Conf.,* Sept. 22, pp. 134–140, 1990.

17. V. Bharghavan et al, MACAW: A media access protocol for wireless LAN's, *Comput. Commun. Rev., 24,* 4, 212–225, Oct. 1994.

18. C. Lin and M. Gerla, Real-time support in multihop wireless networks, *ACM/Baltzer Wireless Networks, 5,* 2, 125–135, 1999.

19. F. Talucci and M. Gerla, MACA-BI (MACA by invitation): A wireless MAC protocol for high speed ad hoc networking, *Proc. IEEE ICUPC'97,* vol. 2, pp. 913–917, San Diego, CA, Oct. 1997.

20. I. Chlamtac and A. Faragó, Making transmission schedules immune to topology changes in multihop packet radio networks, *IEEE/ACM Trans. Networking, 2,* 1, 23–29, Feb. 1994.

21. R. Lidl and H. Niederreiter, *Introduction to Finite Fields and Their Applications,* Cambridge, MA: Cambridge University Press, 1994.

22. S. Basagni and D. Bruschi, A logarithmic lower bound for time-spread multiple-access (TSMA) protocols, *ACM/Kluwer Wireless Networks, 6,* 2, 161–163.

23. S. Basagni, D. Bruschi, and I. Chlamtac, A mobility transparent deterministic broadcast mechanism for ad hoc networks, *ACM/IEEE Transactions on Networking, 7,* 6, 799–809, Dec. 1999.

24. S. Basagni, A. D. Myers, and V. R. Syrotiuk, Mobility-independent flooding for real-time, multimedia applications in ad hoc networks, in *Proceedings of 1999 IEEE Emerging Technologies Symposium on Wireless Communications and Systems,* Richardson, TX, April 12–13 1999.

25. D. Bruschi and M. Del Pinto, Lower bounds for the broadcast problem in mobile radio networks, *Distributed Computing 10,* 3, 129–135, April 1997.

26. I. Cidon and M. Sidi, Distributed assignment algorithms for multihop packet radio networks, *IEEE Trans. on Comput., 38,* 10, 1353–1361, Oct. 1989.

27. L. Pond and V. Li, A distributed timeslot assignment protocol for mobile multi-hop broadcast packet radio networks, *Proc. IEEE MILCOM'89,* vol. 1, pp. 70–74, Boston, MA, Oct. 1989.

28. A. Ephremides and T. Truong, Scheduling broadcasts in multihop radio networks, *IEEE Trans. Commun., 38,* 4, 456–460, April 1990.

29. C. Zhu and M. Corson, A five-phase reservation protocol (FPRP) for mobile ad hoc networks, *Proc. IEEE INFOCOM'98,* vol. 1, pp. 322–331, San Francisco, CA, Mar. /Apr. 1998.

30. B. Sharp, A. Grindrod, and D. Camm, Hybrid TDMA/CDMA protocol self-managing packet radio networks, *Proc. IEEE ICUPC'95,* pp. 929–933, Tokyo, Japan, Nov. 1995.

31. I. Chlamtac et al., ADAPT: A dynamically self-adjusting media access control protocol for ad hoc networks, *Proc. IEEE GLOBECOM'99,* vol. 1a, pp. 11–15, Rio De Janeiro, Brazil, Dec. 1999.

32. D. Jeong and W. Jeon, Performance of an exponential backoff scheme for the slotted-ALOHA protocol in local wireless environment, *Proc. IEEE Trans. Veh. Tech., 44,* 3, 470–479, Aug. 1995.

33. I. Chlamtac et al., A performance comparison of hybrid and conventional MAC protocols for wireless networks, *Proc. IEEE VTC'00-Spring,* vol. 1, pp. 201–205, Tokyo, Japan, May 2000.

34. I. Chlamtac et al., An adaptive medium access control (MAC) protocol for reliable broadcast in wireless networks, *Proc. IEEE ICC'00,* vol. 3, pp. 1692–1696, New Orleans, LA, June 2000.

35. A. Myers, G. Záruba, and V. R. Syrotiuk, An adaptive generalized transmission protocol for ad hoc networks, to appear in *ACM/Kluwer Mobile Networks and Applications.*

36. A. Faragó et al., Meta-MAC protocols: Automatic combination of MAC protocols to optimize performance for unknown conditions, *IEEE JSAC, 18,* 9, 1670–1681, Sept. 2000.

37. A. Faragó et al., A new approach to MAC protocol optimization, *Proc. IEEE GLOBECOM'01,* vol. 3, pp. 1742–1746, San Francisco, CA, Nov./Dec. 2001.

CHAPTER 7

Traffic Integration in Personal, Local, and Geographical Wireless Networks

RAFFAELE BRUNO, MARCO CONTI, and ENRICO GREGORI
CNR, Istituto CNUCE, Pisa, Italy

7.1   INTRODUCTION

Currently, users identify wireless networks with first- and second-generation cellular telephony networks. Although voice and short messaging have driven the success of these networks so far, data and more sophisticated applications are emerging as the future driving forces for the extensive deployment of new wireless technologies.

In this chapter, we will consider future wireless technologies that will provide support to different types of traffic including legacy voice applications, Internet data traffic, and sophisticated multimedia applications.

In the near future, wireless technologies will span from broadband wide-area technologies (such as satellite-based networks and cellular networks) to local and personal area networks. In this chapter, for each class of network, we will present the emerging wireless technologies for supporting service integration. Our overview will start by analyzing the Bluetooth technology [30] that is the de facto standard for wireless personal area networks (WPANs), i.e., networks that connect devices placed inside a circle with radius of 10 meters. Two main standards exist for wireless local area networks (WLANs): IEEE 802.11 [21] and HiperLAN [15]. In this chapter we focus on the IEEE 802.11 technology, as it is the technology currently available on the market. After a brief description of the IEEE 802.11 architecture, we will focus on the mechanisms that have been specifically designed to support delay-sensitive traffic.

For wireless wide area networks, we will focus on the technology for third-generation mobile radio networks. Two standards are emerging worldwide for this technology: the Universal Mobile Telecommunication System (UMTS) of the European Telecommunication Standard Institute (ETSI), and the International and Mobile Telecommunications-2000 (IMT-2000) of the International Telecommunication Union (ITU). The differences between these two standards are not relevant for the discussion in this chapter. Whenever necessary, we will use UMTS as the reference technology [1, 32].

All the network technologies analyzed in this chapter operate according to the infrastructure-based approach (see Figure 7.1). An infrastructure-based architecture imposes the existence of a centralized controller for each cell, which takes different names depend-

Handbook of Wireless Networks and Mobile Computing, Edited by Ivan Stojmenović.   **145**
ISBN 0-471-41902-8   © 2002 John Wiley & Sons, Inc.

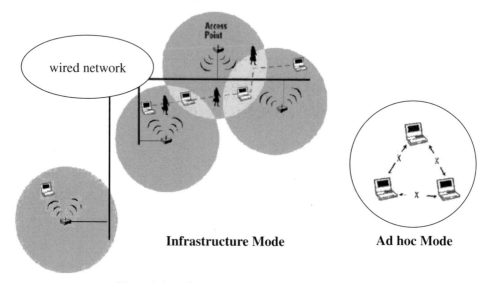

Infrastructure Mode　　　　　**Ad hoc Mode**

Figure 7.1　Infrastructure-based and ad hoc networks.

ing on the technology: master, access point, base station, etc. The cell identifies the area covered by the centralized controller, i.e., the area inside which a mobile terminal can directly communicate with the centralized controller. The cell size, as said before, depends on the technology, e.g., from 10 meters in Bluetooth up to kilometers in UMTS. Furthermore, inside UMTS, cells of different sizes can be used to accommodate different classes of users.

The centralized controller is connected to the wired network so as to have both intercell communication and access to other networks such as Internet.

WPANs and WLANs may also operate in the ad hoc mode [29]. An ad hoc network is a set of mobile terminals within the range of each other that dynamically configure themselves to set up a temporary network (see Figure 7.1). In this configuration, no fixed controller is required, but a controller is dynamically elected among all the stations participating in the communication.

Both in the infrastructure-based and ad hoc modes, the centralized controller is in charge to manage the radio resources of its cell. To achieve this, the following functionalities are implemented in all the network technologies we analyze: a medium access control mechanism, a scheduling algorithm, and a signaling channel for the communications from the centralized controller to the mobile terminals (downlink signaling channel).

The medium access control mechanism is required for managing the communications from the mobile terminals to the controller, and it is used by the mobile terminals for requesting transmission resources. In all technologies, this mechanism is used when a mobile terminal needs to start a communication and hence does not yet have any transmission resources allocated to it. In this case, the mobile terminal transmits on a channel that is shared among all the terminals in the cell. Protocols belonging to the random access class are typically used to implement the medium access control mechanisms [18]. Once the centralized controller receives the mobile terminal requests, it assigns the transmission resources according to the rules defined by its scheduling algorithm. Finally, the assigned resources are communicated to the terminals through the downlink signaling channel.

As the emphasis of this chapter is on the integration of different types of traffic, we will primarily focus on the medium access control mechanisms, the scheduling algorithms, and the downlink signaling channels adopted by these technologies.

7.2 A TECHNOLOGY FOR WPAN: BLUETOOTH

Bluetooth wireless technology is a de facto standard for low-cost, short-range, radio links between mobile PCs, mobile phones, and other portable devices. The Bluetooth specifications are released by the Bluetooth Special Interest Group (SIG), an industry group consisting of industrial leaders in the telecommunications, computing, and networking [11]. In addition, the IEEE 802.15 Working Group for Wireless Personal Area Networks has started a project to publish and approve a standard derived from the Bluetooth specification [20].

The Bluetooth system operates in the 2.4 GHz industrial, scientific, and medicine (ISM) band. It is based on a low-cost, short-range radio link integrated into a microchip, enabling protected ad hoc connections for wireless communication of voice and data in stationary and mobile environments. It enables use of mobile data in different ways for different applications. Due to its low-cost target, it can be envisaged that Bluetooth microchips will be embedded in all consumer electronic devices.

The characteristics of the Bluetooth technology offer wide room for innovative solutions and applications that could bring radical changes to everyday life. Let us imagine a PDA (with a Bluetooth microchip) that automatically synchronizes with all the electronic devices in its 10 meter range when you arrive at your home. Your PDA can, for example, automatically unlock the door, turn on the house lights while you are getting in, and adjust the heat or air conditioning to your preset preferences. But not only the home can become a more comfortable environment when the access to information is fast and easy. Let us imagine arriving at the airport and finding a long queue at the check-in desk for seat assignment. You can avoid the queue using a hand-held device to present an electronic ticket and automatically select your seat.

7.2.1 The Bluetooth Network

From a logical standpoint, Bluetooth belongs to the contention-free, token-based multiaccess networks [18]. In a Bluetooth network, one station has the role of master and all other Bluetooth stations are slaves. The master decides which slave is the one to have access to the channel. The units that share the same channel (i.e., are synchronized to the same master) form a piconet, the fundamental building block of a Bluetooth network. A piconet has a gross bit rate of 1 Mbps that represents the channel capacity before considering the overhead introduced by the adopted protocols and polling scheme. A piconet contains a master station and up to seven active (i.e., participating in data exchange) slaves simultaneously. Independent piconets that have overlapping coverage areas may form a scatternet.

A scatternet exists when a unit is active in more than one piconet at the same time (a unit can be master in only one piconet). A slave may communicate with the different piconets it belongs to only in a time-multiplexing mode. This means that, for any time instant, a station can only transmit on the single piconet to which its clock is synchronized at that time. To transmit on another piconet, it has to change the synchronization parameters. More details on construction procedures for piconets and scatternets can be found in Chapter 27 of this handbook.

7.2.2 The Bluetooth Architecture

The complete protocol stack contains a Bluetooth core of Bluetooth-specific protocols: Bluetooth radio, baseband, link manager protocol (LMP), logical link control and adaptation protocol (L2CAP), service discovery protocol (SDP) as shown in Figure 7.2. In addition, examples of higher-layer non-Bluetooth-specific protocols are also shown in the figure; these can be implemented on top of the Bluetooth technology.

Bluetooth radio provides the physical links among Bluetooth devices and the baseband layer provides a transport service of packets on the physical links. In the next subsections these layers will be presented in detail.

The LMP protocol is responsible for the set-up and management of physical links. The management of physical links consists of several activities: putting a slave in a particular operating state (i.e., sniff, hold, or park modes [30]), monitoring the status of the physical channel, and assuring a prefixed quality of service (e.g., LMP defines transmission power, maximum poll interval, etc.). LMP also implements security capabilities at link level.

The radio, baseband, and LMP may be implemented in the Bluetooth device. The device will be attached to a host, thus providing that host with Bluetooth wireless communi-

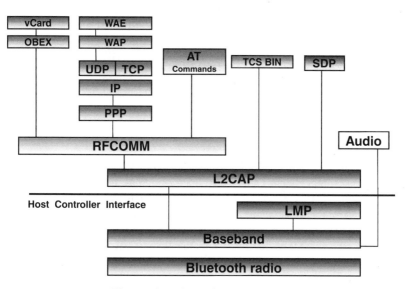

Figure 7.2 Bluetooth protocol stack.

cation. L2CAP layer and the other high-layer protocols are in the host. The host controller interface is a standard interface that enables high-layer protocols to access the services provided by the Bluetooth device.

The L2CAP services are used only for data transmissions. The main features supported by L2CAP are: protocol multiplexing (the L2CAP uses a protocol-type field to distinguish between upper-layer protocols) and segmentation and reassembly. The latter feature is required because the baseband packet size is smaller than the usual size of packets used by higher-layer protocols.

In legacy LANs, users locate services such as file server, print server, and name server by some static configuration. The configuration is usually established and maintained by a system administrator who manually configures the client devices. For dynamic ad hoc networks, this static configuration is not adequate. The SDP protocol is used to find the type of services that are available in the network.

Finally, RFCOMM is a serial line emulation protocol, i.e., a cable replacement protocol. It emulates RS-232 control and data signals over Bluetooth baseband, providing transport capabilities for upper-level services that use serial lines as their transport mechanism.

7.2.3 The Bluetooth Device

A Bluetooth unit consists of a radio unit operating in the 2.4 GHz band. In this band, 79 different radio frequency (RF) channels that are spaced 1 MHz apart are defined. The radio layer utilizes the frequency hopping spread spectrum (FHSS) as its transmission technique. The hopping sequence is a pseudorandom sequence of 79 hop length, and it is unique for each piconet. It is enabled by exploiting the actual value of the master clock and its unique Bluetooth device address, a 48 bit address compliant with the IEEE 802 standard addressing scheme [30]. The FHSS system has been chosen to reduce the interference of nearby systems operating in the same frequency range (for example, IEEE 802.11 WLAN) and make the link robust [12, 17]. The nominal rate of hopping between two consecutive RF is 1600 hop/sec.

A time division duplex (TDD) scheme of transmission is adopted. The channel is divided into time slots, each 625 μs in length, and each slot corresponds to a different RF hop frequency. The time slots are numbered according to the Bluetooth clock of the master. The master has to begin its transmissions in even-numbered time slots. Odd-numbered time slots are reserved for the beginning of the slaves' transmissions.

The transmission of a packet nominally covers a single slot, but it may last up to five consecutive time slots (see Figure 7.3). For multislot packets, the RF hop frequency to be used for the entire packet is the RF hop frequency assigned to the time slot in which the transmission has begun. The RF change reduces the interference from signals coming from other radio modules.

There are two types of physical links that can be established between Bluetooth devices: a synchronous connection-oriented (SCO) link, and an asynchronous connectionless (ACL) link. The first type of physical link is a point-to-point, symmetric connection between the master and a specific slave. It is used to deliver delay-sensitive traffic, mainly voice. In fact, the SCO link rate is 64 Kbit/s and it is settled by reserving a couple of consecutive slots for master-to-slave transmission and immediate slave-to-master response.

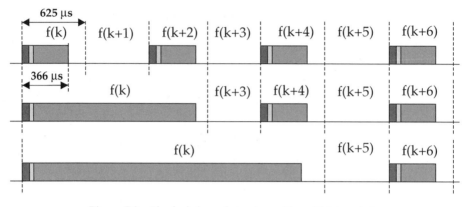

Figure 7.3 Physical channel structure with multislot packets.

The SCO link can be considered a circuit-switched connection between the master and the slave. The second kind of physical link, ACL, is a connection between the master and all slaves participating in the piconet. It can be considered a packet-switched connection between the Bluetooth devices and can support the reliable delivery of data: a fast automatic repeat request (ARQ) scheme is adopted to assure data integrity. An ACL channel supports point-to-multipoint transmissions from the master to the slaves.

As stated above, channel access is managed according to a polling scheme. The master decides which slave is the only one to have access to the channel by sending it a packet. The master packet may contain data or can simply be a polling packet. When the slave receives a packet from the master, it is authorized to transmit in the next time slot. For SCO links, the master periodically polls the corresponding slave. Polling is asynchronous for ACL links. Figure 7.4 presents a possible pattern of transmissions in a piconet with a master and two slaves. Slave 1 has both a SCO (packets filled with diagonal lines) and an ACL (packets filled with horizontal lines) link with the master, whereas Slave 2 has an ACL link only (packets filled with vertical lines). In this example, the SCO link is periodically polled by the master every six slots, whereas ACL links are polled asynchronously. Furthermore, the size of the packets on an ACL link is constrained by the presence of SCO links. For example, in Figure 7.4 the master sends a multislot packet to Slave 2, which, in turn, can reply with a single-slot packet only, because the successive slots are reserved for the SCO link.

As stated above, a piconet has a gross bit rate of 1 Mbps. The polling scheme and the protocols control information, obviously reducing the amount of user data that can be delivered by a piconet. We analyze the limiting performance of a piconet below. This analysis is performed by assuming a single master–slave link in which both stations operate under asymptotic conditions, i.e., the stations always have a packet ready for transmission. The results of this analysis are summarized in Tables 7.1 and 7.2 for SCO and ACL links, respectively. To enhance the reliable delivery of the packets, forward error correction (FEC) and cyclic redundancy check (CRC) algorithms may be used. The possible presence of FEC, CRC, and multislot transmission results in different payload lengths, as summarized in the tables.

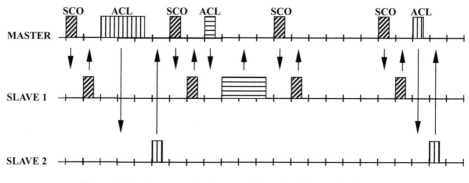

Figure 7.4   An example of transmissions in a Bluetooth piconet.

The SCO packets (see Table 7.1), denoted by HVy, are never retransmitted and the payload is not protected by a CRC. The y indicates the FEC level and it also identifies how many SCO connections may be concurrently active in a piconet. In addition to the three pure SCO packets, a DV packet is defined that can also carry asynchronous data but is still recognized on SCO links. In the Table 7.1, the items followed by "D" relate to the data field only. The ACL packets (see Table 7.2) are of two different groups, one denoted DMx (medium-speed data) and the other one denoted DHx (high-speed data). The former has a payload encoded with a 2/3 FEC and the latter has no FEC encoding. The subscript x

TABLE 7.1   SCO packets

Type	User payload (bytes)	FEC	CRC	Symmetric maximum rate (kbps)
HV1	10	1/3	no	64.0
HV2	20	2/3	no	64.0
HV3	30	no	no	64.0
DV	10 + (0–9)D	2/3 D	yes D	64.0 + 57.6 D

TABLE 7.2   ACL packets

Type	User payload (bytes)	FEC	CRC	Symmetric maximum rate (kbps)	Asymmetric maximum rate (kbps) Forward	Asymmetric maximum rate (kbps) Reverse
DM1	0–17	2/3	yes	108.8	108.8	108.8
DM3	0–121	2/3	yes	258.1	387.2	54.4
DM5	0–224	2/3	yes	286.7	477.8	36.3
DH1	0–27	no	yes	172.8	172.8	172.8
DH3	0–183	no	yes	390.4	585.6	86.4
DH5	0–339	no	yes	433.9	723.2	57.6

stands for the number of slots that are necessary to transmit the packet. All ACL packets have a CRC field for checking the payload integrity. Tables 7.1 and 7.2 summarize SCO and ACL packet characteristics, respectively. In addition, the tables report, assuming a piconet with two only devices, the maximum aggregate piconet throughput for symmetric and asymmetric communications. In the asymmetric case, the throughput corresponding to DM_x is computed by assuming that forward and the reverse traffic is transmitted using DM_x and DM1 packets, respectively.

7.2.4 Scheduling Algorithms for the ACL Traffic

In the previous section, we examined the limiting performance of a Bluetooth piconet in the simple two-station configuration. In this configuration, Bluetooth is simply used as a cable replacement. However, as explained before, this technology is designed to operate in a more general piconet setting where there are several active slaves. In this case, the master must implement a scheduling algorithm to decide the slaves' polling order. The Bluetooth specification indicates as a possible solution the round robin polling algorithm: slaves are polled in a cyclic order. Below, we evaluate Bluetooth performance via simulation, assuming a round robin scheduler. The simulated network topology is constituted by a single piconet with a master and six slaves.

We have modeled the intrapiconet communications, i.e., no traffic comes (goes) from (to) the outside of the piconet. Each slave is a source of IP packets and the interarrival times between consecutive packet generations are exponentially distributed, hence the IP packet arrival process is Poissonian. The packet length is uniformly distributed in the range from 500 to 1500 bytes. Each IP packet is encapsulated into an L2CAP packet that adds the 4 bytes L2CAP header and sent to the Bluetooth device local transmission queue. This local queue has a finite size B_S and the queued packets are served according to a first come first served (FCFS) policy. Large L2CAP packets must be segmented into smaller baseband packets before transmission. A new L2CAP packet cannot be served until all fragments (generated during the segmentation) of the previous L2CAP packet have been successfully transmitted. The segmentation procedure is accomplished, just before the transmission, in such a way as to generate the minimum number of baseband packets.

Within the master, N local transmission queues are implemented, where N is the number of active slaves. Each master local queue has a finite size B_M and the queued packets are served according to a FCFS policy. When an L2CAP packet is completely received by the master, the master accomplishes the reassembly procedure and forwards it on the transmission queue related to the slave, to which the packet is addressed.

In the transmission phase, the master behaves the same way as a slave. The master and the slaves transmit the ACL packets according to the Bluetooth transmission scheme described in the previous sections.

During the simulations we performed, we considered two traffic patterns: symmetric and asymmetric. In the former, all slaves contribute the same percentage to the offered load, while in the asymmetric case, Slave 1 produces the 90% of the overall load. In both traffic patterns, the destination address is sampled in a uniform way among the other slaves.

Simulative results presented in this section have been obtained by applying the independent replication technique with a 90% confidence level. Furthermore, we assumed an ideal

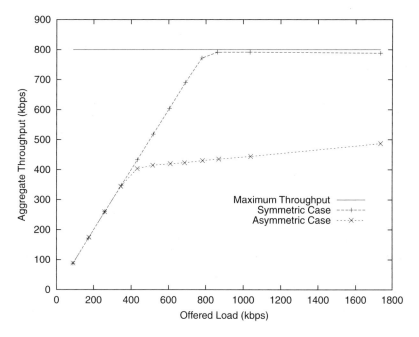

Figure 7.5   Throughput performance in a single piconet.

channel with no transmission errors [26]. Within each simulation, we have utilized the DH type for ACL packets, and the buffer sizes (B_S and B_M) are 15,000 bytes. The use of buffers with a finite size is necessary to perform steady-state simulations in overload conditions.

In Figure 7.5 we plot the aggregate throughput that is achievable in the symmetric and asymmetric cases. It is known that the round robin polling algorithm is the best policy to use when the system is symmetric and completely loaded, and the plotted curves confirm that. However, it is also clear that the round robin polling algorithm is very inefficient under asymmetric conditions because the master continuously polls slaves that have no traffic to send, and this behavior implies bandwidth wastage. In the asymmetric scenario, the Slave 1 local queue saturates, i.e., there are packet losses due to buffer overflow, when the offered load is equal to 400 kbps. By increasing the offered load beyond 400 kbps, the throughput performance increases very slowly.

These results point out the ineffectiveness of round robin scheduling in meeting the requirements of a WPAN highly dynamic scenario. The definition of an efficient scheduling algorithm for Bluetooth is an open research issue. This issue is discussed in [8, 9, 23].

7.3 TECHNOLOGIES FOR HIGH-SPEED WLANs

In the past few years, the use of wireless technologies in the LAN environment has become more and more important, and it is easy to foresee that wireless LANs (WLANs) will be the solution for home and office automation. WLANs offer high flexibility and ease of network installation with respect to wired LAN infrastructures. A WLAN should satisfy the same requirements typical of any LAN, including high capacity, full connectivity among attached stations, and broadcast capability. However, to meet these objectives, WLANs should be designed to face some issues specific to the wireless environment, like security, power consumption, mobility, and bandwidth limitation of the air interface.

Two main standards exist for WLAN: IEEE 802.11 and HiperLAN. HiperLAN (high-performance radio local area network) is a family of standards promoted by the European Telecommunication Standard Institute (ETSI) [15]. The most interesting standard for WLAN is HiperLAN/2. The HiperLAN/2 technology addresses high-speed wireless networks, i.e., those in which data rates range from 6 to 54 Mbit/s. Thus, the technology is suitable for interconnecting portable devices to each other and to broadband core networks such as IP, ATM, and UMTS. Infrastructure-based and ad hoc networking configurations are both supported in HiperLAN/2. HiperLAN/2 is designed to appropriately support data transport characterized by a quality of service (QoS). More details on this technology can be found in [27].

In this chapter, we focus on the IEEE 802.11 technology, as it is mature from an industrial standpoint: IEEE 802.11 cards and access points (both for PC and PDA) are produced by several manufacturers. On the other hand, to the best of our knowledge, HiperLAN is still at the prototype level.

IEEE 802.11 is the standard for wireless local area networks promoted by the Institute of Electrical and Electronics Engineers (IEEE).

The IEEE 802.11 technology operates in the 2.4 GHz industrial, scientific, and medicine (ISM) band and provides wireless connectivity for fixed, portable, and mobile stations within a local area. The IEEE 802.11 technology can be utilized to implement both wireless infrastructure networks and wireless ad hoc networks.

Mandatory support for asynchronous data transfer is specified as well as optional support for distributed time-bounded services, i.e., traffic that is bounded by specified time delays to achieve an acceptable quality of service (QoS).

7.3.1   IEEE 802.11 Architecture and Protocols

The IEEE 802.11 standard defines a MAC layer and a physical layer for WLANs (see Figure 7.6). The MAC layer provides to its users both contention-based and contention-free access control on a variety of physical layers. The standard provides two physical layer specifications for radio (frequency hopping spread spectrum, direct sequence spread spectrum), operating in the 2400–2483.5 MHz band (depending on local regulations), and one for infrared. The physical layer provides the basic rates of 1 Mbit/s and 2 Mbit/s. Two projects are currently ongoing to develop higher-speed PHY extensions to 802.11 operating in the 2.4 GHz band (Project 802.11b, handled by TGb) and in the 5 GHz band (Project 802.11a, handled by TGa); see [19].

The basic access method in the IEEE 802.11 MAC protocol is the distributed coordination function (DCF), which is a carrier sense multiple access with collision avoidance (CSMA/CA) MAC protocol. Besides the DCF, the IEEE 802.11 also incorporates an optional/additional access method known as the point coordination function (PCF). PCF is an access method similar to a polling system and uses a point coordinator to determine

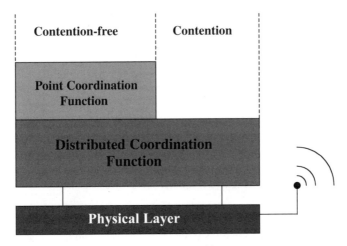

Figure 7.6 IEEE 802.11 architecture.

which station has the right to transmit. The basic access mechanism is designed to support best effort traffic, like Internet data, that does not require any service guarantees. In scenarios in which service guarantees are also required, the PCF access method must be used. Below, we first describe the DCF access method, and then we present the PCF extension.

IEEE 802.11 DCF

The DCF access method, hereafter referred to as "basic access," is summarized in Figure 7.7. When using the DCF, before a station initiates a transmission, it senses the channel to determine whether another station is transmitting. If the medium is found to be idle for an interval that exceeds the distributed interframe space (DIFS), the station continues with its transmission.* On the other hand (when the medium is busy), the transmission is deferred until the end of the ongoing transmission. A random interval, henceforth referred to as the "backoff interval," is then selected, which is used to initialize the "backoff timer." The backoff timer is decreased for as long as the channel is sensed to be idle, stopped when a transmission is detected on the channel, and reactivated when the channel is sensed to be idle again for more than a DIFS. The station transmits when the backoff timer reaches zero.

The DCF adopts a slotted binary exponential backoff technique. In particular, the time immediately following an idle DIFS is slotted, and a station is allowed to transmit only at the beginning of each slot time, which is equal to the time needed at any station to detect the transmission of a packet from any other station. The backoff time is uniformly chosen in the interval $(0, CW-1)$ defined as the "backoff window," also referred to as the "contention window." At the first transmission attempt, $CW = CW_{min}$, and it is doubled at each retransmission up to CW_{max}. In the standard [21] the CW_{min} and CW_{max} values depend on the physical layer adopted. For example, for frequency hopping, CW_{min} and CW_{max} are 16

---

*To guarantee fair access to the shared medium, a station that has just transmitted a packet and has another packet ready for transmission must perform the backoff procedure before initiating the second transmission.

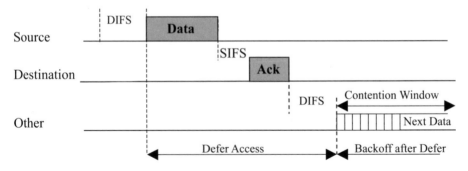

Figure 7.7 Basic access mechanism.

and 1024, respectively (note that CSMA/CA does not rely on the capability of the stations to detect a collision by hearing their own transmission). Immediate positive acknowledgements are employed to ascertain the successful reception of each packet transmission. This is accomplished by the receiver (immediately following the reception of the data frame), which initiates the transmission of an acknowledgment (ACK) frame after a time interval, the short interframe space (SIFS), which is less than the DIFS. If an acknowledgment is not received, the data frame is presumed to have been lost and a retransmission is scheduled. The ACK is not transmitted if the received packet is corrupted. A cyclic redundancy check (CRC) algorithm is adopted to discover transmission errors.

After an erroneous frame is detected (due to collisions or transmission errors), the channel must remain idle for at least an extended interframe space (EIFS) interval before the stations reactivate the backoff algorithm.

The MAC layer also defines virtual carrier sensing: the messages convey the amount of time the channel will be utilized to complete the successful transmission of the data. This information is used by each station to adjust a network allocation vector (NAV) containing the period of time the channel will remain busy.

The basic access mechanism can be extended by a medium reservation mechanism, also referred to as a floor acquisition mechanism, named "request to send/clear to send" (RTS/CTS). In this case, after gaining access to the medium and before starting the transmission of a data packet itself, a short control packet (RTS) is sent to the receiving station announcing the upcoming transmission. The receiver replies to this with a CTS packet to indicate readiness to receive the data. This mechanism can be used to capture the channel control before the transmission of long packets, thus avoiding "long collisions." In addition, the RTS/CTS mechanism solves the hidden station problem during the transmission of the user data [21]. Further considerations on the protection provided by the RTS/CTS mechanism against the hidden terminal problem can be found in Chapter 27 of this handbook.

7.3.2 IEEE 802.11 Performance

The physical layer technology determines some network parameter values, e.g., SIFS, DIFS, and backoff slot time. Results presented below are obtained by assuming the fre-

TABLE 7.3 WLAN configuration

SIFS	DIFS	Backoff slot time	Bit rate	Propagation delay	Stations	CW_{min}	CW_{max}
28 μsec	128 μsec	50 μsec	2 Mbps	1 μsec	10, 50, 100	32	256

quency hopping, spread spectrum technology at 2 Mbps transmission rate. Table 7.3 shows the configuration parameter values of the IEEE 802.11 WLAN analyzed below.

IEEE 802.11 Protocol Capacity

The IEEE 802.11 protocol capacity was extensively investigated in [13]. In the following, the main results of that analysis will be summarized. Specifically, in [13] the theoretical throughput limit for the IEEE 802.11 network is analytically derived (i.e., the maximum throughput that can be achieved by adopting the IEEE 802.11 MAC), and compared with the real protocol capacity. These results show that, depending on the network configuration, the standard protocol can operate very far from its theoretical limits. Specifically, as shown in Figure 7.8, the distance between the IEEE 802.11 and the analytical bound increases with the number of active networks, M.

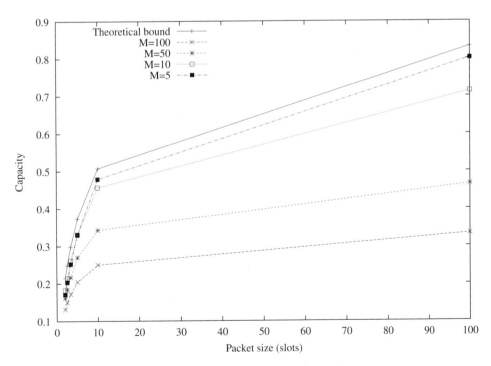

Figure 7.8 IEEE 802.11 protocol capacity.

Results presented in Figure 7.8 show that the performance of IEEE 802.11 is negatively affected by an increase in network congestion. This is a typical behavior of random access algorithms that can be partially solved by using stabilization algorithms. These algorithms tune the protocol parameters using feedback from the network. One of the most well-known algorithms of this class is named pseudo-Bayesian [28]. Extending the Rivest approach [28], stabilization algorithms for the IEEE 802.11 have been proposed in [12], [8], and [7]. These works propose different approaches to maintaining the IEEE 802.11 capacity level close to the theoretical bound for all network congestion levels.

The IEEE 802.11 capacity analysis presented above is performed by assuming that the network operates under asymptotic conditions (i.e., each LAN station always has a packet ready for transmission). LANs generally operate under normal conditions, i.e., the network stations generate an aggregate traffic that is lower (or slightly higher) than the maximum traffic the network can support. Under these load conditions, the most meaningful performance figure is the MAC delay, i.e., the time required for a station to successfully transmit the packet at the head of its transmission queue [14]. Results below are obtained by assuming that a station alternates between idle and busy states. State changes occur according to an on/off Markov chain. Specifically, after each successful transmission, a station remains in the on state (i.e., busy state) with probability 0.9. At the end of a transmission, a station in the off state (i.e., idle state) changes its state to on with probability x. By increasing the average sojourn time in the off state, we model a decrease in the network load.

Two sets of experiments were performed corresponding to a traffic generated by 50 stations, made up of short (2 slots) and long (100 slots) messages, respectively. Figure 7.9 (which plots the average MAC delay versus the channel utilization) highlights that, for light load conditions, the IEEE 802.11 exhibits very low MAC delays. However, as the offered load approaches the capacity of the protocol, the MAC delay sharply increases and becomes unbounded. This behavior is due to the CSMA/CA protocol. Under light-load conditions, the protocol introduces almost no overhead (a station can immediately transmit as soon as it has a packet ready for transmission). On the other hand, when the load increases, the collision probability increases as well, and most of the time a transmission results in a collision. Several transmission attempts are necessary before a station is able to transmit a packet, and delays tend to be unbounded.

For this reason, the IEEE 802.11 DCF mode is not suitable for the transmission of delay-sensitive data. Support for users that require quality of service guarantees is provided in IEEE 802.11 by the PCF operational mode. PCF is designed to coexist with the DCF. Best effort users still transmit data using the DCF mode, whereas QoS-sensitive users exploit the PCF mode.

Point Coordination Function

The point coordination function guarantees frame transmissions in a contention-free way. This functionality, as shown in Figure 7.6, must be implemented on top of the DCF, and can be used only in infrastructure networks. To determine which station can transmit, the PCF uses a point coordinator (PC) that it is usually implemented in the access point. Stations that use PCF (stations CF_Aware) are recorded in a list managed by the point coordi-

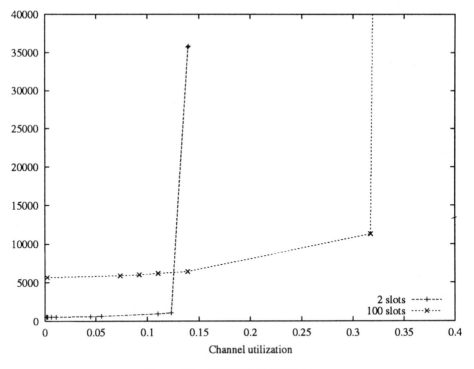

Figure 7.9 IEEE 802.11 MAC delay.

nator, which, through polling techniques, guarantees to these stations a contention-free access to the channel.

In an IEEE 802.11 WLAN, periods under the DCF functionality can be interleaved to periods in which the control is entrusted to the PCF modality. The frequency with which these periods alternate is specified by the CFP_Rate parameter, whose value is selected by the point coordinator. Every contention-free period begins with the transmission of a beacon frame (by the point coordinator), whose main target is the stations' synchronization. The beacon transmission has higher priority than data transmission. This is obtained by adopting for the beacon transmission an interframe space, named PIFS, that is shorter than the DIFS.

The point coordinator, with the beacon frame, transmits the estimated length of the contention-free period, CFP_Max_Duration, which is used by the stations in the cell to disable the DCF transmissions. This is achieved by setting the NAV to the CFP_Max_ Duration value. At the end of the contention-free period, the point coordinator sends a special message that clears the NAV in all stations; hence, it implies switching to the DCF modality.

During the contention-free period, the point coordinator sends polling messages to the CF_Aware stations, enabling contention-free transmission. Each polled station after a SIFS can access the medium and it may choose to transmit a frame to the PC or to another

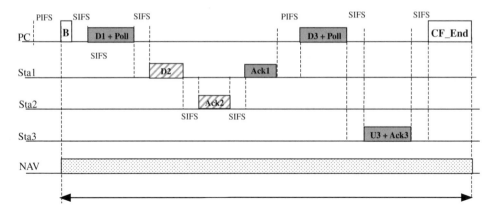

Figure 7.10 Data transmission and related acknowledgment between stations operating in the PCF mode.

station in the cell. If the polled station does not reply, the point coordinator, after a PIFS, issues a poll to the next station to be polled according to its scheduling algorithm. The scheduler in the point coordinator is not defined in the standard and is an open research issue.

As in DCF, all data transmissions are acknowledged by the receiving station. For example, as shown in Figure 7.10, Station 1, after receiving the poll from the point coordinator, waits a SIFS and accesses the medium to transmit data to Station 2. Station 2, after receiving the frame, will send, as in DCF mode, the ACK to Station 1. At the end of this station-to-station transmission, Station 1 has to send back to the PC the ACK of the last data message received from the PC. In Figure 7.10, the case of a direct communication between the PC and Station 3 is shown.

To prevent that the point coordinator lockout all DCF traffic (by repeatedly issuing polls), IEEE 802.11 defines a superframe structure. During the first part of this interval, the point coordinator may issue polls, then it idles for the remaining part of the superframe, allowing DCF-based transmissions.

7.4 THIRD-GENERATION CELLULAR SYSTEMS: UMTS

The growing demand for cellular networks providing both high-rate data services and better spectrum efficiency is the main driver for the deployment of third-generation mobile radio networks, often called "3G." Considerable efforts toward 3G network standardization have been carried out simultaneously in Europe and the United States. Two main standards have been developed. In Europe, the ETSI is developing the UMTS standard for 3G systems and the ITU is developing the IMT-2000 standard for 3G systems, with small differences in the specification of radio interface.

The main objectives for the IMT-2000/UMTS systems are [32]:

- Full coverage and mobility for rates up to 144 Kb/s. Up to 2 Mb/s rates for low mobility and limited coverage.
- Use of different sized cells (macro, micro, and pico) for indoor and outdoor applications, with seamless handover between them.
- high spectrum efficiency compared to existing systems.

To achieve these targets, extensive investigations have identified the code division multiple access (CDMA) as the multiple access scheme for the 3G air interface.

CDMA assigns to each user a unique code sequence that is used to code data before transmission. If a receiver knows the code sequence related to a user, it is able to decode the received data. Several users can simultaneously transmit on the same frequency channel by adopting different code sequences. A low cross-correlation among these codes is the main requirement for enabling a receiver to successfully decode the user-generated data. Codes with zero cross-correlation are referred to as orthogonal codes. In particular, the most promising CDMA technique for third-generation systems is the direct sequence (DS)-CDMA, in which the original digital data to be transmitted at time t on a sender–receiver connection, say $b(t)$, is multiplied by a wide-band digital code $c(t)$, which represents the code sequence to be used for that particular connection at time t (see Figure 7.11).

The number of code bits used to represent a single information bit, i.e., the ratio between the chip rate [the bit rate of $c(t)$] and the bit rate of $b(t)$, is known as spreading factor (SF).

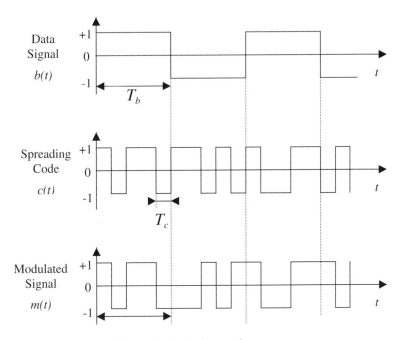

Figure 7.11 Basic spread spectrum.

The different standardization groups have proposed two multiple access schemes based on the DS-CDMA principle for the air interface: the wideband CDMA (W-CDMA) and the time-division CDMA (TD-CDMA). The W-CDMA adopts a DS-CDMA in which all users transmit in the same frequency channel. In W-CDMA systems, the SF can be very large (up to 512), and this is the reason why this technique is called wideband. The TD-CDMA is based on a hybrid access scheme in which each frequency channel is structured in frame and time slots. Within each time slots more channels can be allocated and separated from each other by means of the DS-CDMA. The number of codes in a time slot is not fixed but depends on the rate and SF of each physical channel.

The multiplexing of the downlink and uplink traffic is implemented with different mechanisms in the W-CDMA and in TD-CDMA. The W-CDMA implements a frequency division duplexing (FDD) mode, in which the uplink and downlink traffic are separated in frequency by using different bands. In this case, a physical channel is identified by a code and one frequency. The TD-CDMA implements a time division duplexing (TDD) mode, in which the uplink and downlink traffic are separated by different time slots assigned to them within the frame.

Figure 7.12 shows the frequencies allocated in Europe for UMTS. The figure clearly indicates that there are two paired 60 MHz bands reserved for W-CDMA. A 35 MHz band, subdivided in two unpaired bands, is reserved for TD-CMDA. Finally, the figure also shows bands reserved for satellite services (SAT).

In the rest of this chapter, we focus on the TD-CDMA technique defined by the UMTS standard. This technique is the most suitable and flexible mechanism for the integration of Internet services in future 3G systems. In fact, the frame structure is tailored to the asymmetry of uplink and downlink Internet traffic, with respect to the FDD, in which the same bandwidth is assigned to the downlink and uplink directions.

7.4.1 UMTS Terrestrial Radio Access Network

Three main segments constitute the UMTS system: the core network (CN), the UMTS terrestrial radio access network (UTRAN), and the user equipment (UE), as shown in Figure 7.13.

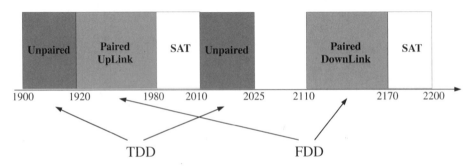

Figure 7.12   UMTS frequencies.

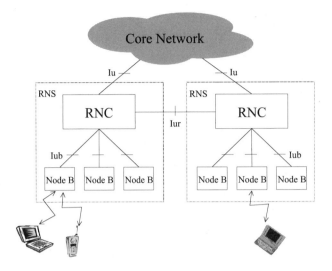

Figure 7.13 UMTS general architecture.

The CN is the fixed infrastructure, also called backbone, and it is responsible for the set-up and the control of communication, and the overall management of the users, from mobility to billing. Moreover, the CN is designed to be radio-technology-independent, in the sense that it remains unchanged, whatever the radio access technique.

The UTRAN accomplishes all the radio-dependent functions characterizing the UMTS system, and it represents the radio interface between the mobile user and the network. In particular, UTRAN is constituted by a set of radio network controllers (RNCs) that are connected to the CN. Each RNC is the controller for a group of adjacent base stations (named Node B in the UMTS terminology), e.g., it accomplishes the procedures for handover decisions and macrodiversity management. The macrodiversity mechanism permits a mobile user to have the same connection active through more than one base station with different codes. This functionality enables soft handover, in which the connection continuity is guaranteed through the path multiplicity between the mobile terminal and the "bridging point" in the network. Another particular functionality of the UMTS system is the interfrequency handover. As stated in Section 7.1, the UMTS system is organized in a hierarchical cell structure, with picocells for indoor environments, microcells for urban environments, and macrocells for rural environments. This structure can guarantee maximum area coverage with different mobile user densities. Each layer of this hierarchy has a different frequency assigned to avoid interlayer interference. Hence, the UMTS system has to locate the user in the appropriate cell, according to its mobility pattern, and eventually manage the change of level hierarchy when the user's mobility pattern varies.

The base station is responsible for the management of radio resources within a single cell, and it generates the radio signal delivered to each user located in its coverage area.

In the following subsection, we concentrate on the logical structure of radio interface between mobile users and base stations with the aim of introducing the mechanisms and the services that the MAC layer provides to realize the radio resource allocation.

The Radio Interface

The radio interface specifies how both user data and signaling information has to be exchanged between the mobile user and the network [1]. Depending on the user–data transfer requirements, three different operational modes have been defined:

1. Transparent data transfer—provides only segmentation and reassembly procedures
2. Unacknowledged data transfer—provides error and duplicate detection, but no attempts at recovering corrupted messages
3. Acknowledged data transfer—provides a guaranteed delivery of messages from/to upper layers

Below, we will focus on the radio interface adopted in the TD-CDMA system. This interface is named UMTS terrestrial radio access—time division duplex (UTRA-TDD). To support data connections with different bit rates, the TD-CDMA system utilizes coding sequences with variable spreading factor (SF). Since the chip rate is fixed at 3.84 Mchip/s, the lower the SF value, the higher the data rate. In TD-CDMA, the spreading factor may take values 1, 2, 4, 8, and 16. To limit the interference between users transmitting in the same time slot, we need to assign them orthogonal codes, i.e., with zero cross-correlation. This is obtained in UMTS by adopting orthogonal variable spreading factor (OVSF) codes [3, 4]. By using codes with SF = 16, we can have, in principle, up to 16 simultaneous transmissions in the same time slot. Each transmission can deliver a unit quota of traffic, referred to as a resource unit (RU). In general, with SF = x we can have (in the same time slot) only x simultaneous transmissions, which can deliver data corresponding to up to 16/x RUs. To simplify the presentation, hereafter we will always assume SF = 16. Whenever, we wish to assign to a connection a SF less than 16, say x, from a logical standpoint, it is equivalent to assigning to that connection x orthogonal codes with SF = 16.

In the TD-CDMA access mode, the channel is structured in frames of 10 msec length, and each frame contains 15 time slots. Therefore, the radio channel can be modeled by the time-code matrix shown in Figure 7.14. In this matrix, the (i, j) element corresponds to the RU associated to the i-th code (with SF = 16) in the j-th time slot of the frame.

The RUs of the matrix are used to transmit signaling traffic and users' data both in the uplink and downlink directions. UTRA-TDD has several signaling channels [2, 5], but for the purpose of the following discussion we only introduce the following:

- Synchronization Channel (SCH): downlink channel that delivers all the necessary information to guarantee the synchronism between mobile users and the base station. This synchronism is fundamental to correctly interpreting the frame structure and to identifying the location of the broadcast channel within the frame.
- Broadcast Channel (BCH): downlink channel that delivers specific information related to the cell, such as the frame structure and random access channel location within the frame.

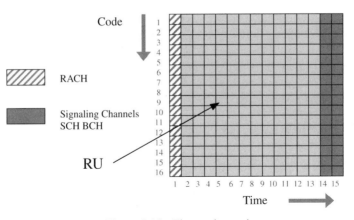

Figure 7.14   Time code matrix.

- Random Access Channel (RACH): uplink channel that delivers the users' requests for a new connection. This channel is shared among all the users located in the cell; hence, an appropriate contention control mechanism is needed.
- Forward Access Channel (FACH): downlink channel that delivers control information to a mobile user. The control information is mainly related to the RUs assigned (by the scheduler in the base station) to that user for data transmission.

As it is clear from the channel description, only the SCH channel must have a fixed position inside the frame. For the purposes of our discussion on TD-CDMA, we will assume that signaling channels will have a fixed position inside the matrix corresponding to the first and last two slots of each frame (see Figure 7.14). The assignment of the remaining RUs to transmit the user traffic is managed by the scheduling algorithm that is implemented in the base station.

In the following, we will consider two traffic classes: voice and Internet data. The former requires a connection-oriented service with low delay (20 msec) and low bit error rate (BER) requirements (10E-3). Internet data is well delivered by a connectionless service with no stringent delay requirements.

Each time a new voice connection must be activated, the voice terminal issues a request to the base station using the shared RACH channel. Once the request is received by the base station and the UMTS network has accepted the new connection, the resources allocated to the new connection on the UTRA-TDD access channel remain reserved until the connection is closed. On the other hand, the Internet traffic is highly bursty and to manage the channel in an efficient way, resources must be assigned to an Internet user only when it has data to transmit. Several allocation policies can be adopted for Internet traffic. In the following, we follow the approach proposed in [6]. According to this approach, RUs are allocated to the Internet traffic on a frame-by-frame basis. In each frame, RUs not reserved for voice traffic are fairly assigned to active data users (users with data waiting to be transmitted), i.e., each active user receives the same number of RUs. Therefore, Internet users access the RACH to request RU allocation only at the beginning of each busy period of their transmission buffer [25]. When this request is received, the base station will assign RUs to this user in all subsequent frames unless it receives an empty buffer indication.

According to our assumptions, the first time slot in each matrix is reserved for the RACH and the users transmit on this channel randomly, choosing one of the 16 possible orthogonal (SF = 16) codes. Hence, collisions may occur. An Aloha-like algorithm is used to manage this shared channel [6].

Scheduling Algorithm for UTRA-TDD

Once the RU allocation requests have been received by the base station, the scheduling algorithm assigns the available resources among the requesting users. The first big problem that a scheduler has to cope with (in a TD-CDMA environment) is soft degradation. Soft degradation makes the number of RUs that can be assigned in a time slot lower than the number of available codes, i.e., 16 with our assumption of SF = 16. This is a characteristic of CDMA systems. In these systems, there is no hard limitation of resources but a soft degradation of transmission quality. A new connection can always be set up if there is an available code because there is no a priori fixed capacity limit. The only bound is provided by the quality criteria adopted by the system, which assesses the maximum interference level acceptable. That is, the simultaneous transmission of different signals over the same bandwidth can take place as long as the interference level does not exceed a given threshold. It is worth noting that in a real environment, it is possible to observe interference between users at the receiving side, even if orthogonal codes are assigned to the users.

Therefore, an UTRA-TDD scheduling algorithm must be both traffic- and interference-adaptable. The latter requirement is tightly connected with soft degradation. The target of the scheduling algorithm is to be fair and efficient. "Fair" means equal sharing of the transmission resources among users of the same class. "Efficient" means that it must optimize some performance figure. For example, for Internet traffic we have chosen to maximize the throughput per frame, i.e., the amount of data successfully transmitted on the radio channel in a frame period.

The most challenging part of the scheduling algorithm is that related to Internet data traffic. For this reason, in the following we assume that we have only Internet data traffic to transmit on the radio channel. In the general case in which voice traffic (and other high-priority traffic) is present, the RUs assigned to the Internet data are those not reserved for the high-priority traffic.

The scheduling algorithm proposed and analyzed in [6] is based on the three steps shown in Figure 7.15. In the first step of the algorithm, the time slots available for Internet data are partitioned in two subsets, UL and DL, for transmission in the uplink and downlink directions, respectively. This partition is created according to a fairness criterion by taking into consideration the number of active users (or, equivalently, nonempty transmission buffers) in the uplink and downlink directions.

Once this partition is generated, for both the uplink and downlink directions, the second step of the algorithm computes (independently for each direction) the number of RUs per time slot (see the second step of Figure 7.15) that can be used for data transmission, taking into consideration the soft degradation phenomenon.

For ease of presentation, let us assume that we know the characteristics of the system interference when k ($k \leq$ SF, assuming SF = 16) codes are used. Specifically, let us indi-

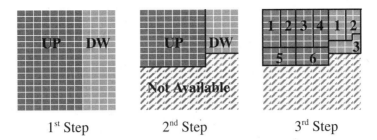

Figure 7.15 Scheduling algorithm steps.

cate with $Pe(k)$ the probability that a RU is discarded at the receiver due to transmission errors when k codes are used in the same slot.

From the $Pe(k)$ knowledge, the algorithm selects the optimal value of k, say k^*, that maximizes the throughput (see the second step of Figure 7.15) according to the following formula:

$$T(k^*) = \max\{T(i), i = 1, 2, 4, 8, 16\}$$

where $T(i) = E$(RUs correctly delivered when i codes are used) $= [1 - Pe(i)] \times i$.

Finally, the third step of the scheduling algorithm assigns the same number of RUs to all active users.

Note that hereafter we do not discuss the cases in which the number of RUs per user is not an integer number. The algorithm can be easily extended to manage these cases.

Unfortunately, the assumption that we know a priori the characteristics of the system interference is very far from the real cases. In a CDMA system, the overall system interference depends on a multiplicity of factors:

- The users' mobility pattern, since the system shows a different behavior depending on the user speed
- The coverage area of each base station
- The intercell interference due to a reuse factor equal to one. It means that each base station utilizes all the radio resources of the network, and it could happen that two adjacent base stations have users that either transmit with the same code, or receive on the same code. To minimize this kind of interference, each station uses a different scrambling sequence to make the signals coming from different cells orthogonal [6]
- The intracell interference due to the simultaneous use over the same radio channel of a variable number of codes, depending on the rate and SF of each physical channel.

Therefore, it is not possible to analytically characterize the system interference; at best we can try to estimate the $Pe(k)$ function by observing the number of RUs correctly received. The estimation of the $Pe(k)$ function is extensively studied and evaluated in [6].

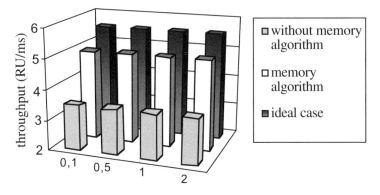

mean channel persistence time (sec)

Figure 7.16   Throughput performance in the linear interference scenario.

Two main classes of estimation algorithms have been proposed: worst-case and moving-average estimators. The former are very simple, as they use the $Pe(k)$ value related to the last frame. The latter are real estimators, as all the system history contributes to the current $Pe(k)$ estimates.

For example, Figure 7.16 shows the system throughput by assuming that the system interference characteristics generate linear $Pe(k)$ values, i.e., $Pe(0) = 0$, $Pe(16) = 1$, and that the function increases linearly among these two extremes. In the figure, we also show the ideal case results that have been analytically derived by using the $Pe(k)$ formula. As shown in the figure, it is possible to design $Pe(k)$ estimators that drive the system close to its ideal behavior, and that also work well with a channel that shows a rapid change of the interference levels.

ACKNOWLEDGMENTS

The authors wish to thank Graziano Bini for his valuable comments on the manuscript.

REFERENCES

1. 3G TS 25.301, Radio Interface Protocol Architecture, 3rd Generation Partnership Project, Technical Specification Group Radio Access Network, version 3.4.0 (2000-03).

2. 3G TS 25.221, Physical Channels and Mapping of Transport Channels onto Physical Channels (TDD), 3rd Generation Partnership Project, Technical Specification Group Radio Access Network, version 3.1.1 (1999-12).

3. 3G TS 25.222 Multiplexing and Channel Coding (TDD), 3rd Generation Partnership Project, Technical Specification Group Radio Acces Network, version 3.1.1 (1999-12).

4. 3G TS 25.223, Spreading and Modulation (TDD), 3rd Generation Partnership Project, Technical Specification Group Radio Access Network, version 3.1.1 (1999-12).

5. 3G TS 25.321 MAC Protocol Specification, 3rd Generation Partnership Project, Technical Specification Group Radio Access Network, Working Group 2, version 2.0.0 (1999-04).

6. G. Bini, M. Conti, and E. Gregori, Scheduling of internet traffic on UTRA-TDD, CNUCE Technical Report, CNUCE-B4-2000-027, 2000.

7. L. Bononi, M. Conti, and E. Gregori, Design and performance evaluation of an asymptotically optimal backoff algorithm for IEEE 802.11 Wireless LANs, *Proceedings HICSS-33,* Maui, Hawaii, January 4–7, 2000.

8. R. Bruno, M. Conti, and E. Gregori, A simple protocol for the dynamic tuning of the backoff mechanism in IEEE 802 networks, *Proceedings European Wireless 2000,* Dresden, Germany, September, 2000.

9. R. Bruno, M. Conti, and E. Gregori, WLAN Technologies for mobile ad hoc networks, *Proceedings HICSS-34,* Maui, Hawaii, January 3–6, 2001.

10. R. Bruno, M. Conti, and E. Gregori, Bluetooth: Architecture, protocols and scheduling algorithms, *Cluster Computing* (to appear).

11. Website of the Bluetooth Special Interest Group: http://www.bluetooth.com/.

12. F. Calì, M. Conti, and E. Gregori, Dynamic IEEE 802.11: Design, modeling and performance evaluation, *IEEE Journal on Selected Areas in Communications, 18*(9), 1774–1786, September 2000.

13. F. Calì, M. Conti, and E. Gregori, Dynamic tuning of the IEEE 802.11 Protocol to achieve a theoretical throughput limit, *IEEE/ACM Transactions on Networking, 8,* 6, 785–799, (December 2000).

14. M. Conti, E. Gregori, and L. Lenzini, *Metropolitan Area Networks,* New York: Springer Verlag, 1997.

15. ETSI Technical Report 101 683, V1.1.1, Broadband radio access networks (BRAN): High performance local area network (HiperLAN) Type 2; System Overview.

16. S. Galli, K. D. Wong, B. J. Koshy, and M. Barton, Bluetooth technology: Link performance and networking issues, *Proceedings European Wireless 2000,* Dresden, Germany, September 2000.

17. J. C. Haartsen and S. Zurbes, Bluetooth voice and data performance in 802.11 DS WLAN environment, Technical Report, Ericsson, May 1999.

18. J. L. Hammond and P. J. P. O'Reilly, *Performance Analysis of Local Computer Networks,* Reading, MA: Addison-Wesley, 1988.

19. Website of the IEEE 802.11 WLAN: http://grouper.ieee.org/grups/802/11/main.html.

20. Website of the IEEE 802.15 WPA.N Task Group 1: http://www.ieee802.org/15/pub/TG1.html.

21. IEEE Standard for Wireless LAN— Medium Access Control and Physical Layer Specification, P802.11, November 1997.

22. N. Johansson, U. Korner, and P. Johansson, Wireless ad-hoc networking with Bluetooth, *Proceedings of Personal Wireless Communications,* Copenhagen, March 1999.

23. N. Johansson, U. Korner, and P. Johansson, Performance evaluation of scheduling algorithm for Bluetooth, *Proceedings IFIP Broadband Communications,* Hong Kong, November 1999.

24. N. Johansson, M. Kihl, and U. Korner, TCP/IP over Bluetooth wireless ad-hoc network, *Proceedings IFIP Networking 2000,* Paris 1999, pp. 799–810.

25. L. Kleinrock, *Queueing Systems,* Vol. 1, New York: Wiley, 1975.

26. A. M. Law and W. D. Kelton, *Simulation Modeling and Analysis,* New York: McGraw Hill International Editions, 1991.

27. E. Mingozzi, QoS Support By The HiperLAN/2 MAC protocol: A performance evaluation, *Cluster Computing* (to appear).

28. R. L. Rivest, Network control by Bayesian broadcast, *IEEE Trans on Information Theory, 33,* 323–328, 1987,.

29. M. Scott Corson, J. P. Macker, and G. H. Cirincione, Internet-based mobile ad hoc networking, *IEEE Internet Computing,* 63–70, July-August 1999.

30. Specification of the Bluetooth System, Version 1.0B, December 1999.

31. W. Stallings, *Local and Metropolitan Area Networks,* Upper Saddle River, NJ: Prentice Hall, 1996.

32. B. H. Walke, *Mobile Radio Networks Networking and Protocols,* New York: Wiley, 2000.

33. J. Weinmiller, M. Schläger, A. Festag, and A. Wolisz, Performance study of access control in wireless LANs-IEEE 802.11 DFWMAC and ETSI RES 10 HIPERLAN, *Mobile Networks and Applications, 2,* 55–67, 1997.

CHAPTER 8

Fair Scheduling in Wireless Packet Data Networks

THYAGARAJAN NANDAGOPAL and XIA GAO

Coordinated Science Laboratory, University of Illinois at Urbana-Champaign

8.1 INTRODUCTION

Recent years have witnessed a tremendous growth in the wireless networking industry. The growing use of wireless networks has brought the issue of providing fair wireless channel arbitration among contending flows to the forefront. Fairness among users implies that the allocated channel bandwidth is in proportion to the "weights" of the users. The wireless channel is a critical and scarce resource that can fluctuate widely over a period time. Hence, it is imperative to provide fair channel access among multiple contending hosts. In wireline networks, fluid fair queueing has long been a popular paradigm for achieving instantaneous fairness and bounded delays in channel access. However, adapting wireline fair queueing algorithms to the wireless domain is nontrivial because of the unique problems in wireless channels such as location-dependent and bursty errors, channel contention, and joint scheduling for uplink and downlink in a wireless cell. Consequently, the fair queueing algorithms proposed in literature for wireline networks do not apply directly to wireless networks.

In the past few years, several wireless fair queueing algorithms have been developed [2, 3, 6, 7, 10, 11, 16, 19, 20, 22] for adapting fair queueing to the wireless domain. In fluid fair queueing, during each infinitesimally small time window, the channel bandwidth is distributed fairly among all the backlogged flows, where a flow is defined to be a logical stream of packets between applications. A flow is said to be backlogged if it has data to transmit at a given time instant. In the wireless domain, a packet flow may experience location-dependent channel error and hence may not be able to transmit or receive data during a given time window. The goal of wireless fair queueing algorithms is to make short bursts of location-dependent channel error transparent to users by a dynamic reassignment of channel allocation over small time scales. Specifically, a backlogged flow f that perceives channel error during a time window $[t_1, t_2]$ is compensated over a later time window $[t_1', t_2']$ when f perceives a clean channel. Compensation for f involves granting additional channel access to f during $[t_1', t_2']$ in order to make up for the lost channel access during $[t_1, t_2]$, and this additional channel access is granted to f at the expense of flows that were granted additional channel access during $[t_1, t_2]$ while f was unable to transmit any data.

Handbook of Wireless Networks and Mobile Computing, Edited by Ivan Stojmenović.
ISBN 0-471-41902-8   © 2002 John Wiley & Sons, Inc.

Essentially, the idea is to swap channel access between a backlogged flow that perceives channel error and backlogged flows that do not, with the intention of reclaiming the channel access for the former when it perceives a clean channel. The different proposals differ in terms of how the swapping takes place, between which flows the swapping takes place, and how the compensation model is structured.

Although fair queueing is certainly not the only paradigm for achieving fair and bounded delay access in shared channels, this chapter focuses exclusively on the models, policies, and algorithms for wireless fair queueing. In particular, we explore the mechanisms of the various algorithms in detail using a wireless fair queueing architecture [15]. In Section 8.2, we describe the network and wireless channel model, and give a brief introduction to fluid fair queueing. We also present a model for fairness in wireless data networks, and outline the major issues in channel-dependent fair scheduling. In Section 8.3, we discuss the wireless fair queueing architecture and describe the different policies and mechanisms for swapping, compensation, and achieving short-term and long-term fairness. In Section 8.4, we provide an overview of several contemporary algorithms for wireless fair queueing. Section 8.5 concludes this chapter with a look at future directions.

8.2 MODELS AND ISSUES

In this section, we first describe the network and channel model, and provide a brief overview of wireline fluid fair queueing. We then define a service model for wireless fair queueing, and outline the key issues that need to be addressed in order to adapt fluid fair queueing to the wireless domain.

8.2.1 Network and Channel Model

The technical discussions presented in this chapter are specific to a packet cellular network consisting of a wired backbone and partially overlapping wireless cells. Other wireless topologies are briefly discussed in Section 8.5. Each cell is served by a base station that performs the scheduling of packet transmissions for the cell (see Figure 8.1). Neighboring cells are assumed to transmit on different logical channels. All transmissions are either uplink (from a mobile host to a base station) or downlink (from a base station to a mobile host). Each cell has a single logical channel that is shared by all mobile hosts in the cell. (This discussion also applies to multi-channel cellular networks, under certain restrictions.) Every mobile host in a cell can communicate with the base station, though it is not required for any two mobile hosts to be within range of each other. Each flow of packets is identified by a <host, uplink/downlink flag, flow id> triple, in addition to other packet identifiers.

The distinguishing characteristics of the model under consideration are:

- Channel capacity is dynamically varying
- Channel errors are location-dependent and bursty in nature [5]
- There is contention for the channel among multiple mobile hosts

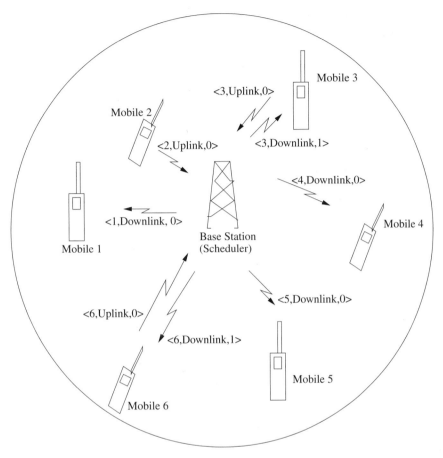

Figure 8.1 Cellular architecture.

- Mobile hosts do not have global channel status (in terms of which other hosts are contending for the same channel, etc.)
- The scheduling must take care of both uplink and downlink flows
- Mobile hosts are often constrained in terms of processing power and battery power

Thus, any wireless scheduling and channel access algorithm must consider the constraints imposed by this environment.

In terms of the wireless channel model, we consider a single channel for both uplink and downlink flows, and for both data and signaling. Even though all the mobiles and the base station share the same channel, stations may perceive different levels of channel error patterns due to location-dependent physical layer impairments (e.g., cochannel interference, hidden terminals, path loss, fast fading, and shadowing). User mobility also results in different error characteristics for different users. In addition, it has been shown in [5] that errors in wireless channels occur in bursts of varying lengths. Thus, channel errors are location-dependent and bursty. This means that different flows perceive different channel capacities. Note that channel errors result in both data loss and reduce channel capacity. Although data loss can be addressed using a range of techniques, such as forward error correction (FEC), the important issue is to address capacity loss, which is the focus of all wireless fair queueing algorithms.

A flow is said to perceive a clean channel if both the communicating endpoints perceive clean channels and the handshake can take place. A flow is said to perceive a dirty channel if either endpoint perceives a channel error. We assume a mechanism for the (possibly imperfect) prediction of channel state. This is reasonable, since typically channel errors, being bursty, are highly correlated between successive slots. Hence, every host can listen to the base station, and the base station participates in every data transmission by sending either data or an acknowledgement. Thus, every host that perceives a clean channel must be able to overhear some packet from the base station during each transmission.

We assume that time is divided into slots, where a slot is the time for one complete packet transmission including control information. For simplicity of discussion, we consider packets to be of fixed size. However, all wireless fair queueing algorithms can handle variable size packets as well. Following the popular CSMA/CA paradigm [9], we assume that each packet transmission involves a RTS-CTS handshake between the mobile host and the base station that precedes the data transmission. Successful receipt of a data packet is followed by an acknowledgement. At most one packet transmission can be in progress at any time in a cell.

Note that although we use the CSMA/CA paradigm as a specific instance of a wireless medium access protocol, this is not a requirement in terms of the applicability of the wireless fair queueing algorithms described in this chapter. The design of the medium access protocol is tied very closely to that of the scheduler; however, the issues that need to be addressed in the medium access protocol do not limit the generality of the issues that need to be addressed in wireless fair queueing [10, 11]. The design of a medium access protocol is a subject requiring detailed study and, in this chapter, we will merely restrict our attention to the impact a scheduling algorithm has on the medium access protocol.

8.2.2 Fluid Fair Queueing

We now provide a brief overview of fluid fair queueing in wireline networks. Consider a unidirectional link that is being shared by a set F of data flows. Consider also that each flow $f \in F$ has a rate weight r_f. At each time instant t, the rate allocated to a backlogged flow f is $r_f C(t)/\Sigma_{i \in B(t)} r_i$, where $B(t)$ is the set of nonempty queues and $C(t)$ is the link capacity at time t. Therefore, fluid fair queueing serves backlogged flows in proportion to their rate weights. Specifically, for any time interval $[t_1, t_2]$ during which there is no change in the set of backlogged flows $B(t_1, t_2)$, the channel capacity granted to each flow i, $W_i(t_1, t_2)$, satisfies the following property:

$$\forall i, j \in B(t_1, t_2), \left| \frac{W_i(t_1, t_2)}{r_i} - \frac{W_j(t_1, t_2)}{r_j} \right| = 0. \tag{8.1}$$

The above definition of fair queueing is applicable to both channels with constant capacity and channels with time varying capacity.

Since packet switched networks allocate channel access at the granularity of packets rather than bits, packetized fair queueing algorithms must approximate the fluid model. The goal of a packetized fair queueing algorithm is to minimize $|W_i(t_1, t_2)/r_i - W_j(t_1, t_2)/r_j|$ for any two backlogged flows i and j over an arbitrary time window $[t_1, t_2]$. For example, weighted fair queueing (WFQ) [4] and packet generalized processor sharing (PGPS) [18] are nonpreemptive packet fair queueing algorithms that simulate fluid fair queueing and transmit the packet whose last bit would be transmitted earliest according to the fluid fair queueing model.

In WFQ, each packet is associated with a start tag and finish tag, which correspond respectively to the "virtual time" at which the first bit of the packet and the last bit of the packet are served in fluid fair queueing. The scheduler then serves the packet with the minimum finish tag in the system. The kth packet of flow i that arrives at time $A(p_i^k)$ is allocated a start tag, $S(p_i^k)$, and a finish tag, $F(p_i^k)$, as follows:

$$S(p_i^k) = \max\{V[A(p_i^k)], F(p_i^{k-1})\}$$

where $V(t)$, the virtual time at time t, denotes the current round of service in the corresponding fluid fair queueing service.

$$F(p_i^k) = S(p_i^k) + L_i^k/r_i$$

where L_i^k is the length of the kth packet of flow i.

The progression of the virtual time $V(t)$ is given by

$$\frac{dV(t)}{dt} = \frac{C(t)}{\Sigma_{i \in B(t)} r_i}$$

where $B(t)$ is the set of backlogged flows at time t. As a result of simulating fluid fair queueing, WFQ has the property that the worst-case packet delay of a flow compared to the fluid service is upper bounded by one packet. A number of optimizations to WFQ, including closer approximations to the fluid service and reductions in the computational complexity, have been proposed in literature (see [22] for an excellent survey).

8.2.3 Service Model for Fairness in Wireless Networks

Wireless fair queueing seeks to provide the same service to flows in a wireless environment as traditional fair queueing does in wireline environments. This implies providing bounded delay access to each flow and providing full separation between flows. Specifically, fluid fair queueing can provide both long-term fairness and instantaneous fairness among backlogged flows. However, we show in Section 8.2.4 that in the presence of location-dependent channel error, the ability to provide both instantaneous and long-term fairness will be violated. Channel utilization can be significantly improved by swapping channel access between error-prone and error-free flows at any time, or by providing error correction (FEC) in the packets. This will provide long-term fairness but not instantaneous fairness, even in the fluid model in wireless environments. Since we need to compromise on complete separation (the degree to which the service of one flow is unaffected by the behavior and channel conditions of another flow} between flows in order to improve efficiency, wireless fair queueing necessarily provides a somewhat less stringent quality of service than wireline fair queueing.

We now define the wireless fair service model that wireless fair queueing algorithms typically seek to satisfy, and defer the discussion of the different aspects of the service model to subsequent sections. The wireless fair service model has the following properties:

- Short-term fairness among flows that perceive a clean channel and long-term fairness for flows with bounded channel error
- Delay bounds for packets
- Short-term throughput bounds for flows with clean channels and long-term throughput bounds for all flows with bounded channel error
- Support for both delay-sensitive and error-sensitive data flows

We define the error-free service of a flow as the service that it would have received at the same time instant if all channels had been error-free, under identical offered loads. A flow is said to be leading if it has received channel allocation in excess of its error-free service. A flow is said to be lagging if it has received channel allocation less than its error-free service. If a flow is neither leading nor lagging, it is said to be "in sync," since its channel allocation is exactly the same as its error-free service. If the wireless scheduling algorithm explicitly simulates the error-free service, then the lead and lag can be easily computed by computing the difference of the queue size of a flow in the error-free service and the actual queue size of the flow. If the queue size of a flow in the error-free service is larger, then the flow is leading. If the queue size of a flow in the error-free service is smaller, then the flow is lagging. If the two queue sizes are the same, then the flow is in sync.

8.2.4 Issues in Wireless Fair Queueing

From the description of fair queueing in wireline networks in Section 8.2.2 and the description of the channel characteristics in Section 8.2.3, it is clear that adapting wireline fair queueing to the wireless domain is not a trivial exercise. Specifically, wireless fair queueing must deal with the following issues that are specific to the wireless environment.

- The failure of traditional wireline fair queueing in the presence of location-dependent channel error.
- The compensation model for flows that perceive channel error: how transparent should wireless channel errors be to the user?
- The trade off between full separation and compensation, and its impact on fairness of channel access.

- The trade-off between centralized versus distributed scheduling and the impact on medium access protocols in a wireless cell.
- Limited knowledge at the base stations about uplink flows: how does the base station discover the backlogged state and arrival times of packets at the mobile host?
- Inaccuracies in monitoring and predicting the channel state, and its impact on the effectiveness of the compensation model.

We now address all of the issues listed above, except the compensation model for flows perceiving channel error, which we describe in the next section.

8.2.4.1 Why Wireline Fair Queueing Fails over Wireless Channels

Consider three backlogged flows during the time interval [0, 2] with $r_1 = r_2 = r_3$. Flow 1 and flow 2 have error-free channels, whereas flow 3 perceives a channel error during the time interval [0, 1). By applying equation (1.1) over the time periods [0, 1) and [1, 2], we arrive at the following channel capacity allocation:

$$W_1[0, 1) = W_2[0,1) = \tfrac{1}{2}, \; W_1[1, 2] = W_2[1, 2] = W_3[1, 2] = \tfrac{1}{3}$$

Now, over the time window [0, 2], the allocation is

$$W_1[0, 2] = W_2[0, 2] = \tfrac{5}{6}, \; W_3[0, 2] = \tfrac{1}{3}$$

which does not satisfy the fairness property of equation (8.1). Even if we had assumed that flow 3 had used forward error correction to overcome the error in the interval [0, 1), and shared the channel equally with the other two flows, it is evident that its application-level throughput will be less than that of flows 1 and 2, since flow 3 experiences some capacity loss in the interval [0, 1). This simple example illustrates the difficulty in defining fairness in a wireless network, even in an idealized model. In general, due to location-dependent channel errors, server allocations designed to be fair over one time interval may be inconsistent with fairness over a different time interval, though both time intervals have the same backlogged set.

In the fluid fair queueing model, when a flow has nothing to transmit during a time window $[t, t + \Delta]$, it is not allowed to reclaim the channel capacity that would have been allocated to it during $[t, t + \Delta]$ if it were backlogged at t. However, in a wireless channel, it may happen that the flow is backlogged but unable to transmit due to channel error. In such circumstances, should the flow be compensated at a later time? In other words, should channel error and empty queues be treated the same or differently? In particular, consider the scenario when flows f_1 and f_2 are both backlogged, but f_1 perceives a channel error and f_2 perceives a good channel. In this case, f_2 will additionally receive the share of the channel that would have been granted to f_1 in the error-free case. The question is whether the fairness model should readjust the service granted to f_1 and f_2 in a future time window in order to compensate f_1. The traditional fluid fair queueing model does not need to address this issue since in a wireline model, either all flows are permitted to transmit or none of them is.

In order to address this issue, wireless fair queueing algorithms differentiate between a nonbacklogged flow and a backlogged flow that perceives channel error. A flow that is not backlogged does not get compensated for lost channel allocation. However, a backlogged flow f that perceives channel error is compensated in future when it perceives a clean channel, and this compensation is provided at the expense of those flows that received additional channel allocation when f was unable to transmit. Of course, this compensation model makes channel errors transparent to the user to some extent, but only at the expense of separation of flows. In order to achieve a trade-off between compensation and separation, we bound the amount of compensation that a flow can receive at any time. Essentially, wireless fair queueing seeks to make short error bursts transparent to the user so that long-term throughput guarantees are ensured, but exposes prolonged error bursts to the user.

8.2.4.2 Separation versus Compensation

Exploring the trade-off between separation and compensation further, we illustrate a typical scenario and consider several possible compensation schemes. Let flows f_1, f_2, and f_3 be three flows with equal weights that share a wireless channel. Let f_1 perceive a channel error during a time window $[0, 1)$, and during this time window, let f_2 receive all the additional channel allocation that was scheduled for f_1 (for example, because f_2 has packets to send at all times, while f_3 has packets to send only at the exact time intervals determined by its rate). Now, suppose that f_1 perceives a clean channel during $[1, 2]$. What should the channel allocation be?

During $[0, 1]$, the channel allocation was as follows:

$$W_1[0, 1) = 0, \ W_2[0, 1) = \tfrac{2}{3}, \ W_3[0, 1) = \tfrac{1}{3}$$

Thus, f_2 received one-third units of additional channel allocation at the expense of f_1, while f_3 received exactly its contracted allocation. During $[1, 2]$, what should the channel allocation be? In particular, there are two questions that need to be answered:

1. Is it acceptable for f_3 to be impacted due to the fact that f_1 is being compensated even though f_3 did not receive any additional bandwidth?
2. Over what time period should f_1 be compensated for its loss?

In order to provide separation for flows that receive exactly their contracted channel allocation, flow f_3 should not be impacted at all by the compensation model. In other words, the compensation should only be between flows that lag their error-free service and flows that lead that error-free service, where error-free service denotes the service that a flow would have received if all the channels were error-free.

The second question is how long it takes for a lagging flow to recover from its lag. Of course, a simple solution is to starve f_2 in $[1, 2]$ and allow f_1 to catch up with the following allocation:

$$W_1[1, 2] = \tfrac{2}{3}, \ W_2[1, 2] = 0, \ W_3[1, 2) = \tfrac{1}{3}$$

However, this may end up starving flows for long periods of time when a backlogged flow perceives channel error for a long time. Of course, we can bound the amount of compensation that a flow can receive, but that still does not prevent pathological cases in which a single backlogged flow among a large set of backlogged flows perceives a clean channel over a time window, and is then starved out for a long time until all the other lagging flows catch up. In particular, the compensation model must provide for a graceful degradation of service for leading flows while they give up their lead.

8.2.4.3 Centralized versus Distributed Scheduling

In a cell, hosts are only guaranteed to be within the range of the base station and not other hosts, and all transmissions are either uplink or downlink. Thus, the base station is the only logical choice for the scheduling entity in a cell, making the scheduling centralized. However, although the base station has full knowledge of the current state of each downlink flow (i.e., whether it is backlogged, and the arrival times of the packets), it has limited and imperfect knowledge of the current state of each uplink flow. In a centralized approach, the base station has to rely on the mobile hosts to convey uplink state information for scheduling purposes, which adds to control overhead for the underlying medium access protocol.

In a distributed approach, every host with some backlogged flows (including the base station) will have imperfect knowledge of other hosts' flows. Thus, the medium access protocol will also have to be decentralized, and the MAC must have a notion of priority for accessing the channel based on the eligibility of the packets in the flow queues at that host (e.g., backoffs). Since the base station does not have exclusive control over the scheduling mechanism, imprecise information sharing among backlogged uplink and downlink flows will result in poor fairness properties, both in the short term and in the long term.

In our network model, since the base station is involved in every flow, a centralized scheduler gives better fairness guarantees than a distributed scheduler. All wireless fair scheduling algorithms designed for cellular networks follow this model. Distributed schedulers, however, are applicable in different network scenarios, as will be discussed in Section 8.5. The important principle here is that the design of the medium access control (MAC) protocol is closely tied to the type of scheduler chosen.

8.2.4.4 Incomplete State at the Base Station for Uplink Scheduling

When the base station is the choice for the centralized scheduler, it has to obtain the state of all uplink flows to ensure fairness for such flows. As discussed above, it is impossible for the centralized scheduler to have perfect knowledge of the current state for every uplink flow. In particular, the base station may not know precisely when a previously non-backlogged flow becomes backlogged, and the precise arrival times of uplink packets in this case. The lack of such knowledge has an impact on the accuracy of scheduling and delay guarantees that can be provided in wireless fair queueing.

This problem can be alleviated in part by piggybacking flow state on uplink transmissions, but newly backlogged flows may still not be able to convey their state to the base station. For a backlogged flow, the base station only needs to know if the flow will continue to remain backlogged even after it is allocated to a channel. This information can be easily obtained by the base station by adding a one bit field in the packet header. For a nonbacklogged flow, the base station needs to know precisely when the flow becomes backlogged. As far as we know, there exists no way to guarantee up-to-date flow state for uplink flows at the base station except for periodic polling, which may be wasteful in terms of consuming excessive signaling bandwidth. In related work [10, 11], two alternative mechanisms are proposed for a base station to obtain this information, but these mechanisms do not guarantee that the base station will indeed obtain the precise state of uplink flows.

8.2.4.5 Channel State Monitoring and Prediction

Perfect channel-dependent scheduling is only possible if the scheduler has accurate information about the channel state of each backlogged flow. The location-dependent nature of channel error requires each backlogged flow to monitor its channel state continuously, based on which the flow may predict its future channel state and send this information to the scheduler. In CDMA cellular networks, a closed power-control loop provides the signal gain for a host to the base station, accurate to a few milliseconds. However, this may not be sufficient for error bursts of a shorter duration. In order to complement channel state monitoring techniques, we need to predict the channel state based on previous known state, in a fairly accurate manner.

Errors in the wireless channel typically occur over bursts and are highly correlated in successive slots, but possibly uncorrelated over longer time windows [5]. Thus, fairly accurate channel prediction can be achieved using an n-state Markov model. In fact, it has been noted that even using a simple one step prediction algorithm (predict slot $i + 1$ is good if slot i is observed to be good, and bad otherwise) results in an acceptable first cut solution to this problem [11].

A wireless fair scheduler needs precise state information to provide tight fairness guarantees to flows. If the scheduler has perfect state information, it can try to swap slots between flows and avoid capacity loss. However, if all flows perceive channel errors or the scheduler has imperfect channel state, then capacity loss is unavoidable. In this sense, wireless fair queueing algorithms do not make any assumptions about the exact error model, though they assume an upper bound on the number of errors during any time window of size T_i, i.e., flow i will not perceive more than e_i errors in any time window of size T_i, where e_i and T_i are per-flow parameters for flow i. The delay and throughput properties that are derived for the wireless fair queueing algorithms are typically "channel-conditioned," i.e. conditioned on the fact that flow i perceives no more than e_i errors in any time window of size T_i [10, 11].

8.3 WIRELESS FAIR QUEUEING ARCHITECTURE

In this section, we present a generic framework for wireless fair queueing, identify the key components of the framework, and discuss the choices for the policies and mechanisms for each of the components. The next section provides instantiations of these choices with specific wireless fair queueing algorithms from contemporary literature.

Wireless fair queueing involves the following five components:

- Error-free service model: defines an ideal fair service model assuming no channel errors. This is used as a reference model for channel allocation.
- Lead and lag model: determines which flows are leading or lagging their error-free service, and by how much.
- Compensation model: compensates lagging flows that perceive an error-free channel at the expense of leading flows, and thus addresses the key issues of bursty and location-dependent channel error in wireless channel access.
- Slot queue and packet queue decoupling: allows for the support of both delay-sensitive and error-sensitive flows in a single framework and also decouples connection-level packet management policies from link-level packet scheduling policies.
- Channel monitoring and prediction: provides a (possibly inaccurate) measurement and estimation of the channel state at any time instant for each backlogged flow.

Figure 8.2 shows the generic framework for wireless fair queueing. The different components in the framework interact as follows. The error-free service is used as the reference model for the service that each flow should receive. Since a flow may perceive location-dependent channel error during any given time window, the lead and lag model specifies how much additional service the flow is eligible to receive in the future (or how much service the flow must relinquish in the future). The goal of wireless fair queueing is to use the compensation model in order to make short location-dependent error bursts transparent to the lagging flows while providing graceful service degradation for leading flows. In order to support both delay-sensitive and error-sensitive flows, the scheduler only allocates slots to flows and does not determine which packet will be transmitted when a flow is allocated a slot. Finally, the channel prediction model is used to determine whether a flow perceives a clean or dirty channel during each slot. (If the channel is dirty, we assume that the channel prediction model can also predict the amount of FEC required, if error correction is used.)

Once a flow is allocated a slot, it still needs to perform the wireless medium access algorithm in order to gain access to the channel and transmit a packet. We do not explore the interactions between the scheduling algorithm and the medium access algorithm in this chapter. We now proceed to describe the components of the architecture, except channel monitoring and prediction, which have been described earlier.

8.3.1   Error-Free Service Model

The error-free service model provides a reference for how much service a flow should receive in an ideal error-free channel environment. As mentioned above, the goal of wireless fair queueing is to approximate the error-free service model by making short error bursts transparent to a flow, and only expose prolonged channel error to the flow.

Most contemporary wireless fair queueing algorithms use well-known wireline fair queueing algorithms for their error-free service model. Three choices have typically been used:

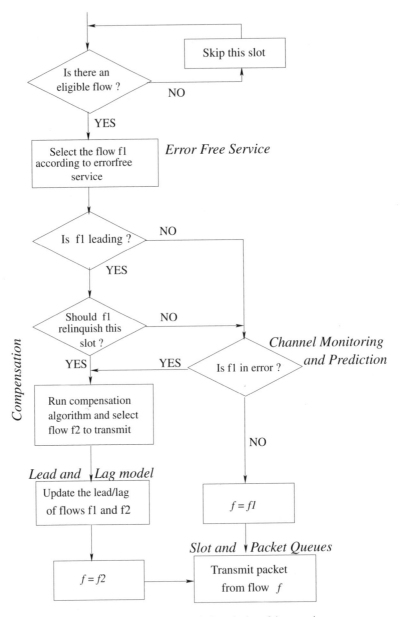

Figure 8.2   Generic framework for wireless fair queueing.

1. Wireline fair queueing algorithms such as WFQ [4] or PGPS [18], in which the rate of change of the virtual time (dV/dt) is explicitly simulated. Simulating the virtual time explicitly can be computationally expensive. Idealized wireless fair queueing (IWFQ) [10] uses WFQ or WF^2Q [1] to compute its error-free service.

2. Wireline fair queueing algorithms such as start-time fair queueing (STFQ) [8], in which the virtual time is not explicitly simulated. In STFQ, for example, the virtual time is set to the start tag of the packet that is currently being served. Channel-condition-independent fair-queueing (CIF-Q) [16] uses STFQ to compute its error free service.

3. A variation of fluid fair queueing that allows for a decoupling of delay and rate in the scheduler. This is achieved by allocating a rate weight r_i and a delay weight ϕ_i for each flow i, and modifying the tagging mechanism described in Section 8.2.2 as follows:

$$S(p_i^k) = \max\{V(A[p_i^k]), S(p_i^{k-1}) + L_i^{k-1}/r_i\}$$

$$F(p_i^k) = S(p_i^k) + L_i^k/\phi_i$$

This algorithm was proposed as part of the wireless fair service (WFS) [11] proposal. In a conventional fair queueing scheme described in Section 8.2.2, we can think of the scheduler as a leaky bucket, and assign tags to packets. By assigning start tags to packets, we admit them into the bucket, which is done according to the rate weight r_i of the flow. The order in which packets are drained out of the bucket is the same order as which they are admitted into the bucket. Thus, the delay of a packet is inversely proportional to the rate weight r_i of the flow to which it belongs. In the variation of fluid fair queueing described here, the order in which the packets are served can be modified from the order in which they were admitted by using the delay weight ϕ_i of the flows. This allows the scheduler to support flows with very low rate and delay requirements. We say that the scheduler has a larger schedulable region.

These choices are equally applicable to almost all wireless fair queueing algorithms. While some algorithms such as the server-based fairness approach (SBFA) [19] and effort-limited fair scheduling (ELF) [6] explicitly specify that any wireline fair scheduling algorithm can be used for their error-free service, in general, any of the above three variants of wireline fair queueing can be used for the error-free service of wireless fair queueing algorithms. The wireless packet scheduler (WPS) proposed in [10], however, uses only a round robin version of WFQ for its error-free service.

8.3.2 Lead and Lag Model

In Section 8.2.3, we described the lag and lead of lagging flows and leading flows in terms of the difference in service received by the actual flow compared to its idealized service. We now refine this definition: the lag of a lagging flow denotes the amount of additional service to which it is entitled in the future in order to compensate for lost service in the past, whereas the lead of a leading flow denotes the amount of additional service that the flow has to relinquish in the future in order to compensate for additional service received in the past.

There are two distinct approaches to computing lag and lead.

1. The lag of a flow is the difference between the error-free service and real service received by the flow. In this case, a flow that falls behind its error-free service is compensated irrespective of whether its lost slots were utilized by other flows. SBFA [19] and ELF [6] use this approach.

2. The lag of a flow is the number of slots allocated to the flow during which it could not transmit due to channel error and another backlogged flow that had no channel error transmitted in its place and increased its lead. In this case, the lag of a flow is incremented upon a lost slot only if another flow that took this slot is prepared to relinquish a slot in the future. IWFQ, WPS [10], WFS [11], and CIF-Q [16] use this approach.

Lead and lag may be upper bounded by flow-specific parameters. An upper bound on lag is the maximum error burst that can be made transparent to the flow, whereas an upper bound on lead is the maximum number of slots that the flow must relinquish in the future in order to compensate for additional service received in the past.

8.3.3 Compensation Model

The compensation model is the key component of wireless fair queueing algorithms. It determines how lagging flows make up their lag and how leading flows give up their lead. Thus, the compensation model has to address three main issues: (a) When does a leading flow relinquish the slots that are allocated to it? (b) When are slots allocated for compensating lagging flows? (c) How are compensation slots allocated among lagging flows? We now explore the design choices for each issue.

Leading flows are required to give up some of the slots that are allocated to them in error-free service so that lagging flows can use these slots to reduce their lag. There are three possible choices for a leading flow to relinquish its lead.

1. The first choice, adopted by IWFQ, WPS [10], and ELF [6], is for a leading flow to relinquish all slots until it becomes in sync. The problem with this approach is that a leading flow that has accumulated a large lead because other flows perceive large error bursts may end up being starved of channel access at a later time when all lagging flows start to perceive clean channels.

2. The second choice is for a leading flow to relinquish a fraction of the slots allocated to it. The fraction of slots relinquished may be constant, as in CIF-Q [16], or may be proportional to the lead of the flow, as in WFS [11]. The advantage of relinquishing a fraction of the allocated slots is that service degradation is graceful. In WFS, for example, the degradation in service decreases exponentially as the lead of a flow decreases.

3. The third choice is for a leading flow to never relinquish its lead. In this case, we assume that there is a separate reserved portion of the channel bandwidth that is dedicated for the compensation of lagging flows. SBFA [19] uses this approach.

Lagging flows must receive additional slots in excess of their error-free service in order to make up for lost service in the past. We call these additional slots "compensation slots." There are three choices for allocating compensation slots to lagging flows:

1. Compensation slots are preferentially allocated until there are no lagging flows that perceive a clean channel, as in IWFQ, WPS [10], and ELF [6]. As a result, lagging flows take precedence in channel allocation over in-sync and leading flows.
2. Compensation slots are allocated only when leading flows relinquish slots, as in CIF-Q [16] and WFS [11].
3. Compensation slots are allocated from a reserved fraction of the channel bandwidth that is set aside specifically to compensate lagging flows, as in SBFA [19].

Giving lagging flows precedence in channel allocation may disturb in-sync flows and cause them to lag even if they perceive no channel error. On the other hand, allocating a separate reserved portion of the channel statically bounds the amount of compensation that can be granted. The second approach, in which slots are swapped explicitly between leading and lagging flows, does not disturb in-sync flows, but compensates lagging flows slightly more slowly than the other two choices. The exact choice of the compensation technique is thus left to the network designer, by considering the QoS requirements of the applications that will be used by mobile hosts in the network.

The final question in the compensation model is how to distribute compensation slots among lagging flows. Three design choices have been explored in contemporary algorithms:

1. The lagging flow with the largest normalized lag is allocated the compensation slot, as in CIF-Q [16] and ELF [6].
2. The history of when flows begin lagging is maintained, and the flows are compensated according to the order in which they became backlogged, as in IWFQ [10] and SBFA [19].
3. The lagging flows are compensated fairly, i.e., each lagging flow receives a number of compensation slots in proportion to its lag, as in WPS [10] and WFS [11].

Among these options, fair compensation achieves the goal of short-term fairness in wireless fair service, but is computationally more expensive than the other two options.

8.3.4 Slot Queues and Packet Queues

Typically, wireline fair queueing algorithms assign tags to packets as soon as they arrive. This works well if we assume no channel error, i.e., a scheduled packet will always be transmitted and received successfully. However, in a wireless channel, packets may be corrupted due to channel error, and an unsuccessfully transmitted packet may need to be re-transmitted for an error-sensitive flow. Retagging the packet will cause it to join the end of the flow queue and thus cause packets to be delivered out of order.

Fundamentally, there needs to be a separation between "when to send the next packet," and "which packet to send next." The first question should be answered by the scheduler, whereas the second question is really a flow-specific decision and should be beyond the scope of the scheduler. In order address these two questions, one additional level of abstraction can be used in order to decouple "slots," the units of channel allocation, from "packets," the units of data transmission. When a packet arrives in the queue of a flow, a corresponding slot is generated in the slot queue of the flow and tagged according to the wireless fair queueing algorithm. At each time, the scheduler determines which slot will get access to the channel, and the head-of-line packet in the corresponding flow queue is then transmitted. The number of slots in the slot queue at any time is exactly the same as the number of packets in the flow queue.

Providing this additional level of abstraction enables the scheduler to support both error-sensitive flows and delay-sensitive flows according to the wireless fair service model. Error-sensitive flows will not delete the head-of-line packet upon channel error during transmission, but delay-sensitive flows may delete the head-of-line packet once it violates its delay bound. Likewise, the flow may have priorities in its packets, and may choose to discard an already queued packet in favor of an arriving packet when its queue is full. Essentially, the approach is to limit the scope of the scheduler to determine only which flow is allocated the channel next, and let each flow make its own decision about which packet in the flow it wishes to transmit. In our scheduling model, we support any queueing and packet dropping policy at the flow level because we decouple slot queues from packet queues.*

8.4   ALGORITHMS FOR WIRELESS FAIR QUEUEING

In the last section, we described the key components of a generic wireless fair queueing algorithm and discussed possible design choices for each of the components. In this section, we consider six contemporary wireless fair queueing algorithms and compare their characteristics. A detailed performance evaluation of many of these algorithms can be found in [15].

Among the algorithms proposed in contemporary literature, we choose six representative algorithms for discussion. The algorithms that we choose not to describe behave very similarly to one of the algorithms described here. The six algorithms chosen are the idealized wireless fair queueing algorithm (IWFQ) [10], the wireless packet scheduling algorithm [10], the channel-condition-independent fair queueing algorithm (CIF-Q) [16], the server-based fairness approach (SBFA) [19], the wireless fair service algorithm (WFS) [11], and the effort-limited fair scheduling algorithm (ELF) [6].

---

*The slot queue and packet queue decoupling described in this section are applicable for fixed size packets only. Adapting this mechanism for variable size packets involves solving several subtle issues, which are beyond the scope of this discussion.

8.4.1   Idealized Wireless Fair Queueing (IWFQ)

IWFQ was the first algorithm to propose a structured adaptation of fair queueing to the wireless domain. In this algorithm, the error-free service is simulated by WFQ [1] or WF^2Q [4]. The start tag and finish tag of each slot are assigned as in WFQ. The service tag of a flow is set to the finish tag of its head of line slot. In order to schedule a transmission, IWFQ selects the flow with the minimum service tag among the backlogged flows that perceive a clean channel.

Each flow i has a lead bound of l_i and a lag bound of b_i. The service tag of flow i is not allowed to increase by more than l_i above, or decrease by more than b_i below, the service tag of its error-free service. The lag of a flow depends on the number of slots in which a flow was unable to transmit, but in which another flow was able to transmit in its place.

The compensation model in IWFQ is implicit. If a flow perceives channel error, it retains its tag (and, hence, precedence for transmission when it becomes error free). Likewise, if a flow receives additional service, its service tag increases. Consequently, lagging flows end up having lower service tags than flows that are in sync or leading and, hence, have precedence in channel access when they become error free.

As a consequence of the compensation model in IWFQ, a flow that is lagging for a long time will be able to capture the channel once it becomes error free. Likewise, a leading flow may be starved out of channel access for long periods of time. Thus, the compensation model in IWFQ does not support graceful degradation of service. Additionally, in-sync flows will be starved of service when compensation is granted to lagging flows. Thus, in the short term, a flow may not receive any service even if it has a clean channel and has not received any excess service.

8.4.2   Wireless Packet Scheduling (WPS)

WPS was proposed as a more practical version of IWFQ in [10]. The error-free service of WPS uses a variant of weighted round robin and WFQ, and is called WRR with spreading. To illustrate this mechanism, consider three flows f_1, f_2, and f_3 with weights of 2, 3, and 5, respectively. While the slot allocation in standard WRR would be according to the schedule $\langle f_1, f_1, f_2, f_2, f_2, f_3, f_3, f_3, f_3, f_3 \rangle$, WRR with spreading allocates slots according to the schedule $\langle f_3, f_2, f_3, f_1, f_3, f_2, f_3, f_1, f_2, f_3 \rangle$, which is identical to the schedule generated by WFQ if all flows are backlogged. The mechanism used to achieve this spreading is described in [10].

In WPS, the lead and lag of a flow are used to adjust the weights of the flow in the WRR spreading allocation. The lead is treated as negative lag. Thus, WPS generates a "frame" of slot allocation from the WRR spreading algorithm. At the start of a frame, WPS computes the effective weight of a flow equal to the sum of its default weight and its lag, and resets the lag to 0. The frame is then generated based on the effective weights of flows. The lag and the lead are bounded by a threshold.

In each slot of the frame, if the flow that is allocated the slot is backlogged but perceives a channel error, then WPS tries to swap the slot with a future slot allocation within the same frame. If this is not possible (i.e., there is no backlogged flow perceiving a clean channel with a slot allocation later in the frame), then WPS increments the lag of the flow if another flow can transmit in its place (i.e., there is a backlogged flow with clean channel but it has been served its slot allocations for this frame), and the lead of this new alternate flow is incremented.

The lag/lead accounting mechanism described above maintains the difference between the real service and the error-free service across frames. By changing the effective weight in each frame depending on the result of the previous frame, WPS tries to provide additional service to lagging flows at the expense of leading flows. In the ideal case, in-sync flows are unaffected at the granularity of frames, though their slot allocations may change within the frame.

WPS is a practical variant of IWFQ, and so its performance is also similar to that of IWFQ. In particular, it is susceptible to a lagging flow accumulating a large lag and starving other flows when it begins to perceive a clean channel. However, unlike IWFQ, an in-sync flow that perceives a clean channel will always be able to access the channel within a frame. This cannot be said of leading flows, whose effective weight could be zero for the frame even if they are backlogged. Thus, WPS does not disturb in-sync flows, even though it provides poor fairness guarantees in the short term. Since a lagging flow will eventually catch up with its lag, WPS provides bounds on the fairness and throughput in the long term.

8.4.3 Channel-Condition-Independent Fair Queueing (CIF-Q)

In CIF-Q, the error-free service is simulated by STFQ [8]. The lag or lead of a flow are maintained just as in IWFQ. In other words, the lag of a backlogged flow is incremented only when some other flow is able to transmit in its place. Lead is maintained as negative lag.

When a lagging or in-sync flow i is allocated the channel, it transmits a packet if it perceives a clean channel. Otherwise, if there is a backlogged flow j that perceives a clean channel and transmits instead of i, then the lag of i is incremented and the lag of j is decremented.

A leading flow i retains a fraction α of its service and relinquishes a fraction $1 - \alpha$ of its service, where α is a system parameter that governs the service degradation of leading flows. When a leading flow relinquishes a slot, it is allocated to the lagging flow with a clean channel and the largest normalized lag, where the normalization is done using the rate weight of the flow. Thus, lagging flows receive additional service only when leading flows relinquish slots.

As a consequence of its compensation model, CIF-Q provides a graceful linear degradation in service for leading flows. Additionally, it performs compensation of lagging flows by explicitly swapping slots with leading flows, thus ensuring that in-sync flows are not affected. CIF-Q thus overcomes two of the main drawbacks of IWFQ, and is able to satisfy the properties of the wireless fair service model described in Section 8.2.3.

8.4.4 Server-Based Fairness Approach (SBFA)

SBFA provides a framework in which different wireline scheduling algorithms can be adapted to the wireless domain. The error-free service in SBFA is the desired wireline scheduling algorithm that needs to be adapted to the wireless domain. For example, we can choose WFQ or WRR to be the error-free service.

SBFA statically reserves a fraction of the channel bandwidth for compensating lagging flows. This reserved bandwidth is called a virtual compensation flow or a long-term fairness server (LTFS). When a backlogged flow is unable to transmit due to channel error, a slot request corresponding to that flow is queued in the LTFS. The LTFS is allocated a rate weight that reflects the bandwidth reserved for compensation. The scheduling algorithm treats LTFS on a par with other packet flows for channel allocation.

When the LTFS flow is selected by the scheduler, the flow corresponding to the head-of-line slot in the LTFS is selected for transmission. Thus, in contrast with other wireless fair queueing algorithms, SBFA tries to compensate the lagging flows using the reserved bandwidth rather than swapping slots between leading and lagging flows.

There is no concept of leading flows in SBFA. The lag of a flow is not explicitly bounded, and the order of compensation among lagging flows is according to the order in which their slots are queued in the LTFS.

When the reserved bandwidth is not used, it is distributed among other flows according to the error-free scheduling policy. This excess service is essentially free since lead is not maintained.

As a consequence of the compensation model, SBFA provides fairness guarantees as a function of the statically reserved LTFS bandwidth. The bounds are very sensitive to this reserved fraction. For example, a single flow could perceive lots of errors, thereby utilizing all the bandwidth of the LTFS flow. Other flows experiencing errors may not get enough compensation, resulting in unfair behavior for the system. However, if the reserved fraction is large enough, then this situation does not arise. Thus, the rate of compensation is bounded by the reserved portion of the channel bandwidth. The service degradation for leading and in-sync flows is graceful and the available service is lower-bounded by the minimum rate contracts established for the flow.

8.4.5 Wireless Fair Service (WFS)

In WFS, the error free service is computed by the modified fair queueing algorithm described in Section 8.3.1 in order to achieve a delay–bandwidth decoupling in the scheduler. This decoupling expands the schedulable region for WFS. Unlike traditional fair queueing algorithms, WFS can support flows with high bandwidth and high delay requirements, as well as flows with low bandwidth and low delay requirements, due to the use of this modified scheduler.

The notion of lag and lead in WFS is the same as in CIF-Q. A flow can increase its lag only when another flow can transmit in its slot. Each flow i has a lead bound of l_i^{max} and a lag bound of b_i^{max}. A leading flow with a current lead of l_i relinquishes a fraction l_i/l_i^{max} of its slots, whereas a lagging flow with a current lag of b_i receives a fraction $b_i/\Sigma_{j \in S} b_j$ of all the relinquished slots, where S is the set of backlogged flows. Effectively, leading flows relinquish their slots in proportion to their lead, and relinquished slots are fairly distributed among lagging flows.

As a consequence of the compensation model, service degradation is graceful for leading flows and the fraction of slots relinquished by leading flows decreases exponentially. WFS maintains a WPS-like "WRR with spreading" mechanism for determining which lagging flow will receive a relinquished slot. The weight of a lagging flow in the WRR is equal to its lag. As a result of this compensation model, compensation slots are fairly allocated among lagging flows.

WFS achieves all the properties of the fair service model described in Section 8.2.3. It achieves both short-term and long-term fairness, as well as delay and throughput bounds. The error-free service of WFS allows it to decouple delay and bandwidth requirements.

8.4.6 Effort-Limited Fair Queueing (ELF)

ELF uses any wireline fair queueing algorithm as its error-free service. It is similar to SBFA in the sense that it provides a general architecture for adapting different fair queueing schemes to wireless networks.

In ELF, the lag of a flow is the difference between the actual service received and the error-free service. The lead is maintained as negative lag. Whenever a flow is unable to transmit due to channel error, it retains its precedence in terms of a parameter called "deserve," which is similar to the precedence of tags in IWFQ. Among the set of backlogged flows with a clean channel, the flow with the largest normalized value of the deserve parameter accesses the channel first; the normalization is done using the rate weight of the flows. Thus, the flow with the highest precedence gets to transmit in each slot. The lag of a flow is bounded by an effort parameter P_i, which is flow-specific. The lead is not bounded.

The compensation model for ELF is similar to that of IWFQ. The flow with the highest precedence, defined by deserve/r_i, is chosen to be the next eligible flow is chosen for transmission. Note that lagging flows have precedence over in-sync flows, which have precedence over leading flows. Thus, compensation comes at the expense of leading and in-sync flows.

As a result of this compensation model, ELF can provide long-term fairness to flows since all lagging flows will eventually eliminate their lag as long as they have packets to send. However, backlogged leading flows with a clean channel will be starved of service until the lagging flows give up their lag. Note that when an in-sync flow is starved of service, it immediately becomes a lagging flow. Thus, the service degradation is not graceful, and short-term fairness is not ensured for flows with clean channels.

All the algorithms described in this section share several common features. First, they all specify an error-free service model and then try to approximate the error-free service, even when some flows perceive location-dependent error, by implicitly or explicitly compensating lagging flows at the expense of leading flows. Second, they all have similar computational complexity. Third, they all provide mechanisms to bound the amount of compensation that can be provided to any flow, thereby controlling the amount of channel error that can be made transparent to error-prone flows. Finally, all of them try to achieve at least some degree of wireless fair service. Among the algorithms described, CIF-Q and WFS achieve all the properties of wireless fair service.

8.5 ISSUES AND FUTURE DIRECTIONS

In this section, we consider future research directions in wireless fair queueing. We investigate three issues:

1. We have assumed that all flows are treated as best-effort flows until now. In practice, networks classify services into different classes, such as guaranteed and best-effort services [17]. Wireless fair queueing schemes have to accommodate these multiple classes of service.

2. The use of error-correcting schemes has been proposed as a means of addressing channel error. The impact of such schemes on the compensation mechanisms of wireless fair scheduling algorithms needs further investigation.

3. A growing class of wireless networks do not have a coordinating central node, such as base station. These networks are, in general, referred to as ad hoc networks. There are two questions that arise when dealing with fairness in networks: (a) what is the notion of fairness in an ad hoc network? (b) How do we ensure fairness in the absence of centralized control?

We briefly discuss these issues in this section, providing pointers to ongoing work in these areas, and conclude the chapter.

8.5.1 Multiple Service Classes

The differentiated services architecture proposed for the Internet has different service classes, such as guaranteed service, predictive service, and best effort service [17], to provide varying levels of QoS to paying users. This classification is also expected to become the norm for wireless data networks. Different service classes have an inherent notion of priority; for example, flows with guaranteed service must be treated preferentially when compared to best-effort flows. Although many wireless scheduling algorithms treat all flows equally, some wireless scheduling algorithms have been proposed with a multiple service class model. Class-based queueing with channel-state dependent scheduling [20] and ELF [6] use multiple service class schedulers.

The approach followed in these algorithms is very simple, and it can be easily extended to all wireless fair queueing algorithms discussed in this chapter. Bandwidth is at first reserved for the flows in the highest service class, and the remaining bandwidth is given to the lower service classes. Once the bandwidth is assigned to the different service classes for a given flow set, scheduling is performed on individual flows within a service class, using the bandwidth for that service class. This ensures that service obtained by all flows is in accordance with the nature of the service class to which they belong. However, when the order of priority is not explicitly clear among the different service classes, the above approach is not sufficient.

8.5.2 Error Correction

Forward error correction (FEC) schemes can be used to protect against data loss due to channel error. For a channel error rate of e_i, the packet has to include a redundancy of $\lambda(e_i)$ per bit. Given a packet size p_i for flow i, the useful throughput for the flow is $p_i[1 - \lambda(e_i)]$. This tells us that even if all flows are given fair channel access, different users perceive different rates of channel error and, hence, the actual throughput for different users is not fair. In other words, when we use FEC, fairness in the MAC layer does not translate to the desired fairness in the application layer. Therefore, wireless fair scheduling algorithms must keep track of the actual throughput and update the lag or the lead of flows accordingly.

FEC schemes can improve channel capacity utilization in the absence of perfect channel state information. The MAC layer can include additional redundancy in the packet to be transmitted, resulting in increased number of successful transmissions. There is a trade-off between the robustness and the loss of channel capacity due to this additional redundancy. In [7], an adaptive control algorithm is proposed to optimize the gain in the channel capacity by using varying degrees of redundancy in the transmitted packet. This algorithm can be used in conjunction with any wireless scheduling algorithm to obtain better performance. We believe that this area needs further investigation.

8.5.3 Scheduling in Multihop Wireless (Ad Hoc) Networks

In ad hoc networks, mobile hosts are distributed over a given area, where each mobile host is not always within range of all hosts. Communication between two hosts is done by a series of hops between neighboring nodes. Such networks are characterized by the absence of a coordinating host, and as a result, no host has global information. A simple example of such a network is shown in Figure 8.3.

In this figure, host D can hear hosts A, B, C, and E, whereas host F can hear only host E. Thus, D has to contend for channel access among its four neighbors, while F has only one contending neighbor. If we assume that each host obtains a bandwidth share that is inversely proportional to the number of hosts within its range, then D gets one-fifth of the channel capacity, whereas F gets half of the capacity. The channel share is dependent on the location of the host. Another way of assigning the channel bandwidth is to consider flows, i.e., pairs of communicating nodes, and divide the bandwidth among flows in a

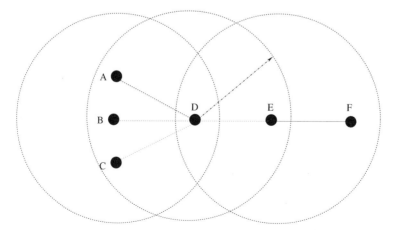

Figure 8.3   Ad hoc network.

neighborhood. In this case, the channel share depends on the location of the host and the neighbors with which it communicates. Thus, the notion of fairness has to be defined precisely at first before we attempt to design a scheduling algorithm to obtain the fairness model. In [12, 13, 14], different fairness models are proposed and distributed scheduling algorithms developed to achieve the fairness models.

As a special case of an ad hoc network, the authors in [21] consider a wireless local area network in which all hosts are in range of each other. A distributed fair scheduling algorithm is proposed for such a network. The base station is treated as a host that takes part in the distributed scheduling. However, this work cannot be generalized to other ad hoc networks.

In this chapter, we have identified the issues that need to be solved in order to achieve wireless fair queueing, and we have described some state-of-the-art solutions in this area. Many of these wireless fair queueing algorithms can effectively provide channel-conditioned guarantees on the fairness and throughput that can be achieved for flows. We have also identified a few directions for future research in this area and have described ongoing work along these directions.

REFERENCES

1. J. C. R. Bennett and H. Zhang, WF^2Q: Worst-case fair weighted fair queueing, in *Proceedings of IEEE INFOCOM,* pp. 120–128, San Francisco, CA, March 1996.

2. P. Bhagwat, P. Bhattacharya, A. Krishma, and S. Tripathi, Enhanc-ing throughput over wireless LANs using channel state dependent packet scheduling, in *Proceedings of IEEE INFOCOM,* pp. 113–1140, San Francisco, CA, March 1996.

3. G. Bianchi, A. Campbell, and R. Liao, On utility-fair adaptive services in wireless packet networks, in *Proceedings of IEEE/ IFIP International Workshop on Quality of Service,* pp. 256–267, Napa, CA, May 1998.

4. A. Demers, S. Keshav, and S, Shenker. Analysis and simulation of a fair queueing algorithm, in *Proceedings of ACM SIGCOMM '89,* pp. 1–12, Austin, TX, September 1989.

5. D. Eckhardt and P. Steenkiste, Improving wireless LAN performance via adaptive local error control, in *Proceedings of the IEEE International Conference on Network Protocols,* pp. 327–338, Austin, TX, October 1998.

6. D. Eckhardt and P. Steenkiste, Effort-limited Fair (ELF) scheduling for wireless networks, in *Proceedings of IEEE INFOCOM,* pp. 1097–1106, Tel Aviv, Israel, March 2000.

7. X. Gao, T. Nandagopal, and V. Bharghavan, On improving the perfor-mance of utility-based wireless fair scheduling through a combination of adaptive FEC and ARQ, *Journal of High Speed Networks, 10*(2), 2001.

8. P. Goyal, H.M. Vin, and H. Chen, Start-time fair queueing: A scheduling algorithm for integrat-ed service access, in *Proceedings of ACM SIGCOMM '96,* pp. 157–168, Palo Alto, CA, August 1996.

9. IEEE. Wireless LAN Medium Access Control(MAC) and Physical Layer(PHY) Specifications. IEEE Standard 802.11, June 1997.

10. 5. Lu, V. Bharghavan, and R. Srikant, Fair queuing in wireless packet networks, in *Proceedings of ACM SIGCOMM '97,* pp. 63–74, Cannes France, September 1997.

11. S. Lu, T. Nandagopal, and V. Bharghavan, Fair scheduling in wireless packet networks, in *Proceedings of the ACM/IEEE International Conference on Mobile Computing and Networking,* pp. 10–20, Dallas, TX, October 1998.

12. H. Luo and S. Lu, A self-coordinating approach to distributed fair queue-ing in adhoc wireless networks, in *Proceedings of IEEE INFOCOM,* pp. 1370–1379, Anchorage Alaska, April 2001.

13. H. Luo, S. Lu, and V. Bharghavan, A new model for packet scheduling in multihop wireless networks, in *Proceedings of the ACM/IEEE International Conference on Mobile Computing and Networking,* pp. 76–86, Boston, MA, August 2000.

14. T. Nandagopal, T. Kim, X. Gao, and V. Bharghavan, Achieving MAC layer fairness in wireless packet networks, in *ACM/IEEE International Conference on Mobile Computing and Networking,* pp. 87–98, Boston, MA, August 2000.

15. T. Nandagopal, S. Lu, and V. Bharghavan, A unified architecture for the design and evaluation of wireless fair queueing algorithms, in *Proceedings of the ACM/IEEE International Conference on Mobile Computing and Networking,* pp. 132–142, Seattle, WA, August 1999.

16. T.S. Ng, I. Stoica, and H. Zhang, Packet fair queueing algorithms for wireless networks with location-dependent errors, in *Proceedings of IEEE INFOCOM,* pp. 1103–1111, San Francisco, CA, March 1998.

17. K. Nichols, S. Blake, F. Baker, and D. L. Black, Definition of the Differ-entiation Services Field (DS Field) in the IPv4 and IPv6 Headers. RFC 2474, December 1998.

18. A. Parekh and R. Gallager, A generalized processor sharing approach to flow control in integrated services networks: the single node case. *IEEE/ACM Transactions on Networking,* 1(3):344–357, June 1993.

19. P. Ramanathan and P. Agrawal, Adapting packet fair queueing algorithms to wireless networks, in *Proceedings of the ACM/IEEE International Conference on Mobile Computing and Networking,* pp. 1–9, Dallas, TX, October 1998.

20. M. Srivastava, C. Fragouli, and V. Sivaraman, Controlled multimedia wireless link sharing via enhanced class-based queueing with channel-state-dependent packet scheduling, in *Proceedings of IEEE INFOCOM,* pp. 572–580, San Francisco, March 1998.

21. N. Vaidya, P. Bahi, and S. Gupta, Distributed fair scheduling in a wireles LAN, in *Proceedings of the ACM/IEEE International Conference on Mobile Computing and Networking,* pp. 167–178, Boston, MA, August 2000.

22. H. Zhang, Service disciplines for guaranteed performance service in packet-switching networks, *Proceedings of the IEEE, 83*(10):1374–1396, October 1995.

CHAPTER 9

Randomized Initialization Protocols for Radio Networks

KOJI NAKANO

Japan Advanced Institute for Science and Technology

STEPHAN OLARIU

Department of Computer Science, Old Dominion University, Norfolk

9.1 INTRODUCTION

In recent years, wireless and mobile communications have seen explosive growth both in terms of the number of services provided and the types of technologies that have become available. Indeed, cellular telephony, radio paging, cellular data, and even rudimentary multimedia services have become commonplace and the demand for enhanced capabilities will continue to grow into the foreseeable future [6, 12, 43, 46]. It is anticipated that in the not-so-distant future, mobile users will be able to access, while on the move, their data and other services such as electronic mail, video telephony, stock market news, map services, and electronic banking, among many others [12, 21, 41].

A radio network (RN, for short) is a distributed system with no central arbiter, consisting of n radio transceivers, henceforth referred to as stations. We assume that the stations are bulk-produced hand-held devices running on batteries and that it is impossible or impractical to distinguish them by serial or manufacturing numbers. Unlike the well-studied cellular systems that assume the existence of a robust infrastructure, the RNs are self-organizing, rapidly deployable, possibly multihop, and do not rely on an existing infrastructure. These networks find applications in disaster relief, interactive mission planning, search-and-rescue, law enforcement, multimedia classroom, and collaborative computing, among other special-purpose applications [16, 18, 20, 23, 26, 28]. At the system level, scalability and topology management concerns suggest a hierarchical organization of RN systems [20, 23, 26, 36, 41, 43], with the lowest level in the hierarchy being a cluster, typically a single-hop subsystem. As argued in [20, 23, 26, 36, 40, 41, 43], in addition to helping with scalability and robustness, aggregating stations into clusters and, further, into superclusters has the added benefit of concealing the details of global network topology from individual stations.

An important task to perform is that of assigning the n stations of the radio network distinct ID numbers (vaguely similar to IP addresses) in the range 1 to n. This task is known as initialization and, we argue, is fundamental, as many of the existing protocols

Handbook of Wireless Networks and Mobile Computing, Edited by Ivan Stojmenović.
ISBN 0-471-41902-8   © 2002 John Wiley & Sons, Inc.

for radio networks tacitly assume that the stations already have IDs. The initialization problem is nontrivial since the stations are assumed to be indistinguishable. Further, since the stations are power-limited, it is of importance to design energy-efficient initialization protocols for single-hop RNs both in the case where the system has a collision detection capability and in the case where this capability is not present.

As customary, time is assumed to be slotted and all the stations have a local clock that keeps synchronous time by interfacing with a global positioning system (GPS, for short) [15, 24]. We note here that under current technology, the commercially available GPS system (GPS systems using military codes achieve an accuracy that is orders of magnitude better than commercial codes) provides location information accurate within 22 meters as well as time information accurate to within 100 nanoseconds [15]. This is more than sufficient for the stations to synchronize. The stations are assumed to have the computing power of a laptop computer; in particular, they all run the same protocol and can generate random bits that provide local data on which the stations may perform computations.

The stations communicate using k, ($k \geq 1$), radio frequencies channels. We assume that in a time slot, a station can tune to one radio channel and/or transmit on at most one (possibly the same) channel. A transmission involves a data packet whose length is such that the transmission can be completed within one time slot. We employ the commonly accepted assumption that when two or more stations are transmitting on a channel in the same time slot, the corresponding packets collide and are garbled beyond recognition. We distinguish between RN systems based on their capability to detect collisions. Specifically, in the RN with collision detection (CD, for short), at the end of a time slot the status of a radio channel is:

- NULL—no transmission on the channel
- SINGLE—exactly one transmission on the channel
- COLLISION—two or more transmissions on the channel

In the RN with no collision detection (no-CD, for short), at the end of a time slot the status of a radio channel is:

- NOISE—ambient noise: either no transmission or collision of several transmissions on the channel
- SINGLE—exactly one transmission on the channel

In other words, the RN with no-CD cannot distinguish between ambient noise and two or more transmissions colliding on the channel. A number of radio and cellular networks including AMPS, GSM, ALOHA-net, as well as the well-known Ethernet are known to rely on sophisticated collision detection capabilities [1, 2, 10, 11, 12, 29]. However, several workers have pointed out that from a practical standpoint the no-CD assumption makes a lot of sense, especially in the presence of noisy channels, which, we argue, tends to be the norm rather than the exception. Given the additional limitations, it is far more challenging to design efficient protocols for RNs with no-CD than for those with collision detection capabilities [8, 9].

It is very important to realize that since the stations of the RN are running on batteries, saving battery power is exceedingly important, as recharging batteries may not be an option while on mission. It is well known that a station expends power while its transceiver is active, that is, while transmitting or receiving a packet. It is perhaps surprising at first that a station expends power even if it receives a packet that is not destined for it [7, 19, 21, 39, 42, 44, 45]. Consequently, we are interested in developing protocols that allow stations to power their transceiver off (i.e., "go to sleep") to the largest extent possible. Accordingly, we judge the goodness of a protocol by the following two yardsticks:

1. The overall number of time slots required by the protocol to terminate
2. For each individual station, the total number of time slots in which it has to be awake in order to transmit/receive packets

The individual goals of optimizing these parameters are, of course, conflicting. It is relatively straightforward to minimize overall completion time at the expense of energy consumption. Similarly, one can minimize energy consumption at the expense of completion time [44, 45, 46]. The challenge is to strike a sensible balance between the two by designing protocols that take a small number of time slots to terminate while being, at the same time, as energy-efficient as possible.

The main goal of this chapter is to survey some of the recent initialization protocols for single-hop RN. The remainder of this chapter is organized as follows. Section 9.2 surveys the state of the art. Section 9.3 reviews basic probability theory necessary to analyze the initialization protocols. Section 9.4 discusses a number of energy-efficient prefix sum protocols that will turn out to be key ingredients in the remainder of this chapter. In Section 9.5 we present known initialization protocols for single-channel radio networks. Section 9.6 provides an extension of the single-channel initialization protocols to the case where k channels are available. Section 9.7 presents a number of energy-efficient initialization protocols for k channel RNs. Finally, Section 9.8 offers concluding remarks and open problems.

9.2 STATE OF THE ART

As stated previously, the initialization problem involves assigning each of the n stations of an RN an integer ID number in the range 1 to n such that no two stations share the same ID.

The initialization problem is fundamental in both network design and in multiprocessor systems [32, 37]. Recent advances in wireless communications and mobile computing have exacerbated the need for efficient protocols for RNs. As a result, a large number of such protocols have been reported in the literature [3, 17, 32, 33]. However, virtually all these protocols function under the assumption that the n stations in the RN have been initialized in advance. The highly nontrivial task of assigning the stations distinct ID numbers, i.e., initializing the stations, is often ignored in the literature. It is, therefore, of importance to design energy-efficient initialization protocols for RNs both in the case where the system has a collision detection capability and for the case where this capability is not present.

In the broad area of distributed computing, the initialization problem is also known as the processor identity or the processor naming problem. The processor identity problem and its variants, including renaming processors, has been addressed in the literature. We refer the interested reader to [4, 5, 14, 25, 27, 38] and to the various other references therein.

In the context of radio networks, Hayashi et al. [22] presented a protocol that initializes a single-channel, n-station RN with CD in $O(n)$ time slots with probability at least $1 - 1/2^{O(n)}$. The protocol repeatedly partitions the stations of the RN into nonempty subsets until, eventually, every subset consists of a single station. Further, Nakano and Olariu [34] have presented an initialization protocol for k channel, n station RNs with CD terminating, with probability exceeding $1 - 1/n$, in $10n/3k + O(\sqrt{(n \ln n)}/k)$ time slots. They also showed that if the collision detection capability is not present, the RN can be initialized, with high probability, in $5.67n/k + O(\sqrt{(n \ln n)}/k)$ time slots. More recently, Micić and Stojmenović [30] improved the constant factor of the time slots necessary to initialize a single-channel, n station RN with CD.

Bordim et al. [13] showed that, if the number n of stations is known beforehand, a single-channel n station RN with CD can be initialized, with probability exceeding $1 - 1/n$, in $O(n)$ time slots with no station being awake for more than $O(\log n)$ time slots. This protocol uses the initialization protocol of [22] as follows: having partitioned the n stations into $n/\log n$ subsets of roughly $\log n$ stations, each subset is initialized individually. The key observation is that a station needs to be awake only for the time necessary to initialize the subset to which it belongs. By using the protocol of [22], each subset can be initialized, with probability exceeding $1 - 1/2^{O(\log n)}$, in $O(\log n)$ time slots and, thus, no station has to be awake for more than $O(\log n)$ time slots. Once each subset has been initialized, a simple prefix sum computation allows the stations to update their local ID to the desired ID. Bordim et al. [13] went on to show how to use the single-channel initialization protocol to initialize, with probability exceeding $1 - 1/n$, a k channel, ($k \leq n/\log n$), RN with CD in $O(n/k)$ time slots with no station being awake for more than $O(\log n)$ time slots. More recently, Nakano and Olariu [35] presented an initialization protocol for k channel, n station RNs with no-CD terminating, with probability exceeding $1 - 1/n$, in $O(n/k + \log n)$ time slots, with no station being awake for more than $O(\log \log n)$ time slots.

9.3 A REFRESHER OF BASIC PROBABILITY THEORY

The main goal of this section is to review elementary probability theory results that are useful for analyzing the performance of our protocols. For a more detailed discussion of background material we refer the reader to [31].

Throughout, Pr[A] will denote the probability of event A. Let $E_1, E_2, \ldots, E_m$ be arbitrary events over a sample space. The well-known De Morgan law states that

$$\overline{\bigcap_{i=1}^{m} E_i} = \bigcup_{i=1}^{m} \overline{E_i} \qquad (9.1)$$

where $\overline{E}_i$ is the event that occurs if and only if E_i does not. In addition, it is known that

$$\Pr\left[\bigcup_{i=1}^{m} E_i\right] \le \sum_{i=1}^{m} \Pr[E_i] \tag{9.2}$$

with equality holding if the events E_is are disjoint.

For example, assume that the stations of an RN have been partitioned into k groups G_1, $G_2, \ldots, G_k$ and that for a given i, $(1 \le i \le k)$, the probability of the event $\overline{E}_i$ that group G_i fails to satisfy a predicate $\mathcal{P}$ is p_i. Now, (9.1) and (9.2) combined guarantee that the probability of the event that all the groups satisfy predicate $\mathcal{P}$ is:

$$\Pr[E_1 \cap E_2 \cap \cdots \cap E_k] = 1 - \Pr[\overline{E_1 \cap E_2 \cap \cdots \cap E_k}]$$

$$= 1 - \Pr[\overline{E}_1 \cup \overline{E}_2 \cup \cdots \cup \overline{E}_k] \ge 1 - \sum_{i=1}^{m} p_i \tag{9.3}$$

Notice that (3) holds regardless of whether or not the events $\overline{E}_i$ are independent.

For a random variable X, $E[X]$ denotes the expected value of X. Let X be a random variable denoting the number of successes in n independent Bernoulli trials with parameters p and $1 - p$. It is well known that X has a binomial distribution and that for every r, $(0 \le r \le n)$,

$$\Pr[X = r] = \binom{n}{r} p^r (1 - p)^{n-r} \tag{9.4}$$

Further, the expected value of X is given by

$$E[X] = \sum_{r=0}^{n} r \cdot \Pr[X = r] = np \tag{9.5}$$

To analyze the tail of the binomial distribution, we shall make use of the following estimate, commonly referred to as Chernoff bound [31]:

$$\Pr\{X > (1 + \delta)E[X]\}$$

$$< \left(\frac{e^{\delta}}{(1 + \delta)^{(1+\delta)}}\right)^{E[X]} \qquad (0 \le \delta) \tag{9.6}$$

We will also rely on the following estimates that can be derived from (9.6):

$$\Pr\{X \le (1 - \epsilon)E[X]\} \le e^{-(\epsilon^2/2)E[X]} \qquad (0 \le \epsilon \le 1) \tag{9.7}$$

$$\Pr\{X \ge (1 + \epsilon)E[X]\} \le e^{-(\epsilon^2/3)E[X]} \qquad (0 \le \epsilon \le 1) \tag{9.8}$$

Let X be the random variable denoting the number of successes in a number $\alpha(n)$ of independent Bernoulli trials, each succeeding with probability p. Clearly, $E[X] = p \cdot \alpha(n)$.

Our goal is to determine the values of $E[X]$ and $\alpha(n)$ in such a way that, for any fixed $f \geq 1$, equation (9.7) yields:

$$\Pr[X < n] = \Pr\{X < (1 - \epsilon)E[X]\} < e^{-(\epsilon^2/2)E[X]} = \frac{1}{f} \tag{9.9}$$

It is easy to verify that (9.9) holds whenever*

$$\begin{cases} (1 - \epsilon)E[X] = n \\ (\epsilon^2/2)E[X] = \ln f \end{cases} \tag{9.10}$$

hold true. From (9.10), we have

$$(E[X])^2 - 2(n + \ln f)E[X] + n^2 = 0 \tag{9.11}$$

Solving for $E[X]$ in (9.11) we obtain:

$$E[X] = n + \ln f + \sqrt{2n \ln f + (\ln f)^2} < n + 2\ln f + o(n + \ln f) \tag{9.12}$$

Equation (9.12) allows the desired determination of $\alpha(n)$. That is,

$$\alpha(n) = pE[X] < pn + 2p \ln f + o[p(n + \ln f)] \tag{9.13}$$

We note here that (9.13) will be used repeatedly in the remainder of this chapter to bound the tail of various binomial distributions.

Finally, we take note of following classic double inequality that will be used frequently in the remainder of this work.

Lemma 3.1   For every natural number n, $(n \geq 2)$, $(1 - 1/n)^n < 1/e < 1 - (1/n)^{n-1}$.

9.4 ENERGY-EFFICIENT PREFIX SUMS PROTOCOLS

The purpose of this section is to discuss energy-efficient prefix sums protocols for single-hop radio stations.

Consider first the case of a single-hop, single-channel RN with n $(n \leq m)$ stations each of which have a unique ID in the range $[1, m]$. Let S_i $(1 \leq i \leq m)$ denote the station with ID i. Note that for some i, S_i may not exist.

We assume that every station S_i stores a number x_i. The well-known prefix sums problem seeks to determine for every S_i the sum of x_js with indices no larger than i, that is,

$$\sum \{x_j \mid 1 \leq j \leq i \text{ and } S_j \text{ exists}\}$$

---

*In this work we let $\ln n$ and $\log n$ denote the natural logarithm and the logarithm to base 2, respectively.

A naive protocol to solve the prefix sums problem in $m - 1$ time slots proceeds as follows: in time slot j, $(1 \leq j \leq m - 1)$, station S_j transmits x_j on the channel, and every station S_i $(j < i)$ monitors the channel. By summing the numbers transmitted, each station can determine the corresponding prefix sum. Observe that this simple protocol is not energy efficient, because the last station S_m has to be awake for $m - 1$ time slots.

We now introduce an energy-efficient protocol to solve the prefix sums problem. When our protocol terminates, the following three conditions are satisfied:

1. Every active station S_i, $(1 \leq i \leq n)$, stores its prefix sum.
2. The last station S_k, such that no station S_i with $i > k$ exists, has been identified.
3. The protocol takes $2m - 2$ time slots and no station is awake for more than $2 \log m$ time slots.

If $m = 1$, then S_1 knows x_1 and the above conditions are verified. Now, assume that $m \geq 2$ and partition the n stations into two groups $\mathcal{P}_1 = \{S_i \mid 1 \leq i \leq m/2\}$ and $\mathcal{P}_2 = \{S_i \mid m/2 + 1 \leq i \leq m\}$. Recursively solve the prefix sums problem in $\mathcal{P}_1$ and $\mathcal{P}_2$. By the induction hypothesis, conditions (1)–(3) above are satisfied and, therefore, each of the two subproblems can be solved in $m - 2$ time slots, with no station being awake for more than $2 \log m - 2$ time slots.

Let S_j and S_k be the last active stations in $\mathcal{P}_1$ and in $\mathcal{P}_2$, respectively. In the next time slot, station S_j transmits the sum $\Sigma\{x_i \mid 1 \leq i \leq j$ and $S_i \in \mathcal{P}_1$ exists$\}$ on the channel. Every station in $\mathcal{P}_2$ monitors the channel and updates accordingly the value of its prefix sum. In one additional time slot, station S_k reveals its identity.

The reader should have no difficulty confirming that when the protocol terminates, conditions (1)–(3) above are satisfied. To summarize, we have proved the following result.

Lemma 4.1 Assuming that the n $(n \leq m)$ stations of a single-hop, single-channel, radio network have unique IDs in the range $[1, m]$, the prefix sums problem can be solved in $2m - 2$ time slots, with no station being awake for more than $2\log m$ time slots.

We next extend the energy-efficient prefix sums protocol for single-channel RNs to the case where k $(k \geq 1)$ channels are available. We begin by partitioning the stations into k equal-sized groups $G_1, G_2, \ldots, G_k$ such that $G_i = \{S_j \mid (i - 1) \cdot m/k + 1 \leq j \leq i \cdot m/k$ and S_j exists$\}$. By assigning one channel to each such group, the instance of the prefix sums problem local to each group G_i can be solved using the protocol for the single-channel case discussed above. By Lemma 4.1, this task can be completed in $2m/k - 2$ time slots, with no station being awake for more than $2 \log m/k$ time slots.

At this point, we have the local sum $\text{sum}(G_i)$ of each G_i and we need to compute the prefix sums of $\text{sum}(G_1), \text{sum}(G_2), \ldots, \text{sum}(G_k)$. This can be done by modifying slightly the protocol described for the single-channel RN. Recall that in the single-channel protocol, the prefix sums of $\mathcal{P}_1$ are computed recursively, and those for $\mathcal{P}_2$ are computed recursively. Since k channels are available, the prefix sums of $\mathcal{P}_1$ and $\mathcal{P}_2$ are computed simultaneously by allocating $k/2$ channels to each of them. After that, the overall solution can be obtained in two more time slots. Using this idea, the prefix sums problem can be solved in

$2m/k + 2 \log k - 2$ time slots, with no station being awake for more than $2 \log m/k + 2 \log k = 2 \log m$ time slots. To summarize, we have proved the following result.

Lemma 4.2 Assuming that the n ($n \leq m$) stations of a single-hop, k channel radio network have unique IDs in the range $[1, m]$, the prefix sums problem can be solved in $2m/k + 2 \log k - 2$ time slots, with no station being awake for more than $2 \log m$ time slots.

The next result specializes Lemma 4.2 to the case of a single-hop, k channel radio network with at most k stations with distinct IDs in the range $[1, k]$.

Corollary 4.3 Assuming that the k stations of a single-hop, k channel radio network have unique IDs in the range $[1, k]$, the prefix sums problem can be solved in $2 \log k$ time slots.

9.5 INITIALIZING A SINGLE-CHANNEL RN

This section presents initialization protocols for single-hop, single-channel, n station radio networks. In Subsection 9.5.1, we focus on the task of initializing a radio network with no collision detection capabilities, where the number n of stations is known in advance. This first protocol terminates, with probability exceeding $1 - 1/f$, in $en + 2e \ln f + o(n + \ln f)$ time slots. In Subsections 9.5.2 and 9.5.3, we turn to the more realistic case where the number n of stations is not known in advance. Specifically, in Subsection 9.5.2 we show that if the collision detection capability is present, an n station radio network can be initialized by a protocol terminating, with probability exceeding $1 - 1/f$, in $4n + 8 \ln f + o(n + \ln f)$ time slots. Finally, in Subsection 9.5.3 we show that if the stations lack collision detection, initialization can be performed, with probability exceeding $1 - 1/f$, in $12n + O[(\log f)^2] + o(n)$ time slots.

9.5.1 Protocol for Known *n* and No CD

Consider a single-hop, single-channel n station RN where the number n of stations is known in advance. The idea of the initialization protocol is quite simple and intuitive. To begin, each station transmits on the channel with probability $1/n$ until the status of the channel is single. At this point, the station that has transmitted receives the ID of 1 and leaves the protocol. Next, the remaining stations transmit on the channel with probability $1/n - 1$ until the status of the channel is single. Again, the unique station that has transmitted in the last time slot receives the ID of 2 and leaves the protocol. This is then continued until all the stations have received their IDs. The details are spelled out as follows.

Protocol `Initialization-for-known-n`
for $m \leftarrow n$ **downto** 1 **do**
   repeat
      each station transmits on the channel with probability $1/m$ ($\star$)
   until the status of the channel is SINGLE;

the unique station that has transmitted in the previous time slot
receives ID number $n - m + 1$ and leaves the protocol
endfor

The correctness of protocol `Initialization-for-known-n` being easily seen,
we now turn to the task of evaluating the number of time slots it takes the protocol to terminate. We say that the current time slot in step ($\star$) is successful if the status of the channel is single. Let X be the random variable denoting the number of stations transmitting in
a given time slot. Then, by virtue of (9.4) and of Lemma 3.1, at the end of this time slot the
status of the channel is single with probability

$$\Pr[X = 1] = \binom{m}{1}\left(\frac{1}{m}\right)^1\left(1 - \frac{1}{m}\right)^{m-1}$$

$$= \left(1 - \frac{1}{m}\right)^{m-1} > \frac{1}{e} \qquad \text{(by Lemma 3.1)}$$

Clearly, protocol `Initialization-for-known-n` requires n successful time slots
to terminate. Let Y be the random variable denoting the number of successful time slots
among the first $\alpha(n)$ time slots in step ($\star$) of the protocol. It is clear that $E[Y] > \alpha(n)/e$.
We wish to determine $\alpha(n)$ such that for every $f \geq 1$

$$\Pr[Y < n] = \Pr\{Y < (1 - \epsilon)E[Y]\} < \frac{1}{f}$$

Now, using (9.13) we obtain $E[Y] = n + 2 \ln f + o(n + \ln f)$ and, therefore, $\alpha(n) = en + 2e \ln f + o(n + \ln f)$.

We just proved that with probability exceeding $1 - 1/f$, among the first $en + 2e \ln f + o(n + \ln f)$ time slots there are at least n successful ones.

Importantly, our protocol does not rely on the existence of the collision detection capability. Therefore, we have the following result.

Theorem 5.1 The task of initializing a single-hop, single-channel n station radio net-
work with known n terminates, with probability exceeding $1 - 1/f$ ($f \geq 1$), in $en + 2e \ln f + o(n + \ln f)$ time slots, regardless of whether or not the system has collision detection capabilities.

9.5.2 Protocol for Unknown n: The CD Case

The idea behind the initialization protocol for the single-channel RN with CD is to construct a full binary tree (each of whose internal nodes has exactly two children) that we
call a partition tree. As it turns out, the leaves of the partition tree are, with high probability, individual stations of the RN. Some leaves may be empty but, as we shall see, this
event has a small probability. The internal nodes of the partition tree are associated with
groups of two or more stations. By flipping coins, these stations will be assigned to the

left or right subtree rooted at that node. For an illustration of a partition tree corresponding to a five-station RN we refer the reader to Figure 9.1.

Each station maintains local variables l, L, and N. Let $\mathcal{P}_i$ denote the group of stations whose local variable l has value i. Notice that the collision detection capability allows us to determine whether a given node is a leaf or an internal node. This is done simply by mandating the stations associated with that node to transmit and by recording the corresponding status of the channel. The details of the initialization protocol follow.

Protocol `Initialization-with-CD`;
each station sets $l \leftarrow L \leftarrow N \leftarrow 1$;
// initialize $\mathcal{P}_1 \leftarrow$ all stations;
while $L \geq 1$ **do**
    all stations in $\mathcal{P}_L$ transmit on the channel;
    if Channel_status = COLLISION **then**
        each station in $\mathcal{P}_L$ flips a fair coin;
        all stations set $L \leftarrow L + 1$;
        all stations that flipped "heads" set $l \leftarrow L$
    else
        if Channel_status = SINGLE **then**
            the unique station in $\mathcal{P}_L$ sets ID $\leftarrow N$ and leaves the protocol;
            all stations set $N \leftarrow N + 1$;
        endif
        all stations set $L \leftarrow L - 1$
    endif
endwhile

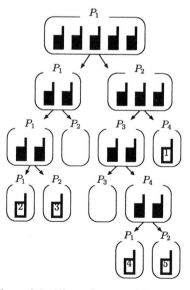

Figure 9.1 Illustrating a partition tree.

To address the correctness of protocol `Initialization-with-CD` we note that no station is associated with more than one node at each level in the partition tree. Moreover, if a station is associated with an internal node of the partition tree, then it is associated with all the nodes along the unique path to the root. Consequently, each station will end up in exactly one leaf of the tree. Since the partition tree is traversed in a depth-first fashion, each station is guaranteed to eventually receive an ID. The fact that N is only incremented when the status of the channel is single guarantees that no two stations will receive the same ID and that the IDs are consecutive numbers from 1 to n.

Next, we now turn to the task of evaluating the number of time slots it takes the protocol to terminate. It should be clear that the total number of nodes in the partition tree is equal to the number of time slots. Thus, we are going to evaluate the number of nodes. Call an internal node of the partition tree successful if both its left and right subtrees are nonempty. It is clear that every partition tree of an n station RN must have exactly $n - 1$ successful internal nodes.

Consider an internal node u of the partition tree that has m ($m \geq 2$) stations associated with it. The probability that an internal node with m stations is partitioned into two subsets is at least

$$1 - \frac{1}{2^{m-1}} \geq \frac{1}{2} \tag{9.14}$$

Let Z be the random variable denoting the number of successes in $g(n)$ of independent Bernoulli trials, each succeeding with probability $\frac{1}{2}$. We wish to determine $g(n)$ such that

$$\Pr[Z < n] = \Pr\{Y < (1 - \epsilon)E[Z]\} < \frac{1}{f}$$

Now, using (9.13) we obtain $E[Z] = n + 2 \ln f + o(n + \ln f)$ and, therefore, $g(n) = 2n + 4 \ln f + o(n + \ln f)$. It follows that, for every $f \geq 1$, with probability at least $1 - 1/f$, the partition tree has at most $2n + 4 \ln f + o(n + \ln f)$ internal nodes. Further, it is well known that a full binary tree with N internal nodes has exactly $N + 1$ leaf nodes. Therefore, with probability exceeding $1 - 1/f$, the partition tree has $4n + 8 \ln f + o(n + \ln f)$ nodes. Consequently, we have proved the following result.

Theorem 5.2   Even if n is not known beforehand, a single-hop, single-channel, n station radio network with CD can be initialized, with probability exceeding $1 - 1/f$, for every $f \geq 1$, in $4n + 8 \ln f + o(n + \ln f)$ time slots.

9.5.3   Protocol for Unknown *n*: The No-CD Case

Suppose that the stations in a subset $\mathcal{P}$ transmit on the channel. If the stations can detect collisions, then every station can determine whether $|\mathcal{P}| = 0$, $|\mathcal{P}| = 1$, or $|\mathcal{P}| \geq 2$. On the other hand, if the stations lack the collision detection capability, then they can only determine whether $|\mathcal{P}| = 1$ or $|\mathcal{P}| \neq 1$.

Next, we show that once a leader is elected, the RN with no-CD can simulate one time slot of the RN with CD in three time slots. In other words, the RN with no-CD can determine whether $|\mathcal{P}| = 0$, $|\mathcal{P}| = 1$, or $|\mathcal{P}| \geq 2$. Let p be a leader.

First, the leader p informs all the remaining stations whether $p \in \mathcal{P}$ or not. After that, the following protocol is executed:

Case 1: $p \in \mathcal{P}$. Since $|\mathcal{P}| \geq 1$, it is sufficient to check whether $|\mathcal{P}| = 1$ or $|\mathcal{P}| \geq 2$. The stations in $\mathcal{P}$ transmit on the channel. If the status of the channel is single, then $|\mathcal{P}| = 1$, otherwise, it must be that $|\mathcal{P}| \geq 2$.

Case 2: $p \notin \mathcal{P}$. By mandating the stations in $\mathcal{P}$ to transmit on the channel we can determine if $|\mathcal{P}| = 1$ or $|\mathcal{P}| \neq 1$. Similarly, by mandating the stations in $\mathcal{P} \cup \{p\}$ to transmit, we can determine if $|\mathcal{P}| = 0$ or $|\mathcal{P}| \neq 0$. These two results combined allow the stations to determine whether $|\mathcal{P}| = 0$, $|\mathcal{P}| = 1$, or $|\mathcal{P}| \geq 2$.

Thus, three time slots are sufficient to simulate the RN with CD if a leader is elected beforehand. For the sake of completeness we now present a leader election protocol for single-hop, single-channel radio networks with no-CD.

Protocol `Election-with-no-CD`
for $i \leftarrow 0$ **to** ∞ **do**
  for $j \leftarrow 0$ **to** i **do**
      each station transmits on the channel with probability $1/2^j$;
      if Channel_status = SINGLE **then**
         the unique station that has transmitted is declared the leader
      endif
  end for
end for

It is clear that protocol `Election-with-no-CD` terminates with the correct election of a leader. Let s be the unique integer satisfying $2^s \leq n < 2^{s+1}$. We say that a time slot is good if $j = s$, that is, if $2^j \leq n < 2^{j+1}$. A good time slot succeeds in finding a leader with probability

$$\binom{n}{1}\left(\frac{1}{2^s}\right)^1\left(1 - \frac{1}{2^s}\right)^{n-1} \geq \left(1 - \frac{1}{2^s}\right)^{2^{s+1}-1} > \frac{1}{e^2} \qquad \text{(by Lemma 3.1)}$$

Thus, by Lemma 3.1 the first t good time slots fail to elect a leader with probability at most

$$\left(1 - \frac{1}{e^2}\right)^t < e^{-t/e^2}$$

On the other hand, the first $s + t$ iterations of the outer **for**-loop, corresponding to values of i between 0 and $s + t - 1$, are guaranteed to contain t good time slots. It follows that the first $1 + 2 + \cdots + (s + t) = O(s + t)^2$ time slots must contain t good ones. Since $s = \lfloor \log n \rfloor$ we have proved the following result.

Theorem 5.3 Protocol `Election-with-no-CD` terminates, with probability exceeding $1 - e^{-t/e^2}$, in $O[t^2 + (\log n)^2]$ time slots.

By taking $t = e^2 \ln f$, we obtain the following result.

Corollary 5.4 Protocol `Election-with-no-CD` terminates, with probability exceeding $1 - (1/f)$, in at most $0.5 \, (\log n)^2 + 3.7 \log n \log f + 13.12 \, (\log f)^2 + o(\log n + \log f)$ time slots.

Corollary 5.4 can be stated more succinctly by absorbing the constants in the big-O notation as follows.

Corollary 5.5 Protocol `Election-with-no-CD` terminates, with probability exceeding $1 - 1/f$, in $O[(\log n)^2 + (\log f)^2]$ time slots.

Recall that, as we just showed, once a leader is available, each time slot of a radio network with CD can be simulated by a radio network with no-CD in three time slots. Thus, Theorem 5.2 and Corollary 5.5 combined imply the following result.

Theorem 5.6 Even if n is not known beforehand, a single-hop, single-channel, n station radio network with no-CD can be initialized, with probability exceeding $1 - 1/f$, in $12n + O[(\log f)^2] + o(n)$ time slots.

9.6 INITIALIZING A *k*-CHANNEL RN

The main goal of this section to provide a natural extension of the results in the previous sections to the case of single-hop, n station radio networks endowed with k ($k \geq 1$) channels. The basic idea is to partition the n stations into k groups of roughly the same size. Each such group is assigned to a channel and initialized independently. Once local IDs within each group are available, a simple prefix sums computation allows the stations to update their local IDs to the desired global IDs. The details of the protocol follow.

Protocol `Initialization-with-k-channels`
Step 1. Each station selects uniformly at random an integer i in the range $[1, k]$. Let $G(i)$ ($1 \leq i \leq k$) denote the stations that have selected i.
Step 2. Use channel i to initialize the stations in group $G(i)$. Let n_i denote the number of stations in $G(i)$ and let $S_{i,j}$ denote the j-th ($1 \leq j \leq n_i$) station in $G(i)$.
Step 3. Compute the prefix sums of $n_1, n_2, \ldots, n_k$ using the first station in each group $G(i)$.
Step 4. Each station $S_{i,j}$, ($1 \leq j \leq n_i$), determines its ID by adding $n_1 + n_2 + \cdots n_{i-1}$ to j.

The correctness of the protocol being easy to see, we now turn to the complexity. Recall that $G(i)$ ($1 \leq i \leq k$) is the group of stations that have selected integer i in Step 1 and let X_i be the random variable denoting the number of stations in group $G(i)$. A particular station belongs to group $G(i)$ with probability $1/k$. Clearly, $E[X_i] = n/k$. Our goal is to determine the value of ϵ in such a way that, for any $f \geq 1$, equation (9.7) yields:

$$\Pr\{X < (1 + \epsilon)E[X_i]\} < e^{-(\epsilon^2/3)(n/k)} = \frac{1}{f} \tag{9.15}$$

It is easy to verify that (9.15) holds when

$$\epsilon = \sqrt{\frac{3k \ln f}{n}} \tag{9.16}$$

Thus, for every $f \geq 1$, with probability exceeding $1 - 1/f$, group $G(i)$ contains at most $(1 + \epsilon)E[X] = n/k + \sqrt{(3n \ln f)/k}$ stations. Now, Theorem 5.2 guarantees that $G(i)$ can be initialized, with probability exceeding $1 - 1/f$, in $4(n/k + \sqrt{(3n \ln f)/k}) + 8 \ln f + o(n + \sqrt{(3n \ln f)/k} + \ln f) = O(n/k + \log f)$ time slots. Put differently, the probability that $G(i)$ cannot be initialized in $O[n/k + \log(fk)] = O(n/k + \log k + \log f)$ time slots is less than $1/fk$.

By (9.3), all the groups can be initialized, with probability exceeding $1 - 1/f$, in $O(n/k + \log k + \log f)$ time slots. Thus, Step 2 terminates, with probability exceeding $1 - 1/f$, in $O(n/k + \log k + \log f)$ time slots. By Corollary 4.3, Step 3 terminates in $2 \log k$ time slots. Further, Step 4 can be completed in one time slot. Thus, we have proved the following result.

Theorem 6.1   The task of initializing a single-hop, k channel, n station radio network with CD terminates, with probability exceeding $1 - 1/f$, $(f \geq 1)$ in $O(n/k + \log k + \log f)$ time slots.

To extend the result of Theorem 6.1 to radio networks with no-CD we note that in Step 2 we need to use an initialization protocol for radio networks with no-CD. The complexity of all the other steps remains the same. Recall that group $G(i)$ has at most $n/k + \sqrt{(3n \ln f)/k}$ stations with probability exceeding $1 - 1/f$. By Theorem 5.6, group $G(i)$ can be initialized, with probability exceeding $1 - 1/f$, in $12(n/k + \sqrt{(3n \ln f)/k]} + O[(\log f)^2] + o[n/k + \sqrt{(3n \ln f)/k]} = O[n/k + (\log f)^2]$ time slots. Steps 3 and 4 can be completed in $O(\log k)$ time slots. Thus, we have the following corollary of Theorem 6.1.

Corollary 6.2   The task of initializing a single-hop, k channel, n station radio network terminates, with probability exceeding $1 - 1/f$, in $O[n/k + \log k + (\log f)^2]$ time slots, even if the system does not have collision detection capabilities.

9.7   ENERGY-EFFICIENT INITIALIZATION PROTOCOLS

The main goal of this section is to present a number of energy-efficient initialization protocols for single-hop, k channel, n station radio networks with collision detection. A key ingredient of these protocols is the energy-efficient prefix sums protocol presented in Section 9.4.

In Subsection 9.7.1 we discuss the details of an energy-efficient initialization protocol for the case where the number n of stations is known beforehand. In Subsection 9.7.2 we develop an energy-efficient protocol that approximates the number of stations in a radio network. This protocol is a key ingredient of the initialization protocol of Subsection 9.7.3. Finally, in Subsection 9.7.4 we extend the results of Subsection 9.7.3 to the case where k ($k \geq 1$), channels are available.

9.7.1 An Energy-Efficient Initialization for Known *n*

The basic assumption adopted in this subsection is that the number n of stations is known beforehand. We show that if this is the case, then with probability exceeding $1 - (1/n)$, a single-hop, single-channel, n station RN can be initialized in $O(n)$ time slots, with no station being awake for more than $O(\log n)$ time slots.

Let $t(n, f)$ be a function such that `Initialization-with-CD` in Section 9.5 terminates, with probability exceeding $1 - 1/f$, in at most $t(n, f)$ time slots. Theorem 5.2 guarantees that

$$t(n, f) \leq 4n + 8 \ln f + o(n + \ln f) \tag{9.17}$$

In outline, our protocol proceeds as follows. Since n is known, the n stations are partitioned into $n/\log n$ groups and each such group is initialized individually. Once the groups have been initialized the exact number of stations in each group is also known. At this point by solving the instance of the prefix sums problem consisting of the number of stations in each group, the stations can update their local ID within their own group to the desired ID. The details are spelled out as follows.

Protocol `Energy-efficient-initialization`
Step 1. Each station selects uniformly at random an integer i in the range $[1, (n/\log n)]$.
Let $G(i)$ denote the group of stations that have selected integer i.
Step 2. Initialize each group $G(i)$ individually in $t(4 \log n, n^2)$ time slots.
Step 3. Let N_i denote the number of stations in group $G(i)$. By computing the prefix sums of $N_1, N_2, \ldots, N_{(n/\log n)}$ every station determines, in the obvious way, its global ID within the RN.

Clearly, Step 1 needs no transmissions. Step 2 can be performed in $(n/\log n)t(4 \log n, n^2)$ time slots using protocol `Initialization-with-CD` as follows: the stations in group $G(i)$, ($1 \leq i \leq n/\log n$), are awake for $t(4 \log n, n^2)$ time slots from time slot $(i - 1) \cdot t(4 \log n, n^2) + 1$ to time slot $i \cdot t(4 \log n, n^2)$. Outside of this time interval, the stations in group $G(i)$ are asleep and consume no power.

As we are going to show, with high probability, no group $G(i)$ contains more than $4 \log n$ stations. To see that this is the case, observe that the expected number of stations in $G(i)$ is $E[N_i] = n \times \log n/n = \log n$. Now, using the Chernoff bound in (9.6), we can write

$$\Pr[N_i > 4 \log n]$$

$$= \Pr[N_i > (1 + 3)E[N_i]]$$

$$< \left(\frac{e^3}{4^4}\right)^{E[N_i]} \qquad \text{(by (6) with } \delta = 3)$$

$$< n^{-3.67} \qquad \text{(since } \log e^3/4^4 = -3.67\ldots)$$

It follows that the probability that group $G(i)$ contains more than $4 \log n$ stations is less than $n^{-3.67}$. Now, (9.3) implies that with probability exceeding $1 - n \cdot n^{-3.67} = 1 - n^{-2.67}$, none of the groups $G(1), G(2), \ldots, G(n/\log n)$ contains more than $4 \log n$ stations. If this is the case, a particular group $G(i)$ can be initialized, with probability exceeding $1 - 1/n^2$), in at most $t(4 \log n, n^2)$ time slots. We note that by (9.17) we have

$$t(4 \log n, n^2) = 16 \log n + 16 \ln f + o(\log n) < 16 \log n + 11.1 \log n + o(\log n)$$

$$= 27.1 \log n + o(\log n)$$

Thus, by (9.3), with probability exceeding $1 - 1/n^2 \cdot n/\log n - n^{-2.67} > 1 - 1/n$, all the groups $G(i)$ will be initialized individually in $t(4 \log n, n^2) \times n/\log n < 27.1 \, n + o(n)$ time slots, with no station being awake for more than $t(4 \log n, n^2) < 27.1 \log n + o(\log n)$ time slots.

Let P_i, $(1 \le i \le n/\log n)$, denote the last station in group $G(i)$. It is clear that as a byproduct of the initialization protocol, at the end of Step 2, each station P_i knows the number N_i of stations in $G(i)$. Step 3 involves solving the instance of the prefix sums problem involving $N_1, N_2, \ldots, N_{(n/\log n)}$. In each group $G(i)$ only station P_i participates in the prefix sums protocol. The prefix sums protocol discussed in Section 9.4 will terminate in $2n/\log n - 2 = o(n)$ time slots, and no station needs to be awake for more than $2 \log n/\log n < 2 \log n$ time slots. To summarize, we have proved the following result.

Theorem 7.1 If the number n of stations is known beforehand, a single-hop, single-channel radio network can be initialized, with probability exceeding $1 - 1/n$, in $27.1 \, n + o(n)$ time slots, with no station being awake for more than $29.1 \log n + o(\log n)$ time slots.

9.7.2 Finding a Good Approximation for $n/\log n$

At the heart of our energy-efficient initialization protocol of an RN where the number n of stations is not known beforehand lies a simple and elegant approximation protocol for $n/\log n$. In addition to being a key ingredient in our subsequent protocols, the task of finding a tight approximation for $n/\log n$ is of an independent interest.

To be more precise, our approximation protocol returns an integer I satisfying, with probability at least $1 - O(n^{-1.83})$, the double inequality

$$\frac{n}{16 \log n} < 2^I < \frac{2n}{\log n} \tag{9.18}$$

It is clear that (9.18) can be written in the equivalent form

$$\log n - \log \log n - 4 < I < \log n - \log \log n + 1 \tag{9.19}$$

Notice that the main motivation for finding a good approximation for $n/\log n$ comes from the fact that protocol `Energy-efficient-initialization` discussed in Subsection 9.7.1 partitions the n stations into $n/\log n$ groups and initializes each group independently. If n is not known beforehand, this partitioning cannot be done. However, once a good approximation of $n/\log n$ is available, protocol `Energy-efficient-initialization` can be used.

Before getting into the technical details of the approximation protocol it is, perhaps, appropriate to give the reader a rough outline of the idea of the protocol. To begin, each station is mandated to generate uniformly at random a number in the interval $(0,1]$. We then partition the stations into (an infinite number of) groups such that group $G(i)$ contains the stations that have generated a number in the interval $(1/2^i, 1/2^{i-1}]$. It is clear that the expected number of stations in group $G(i)$ is $n/2^i$. Now, we let protocol `Initialization-with-CD` run on group $G(i)$ for $t(8i, e^{8i})$ time slots. Clearly, as i increases the number of stations in group $G(i)$ decreases, while the time protocol `Initialization-with-CD` is larger and larger. The intuition is that for some integer i, the number of stations in $G(i)$ is bounded by $8i$ and `Initialization-with-CD` will terminate within the allocated time. We let I be the smallest such integer i. The details of the approximation protocol follow.

Protocol `Approximation`
each station generates uniformly at random a number x in $(0, 1]$
and let $G(i)$, $(i \geq 1)$, denote the group of stations for which $1/2^i < x \leq 1/2^{i-1}$.
for $i \leftarrow 1$ **to** ∞ **do**
    run protocol `Initialization-with-CD` on group $G(i)$ for $t(8i, e^{8i})$ time slots;
    if (the initialization is complete) **and** ($G(i)$ contains at most $8i$ stations) **then**
        the first station in group $G(i)$ transmits an "exit" signal
endfor

We begin by evaluating the number of time slots it takes protocol `Approximation` to terminate. Let I be the value of i when the **for**-loop is exited. One iteration of the **for**-loop takes $t(8i, e^{8i}) + 1$ time slots. By (17), we can write $t(8i, e^{8i}) + 1 < 32i + 64i + o(i) + 1 = 96i + o(i)$. Thus, the total number of time slots needed by the protocol to terminate is at most

$$\sum_{i=1}^{I} [t(8i, e^{8i}) + 1] = \sum_{i=1}^{I} [96i + o(i)] < 48I^2 + o(I^2)$$

Next, we evaluate for each station the maximum number of time slots during which it has to be awake. Clearly, each station belongs to exactly one of the groups $G(i)$ and, therefore, every station is awake for at most $t(8I, e^{8I}) < 96I + o(I)$ time slots. Further, all the stations must monitor the channel to check for the "exit" signal. Of course, this takes I additional time slots. Thus, no station needs to be awake for more than $97I + o(I)$ time slots.

Our next task is to show that I satisfies, with high probability, condition (9.19). For this purpose, we rely on the following technical results.

Lemma 7.2 If i satisfies $1 \le i \le \log n - \log \log n - 4$ then $\Pr[|G(i)| > 8i] > 1 - n^{-2.88}$

Proof: Clearly, $i \le \log n - \log \log n - 4$ implies that

$$2^i \le \frac{n}{16 \log n}$$

and similarly

$$16i < 16\log n \le \frac{n}{2^i}$$

Since the group $G(i)$ consists of those stations for which $1/2^i < x \le 1/2^{i-1}$, the expected number of stations is $E[|G(i)|] = n/2^i$. Using (7) with $\epsilon = \frac{1}{2}$, we can evaluate the probability $\Pr[|G(i)| \le 8i]$ that group $G(i)$ contains at most $8i$ stations as follows:

$$
\begin{aligned}
&\Pr[|G(i)| \le 8i] \\
&< \Pr\left[|G(i)| \le \left(1 - \frac{1}{2}\right)\frac{n}{2^i}\right] &&\text{(since } 16i < n/2^i) \\
&< e^{-(1/2)^3(n/2^i)} &&\text{(by (9.7) with } \epsilon = \frac{1}{2}) \\
&< e^{-2\log n} &&\text{(since } 16\log n \le n/2^i) \\
&< n^{-2.88} &&\text{(since } \log(e^{-2}) = -2.88 \ldots)
\end{aligned}
$$

Thus, $\Pr[|G(i)| > 8i] > 1 - n^{-2.88}$, as claimed. $\square$

Lemma 7.3 If $i = \lfloor \log n - \log \log n \rfloor + 1$ then $\Pr[|G(i)| < 8i] > 1 - n^{-1.83}$.

Proof: If $i = \lfloor \log n - \log \log n \rfloor + 1$ then clearly

$$\log n - \log \log n < i \le \log n - \log \log n + 1$$

This also implies that

$$\frac{n}{\log n} < 2^i \le \frac{2n}{\log n}$$

and that

$$\frac{i}{2} \le \frac{\log n}{2} \le \frac{n}{2^i} < \log n < i + \log \log n < 2i$$

Using these observations, we can evaluate the probability $\Pr[|G(i)| \geq 8i]$ that group $G(i)$ contains at least $8i$ stations as follows:

$$\Pr[|G(i)| \geq 8i]$$

$$< \Pr\left[|G(i)| \geq 4\frac{n}{2^i}\right] \qquad \text{(since } n/2^i < 2i\text{)}$$

$$< \left(\frac{e^3}{4^4}\right)^{n/2^i} \qquad \text{(from (6) with } \delta = 3\text{)}$$

$$\leq \left(\frac{e^3}{4^4}\right)^{\log n/2} \qquad \text{(from } (\log n/2\} \leq (n/2^i)\text{)}$$

$$< n^{-1.83} \qquad \text{(from } \log(e^3/4^4)^{1/2} = -1.83\ldots\text{)}$$

Thus, $\Pr[|G(i)| < 8i] > 1 - n^{-1.83}$ and the proof of the lemma is complete. $\qquad \square$

Lemmas 7.2 and 7.3 combined, imply the following result.

Lemma 7.4 The value I of i when the **for**-loop is exited satisfies, with probability at least $1 - n^{-1.83}$, condition (9.19).

Thus, we have proved the following important result.

Theorem 7.5 Protocol `Approximation` terminates, with probability exceeding $1 - n^{-1.83}$, in $48(\log n)^2 + o(\log n^2)$ time slots, and no station has to be awake for more than $97 \log n + o(\log n)$ time slots. In addition, the integer I returned by the protocol satisfies condition (9.19).

At this point we are interested in extending protocol `Approximation` to the case where k ($k \geq 1$) channels $C(1), C(2), \ldots, C(k)$ are available. The idea of the extension is simple. Having determined the groups $G(1), G(2), \ldots$, we allocate channels to groups as follows. For every i ($1 \leq i \leq k$) we allocate channel $C(i)$ to group $G(i)$ and, as before, attempt to initialize the stations in group $G(i)$. However, this time we allow protocol `Initialization-with-CD` to run for $t(8i, e^{8i}) + 1 = O(i)$ time slots. If none of these attempts is successful, we allocate the channels in a similar fashion to the next set of k groups $G(k+1), G(k+2), \ldots, G(2k)$. This is then continued, as described, until eventually one of the groups is successfully initialized.

We now estimate the number of time slots required to obtain the desired value of I. Let c be the integer satisfying $ck + 1 \leq I < (c+1)k$. In other words, in the c-th iteration, I is found. Then, if $c \geq 1$, the total number of time slots is

$$O(k) + O(2k) + O(3k) + \cdots + O(ck) = O(c^2 k) = O\left(\frac{I^2}{k}\right) = O\left(\frac{(\log n)^2}{k}\right)$$

If $c = 0$, the total number of time slots is $128I = O(\log n)$. To summarize, we state the following result.

Lemma 7.6 In case k channels are available, protocol `Approximation` terminates, with high probability, in $O[(\log n)^2/k + \log n]$ time slots, with no station being awake for more than $O(\log n)$ time slots.

9.7.3 An Energy-Efficient Initialization for Unknown n

The main goal of this subsection is to present an energy-efficient initialization protocol for single-hop, single-channel radio stations where the number n of stations is not known beforehand.

Recall that protocol `Energy-efficient-initialization` partitions the n stations into $n/\log n$ groups and initializes each group individually. Unfortunately, when n is not known, this partitioning cannot be done. Instead, using protocol `Approximation`, we find an integer I which, by Theorem 7.5 satisfies, with probability exceeding $1 - n^{-1.83}$, condition (9.19) and therefore also (9.18). In other words, 2^I is a good approximation of $n/\log n$. Once this approximation is available, we perform protocol `Energy-efficient-initialization` by partitioning the stations into 2^{I+4} groups $H(1), H(2), \ldots, H(2^{I+4})$. Clearly, the expected number of stations per group is $n/2^{I+4}$. If condition (9.19) is satisfied, then we have

$$\frac{\log n}{32} < \frac{n}{2^{I+4}} < \log n$$

In this case, with probability exceeding $1 - 1/n^2$, $t(\log n, n^2) < 15.1 \log n + o(\log n)$ time slots suffice to initialize a particular group $H(i)$.

The obvious difficulty is that, since n is not known, we cannot allocate $t(\log n, n^2)$ time slots to each group. Instead, we allocate $t[2(I + 4), 2^{2I+4}]$ time slots. Note that, if (9.19) is satisfied then $2(I + 4) > \log n$ holds. As a result, with probability at least $1 - (1/n)$, all of the groups can be initialized individually in at most $2^{I+4} \cdot t[2(I + 4), 2^{2I+4}] = O(n)$ time slots, with no station being awake for more than $t[2(I + 4), 2^{2I+4}] = O(\log n)$ time slots.

Of course, once the individual groups have been initialized, we still need to solve an instance of the the prefix sums problem that will allow stations to update their local IDs. By Lemma 4.1 the corresponding prefix sums problem can be solved in $2 \cdot 2^{I+4} - 2 = O(n/\log n)$ time slots, with no station being awake for more than $2 \log (2^{I+4}) = O(\log n)$ time slots. Since condition (9.19) is satisfied with probability at least $1 - O(n^{-1.83})$, we have proved the following important result.

Theorem 7.7 Even if the number n of stations is not known beforehand, an n station, single-channel radio network can be initialized by a protocol terminating, with probability exceeding $1 - 1/n$, in $O(n)$ time slots and no station has to be awake for more than $O(\log n)$ time slots.

9.7.4   An Energy-Efficient Initialization for the *k*-Channel RN and Unknown *n*

The main purpose of this subsection is to present an energy-efficient initialization protocol for single-hop, *k*-channel *n* station radio networks where the number *n* of stations is not known beforehand. Let $C(1), C(2), \ldots, C(k)$ denote the *k* channels available in the RN.

The idea is to extend protocol in Subsection 9.7.3 to take advantage of the *k* channels. Recall that this initialization protocol first runs protocol `Approximation` to obtain a good approximation of $n/\log n$. Once this approximation is available, protocol `Energy-efficient-initialization` is run.

Recall that by Lemma 7.6 in the presence of *k* channels, protocol `Approximation` terminates, with high probability, in $O\{[(\log n)^2/k] + \log n\}$ time slots, with no station being awake for more than $O(\log n)$ time slots.

We can extend the energy-efficient initialization protocol for single-channel RNs discussed in Subsection 9.7.3 to the case of a *k* channel radio network as follows. Recall that we need to initialize each of the groups $H(1), H(2), \ldots, H(2^{I+4})$. This task can be performed as follows: since we have *k* channels, $2^{I+4}/k$ groups can be assigned to each channel and be initialized efficiently. Since each group $H(j)$ can be initialized in $O(I + 4)$ time slots, all the 2^{I+4} groups can be initialized in $O(I + 4) \cdot (2^{I+4}/k) = O(n/k)$ time slots, with no station being awake no more than $O(\log n)$ time slots. After that we use the *k* channel version of the prefix sums protocol discussed in Section 9.4. This takes $2(2^{I+4}/k) + 2 \log k - 2 < (64n/k \log n) + 2 \log k$ time slots, with no station being awake for more than $2 \log(2^{I+4}/k) + 2 \log k$ time slots. Therefore, we have the following result.

Theorem 7.8   Even if the number *n* of stations is not known in advance, a single-hop, *k*-channel *n* station radio network can be initialized, with probability exceeding $1 - O(n^{-1.83})$, in $O[(n/k) + \log n]$ time slots, with no station being awake for more than $O(\log n)$ time slots.

9.8   CONCLUDING REMARKS AND OPEN PROBLEMS

A radio network is a distributed system, with no central arbiter, consisting of *n* mobile radio transceivers, referred to as stations. Typically, these stations are small, inexpensive, hand-held devices running on batteries that are deployed on demand in support of various events including disaster relief, search-and-rescue, or law enforcement operations.

In this chapter, we have surveyed a number of recent results involving one of the fundamental tasks in setting up a radio network, namely that of initializing the network both in the case where collision detection is available and when it is not. The task of initializing a radio network involves assigning each of the *n* stations a distinct ID number in the range from1 to *n*.

A large number of natural problems remains open. First, in practical situations one may relax the stringent requirement of assigning IDs in the exact range 1 to *n* and settle for a somewhat larger range 1 to *m*. This makes sense if *n* is not known and if a tight upper bound m on n is somehow available. It would be of great interest to look at the resulting relaxed initialization problem.

The second way of extending the initialization problem that we discussed is to allow duplicate IDs. This extension is motivated by the fact that in multihop radio networks what is really important is that in some local sense the stations should have unique IDs. Of course, the problem at hand can be stated as a planar graph coloring problem.

Addressing these and other related problems promises to be an exciting area of further work.

ACKNOWLEDGMENTS

This work was supported, in part, by ONR grant N00014-97-1-0526 and by Grant-in-Aid for Encouragement of Young Scientists (12780213) from the Ministry of Education, Science, Sports, and Culture of Japan.

REFERENCES

1. N. Abramson, *Multiple Access Communications: Foundations for Emerging Technologies,* IEEE Press, New York, 1993.

2. N. Abramson, Multiple access in wireless digital networks, *Proceedings of the IEEE, 82,* 1360–1370, 1994.

3. N. Alon, A. Bar-Noy, N. Linial, and D. Peleg, Single-round simulation on radio networks, *Journal of Algorithms, 13,* 188–210, 1992.

4. D. Angluin, Global and local properties in networks of processors, *Proceedings 12th ACM Symposium on Theory of Computing*, 1980, pp. 82–93.

5. H. Attiya, A. Bar-Noy, D. Dolev, D. Peleg, and R. Reischuk, Renaming in an asynchronous environment, *Journal of the ACM, 37,* 524–548, 1990.

6. D. J. Baker, Data/voice communication over a multihop, mobile, high frequency network, *Proceedings MILCOM'97*, Monterey, CA, 1997, pp. 339–343.

7. N. Bambos and J. M. Rulnick, Mobile power management for wireless communication networks, *Wireless Networks, 3,* 3–14, 1997.

8. R. Bar-Yehuda, O. Goldreich, and A. Itai, Efficient emulation of single-hop radio network with collision detection on multi-hop radio network with no collision detection, *Distributed Computing, 5,* 67–71, 1991.

9. R. Bar-Yehuda, O. Goldreich, and A. Itai, On the time-complexity of broadcast in multi-hop radio networks: An exponential gap between determinism and randomization, *Journal of Computer and Systems Sciences, 45,* 104–126, 1992.

10. D. Bertzekas and R. Gallager, *Data Networks*, Second Edition, Prentice-Hall, Upper Saddle River, NJ, 1992.

11. R. Binder, N. Abramson, F. Kuo, A. Okinaka, and D. Wax, ALOHA packet broadcasting—a retrospect, *AFIPS Conference Proceedings*, May 1975, pp. 203–216.

12. U. Black, *Mobile and Wireless Networks*, Prentice-Hall, Upper Saddle River, NJ, 1996.

13. J. L. Bordim, J.Cui, T. Hayashi, K. Nakano, and S. Olariu, Energy-efficient initialization protocols for ad-hoc radio networks, *IEICE Trans. Fundamentals, E-83-A,* 9, 1796–1803, (2000.

14. F. Cristian, Reaching agreement on processor-group membership in synchronous distributed systems, *Distributed Computing, 4,* 54–264 (1991.

15. P. H. Dana, The geographer's craft project, Deptartment of Geography, University of Texas, Austin, Sept. 1999, http://www.utexas.edu/depts/grg/gcraf/notes/gps/gps.html.

16. B. H. Davies and T. R. Davies, Applications of packet switching technology to combat net radio, *Proceedings of the IEEE, 75,* 43–55, 1987.

17. R. Dechter and L. Kleinrock, Broadcast communication and distributed algorithms, *IEEE Transactions on Computers, C-35,* 210–219, 1986.

18. D. Duchamp, S. K. Feiner, and G. Q. Maguire, Software technology for wireless mobile computing, *IEEE Network Magazine,* Nov., 12–18, 1991.

19. W. C. Fifer and F. J. Bruno, Low cost packet radio, *Proceedings of the IEEE, 75,* 33–42, 1987.

20. M. Gerla and T.-C. Tsai, Multicluster, mobile, multimedia radio network, *Wireless Networks, 1,* 255–265, 1995.

21. E. P. Harris and K. W. Warren, Low power technologies: a system perspective, *Proceedings 3rd International Workshop on Multimedia Communications,* Princeton, NJ 1996.

22. T. Hayashi, K. Nakano, and S. Olariu, Randomized initialization protocols for packet radio networks, *Proceedings 13th International Parallel Processing Symposium,* 1999, pp. 544–548.

23. A. Iwata, C.-C. Chiang, G. Pei, M. Gerla, and T.-W. Chen, Scalable routing strategies for ad-hoc networks, *IEEE Journal on Selected Areas in Communications, 17,* 1369–1379, 1999.

24. E. D. Kaplan, *Understanding GPS: Principles and Applications,* Artech House, Boston, 1996.

25. S. Kutten, R. Ostrovsky, and B. Patt-Shamir, The Las Vegas processor identity problem, *Proceedings Second Israel Symposium on Theory of Computing and Systems,* 1993.

26. C. R. Lin and M. Gerla, Adaptive clustering in mobile wireless networks, *IEEE Journal on Selected Areas in Communications, 16,* 1265–1275, 1997.

27. R. J. Lipton and A. Park, The processor identity problem, *Information Processing Letters, 36,* 91–94, 1990.

28. W. Mangione-Smith and P. S. Ghang, A low power medium access control protocol for portable multimedia devices, *Proceedings Third International Workshop on Mobile Multimedia Communications,* Princeton, NJ, September 1996.

29. R. M. Metcalfe and D. R. Boggs, Ethernet: Distributed packet switching for local computer networks, *Communications of the ACM, 19,* 395–404, 1976.

30. A. Micić and I. Stojmenović, A hybrid randomized initialization protcol for TDMA in single-hop wireless networks, unpublished manuscript, 2001.

31. R. Motwani and P. Raghavan, *Randomized Algorithms,* Cambridge: Cambridge University Press, 1995.

32. K. Nakano, Optimal initializing algorithms for a reconfigurable mesh, *Journal of Parallel and Distributed Computing, 24,* 218–223, 1995.

34. K. Nakano, S. Olariu, and J. L. Schwing, Broadcast-efficient protocols for mobile radio networks, *IEEE Transactions on Parallel and Distributed Systems, 10,* 1276–1289, 1999.

35. K. Nakano, and S. Olariu, Energy-efficient initialization protocols for single-hop radio networks with no Collision Detection, *IEEE Transactions on Parallel and Distributed Systems, 11,* 851–863, (2000.

36. M. Joa-Ng and I.-T. Lu, A peer-to-peer zone-based two-level link state routing for mobile ad-hoc networks, *IEEE Journal of Selected Areas in Communications, 17,* 1415–1425, 1999.

37. S. Olariu, I. Stojmenović, and A. Zomaya, On the dynamic initialization of parallel computers, *Journal of Supercomputing, 15,* 5–24, (2000.

38. A. Panconesi, M. Papatriantafilou, P. Tsiagas, and P. Vitányi, Randomized wait-free naming, *Proceedings ISAAC'94*, New York: Springer-Verlag, 1994, pp. 83–91.

39. R. A. Powers, Batteries for low-power electronics, *Proceedings of the IEEE, 83,* 687–693, 1995.

40. R. Ramanathan and M. Steenstrup, Hierarchically organized, multihop wireless networks for quality-of-service support, *Mobile Networks and Applications, 3,* 10–119, 1998.

41. D. Raychaudhuri and N. D. Wilson, ATM-based transport architecture for multiservice wireless PCN, *IEEE Journal on Selected Areas in Communications, 12,* 1401–1414, 1994.

42. A. K. Salkintzis and C. Chamzas, An in-band power-saving protocol for mobile data networks, *IEEE Transactions on Communications, COM-46,* 1194–1205, 1998.

43. R. Sanchez, J. Evans, and G. Minden, Networking on the battlefield: challenges in highly dynamic multihop wireless networks, *Proceedings IEEE MILCOM'99*, Atlantic City, NJ, October 1999.

44. K. Sivalingam, M. B. Srivastava, and P. Agrawal, Low power link and access protocols for wireless multimedia networks, *Proceedings IEEE Vehicular Technology Conference VTC'97*, Phoenix, AZ, May, 1997.

45. M. Stemm, P. Gauthier, and D. Harada, Reducing power consumption on network interfaces in hand-held devices, *Proceedings 3rd International Workshop on Multimedia Communications*, Princeton, NJ, 1996.

46. J. E. Wieselthier, G. D. Nguyen, and A. Ephremides, Multicasting in energy-limited ad-hoc wireless networks, *Proceedings MILCOM'98*, 1998.

CHAPTER 10

Leader Election Protocols for Radio Networks

KOJI NAKANO
Japan Advanced Institute for Science and Technology

STEPHAN OLARIU
Department of Computer Science, Old Dominion University, Norfolk

10.1 INTRODUCTION

A radio network (RN, for short) is a distributed system with no central arbiter, consisting of n radio transceivers, henceforth referred to as stations. In a single-channel RN, the stations communicate over a unique radio frequency channel known to all the stations. A RN is said to be single-hop when all the stations are within transmission range of each other. In this chapter, we focus on single-channel, single-hop radio networks. Single-hop radio networks are the basic ingredients from which larger, multi-hop radio networks are built [3, 22].

As customary, time is assumed to be slotted and all transmissions are edge-triggered, that is, they take place at time slot boundaries [3, 5]. In a time slot, a station can transmit and/or listen to the channel. We assume that the stations have a local clock that keeps synchronous time, perhaps by interfacing with a global positioning system (GPS, for short) [6, 8, 18, 20]. It is worth noting that, under current technology, the commercially available GPS systems provide location information accurate to within 22 meters as well as time information accurate to within 100 nanoseconds [6]. It is well documented that GPS systems using military codes achieve a level of accuracy that is orders of magnitude better than their commercial counterparts [6, 8]. In particular, this allows the stations to detect time slot boundaries and, thus, to synchronize.

Radio transmission is isotropic, that is, when a station is transmitting, all the stations in its communication range receive the packet. We note here that this is in sharp contrast with the basic point-to-point assumption in wireline networks in which a station can specify a unique destination station. We employ the commonly accepted assumption that when two or more stations are transmitting on a channel in the same time slot, the corresponding packets collide and are garbled beyond recognition. It is customary to distinguish among radio networks in terms of their collision detection capabilities. In the RN with collision detection, the status of a radio channel in a time slot is:

NULL if no station transmitted in the current time slot

SINGLE if exactly one station transmitted in the current time slot

Handbook of Wireless Networks and Mobile Computing, Edited by Ivan Stojmenović.
ISBN 0-471-41902-8   © 2002 John Wiley & Sons, Inc.

COLLISION if two or more stations transmitted the channel in the current time slot

The problem that we survey in this chapter is the classical leader election problem, which asks the network to designate one of its stations as leader. In other words, after executing the leader election protocol, exactly one station learns that it was elected leader, whereas the remaining stations learn the identity of the leader. Historically, the leader election problem has been addressed in wireline networks [1, 2, 9, 10, 21], in which each station can specify a destination station.

The leader election problem can be studied in the following three scenarios:

Scenario 1: The number n of stations is known in advance

Scenario 2: The number n of stations is unknown, but an upper bound u on n is known in advance

Scenario 3: Neither the number of stations nor an upper bound on this number is known in advance

It is intuitively clear that the task of leader election is the easiest in Scenario 1 and hardest in Scenario 3, with Scenario 2 being in between the two.

Randomized leader election protocols designed for single-channel, single-hop radio networks work as follows. In each time slot, the stations transmit on the channel with some probability. As we will discuss shortly, this probability may or may not be the same for individual stations. If the status of the channel is SINGLE, the unique station that has transmitted is declared the leader. If the status is not SINGLE, the above is repeated until, eventually, a leader is elected. Suppose that a leader election protocol runs for t time slots and a leader has still not been elected at that time. The history of a station up to time slot t is captured by

The status of the channel—The status of the channel in each of the t time slots, that is, a sequence of {NULL,COLLISION} of length t.

Transmit/not-transmit—The transmission activity of the station in each of the t time slots, that is, a sequence of {transmit,not-transmit} of length t.

It should be clear that its history contains all the information that a station can obtain in t time slots. From the perspective of how much of the history information is used, we identify three types of leader election protocols for single-channel, single-hop radio networks:

1. Oblivious. In time slot i, $(1 \leq i)$, every station transmits with probability p_i. The probability p_i is fixed beforehand and does not depend on the history.

2. Uniform. In time slot i $(1 \leq i)$, all the stations transmit with the same probability p_i. Here p_i is a function of the history of the status of channel in time slots 1, 2, . . . , $i - 1$.

3. Non-uniform:In each time slot, every station determines its transmission probability, depending on its own history.

An oblivious leader election protocol is uniquely determined by a sequence $P = \langle p_1,$

$p_2, \ldots \rangle$ of probabilities. In time slot i ($1 \leq i$), every station transmits with probability p_i. A leader is elected if the status of the channel is SINGLE. Clearly, oblivious leader election protocols also work for radio networks with no collision detection, in which the stations cannot distinguish between NULL and COLLISION.

A uniform leader election protocol is uniquely determined by a binary tree T of probabilities. T has nodes $p_{i,j}$ ($1 \leq i$; $1 \leq j \leq 2^{i-1}$), each corresponding to a probability. Node $p_{i,j}$ has left child $p_{i+1,2j-1}$ and right child $p_{j+1,2j}$. The leader election protocol traverses T from the root as follows. Initially, the protocol is positioned at the root $p_{1,1}$. If in time slot i the protocol is positioned at node $p_{i,j}$, then every station transmits on the channel with probability $p_{i,j}$. If the status of the channel is SINGLE, the unique station that has transmitted becomes the leader and the protocol terminates. If the status of channel is NULL, the protocol moves to the left child $p_{i+1,2j-1}$; if the status is COLLISION, the protocol moves to the right child $p_{i+1,2j}$.

Similarly, a nonuniform leader election protocol is captured by a ternary tree T with nodes $p_{i,j}$ ($1 \leq i$; $1 \leq j \leq 3^{i-1}$), each corresponding to a probability. The children of node $p_{i,j}$ are, in left to right order, $p_{i+1,3j-2}, p_{i+1,3j-1}$, and $p_{i+1,3j}$. Each station traverses T from the root as follows. Initially, all the stations are positioned at the root $p_{1,1}$. If in time slot i a station is positioned at node $p_{i,j}$ then it transmits with probability $p_{i,j}$. If the status of the channel is SINGLE, the unique station that has transmitted becomes the leader and the protocol terminates. If the status of the channel is NULL, the station moves to $p_{i+1,3j-2}$. If the status of channel is COLLISION, then the station moves to $p_{i+1,3j-1}$ or $p_{i+1,3j}$ depending on whether or not is has transmitted in time slot i. Figure 10.1 illustrates the three types of leader election protocols.

Several randomized protocols for single-channel, single-hop networks have been presented in the literature. Metcalfe and Boggs [12] presented an oblivious leader election protocol for Scenario 1 that is guaranteed to terminate in $O(1)$ expected time slots. Their protocol is very simple: every station keeps transmitting on the channel with probability $1/n$. When the status of channel becomes SINGLE, the unique station that has transmitted is declared the leader. Recently, Nakano and Olariu [14] presented two nonuniform leader election protocols for Scenario 3. The first one terminates, with probability $1 - 1/n$ in $O(\log n)$ time slots. (In this chapter, log and ln are used to denote the logarithms to the base 2 and e, respectively.) The second one terminates with probability $1 - 1/\log n$ in $O(\log \log n)$ time slots. The main drawback of these protocols is that the "high probabili-

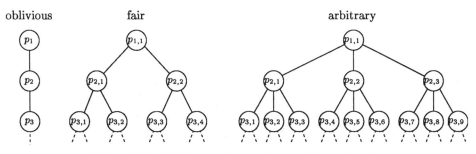

Figure 10.1 Oblivious, uniform, and nonuniform protocols.

TABLE 10.1 A summary of known leader election protocols

Protocol	Scenario	Time slots with probability $1 - 1/f$	Time slots, average
Oblivious	1	$e \ln f$	e
Oblivious	2	$\log u \log f$	$O(\log u)$
Oblivious	3	$O[(\log n)^2 + (\log f)^2]$	$O[(\log n)^2]$
Oblivious	3	$O(f^\epsilon \log n)$	$O(\log n)$
Oblivious	3	$O\{\min[(\log n)^2 + (\log f)^2, f^\epsilon \log n]\}$	$O(\log n)$
Uniform	3	$\log \log n + o(\log \log n) + O(\log f)$	$\log \log n + o(\log \log n)$
Nonuniform	3	$\log \log n + 2.78 \log f + o(\log \log n + \log f)$	$\log \log n + o(\log \log n)$

ty" expressed by either $1 - 1/n$ or $1 - 1/\log n$ becomes meaningless for small values of n. For example, the $O(\log \log n)$ time protocol may take a very large number of time slots to terminate. True, this only happens with probability at most $1/\log n$. However, when n is small, this probability is nonnegligible. To address this shortcoming, Nakano and Olariu [15] improved this protocol to terminate, with probability exceeding $1 - 1/f$ in $\log \log n + 2.78 \log f + o(\log \log n + \log f)$ time slots. Nakano and Olariu [16] also presented an oblivious leader election protocol for Scenario 3 terminating with probability at least $1 - 1/f$ in $O\{\min[(\log n)^2 + (\log f)^2, f^{3/5} \log n]\}$ time slots.

In a landmark paper, Willard [22] presented a uniform leader election protocol for the conditions of Scenario 2 terminating in $\log \log u + O(1)$ expected time slots. Willard's protocol involves two stages: the first stage, using binary search, guesses in $\log \log u$ time slots a number i $(0 \leq i \leq \log u)$, satisfying $2^i \leq n < 2^{i+1}$. Once this approximation for n is available, the second stage elects a leader in $O(1)$ expected time slots using the protocol of [12]. Thus, the protocol elects a leader in $\log \log u + O(1)$ expected time slots. Willard \citeWIL86 went on to improve this protocol to run under the conditions of Scenario 3 in $\log \log n + o(\log \log n)$ expected time slots. The first stage of the improved protocol uses the technique presented in Bentley and Yao [4], which finds an integer i satisfying $2^i \leq n < 2^{i+1}$, bypassing the need for a known upper bound u on n. More recently, Nakano and Olariu with probability exceeding $1 - 1/f$, in $\log \log n + o(\log \log n) + O(\log f)$ time slots. Our uniform leader election features the same performance as the nonuniform leader election protocol of [15] even though all the stations transmit with the same probability in each time slot.

In this chapter, we survey known leader election protocols. See Table 10.1 for the characteristics of these protocols.

10.2 A BRIEF REFRESHER OF PROBABILITY THEORY

The main goal of this section is to review elementary probability theory results that are useful for analyzing the performance of our protocols. For a more detailed discussion of background material we refer the reader to [13].

For a random variable X, $E[X]$ denotes the expected value of X. Let X be a random variable denoting the number of successes in n independent Bernoulli trials with parameter p. It is well known that X has a binomial distribution and that for every integer r $(0 \leq r \leq n)$

$$\Pr[X = r] = \binom{n}{r} p^r (1 - p)^{n-r}$$

Further, the expected value of X is given by

$$E[X] = \sum_{r=0}^{n} r \cdot \Pr[X = r] = np$$

To analyze the tail of the binomial distribution, we shall make use of the following estimates, commonly referred to as Chernoff bounds [13]:

$$\Pr[X > (1 + \delta)E[X]] < \left(\frac{e^{\delta}}{(1 + \delta)^{(1+\delta)}} \right)^{E[X]} \qquad (0 \leq \delta) \tag{10.1}$$

$$\Pr[X > (1 + \epsilon)E[X]] < e^{-(\epsilon^2/3)E[X]} \qquad (0 \leq \epsilon \leq 1) \tag{10.2}$$

$$\Pr[X < (1 - \epsilon)E[X]] < e^{-(\epsilon^2/3)E[X]} \qquad (0 \leq \epsilon \leq 1) \tag{10.3}$$

Let X be a random variable assuming only nonnegative values. The following inequality, known as the Markov inequality, will also be used:

$$\Pr[X \geq c \cdot E[X]] \leq \frac{1}{c} \qquad \text{for all } c \geq 1 \tag{10.4}$$

To evaluate the expected value of a random variable, we state the following lemma.

Lemma 2.1   Let X be a random variable taking a value smaller than or equal to $T(F)$ with probability at least F $(0 \leq F \leq 1)$, where T is a nondecreasing function. Then, $E[X] \leq \int_0^1 T(F)dF$.

Proof: Let k be any positive integer. Clearly, X is no more than $T(i/k)$ with probability i/k for every i $(1 \leq i \leq k)$. Thus, the expected value of X is bounded by

$$E[X] \leq \sum_{i=1}^{k} \left(\frac{i}{k} - \frac{i-1}{k} \right) T\left(\frac{i}{k} \right) = \sum_{i=1}^{k} \frac{1}{k} T\left(\frac{i}{k} \right).$$

As $k \to \infty$ we have $E[X] \leq \int_0^1 T(F)dF$. $\square$

For later reference, we state the following corollary.

Corollary 2.2   Let X be a random variable taking a value no more than $\ln f$ with probability at least $1 - 1/f$. Then, $E[X] \leq 1$.

Proof: Let $F = 1 - 1/f$ and apply Lemma 2.1. We have

$$E[X] \le \int_0^1 \ln \frac{1}{F} \, dF = [F - F \ln F]_0^1 = 1$$

$\square$

10.3   OBLIVIOUS LEADER ELECTION PROTOCOLS

The main goal of this section is to discuss oblivious leader election protocols for radio networks for Scenarios 1, 2, and 3.

10.3.1   Oblivious Leader Election for Scenario 1

Let $P = \langle p_1, p_2, p_3, \ldots \rangle$ be an arbitrary sequence of probabilities and suppose that in time slot i each of the n stations of the RN is transmitting on the channel with probability p_i. If the status of the channel is SINGLE, the unique station that has transmitted becomes the leader. Otherwise, in time slot $i + 1$ every station transmits with probability p_{i+1}. This is repeated until either the sequence P is exhausted or the status of the channel is, eventually, SINGLE. The details are spelled out in the following protocol.

Protocol Election(P)
for $i \leftarrow 1$ to $|P|$ **do**
    each station transmits with probability p_i and all stations monitor the channel;
    if the status of the channel is SINGLE **then**
        the station that has transmitted becomes the leader and the protocol terminates
endfor

Clearly, since every station transmits with the same probability p_i in time slot i, Election(P) is oblivious for any sequence P of probabilities. Since correctness is easy to see, we now turn to the task of evaluating the number of time slots it takes protocol Election(P) to terminate. Let X be the random variable denoting the number of stations that transmit in the i-th time slot. Then, the status of the channel is SINGLE with probability

$$\Pr[X = 1] = \binom{n}{1} p_i (1 - p_i)^{n-1}$$

Simple calculations show that if we choose $p_i = 1/n$, the probability $\Pr[X = 1]$ is maximized. In this case,

$$\Pr[X = 1] = \left(1 - \frac{1}{n}\right)^{n-1} > \frac{1}{e}$$

Therefore, we choose $P = \langle 1/n, 1/n, 1/n, \ldots \rangle$. Now, each iteration of the **for** loop in protocol Election($P = \langle 1/n, 1/n, 1/n, \ldots \rangle$) succeeds in electing a leader with probability exceeding $1/e$. Hence, t trials fails to elect a leader with probability

$$\left(1 - \frac{1}{e}\right)^t < e^{-(t/e)}$$

Let f be a parameter satisfying $1/f = e^{-(t/e)}$. Then, we have $t = e \ln f$. Therefore, we have the following lemma:

Lemma 3.1 An oblivious protocol `Election` $(\langle 1/n, 1/n, 1/n, \ldots \rangle)$ elects a leader in e $\ln f$ time slots with probability at least $1 - 1/f$ for any $f \geq 1$.

Note that the value of n must be known to every station in order to perform `Election` $(\langle 1/n, 1/n, 1/n, \ldots \rangle)$.

10.3.2 Oblivious Leader Election for Scenario 2

The main purpose of this subsection is to discuss a randomized leader election protocol for an n-station RN under the assumption that an upper bound u of the number n of stations is known beforehand. However, the actual value of n itself is not known.

Let D_i $(1 \geq 1)$ be the sequence of probabilities of length i defined as

$$D_i = \left\langle \frac{1}{2^1}, \frac{1}{2^2}, \ldots, \frac{1}{2^i} \right\rangle$$

We propose to investigate the behavior of protocol `Election` when run with the sequence D_i. Can we expect `Election`(D_i) to terminate with the election of a leader? The answer is given by the following result.

Lemma 3.2 For every n, protocol `Election`(D_i) succeeds in electing a leader with probability at least 1–2 whenever $i \geq \log n$.

Proof: The proof for $n = 2, 3, 4$ is easy. For example, if $n = 3$, `Election`(D_2) fails to elect a leader with probability

$$\left[1 - \binom{3}{1}\left(1 - \frac{1}{2}\right)^2\left(\frac{1}{2}\right)^1\right]\left[1 - \binom{3}{1}\left(1 - \frac{1}{4}\right)^2\left(\frac{1}{4}\right)^1\right] = \frac{185}{512} < \frac{1}{2}$$

Hence, `Election`(D_2) elects a leader with probability exceeding $\frac{1}{2}$ for $n = 3$. The reader should have no difficulty to confirm for $n = 2$ and 4. Next, assume that $n > 4$ and let $j = \lceil \log n \rceil$. Clearly, $i \geq j \geq 3$ and thus sequence D_i includes $1/2^{j-2}$, $1/2^{j-1}$, and $1/2^j$. `Election`$(\langle 1/2^{j-2}\rangle)$ succeeds in electing a leader with probability

$$\binom{n}{1}\left(1 - \frac{1}{2^{j-2}}\right)^{n-1}\left(\frac{1}{2^{j-2}}\right) > e^{-n/2^{j-2}}\frac{n}{2^{j-2}} \qquad \left[\text{from } \left(1 - \frac{1}{x}\right)^{x-1} > e^{-1} \text{ for every } x \geq 2\right]$$

$$> \frac{1}{4}e^{-1/4} \qquad \left[\text{from } \frac{n}{2^{j-2}} > \frac{1}{4}\right].$$

Similarly, we can prove that Election($\langle 1/2^{j-1} \rangle$) and Election($\langle 1/2^{j} \rangle$) succeed in electing a leader with probability at least $\frac{1}{2}e^{-1/2}$ and $2e^{-2}$, respectively. Therefore, Election(D_i) fails to elect a leader with probability at most

$$\left(1 - \frac{1}{4}e^{-1/4}\right)\left(1 - \frac{1}{2}e^{-1/2}\right)(1 - 2e^{-2}) < \frac{1}{2}.$$

This completes the proof.   □

Let $D_i^{\infty} = D_i \cdot D_i \cdot D_i \cdots$ be an infinite sequence, where "$\cdot$" denotes the concatenation of sequences. For example, $D_2^{\infty} = \langle \frac{1}{2}, \frac{1}{4}, \frac{1}{2}, \frac{1}{4}, \frac{1}{2}, \frac{1}{4}, \ldots \rangle$. Suppose that every station knows the upper bound u of the number n of the station. Since Election($D_{\lceil \log u \rceil}^{\infty}$) elects a leader with probability at least $\frac{1}{2}$ from Lemma 3.2, t times iteration of Election($D_{\lceil \log u \rceil}^{\infty}$) fails to elect a leader with probability $1/2^t$. Also, the t times iteration runs in $t\lceil \log u \rceil$ time slots. Therefore, we have:

Lemma 3.3   An oblivious protocol Election($D_{\lceil \log u \rceil}^{\infty}$) elects a leader in $\log f \lceil \log u \rceil$ time slots with probability at least $1 - 1/f$ for any $f \geq 1$.

10.3.3   Oblivious Leader Election for Scenario 3

Let $V = \langle v(1), v(2), \ldots \rangle$ be a nondecreasing sequence of positive integers such that $1 \leq v_1 \leq v_2 \leq \cdots$ holds. For such sequence V, let $P(V) = D_{v(1)} \cdot D_{v(2)} \cdot D_{v(3)} \cdots$ be the infinite sequence of probabilities. For example, if $V = \langle 1, 2, 3, \ldots \rangle$, then $P(V) = D_1 \cdot D_2 \cdot D_3 \cdots = \langle \frac{1}{2}, \frac{1}{2}, \frac{1}{4}, \frac{1}{2}, \frac{1}{4}, \frac{1}{8}, \ldots \rangle$. We are going to evaluate the performance Election($P(V)$) for various sequences V.

For a sequence $V = \langle v(1), v(2), \ldots \rangle$, let $l(V)$ denote the minimum integer satisfying $v[l(V)] \geq \lceil \log n \rceil$. In other words

$$1 \leq v(1) \leq v(2) \leq \cdots < v[l(V)] \leq \lceil \log n \rceil \leq v[l(V) + 1] \leq v[l(V) + 2] \leq \cdots$$

holds. Notice that, from Lemma 3.2, each call of Election($D_{v[l(V)]}$), Election($D_{v[l(V)+1]}$), $\ldots$, elects a leader with probability at least $\frac{1}{2}$. Thus, $l(V) + t - 1$ calls Election($D_{v(1)}$), Election($D_{v(2)}$), $\ldots$, Election($D_{v[l(V)+t]}$) elect a leader with probability at least $1/2^t$. Further, the $l(V) + t - 1$ calls run in $v(1) + v(2) \cdots + v[l(V) + t - 1]$ time slots. Consequently, Election($P(V)$) runs in $v(1) + v(2) \cdots + v[l(V) + \log f - 1]$ time slots with probability $1 - 1/f$.

We conclude the following important lemma:

Lemma 3.4   For any sequence $V = \langle v(1), v(2), \ldots \rangle$, Election[$P(V)$] elects a leader, with probability at least $1 - 1/f$ for any $f \geq 1$ in $v(1) + v(2) \cdots + v[l(V) + \log f - 1]$ time slots.

Let $V_1 = \langle 1, 2, 3, \ldots \rangle$ be a sequence of integers. We are going to evaluate the performance of Election[$P(V_1)$] using Lemma 3.4. Recall that

$$P(V_1) = D_1 \cdot D_2 \cdot D_3 \cdots = \langle \tfrac{1}{2}, \tfrac{1}{2}, \tfrac{1}{4}, \tfrac{1}{2}, \tfrac{1}{4}, \tfrac{1}{8}, \ldots \rangle$$

Since $l(V_1) = \lceil \log n \rceil$, Election($P(V_1)$) elects a leader with probability $1 - 1/f$ in $O(1 + 2 + \cdots + [\log n + \log f - 1]) = O[(\log n)^2 + (\log f)^2]$ time slots. Thus, we have the following lemma.

Lemma 3.5   Protocol Election[$P(V_1)$] elects a leader in $O[(\log n)^2 + (\log f)^2]$ time slots with probability at least $1 - 1/f$ for any $f \geq 1$.

For any fixed real number c ($1 < c < 2$) let $V_c = \langle \lceil c^0 \rceil, \lceil c^1 \rceil, \lceil c^2 \rceil, \ldots \rangle$ be a sequence of integers. Clearly, $l(V_c) \leq \lceil \log \log n / \log c \rceil$. Thus, from Lemma 3.4, Election[$P(V_c)$] elects a leader with probability $1 - 1/f$ in

$$O(c^0 + c^1 + \cdots + c^{\lceil \log \log n / \log c \rceil + \log f}) = O(f^{\log c} \log n)$$

time slots. Thus we have:

Lemma 3.6   Oblivious protocol Election[$P(V_c)$] ($1 < c < 2$) elects a leader in $O(f^{\log c} \log n)$ time slots with probability at least $1 - 1/f$ for any $f \geq 1$.

For any two sequences $P = \langle p_1, p_2, \ldots \rangle$ and $P' = \langle p_1', p_2', \ldots \rangle$, let $P \oplus P' = \langle p_1, p_1', p_2, p_2', \ldots \rangle$ denote the combined sequence of P and P'. We are going to evaluate the performance of Election[$P(V_1) \oplus P(V_c)$].

Let Z be a sequence of probabilities such that $Z = \langle 0, 0, 0, \ldots \rangle$. Clearly, Election[$P(V_1) \oplus Z$] and Election[$Z \oplus P(V_c)$] run, with probability at least $1 - 1/f$, in $O[(\log n)^2 + (\log f)^2]$ and $O(f^{\log c} \log n)$ time slots, respectively, from Lemmas 3.5 and 3.6. Thus, Election[$P(V_1) \oplus P(V_c)$] runs in $O\{\min[(\log n)^2 + (\log f)^2, f^{\log c} \log n]\}$ time slots. Therefore, we have:

Theorem 3.7   An oblivious leader election protocol Election[$P(V_1) \oplus P(V_c)$] elects a leader in $O\{\min[(\log n)^2 + (\log f)^2, f^{\log c} \log n]\}$ time slots with probability at least $1 - 1/f$ for any $f \geq 1$.

Note that for a fixed c such that $1 < c < 2$, we have $0 < \log c < 1$. Thus, by choosing small $\epsilon = \log c$, we have,

Corollary 3.8   With probability at least $1 - 1/f$ for any $f \geq 1$, oblivious protocol Election[$P(V_1) \oplus P(V_c)$] elects a leader in $O\{\min[(\log n)^2 + (\log f)^2, f^{\epsilon} \log n]\}$ for any fixed small $\epsilon > 0$.

10.4   UNIFORM LEADER ELECTION PROTOCOLS

The main purpose of this section is to discuss a uniform leader election protocol that terminates, with probability exceeding $1 - 1/f$ for every $f \geq 1$, in $\log \log n + o(\log \log n) + O(\log f)$ time slots We begin by presenting a very simple protocol that is the workhorse of all subsequent leader election protocols.

Protocol Broadcast (p)
   every station transmits on the channel with probability $1/2^p$;
   if the status of the channel is SINGLE **then**
      the unique station that has transmitted becomes the leader and
      all stations exit the (main) protocol

10.4.1   A Uniform Leader Election Protocol Terminating in 2 log log n Time Slots

In outline, our leader election protocol proceeds in three phases. In Phase 1 the calls Broadcast (2^0), Broadcast (2^1), Broadcast (2^2), ..., Broadcast (2^t) are performed until, for the first time, the status of the channel is NULL in Broadcast (2^t). At this point Phase 2 begins. Phase 2 executes a variant of binary search on the interval [0, 2^t] using the protocol Broadcast as follows:

- First, Broadcast ($2^t/2$) is executed. If the status of the channel is SINGLE then the unique station that has transmitted becomes the leader.

- If the status of channel is NULL then binary search is performed on the interval [0, ($2^t/2$)], that is, Broadcast($2^t/4$) is executed.

- If the status of channel is COLLISION then binary search is performed on the interval [($2^t/2$), 2^t], that is, Broadcast ($\frac{3}{4} \cdot 2^t$) is executed.

This procedure is repeated until, at some point, binary search cannot further split an interval. Let u be the integer such that the last call of Phase 2 is Broadcast(u). Phase 3 repeats the call Broadcast(u) until, eventually, the status of the channel is SINGLE, at which point a leader has been elected. It is important to note that the value of u is continuously adjusted in Phase 3 as follows: if the status of the channel is NULL, then it is likely that 2^u is larger than n. Thus, u is decreased by one. By the same reasoning, if the status of the channel is COLLISION, u is increased by one.

   With this preamble out of the way, we are now in a position to spell out the details of our uniform leader election protocol.

Protocol Uniform-election
Phase 1:
   $i \leftarrow -1$;
   repeat
      $i \leftarrow i + 1$;
      Broadcast(2^i)
   until the status of the channel is NULL;
Phase 2:
   $l \leftarrow 0; u \leftarrow 2^i$;
   while $l + 1 < u$ **do**
      $m \leftarrow \lceil (l + u)/2 \rceil$;
      Broadcast(m);

if the status of channel is NULL **then**
    $u \leftarrow m$
else
    $l \leftarrow m$
endwhile
Phase 3:
  repeat
    Broadcast(u);
    if the status of channel is NULL **then**
      $u \leftarrow \max(u - 1, 0)$
    else
      $u \leftarrow u + 1$
  forever

We now turn to the task of evaluating the number of time slots it takes the protocol to terminate. In Phase 1, once the status of the channel is NULL the protocol exits the repeat-until loop. Thus, there exist an integer t such that the status of the channel is:

- SINGLE or COLLISION in the calls Broadcast(2^0), Broadcast(2^1), Broadcast(2^2), ..., Broadcast($2^t - 1$), and
- NULL in Broadcast (2^t).

Let $f \geq 1$ be arbitrary and write

$$s = \lceil \log \log (4nf) \rceil \tag{10.5}$$

To motivate the choice of s in (10.5) we show that with probability exceeding $1 - 1/4f$, s provides an upper bound on t. Let X be the random variable denoting the number of stations that transmit in Broadcast(2^s). The probability that a particular station is transmitting in the call Broadcast(2^s) is less than $1/2^{2^s}$. Thus, the expected value $E[X]$ of X is upper-bounded by

$$E[X] < \frac{n}{2^{2^s}} \leq \frac{n}{4nf} = \frac{1}{4f} \tag{10.6}$$

Using the Markov inequality (10.4) and (10.6) combined, we can write

$$\Pr[X \geq 1] < \Pr[X \geq 4fE[X]] \leq \frac{1}{4f} \tag{10.7}$$

Equation (7) implies that with probability exceeding $1 - 1/4f$, the status of the channel at the end of the call Broadcast(2^s) is NULL confirming that

$$t \leq s \text{ holds with probability exceeding } 1 - \frac{1}{4f} \tag{10.8}$$

Thus, with probability exceeding $1 - 1/4f$, Phase 1 terminates in

$$t + 1 \leq s + 1 = \lceil \log \log(4nf) \rceil + 1 = \log \log n + O(\log \log f)$$

time slots. Since Phase 2 terminates in at most $s + 1 = \log \log n + O(\log \log f)$ time slots, we have proved the following result.

Lemma 4.1 With probability exceeding $1 - 1/4f$, Phase 1 and Phase 2 combined take at most $2 \log \log n + O(\log \log f)$ time slots.

Our next goal is to evaluate the value of u at the end of Phase 2. For this purpose, we say that the call `Broadcast(m)` executed in Phase 2 fails

- if $n \leq 2^m/4(s + 1)f$ and yet the status of the channel is COLLISION, or
- if $n \geq 2^m \cdot \ln[4(s + 1)f]$ and yet the status of the channel is NULL.

We are interested in evaluating the probability that `Broadcast(m)` fails. Let Y be the random variable denoting the number of stations transmitting in the call `Broadcast(m)`. First, if $n \leq 2^m/4(s + 1)f$, then $E[Y] = n/2^m \leq 1/4(s + 1)f$ holds. By using the Markov inequality (4), we have

$$\Pr[Y > 1] \leq \Pr[Y > 4(s + 1)f \cdot E[Y]] < \frac{1}{4(s + 1)f}$$

It follows that the status of the channel is COLLISION with probability at most $1/4(s + 1)f$.
Next, suppose that $n \geq 2^m \cdot \ln[4(s + 1)f]$ holds. The status of the channel is NULL with probability at most

$$\Pr[Y = 0] = \left(1 - \frac{1}{2^m}\right)^n$$

$$< e^{-n/2m}$$

$$\leq e^{-\ln[4(s+1)f]} = \frac{1}{4(s + 1)f}$$

Clearly, in either case, the probability that the call `Broadcast(m)` fails is at most $1/4(s + 1)f$. Importantly, this probability is independent of m. Since the protocol `Broadcast` is called at most $s + 1$ times in Phase 2, the probability that none of these calls fails is at least $1 - 1/4f$. On the other hand, recall that the probability that `Broadcast` is called at most $s + 1$ times exceeds $1 - 1/4f$. Now a simple argument shows that the probability that Phase 2 involves at most $s + 1$ calls to `Broadcast` and that none of these calls fail exceeds $1 - 1/2f$. Thus, we have proved the following result.

Lemma 4.2 With probability exceeding $1 - 1/2f$, when Phase 2 terminates u satisfies the double inequality $\{n/\ln[4(s + 1)f]\} \leq 2^u \leq 4(s + 1)fn$.

Finally, we are interested in getting a handle on the number of time slots involved in Phase 3. For this purpose, let v ($1 \leq v$) be the integer satisfying the double inequality

$$2^{v-1} < n \leq 2^v \qquad (10.9)$$

A generic call $\texttt{Broadcast}(u)$ performed in Phase 3 is said to

- Fail to decrease if $u \geq v + 2$ and yet the status of the channel is COLLISION
- Succeed in decreasing if $u \geq v + 3$ and yet the status of the channel is NULL
- Fail to increase if $u \leq v - 2$ and yet the status of the channel is NULL
- Succeed in increasing if $u \leq v - 3$ and yet the status of the channel is COLLISION
- Be good, otherwise

More generally, we say that the call $\texttt{Broadcast}(u)$ fails if it fails either to increase or to decrease; similarly, the call $\texttt{Broadcast}(u)$ is said to succeed if it succeeds either to increase or to decrease. Referring to Figure 10.2, the motivation for this terminology comes from the observation that if $\texttt{Broadcast}(u)$ succeeds then, u is updated so that u approaches v.

Assume that the call $\texttt{Broadcast}(u)$ is good. Clearly, if such is the case, the double inequality $v - 2 \leq u \leq v + 2$ holds at the beginning of the call. The status of the channel in $\texttt{Broadcast}(u)$ is SINGLE with probability at least

$$\binom{n}{1} \frac{1}{2^u} \left(1 - \frac{1}{2^u} \right)^{n-1} > \frac{n}{2^u} e^{-n/2^u}$$

$$> \min \left(\frac{2^{u+2}}{2^u} e^{-2^{u+2}/2^u}, \frac{2^{u-3}}{2^u} e^{-2^{u-3}/2^u} \right)$$

$$> \min \left(\frac{4}{e^4}, \frac{1}{8e^{1/8}} \right) = \frac{4}{e^4}$$

We note that this probability is independent of u. Thus, if a good call is executed $e^4/4$ $\ln(4f)$ times, a leader is elected with probability at least

$$1 - \left(1 - \frac{4}{e^4} \right)^{(e^4/4)\ln(4f)} > 1 - e^{-\ln(4f)} = 1 - \frac{1}{4f}$$

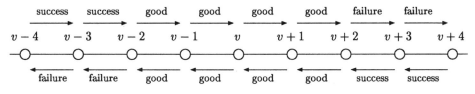

Figure 10.2 The terminology used in Phase 3.

As we are about to show, good calls occur quite frequently in Phase 3. To this end, we prove an upper bound on the probability that the call $\texttt{Broadcast}(u)$ fails. Let Z denote the number of stations that transmit in $\texttt{Broadcast}(u)$. Clearly, $E[Z] = n/2^u$. Thus, if $u \geq v + 2$ then the call $\texttt{Broadcast}(u)$ fails to decrease with probability at most

$$\Pr[Z > 1] = \Pr\left[Z > \frac{2^u}{n} E[Z]\right]$$

$$< \Pr\left[Z > \frac{2^u}{2^v} E[Z]\right] \qquad \text{(from } n \leq 2^v\text{)}$$

$$< \Pr[Z > 4E[Z]] \qquad \text{(from } u \geq v + 2\text{)}$$

$$< \tfrac{1}{4} \qquad \text{[by Markov's inequality (10.4)]}$$

On the other hand, if $u \leq v - 2$ then the probability that $\texttt{Broadcast}(u)$ fails to increase is at most

$$\Pr[Z = 0] = \left(1 - \frac{1}{2^u}\right)^n$$

$$< e^{-n/2^u}$$

$$< e^{-2^{v-1}/2^u} \qquad \text{(from } 2^{v-1} < n\text{)}$$

$$< e^{-2} \qquad \text{(from } u \leq v - 2\text{)}$$

$$< \tfrac{1}{4}$$

Therefore, the call $\texttt{Broadcast}(u)$ fails with probability at most $\tfrac{1}{4}$.

Suppose that $\texttt{Broadcast}(u)$ is executed $\tfrac{8}{3}e^4[\ln(4f) + \log\log\log n]$ times in Phase 3 and let N_s, N_f, and N_g be, respectively, the number of times $\texttt{Broadcast}(u)$ succeeds, fails, and is good among these $\tfrac{8}{3}e^4[\ln(4f) + \log\log\log n]$ calls. Clearly

$$N_s + N_f + N_g = 4e^4(\ln f + \log\log\log n) \qquad (10.10)$$

If at the end of Phase 2 u satisfies the double inequality of Lemma 4.2, we have

$$u \geq \log\left(\frac{n}{4(s+1)f}\right) > \log n - \log(s+1) - \log\log f - 2$$

$$> v - \log\log f - \log\log\log n - \log\log\log f - 4$$

and, similarly,

$$u \leq \log\{n[\ln(4(s+1)f)]\} < \log n + \log\ln(s+1) + \log\ln f + 2$$

$$< v + \log\log f + \log\log\log\log n + \log\log\log\log f + 3$$

Thus, we have,

$$|u - v| < 2 \log \log f + \log \log \log n + 4 \tag{10.11}$$

Referring to Figure 10.2, we note that if $|u - v| \leq 2$ holds at the end of Phase 2, then $N_s \leq N_f$. By the same reasoning, it is easy to see that if (10.11) holds at the end of Phase 2, we have

$$N_s < N_f + 2 \log \log f + \log \log \log n + 2 \tag{10.12}$$

Since a particular call Broadcast(u) fails with probability at most $\frac{1}{4}$, we have

$$E[N_f] \leq \frac{2e^4}{3}[\ln(4f) + \log \log \log n]$$

Thus, the probability that more than $e^4[\ln(4f) + \log \log \log n]$ calls fail is at most

$$\Pr[N_f > e^4(\ln(4f) + \log \log \log n)] < \Pr[N_f > (1 + \tfrac{1}{2})E[N_f]]$$
$$< e^{-1/2^2 \cdot 3E[N_f]}$$
$$< e^{-e^4/24[\ln(4f)+\log \log \log n]}$$
$$< \frac{1}{4f}$$

Suppose that $N_f \leq e^4[\log(4f) + \log \log \log n]$ is satisfied. Then, we have

$$N_g = \tfrac{8}{3}e^4[\ln(4f) + \log \log \log n] - (N_s + N_f)$$
$$\geq \tfrac{8}{3}e^4[\ln(4f) + \log \log \log n] - 2N_f - (2 \log f + \log \log \log n + 2)$$
$$> \frac{e^4}{2} \ln(4f)$$

Therefore, with probability at least $1 - 1/4f$, among $e^4/2[\log (4f) + \log \log \log n]$ calls Broadcast(u) there are at least $\frac{2}{3}e^4 \ln(4f)$ good ones. It follows that if at the end of Phase 2 u satisfies the double in equality in Lemma 4.2, then with probability $1 - 1/2f$, Phase 3 terminates in at most $e^4/2(\log f + \log \log \log n)$ time slots. To summarize, we have proved the following result.

Lemma 4.3 Protocol Uniform-election terminates, with probability at least $1 - 1/f$, in at most $2 \log \log n + o(\log \log n) + O(\log f)$ time slots.

10.4.2 Uniform Leader Electing Protocol Terminating in log log n Time Slots

The main goal of this subsection is to outline the changes that will make protocol Uniform-election terminate, with probability exceeding $1 - 1/f$, in log log $n + o($log

log n) + $O(\log f)$ time slots. The modification is essentially the same as that of `arbitrary-election`.

In Phase 1 the calls `Broadcast`(2^{0^2}), `Broadcast`(2^{1^2}), `Broadcast`(2^{2^2}), ..., `Broadcast`(2^{t^2}) are performed until, for the first time, the status of the channel is NULL in `Broadcast`(2^{t^2}). Phase 2 performs binary search on $[0, 2^{t^2}]$ using `Broadcast` as discussed in Subsection 10.4.1. The reader should be in a position to confirm that $t \leq \lceil \sqrt{\log \log (4nf)} \rceil$ is satisfied with probability at least $1 - 1/f$, for any $f \geq 1$. Thus, Phase 1 terminates in $\lceil \sqrt{\log \log (4nf)} \rceil + 1$ time slots, while Phase 2 terminates in $(\lceil \sqrt{\log \log (4nf)} \rceil + 1)^2$ time slots. Therefore, with probability at least $1 - 1/f$, Phase 1 and 2 combined terminate in $\log \log n + o(\log \log n) + O(\log \log f)$ time slots. Thus, we have the following result.

Theorem 4.4   There exists a uniform leader election protocol that terminates, with probability at least $1 - 1/f$, in $\log n + o(\log \log n) + O(\log f)$ time slots, for every $f \geq 1$.

10.5 NONUNIFORM LEADER ELECTION PROTOCOL

The main goal of this section is to present a nonuniform leader election protocol for single-hop, single-channel radio networks that runs in $\log n + 2.78 \log f + o(\log \log n + \log f)$ time slots. The workhorse of our leader election protocols is the protocols `Sieve` whose details follow.

Protocol `Sieve`(p)
every active station transmits on the channel with probability $1/2^{2p}$;
if the status of the channel is SINGLE **then**
    the unique station that has transmitted becomes the leader and
    all stations exit the (main) protocol
else if the status of the channel is COLLISION **then**
    the stations that have not transmitted become inactive
endif

Using `Sieve`(p), we first discuss a nonuniform leader election protocol terminating in $2 \log \log n + 2.78 \log f + o(\log \log n + \log f)$ time slots. We then go on to modify this protocol to run in $\log \log n + 2.78 \log f + o(\log \log n + \log f)$ time slots.

10.5.1 Nonuniform Leader Election in 2 log log *n* Time Slots

In outline, our leader election protocol proceeds in three phases. In Phase 1 the calls `Sieve`(0), `Sieve`(1), `Sieve`(2), ..., `Sieve`(t) are performed until, for the first time, the status of the channel is NULL in `Sieve`(t). At this point Phase 2 begins. In Phase 2 we perform the calls `Sieve`($t - 1$), `Sieve`($t - 2$), ..., `Sieve`(0). Finally, Phase 3 repeats the call `Sieve`(0) until, eventually, the status of the channel is SINGLE, at which point a leader has been elected.

With this preamble out of the way, we are now in a position to spell out the details of our leader election protocol.

Protocol Nonuniform-election
initially all the stations are active;
Phase 1:
    for $i \leftarrow 0$ **to** ∞
        Sieve(i);
        exit for-loop if the status of the channel is NULL;
Phase 2:
    $t \leftarrow i - 1$;
    for $i \leftarrow t$ **downto** 0
        Sieve(i);
Phase 3:
    repeat
        Sieve(0);
    forever

We now turn to the task of evaluating the number of time slots it takes the protocol to terminate. In Phase 1, once the status of the channel is NULL the protocol exits the for loop. Thus, there must exist an integer t such that the status of the channel is:

- SINGLE or COLLISION in Sieve(0), Sieve(1), Sieve(2), ..., Sieve($t-1$)
- NULL in Sieve(t)

Let $f \geq 1$ be an arbitrary real number. Write

$$s = \lceil \log \log (4nf) \rceil \tag{10.13}$$

Equation (10.13) guarantees that $2^{2^s} \geq 4nf$. Assume that Sieve(0), Sieve(1), ..., Sieve(s) are performed in Phase 1 and let X be the random variable denoting the number of stations that transmitted in Sieve(s). Suppose that we have at most n active stations, and Sieve(s) is performed. Let X denote the number of stations that transmits in Sieve(s). Clearly, the expected value $E[X]$ of X is

$$E[X] \leq \frac{n}{2^{2^s}} \leq \frac{n}{4nf} = \frac{1}{4f} \tag{10.14}$$

Using the Markov inequality (10.4) and (10.14), we can write

$$\Pr[X \geq 1] \leq \Pr[X \geq 4fE[X]] \leq \frac{1}{4f} \tag{10.15}$$

Equation (15) guarantees that with probability at least $1 - 1/4f$, the status of the channel in Sieve(s) is NULL. In particular, this means that

$$t \leq s \text{ holds with probability at least } 1 - \frac{1}{4f} \qquad (10.16)$$

and, therefore, Phase 1 terminates in

$$t + 1 \leq s + 1 = \lceil \log \log (4nf) \rceil + 1 = \log \log n + O(\log \log f)$$

time slots. In turn, this implies that Phase 2 also terminates in $\log \log n + O(\log \log f)$ time slots. Thus, we have the following result.

Lemma 5.1   With probability exceeding $1 - 1/4f$, Phase 1 and Phase 2 combined take at most $2 \log \log n + O(\log \log f)$ time slots.

Recall that Phase 2 involves t calls, namely $\texttt{Sieve}(t - 1)$, $\texttt{Sieve}(t - 2), \ldots,$ $\texttt{Sieve}(0)$. For convenience of the analysis, we regard the last call, $\texttt{Sieve}(t)$, of Phase 1 as the first call of Phase 2. For every i $(0 \leq i \leq t^2)$ let N_i denote the number of active stations just before the call $\texttt{Sieve}(i)$ is executed in Phase 2. We say that $\texttt{Sieve}(i)$ is in failure if

$$N_i > 2^{2^i} \ln(4f(s + 1)) \text{ and the status of the channel is NULL in } \texttt{Sieve}(i)$$

and, otherwise, successful. Let us evaluate the probability of the event F_i that $\texttt{Sieve}(i)$ is failure. From $[1 - (1/n)]^n \leq (1/e)$ we have

$$\Pr[F_i] = \left(1 - \frac{1}{2^{2^i}}\right)^{N_i} < e^{-N_i/2^{2^i}} < e^{-\ln[4f(s^2+1)]} = \frac{1}{4f(s^2 + 1)}$$

In other words, $\texttt{Sieve}(i)$ is successful with probability exceeding $1 - [1/4f(s + 1)]$. Let F be the event that all t calls to $\texttt{Sieve}$ in Phase 2 are successful. Clearly,

$$F = \overline{F_0} \cap \overline{F_1} \cap \cdots \cap \overline{F_t} = \overline{F_0 \cup F_1 \cup \cdots \cup F_t}$$

and, therefore, we can write

$$\Pr[F] = \Pr[\overline{F_0 \cup F_1 \cup \cdots \cup F_t}] > 1 - \sum_{i=0}^{t} \frac{1}{4f(s + 1)} \geq 1 - \frac{1}{4f} \qquad (10.17)$$

Thus, the probability that all the t^2 calls in Phase 2 are successful exceeds $1/4f$, provided that $t \leq s$. Recall, that by (10.16), $t \leq s$ holds with probability at least $1 - 1/4f$. Thus, we conclude that with probability exceeding $1 - 1/2f$ all the calls to $\texttt{Sieve}$ in Phase 2 are successful.

Assume that all the calls to $\texttt{Sieve}$ in Phase 2 are successful and let t' $(0 \leq t' \leq t)$ be the smallest integer for which the status of the channel is NULL in $\texttt{Sieve}(t')$. We note that since, by the definition of t, the status of the channel in NULL in $\texttt{Sieve}(t)$, such an integer t' always exists. Our choice of t' guarantees that the status of the channel must be COLLISION in each of the calls Sieve(j), with $0 \le j \le t' - 1$.

Now, since we assumed that all the calls to Sieve in Phase 2 are successful, it must be the case that

$$N_{t'} \le 2^{2^{t'}} \ln[4f(s + 1)] \tag{10.18}$$

Let Y be the random variable denoting the number of stations that are transmitting in Sieve(0) of Phase 2. To get a handle on Y, observe that for a given station to transmit in Sieve(0) it must have transmitted in each call Sieve(j) with $0 \le j \le t' - 1$. Put differently, for a given station the probability that it is transmitting in Sieve(0) is at most

$$\frac{1}{2^{2^{t'}-1} 2^{2^{t'}-2} \cdots 2^{2^0}} = \frac{1}{2^{2^{t'}-1}} = \frac{2}{2^{2^{t'}}}$$

Therefore, we have

$$E[Y] \le \frac{2N_{t'}}{2^{2^{t'}}} \le \frac{2 \cdot 2^{2^{t'}} \ln[4f(s^2 + 1)]}{2^{2^{t'}}} = 2 \ln[4f(s + 1)] \tag{10.19}$$

Select the value $\delta > 0$ such that

$$(1 + \delta)E[Y] = 7 \ln[4f(s + 1)] \tag{10.20}$$

Notice that by (19) and (20) combined, we have

$$1 + \delta = \frac{7 \ln[4f(s + 1)]}{E[Y]} \ge \frac{7 \ln[4f(s + 1)]}{2 \ln[4f(s + 1)]} = \frac{7}{2}$$

In addition, by using the Chernoff bound (1) we bound the tail of Y, that is,

$$\Pr[Y > 7 \ln[4f(s + 1)]] = \Pr[Y > (1 + \delta)E[Y]]$$

as follows:

$$\Pr[Y > (1 + \delta) E[Y]] < \left(\frac{e}{1 + \delta}\right)^{(1+\delta)E[Y]} = \left(\frac{2e}{7}\right)^{7\ln[4f(s+1)]} < e^{-\ln[4f(s+1)]} < \frac{1}{4f}$$

We just proved that, as long as all the calls to Sieve are successful, with probability exceeding $1 - 1/4f$, at the end of Phase 2 no more than $7 \ln[4f(s + 1)]$ stations remain active. Recalling that all the calls to Sieve are successful with probability at least $1 - 1/2f$, we have the following result.

Lemma 5.2 With probability exceeding $1 - 3/4f$, the number of remaining active stations at the end of Phase 2 does not exceed $7 \ln[4f(s + 1)]$.

Let N be the number of remaining active stations at the beginning of Phase 3 and assume that $N \le 7 \ln[4f(s + 1)]$. Recall that Phase 3 repeats `Sieve`(0) until, eventually, the status of channel becomes SINGLE.

For a particular call `Sieve`(0) in Phase 3, we let N', ($N' \ge 2$), be the number of active stations just before the call. We say that `Sieve`(0) is successful if

- Either the status of the channels is SINGLE in `Sieve`(0), or
- At most $\lceil N'/2 \rceil$ stations remain active after the call.

The reader should have no difficulty confirm that the following inequality holds for all $N' \ge 2$

$$\frac{\binom{N'}{1} + \binom{N'}{2} + \cdots + \binom{N'}{\lceil \frac{N'}{2} \rceil}}{2^{N'}} \ge \frac{1}{2}$$

It follows that a call is successful with probability at least $\frac{1}{2}$. Since N stations are active at the beginning of Phase 3, $\lceil \log N \rceil$ successful calls suffice to elect a leader.

Let Z be the random variable denoting the number of successes in a number α of independent Bernoulli trials, each succeeding with probability $\frac{1}{2}$. Clearly, $E[Z] = \alpha/2$. Our goal is to determine the values of ϵ and α in such a way that equation (10.3) yields

$$\Pr[Z < \lceil \log N \rceil] = \Pr[Z < (1 - \epsilon)E[Z]] < e^{-(\epsilon^2/2)E[Z]} = \frac{1}{4f} \qquad (10.21)$$

It is easy to verify that (21) holds whenever

$$\begin{cases} (1 - \epsilon)E[Z] = \lceil \log N \rceil \\ \frac{\epsilon^2}{2} E[Z] = \ln(4f) \end{cases} \qquad (10.22)$$

hold true. Write

$$A = \frac{\lceil \log N \rceil}{2 \ln(4f)}$$

Solving for ϵ and $E[Z]$ in (22) we obtain:

$$0 < \epsilon = \frac{2}{1 + \sqrt{4A + 1}} < 1$$

and

$$E[Z] = \ln(4f)[2A + 1 + \sqrt{4A + 1}] < \ln(4f)(6A + 2) = 3\lceil \log N \rceil + 2 \ln(4f).$$

If we assume, as we did before, that $N \leq 7 \ln[4f(s + 1)]$, it follows that

$$\lceil \log N \rceil \leq 3 + \log \ln(4f(s + 1)) = O(\log \log \log n + \log \log f)$$

Thus, we can write

$$\alpha = 2E[Z] = 4 \ln f + O(\log \log \log \log n + \log \log f)$$

Therefore, if $N \leq 7 \ln[4f(s + 1)]$ then Phase 3 takes $4 \ln f + O[\log \log \log \log n + \log \log f]$ time slots with probability at least $1 - 1/4f$. Noting that $N \leq 7 \ln[4f(s + 1)]$ holds with probability at least $1 - 3/4f$, we have obtained the following result.

Lemma 5.3 With probability at least $1 - 1/f$, Phase 3 terminates in at most $4 \ln f + O(\log \log \log n + \log f)$ time slots.

Now Lemmas 5.1 and 5.3 combined imply that with probability exceeding $1 - 3/4f - 1/4f = 1 - 1/f$ the protocol Nonuniform-election terminates in

$$2 \log \log n + O(\log \log f) + 4 \ln f + O(\log \log \log n + \log \log f)$$
$$= 2 \log \log n + 4 \ln f + o(\log \log n + \log f)$$
$$< 2 \log \log n + 2.78 \log f + o(\log \log n + \log f)$$

time slots. Thus, we have

Lemma 5.4 Protocol Leader-election terminates, with probability exceeding $1 - 1/f$, in $2 \log \log n + 2.78 \log f + o(\log \log n + \log f)$ time slots for every $f \geq 1$.

10.5.2 Nonuniform Leader Election in log log *n* Time Slots

In this subsection, we modify Nonuniform-election to run in $\log \log n + O(\log f) + o(\log \log n)$ time slots with probability at least $1 - 1/f$. The idea is to modify the protocol such that Phase 1 runs in $o(\log \log n)$ time slots as follows. In Phase 1 the calls Sieve(0^2), Sieve(1^2), Sieve(2^2), ..., Sieve(t^2) are performed until, for the first time, the status of the channel is NULL in Sieve(t^2). At this point Phase 2 begins. In Phase 2 we perform the calls Sieve($t^2 - 1$), Sieve($t^2 - 2$), ..., Sieve(0). Phase 3 repeats Sieve(0) in the same way.

Similarly to subsection 10.4.2 we can evaluate the running time slot of the modified Nonuniform-election as follows. Let $f \geq 1$ be any real number and write

$$s = \lceil \sqrt{\log \log (4nf)} \rceil. \tag{10.23}$$

The reader should have no difficulty to confirm that

$$t \leq s \text{ holds with probability at least } 1 - \frac{1}{4f} \tag{10.24}$$

Therefore, Phase 1 terminates in

$$t + 1 \leq s + 1 = \lceil \sqrt{\log \log (4nf)} \rceil + 1 = O(\sqrt{\log \log n} + \sqrt{\log \log f})$$

time slots. In turn, this implies that Phase 2 terminates in at most

$$t^2 \leq s^2 < (\sqrt{\log \log (4nf)} + 1)^2 \leq \log \log n + \log \log f + O(\sqrt{\log \log n} + \sqrt{\log \log f})$$

time slots. Thus, we have the following result.

Lemma 5.5   With probability exceeding $1 - 1/4f$, Phase 1 and Phase 2 combined take at most $\log \log n + \log \log f + O(\sqrt{\log \log n} + \sqrt{\log \log f})$ time slots.

Also, it is easy to prove the following lemma in the same way.

Lemma 5.6   With probability exceeding $1 - 3/4f$, the number of remaining active stations at the end of Phase 2 does not exceed $7 \ln[4f(s^2 + 1)]$.

Since Phase 3 is the same as `Nonuniform-election`, we have the following theorem.

Theorem 5.7   There exists a nonuniform leader election protocol terminating in $\log \log n + 2.78 \log \log f + o(\log \log n + \log f)$ time slots with probability at least $1 - 1/f$ for any $f \geq 1$.

10.6   CONCLUDING REMARKS AND OPEN PROBLEMS

A radio network is a distributed system with no central arbiter, consisting of n radio transceivers, referred to as stations. The main goal of this chapter was to survey a number of recent leader election protocols for single-channel, single-hop radio networks.

Throughout the chapter we assumed that the stations are identical and cannot be distinguished by serial or manufacturing number. In this set-up, the leader election problem asks to designate one of the stations as leader.

In each time slot, the stations transmit on the channel with some probability until, eventually, one of the stations is declared leader. The history of a station up to time slot t is captured by the status of the channel and the transmission activity of the station in each of the t time slots.

From the perspective of how much of the history information is used, we identified three types of leader election protocols for single-channel, single-hop radio networks: oblivious if no history information is used, uniform if only the history of the status of the channel is used, and nonuniform if the stations use both the status of channel and the transmission activity.

We noted that by extending the leader election protocols for single-hop radio networks discussed in this chapter, one can obtain clustering protocols for multihop radio networks, in which every cluster consists of one local leader and a number of stations that are one hop away from the leader. Thus, every cluster is a two-hop subnetwork [18]. We note that a number of issues are still open. For example, it is highly desirable to elect as a leader of a cluster a station that is "optimal" in some sense. One optimality criterion would be a central position within the cluster. Yet another nontrivial and very important such criterion is to elect as local leader a station that has the largest remaining power level.

ACKNOWLEDGMENTS

Work was supported, in part, by the NSF grant CCR-9522093, by ONR grant N00014-97-1-0526, and by Grant-in-Aid for Encouragement of Young Scientists (12780213) from the Ministry of Education, Science, Sports, and Culture of Japan.

REFERENCES

1. H. Abu-Amara, Fault-tolerant distributed algorithms for election in complete networks, *IEEE Transactions on Computers, C-37,* 449–453, 1988.

2. Y. Afek and E. Gafni, Time and message bounds for election in synchronous and asynchronous complete networks, *SIAM Journal on Computing, 20,* 376–394, 1991.

3. R. Bar-Yehuda, O. Goldreich, and A. Itai, Efficient emulation of single-hop radio network with collision detection on multi-hop radio network with no collision detection, *Distributed Computing, 5,* 67–71, 1991.

4. J. Bentley and A. Yao, An almost optimal algorithm for unbounded search, *Information Processing Letters, 5,* 82–87, 1976.

5. D. Bertzekas and R. Gallager, *Data Networks,* 2nd Edition, Upper Saddle River, NJ: Prentice-Hall, 1992.

6. P. H. Dana, The geographer's craft project, Deptartment of Geography, University of Texas, Austin, Sept. 1999, http://www.utexas.edu/depts/grg/gcraf/notes/gps/gps.html.

7. H. El-Rewini and T. G. Lewis, *Distributed and Parallel Computing,* Greenwich: Manning, 1998.

8. E. D. Kaplan, *Understanding GPS: Principles and Applications,* Boston: Artech House, 1996.

9. E. Korach, S. Moran, and S. Zaks, Optimal lower bounds for some distributed algorithms for a complete network of processors, *Theoretical Computer Science, 64,* 125–132, 1989.

10. M. C. Loui, T. A. Matsushita, and D. B. West, Election in complete networks with a sense of direction, *Information Processing Letters, 22,* 185–187, 1986.

11. N. Lynch, *Distributed Algorithms,* Morgan Kaufmann Publishers, 1996.

12. R. M. Metcalfe and D. R. Boggs, Ethernet: distributed packet switching for local computer networks, *Communications of the ACM, 19,* 395–404, 1976.

13. R. Motwani and P. Raghavan, *Randomized Algorithms,* Cambridge: Cambridge University Press, 1995.

14. K. Nakano and S. Olariu, Randomized $O(\log \log n)$-round leader election protocols in radio networks, *Proceedings of International Symposium on Algorithms and Computation* (LNCS 1533), 209–218, 1998.

15. K. Nakano and S. Olariu, Randomized leader election protocols for ad-hoc networks, *Proceedings of Sirocco 7,* June 2000, 253–267.

16. K. Nakano and S. Olariu, Randomized leader election protocols in radio networks with no collision detection, *Proceedings of International Symposium on Algorithms and Computation,* 362–373, 2000.

17. K. Nakano and S. Olariu, Uniform leader election protocols for radio networks, unpublished manuscript.

18. M. Joa-Ng and I.-T. Lu, A peer-to-peer zone-based two-level link state routing for mobile ad-hoc networks, *IEEE Journal of Selected Areas in Communications, 17,* 1415–1425, 1999.

19. B. Parhami, *Introduction to Parallel Processing,* New York: Plenum Publishing, 1999.

20. B. Parkinson and S. Gilbert, NAVSTAR: global positioning system—Ten years later, *Proceedings of the IEEE,* 1177–1186, 1983.

21. G. Singh, Leader election in complete networks, *Proc. ACM Symposium on Principles of Distributed Computing,* 179–190, 1992.

22. D. E. Willard, Log-logarithmic selection resolution protocols in a multiple access channel, *SIAM Journal on Computing, 15,* 468–477, 1986.

CHAPTER 11

Data Broadcast

JIANLIANG XU and DIK-LUN LEE
Department of Computer Science, Hong Kong University of Science and Technology

QINGLONG HU
IBM Silicon Valley Laboratory, San Jose, California

WANG-CHIEN LEE
Verizon Laboratories, Waltham, Massachusetts

11.1 INTRODUCTION

We have been witnessing in the past few years the rapid growth of wireless data applications in the commercial market thanks to the advent of wireless devices, wireless high-speed networks, and supporting software technologies. We envisage that in the near future, a large number of mobile users carrying portable devices (e.g., palmtops, laptops, PDAs, WAP phones, etc.) will be able to access a variety of information from anywhere and at any time. The types of information that may become accessible wirelessly are boundless and include news, stock quotes, airline schedules, and weather and traffic information, to name but a few.

There are two fundamental information delivery methods for wireless data applications: point-to-point access and broadcast. In point-to-point access, a logical channel is established between the client and the server. Queries are submitted to the server and results are returned to the client in much the same way as in a wired network. In broadcast, data are sent simultaneously to all users residing in the broadcast area. It is up to the client to select the data it wants. Later we will see that in a special kind of broadcast system, namely on-demand broadcast, the client can also submit queries to the server so that the data it wants are guaranteed to be broadcast.

Compared with point-to-point access, broadcast is a more attractive method for several reasons:

- A single broadcast of a data item can satisfy all the outstanding requests for that item simultaneously. As such, broadcast can scale up to an arbitrary number of users.

- Mobile wireless environments are characterized by asymmetric communication, i.e., the downlink communication capacity is much greater than the uplink communication capacity. Data broadcast can take advantage of the large downlink capacity when delivering data to clients.

Handbook of Wireless Networks and Mobile Computing, Edited by Ivan Stojmenović.
ISBN 0-471-41902-8   © 2002 John Wiley & Sons, Inc.

- A wireless communication system essentially employs a broadcast component to deliver information. Thus, data broadcast can be implemented without introducing any additional cost.

Although point-to-point and broadcast systems share many concerns, such as the need to improve response time while conserving power and bandwidth consumption, this chapter focuses on broadcast systems only.

Access efficiency and power conservation are two critical issues in any wireless data system. Access efficiency concerns how fast a request is satisfied, and power conservation concerns how to reduce a mobile client's power consumption when it is accessing the data it wants. The second issue is important because of the limited battery power on mobile clients, which ranges from only a few hours to about half a day under continuous use. Moreover, only a modest improvement in battery capacity of 20–30% can be expected over the next few years [30]. In the literature, two basic performance metrics, namely access time and tune-in time, are used to measure access efficiency and power conservation for a broadcast system, respectively:

- Access time is the time elapsed between the moment when a query is issued and the moment when it is satisfied.
- Tune-in time is the time a mobile client stays active to receive the requested data items.

Obviously, broadcasting irrelevant data items increases client access time and, hence, deteriorates the efficiency of a broadcast system. A broadcast schedule, which determines what is to be broadcast by the server and when, should be carefully designed. There are three kinds of broadcast models, namely push-based broadcast, on-demand (or pull-based) broadcast, and hybrid broadcast. In push-based broadcast [1, 12], the server disseminates information using a periodic/aperiodic broadcast program (generally without any intervention of clients); in on-demand broadcast [5, 6], the server disseminates information based on the outstanding requests submitted by clients; in hybrid broadcast [4, 16, 21], push-based broadcast and on-demand data deliveries are combined to complement each other. Consequently, there are three kinds of data scheduling methods (i.e., push-based scheduling, on-demand scheduling, and hybrid scheduling) corresponding to these three data broadcast models.

In data broadcast, to retrieve a data item, a mobile client has to continuously monitor the broadcast until the data item of interest arrives. This will consume a lot of battery power since the client has to remain active during its waiting time. A solution to this problem is air indexing. The basic idea is that by including auxiliary information about the arrival times of data items on the broadcast channel, mobile clients are able to predict the arrivals of their desired data. Thus, they can stay in the power saving mode and tune into the broadcast channel only when the data items of interest to them arrive. The drawback of this solution is that broadcast cycles are lengthened due to additional indexing information. As such, there is a trade-off between access time and tune-in time. Several indexing techniques for wireless data broadcast have been introduced to conserve battery power while maintaining short access latency. Among these techniques, index tree [18] and signature [22] are two representative methods for indexing broadcast channels.

The rest of this chapter is organized as follows. Various data scheduling techniques are discussed for push-based, on-demand, and hybrid broadcast models in Section 11.2. In Section 11.3, air indexing techniques are introduced for single-attribute and multiattribute queries. Section 11.4 discusses some other issues of wireless data broadcast, such as semantic broadcast, fault-tolerant broadcast, and update handling. Finally, this chapter is summarized in Section 11.5.

11.2 DATA SCHEDULING

11.2.1 Push-Based Data Scheduling

In push-based data broadcast, the server broadcasts data proactively to all clients according to the broadcast program generated by the data scheduling algorithm. The broadcast program essentially determines the order and frequencies that the data items are broadcast in. The scheduling algorithm may make use of precompiled access profiles in determining the broadcast program. In the following, four typical methods for push-based data scheduling are described, namely flat broadcast, probabilistic-based broadcast, broadcast disks, and optimal scheduling.

11.2.1.1 Flat Broadcast
The simplest scheme for data scheduling is flat broadcast. With a flat broadcast program, all data items are broadcast in a round robin manner. The access time for every data item is the same, i.e., half of the broadcast cycle. This scheme is simple, but its performance is poor in terms of average access time when data access probabilities are skewed.

11.2.1.2 Probabilistic-Based Broadcast
To improve performance for skewed data access, the probabilistic-based broadcast [38] selects an item i for inclusion in the broadcast program with probability f_i, where f_i is determined by the access probabilities of the items. The best setting for f_i is given by the following formula [38]:

$$f_i = \frac{\sqrt{q_i}}{\sum_{j=1}^{N} \sqrt{q_j}} \tag{11.1}$$

where q_j is the access probability for item j, and N is the number of items in the database. A drawback of the probabilistic-based broadcast approach is that it may have an arbitrarily large access time for a data item. Furthermore, this scheme shows inferior performance compared to other algorithms for skewed broadcast [38].

11.2.1.3 Broadcast Disks
A hierarchical dissemination architecture, called broadcast disk (Bdisk), was introduced in [1]. Data items are assigned to different logical disks so that data items in the same range of access probabilities are grouped on the same disk. Data items are then selected from the disks for broadcast according to the relative broadcast frequencies assigned to the disks. This is achieved by further dividing each disk into smaller, equal-size units

called chunks, broadcasting a chunk from each disk each time, and cycling through all the chunks sequentially over all the disks. A minor cycle is defined as a subcycle consisting of one chunk from each disk. Consequently, data items in a minor cycle are repeated only once. The number of minor cycles in a broadcast cycle equals the least common multiple (LCM) of the relative broadcast frequencies of the disks. Conceptually, the disks can be conceived as real physical disks spinning at different speeds, with the faster disks placing more instances of their data items on the broadcast channel. The algorithm that generates broadcast disks is given below.

Broadcast Disks Generation Algorithm {
   Order the items in decreasing order of access popularities;
   Allocate items in the same range of access probabilities on a different *disk*;
   Choose the relative broadcast frequency *rel_freq(i)* (in integer) for each disk i;
   Split each disk into a number of smaller, equal-size chunks:
      Calculate *max_chunks* as the LCM of the relative frequencies;
      Split each disk i into *num_chunk(i)* = *max_chunks/rel_freq(i)* chunks; let C_{ij} be the
      jth chunk in disk i;
   Create the broadcast program by interleaving the chunks of each disk:
   for i = 0 to *max_chunks* − 1
   {
      for j = 0 to *num_disks*
         broadcast chunk $C_{j,(i \bmod num\_chunks(j))}$;
   }

Figure 11.1 illustrates an example in which seven data items are divided into three groups of similar access probabilities and assigned to three separate disks in the broad-

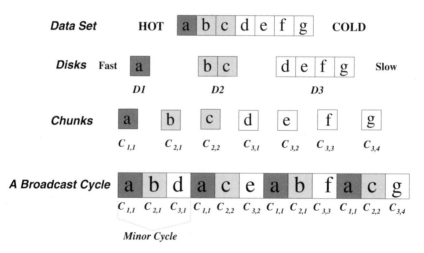

Figure 11.1   An Example of a seven-item, three-disk broadcast program.

cast. These three disks are interleaved in a single broadcast cycle. The first disk rotates at a speed twice as fast as the second one and four times as fast as the slowest disk (the third disk). The resulting broadcast cycle consists of four minor cycles.

We can observe that the Bdisk method can be used to construct a fine-grained memory hierarchy such that items of higher popularities are broadcast more frequently by varying the number of the disks, the size, relative spinning speed, and the assigned data items of each disk.

11.2.1.4 Optimal Push Scheduling

Optimal broadcast schedules have been studied in [12, 34, 37, 38]. Hameed and Vaidya [12] discovered a square-root rule for minimizing access latency (note that a similar rule was proposed in a previous work [38], which considered fixed-size data items only). The rule states that the minimum overall expected access latency is achieved when the following two conditions are met:

1. Instances of each data item are equally spaced on the broadcast channel
2. The spacing s_i of two consecutive instances of each item i is proportional to the square root of its length l_i and inversely proportional to the square root of its access probability q_i, i.e.,

$$s_i \propto \sqrt{l_i/q_i} \qquad (11.2)$$

or

$$s_i^2 \frac{q_i}{l_i} = \text{constant} \qquad (11.3)$$

Since these two conditions are not always simultaneously achievable, the online scheduling algorithm can only approximate the theoretical results. An efficient heuristic scheme was introduced in [37]. This scheme maintains two variables, B_i and C_i, for each item i. B_i is the earliest time at which the next instance of item i should begin transmission and $C_i = B_i + s_i$. C_i could be interpreted as the "suggested worse-case completion time" for the next transmission of item i. Let N be the number of items in the database and T be the current time. The heuristic online scheduling algorithm is given below.

Heuristic Algorithm for Optimal Push Scheduling {
 Calculate optimal spacing s_i for each item i using Equation (11.2);
 Initialize $T = 0$, $B_i = 0$, and $C_i = s_i$, $i = 1, 2, \ldots, N$;
 While (the system is not terminated){
  Determine a set of item $S = \{i | B_i \leq T, 1 \leq i \leq N\}$;
  Select to broadcast the item $i_{\min}$ with the min C_i value in S (break ties arbitrarily);
  $B_{i_{\min}} = C_{i_{\min}}$;
  $C_{i_{\min}} = B_{i_{\min}} + s_{i_{\min}}$;
  Wait for the completion of transmission for item $i_{\min}$;
  $T = T + l_{i_{\min}}$;
 }
}

This algorithm has a complexity of $O(\log N)$ for each scheduling decision. Simulation results show that this algorithm performs close to the analytical lower bounds [37].

In [12], a low-overhead, bucket-based scheduling algorithm based on the square root rule was also provided. In this strategy, the database is partitioned into several buckets, which are kept as cyclical queues. The algorithm chooses to broadcast the first item in the bucket for which the expression $[T - R(I_m)]^2 q_m / l_m$ evaluates to the largest value. In the expression, T is the current time, $R(i)$ is the time at which an instance of item i was most recently transmitted, I_m is the first item in bucket m, and q_m and l_m are average values of q_i's and l_i's for the items in bucket m. Note that the expression $[T - R(I_m)]^2 q_m / l_m$ is similar to equation (11.3). The bucket-based scheduling algorithm is similar to the Bdisk approach, but in contrast to the Bdisk approach, which has a fixed broadcast schedule, the bucket-based algorithm schedules the items online. As a result, they differ in the following aspects. First, a broadcast program generated using the Bdisk approach is periodic, whereas the bucket-based algorithm cannot guarantee that. Second, in the bucket-based algorithm, every broadcast instance is filled up with some data based on the scheduling decision, whereas the Bdisk approach may create "holes" in its broadcast program. Finally, the broadcast frequency for each disk is chosen manually in the Bdisk approach, whereas the broadcast frequency for each item is obtained analytically to achieve the optimal overall system performance in the bucket-based algorithm. Regrettably, no study has been carried out to compare their performance.

In a separate study [33], the broadcast system was formulated as a deterministic Markov decision process (MDP). Su and Tassiulas [33] proposed a class of algorithms called priority index policies with length (PIPWL-γ), which broadcast the item with the largest $(p_i/l_i)^\gamma [T - R(i)]$, where the parameters are defined as above. In the simulation experiments, PIPWL-0.5 showed a better performance than the other settings did.

11.2.2 On-Demand Data Scheduling

As can be seen, push-based wireless data broadcasts are not tailored to a particular user's needs but rather satisfy the needs of the majority. Further, push-based broadcasts are not scalable to a large database size and react slowly to workload changes. To alleviate these problems, many recent research studies on wireless data dissemination have proposed using on-demand data broadcast (e.g., [5, 6, 13, 34]).

A wireless on-demand broadcast system supports both broadcast and on-demand services through a broadcast channel and a low-bandwidth uplink channel. The uplink channel can be a wired or a wireless link. When a client needs a data item, it sends to the server an on-demand request for the item through the uplink. Client requests are queued up (if necessary) at the server upon arrival. The server repeatedly chooses an item from among the outstanding requests, broadcasts it over the broadcast channel, and removes the associated request(s) from the queue. The clients monitor the broadcast channel and retrieve the item(s) they require.

The data scheduling algorithm in on-demand broadcast determines which request to service from its queue of waiting requests at every broadcast instance. In the following, on-demand scheduling techniques for fixed-size items and variable-size items, and energy-efficient on-demand scheduling are described.

11.2.2.1 On-Demand Scheduling for Equal-Size Items

Early studies on on-demand scheduling considered only equal-size data items. The average access time performance was used as the optimization objective. In [11] (also described in [38]), three scheduling algorithms were proposed and compared to the FCFS algorithm:

1. First-Come-First-Served (FCFS): Data items are broadcast in the order of their requests. This scheme is simple, but it has a poor average access performance for skewed data requests.

2. Most Requests First (MRF): The data item with the largest number of pending requests is broadcast first; ties are broken in an arbitrary manner.

3. MRF Low (MRFL) is essentially the same as MRF, but it breaks ties in favor of the item with the lowest request probability.

4. Longest Wait First (LWF): The data item with the largest total waiting time, i.e., the sum of the time that all pending requests for the item have been waiting, is chosen for broadcast.

Numerical results presented in [11] yield the following observations. When the load is light, the average access time is insensitive to the scheduling algorithm used. This is expected because few scheduling decisions are required in this case. As the load increases, MRF yields the best access time performance when request probabilities on the items are equal. When request probabilities follow the Zipf distribution [42], LWF has the best performance and MRFL is close to LWF. However, LWF is not a practical algorithm for a large system. This is because at each scheduling decision, it needs to recalculate the total accumulated waiting time for every item with pending requests in order to decide which one to broadcast. Thus, MRFL was suggested as a low-overhead replacement of LWF in [11].

However, it was observed in [6] that MRFL has a performance as poor as MRF for a large database system. This is because, for large databases, the opportunity for tie-breaking diminishes and thus MRFL degenerates to MRF. Consequently, a low-overhead and scalable approach called $R \times W$ was proposed in [6]. The $R \times W$ algorithm schedules for the next broadcast the item with the maximal $R \times W$ value, where R is the number of outstanding requests for that item and W is the amount of time that the oldest of those requests has been waiting for. Thus, $R \times W$ broadcasts an item either because it is very popular or because there is at least one request that has waited for a long time. The method could be implemented inexpensively by maintaining the outstanding requests in two sorted orders, one ordered by R values and the other ordered by W values. In order to avoid exhaustive search of the service queue, a pruning technique was proposed to find the maximal $R \times W$ value. Simulation results show that the performance of the $R \times W$ is close to LWF, meaning that it is a good alternative for LWF when scheduling complexity is a major concern.

To further improve scheduling overheads, a parameterized algorithm was developed based on $R \times W$. The parameterized $R \times W$ algorithm selects the first item it encounters in the searching process whose $R \times W$ value is greater than or equal to $\alpha \times$ threshold, where

α is a system parameter and threshold is the running average of the $R \times W$ values of the requests that have been serviced. Varying the α parameter can adjust the performance tradeoff between access time and scheduling overhead. For example, in the extreme case where $\alpha = 0$, this scheme selects the top item either in the R list or in the W list; it has the least scheduling complexity but its access time performance may not be very good. With larger α values, the access time performance can be improved, but the scheduling complexity is increased as well.

11.2.2.2 On-Demand Scheduling for Variable-Size Items

On-demand scheduling for applications with variable data item sizes was studied in [5]. To evaluate the performance for items of different sizes, a new performance metric called stretch was used. Stretch is the ratio of the access time of a request to its service time, where the service time is the time needed to complete the request if it were the only job in the system.

Compared with access time, stretch is believed to be a more reasonable metric for items of variable sizes since it takes into consideration the size (i.e., service time) of a requested data item. Based on the stretch metric, four different algorithms have been investigated [5]. All four algorithms considered are preemptive in the sense that the scheduling decision is reevaluated after broadcasting any page of a data item (it is assumed that a data item consists of one or more pages that have a fixed size and are broadcast together in a single data transmission).

1. Preemptive Longest Wait First (PLWF): This is the preemptive version of the LWF algorithm. The LWF criterion is applied to select the subsequent data item to be broadcast.

2. Shortest Remaining Time First (SRTF): The data item with the shortest remaining time is selected.

3. Longest Total Stretch First (LTSF): The data item which has the largest total current stretch is chosen for broadcast. Here, the current stretch of a pending request is the ratio of the time the request has been in the system thus far to its service time.

4. MAX Algorithm: A deadline is assigned to each arriving request, and it schedules for the next broadcast the item with the earliest deadline. In computing the deadline for a request, the following formula is used:

$$\text{deadline} = \text{arrival time} + \text{service time} \times S_{max} \qquad (11.4)$$

where S_{max} is the maximum stretch value of the individual requests for the last satisfied requests in a history window. To reduce computational complexity, once a deadline is set for a request, this value does not change even if S_{max} is updated before the request is serviced.

The trace-based performance study carried out in [5] indicates that none of these schemes is superior to the others in all cases. Their performance really depends on the system settings. Overall, the MAX scheme, with a simple implementation, performs quite well in both the worst and average cases in access time and stretch measures.

11.2.2.3 Energy-Efficient Scheduling

Datta et al. [10] took into consideration the energy saving issue in on-demand broadcasts. The proposed algorithms broadcast the requested data items in batches, using an existing indexing technique [18] (refer to Section 11.3 for details) to index the data items in the current broadcast cycle. In this way, a mobile client may tune into a small portion of the broadcast instead of monitoring the broadcast channel until the desired data arrives. Thus, the proposed method is energy efficient. The data scheduling is based on a priority formula:

$$\text{Priority} = IF^{ASP} \times PF \tag{11.5}$$

where IF (ignore factor) denotes the number of times that the particular item has not been included in a broadcast cycle, PF (popularity factor) is the number of requests for this item, and ASP (adaptive scaling factor) is a factor that weights the significance of IF and PF. Two sets of broadcast protocols, namely constant broadcast size (CBS) and variable broadcast size (VBS), were investigated in [10]. The CBS strategy broadcasts data items in decreasing order of the priority values until the fixed broadcast size is exhausted. The VBS strategy broadcasts all data items with positive priority values. Simulation results show that the VBS protocol outperforms the CBS protocol at light loads, whereas at heavy loads the CBS protocol predominates.

11.2.3 Hybrid Data Scheduling

Push-based data broadcast cannot adapt well to a large database and a dynamic environment. On-demand data broadcast can overcome these problems. However, it has two main disadvantages: i) more uplink messages are issued by mobile clients, thereby adding demand on the scarce uplink bandwidth and consuming more battery power on mobile clients; ii) if the uplink channel is congested, the access latency will become extremely high. A promising approach, called hybrid broadcast, is to combine push-based and on-demand techniques so that they can complement each other. In the design of a hybrid system, three issues need to be considered:

1. Access method from a client's point of view, i.e., where to obtain the requested data and how
2. Bandwidth/channel allocation between the push-based and on-demand deliveries
3. Assignment of a data item to either push-based broadcast, on-demand broadcast or both

Concerning these three issues, there are different proposals for hybrid broadcast in the literature. In the following, we introduce the techniques for balancing push and pull and adaptive hybrid broadcast.

11.2.3.1   Balancing Push and Pull

A hybrid architecture was first investigated in [38, 39]. The model is shown in Figure 11.2. In the model, items are classified as either frequently requested (f-request) or infrequently requested (i-request). It is assumed that clients know which items are f-requests and which are i-requests. The model services f-requests using a broadcast cycle and i-requests on demand. In the downlink scheduling, the server makes K consecutive transmissions of f-requested items (according to a broadcast program), followed by the transmission of the first item in the i-request queue (if at least one such request is waiting). Analytical results for the average access time were derived in [39].

In [4], the push-based Bdisk model was extended to integrate with a pull-based approach. The proposed hybrid solution, called interleaved push and pull (IPP), consists of an uplink for clients to send pull requests to the server for the items that are not on the push-based broadcast. The server interleaves the Bdisk broadcast with the responses to pull requests on the broadcast channel. To improve the scalability of IPP, three different techniques were proposed:

1. Adjust the assignment of bandwidth to push and pull. This introduces a trade-off between how fast the push-based delivery is executed and how fast the queue of pull requests is served.
2. Provide a pull threshold T. Before a request is sent to the server, the client first monitors the broadcast channel for T time. If the requested data does not appear in the broadcast channel, the client sends a pull request to the server. This technique avoids overloading the pull service because a client will only pull an item that would otherwise have a very high push latency.
3. Successively chop off the pushed items from the slowest part of the broadcast schedule. This has the effect of increasing the available bandwidth for pulls. The disadvantage of this approach is that if there is not enough bandwidth for pulls, the performance might degrade severely, since the pull latencies for nonbroadcast items will be extremely high.

11.2.3.2   Adaptive Hybrid Broadcast

Adaptive broadcast strategies were studied for dynamic systems [24, 32]. These studies are based on the hybrid model in which the most frequently accessed items are delivered

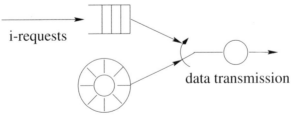

Figure 11.2   Architecture of hybrid broadcast.

to clients based on flat broadcast, whereas the least frequently accessed items are provided point-to-point on a separate channel. In [32], a technique that continuously adjusts the broadcast content to match the hot-spot of the database was proposed. To do this, each item is associated with a "temperature" that corresponds to its request rate. Thus, each item can be in one of three possible states, namely vapor, liquid, and frigid. Vapor data items are those heavily requested and currently broadcast; liquid data items are those having recently received a moderate number of requests but still not large enough for immediate broadcast; frigid data items refer to the cold (least frequently requested) items. The access frequency, and hence the state, of a data item can be dynamically estimated from the number of on-demand requests received through the uplink channel. For example, liquid data can be "heated" to vapor data if more requests are received. Simulation results show that this technique adapts very well to rapidly changing workloads.

Another adaptive broadcast scheme was discussed in [24], which assumes fixed channel allocation for data broadcast and point-to-point communication. The idea behind adaptive broadcast is to maximize (but not overload) the use of available point-to-point channels so that a better overall system performance can be achieved.

11.3   AIR INDEXING

11.3.1   Power Conserving Indexing

Power conservation is a key issue for battery-powered mobile computers. Air indexing techniques can be employed to predict the arrival time of a requested data item so that a client can slip into doze mode and switch back to active mode only when the data of interest arrives, thus substantially reducing battery consumption.

In the following, various indexing techniques will be described. The general access protocol for retrieving indexed data frames involves the following steps:

- Initial Probe: The client tunes into the broadcast channel and determines when the next index is broadcast.
- Search: The client accesses the index to find out when to tune into the broadcast channel to get the required frames.
- Retrieve: The client downloads all the requested information frames.

When no index is used, a broadcast cycle consists of data frames only (called nonindex). As such, the length of the broadcast cycle and hence the access time are minimum. However, in this case, since every arriving frame must be checked against the condition specified in the query, the tune-in time is very long and is equal to the access time.

11.3.1.1   The Hashing Technique

As mentioned previously, there is a trade-off between the access time and the tune-in time. Thus, we need different data organization methods to accommodate different applications. The hashing-based scheme and the flexible indexing method were proposed in [17].

In hashing-based scheme, instead of broadcasting a separate directory frame with each broadcast cycle, each frame carries the control information together with the data that it holds. The control information guides a search to the frame containing the desired data in order to improve the tune-in time. It consists of a hash function and a shift function. The hash function hashes a key attribute to the address of the frame holding the desired data. In the case of collision, the shift function is used to compute the address of the overflow area, which consists of a sequential set of frames starting at a position behind the frame address generated by the hash function.

The flexible indexing method first sorts the data items in ascending (or descending) order and then divides them into p segments numbered 1 through p. The first frame in each of the data segments contains a control index, which is a binary index mapping a given key value to the frame containing that key. In this way, we can reduce the tune-in time. The parameter p makes the indexing method flexible since, depending on its value, we can either get a very good tune-in time or a very good access time.

In selecting between the hashing scheme and the flexible indexing method, the former should be used when the tune-in time requirement is not rigid and the key size is relatively large compared to the record size. Otherwise, the latter should be used.

11.3.1.2 The Index Tree Technique

As with a traditional disk-based environment, the index tree technique [18] has been applied to data broadcasts on wireless channels. Instead of storing the locations of disk records, an index tree stores the arrival times of information frames.

Figure 11.3 depicts an example of an index tree for a broadcast cycle that consists of 81 information frames. The lowest level consists of square boxes that represent a collection of three information frames. Each index node has three pointers (for simplicity, the three pointers pointing out from each leaf node of the index tree are represented by just one arrow).

To reduce tune-in time while maintaining a good access time for clients, the index tree can be replicated and interleaved with the information frames. In distributed indexing, the index tree is divided into replicated and nonreplicated parts. The replicated part consists of the upper levels of the index tree, whereas the nonreplicated part consists of the lower levels. The index tree is broadcast every $1/d$ of a broadcast cycle. However, instead of replicating the entire index tree d times, each broadcast only consists of the replicated part and the nonreplicated part that indexes the data frames immediately following it. As such, each node in the nonreplicated part appears only once in a broadcast cycle. Since the lower levels of an index tree take up much more space than the upper part (i.e., the replicated part of the index tree), the index overheads can be greatly reduced if the lower levels of the index tree are not replicated. In this way, tune-in time can be improved significantly without causing much deterioration in access time.

To support distributed indexing, every frame has an offset to the beginning of the root of the next index tree. The first node of each distributed index tree contains a tuple, with the first field containing the primary key of the data frame that is broadcast last, and the second field containing the offset to the beginning of the next broadcast cycle. This is to guide the clients that have missed the required data in the current cycle to tune to the next broadcast cycle. There is a control index at the beginning of every replicated index to direct clients to a proper branch in the index tree. This additional index information for nav-

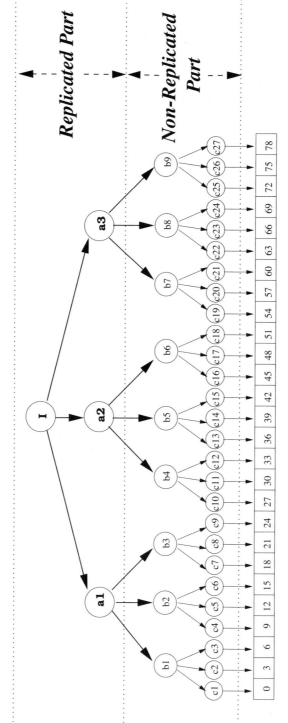

Figure 11.3 A full index tree.

igation together with the sparse index tree provides the same function as the complete index tree.

11.3.1.3   The Signature Technique

The signature technique has been widely used for information retrieval. A signature of an information frame is basically a bit vector generated by first hashing the values in the information frame into bit strings and then superimposing one on top of another [22]. Signatures are broadcast together with the information frames. A query signature is generated in a similar way based on the query specified by the user. To answer a query, a mobile client can simply retrieve information signatures from the broadcast channel and then match the signatures with the query signature by performing a bitwise AND operation. If the result is not the same as the query signature, the corresponding information frame can be ignored. Otherwise, the information frame is further checked against the query. This step is to eliminate records that have different values but also have the same signature due to the superimposition process.

The signature technique interleaves signatures with their corresponding information frames. By checking a signature, a mobile client can decide whether an information frame contains the desired information. If it does not, the client goes into doze mode and wakes up again for the next signature. The primary issue with different signature methods is the size and the number of levels of the signatures to be used.

In [22], three signature algorithms, namely simple signature, integrated signature, and multilevel signature, were proposed and their cost models for access time and tune-in time were given. For simple signatures, the signature frame is broadcast before the corresponding information frame. Therefore, the number of signatures is equal to the number of information frames in a broadcast cycle. An integrated signature is constructed for a group of consecutive frames, called a frame group. The multilevel signature is a combination of the simple signature and the integrated signature methods, in which the upper level signatures are integrated signatures and the lowest level signatures are simple signatures.

Figure 11.4 illustrates a two-level signature scheme. The dark signatures in the figure are integrated signatures. An integrated signature indexes all data frames between itself and the next integrated signature (i.e., two data frames). The lighter signatures are simple signatures for the corresponding data frames. In the case of nonclustered data frames, the number of data frames indexed by an integrated signature is usually kept small in order to maintain the filtering capability of the integrated signatures. On the other hand, if similar

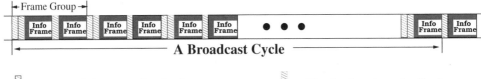

Figure 11.4   The multilevel signature technique.

data frames are grouped together, the number of frames indexed by an integrated signature can be large.

11.3.1.4 The Hybrid Index Approach

Both the signature and the index tree techniques have some advantages and disadvantages. For example, the index tree method is good for random data access, whereas the signature method is good for sequentially structured media such as broadcast channels. The index tree technique is very efficient for a clustered broadcast cycle, and the signature method is not affected much by the clustering factor. Although the signature method is particularly good for multiattribute retrieval, the index tree provides a more accurate and complete global view of the data frames. Since clients can quickly search the index tree to find out the arrival time of the desired data, the tune-in time is normally very short for the index tree method. However, a signature does not contain global information about the data frames; thus it can only help clients to make a quick decision regarding whether the current frame (or a group of frames) is relevant to the query or not. For the signature method, the filtering efficiency depends heavily on the false drop probability of the signatures. As a result, the tune-in time is normally long and is proportional to the length of a broadcast cycle.

A new index method, called the hybrid index, builds index information on top of the signatures and a sparse index tree to provide a global view for the data frames and their corresponding signatures. The index tree is called sparse because only the upper t levels of the index tree (the replicated part in the distributed indexing) are constructed. A key search pointer node in the t-th level points to a data block, which is a group of consecutive frames following their corresponding signatures. Since the size of the upper t levels of an index tree is usually small, the overheads for such additional indexes are very small. Figure 11.5 illustrates a hybrid index. To retrieve a data frame, a mobile client first searches the sparse index tree to obtain the approximate location information about the desired data frame and then tunes into the broadcast to find out the desired frame.

Since the hybrid index technique is built on top of the signature method, it retains all of the advantages of a signature method. Meanwhile, the global information provided by the sparse index tree considerably improves tune-in time.

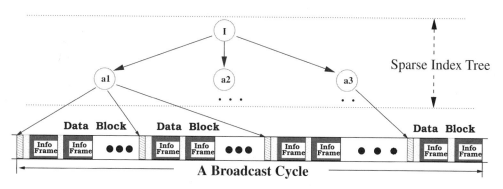

Figure 11.5 The hybrid index technique.

11.3.1.5 The Unbalanced Index Tree Technique

To achieve better performance with skewed queries, the unbalanced index tree technique was investigated [9, 31]. Unbalanced indexing minimizes the average index search cost by reducing the number of index searches for hot data at the expense of spending more on cold data.

For fixed index fan-outs, a Huffman-based algorithm can be used to construct an optimal unbalanced index tree. Let N be the number of total data items and d the fan-out of the index tree. The Huffman-based algorithm first creates a forest of N subtrees, each of which is a single node labeled with the corresponding access frequency. Then, the d subtrees with the smallest labels are attached to a new node, and the resulting subtree is labeled with the sum of all the labels from its d child subtrees. This procedure is repeated until there is only one subtree. Figure 11.6 demonstrates an index tree with a fixed fan-out of three. In the figure, each data item i is given in the form of (i, q_i), where q_i is the access probability for item i.

Given the data access patterns, an optimal unbalanced index tree with a fixed fan-out is easy to construct. However, its performance may not be optimal. Thus, Chen et al. [9] discussed a more sophisticated case for variable fan-outs. In this case, the problem of optimally constructing an index tree is NP-hard [9]. In [9], a greedy algorithm called variant fan-out (VF) was proposed. Basically, the VF scheme builds the index tree in a top-down manner. VF starts by attaching all data items to the root node. Then, after some evaluation, VF it groups the nodes with small access probabilities and moves them to one level lower so as to minimize the average index search cost. Figure 11.7 shows an index tree built using the

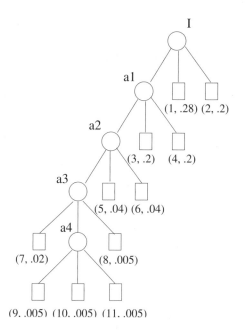

Figure 11.6 Index tree of a fixed fan-out of three.

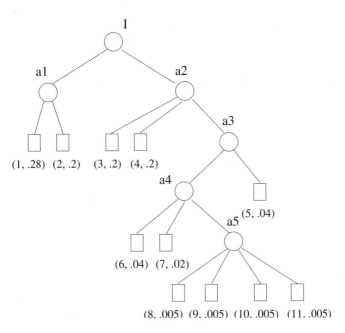

Figure 11.7 Index tree of variable fan-outs.

VF method, in which the access probability for each data is the same as in the example for fixed fan-outs. The index tree with variable fan-outs in Figure 11.7 has a better average index search performance than the index tree with fixed fan-outs in Figure 11.6 [9].

11.3.2 Multiattribute Air Indexing

So far, the index techniques considered are based on one attribute and can only handle single attribute queries. In real world applications, data frames usually contain multiple attributes. Multiattribute queries are desirable because they can provide more precise information to users.

Since broadcast channels are a linear medium, when compared to single attribute indexing and querying, data management and query protocols for multiple attributes appear much more complicated. Data clustering is an important technique used in single-attribute air indexing. It places data items with the same value under a specific attribute consecutively in a broadcast cycle [14, 17, 18]. Once the first data item with the desired attribute value arrives, all data items with the same attribute value can be successively retrieved from the broadcast. For multiattribute indexing, a broadcast cycle is clustered based on the most frequently accessed attribute. Although the other attributes are nonclustered in the cycle, a second attribute can be chosen to cluster the data items within a data cluster of the first attribute. Likewise, a third attribute can be chosen to cluster the data items within a data cluster of the second attribute. We call the first attribute the clustered attribute and the other attributes the nonclustered attributes.

For each nonclustered attribute, a broadcast cycle can be partitioned into a number of segments called metasegments [18], each of which holds a sequence of frames with non-decreasing (or nonincreasing) values of that attribute. Thus, when we look at each individual metasegment, the data frames are clustered on that attribute and the indexing techniques discussed in the last subsection can still be applied to a metasegment. The number of metasegments in the broadcast cycle for an attribute is called the scattering factor of the attribute. The scattering factor of an attribute increases as the importance of the attribute decreases.

The index tree, signature, and hybrid methods are applicable to indexing multiattribute data frames [15]. For multiattribute indexing, an index tree is built for each index attribute, and multiple attribute values are superimposed to generate signatures.

When two special types of queries, i.e., queries with all conjunction operators and queries with all disjunction operators, are considered, empirical comparisons show that the index tree method, though performing well for single-attribute queries, results in poor access time performance [15]. This is due to its large overheads for building a distributed index tree for each attribute indexed. Moreover, the index tree method has an update constraint, i.e., updates of a data frame are not reflected until the next broadcast cycle. The comparisons revealed that the hybrid technique is the best choice for multiattribute queries due to its good access time and tune-in time. The signature method performs close to the hybrid method for disjunction queries. The index tree method has a similar tune-in time performance as the hybrid method for conjunction queries, whereas it is poor in terms of access time for any type of multiattribute queries.

11.4 OTHER ISSUES

11.4.1 Semantic Broadcast

The indexing techniques discussed in Section 11.3 can help mobile clients filter information and improve tune-in time for data broadcast. This type of broadcast is called item-based. One major limitation of such item-based schemes is their lack of semantics associated with a broadcast. Thus, it is hard for mobile clients to determine if their queries could be answered from the broadcast entirely, forcing them to contact the server for possibly additional items. To remedy this, a semantic-based broadcast approach was suggested [20]. This approach attaches a semantic description to each broadcast unit, called a chunk, which is a cluster of data items. This allows clients to determine if a query can be answered based solely on the broadcast and to define precisely the remaining items in the form of a "supplementary" query.

Consider a stock information system containing stock pricing information. The server broadcasts some data, along with their indexes. A mobile client looking for an investment opportunity issues a query for the list of companies whose stock prices are between $30 and $70 (i.e., $30 \leq \text{price} \leq 70$). Employing a semantic-based broadcast scheme as shown in Figure 11.8, data items are grouped into chunks, each of which is indexed by a semantic descriptor. A client locates the required data in the first two chunks since together they can satisfy the query predicate completely. For the first chunk, it drops the item Oracle, 28 and keeps the item Dell, 44. For the second chunk, both items Intel, 63 and Sun, 64 are re-

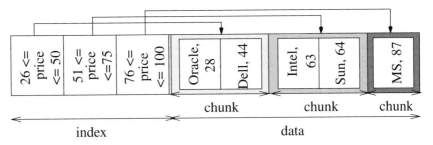

Figure 11.8   An example of semantic broadcast.

tained. In case the server decides not to broadcast the first chunk (i.e., the stocks whose prices are between $26 and $50), a client could assert that the missing data can be loaded from the server using a query with predicate $30 \leq \text{price} \leq 50$.

11.4.2   Fault-Tolerant Broadcast

Wireless transmission is error-prone. Data might be corrupted or lost due to many factors such as signal interference, etc. When errors occur, mobile clients have to wait for the next copy of the data if no special precaution is taken. This will increase both access time and tune-in time. To deal with unreliable wireless communication, the basic idea is to introduce controlled redundancy in the broadcast program. Such redundancy allows mobile clients to obtain their data items from the current broadcast cycle even in the presence of errors. This eliminates the need to wait for the next broadcast of the data whenever any error occurs. Studies on fault-tolerant broadcast disks and air indexing have been performed in [8] and [36], respectively.

11.4.3   Data and Index Allocation over Multiple Broadcast Channels

It is argued in [28] that multiple physical channels cannot be coalesced into a single high-bandwidth channel. Hence, recent studies have been undertaken on data and index allocation over multiple broadcast channels [25, 26, 28]. In [26], to minimize the average access delay for data items in the broadcast program, a heuristic algorithm VF^k was developed to allocate data over a number of channels. While previous studies addressed data scheduling and indexing separately, these authors [25, 28] considered the allocation problem of both data and index over multiple channels. Various server broadcast and client access protocols were investigated in [28]. In [25], the allocation problem aimed at minimizing both the average access time and the average tune-in time. It was mapped into the personnel assignment problem from which the optimization techniques were derived to solve the problem.

11.4.4   Handling Updates for Data Broadcast

In reality, many applications that can best profit from a broadcast-based approach are required to update their data frequently over time (e.g., stock quotation systems and traffic reports). Acharya et al. [2] discussed methods for keeping clients' caches consistent with the updated data values at the server for the Bdisk systems. The techniques of invalidating or updating cached copies were investigated.

Data consistency issues for transactional operations in push-based broadcast were explored in [27, 29]. For a wireless broadcast environment, the correctness criteria of ACID transactions might be too restrictive. Thus, these studies relaxed some of the requirements and new algorithms have been developed. In [27], the correctness criterion for read-only transactions is that each transaction reads consistent data, i.e., the read set of each read-only transaction must form a subset of a consistent database state. The proposed schemes maintain multiple versions of items either on air or in a client cache to increase the concurrency of client read-only transactions. In [29], the correctness criterion employed is update consistency, which ensures (1) the mutual consistency of data maintained by the server and read by clients; and (2) the currency of data read by clients. Two practical schemes, F-Matrix and R-Matrix, were proposed to efficiently detect update consistent histories by broadcasting some control information along with data.

11.4.5 Client Cache Management

An important issue relating to data broadcast is client data caching. Client data caching is a common technique for improving access latency and data availability. In the framework of a mobile wireless environment, this is much more desirable due to constraints such as limited bandwidth and frequent disconnections. However, frequent client disconnections and movements between different cells make the design of cache management strategies a challenge. The issues of cache consistency, cache replacement, and cache prefetching have been explored in [3, 7, 19, 40, 41].

11.5 SUMMARY

This chapter has presented various techniques for wireless data broadcast. Data scheduling and air indexing were investigated with respect to their performance in access efficiency and power consumption. For data scheduling, push-based, on-demand, and hybrid scheduling were discussed. Push-based broadcast is attractive when access patterns are known a priori, whereas on-demand broadcast is desirable for dynamic access patterns. Hybrid data broadcast offers more flexibility by combining push-based and on-demand broadcasts. For air indexing, several basic indexing techniques, such as the hashing method, the index tree method, the signature method, and the hybrid method, were described. Air indexing techniques for multiattribute queries were also discussed. Finally, some other issues of wireless data broadcast, such as semantic broadcast, fault-tolerant broadcast, update handling, and client cache management, were briefly reviewed.

ACKNOWLEDGMENTS

The writing of this chapter was supported by Research Grants Council of Hong Kong, China (Project numbers HKUST-6077/97E and HKUST-6241/00E).

REFERENCES

1. S. Acharya, R. Alonso, M. Franklin, and S. Zdonik, Broadcast disks: Data management for asymmetric communications environments, in *Proceedings of ACM SIGMOD Conference on Management of Data,* pp. 199–210, San Jose, CA, USA, May 1995.

2. S. Acharya, M. Franklin, and S. Zdonik, Disseminating updates on broadcast disks, in *Proceedings of the 22nd International Conference on Very Large Data Bases (VLDB'96),* pp. 354–365, Mumbai (Bombay), India, September 1996.

3. S. Acharya, M. Franklin, and S. Zdonik, Prefetching from a broadcast disk, in *Proceedings of the 12th International Conference on Data Engineering (ICDE'96),* pp. 276–285, New Orleans, LA, USA, February 1996.

4. S. Acharya, M. Franklin, and S. Zdonik, Balancing push and pull for data broadcast, in *Proceedings of ACM SIGMOD Conference on Management of Data,* pp. 183–194, Tucson, AZ, USA, May 1997.

5. S. Acharya and S. Muthukrishnan, Scheduling on-demand broadcasts: New metrics and algorithms, in *Proceedings of the 4th Annual ACM/IEEE International Conference on Mobile Computing and Networking (MobiCom'98),* pp. 43–54, Dallas, TX, USA, October 1998.

6. D. Aksoy and M. Franklin, R × W: A scheduling approach for large-scale on-demand data broadcast. *IEEE/ACM Transactions on Networking, 7*(6): 846–860, December 1999.

7. D. Barbara and T. Imielinski, Sleepers and workaholics: Caching strategies for mobile environments, in *Proceedings of ACM SIGMOD Conference on Management of Data,* pp. 1–12, Minneapolis, MN, USA, May 1994.

8. S. K. Baruah and A. Bestavros, Pinwheel scheduling for fault-tolerant broadcast disks in real-time database systems, in *Proceedings of the 13th International Conference on Data Engineering (ICDE'97),* pp. 543–551, Birmingham, UK, April 1997.

9. M.-S. Chen, P. S. Yu, and K.-L. Wu, indexed sequential data broadcasting in wireless mobile computing, in *Proceedings of the 17th International Conference on Distributed Computing Systems (ICDCS'97),* pp. 124–131, Baltimore, MD, USA, May 1997.

10. A. Datta, D. E. VanderMeer, A. Celik, and V. Kumar, Broadcast protocols to support efficient retrieval from databases by mobile users, *ACM Transactions on Database Systems (TODS), 24*(1): 1–79, March 1999.

11. H. D. Dykeman, M. Ammar, and J. W. Wong, Scheduling algorithms for videotex systems under broadcast delivery, in *Proceedings of IEEE International Conference on Communications (ICC'86),* pp. 1847–1851, Toronto, Canada, June 1986.

12. S. Hameed and N. H. Vaidya, Efficient algorithms for scheduling data broadcast, *ACM/Baltzer Journal of Wireless Networks (WINET), 5*(3): 183–193, 1999.

13. Q. L. Hu, D. L. Lee, and W.-C. Lee, Performance evaluation of a wireless hierarchical data dissemination system, in *Proceedings of the 5th Annual ACM/IEEE International Conference on Mobile Computing and Networking (MobiCom'99),* pp. 163–173, Seattle, WA, USA, August 1999.

14. Q. L. Hu, W.-C. Lee, and D. L. Lee, A hybrid index technique for power efficient data broadcast, *Journal of Distributed and Parallel Databases (DPDB), 9*(2), 151–177, 2001.

15. Q. L. Hu, W.-C. Lee, and D. L. Lee, Power conservative multi-attribute queries on data broadcast, in *Proceedings of the 16th International Conference on Data Engineering (ICDE'2000),* pp. 157–166, San Diego, CA, USA, February 2000.

16. T. Imielinski and S. Viswanathan, Adaptive wireless information systems, in *Proceedings of the*

Special Interest Group in DataBase Systems (SIGDBS) Conference, Tokyo, Japan, October 1994.

17. T. Imielinski, S. Viswanathan, and B. R. Badrinath, Power efficient filtering of data on air, in *Proceedings of the 4th International Conference on Extending Database Technology (EDBT'94),* pp. 245–258, Cambridge, UK, March 1994.

18. T. Imielinski, S. Viswanathan, and B. R. Badrinath, Data on air—organization and access, *IEEE Transactions of Knowledge and Data Engineering (TKDE), 9*(3): 353–372, May-June 1997.

19. J. Jing, A. K. Elmagarmid, A. Helal, and R. Alonso, Bit-sequences: A new cache invalidation method in mobile environments, *ACM/Baltzer Journal of Mobile Networks and Applications (MONET), 2*(2): 115–127, 1997.

20. K. C. K. Lee, H. V. Leong, and A. Si, A semantic broadcast scheme for a mobile environment based on dynamic chunking, in *Proceedings of the 20th IEEE International Conference on Distributed Computing Systems (ICDCS'2000),* pp. 522–529, Taipei, Taiwan, April 2000.

21. W.-C. Lee, Q. L. Hu, and D. L. Lee, A study of channel allocation methods for data dissemination in mobile computing environments, *ACM/Baltzer Journal of Mobile Networks and Applications (MONET), 4*(2): 117–129, 1999.

22. W.-C. Lee and D. L. Lee, Using signature techniques for information filtering in wireless and mobile environments, *Journal of Distributed and Parallel Databases (DPDB), 4*(3): 205–227, July 1996.

23. W.-C. Lee and D. L. Lee, Signature caching techniques for information broadcast and filtering in mobile environments, *ACM/Baltzer Journal of Wireless Networks (WINET), 5*(1): 57–67, 1999.

24. C. W. Lin and D. L. Lee, Adaptive data delivery in wireless communication environments, in *Proceedings of the 20th IEEE International Conference on Distributed Computing Systems (ICDCS'2000),* pp. 444–452, Taipei, Taiwan, April 2000.

25. S.-C. Lo and A. L. P. Chen, Optimal index and data allocation in multiple broadcast channels, in *Proceedings of the 16th IEEE International Conference on Data Engineering (ICDE'2000),* pp. 293–302, San Diego, CA, USA, February 2000.

26. W.-C. Peng and M.-S. Chen, Dynamic generation of data broadcasting programs for a broadcast disk array in a mobile computing environment, in *Proceedings of the 9th ACM International Conference on Information and Knowledge Management (CIKM'2000),* pp. 38–45, McLean, VA, USA, November 2000.

27. E. Pitoura and P. K. Chrysanthis, Exploiting versions for handling updates in broadcast disks, in *Proceedings of the 25th International Conference on Very Large Data Bases (VLDB'99),* pp. 114–125, Edinburgh, Scotland, UK, September 1999.

28. K. Prabhakara, K. A. Hua, and J. Oh, Multi-level multi-channel air cache designs for broadcasting in a mobile environment, in *Proceedings of the 16th IEEE International Conference on Data Engineering (ICDE'2000),* pp. 167–176, San Diego, CA, USA, February 2000.

29. J. Shanmugasundaram, A. Nithrakashyap, R. M. Sivasankaran, and K. Ramamritham, Efficient concurrency control for broadcast environments, in *Proceedings of ACM SIGMOD International Conference on Management of Data,* pp. 85–96, Philadelphia, PA, USA, June 1999.

30. S. Sheng, A. Chandrasekaran, and R. W. Broderson, A portable multimedia terminal, *IEEE Communications Magazine, 30*(12): 64–75, December 1992.

31. N. Shivakumar and S. Venkatasubramanian, Energy-efficient indexing for information dissemination in wireless systems, *ACM/Baltzer Journal of Mobile Networks and Applications (MONET), 1*(4): 433–446, 1996.

32. K. Stathatos, N. Roussopoulos, and J. S. Baras, Adaptive data broadcast in hybrid networks, in *Proceedings of the 23rd International Conference on Very Large Data Bases (VLDB'97)*, pp. 326–335, Athens, Greece, August 1997.

33. C. J. Su and L. Tassiulas, Broadcast scheduling for the distribution of information items with unequal length, in *Proceedings of the 31st Conference on Information Science and Systems (CISS'97)*, March 1997.

34. C. J. Su, L. Tassiulas, and V. J. Tsotras, Broadcast scheduling for information distribution, *ACM/Baltzer Journal of Wireless Networks (WINET)*, 5(2): 137–147, 1999.

35. K. L. Tan and J. X. Yu, Energy efficient filtering of nonuniform broadcast, in *Proceedings of the 16th International Conference on Distributed Computing Systems (ICDCS'96)*, pp. 520–527, Hong Kong, May 1996.

36. K. L. Tan and J. X. Yu, On selective tuning in unreliable wireless channels, *Journal of Data and Knowledge Engineering (DKE)*, 28(2): 209–231, November 1998.

37. N. H. Vaidya and S. Hameed, Scheduling data broadcast in asymmetric communication environments, *ACM/Baltzer Journal of Wireless Networks (WINET)*, 5(3): 171–182, 1999.

38. J. W. Wong, Broadcast delivery, *Proceedings of the IEEE*, 76(12): 1566–1577, December 1988.

39. J. W. Wong and H. D. Dykeman, Architecture and performance of large scale information delivery networks, in *Proceedings of the 12th International Teletraffic Congress*, pp. 440–446, Torino, Italy, June 1988.

40. J. Xu, Q. L. Hu, D. L. Lee, and W.-C. Lee, SAIU: An efficient cache replacement policy for wireless on-demand broadcasts, in *Proceedings of the 9th ACM International Conference on Information and Knowledge Management (CIKM'2000)*, pp. 46–53, McLean, VA, USA, November 2000.

41. J. Xu, X. Tang, D. L. Lee, and Q. L. Hu, Cache coherency in location-dependent information services for mobile environment, in *Proceedings of the 1st International Conference on Mobile Data Management*, pp. 182–193, Hong Kong, December 1999.

42. G. K. Zipf, *Human Behaviour and the Principle of Least Effort*. Boston: Addison-Wesley, 1949.

CHAPTER 12

Ensemble Planning for Digital Audio Broadcasting

ALBERT GRÄF and THOMAS McKENNEY

Department of Music Informatics, Johannes Gutenberg University, Mainz, Germany

12.1 INTRODUCTION

It is expected that in many countries digital broadcasting systems will mostly replace current FM radio and television technology in the course of the next one or two decades. The digital media not only offer superior image and audio quality and interesting new types of multimedia data services "on the air," but also have the potential to employ the scarce resource of broadcast frequencies much more efficiently. Thus, broadcast companies and network providers have a demand for new planning methods that help to fully exploit these capabilities in the large-scale digital broadcasting networks of the future.

In this chapter, we consider in particular the design of DAB (digital audio broadcasting) networks. Although channel assignment methods for analog networks, which are usually based on graph coloring techniques (see, e.g., [3, 9, 11, 19, 21]), are also applicable to DAB planning, they are not by themselves sufficient for the effective planning of large DAB networks. This is due to the fact that, in contrast to classical radio networks, the DAB system transmits whole "ensembles" consisting of multiple radio programs and other (data) services, and allows an ensemble to be transmitted on a single channel even if the corresponding transmitters may interfere. Hence, one can span large areas with so-called single frequency networks, which makes it possible to utilize electromagnetic spectrum much more efficiently. To make the best use of this feature, however, it is necessary to integrate the planning of the ensembles with the frequency assignment step. This is not possible with existing methods, which are all simply adaptions of known graph coloring techniques that are applied to a prescribed ensemble collection.

We first show how to formulate this generalized planning problem, which we call the ensemble planning problem, as a combined bin packing/graph coloring problem. We then discuss some basic solution techniques and algorithms to compute lower bounds in order to assess the quality of computed solutions. Finally, we develop, in some detail, a more advanced tabu search technique for the problem. Experimental results are used to point out the strengths and weaknesses of current solution approaches.

Handbook of Wireless Networks and Mobile Computing, Edited by Ivan Stojmenović.
ISBN 0-471-41902-8   © 2002 John Wiley & Sons, Inc.

12.1.1   Mathematical Preliminaries

We assume familiarity with the basic notions of graph theory (see, e.g., [8] or [14]) and NP-completeness [7]. All graphs are simple, undirected, and loopless. The subgraph of a graph $G = (V, E)$ induced by a subset of vertices $W \subseteq V$ is denoted G_W; it consists of the vertex set W and all edges of G between the vertices in W. A coloring of a graph $G = (V, E)$ is a function f mapping vertices to "colors" in such a manner that $f(v) \neq f(w) \; \forall \; vw \in E$. If $|f(V)| \leq k$ then f is also called a k-coloring. The chromatic number $\chi(G)$ of G is defined to be the minimum k for which such a k-coloring exists. The graph coloring problem is, given $G = (V, E)$ and integer $k \geq 0$, to decide whether G has a k-coloring. A clique of a graph $G = (V, E)$ is a subset W of V s.t. G_W is complete, i.e., $vw \in E \; \forall \; v, w \in W : v \neq w$. The clique number $\omega(G)$ is the maximum number of vertices in a clique of G, and the clique problem is, given G and integer $k \geq 0$, to decide whether G has a clique of size at least k. The clique number is an obvious lower bound on the chromatic number of a graph, since all vertices in a clique must be colored differently (this bound is not tight as there are graphs G for which the gap between $\omega(G)$ and $\chi(G)$ becomes arbitrarily large [8]). It is well known that both the coloring and the clique problem are NP-complete. Moreover, both problems are also difficult to approximate: the problem of determining a coloring using at most $|V|^{1/7-\varepsilon}\chi(G)$ colors, and the problem of finding a clique of size at least $|V|^{\varepsilon-1/4}\omega(G)$, are NP-hard for each $\varepsilon > 0$ [6]. This implies, in particular, that it is not possible to approximate the optimization versions of these problems within constant performance ratio in polynomial time, unless P = NP.

Another type of NP-complete problem we deal with in this chapter is the bin packing problem. Given a set X with positive element sizes μ_x, $x \in X$, and $M > 0$, an M-packing of X is a set $\mathcal{B}$ of mutually disjoint subsets of X s.t. $X = \cup_{B \in \mathcal{B}} B$ and the total size $\mu_B = \Sigma_{x \in B}\mu_x$ of each "bin" $B \in \mathcal{B}$ is at most M. The bin packing problem is, given X, μ, M and a nonnegative integer k, to decide whether X has an M-packing $\mathcal{B}$ of size at most k. We also let $p_M(X)$ denote the minimum size of an M-packing of X, called the M-packing number of X. In contrast to the chromatic and clique numbers, the packing number can be approximated with good performance quite easily, using a simple kind of "greedy" procedure known as the first-fit packing algorithm [7].

12.2   THE ENSEMBLE PLANNING PROBLEM

Two special aspects of the DAB technology motivate the problem discussed in this chapter: First, a DAB frequency block usually carries several different radio programs and additional data services. Therefore we have to deal with service ensembles instead of single radio programs. Each service needs a certain bandwidth, and the total bandwidth of all services forming an ensemble must not exceed the bandwidth available in a DAB frequency block.

Second, an ensemble may be transmitted on a single frequency block channel, even by potentially interfering transmitters; collections of transmitters that all broadcast the same ensemble on the same channel are called single frequency networks (SFNs). By making a judicious choice of SFNs, one can often save a considerable amount of frequency resources compared to conventional broadcast networks in which interfering transmitters must always be given different channels, even if they transmit the same signal. However, to fully exploit the potential frequency savings, new planning algorithms are needed.

Therefore, in our approach to DAB network planning we not only consider the channel assignment aspect, but also the search for ensemble collections that help to reduce the overall frequency demand. In our model, the network is described by a graph whose vertices correspond to the (geographical) areas for which a certain service supply is to be provided. Two vertices are connected by an edge if transmitters in the corresponding areas may interfere. (In practice, the areas are usually polygons on the earth's surface, and edges connect areas that are within a given geometric distance, the so-called block repetition distance.)

The goal is to find ensembles that realize the desired service supply, and a corresponding assignment of frequency blocks that prevents interference and minimizes frequency requirements. We call this the ensemble planning problem. Thus an instance of the ensemble planning problem consists of the following items:

- A set S of services, where each service $s \in S$ has a positive bandwidth μ_s
- The area graph $G = (V, E)$, where V is the set of areas and the edge set E is interpreted as the interference relationship between areas
- The requirements R_v, $v \in V$, which denote, for each area $v \in V$, the set of services to be supplied in that area
- The maximum ensemble size $M > 0$

We generally assume (w.l.o.g.) that all bandwidths and the ensemble size are positive integers. R and μ are considered as functions $R : V \mapsto 2^S$ and $\mu : S \mapsto \mathbb{N}$. In the following we usually only specify the parameters G, R, and M and assume a corresponding service set S with bandwidths μ without further notice.

A solution to the ensemble planning problem consists of two items, an ensemble assignment and a corresponding block assignment. An ensemble assignment is a relation $\mathcal{B} \subseteq V \times 2^S$, which assigns to each $v \in V$ a set $\mathcal{B}_v = \{B : (v, B) \in \mathcal{B}\}$ of ensembles (service sets) that are to be transmitted in the corresponding area. For an ensemble assignment $\mathcal{B}$ to be admissible, it must satisfy the supply requirements, and the individual ensembles must not exceed the maximum ensemble size:

$$R_v \subseteq \bigcup_{B \in \mathcal{B}_v} B \; \forall \, v \in V \tag{12.1}$$

$$\mu_B \leq M \; \forall \, B \in \mathcal{B}_v, v \in V \tag{12.2}$$

where the total bandwidth μ_B of an ensemble $B \subseteq S$ is defined by $\mu_B = \Sigma_{s \in B} \mu_s$.

The second part of the solution is the block assignment f, which maps each $(v, B) \in B$ to a corresponding frequency block or "color" $f(v, B)$. To be admissible, the block assignment must not introduce any interferences, i.e., different ensembles in the same or interfering areas must always be assigned different frequency blocks:

$$f(v, B) \neq f(w, C) \; \forall \, (v, B), (w, C) \in \mathcal{B} : B \neq C \wedge (v = w \vee vw \in E) \tag{12.3}$$

Finally, the target function to be minimized is the number of distinct frequency blocks, i.e., $|f(\mathcal{B})| = |\{f(v, B) : (v, B) \in \mathcal{B}\}|$. We can now formulate the ensemble planning problem in the usual decision format as follows:

Problem 1 (Ensemble Planning Problem)   Given $G = (V, E)$, $R : V \mapsto 2^S$, $M \in \mathbb{N}$ and $K \in \mathbb{N}$, decide whether there is an admissible ensemble assignment $\mathcal{B}$ and corresponding admissible block assignment f s.t. $|f(\mathcal{B})| \le K$.

In the following, for given G, R, and M, by $\chi_M^R(G)$ we denote the minimum number of frequency blocks in any admissible solution. It is not difficult to see that the admissible block assignments f for a given ensemble assignment $\mathcal{B}$ actually are in one-to-one correspondence to the valid colorings of an associated ensemble graph $G^{\mathcal{B}}$ which has $\mathcal{B}$ as its set of vertices and whose edges are precisely those pairs $(v, B)(w, C)$ for which $B \ne C \wedge (v = w \vee vw \in E)$; cf. Equation (12.3). Consequently we have that

$$\chi_M^R(G) = \min\{\chi(G^{\mathcal{B}}) : \mathcal{B} \text{ admissible}\} \tag{12.4}$$

Hence the ensemble planning problem is nothing but a graph coloring problem on top of a kind of packing problem. We further explore this in the following sections.

Example 1   Consider the problem instance in Figure 12.1, which involves five areas I–V and eight services A–H. We assume that only adjacent areas (such as I and V, or II and IV, but not I and IV) interfere. Thus, the area graph in this case is W_4, the wheel with 4 spokes, where area V forms the hub of the wheel. The requirements R_v and service bandwidths μ_s are given in the figure. The maximum ensemble size is $M = 9$.

Our task is (1) to arrange the services into a collection of ensembles for each area (this is what we call the ensemble assignment), and (2) to assign channels to the resulting en-

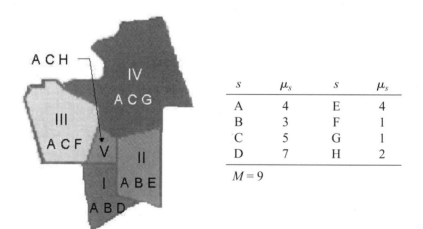

s	μ_s	s	μ_s
A	4	E	4
B	3	F	1
C	5	G	1
D	7	H	2
$M = 9$			

Figure 12.1   Ensemble planning problem.

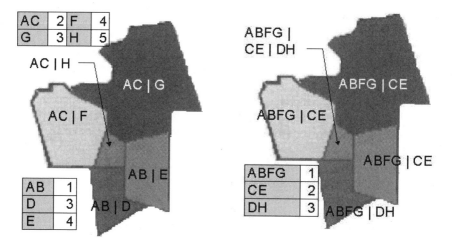

Figure 12.2 Two ensemble/block assignments.

sembles (this is the block assignment). We want to do this in such a manner that the conditions (12.1), (12.2), and (12.3) are satisfied. And, of course, we want the number of required frequency blocks to be as small as possible. (This is the hard part.)

Figure 12.2 shows two different solutions. The first solution (on the left-hand side) is fairly straightforward: we simply pack the services required for each area into a minimum number of ensembles. We call such an assignment, which supplies each area exactly with the requested services, a strict ensemble assignment. It is easy to see that this solution requires five frequency blocks in order to avoid interference and, in fact, one can show that in this example each strict ensemble assignment needs at least five frequencies.

It is possible to do better than this, but only if we allow a certain degree of "oversupply," as shown in the second solution. Here, we packed the entire service collection into three different ensembles, which can then be transmitted using three frequency blocks. It can be shown that this solution is indeed optimal. Thus we see that in DAB networks it is possible to save frequencies through oversupply.

12.3 BASIC SOLUTION TECHNIQUES

It is not difficult to see that the ensemble planning problem is NP-complete; in fact it contains both the graph coloring and the bin packing problem as special cases. (For the graph coloring problem, take $S = V$, $R_v = \{v\}$ $\forall$ $v \in V$ and $\mu \equiv 1 = M$; for the bin packing problem, let G be a one-vertex graph.) So we know that Problem 1 is not only NP-complete, but also difficult to approximate and, hence, we will be interested in heuristic solutions.

How can we approach this problem? We have already mentioned that the problem reduces to an ordinary graph coloring problem once we have obtained a suitable ensemble assignment. Thus a straightforward approach is to solve the problem in two optimization stages:

- Find an admissible ensemble assignment $\mathcal{B}$.
- Color $G^{\mathcal{B}}$ using some heuristic graph coloring procedure.

For the second stage, a plethora of different graph coloring algorithms is already available. In fact, it turns out that fairly simple "sequential" coloring methods like Brélaz' DSATUR [2] or Matula/Beck's smallest-last algorithm [16] usually perform very well on the kind of "geometric" graphs arising as models of broadcast networks. So we can concentrate on the first step, which is a kind of simultaneous bin packing problem. The difficult part here is to devise a packing strategy that reduces the global number of required colors instead of merely optimizing the packings for individual areas. Of course, no single strategy will work with all area graphs equally well, so let us take a look at the two extreme cases:

- Independent (edgeless) graphs. In this case the problem decomposes into $|V|$ independent bin packing problems, one for each vertex of G, and we have that $\chi_M^R(G) = \max\{p_M(R_v) : v \in V\}$.
- Complete graphs. In this case, all distinct ensembles will have to be assigned different frequency blocks, hence $\chi_M^R(G) = p_M(R_V)$.

(Here and in the following, by R_W we denote the set of all requested services in a set of areas $W \subseteq V$, i.e., $R_W = \cup_{w \in W} R_w$. Thus, in particular, R_V is the set of all requested services.)

This suggests two different types of ensemble packing heuristics that we would expect to work reasonably well with sparse and dense graphs, respectively. For sparse graphs, we will pack the individual requirement sets independently of each other. For dense graphs, we will pack the entire collection of requested services, and then assign to each vertex those ensembles that are needed to satisfy the supply requirements at that vertex. For an arbitrary graph, we might try both approaches and see which one works best.

Since the bin packing problem is NP-complete, we need some heuristic for solving it. A simple method, which works reasonably well, is the so-called first-fit (FF) algorithm, which considers the items (a.k.a. services) to be packed in some order, and puts each item into the first "bin" (a.k.a. ensemble) into which it fits. It is well-known that if the items are ordered by decreasing sizes, this method never performs worse than 11/9 times the optimum (asymptotically). (We refer the reader to [7] for the details of this algorithm and its analysis.)

In the following, we use FF(R, M) to denote the set of ensembles returned by the first-fit algorithm when applied to a set of required services $R \subseteq S$ and the ensemble size M. We can employ the first-fit algorithm for packing ensembles using the two strategies sketched out above, as follows:

Simultaneous First-Fit (SFF) Algorithm:

$$\mathcal{B}_v = \text{FF}(R_v, M) \; \forall \; v \in V \tag{12.5}$$

Global First-Fit (GFF) Algorithm:

$$\mathcal{B}_v = \{B \in \text{FF}(R_V, M) : B \cap R_v \neq \emptyset\} \; \forall \, v \in V \tag{12.6}$$

Incidentally, the two algorithms also correspond to the two solution approaches taken in Example 1. The SFF algorithm computes strict solutions (ensemble assignments exactly satisfying the requirements), aiming at "local optimality" by avoiding oversupply. In contrast, the GFF algorithm strives for "global optimality," producing overlap-free solutions in which the constructed ensembles are mutually disjoint (i.e., each service will only be supplied in a single ensemble for all areas where it is requested). As already indicated, we would expect SFF to work best with sparse, and GFF with dense graphs. In fact, the performance bounds for the first-fit bin packing algorithm directly carry over to SFF and GFF solutions. That is, a (properly colored) SFF (resp. GFF) assignment on an independent (resp. complete) area graph using a service order by decreasing bandwidths will at most be about 22% off the optimum (asymptotically).

As pointed out by Schmeisser [22], SFF (when ordering services by decreasing bandwidths) produces ensemble assignments which can be colored using at most $(11/9)\chi(G)$ colors (asymptotically), whereas GFF can perform arbitrarily bad even if the area graphs are acyclic (and hence bipartite). However, in experiments with geometrically defined area graphs [10] we found that GFF usually performs much better than SFF when the area graphs are dense, or when the services have a high average "circulation" (defined as the percentage of areas requiring a given service).

12.4 LOWER BOUNDS

When dealing with heuristics for NP-hard minimization problems, one is always interested in finding a good lower bound on the optimal solution, which allows us to assess the quality of computed solutions. For the ensemble planning problem, a useful bound is provided by an appropriate generalization of the clique number, which we discuss in this section.

As in the preceding section, we let $R_W = \bigcup_{w \in W} R_w \; \forall \, W \subseteq V$. Similarly, the set of all ensembles in a given area set $W \subseteq V$ is denoted $\mathcal{B}_W$, i.e., $\mathcal{B}_W = \bigcup_{w \in W} \mathcal{B}_w$. The quantity we consider, which we call the clique packing number, is defined as follows:

$$\pi_M^R(G) = \max\{p_M(R_W) : W \text{ clique of } G\} \tag{12.7}$$

To see why $\pi_M^R(G)$ is in fact a lower bound on $\chi_M^R(G)$, let $W \subseteq V$. It is easy to see that, if $\mathcal{B}$ is an admissible ensemble assignment w.r.t R and M, then $|\mathcal{B}_W| \geq p_M(R_W)$. Now consider the special case that W is a clique of G. In this case, the subgraph of $G^{\mathcal{B}}$ induced by $\mathcal{B} \cap (W \times \mathcal{B}_W)$ always contains a clique of size $|\mathcal{B}_W|$. (For each $B \in \mathcal{B}_W$ choose some $w_B \in W$ s.t. $B \in \mathcal{B}_{w_B}$. Then $\{(w_B, B) : B \in \mathcal{B}_W\}$ is a clique of the requested size.) Hence

$$p_M(R_W) \leq |\mathcal{B}_W| \leq \omega(G^{\mathcal{B}}) \leq \chi(G^{\mathcal{B}}) \tag{12.8}$$

By taking the maximum over all cliques W of G on the left-hand side of Equation (12.8), and the minimum over all admissible ensemble assignments $\mathcal{B}$ on the right-hand side, we obtain the desired inequality

$$\pi_M^R(G) \leq \chi_M^R(G) \tag{12.9}$$

The clique packing number is a weighted generalization of the clique number which, instead of merely counting the vertices contained in a clique, weights cliques according to the packing number of their requirements. Although computing the clique packing number is NP-hard, in practice it is much easier to approximate than other lower bounds like the minimum $\omega(G^{\mathcal{B}})$, for which we would have to consider all admissible ensemble assignments. Here we can employ a generalized version of the Carraghan/Pardalos algorithm, a branch-and-bound method for computing the clique number of a graph [4], which we have found to work quite well on not too dense graphs with a few hundred vertices. The algorithm can also be terminated at any time to give a lower bound on the clique number. It can easily be adapted to any weight function which is "monotonous" in the sense that if $W \subseteq W'$, then the weight of W is at most the weight of W'.

One complication is that since the bin packing problem is NP-complete, we can only approximate the clique weights. That is, we actually compute a lower bound

$$\varphi_M^R(G) = \max\{f(R_W, M) : W \text{ clique of } G\} \tag{12.10}$$

on the clique packing number, where $f(X, M)$ is a lower bound on $p_M(X)$ that can be computed efficiently. A simple method is to employ the "sum bound"

$$f(X, M) = \lceil \mu_X/M \rceil \tag{12.11}$$

which is always at least half the packing number. A better lower bound for approximating the clique packing number is discussed in [22].

Example 2 In Example 1, the areas I, II, and V form a clique of the area graph whose requested services sum up to a total bandwidth of 25. Hence, the clique packing number for this instance is at least $\lceil 25/9 \rceil = 3$, which proves that the solution with 3 frequency blocks is optimal (and also shows that the clique packing number is exactly 3). Note that in this example we have $\pi_M^R(G) = \chi_M^R(G)$. This is not true in general; just as with chromatic and clique numbers, there may be a "dual gap" between χ_M^R and π_M^R that can be arbitrarily large.

12.5 A TABU SEARCH METHOD

As pointed out in the previous section, the SFF and GFF algorithms represent two basic solution ideas for the ensemble planning problem (EPP), GFF (in contrast to SFF) taking advantage of the possibilities to reduce the demand of frequencies needed by oversupplying some or all of the vertices $v \in V$ of the area graph $G = (V, E)$ with services $s \in S$ not necessarily required ($s \notin R_v$). We will see later that for quite a few problem instances SFF or GFF (but usually not both) can find optimal or near optimal solutions, yet there are many problem instances, for which both SFF and GFF yield rather poor results. In consequence, our goal is to contruct a solution method, the results of which are at least as good as the better of SFF and GFF in all cases, and which takes into account especially those problem instances for which both SFF and GFF fail to deliver good results. In this latter case, we expect considerable improvements in result quality.

We have decided to use tabu search (TS) techniques as the conceptual basis of our solution method due to good experiences made with TS in a wide variety of telecommunication applications and related fields [1, 15, 13], including frequency assignment problems [12]. A complete description of the algorithm is beyond the scope of this chapter; we refer the reader to [17] for further details. Let us start the development of the solution method by having a brief look at the basic conceptual ideas behind TS, including the slight modifications needed for our purposes.

Note that in contrast to the previous section, here f denotes the target function (or cost function) of our application, i.e., $f(\mathcal{B})$ is the number of frequencies needed for the ensemble assignment $\mathcal{B}$.

12.5.1 The Basic Framework

TS is a heuristic technique for solving discrete optimization problems and is regarded as a member of the family of so-called metaheuristics [18, 20]. It can be understood as a form of neighborhood search, expanded by a few components, the most crucial of which is the concept of setting so-called tabus on some transitions, blocking any development in direction of these transitions as long as the tabus set on them are valid. The underlying idea is to avoid a well-known problem arising with classic neighborhood search, which easily gets trapped in a local optimum.

As an expanded variation of neighborhood search, the first step in adapting TS to a given optimization problem is to define a neighborhood suitable for the problem; that is, given a problem instance characterized by a search space T and a cost function f to be optimized, one must define a function $N : T \to 2^T$, where for all $t \in T$ the subset $N(t) \subseteq T$ is interpreted as the neighborhood of t in T.

With a neighborhood defined, we can now run TS by first choosing a suitable initial value $t_0 \in T$ and then at each iteration $i \in \mathbb{N}$ a permissible value $t_i \in N(t_{i-1})$ of greatest possible gain as the next iteration value, continuing in this fashion until some condition terminates the process. To prevent TS from being trapped in a local optimum, a so-called tabu list is introduced, consisting of either the most recent transitions or of fundamental data specifying the most recent transitions or specifying families of similar transitions for each of the most recent transitions. Any entry in the tabu list and, in consequence, any transition described by an entry in the tabu list is said to be tabued, meaning that such a transition is not selectable in any TS iteration as long as the tabu set on it has not expired. Expiration is then naturally expressed by removing the according entry from the tabu list. For each entry in the tabu list, the time of expiration is denoted by a value called the tabu tenure. In classic TS framework, the tabu tenure is a constant $c \in \mathbb{N}$, equally valid for any entry in the tabu list, expressing in number of iterations the duration of the entry's tabu validity, and measuring this from the moment (iteration) the entry was added to the tabu list.

Our adaption of TS to the EPP brought up the necessity for more dynamics in the generation of tabu tenure values, for reasons we will show in detail later. Thus, we calculate the tabu tenure using an adequate periodic function $g : \mathbb{N} \rightarrow \mathbb{N}$, with $g(i)$, $i \in \mathbb{N}$, being the tabu tenure value to be used when TS has reached the i-th iteration.

As a further component of TS, the aspiration criterion is somewhat the dual of the concept of working with tabus, allowing, under certain circumstances, a transition of some kind of global improvement to be made even though it might be prohibited by a tabu. In the most common interpretation of this idea, the aspiration criterion ignores a tabu on any transition that yields an improvement over the best solution obtained so far in a TS search.

The criteria for TS termination are usually kept simple. TS terminates if for a given number of iterations there is no further improvement in the cost function. This termination condition is sufficient in most cases, and we use it as is in the current development state of our TS.

12.5.2 Definition of the Neighborhood

As already pointed out in the description of the basic TS framework, we must first give a definition of the neighborhood. That is, for each instance of Problem 1 and each $\mathcal{B} \in \mathbb{B}$, where $\mathbb{B}$ denotes the set of all possible ensemble assignments, we must define a set $N(\mathcal{B}) \subseteq \mathbb{B}$ representing the neighborhood of $\mathcal{B}$ in $\mathbb{B}$. To simplify matters, we do not define $N(\mathcal{B})$ directly, but rather introduce a set $M(\mathcal{B})$ of admissible elementary moves m on $\mathcal{B}$, with $m(\mathcal{B})$ denoting the resulting ensemble assignment when applying m to $\mathcal{B}$, and then set $N(\mathcal{B}) := \{ m(\mathcal{B}) \mid m \in M(\mathcal{B}) \}$.

In our approach, an elementary move $m \in M(\mathcal{B})$, for an ensemble assignment $\mathcal{B} \in \mathbb{B}$, is specified as a quadrupel $m = (v, u, z, s)$, with $v \in V$, $u \in \{0, \ldots, |\mathcal{B}_v|\}$, $z \in \{0, \ldots, |\mathcal{B}_v| + 1\}$, $u \neq z$ and $s \in S$. Furthermore, in the case that $u \neq 0$ we demand that $s \in B_u$, where $B_u \in \mathcal{B}_v$ is the ensemble of vertex v with index u. (Here we assume for each $v' \in V$ that the ensembles of $\mathcal{B}_{v'}$ carry indices from 1 to $|\mathcal{B}_{v'}|$. Then, for $i = 1, \ldots, |\mathcal{B}_{v'}|$, $B_i \in \mathcal{B}_{v'}$ is the ensemble of v' with index i.)

Under these assumptions, an elementary move $m = (v, u, z, s) \in M(\mathcal{B})$ is interpreted as the transfer of service s, which is an element of the "source ensemble" $B_u \in \mathcal{B}_v$ of m, to the "target ensemble" $B_z \in \mathcal{B}_v$ of m. The following special cases have to be considered separately:

- If $u = 0$ then s is understood to be a nonrequired service not yet an element of any ensemble of v (not broadcasted), which is to be an element of ensemble $B_z \in \mathcal{B}_v$ after the move m has been made.
- If $z = 0$ then s is a service of the ensemble $B_u \in \mathcal{B}_v$, and is not to be an element of any ensemble of v (not broadcasted) after the move m has been made.
- If $z = |\mathcal{B}_v| + 1$ then the move m opens a new ensemble B_z not yet existing for vertex v, which consists exactly of element s after the move m has been made.

Remark: Given an elementary move $m = (v, u, z, s) \in M(\mathcal{B})$ with $u = 0$ or $z = 0$, for reasons of convenience, we introduce a virtual ensemble B_0 of v consisting of all the services not broadcasted on v. Thus, if $u = 0$, we remove the service s from the virtual source ensemble. On the other hand, if $z = 0$, we add the service s to the virtual target ensemble.

12.5.3 The Problem of Move Evaluation

Now, having defined the neighborhood, we could just use the standard design of the tabu concept and the aspiration criterion, and should have a working TS algorithm. Unfortunately, it turns out that the details of a successful TS implementation for the EPP are much more complicated. The following example illustrates the difficulties we face.

Let $\mathcal{B} \in \mathbb{B}$ be an ensemble assignment. Consider the case that for each pair of vertices $v_1, v_2 \in V$ with $v_1 v_2 \in E$ and for each pair of ensembles $B_1 \in \mathcal{B}_{v_1}, B_2 \in \mathcal{B}_{v_2}$, the following two properties are satisfied:

1. $|B_1| > 2$, $|B_2| > 2$. (This ensures that no single elementary move may cause B_1 or B_2 to become the empty set.)

2. $B_1 \neq B_2$, and at least two elementary moves are needed to make B_1 and B_2 equal.

We then obviously have $f(\mathcal{B}) = f(m(\mathcal{B}))$ for all $m \in M(\mathcal{B})$. In effect, if $\mathcal{B}$ occurs as an intermediate result of a TS search, the cost function f gives no hint how TS should proceed, for all possible transitions would appear equally valuable.

We have found that the situation described above, even though it appears to be a rather extreme case, actually arises very frequently. Experiments have shown that given a problem instance of EPP, for many ensemble assignments $\mathcal{B} \in \mathbb{B}$ we have $f(\mathcal{B}) \leq f(m(\mathcal{B}))$ for all elementary moves $m \in M(\mathcal{B})$ and thus no achievable improvement in the cost function. Furthermore, for many ensemble assignments $\mathcal{B} \in \mathbb{B}$ we even have $f(\mathcal{B}) = f(m(\mathcal{B}))$ for most elementary moves $m \in M(\mathcal{B})$ and thus no change in the cost function at all.

This problem-specific phenomenon makes the cost function as is absolutely unsuitable for any kind of guidance of TS. A way to overcome this dilemma is to develop an alternative system for evaluating the elementary moves $m \in M(\mathcal{B})$. Such a system will rely on characteristic features of the problem at hand, but only those aspects will be considered that appear to be relevant for guiding TS into promising directions.

One of these characteristic features of EPP is that for any $v, w \in V, v \neq w$, and any $B \in \mathcal{B}_v, C \in \mathcal{B}_w$, not only may we use the same frequency $f(v, B) = f(w, C)$ in the case that $vw \notin E$ (which, in an analogous form, applies to virtually all kinds of frequency assignment problems), but also in the case that $vw \in E$ but $B = C$. Let us call this latter case the SFN property (SFN = single frequency network). Now, knowing from GFF, which takes exhaustive advantage of the SFN property by oversupplying vertices $v \in V$ with services $s \in S$ not explicitly required, that use of this property may lead to significant reduction in frequency demand, this gives us an idea how to proceed.

12.5.4 Heuristic Move Evaluation

Before going into the details, let us give an overview of where we are heading. We will introduce an equivalence relation "$\equiv$" and an order relation "$\lhd$" for the elementary moves on an ensemble assignment $\mathcal{B} \in \mathbb{B}$. Given $m_1, m_2 \in M(\mathcal{B})$, and assuming $\mathcal{B}$ to be an intermediate result of TS, the equivalence $m_1 \equiv m_2$ will state that in our problem context both moves appear equally valuable in achieving an improvement in result quality during the further course of the TS search. Then given the set

$$\mathcal{T} := \{T \subseteq M(\mathcal{B}) \mid T \text{ is an equivalence class for "} \equiv \text{"}\}$$

for any $m_1, m_2 \in M(\mathcal{B})$, with $m_1 \in T_1, m_2 \in T_2, T_1, T_2 \in \mathcal{T}, T_1 \neq T_2$, the relationship $m_1 \lhd m_2$ expresses that in our problem context the move m_2 is considered to be of greater value than the move m_1 in guiding TS to future improvement in result quality. With "$\equiv$" and "$\lhd$" given, we can then guide any TS search using "$\equiv$" and "$\lhd$" in the way of an alternative cost function.

Underlying the relations "$\equiv$" and "$\lhd$" is a set of values measuring the tendency of a move to take advantage of the SFN property. The original cost function f is also a part of this set of values, but only plays a secondary role. In consequence, the cost function's role will be less to work out future result improvements than to help hinder loss of result quality already achieved.

For lack of space, we can only develop the major values underlying "$\equiv$" and "$\lhd$". We first need to define that given a vertex $v \in V$ and an ensemble $B \in \mathcal{B}_v$, we call an ensemble $\hat{B}$ an adjacent ensemble of B if there exists a vertex $\hat{v} \in V$, $v\hat{v} \in E$, with $\hat{B} \in \mathcal{B}_{\hat{v}}$.

Now, let $\mathcal{B} \in \mathbb{B}$ be an ensemble assignment, and let $m = (v, u, z, s) \in M(\mathcal{B})$ be an elementary move on $\mathcal{B}$. Let B_u be the source and B_z the target ensemble of the move m. If $z = |\mathcal{B}_v| + 1$, assume $B_z := \emptyset$. Set $\mathcal{B}' := m(\mathcal{B})$. Let B'_u be the source and B'_z the target ensemble after the move m has been made. Note that $B'_u = \emptyset$ is possible.

1. To define $b_1(m)$ and $d(m)$, we first need the following definitions.

$$b_u(m) := \begin{cases} (\max\{|B_u \cap B| \mid B \text{ is adjacent to } B_u\})^2, & \text{if } u \neq 0; \\ 0, & \text{otherwise.} \end{cases}$$

$$b_z(m) := \begin{cases} (\max\{|B_z \cap B| \mid B \text{ is adjacent to } B_z\})^2, & \text{if } z \neq 0; \\ 0, & \text{otherwise.} \end{cases}$$

Define $b'_u(m)$ and $b'_z(m)$ in the same way as $b_u(m)$ and $b_z(m)$, except that B'_u and B'_z are used instead of B_u and B_z.

Now define $b_1(m)$ and $d(m)$ as follows:

$$b_1(m) := [b'_z(m) - b_z(m)]$$

$$d(m) := [b'_u(m) - b_u(m)] + [b'_z(m) - b_z(m)]$$

Interpretation: The value $b'_u(m) - b_u(m)$ expresses the change (caused by the elementary move m) in the maximum number of services the source ensemble has in common with any other ensemble which is adjacent to the source ensemble. In the definition of $b_u(m)$ and $b'_u(m)$ we have squared these values in order to stress changes affecting higher numbers of shared services. The same holds for $b'_z(m) - b_z(m)$. The value $d(m)$ combines these two values. Note that $d(m) > 0$ implies $b_1(m) > 0$, because we always have $b'_u(m) - b_u(m) \leq 0$.

2. Define $b_2(m)$ to be:

$$b_2(m) := \begin{cases} b_u(m), & \text{if } u \neq 0 \text{ and } b_u(m) = b'_u(m); \\ 0, & \text{otherwise.} \end{cases}$$

Interpretation: The value $b_2(m)$ corresponds to the value $b_u(m)$, that is, to the maximum number of services the source ensemble B_u shares with adjacent ensembles, if and only if the move m removes a service from the ensemble B_u without changing $b_u(m)$. That is, the move frees bandwidth which becomes available for further "development" of the ensemble B_u.

3. To define $b_3(m)$, for each $v' \in V$ in the case $u \neq 0$ first define:

$$b_{3,v'}(m) := \begin{cases} 1, & \text{if} & vv' \in E \\ & \text{and} & \exists B' \in \mathcal{B}_{v'} : B_u \cap B' \neq \emptyset \\ & \text{and} & \forall B' \in \mathcal{B}_{v'} : B_u \neq B'; \\ 0, & \text{in all other cases.} \end{cases}$$

In the case $u \neq 0$ further define:

$$g := \left| \{ v' \in V \mid vv' \in E, \exists B' \in \mathcal{B}_{v'} : B_u \cap B' \neq \emptyset \} \right|$$

Now set:

$$b_3(m) := \begin{cases} \dfrac{\sum_{v' \in V} b_{3,v'}(m)}{g}, & \text{if } u \neq 0 \text{ and } g > 0; \\ 0, & \text{otherwise.} \end{cases}$$

Interpretation: The value $b_3(m)$ measures the fraction of "potential SFN situations" in the neighborhood of the source ensemble which the algorithm could eventually make use of, but has not yet done so. Here, a "potential SFN situation" is understood as an adjacent vertex in the area graph which has ensembles B' intersecting the source ensemble B_u in a nontrivial way (i.e., neither $B_u \cap B' = \emptyset$ nor $B_u = B'$ holds). We divide the number of such situations by the total number g of (potential or realized) SFN situations, i.e., situations in which $B_u \cap B' \neq \emptyset$. (If there are no SFN situations at all, then the value is simply set to 0.)

Note that for all $m \in M(\mathcal{B})$ we have $b_i(m) \geq 0$, $i = 1, \ldots, 3$.

Having introduced $b_1(m)$, $b_2(m)$, and $b_3(m)$, we can now define the relations "$\equiv$" and "$\lhd$". For this, let again $\mathcal{B}$ be an ensemble assignment, and let $m_1, m_2 \in M(\mathcal{B})$ be two elementary moves on $\mathcal{B}$.

1. We say that m_1 and m_2 are equivalent, $m_1 \equiv m_2$, if $\exists\, i \in \{1, \dots, 3\}$ such that the following property holds:

$$[b_j(m_1) = b_j(m_2) = 0 \text{ for } j = 1, \dots, i-1]$$

$$\text{and } \begin{cases} b_i(m_1) = b_i(m_2) > 0, & \text{if } i < 3 \\ b_i(m_1) = b_i(m_2) \geq 0, & \text{if } i = 3 \end{cases}$$

2. We say that m_1 is smaller than m_2, $m_1 \lhd m_2$, if $\exists\, i \in \{1, \dots, 3\}$ such that the following property holds:

$$[b_j(m_1) = b_j(m_2) = 0 \text{ for } j = 1, \dots, i-1] \text{ and } b_i(m_1) < b_i(m_2)$$

Note that "$\equiv$" and "$\lhd$" are not defined in a lexicographic way. Instead the first entry $\neq 0$ establishes the order. The idea behind this is that to select the move for the actual TS iteration we utilize a hierarchy of "filters" corresponding to the values $b_1(m)$, $b_2(m)$, and $b_3(m)$, where the first filter triggered by a nonzero value is activated and used to choose the next move.

Finally, we wish to remark that the full version of our TS employs some more values besides $b_1(m)$, $b_2(m)$, and $b_3(m)$, but their objective is merely to bring greater refinement into move evaluation.

Furthermore, we have not yet pointed out how the original cost function f is integrated into "$\equiv$" and "$\lhd$". The easiest way to do this would probably be to introduce a fourth value $b_4(m)$, defined as $b_4(m) := f((\mathcal{B}) - f(m(\mathcal{B}))$, and then expand the definition of "$\equiv$" and "$\lhd$" made above by choosing i from the set $\{1, \dots, 4\}$. Unfortunately, calculating $b_4(m)$ would imply coloring the ensemble graphs induced by $\mathcal{B}$ and especially by $m(\mathcal{B})$. In our implementation, we actually only employ the cost function f under certain special conditions, so that the value of the cost function does not have to be computed for all $m \in M(\mathcal{B})$. See [17] for details.

12.5.5 Setting Tabus

As has already been mentioned in the discussion of the basic TS framework, we will stick close to the standard design of working with tabus, with the one exception that we will use a periodic and not a constant function to generate the tabu tenure values. Before we can go into details, we must first define what the elements are in our problem context that are apt to have a tabu set on them. We have decided to set tabus on elements of the form (v, s), where $v \in V$ is a vertex and $s \in S$ is a service. Thus, if we make the iteration implied by the move $m = (v, u, z, s) \in M(\mathcal{B})$, with $\mathcal{B} \in \mathbb{B}$ being the actual ensemble assignment of TS, we afterward set a tabu on the element (v, s), preventing any further move of service s on vertex v for the time the tabu is valid. Note that the ensembles B_u and B_z, which are the source and target ensembles involved in the move m, are of no importance here. Only the action of having moved a service s on a vertex v is taken into account.

Setting a tabu demands assigning it a tabu tenure value. Using a constant function to generate the tabu tenure values, as done in traditional TS design, does not suffice in our application. For on the one hand, choosing a too small constant risks losing the capability to escape a local optimum once caught in it. On the other hand, choosing a too large constant might bring up the problem of iterating near a global optimum without the possibility of ever reaching it, which would be the case if some vital moves are always blocked by tabus. Experiments showed that we would always face the problem of having either chosen a too small or a too large tabu tenure constant, with always some TS runs possible for which the selected tabu tenure constant yields bad results. In consequence, we have decided to use a periodic function (a modified sine function), generating smaller and larger tabu tenure values in alternating phases. The particular choice of tabu tenure function will most likely have quite an impact on the performance of the algorithm, and hence is an interesting topic for future research.

12.5.6 Aspiration Criterion

The most common interpretation of the aspiration criterion, as described in the introduction of the TS framework, must use the cost function f to decide whether an improvement of the best solution obtained so far in a TS search is achievable. In our application, for a given intermediate result $\mathcal{B}$ of TS, this would imply calculating $f(m(\mathcal{B}))$ for all $m \in M(\mathcal{B})$; that is, coloring the induced ensemble graphs for all $m(\mathcal{B})$. This is simply not practical. Instead, and to keep things simple, we reformulate the aspiration criterion ignoring a tabu on any move $m = (v, u, z, s) \in M(\mathcal{B})$ if $z \neq |\mathcal{B}_z| + 1$ and if $d(m) > 0$ [implying $b_1(m) > 0$]. In addition, to prevent the algorithm from looping, we must ensure that the service s of the move m has not previously been removed from B_z, for then it would return to its origin, ignoring the tabu set to avoid situations of this kind. (To simplify matters, this detail is not included in the algorithmic description below.)

12.5.7 Algorithmic Description

The following program code describes the adaption of TS to the EPP:

```
Choose 𝐵₀ ∈ 𝔹;              // Choose initial value.
f̄ := f(𝐵₀);                 // Remember best result so far.
i := 0;                     // Counter for the TS iterations.
TL := ∅;                    // Initialize tabu list.
WHILE (termination condition not satisfied) DO
BEGIN
    // Note that all tabued moves of K₁(𝐵ᵢ) satisfy the aspiration criterion.
    K₁(𝐵ᵢ) := {m = (v, u, z, s) ∈ M(𝐵ᵢ) |(m ∉ TL ⋁ z ≠ |𝐵_z| + 1) ⋀ d(m) > 0};
    K₂(𝐵ᵢ) := {m ∈ M(𝐵ᵢ) |b₂(m) > 0} \ TL;
    K₃(𝐵ᵢ) := {m ∈ M(𝐵ᵢ) |b₃(m) > 0} \ TL;
    K₄(𝐵ᵢ) := M(𝐵ᵢ) \ TL;
    IF (Kⱼ(𝐵ᵢ) = ∅ ∀ j ∈ {1, . . . , 4}) THEN stop;
    Choose smallest j₀ ∈ {1, . . . , 4} such that K_{j₀}(𝐵ᵢ) ≠ ∅;
    Choose m₀ ∈ K_{j₀}(𝐵ᵢ) such that for all m ∈ K_{j₀}(𝐵ᵢ): m ◁ m₀ ⋁ m ≡ m₀;
```

$\mathcal{B}_{i+1} := m_0(\mathcal{B}_i);$
IF $(f(\mathcal{B}_{i+1}) < \bar{f})$ THEN $\bar{f} := f(\mathcal{B}_{i+1});$
$i := i + 1;$
  Update tabu list TL;
END; // of WHILE

  Remarks:

1. $K_j(\mathcal{B}), j = 1, \ldots, 4$, is a system of so-called candidate lists. In our algorithmic context, we have a priority level set on the candidate lists such that the candidate list $K_j(\mathcal{B})$ is of higher priority than all the candidate lists $K_{j+1}(\mathcal{B}), \ldots, K_4(\mathcal{B}), j = 1, \ldots,$ 3. Each candidate list $K_j(\mathcal{B}), j = 1, \ldots, 4$, consists of the moves $m \in M(\mathcal{B})$ relevant for the priority level it represents.

2. In our current implementation, we use SFF to obtain an initial solution $\mathcal{B}_0$.

3. Since it is of no special relevance for the understanding of the algorithmic description of our TS, and to keep things simple, we have not worked out the details of tabu list administration here.

12.5.8   Test Results

To validate our TS solution approach and its behavior in comparison to SFF and GFF, we have implemented and tested the TS sketched out in this section. The test scenario employed here will stay close to the test design, test description, and test procedures as developed in [10], where the characteristics of the SFF and GFF algorithms and their relation to the clique packing number have already been investigated in some detail. Though the test results presented here are still rather preliminary, and will have to be confirmed with more systematic studies in the future, they already show some interesting characteristics on how our TS approach behaves in relation to SFF, GFF and the clique packing number. The tests were performed using randomly generated problem instances. As area graphs we chose so-called unit disk (UD) graphs, which, because of their geometric structure, are commonly employed as a simplified model of broadcast networks [5]. UD graphs are intersection graphs of equal-sized disks in the Euclidean plane. They are usually specified by a point set $V \subseteq \mathbb{R}^2$ and a diameter d. The edges of the graph are then those pairs vw of distinct vertices v, w for which $\|v - w\|_2 \leq d$, where $\|\cdot\|_2$ denotes the Euclidean norm in $\mathbb{R}^2$.

  We performed two series of tests with diameters $d = 2500$ (graph density $\approx 15.6\%$) and $d = 4000$ (graph density $\approx 34.4\%$), where the point coordinates were generated uniformly and independently from the set $\{0, \ldots, 10000\} \times \{0, \ldots, 10000\}$. (This is slightly different from [10], where the point coordinates were 32 bit random floating point values from the set $[0, 1] \times [0, 1]$.) For the requirements we first generated a service set with uniformly distributed integer bandwidths in the interval $[1, 5]$. Then we determined for each $v \in V$ the size of the corresponding requirement set R_v, again uniformly in the range $[1, 5]$, and selected a random set of this size from the service set. The maximum ensemble size was $M = 10$.

In each test series we varied the parameters n (number of vertices) and r (number of services) as follows: $n \in \{50, 100\}$, $r \in \{10, 20, 50, 100, 250\}$. For each of the 10 resulting parameter combinations we generated 20 random problem instances with the same number of vertices and services—i.e., a total of 200 instances in each series—for which we computed the following values:

- *TS*: number of colors calculated for the best ensemble assignment found by TS
- *GFF*: number of colors calculated for a GFF ensemble assignment
- *SFF*: number of colors calculated for a SFF ensemble assignment
- *BEST*: min$\{TS, GFF, SFF\}$
- *S*: lower bound on the clique packing number, using the generalized Carraghan/ Pardalos algorithm [4] with the sum estimate for the packing number [10].

Both the SFF and GFF algorithms were invoked using a service order by decreasing sizes. Coloring was always done using the saturation algorithm [2]. In the case of SFF and GFF, we furthermore employed an iterated version of the saturation algorithm with 100 runs per coloring. Thus, especially for GFF, we can expect slightly better results than given in [10].

For the TS algorithm, we employed the termination criterion discussed earlier, that is, the search was terminated after a prescribed number N of iterations without an improvement on the best known solution. However, the number of iterations was chosen in relation to the size of the problem instance, using the following heuristic formula:

$$N = \left\lfloor \left(c|V|D \sum_{v \in V} |R_v| \right) + 0.5 \right\rfloor$$

where D is the density of the graph,

$$D = \frac{2|E|}{|V|(|V| - 1)}$$

and c is a small extra factor (5 in this test series).

In addition, we computed the following values:

- *STEP*: number of iterations for TS to achieve the best result (i.e., excluding the number N of trailing iterations without further improvement)
- *TIME*: time needed for STEP iterations, in seconds, on a Pentium III 500 MHz

We have not explicitly figured out the time necessary to compute the values *SFF* and *GFF*, for even the iterated version of the saturation algorithm with 100 runs per coloring took usually less than a second, at maximum 2 seconds, to be computed on a Pentium III 500 MHz, even for the largest problem instances in our test. Calculating *S*, on the other hand, could take up to 5 to 20 minutes on the same machine, depending on the problem instance size.

Figures 12.3 and 12.4 show the average "performance ratios" *BEST/S, TS/S, GFF/S,*

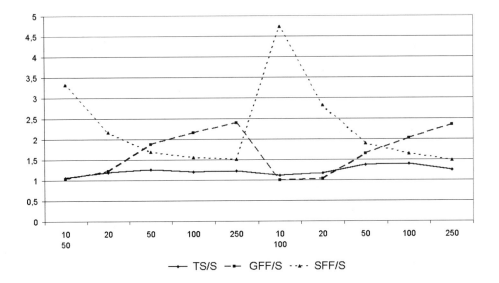

n	r	BEST/S	TS/S	GFF/S	SFF/S	STEP	TIME
50	10	1.03	1.06	1.03	3.32	1828.4	5.3
	20	1.19	1.19	1.23	2.17	2470.6	9.7
	50	1.26	1.26	1.87	1.69	423.4	3.0
	100	1.20	1.20	2.15	1.55	510.2	4.5
	250	1.22	1.22	2.39	1.51	121.4	2.4
100	10	1.00	1.11	1.00	4.74	5974.6	36.8
	20	1.03	1.17	1.03	2.82	10143.9	80.0
	50	1.37	1.37	1.64	1.89	5311.2	75.9
	100	1.39	1.39	2.02	1.64	739.8	13.7
	250	1.25	1.25	2.35	1.48	213.3	10.1

Figure 12.3   Test results for $d = 2500$.

and *SFF/S* for the two test series. Thus, all plotted values are ≥ 1, and a value of 1 indicates that only optimal solutions were computed for the given parameter combination. We have furthermore listed *STEP* and *TIME*, so to give an impression on the amount of effort it takes TS to achieve the best result.

In Table 12.1, for a better understanding of the test results, we give an overview of the percentage of instances ("hits") for which the *BEST* value was obtained.

The behavior of the SFF and GFF solution methods have already been analyzed in [10]; therefore we will only summarize these results, and instead concentrate on TS and its performance. We have pointed out earlier that for quite some problem instances SFF or GFF (but usually not both) can find optimal or near optimal solutions, yet there are many problem instances, for which both SFF and GFF yield rather poor results.

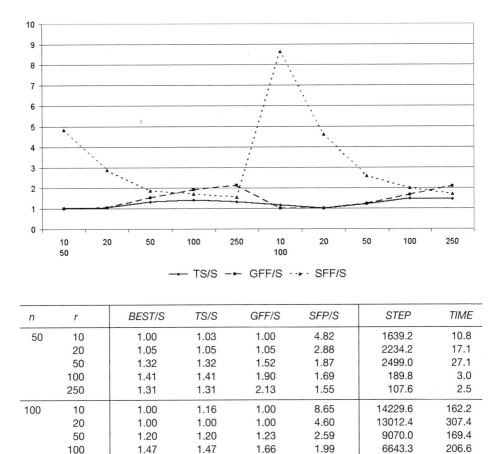

n	r	BEST/S	TS/S	GFF/S	SFP/S	STEP	TIME
50	10	1.00	1.03	1.00	4.82	1639.2	10.8
	20	1.05	1.05	1.05	2.88	2234.2	17.1
	50	1.32	1.32	1.52	1.87	2499.0	27.1
	100	1.41	1.41	1.90	1.69	189.8	3.0
	250	1.31	1.31	2.13	1.55	107.6	2.5
100	10	1.00	1.16	1.00	8.65	14229.6	162.2
	20	1.00	1.00	1.00	4.60	13012.4	307.4
	50	1.20	1.20	1.23	2.59	9070.0	169.4
	100	1.47	1.47	1.66	1.99	6643.3	206.6
	250	1.45	1.45	2.08	1.69	220.5	15.1

Figure 12.4 Test results for $d = 4000$.

Fortunately, there are some systematics in parameter settings, which influence this behavior. As can be seen, GFF finds optimal or near optimal solutions if $r/n \ll 1$. GFF solution quality decreases as r/n increases, and at the same time SFF solution quality improves. At the intersection of these two developments, both solutions are of rather poor quality. Especially in this case we expect and wish TS to achieve improvements in the results computed.

And indeed, as long as $r/n \ll 1$, TS has a hard time generating results which are as good as those of GFF. But as r/n increases, TS begins to dominate SFF and GFF, and this becomes most obvious in the vicinity of the intersection point mentioned above, where SFF and GFF yield results of similar quality.

However, it must be noted that, although TS delivers clearly better results than SFF

TABLE 12.1   Percentage of instances ("hits") for which the BEST value was obtained

$d = 2500$					$d = 4000$				
n	r	TS	GFF	SFF	n	r	TS	GFF	SFF
50	10	80%	95%	0%	50	10	85%	100%	0%
	20	90%	65%	0%		20	100%	100%	0%
	50	100%	0%	5%		50	100%	0%	0%
	100	100%	0%	0%		100	100%	0%	0%
	250	100%	0%	0%		250	100%	0%	5%
100	10	70%	100%	0%	100	10	65%	100%	0%
	20	60%	100%	0%		20	95%	100%	0%
	50	100%	0%	0%		50	95%	70%	0%
	100	100%	0%	0%		100	100%	0%	0%
	250	100%	0%	5%		250	100%	0%	0%

and GFF if $1/2 \le r/n$ (and r/n within the range of our tests), the performance ratio of TS still ranges up to 1.47. Thus, either the results of TS are still not entirely satisfactory, or the lower bound provided by the (approximation of the) clique packing number is not near the optimum for these instances, or both. Some problems concerning the TS design are known, yet not solved. For an example, our TS aims at constructing single frequency networks (SFNs), employing oversupply of services to reach that goal, with a number of criteria to help decide if in a given situation expanding, or cutting back a SFN is advantageous. These criteria are at the moment still under construction. So up to now, in unclear situations, our TS rather tends to build up a SFN, even if the opposite would, eventually in longer terms, bring greater gain.

12.6 CONCLUSION

The ensemble planning problem discussed in this chapter is not only important for the planning of DAB networks, it is also interesting from a theoretical point of view, because it involves complex interactions between different classical NP-hard optimization problems, a feature that pertains to many real-world planning problems in network design and other applications. Further theoretical studies of the problem will probably center around special cases and improved lower-bounding methods, which will help us to better understand the structure of this problem. Some first steps into this direction can be found in [22]. Although the available solution techniques, in particular our tabu search algorithm, already perform fairly well in practice, additional research is needed to further improve these algorithms and to design alternative solution methods.

Beyond the basic problem formulation introduced in this chapter, there are other kinds of constraints and objectives arising in practical network planning that point to additional directions for future research. We sketch out some of these in the following. More details can be found in [10].

12.6.1 Restricted Block Assignments

Just as in classical channel assignment planning, it may be necessary to restrict the set of frequency blocks available at certain vertices. The main reason for this are other types of broadcast services using up certain frequencies in the neighborhood of the corresponding areas. For instance, in most countries, the new DAB network must coexist with existing FM or TV networks for quite some time, and hence it is necessary to protect the frequencies used by these services. This leads to a so-called list coloring problem [14]. Admissible color sets for services instead of vertices are also a practical requirement to be considered, since, e.g., DAB is currently transmitted in different frequency bands, such as the VHF band and the L band, which incur different running costs.

12.6.2 Maximization of Free Bandwidth

In general, there may be many different optimal or good solutions for a given instance of the ensemble planning problem and, hence, we might be interested in finding solutions with certain desirable properties. For instance, even an optimal solution might be further improved by increasing the "free bandwidth" still available in the constructed ensembles for additional services without having to modify the existing block assignment.

12.6.3 Restricting Oversupply

As we have pointed out in Example 1, oversupply is sometimes essential if we want to minimize the overall number of required frequency blocks. However, oversupply also incurs a cost since it will usually increase the number of ensembles per area and hence require a larger number of transmitters to realize the ensemble assignment. In order to restrict the amount of oversupply, we might put a limit on the number of ensembles for a given area. Another possible approach would be to charge for the bandwidth allocated to a service. Yet another type of constraint, which frequently arises in practice, is that we might wish to specify which services must not be supplied in a given area. We call this the ensemble planning problem with forbidden services, which can be interpreted as a special case of "bandwidth prizing." Unfortunately, as proved in [10], this problem is already difficult to approximate in the very simple case of complete area graphs.

ACKNOWLEDGMENTS

This research was supported by the Ministry of Commerce, Transport, Agriculture and Viticulture of Rhineland-Palatinate under the research program of the Association for Research in Media Technology in South-West Germany (FMS).

REFERENCES

1. D. Berger, B. Gendron, J.-Y. Potvin, S. Raghavan, and P. Soriano, Tabu search for a network loading problem with multiple facilities, *Journal of Heuristics, 6*(2): 253–267, 2000.

2. D. Brélaz, New methods to color the vertices of a graph, *Communications of the ACM, 22*(4): 251–256, 1979.

3. H. Breu, *Algorithmic Aspects of Constrained Unit Disk Graphs*, PhD thesis, University of British Columbia, Department of Computer Science, 1996.

4. R. Carraghan and P. M. Pardalos, An exact algorithm for the maximum clique problem, *Operations Research Letters, 9:* 375–382, 1990.

5. B. N. Clark, C. J. Colbourn, and D. S. Johnson, Unit disk graphs, *Discrete Mathematics, 86:* 165–177, 1990.

6. P. Crescenzi and V. Kann, A compendium of NP optimization problems. http:// www.nada.kth. se/theory/problemlist.html.

7. M. R. Garey and D. S. Johnson, *Computers and Intractability. A Guide to the Theory of NP-Completeness*, New York: Freeman, 1979.

8. M. C. Golumbic, *Algorithmic Graph Theory and Perfect Graphs*. Computer Science and Applied Mathematics, New York: Academic Press, 1980.

9. A. Gräf, *Coloring and Recognizing Special Graph Classes*. PhD thesis, Johannes Gutenberg-Universität Mainz, Germany, 1995. Published as Report No. 20/95 in the series Musikinformatik und Medientechnik.

10. A. Gräf, DAB ensemble planning—problems and techniques, *Telecommunication Systems, 18*:137–154, 2001.

11. W. K. Hale, Frequency assignment: Theory and applications, *Proc. IEEE, 68:* 1497–1514, 1980.

12. J.-K. Hao, R. Dorne, and P. Galinier, Tabu search for frequency assignment in mobile radio networks, *Journal of Heuristics, 4:*47–62, 1998.

13. A. Hertz and D. de Werra, Using tabu search techniques for graph coloring, *Computing, 39:* 345–351, 1987.

14. T. R. Jensen and B. Toft, *Graph Coloring Problems*, New York: Wiley, 1995.

15. M. Laguna and F. Glover, Bandwidth packing: a tabu search approach, *Management Science, 39:* 492–500, 1993.

16. D. W. Matula and L. L. Beck, Smallest-last ordering and clustering and graph coloring algorithms, *Journal of the Association of Computing Machinery, 30*(3): 417–427, 1983.

17. T. McKenney, Eine Anpassung der Tabu Search Methode an das DAB Ensemble-Planungsproblem, Band I. Musikinformatik und Medientechnik 41/00, Johannes Gutenberg-Universität Mainz, Musikwissenschaftliches Institut, Bereich Musikinformatik, 2000.

18. I. H. Osman and J. P. Kelly, editors, *Meta-Heuristics: Theory and Applications* 2nd ed., Boston: Kluwer, 1997.

19. A. Quellmalz, *Graphenorientierte Planung von Sendernetzen*, Südwestfunk Schriftenreihe Rundfunktechnik 3. Baden-Baden, Nomos Verlagsgesellschaft, 1993.

20. C. R. Reeves, (Ed.), *Modern Heuristic Techniques for Combinatorial Problems*, New York: McGraw-Hill, 1995.

21. F. S. Roberts, *T*-colorings of graphs: recent results and open problems, *Discrete Mathematics, 93:* 229–245, 1991.

22. K. Schmeisser, Frequency ensemble planning for digital audio broadcasting. Master's thesis, Dalhousie University, Halifax, Canada, 2000.

CHAPTER 13

Transport over Wireless Networks

HUNG-YUN HSIEH and RAGHUPATHY SIVAKUMAR
School of Electrical and Computer Engineering, Georgia Institute of Technology, Atlanta

13.1 INTRODUCTION

The Internet has undergone a spectacular change over the last 10 years in terms of its size and composition. At the heart of this transformation has been the evolution of increasingly better wireless networking technologies, which in turn has fostered growth in the number of mobile Internet users (and vice versa). Industry market studies forecast an installed base of about 100 million portable computers by the year 2004, in addition to around 30 million hand-held devices and a further 100 million "smart phones." With such increasing numbers of mobile and wireless devices acting as primary citizens of the Internet, researchers have been studying the impact of the wireless networking technologies on the different layers of the network protocol stack, including the physical, data-link, medium-access, network, transport, and application layers [13, 5, 15, 18, 4, 17, 16].

Any such study is made nontrivial by the diversity of wireless networking technologies in terms of their characteristics. Specifically, wireless networks can be broadly classified based on their coverage areas as picocell networks (high bandwidths of up to 20 Mbps, short latencies, low error rates, and small ranges of up to a few meters), microcell networks (high bandwidths of up to 10 Mbps, short latencies, low error rates, and small ranges of up to a few hundred meters), macrocell networks (low bandwidths of around 50 kbps, relatively high and varying latencies, high error rates of up to 10% packet error rates, and large coverage areas of up to a few miles), and global cell networks (varying and asymmetric bandwidths, large latencies, high error rates, and large coverage areas of hundreds of miles). The problem is compounded when network models other than the conventional cellular network model are also taken into consideration [11].

The statistics listed above are for current-generation wireless networks, and can be expected to improve with future generations. However, given their projected bandwidths, latencies, error rates, etc., the key problems and solutions identified and summarized in this chapter will hold equally well for future generations of wireless networks [9]. Although the impact of wireless networks can be studied along the different dimensions

Handbook of Wireless Networks and Mobile Computing, Edited by Ivan Stojmenović.
ISBN 0-471-41902-8 © 2002 John Wiley & Sons, Inc.

of protocol layers, classes of wireless networks, and network models, the focus of this chapter is the transport layer in micro- and macrocell wireless networks. Specifically, we will focus on the issue of supporting reliable and adaptive transport over such wireless networks.

The transmission control protocol (TCP) is the most widely used transport protocol in the current Internet, comprising an estimated 95% of traffic; hence, it is critical to address this category of transport protocols. This traffic is due to a large extent to web traffic (HTTP, the protocol used between web clients and servers, uses TCP as the underlying transport protocol). Hence, it is reasonable to assume that a significant portion of the data transfer performed by the mobile devices will also require similar, if not the same, semantics supported by TCP. It is for this reason that most of related studies performed, and newer transport approaches proposed, use TCP as the starting point to build upon and the reference layer to compare against. In keeping with this line of thought, in this chapter we will first summarize the ill effects that wireless network characteristics have on TCP's performance. Later, we elaborate on some of the TCP extensions and other transport protocols proposed that overcome such ill effects.

We provide a detailed overview of TCP in the next section. We identify the mechanisms for achieving two critical tasks—reliability and congestion control—and their drawbacks when operating over a wireless network. We then discuss three different approaches for improving transport layer performance over wireless networks:

1. *Link layer approaches* that enhance TCP's performance without requiring any change at the transport layer and maintain the end-to-end semantics of TCP by using link layer changes

2. *Indirect approaches* that break the end-to-end semantics of TCP and improve transport layer performance by masking the characteristics of the wireless portion of the connection from the static host (the host in the wireline network)

3. *End-to-end approaches* that change TCP to improve transport layer performance and maintain the end-to-end semantics

We identify one protocol each for the above categories, summarize the approach followed by the protocol, and discuss its advantages and drawbacks in different environments. Finally, we compare the three protocols and provide some insights into their behavior vis-à-vis each other.

The contributions of this chapter are thus twofold: (i) we first identify the typical characteristics of wireless networks, and discuss the impact of each of the characteristics on the performance of TCP, and (ii) we discuss three different approaches to either extend TCP or adopt a new transport protocol to address the unique characteristics of wireless networks. The rest of the chapter is organized as follows: In Section 13.2, we provide a background overview of the mechanisms in TCP. In Section 13.3, we identify typical wireless network characteristics and their impact on the performance of TCP. In Section 13.4, we discuss three transport layer approaches that address the problems due to the unique characteristics of wireless networks. In Section 13.5, we conclude the chapter.

13.2 OVERVIEW OF TCP

13.2.1 Overview

TCP is a connection-oriented, reliable byte stream transport protocol with end-to-end congestion control. Its role can be broken down into four different tasks: connection management, flow control, congestion control, and reliability. Because of the greater significance of the congestion control and reliability schemes in the context of wireless networks, we provide an overview of only those schemes in the rest of this section.

13.2.2 Reliability

TCP uses positive acknowledgment (ACK) to acknowledge successful reception of a segment. Instead of acknowledging only the segment received, TCP employs cumulative acknowledgment, in which an ACK with acknowledgment number N acknowledges all data bytes with sequence numbers up to $N-1$. That is, the acknowledgment number in an ACK identifies the sequence number of next byte expected. With cumulative acknowledgment, a TCP receiver does not have to acknowledge every segment received, but only the segment with the highest sequence number. Additionally, even if an ACK is lost during transmission, reception of an ACK with a higher acknowledgment number automatically solves the problem. However, if a segment is received out of order, its ACK will carry the sequence number of the missing segment instead of the received segment. In such a case, a TCP sender may not be able to know immediately if that segment has been received successfully.

At the sender end, a transmitted segment is considered lost if no acknowledgment for that segment is received, which happens either because the segment does not reach the destination, or the acknowledgment is lost on its way back. TCP will not, however, wait indefinitely to decide whether a segment is lost. Instead, TCP keeps a retransmission timeout (RTO) timer that is started every time a segment is transmitted. If no ACK is received by the time the RTO expires, the segment is considered lost, and retransmission of the segment is performed. (The actual mechanisms used in TCP are different because of optimizations. However, our goal here is to merely highlight the conceptual details behind the mechanisms.)

Proper setting of the RTO value is thus important for the performance of TCP. If the RTO value is too small, TCP will timeout unnecessarily for an acknowledgment that is still on its way back, thus wasting network resources to retransmit a segment that has already been delivered successfully. On the other hand, if the RTO value is too large, TCP will wait too long before retransmitting the lost segment, thus leaving the network resources underutilized. In practice, the TCP sender keeps a running average of the segment round-trip times (RTT_{avg}) and the deviation (RTT_{dev}) for all acknowledged segments. The RTO is set to $RTT_{avg} + 4 \cdot RTT_{dev}$.

The problem of segment loss is critical to TCP not only in how TCP detects it, but also how it TCP interprets it. Because TCP was conceived for a wireline network with very low transmission error rate, TCP assumes all losses to be because of congestion. Hence, upon the detection of a segment loss, TCP will invoke congestion control to alleviate the problem, as discussed in the next subsection.

13.2.3 Congestion Control

TCP employs a window-based scheme for congestion control, in which a TCP sender is allowed to have a window size worth of bytes outstanding (unacknowledged) at any given instant. In order to track the capacity of the receiver and the network, and not to overload it either, two separate windows are maintained: a receiver window and a congestion window. The receiver window is a feedback from the receiver about its buffering capacity, and the congestion window is an approximation of the available network capacity. We now describe the three phases of the congestion control scheme in TCP.

Slow Start

When a TCP connection is established, the TCP sender learns of the capacity of the receiver through the receiver window size. The network capacity, however, is still unknown to the TCP sender. Therefore, TCP uses a slow start mechanism to probe the capacity of the network and determine the size of the congestion window. Initially, the congestion window size is set to the size of one segment, so TCP sends only one segment to the receiver and then waits for its acknowledgment. If the acknowledgment does come back, it is reasonable to assume the network is capable of transporting at least one segment. Therefore, the sender increases its congestion window by one segment's worth of bytes and sends a burst of two segments to the receiver. The return of two ACKs from the receiver encourages TCP to send more segments in the next transmission. By increasing the congestion window again by two segments' worth of bytes (one for each ACK), TCP sends a burst of four segments to the receiver. As a consequence, for every ACK received, the congestion window increases by one segment; effectively, the congestion window doubles for each full window worth of segments successfully acknowledged. Since TCP paces the transmission of segments to the return of ACKs, TCP is said to be self-clocking, and we refer to this mechanism as ACK-clocking in the rest of the chapter. The growth in congestion window size continues until it is greater than the receiver window or some of the segments and/or their ACKs start to get lost. Because TCP attributes segment loss to network congestion, it immediately enters the congestion avoidance phase.

Congestion Avoidance

As soon as the network starts to drop segments, it is inappropriate to increase the congestion window size multiplicatively as in the slow start phase. Instead, a scheme with additive increase in congestion window size is used to probe the network capacity. In the congestion avoidance phase, the congestion window grows by one segment for each full window of segments that have been acknowledged. Effectively, if the congestion window equals N segments, it increases by $1/N$ segments for every ACK received.

To dynamically switch between slow start and congestion avoidance, a slow start threshold (*ssthresh*) is used. If the congestion window is smaller than *ssthresh*, the TCP sender operates in the slow start phase and increases its congestion window exponentially; otherwise, it operates in congestion avoidance phase and increases its congestion window linearly. When a connection is established, *ssthresh* is set to 64 K bytes. Whenever a segment gets lost, *ssthresh* is set to half of the current congestion window. If the segment loss is detected through duplicate ACKs (explained later), TCP reduces its congestion window by half. If the segment loss is detected through a time-out, the congestion window is reset to one segment's worth of bytes. In this case, TCP will operate in slow start phase and increase the congestion window exponentially until it reaches *ssthresh*, after which TCP will operate in congestion avoidance phase and increase the congestion window linearly.

Congestion Control

Because TCP employs a cumulative acknowledgment scheme, when the segments are received out of order, all their ACKs will carry the same acknowledgment number indicating the next expected segment in sequence. This phenomenon introduces duplicate ACKs at the TCP sender. An out-of-order delivery can result from either delayed or lost segments. If the segment is lost, eventually the sender times out and a retransmission is initiated. If the segment is simply delayed and finally received, the acknowledgment number in ensuing ACKs will reflect the receipt of all the segments received in sequence thus far. Since the connection tends to be underutilized waiting for the timer to expire, TCP employs a fast retransmit scheme to improve the performance. Heuristically, if TCP receives three or more duplicate ACKs, it assumes that the segment is lost and retransmits before the timer expires. Also, when inferring a loss through the receipt of duplicate ACKs, TCP cuts down its congestion window size by half. Hence, TCP's congestion control scheme is based on the linear increase multiplicative decrease paradigm (LIMD) [8]. On the other hand, if the segment loss is inferred through a time-out, the congestion window is reset all the way to one, as discussed before.

In the next section, we will study the impact of wireless network characteristics on each of the above mechanisms.

13.3 TCP OVER WIRELESS NETWORKS

In the previous section, we described the basic mechanisms used by TCP to support reliability and congestion control. In this section, we identify the unique characteristics of a wireless network, and for each of the characteristics discuss how it impacts TCP's performance.

13.3.1 Overview

The network model that we assume for the discussions on the impact of wireless network characteristics on TCP's performance is that of a conventional cellular network. The mobile hosts are assumed to be directly connected to an access point or base station, which in turn is connected to the backbone wireline Internet through a distribution network. Note that the nature of the network model used is independent of the specific type of wireless network it is used in. In other words, the wireless network can be either a picocell, microcell, or macrocell network and, irrespective of its type, can use a particular network model. However, the specific type of network might have an impact on certain aspects like the available bandwidth, channel access scheme, degree of path asymmetry, etc. Finally, the connections considered in the discussions are assumed to be between a mobile host in the wireless network and a static host in the backbone Internet. Such an assumption is reasonable, given that most of the Internet applications use the client–server model (e.g., http, ftp, telnet, e-mail, etc.) for their information transfer. Hence, mobile hosts will be expected to predominantly communicate with backbone servers, rather than with other mobile hosts within the same wireless network or other wireless networks. However, with the evolution of applications wherein applications on peer entities more often communicate with each other, such an assumption might not hold true.

13.3.2   Random Losses

A fundamental difference between wireline and wireless networks is the presence of random wireless losses in the latter. Specifically, the effective bit error rates in wireless networks are significantly higher than that in a wireline network because of higher cochannel interference, host mobility, multipath fading, disconnections due to coverage limitations, etc. Packet error rates ranging from 1% in microcell wireless networks up to 10% in macrocell networks have been reported in experimental studies [4, 17]. Although the higher packet error rates in wireless networks inherently degrade the performance experienced by connections traversing such networks, they cause an even more severe degradation in the throughput of connections using TCP as the transport protocol.

As described in the previous section, TCP multiplicatively decreases its congestion window upon experiencing losses. The decrease is performed because TCP assumes that all losses in the network are due to congestion, and such a multiplicative decrease is essential to avoid congestion collapse in the event of congestion [8]. However, TCP does not have any mechanisms to differentiate between congestion-induced losses and other random losses. As a result, when TCP observes random wireless losses, it wrongly interprets such losses as congestion losses, and cuts down its window, thus reducing the throughput of the connection. This effect is more pronounced in low bandwidth wireless networks as window sizes are typically small and, hence, packet losses typically result in a retransmission timeout (resulting in the window size being cut down to one) due to the lack of enough duplicate acknowledgments for TCP to go into the fast retransmit phase. Even in high-bandwidth wireless networks, if bursty random losses (due to cochannel interference or fading) are more frequent, this phenomenon of TCP experiencing a timeout is more likely, because of the multiple losses within a window resulting in the lack of sufficient number of acknowledgments to trigger a fast retransmit.

If the loss probability is p, it can be shown that TCP's throughput is proportional to $1/\sqrt{p}$ [14]. Hence, as the loss rate increases, TCP's throughput degrades proportional to $\sqrt{p}$. The degradation of TCP's throughput has been extensively studied in several related works [14, 3, 17].

13.3.3   Large and Varying Delay

The delay along the end-to-end path for a connection traversing a wireless network is typically large and varying. The reasons include:
  • *Low Bandwidths.* When the bandwidth of the wireless link is very low, transmission

delays are large, contributing to a large end-to-end delay. For example, with a packet size of 1 KB and a channel bandwidth of 20 Kbps [representative of the bandwidth available over a wide-area wireless network like CDPD (cellular digital packet data)], the transmission delay for a packet will be 400 ms. Hence, the typical round-trip times for connections over such networks can be in the order of a few seconds.

- *Latency in the Switching Network.* The base station of the wireless network is typically connected to the backbone network through a switching network belonging to the wireless network provider. Several tasks including switching, bookkeeping, etc. are taken care of by the switching network, albeit at the cost of increased latency. Experimental studies have shown this latency to be nontrivial when compared to the typical round-trip times identified earlier [17].

- *Channel Allocation.* Most wide-area wireless networks are overlayed on infrastructures built for voice traffic. Consequently, data traffic typically share the available channel with voice traffic. Due to the real-time nature of the voice traffic, data traffic is typically given lower precedence in the channel access scheme. For example, in CDPD that is overlayed on the AMPS voice network infrastructure, data traffic are only allocated channels that are not in use by the voice traffic. A transient phase in which there are no free channels available can cause a significant increase in the end-to-end delay. Furthermore, since the delay depends on the amount of voice traffic in the network, it can also vary widely over time.

- *Assymmetry in Channel Access.* If the base station and the mobile hosts use the same channel in a wireless network, the channel access scheme is typically biased toward the base station [1]. As a result, the forward traffic of a connection experiences less delay than the reverse traffic. However, since TCP uses ACK-clocking, as described in the previous section, any delay in the receipt of ACKs will slow down the progression of the congestion window size at the sender end, causing degradation in the throughput enjoyed by the connection.

- *Unfairness in Channel Access.* Most medium access protocols in wireless networks use a binary exponential scheme for backing off after collisions. However, such a scheme has been well studied and characterized to exhibit the "capture syndrome" wherein mobile hosts that get access to the channel tend to retain access until they are not backlogged anymore. This unfairness in channel access can lead to random and prolonged delays in mobile hosts getting access to the underlying channel, further increasing and varying the round-trip times experienced by TCP.

Because of the above reasons, connections over wireless networks typically experience large and varying delays. At the same time, TCP relies heavily on its estimation of the round-trip time for both its window size progression (ACK-clocking), and its retransmission timeout (RTO) computation ($RTT_{avg} + 4 \cdot RTT_{dev}$). When the delay is large and varying, the window progression is slow. More critically, the retransmission timeout is artificially inflated because of the large deviation due to varying delays. Furthermore, the RTT estimation is skewed for reasons that we state under the next subsection. Experimental studies over wide-area wireless networks have shown the retransmission timeout values to be as high as 32 seconds for a connection with an average round trip time of just 1 second [17]. This adversely affects the performance of TCP because, on packet loss in the absence of duplicate ACKs to trigger fast retransmit, TCP will wait for an RTO amount of time before inferring a loss, thereby slowing down the progression of the connection.

13.3.4   Low Bandwidth

Wireless networks are characterized by significantly lower bandwidths than their wireline counterparts. Pico- and microcell wireless networks offer bandwidths in the range of 2–10 Mbps. However, macrocell networks that include wide-area wireless networks typically offer bandwidths of only a few tens of kilobits per second. CDPD offers 19.2 Kbps, and the bandwidth can potentially be shared by upto 30 users. RAM (Mobitex) offers a bandwidth of around 8 Kbps, and ARDIS offers either 4.8 Kbps or 19.2 Kbps of bandwidth. The above figures represent the raw bandwidths offered by the respective networks; the effective bandwidths can be expected to be even lower. Such low bandwidths adversely affect TCP's performance because of TCP's bursty nature.

In TCP's congestion control mechanism, when the congestion window size is increased, packets are burst out in a bunch as long as there is room under the window size. During the slow start phase, this phenomenon of bursting out packets is more pronounced since the window size increases exponentially. When the low channel bandwidth is coupled with TCP's bursty nature, packets within the same burst experience increasing round-trip times because of the transmission delays experienced by the packets ahead of them in the mobile host's buffer. For example, when the TCP at the mobile host bursts out a bunch of 8 packets, then packet i among the 8 packets experiences a round-trip time that includes the transmission times for the $i - 1$ packets ahead of it in the buffer. When the packets experience different round-trip times, the average round-trip time maintained by TCP is artificially increased and, more importantly, the average deviation increases. This phenomenon, coupled with the other phenomena described in the previous subsection, results in the retransmission timeout being inflated to a large value. Consequently, TCP reacts to losses in a delayed fashion, reducing its throughput.

13.3.5   Path Asymmetry

Although a transport protocol's performance should ideally be influenced only by the forward path characteristics [17], TCP, by virtue of its ACK-clocking-based window control, depends on both the forward path and reverse path characteristics for its performance. At an extreme, a TCP connection will freeze if acknowledgments do not get through from the receiver to the sender, even if there is available bandwidth on the forward path. Given this nature of TCP, there are two characteristics that negatively affect its performance:

1. *Low Priority for the Path from Mobile Host.* In most wireless networks that use the same channel for upstream and downstream traffic, the base station gains precedence in access to the channel. For example, the CDPD network's DCMA/CD channel access exhibits this behavior [17]. When such a situation arises, assuming the forward path is toward the mobile host, the acknowledgments get lower priority to the data

traffic in the other direction. (If the forward path is from the mobile host, the forward path gains lower precedence and, consequently, the throughput of the connection will again be low.) This will negatively impact the performance of the TCP connection, even though there is no problem with the forward path characteristics.

2. *Channel Capture Effect.* Since most wireless medium access protocols use a binary exponential back-off scheme, mobile hosts that currently have access to the channel are more likely to retain access to the channel. This further increases the time period between two instances at which a mobile host has access to the channel and, hence, can send data or ACKs. Although the channel access schemes might still be long-term fair with respect to the allocations to the different mobile hosts in the network, the short-term unfairness they exhibit can severely degrade TCP's performance [7].

The above two characteristics degrade TCP's performance in two ways. (i) The throughput suffers because of the stunted bandwidth available for the traffic from the mobile host, irrespective of whether it is forward path or reverse path. While it is equally bad in both cases, it can be considered more undesirable for a transport protocol to suffer degraded throughput because of problems with the reverse path. (ii) Because of the short-term unfair access to the channel, when the mobile host sends data, it does so in bursts. This further exacerbates the performance of TCP because of the varying RTT problem identified in the section on low bandwidth.

13.3.6 Disconnections

Finally, given that the stations are mobile, it is likely that they will experience frequent and prolonged disconnections because of phenomena like hand-offs between cells, disruption in the base station coverage (say, when the mobile host is inside a tunnel), or extended fading. In the event of such prolonged disruptions in service, TCP initially experiences a series of retransmission timeouts resulting in its RTO value being exponentially backed-off to a large value, and finally goes into the persistence mode wherein it checks back periodically to determine if the connection is up. When the blackout ends, TCP once again enters the slow start phase and starts with a window size of one. Hence, such frequent blackouts can significantly reduce the throughput enjoyed by TCP flows.

Thus far, we have looked at several unique characteristics of wireless networks. With each characteristic identified, we have also discussed its impact on TCP's performance. In the next section, we discuss three approaches that attempt to improve the performance of the transport protocol over wireless networks.

13.4 APPROACHES TO IMPROVE TRANSPORT LAYER PERFORMANCE

In the previous sections, we have summarized the key mechanisms of TCP, identified the unique characteristics of wireless networks, and discussed how the characteristics impact the performance of TCP. In this section, we examine three different classes of approaches that attempt to provide improved transport layer performance over wireless networks. The approaches that we discuss are: (i) link layer enhancements, (ii) indirect protocols, and

(iii) end-to-end protocols. For each class of approaches, we present an overview, following which we consider an example protocol that belongs to that particular class, describe the protocol, and discuss its performance. Finally, we present a comparative discussion of the three classes of approaches.

13.4.1 Link Layer Enhancements

The approaches that fall under this category attempt to mask the characteristics of the wireless network by having special link layer mechanisms over the wireless link. Such approaches are typically transparent to the overlying transport protocol. Further, the approaches can either be oblivious to the mechanisms of the transport protocol, or make use of the transport layer mechanisms for improved performance. They typically involve buffering of packets at the base station and the retransmission of the packets that are lost due to errors on the wireless link. Consequently, the static host is exposed only to congestion-induced losses. Link layer enhancements thus have the following characteristics: (i) they mask out the unique characteristics of the wireless link from the transport protocol; (ii) they are typically transparent to the transport protocol and, hence, do not require any change in the protocol stack of either the static host or the mobile host; (iii) they can either be aware of the transport protocol's mechanisms or be oblivious to it—the "transport protocol aware" class of protocols can be more effective because of the additional knowledge; (iv) they require added intelligence, additional buffers, and retransmission capability at the base station; (v) they retain the end-to-end semantics of TCP since they do not change the transport protocol. Several schemes including reliable link layer approaches and the snoop protocol [4] belong to this category. We will now provide an overview of the snoop protocol.

13.4.1.1 The Snoop Protocol

The snoop protocol is an approach that enhances the performance of TCP over wireless links without requiring any change in the protocol stacks at either the sender or the receiver. The only changes are made at the base station where code is introduced to cache all transmitted packets and selectively retransmit packets upon the detection of a random wireless loss (or losses). Specifically, the random loss is detected by the receipt of duplicate TCP acknowledgments that arrive from the mobile host at the base station. Hence, the base station in the snoop protocol will need to be TCP-aware and capable of interpreting TCP acknowledgments.

Because of the retransmission of packets at the base station, the static host is kept unaware of the vagaries of the wireless link. In the ideal case, the static host will never realize the existence of the wireless link and its unique characteristics. The snoop protocol is more sophisticated than a simple reliable link layer protocol because it is TCP-aware and hence can perform more optimizations that improve TCP's performance. In particular, at the base station the snoop module, after receiving duplicate ACKs, suppresses the duplicate ACKs in addition to performing the retransmission. This is to avoid the receipt of the duplicate ACKs at the sender, which would trigger another retransmission and undermine the very purpose of having the snoop module at the base station.

Figure 13.1 illustrates the workings of the snoop protocol. Note that the snoop module at the base station can help in improving TCP performance only when the bulk of the data transfer is from the static host to the mobile host. When the data transfer is primarily from the mobile host, the snoop module described thus far cannot provide any substantial improvement in performance, since the mobile host cannot realize whether any packet losses have occurred over the wireless link or in the backbone network because of congestion. The snoop approach solves this problem by employing a negative acknowledgment scheme at the base station that informs the mobile host about losses over the wireless link. The snoop implementation makes use of the TCP-SACK (selective acknowledgments) mechanism to implement the negative acknowledgment scheme. Specifically, selective acknowledgments are sent such that the mobile host realizes losses over the wireless link and retransmits such packets without having to wait for TCP's retransmission timeout (which is typically significantly higher than the round-trip time over the wireless link) to kick in. The snoop approach uses an external multicast scheme to address temporary blackouts because of mobile host handoffs between cells.

We now elaborate on the mechanisms in the snoop approach in terms of the four functionalities of a transport protocol: (i) connection management, (ii) flow control, (iii) congestion control, and (iv) reliability:

- *Connection Management and Flow Control.* The connection management and flow control mechanisms of TCP are unaltered in the snoop approach. However, when the connection is initiated by either end of the connection, appropriate state initializa-

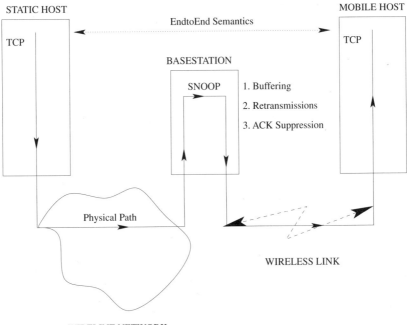

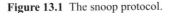

Figure 13.1 The snoop protocol.

tion has to be done at the base station in order to perform the snoop functionality once the data transfer in the connection gets under way.

- *Congestion Control.* The snoop approach does not alter the protocol stack at the static host. The protocol stack at the mobile host is altered to recognize selective acknowledgments sent by the base station in the scenario where the mobile host does the bulk of the data transfer. Finally, explicit schemes are introduced at the base station that influence the congestion control schemes at the end hosts. Specifically, in TCP, when the receiver receives out-of-order packets, it sends back duplicate acknowledgments. When the sender receives three duplicate ACKs, it interprets this as an indication of loss and retransmits the lost packet (identified in the duplicate ACKs) immediately. It also cuts down its congestion window size by half. In snoop, the module at the base station retransmits a lost packet when it observes duplication ACKs and further suppresses the duplicate ACKs, preventing them from reaching the sender. Hence, the connection is less likely to experience fast retransmits (and associated window cut-downs) because of random wireless losses.

- *Reliability.* Except for the selective acknowledgment scheme used by the base station to help identify packets lost in transit from the mobile host, the reliability mechanism of TCP (using cumulative ACKs) is untouched in snoop.

Performance results for the snoop protocol [4] show that it improves TCP's performance in scenarios where bit error rates are greater than $5 \cdot 10^{-7}$. For significantly higher bit rates of about $1.5 \cdot 10^{-5}$, snoop is shown to exceed the performance of TCP by about a factor of 20. The above results have been demonstrated over a wireless network with a data rate of 2 Mbps. For a more detailed treatment of the snoop protocol and its performance, see [4].

13.4.2   Indirect Protocols

Indirect protocols also attempt to mask the characteristics of the wireless portion of a connection from the static host, but do it by splitting the connection at the base station. Specifically, a single transport connection between a static host and a mobile host is split at the base station, and two simultaneous connections are maintained. This allows the second leg of the connection (between the base station and the mobile host) to be customized to address the unique characteristics of the wireless component. They typically involve intelligence at the base station to maintain the simultaneous connections, and have custom protocols to handle the wireless component of the connection. The approaches that belong to this category hence have the following characteristics. (i) There is a split in the end-to-end connection at the base station. (ii) The end-to-end semantics of the TCP protocol are not followed. (iii) Custom congestion control and reliability schemes are employed over the wireless link. (iv) They use state migration from one base station to another upon mobility of mobile host across cells. (v) There is less sophistication at the mobile hosts at the cost of more complexity at the base stations. We now elaborate on I-TCP [2], a transport protocol that belongs to this category.

13.4.2.1 The I-TCP Protocol

The I-TCP protocol uses a split connection approach to handle the characteristics of the wireless component of a TCP connection. Separate transport level connections are used between the static host and the base station, and between the base station and the mobile host. Although TCP is used for the connection between the static host and the base station, a customized transport protocol that is configured to take into consideration the vagaries of the wireless link is used between the base station and the static host. The base station thus exports an "image" of the mobile host to the static host. Through this image, the static host "thinks" that it is communicating with the mobile host and not the base station. When the mobile host undergoes a hand-off across cells, the image is transferred to the base station in the new cell. Since the connection is split at the base station, it is possible for the base station to perform the bulk of the tasks, thus relieving the mobile host of any complex responsibilities.

Figure 13.2 shows a pictorial representation of the I-TCP protocol. A consequence of using the split connection approach is that I-TCP does not conform to the end-to-end semantics of TCP. Instead, two completely different connections are maintained over the two branches. As a result, if there were a base station failure, or if the mobile host remained disconnected from the network for a prolonged period of time, the semantics in I-TCP would be different from that of regular TCP.

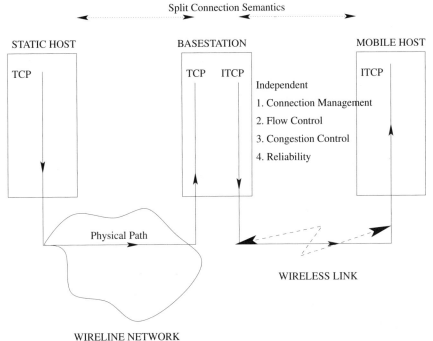

Figure 13.2 The I-TCP protocol.

We now elaborate on the performance of I-TCP in terms of the four functionalities:

- *Connection Establishment and Flow Control.* Both connection establishment and flow control are altered in I-TCP in the sense that they are split across two independent connections. When a mobile host wants to initiate a connection to a static host, it sends a connection request to its base station. The base station creates the appropriate "image" of the mobile host and in turn sends a connection request to the static host. Thus the connection establishment is done explicitly for both the split connections. Similarly, flow control is done independently between the static host and the base station, and the base station and the mobile host.

- *Congestion Control.* Like flow control, congestion control is also done independently along both branches of the split connection. Although the congestion control scheme used over the connection between the static host and the base station is the same as that in regular TCP, a custom congestion control scheme can presumably be used over the connection between the base station and the mobile host. The I-TCP approach does not stipulate the use of a particular congestion control scheme that is suitable for wireless data transfer.

- *Reliability.* Similar to the earlier functions, reliability is also achieved independently over the split connections. When the base station acknowledges a packet to the static host, the static host no longer attempts to send the packet since it believes that the mobile host has received the packet. Then, it is the responsibility of the base station to ensure that the packet is delivered reliably over the second half of the connection. It is because of this two-stage reliability that TCP's end-to-end semantics can be compromised by I-TCP. For example, if there is a base station failure after an acknowledgment is sent back to the sender, the mobile host will never receive all packets that the base station had buffered and acknowledged. However, the sender will believe that all such packets have been delivered to the mobile host. Such an inconsistency will not arise in regular TCP.

Performance results for I-TCP [2] show a marginal performance improvement when operating over a local-area wireless network. On the other hand, over wide-area wireless networks, I-TCP exceeds the performance of TCP by about 100% for different mobility scenarios, and for cases where there are prolonged blackouts (more than 1 second), I-TCP is shown to improve performance by about 200%.

13.4.3 End-to-End Protocols

End-to-end protocols retain the end-to-end semantics of TCP, but require changing the protocol stack at both the sender and the receiver. However, barring the cost of upgrading the protocol stacks, such schemes can typically be much more effective than the previous classes of approaches because of the possibility of a complete revamp of the congestion control and reliability schemes used. For instance, in TCP the congestion control and reliability schemes are closely coupled because of the use of ACKs for both reliability and congestion control. Hence, irrespective of what intermediate scheme is used to improve

TCP's performance, the interplay between reliability and congestion control is not desirable and will negatively influence TCP's performance. However, in a newly designed transport protocol that does not need to conform to TCP's design, such anomalies (at least those that show up when operating over wireless networks) can be removed. Furthermore, since there are no intermediaries as in the case of the previous classes of approaches, there is no chance for the schemes of the end-to-end protocol to interfere with the schemes used by the intermediary. Approaches that belong to this category of approaches have the following characteristics: (i) retention of the end-to-end semantics of TCP; (ii) sophisticated and thoroughly customized congestion control and reliability schemes; and (iii) possibility of a comprehensive solution that addresses most of the problems identified in the previous sections. WTCP [17] is a transport protocol that belongs to this category; we elaborate on it below.

13.4.3.1 The WTCP Protocol

The WTCP protocol is an end-to-end approach to improve transport layer performance over wireless networks. Although the flow control and connection management in WTCP are similar to those in TCP, WTCP uses unique mechanisms for its congestion control and reliability schemes that in tandem enable WTCP to comprehensively overcome the char-

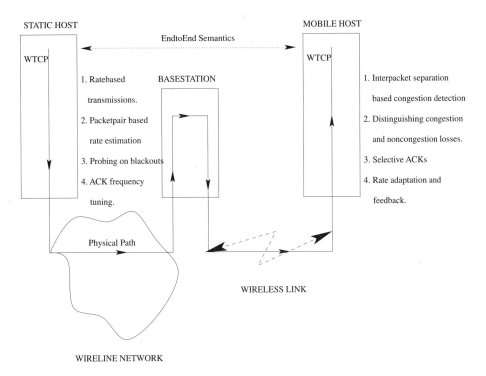

Figure 13.3 The WTCP protocol.

acteristics of wireless networks discussed in Section 13.3. Briefly, WTCP uses rate-based transmissions at the source, interpacket separation at the receiver as the metric for congestion detection, mechanisms for distinguishing between congestion and noncongestion losses, and bandwidth estimation schemes during the start-up phase as part of its congestion control framework. It also uses selective ACKs, no dependence on RTTs and RTOs, and a tunable ACK frequency as part of its approach for achieving reliability. We elaborate subsequently on how each of these mechanisms contribute to improving WTCP's performance over wireless networks.

WTCP requires change of the the protocol stacks at both the sender and the receiver. This is in contrast to the earlier approaches that either require no changes at the end hosts or require changes only at the mobile host. The authors of WTCP argue that although WTCP requires changes at both the sender and the receiver, since most mobile hosts communicate with a proxy server in the distribution network of the wireless network provider, any such changes would need to be done only at the proxy and the mobile host. We now elaborate on each of the mechanisms used in WTCP:

- *Connection Management and Flow Control.* WTCP uses the same connection management and flow control schemes as TCP.
- *Congestion Control.* WTCP uses the following unique schemes for its congestion control:
  - (i) Rate-based transmissions. Since the bursty transmissions of TCP lead to increasing and varying delays, WTCP uses rate-based transmissions and hence spaces out transmissions of packets. This further plays a significant role in WTCP's congestion detection.
  - (ii) Congestion detection based on receiver interpacket separation. Congestion is detected when the interpacket separation at the receiver is greater than the separation at the sender by more than a threshold value. Such a congestion detection scheme is valid because queue buildups that occur because of congestion result in interpacket separations between packets increasing as the packets traverse the network. Further, using such a detection scheme, congestion can be detected before packet losses occur, thereby optimally utilizing the scarce resources of wireless networks.
  - (iii) Computation at the receiver. The receiver does most of the congestion control computation in WTCP. Thus, WTCP effectively removes the effect of reverse path characteristics from the congestion control.
  - (iv) Distinguishing between congestion- and noncongestion-related losses. WTCP uses an interpacket separation-based scheme to distinguish between congestion- and noncongestion-related losses [19]. Thereby, the congestion control scheme in WTCP reacts only to congestion-related losses.
  - (v) Start-up behavior. WTCP uses a packet pair-like approach to estimate the available rate, and sets its initial rate to this value. When the connection experiences a blackout, WTCP uses the same estimation scheme as when it recovers from the blackout.

- *Reliability.* A unique aspect of WTCP is the fact that it decouples the congestion control mechanisms cleanly from the reliability mechanisms. Hence, it uses separate congestion control sequence numbers and reliability sequence numbers in its data transfer. WTCP has the following features in its reliability scheme:

  (i) Use of selective acknowledgments. Unlike TCP which uses only cumulative acknowledgments, WTCP uses a combination of cumulative and selective acknowledgments to retransmit only those packets that are actually lost, thereby saving on unnecessary transmissions.

  (ii) No retransmission timeouts. Although TCP suffers from not being able to accurately measure RTT, and hence experiences inflated RTOs, WTCP does not use retransmission timeouts. Instead, it uses an enhanced selective acknowledgment scheme to achieve reliability.

  (iii) Tunable ACK frequency. The ACK frequency in WTCP is tunable by the sender, depending on the reverse path characteristics.

Performance results (both real-life and simulation experiments) show that WTCP performs significantly better than regular TCP. For packet error rates of around 4%, WTCP shows a performance improvement of about 100% over regular TCP. As the packet error rate increases, the difference in WTCP's performance in comparison with regular TCP keeps increasing.

13.4.4 Comparative Discussion

In order to provide intuition as to how the above-discussed approaches compare with each other, we now provide a high-level discussion on their drawbacks.

- *Link Layer Schemes.* Link layer schemes suffer from the following drawbacks:

  (i) When the delay over the wireless component of the end-to-end path is a significant portion of the end-to-end delay, it is more likely that the retransmissions performed by the enhanced link layer will interfere with the retransmissions at the sender, thereby degrading throughput.

  (ii) When the bandwidths are very low, the delay bandwidth product on the wireless link reduces considerably. In such a scenario, it is unlikely that there will be sufficient number of duplication ACKs for the snoop module to detect a packet loss and perform a local retransmission.

  (iii) The snoop module needs to reside on the base station of the wireless network. However, upgrading the base station is in the hands of the wireless network provider and it is unlikely that a wireless network provider will allow for arbitrary code to be injected into the base stations.

- *Indirect Protocols.* Indirect protocols suffer from the following drawbacks when compared with the other approaches.

  (i) Break in end-to-end semantics. As described earlier, it is possible for the sender and receiver in I-TCP to believe in states inconsistent with each other. This can happen when the mobile host stays disconnected from the base station for a prolonged period of time, or there is a failure at the base station.

(ii) Processing overhead. Since I-TCP is a transport layer mechanism, all packets will have to go up to the transport layer at the point of split, and come down again through the protocol stack. This will introduce unnecessary overheads into the end-to-end data transfer.

(iii) The base station needs to maintain state on a per-connection basis and it is less likely that a wireless network provider will allow for a connection-specific state to reside on the devices inside the wireless network.

- *End-to-End Protocols.* The drawbacks of WTCP are:

(i) WTCP assumes that interpacket separation is a good metric for the detection of congestion. Although this might be true when the bottleneck link is definitely the wireless link, the same is not evident when the bottleneck link can be someplace upstream of the wireless link.

(ii) Loss distinguishing mechanism. The loss detection mechanism currently used by WTCP is a heuristic. However, the heuristic can be shown to fail in several scenarios [6].

(iii) WTCP requires changes in the protocol stack at both the sender and the receiver. Hence, in the absence of proxy servers, static hosts will have to have a dedicated protocol stack for communications with the mobile hosts.

13.5 SUMMARY

Wireless networks are becoming an integral part of the Internet, with the mobile user population increasing at an astronomical rate. Conventional protocols at the different layers of the network protocol stack were designed for a primarily wireline environment, and related studies have shown that they will not suffice for a predominantly wireless environment. In this chapter, we addressed the issue of reliable transport over heterogeneous wireline/wireless networks. We provided a brief overview of the TCP transport protocol, identified the key characteristics of wireless network environments, and discussed the limitations that these characteristics impose on the performance of TCP. We then discussed three broad classes of approaches to support efficient, reliable transport over wireless networks.

However, due to lack of space, we have not touched upon an abundant amount of related work besides those presented in this chapter [3]. Most of the approaches considered in this chapter focus on wireless link characteristics and do not explicitly address the issue of mobility and hand-offs. Several approaches have been proposed in related work that address the hand-off issues in a wireless environment through intelligent network layer schemes [18]. In addition, we have focused only on transport layer problems and solutions in a cellular wireless environment, and have not included the related work in the area of transport over multihop wireless networks in our discussions. For a detailed look at some of the solutions for reliable transport over multihop wireless networks, see [10, 12]. Briefly, the problem of transport over multihop wireless network is made more complicated because of the added dimension of fine-grained mobility. In [10], the authors propose an explicit link failure notification extension to TCP wherein the node upstream of a link failure (because of mobility) sends an ELFN message to the TCP source. The TCP source then freezes its operations until a new route is computed. In [12], the authors argue that in addition to an ELFN mechanism, it is essential to have a hop-by-hop rate control mechanism for effective congestion control over multihop wireless networks.

REFERENCES

1. J. Agosta and T. Russle, *CDPD: Cellular Digital Packet Data Standards and Technology,* McGraw Hill, New York, NY, 1997.

2. A. Bakre and B. R. Badrinath, I-TCP: Indirect TCP for mobile hosts, in *Proceedings of International Conference on Distributed Computing Systems (ICDCS),* Vancouver, Canada, May 1995.

3. H. Balakrishnan, V. N. Padmanabhan, S. Seshan, and R. Katz, A comparison of mechanisms for improving *TCP* performance over wireless links, in *Proceedings of ACM SIGCOMM,* Stanford, CA, August 1996.

4. H. Balakrishnan, S. Seshan, E. Amir, and R. Katz, Improving TCP/IP performance over wireless networks, in *Proceedings of ACM MOBICOM,* Berkeley, CA, November 1995.

5. V. Bharghavan, A. Demers, S. Shenker, and L. Zhang, MACAW: A medium access protocol for wireless LANs, in *Proceedings of ACM SIGCOMM,* London, England, August 1994.

6. S. Biaz and N. H. Vaidya, Discriminating congestion losses from wireless losses using inter-arrival times at the receiver, in *In Proceedings of IEEE Asset,* Richardson, TX, March 1999.

7. H. I. Kassab, C. E. Koksal, and H. Balakrishnan, An analysis of short-term fairness in wireless media access protocols, in *Proceedings of ACM SIGMETRICS,* Santa Clara, CA, June 2000.

8. D. Chiu and R. Jain, Analysis of the increase/decrease algorithms for congestion avoidance in computer networks, *Journal of Computer Networks and ISDN, 17*(1): 1–14, June 1989.

9. Wireless Data Forum. http://www.wirelessdata.org/.

10. G. Holland and N. Vaidya, Analysis of TCP performance over mobile ad-hoc networks, in *Proceedings of ACM MobiCom,* Seattle, WA, August 1999.

11. H-Y. Hsieh and R. Sivakumar, Performance comparison of cellular and multi-hop wireless networks: A quantitative study, in *Proceedings of ACM SIGMETRICS,* Boston, MA, 2001.

12. P. Sinha J. Monks and V. Bharghavan, Limitations of TCP-ELFN for ad hoc networks, in *Proceedings of IEEE International Workshop on Mobile Multimedia Communications,* Tokyo, Japan, October 2000.

13. P. Karn, MACA—A new channel access method for packet radio, in *ARRL/CRRL Amateur Radio 9th Computer Networking Conference,* London, ON, Canada, September 1990.

14. T. V. Lakshman and U. Madhow, The performance of TCP/IP for networks with high bandwidth-delay products and random loss, *IEEE/ACM Trans. Networking, 5*(3):336–350, 1997.

15. S. Lu, V. Bharghavan, and R. Srikant, Fair queuing in wireless packet networks, in *Proceedings of ACM SIGCOMM,* Cannes, France, September 1997.

16. M. Satyanarayanan, Fundamental challenges in mobile computing, in *ACM Symposium on Principles of Distributed Computing,* Philadelphia, PA, May 1996.

17. P. Sinha, N. Venkitaraman, R. Sivakumar, and V. Bharghavan, WTCP: A reliable transport proto-

col for wireless wide-area networks, in *Proceedings of ACM MOBICOM,* Seattle, WA, August 1999.

18. S. Seshan, H. Balakrishnan, and R. H. Katz, Handoffs in cellular wireless networks: The daedalus implementation and experience, *Kluwer International Journal on Wireless Personal Communications, 4*(2):141–162, 1997.

19. P. Sinha, T. Nandagopal, T. Kim and V. Bharghavan, Service differentiation through end-to-end rate control in low bandwidth wireless packet networks, in *Proceedings of IEEE International Workshop on Mobile Multimedia Communications,* San Diego, CA, November 1999.

CHAPTER 14

Security and Fraud Detection in Mobile and Wireless Networks

AZZEDINE BOUKERCHE

Department of Computer Sciences, University of North Texas

14.1 INTRODUCTION

The fusion of computer and telecommunication technologies has heralded the age of information superhighway over wireline and wireless networks. Mobile cellular communication systems and wireless networking technologies are growing at an ever-faster rate, and this is likely to continue in the foreseeable future. Wireless technology is presently being used to link portable computer equipment to corporate distributed computing and other sources of necessary information. Wide-area cellular systems and wireless LANs promise to make integrated networks a reality and provide fully distributed and ubiquitous mobile communications, thus bringing an end to the tyranny of geography. Higher reliability, better coverage and services, higher capacity, mobility management, power and complexity for channel acquisition, handover decisions, security management, and wireless multimedia are all parts of the potpourri.

Further increases in network security are necessary before the promise of mobile telecommunication can be fulfilled. Safety and security management against fraud, intrusions, and cloned mobile phones, just to mention a few, will be one of the major issues in the next wireless and mobile generations. A "safe" system provides protection against errors of trusted users, whereas a "secure" system protects against errors introduced by impostors and untrusted users [1]. Therefore, rather than ignoring the security concerns of potential users, merchants, and telecommunication companies need to acknowledge these concerns and deal with them in a straightforward manner. Indeed, in order to convince the public to use mobile and wireless technology in the next and future generations of wireless systems, telecom companies and all organizations will need to explain how they have addressed the security of their mobile/wireless systems. Manufacturers, M-business, service providers, and entrepreneurs who can visualize this monumental change and effectively leverage their experiences on both wireless and Internet will stand to benefit from it.

Concerns about network security in general (mobile and wired) are growing, and so is research to match these growing concerns. Indeed, since the seminal work by D. Denning [9] in 1981, many intrusion-detection prototypes, for instance, have been created. Intrusion-detection systems aim at detecting attacks against computer systems and wired net-

Handbook of Wireless Networks and Mobile Computing, Edited by Ivan Stojmenović.
ISBN 0-471-41902-8 © 2002 John Wiley & Sons, Inc.

works, or against information systems in general. However, intrusion detection in mobile telecommunication networks has received very little attention. It is our belief that this issue will play a major role in future generations of wireless systems. Several telecom carriers are already complaining about the loss due to impostors and malicious intruders.

In this chapter, we will identify and describe several aspects of wireless and mobile network security. We will discuss the intrusion detection systems in wired and wireless networks and identify the new challenges and opportunities posed by the ad hoc network, a new wireless paradigm for mobile hosts. Unlike traditional mobile wireless networks, ad hoc networks do not rely on any fixed infrastructure. Instead, they rely on each other to keep the network connected. Next, we will examine the authentication problem of mobile users. Finally, we discuss the problems of cloning and fraud detection in mobile phone operations

14.2   NETWORK SECURITY PROBLEMS

Security is an essential part of wired and wireless network communications. Interestingly enough, these systems are designed to provide open access across vast networked environments. Today's technologies are usually network-operation-intrusive, i.e., they often limit the connectivity and inhibit easier access to data and services. With the increasing popularity of wireless networks, the security issue for mobile users could be even more serious than we expect. The traditional analogue cellular phones are very insecure. The 32-bit serial number, the 34-bit phone number, and the conversation in a cell can be scanned easily by an all-band receiver. The widely used advanced mobile phone system (AMPS) is an analogue phone system. Therefore, sending a password or a host name through this system can be a serious security issue. Other security issues in wireless networks that have been studied extensively are anonymity and location privacy in mobile networks; these have received a great deal of interest recently [23]. A typical situation is one in which a mobile user registered in a certain home domain requests services while visiting a foreign domain. Concerned about security and privacy, the user would prefer to remain anonymous with respect to the foreign domain. That is, only the home domain authority should be informed as to the mobile user's real identity, itinerary, whereabouts, etc. Another important issue, namely cloning phones, raises a number of concerns to many telecom carriers. Indeed, many telecommunication companies are losing money due to the use of clones or genuine mobile phones by impostors. One might argue that although it is rather easy to clone an AMPS phone, it is much trickier to clone a D-AMPS, a GSM, or an IS-95 phone. However, the security issue remains, and needs to be resolved in the next wireless network generation. Consequently, there has been a great deal of interest recently in designing mobile phones using new technologies, such as Boot Block flash technology used by Intel Corporation, that will make it much more difficult to clone cellular phones. However, to the best of our knowledge there is very little work being done at the software level. To combat cloning, cellular operators analyze usage to check for unusual patterns. Most obviously, they know that genuine phone cannot be in two places at once. If a phone is making more than one call at a time, it has definitely been cloned. Furthermore, to verify if a call is out of the client patterns, current software (i) does not have an efficient automatic process to warn clients about the impostors using their mobile phones; in most of these systems, human staff are used to do that (only lists of large bills are reviewed to identify cloned phones); (ii) has no efficient ways to control/identify impostors; and (iii) uses an "experimental satisfaction" to prove the correctness of the security framework. Some systems provide the billing process via the Web. However, the identification of a cloned phone is done only at the end of the month. This, unfortunately, is not quite efficient and may lead to a big loss of revenue for the carrier.

The wireless Web opens up many new business opportunities, the most important of which use location-based technology. Ever since the mobile Internet was first suggested, antivirus companies have warned that viruses could attack cellular phones and PDSs. Timofonica was among the first viruses that attacked cell phones. Timofonica was an ordinary virus programmed to send abusive messages to random users of Spanish Telefonica mobile systems. Viruses are a threat to any computing platform and may be a threat to wireless terminals that include processing and memory akin to those of modern computers.

14.3 NETWORK SECURITY MANAGEMENT PLAN

An adequate security system management policy has long been an important issue. A comprehensive network security plan must also consider losses of privacy when we define authentication and authorization as well as losses of performance when we define key management and security protocols. Therefore, a security plan must encompass all of the elements that make up the wireless and/or wired network, and provide important services such as:

1. Access control, i.e., authorization by capability list, wrappers, and firewalls (access control matrix)
2. Confidentiality, i.e., we must ensure that information and transmitted messages are accessible only for reading by authorized parties
3. Authentication, i.e., the receiver must be able to confirm that the message is indeed from the right sender
4. Nonrepudiation, i.e., the sender cannot deny that the message was indeed sent by him/her
5. Integrity, i.e., the message has not been modified in transit
6. Availability, i.e., making sure that the system is available to authorized parties when needed
7. Security administration, i.e., checking audit trails, encryption and password management, maintenance of security equipment and services, and informing users of their responsibilities.

14.4 INTRUSION DETECTION SYSTEMS (IDS)

Intrusion is most probably one of the key issues that wireless and mobile systems will have to deal with. The nature of wireless ad hoc networks makes them very vulnerable to an adversary's malicious attacks. Generally speaking, an intrusion can be defined as an act of a person or proxy attempting to break into or misuse your system in violation of an established policy. Very little research work dealing with the intrusion problem has been done for wireless networks.

In this section, we shall describe the intrusion problem in general. We hope that researchers will pick up what has been done in related areas, and find efficient approaches on how to deal with this problem in an ad hoc network environment.

14.4.1 Current IDS Techniques

Generally speaking, intrusion can be classified as: (i) misuse intrusions, i.e., well-defined attacks against known system vulnerabilities; and (ii) anomaly intrusions, i.e., activities based on deviation from normal system usage patterns. Intrusion detection systems (IDS) are one of the latest security tools in the battle against these attacks. As is well known, it is very difficult to determine exactly which activities provide the best indicators for the established (normal) usage patterns. Thus, researchers have turned to using expert systems or knowledge-based intrusion detection to search for activities known to be indicative of possible intrusive behavior [16]. The motivation behind this approach is to seek a proper behavior as opposed to a normal one. Knowledge-based intrusion detection schemes apply the knowledge they have accumulated about specific attacks and system vulnerabilities. Using this knowledge database, any action that is not explicitly recognized as an attack is considered acceptable. Otherwise, an alarm is triggered by the system.

There are many different intrusion systems available in the marketplace. Expert systems are based on knowledge-based intrusion detection techniques. Each attack is identified by a set of rules. Rule-based languages [13] are used for modeling the knowledge that experts have accumulated about attacks/frauds. Information regarding some intruders has also been added to these systems. A major drawback of knowledge-based intrusion systems is the difficulty of gathering the information on the known attacks (which should be updated regularly) and developing a comprehensive set of rules that can be used to identify intrusive behaviors. Some systems use a combination of several approaches to cover both the normal and proper behavior schemes [17]. We refer to them as behavior-based intrusion detection. Their basic characteristic is that any action that does not match with a previously learned behavior triggers an alarm. The action is considered as intrusive. The main advantages of these systems are that they can exploit new and unforeseen attacks, and contribute to automatically discovering new attacks. However, their high false alarm rate is generally cited as a main drawback of these systems, due basically to the accuracy of the behavior information accumulated during the learning process.

14.5 SECURING DATA TRANSFER IN DIGITAL MOBILE SYSTEMS

All digital mobile systems provide security through some kind of encryption. Data can be encrypted in many ways, but algorithms used for secure data transfer fall into two categories: symmetric and asymmetric. Both rely on performing mathematical operations using a secret number known as a key. The difficulty with symmetric algorithms is that both parties need to have a copy of the key. On the other hand, asymmetric techniques use two separate keys for encryption and decryption. Usually, the encryption key can be publicly distributed, whereas the decryption key is held securely by the recipient.

The most widely used symmetric algorithm in DES (data encryption standard), developed by IBM in 1977. It uses a 56-bit key, which seemed unbreakable at that time. In 1997, a group of Internet users managed to read a DES-coded message. Most organization now use triple-DES, which uses 112 bits. The basic idea is that larger keys mean more possible permutations, and so better encryption. GMS encrypts all data between the phone and the base station using a code called A5 (The A stands for algorithm). The details of the code are kept secret to make it harder to crack. Unfortunately, details have been leaked out over the years and have been posted on hackers' web sites. Thus, we believe there is still much work to be done in the cloning mobile phone area.

Several different asymmetric algorithms have been developed, each using a different type of "one-way" mathematical function. Rivest et al. [32] proposed an efficient algorithm, which they refer to as RSA, that relies on the fact that factorization is more difficult than multiplication. Indeed, multiplying two prime numbers together is easy for a computer, but recovering those two numbers from the product is not. The main drawback of asymmetric schemes is that they use a lot of CPU, and so cannot be used to encrypt an entire message through a mobile phone. Instead, A5 encrypts the message itself using a symmetric algorithm, with a key randomly generated by the network and sent to the handset using an asymmetric algorithm.

14.6 SECURING WIRELESS AD HOC NETWORKS

Many WLANs in use today need an infrastructure network. Infrastructure networks not only provide access to other networks, but also include forwarding functions, medium access control, etc. In these infrastructure-based wireless networks, communication typically takes place only between the wireless nodes and the access point, but not directly between the wireless nodes. Ad hoc wireless networks, however, do not need any infrastructure to work. Each node can communicate with another node; no access point controlling medium access is necessary. Mobile nodes within each other's radio range communicate directly via wireless links, whereas those that are far apart rely on other nodes to relay messages as routers. Node mobility in an ad hoc network causes frequent changes of the network topology.

Since an ad hoc network can be deployed rapidly at relatively low cost, it becomes an attractive option for commercial uses such as sensor networks or virtual classrooms. However, before an ad hoc network becomes a commodity, several security issues must first be resolved. On one hand, the security-sensitive applications of ad hoc networks require a high degree of security; on the other hand, ad hoc networks are inherently vulnerable to security attacks. Therefore, security mechanisms are indispensable for ad hoc networks.

As in any wireless or wired network, traffic across an ad hoc network can be highly vulnerable to security threats. Thus, to secure an ad hoc network, one should consider not only the attributes described in Section 14.3, i.e., availability, confidentiality, integrity, authentication, and nonrepudiation. but also new types of threats that are extended even to the basic structure of the networks. The salient characteristics of ad hoc networks pose both challenges and opportunities in achieving these security goals.

Since ad hoc networks use wireless links, they are susceptible to link attacks ranging from passive eavesdropping to active impersonation, message replay, and message distortion. Active attacks might allow the adversary to delete messages, inject erroneous, modify messages, and impersonate a node, thereby violating availability, integrity, authentication, and nonrepudiation.

14.6.1   Intrusion Detection in Wireless Ad Hoc Networks

Most of the IDS systems developed for wired networks described in previous section cannot be applied to wireless networks. This is mainly due to the fact that today's network-based IDSs, which rely on real-time traffic analysis, can no longer function in the wireless and mobile environments such wireless ad hoc networks. When compared with wired networks, in which traffic monitoring is usually done at switches, routers, and gateways, a wireless ad hoc network does not have traffic concentration points at which IDS can collect audit data for the entire network. Recall that in a wireless ad hoc network, each node can communicate with another node, and no access point controlling medium access is necessary. Mobile nodes within each other's radio range communicate directly via wireless links, whereas those that are far apart rely on other nodes to relay messages as routers.

Recently, Zhang and Lee [31] examined the vulnerability of a wireless ad hoc network. They described an intrusion detection and response mechanism. In their approach, each node is responsible for detecting signs for intrusion locally and independently, but neighboring nodes can collaboratively investigate in a broader range. Individual IDS agents are placed on each and every node. Each IDS agent runs independently and monitors local activities such as user/system activities, communication activities, etc. These IDS agents collectively form the IDS system to protect the wireless ad hoc network against malicious attacks. If an IDS agent detects an intrusion from local data, neighboring IDS agents will collaborate in the global intrusion detection actions. Intrusion detection responses are provided by both the local response initiated by the IDS agent, and global response modules. The type of intrusion response depends on the type of network protocols and applications, and confidence (or certainty) in evidence. For example, the IDS agent can send a "reauthentication" request to all nodes in the network to prompt the end users to authenticate themselves (end hence their wireless nodes), using out-of-bound mechanisms (e,g., visual contacts). Only the reauthenticated nodes may collectively negotiate new communication channels, which in turn recognize each other as legitimate. Thus, the compromised and/or malicious nodes can be excluded. Last but not least, the authors use a secure communication module in their IDS system and provide a high-confidence communication channel among IDS agents. However, this work is still at an early stage, and no experimental data were provided to study the effectiveness of their scheme.

14.6.2   Securing Routing Protocol in Wireless Ad Hoc Networks

Security for any routing protocol [24, 29] is a very difficult problem to deal with. One can take advantage of the redundancies in the network topology, i.e., multiple routes between nodes, to achieve availability. The security of routing protocols is closely tied to the proper distribution of some keys that allow the creation of unforgeable credentials. Thus, designing secure key distribution in ad hoc networks is a challenging problem. Diffie–Hellman key exchange may indeed help to establish some temporary security between particular endpoints. However, they are also vulnerable to the man-in-the-middle attacks that are hard to defeat in an ad hoc network.

Recently, Zhang and Lee [31] defined trace data to describe, for each node, the normal (i.e., legitimate) updates of routing information. Since a legitimate change in the route table can basically be caused by the physical movement(s) of node(s) or network membership changes, and each mobile node should use only reliable information that it can trust, the authors have decided to use data on a node's physical movements and the corresponding change in its routing table as the basis of the trace data. A normal profile on the trace data in effect specifies the correlation of physical movements of the nodes and the changes in the routing table. A classification algorithm is used to compute the classifier and to describe the changes measured by the percentage of changed routes and the percentage of changes in the sum of hops of all routes. A detection model that uses deviation scores distinguishes abnormal from normal updating of the routing table. Unfortunately, no experimental data was provided to study the performance and effectiveness of their scheme.

Public key protocols and symmetric key methods are also devilishly difficult, and without an infrastructure it is very hard to conceive of the use of certificate-based protocols. Multicast data distribution in ad hoc networks poses new types of security problems. Indeed, one should not forget that there will always be many different trust relationships that are hard to maintain between neighbors in a large community. Quality of service (QoS) control could be used to provide a reasonable solution to the multicast data distribution in ad hoc networks.

14.7 AUTHENTICATION OF MOBILE USERS

Some wireless communications systems protocols such as GSM [27, 28] and IS-41 [18, 22] use the secret key crypto-system for authentication. Although the authentication of these systems is only unilateral, and the user's identity and location are not anonymous, the protocols [13, 20] provide more security functions, such as identity, confidentiality, and mutual authentication. The drawback of the above schemes is that they all need a third party, i.e., a third trusted server such as the home location register (HLR) and old visitor location register (VLR). Although HLR creates a record that contains the mobile station's (MS) directory number, profile information, current location, and validation period, etc., whenever the MS subscribes to the service of a mobile system, VLR records the temporal information for the MS when it visits a mobile system other than the home system. HLR acts as the CA; VLR is responsible for authenticating the MS.

Several public key and secret key hybrid schemes have also been proposed in the literature. Brown [7] proposes a hybrid technique to provide privacy and authentication in personnel communication systems. Other authors [10] present a protocol based on Diffie–Hellman scheme to generate a session key, and a mechanism to detect a cloned phone.

Several certificate-based protocols have been proposed for wireless authentication, where the traffic between VLR and HLR is minimized [2, 15, 21]. The basic idea behind these protocols is that when roaming across a domain becomes more frequent, the frequency of long-distance signaling across domains is dramatically reduced. The drawback of these schemes is that incorrect use of certificates in protocols may result in security flaws. For instance, it might be easy to clone a user if its certificate is used as secret information.

To remedy to these drawbacks, other authors [30] propose an authentication procedure consisting of two protocols: a certificate-based authentication (CBA) protocol and a ticket-based authentication (TBA) protocol. Only two parties—mobile station (MS) and visitor location register (VLR)—are involved in executing their scheme. The CBA protocol is used in registration, handover, and when the ticket is invalid.

The certificate contains the user public key and other information and signature information provided by the CA (certificate authority). The ticket is a message authentication code (MAC) $\{TID, Date, L, (TID, Date, L) K_{VLR}\}$, where K_{VLR} is the secret code key of VLR, TID is the temporary identify for MS, $Date$ is the issue date of the ticket, and L is the lifetime of the ticket. Only the user owning the secret key can make a ticket and verify its validity. VLR will save the secret key K, and $(\,.\,)_K$ indicates a secret key crypto-system.

In the authentication suite of protocols [30], HLR issues the certificates $Cert_{VLR}$ and $Cert_{MS}$ to VLR and MS; MS stores the following data: $Cert_{MS}$, $Cert_{HLR}$, and KR_{MS}. VLR saves the following data: $Cert_{VLR}$, $Cert_{HLR}$, KR_{VLR}, and KR_{HLR}; where $Cert_X$ represents the certificate of entity X, and KR_X represents a private key of entity X.

Let us denote by two random numbers R_1 and R_2. Let KU_X be a public key of entity X, K_0 the old session key, and TID a temporary identity. The basic idea of the CBA protocol (shown in Figure 14.1) is the exchange of three type of messages which are described as follows:

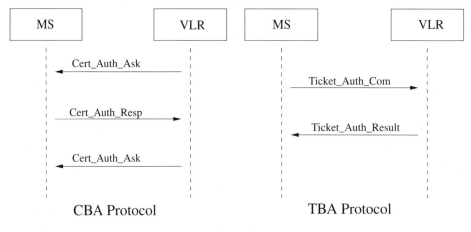

Figure 14.1 CBA and TBA protocols.

1. Cert_Auth_Ask: $Cert_{VLR}$, R_1
2. Cert_Auth_resp: $(K_s)_{KU_{VLR}}$, $[Cert_{MS}||(R_2||R_1)_{KR_{MS}}]_{K_s}$
3. Cert_Auth_Ack: $(K_s)_{KU_{VLR}}$, $[\text{Ticket}||(R_1||R_2)_{KR_{VLR}}]_{K_s}$

where the session key is $R_1 \oplus R_2$.

If the MS stays at the same cell and requests the service several times, we use the TBA protocol. The TBA protocol uses the ticket in the authentication procedure and is described as follows:

1. Ticket_Auth_Com: TID, $(Ticket||R_1)_{K_0}$
2. Ticket_Auth_Result: $(R_2||R_1)_{K_0}$

where the session key is $R_1 \oplus R_2$.

If the ticket is out of date, the MS runs the CBA protocol to get the current ticket. TBA protocol uses a symmetric crypto-system in authenticating the MS. Therefore, the computational cost is lower and the efficiency is higher than that of the CBA protocol.

Since the CBA/TBA suite of protocols do not need a trusted party, entities in these protocols store more information. Nevertheless, Tzeng and Tzeng [30], have proven that the message complexity exchanged between entities the CBA/TBA protocols is less than that of previous UMTS schemes.

Last but not least, an authentication architecture for ad hoc networks has been proposed by Jacob and Corsen [14]. Their scheme presents the formats of all messages together with protocols that are supposed to achieve authentication.

14.8 SUBSCRIPTION AND FRAUD DETECTION IN MOBILE PHONE SYSTEMS

With the increasing popularity of wireless networks, the security issue for mobile users could be even more serious than we expect [5, 12]. Before the mobile phones became widely popular, the greatest threat to the network security in most organizations was dial-up lines. While dial-up lines still merit attention, the risks they pose are minor when compared to wireless and mobile connections. To break the system, one need only buy a piece of portable radio equipment, such as a scanner, to program a mobile cloned to debit calls from genuine mobile phone, and register the frequencies at which mobile phones operate in surrounding areas. Then the person committing the fraud may, for example, park his car in a shopping mall, jot down various frequencies, transfer the data to clones, and then pass them to whomever may be interested in these cloned mobiles. Mobile phones will change many aspects of our lives, but not until potential users become convinced of the security of the mobile networks.

This author and others [4, 26] have presented a distributed security system supported by CORBA that uses on-line telecommunication databases (i.e., CallsFile), as well as database files (i.e., Baseline) created during the training process of the system for the classification of the clients. It uses neural network/pattern recognition techniques.

CORBA and Web/Java security components were added to further secure the system. LOTOS formal specification and validation techniques were embedded in the system to prove its correctness and validate it. The basic framework consists of three main components. The first part protects the security system against cellular cloning (SSCC). The second part uses the security of the Internet and the Web (SETWeb). Finally, the third component, SIPI, protects the system from future impostors that might try to use the mobile phones improperly.

SSCC can be viewed as a black box that interacts with the users via mail or phone, which we refer to as gate-mail, and gate-phone, respectively. The first gate is used by the SSCC to send alarms of possible frauds to the users by "surface" mail, and the second gate allows the SSCC to use mobile phones to send the same alarms. The main purpose of sending alarms by phone is for an immediate notification of possible fraud. Although the "surface" mail is more secure, it is still slower than the notification by phone. The most abstract specification of the SSCC system corresponds to a formalization of the user requirements of this system, and it might be used as a basis for future refinements of the project. Furthermore, using this requirement specification, it will be possible to prove—formally—that it is equivalent to the future final and complete specification. In order to validate the SSCC system, we make use of the CADP tool (Caesar Aldbaran Development Package) [11] available in the Eucalyptus toolbox. The procedure used to obtain the correction proofs between refinements generates the following two automata: SSCC.AUT and SSCC_DET.AUT. These two automata aim at proving the correctness of the system in conformation with ISO 8807 [6] and US DoD ClassA1.

SETWeb, a system phone bill on line via the Web, has been developed to allow clients to consult their phone bill online at any time. The client can then observe if a call from a clone just arrived in his bill, thus avoiding losses. Our system ensures the security and the privacy of the client when he or she tries to access to his/her file [19]. In what follows, we will present the security policy scheme to ensure the security of the carrier site and protect the privacy of the client. Several issues must be maintained, such as access controlling, logging, confidentiality, authentication, and administration of the systems resources, just to mention a few. In their design Notare et al. [26] used all these services to implement the Java security API with the overall goal of protecting the user's information from eavesdropping and tampering. To avoid spoofing attacks and ensure that the user is accessing the right phone carrier site, we made use of digital certificates on the server side.

In this system, the tool "policytool" creates and manages a text file that stores security policy definitions, known as "mypolicy." Those definitions can give special privileges to users having some form of authentication, such as a digital signature. Many security policies can be defined for an environment and its many resources.

14.8.1 SIPI—System to Identify Probable Impostors

The SIPI system has been designed to identify "probable" impostors using cloned phones. Boukerche et al.'s [5, 10, 33] approach to identifying fraudulent calls is to classify the mobile phone users into a set of groups according to their log files [10]. They assume that all relevant characteristics that identify the users will be stored in these files; i.e., where, at what time, and from where the calls were made, etc. Classifying the users into groups will help our system to easily identify if a specific call does not correspond to a mobile phone owner. There are several types of impostors our SIPI system can identify: (i) those who had changed the mobile phone's owner call patterns; (ii) those who bought a mobile phone only for one month (already convinced not to pay); and (iii) those who bought mobile phones using other names. Thus, when the call made using the genuine/cloned phone is terminated, the system will check to see if the characteristics of the call are within the client patterns saved in the file. A warning message could be sent to the client if a fraud was detected. This immediate notification, instead of waiting until the end of monthly bill cycle, will help to reduce losses to the carrier and to the owner of the mobile phone that has been cloned.

To identify these types of impostors as soon as possible instead of at the end of the month, avoiding more losses for the carrier, we propose the use of a radial basis function (RBF) network in its more basic form [25] to partition the users into classes and create the log files that we refer to as baseline files. The architecture of the RBF network consists of an entry layer, a hidden layer, and an output layer. The nodes of the output layer form a linear combination of the radial basis function using the kernel classifier. The RBF function in the hidden layer produces a response for the stimulus of input (pattern). When the input (pattern) is within a small region located in the input space, the RBF function produces a response significantly different from zero. The input is made from the source nodes, i.e., sensorial units. Each activation function requires a center and a scalable parameter. A Gauss function can be used as activator. In this case, the neural network can be used to make decisions of maximum likelihood, i.e., determining which one of the various centers is more likely to be similar to the input vector.

Given $X - C$ as an input vector, the output of a simple node could be defined as follows:

$$F(X - C) = \frac{1}{(2\pi)^{\pi/2} \sigma_1, \sigma_2, \cdots, \sigma n} \exp\left[-\frac{1}{2} \sum_{j=1}^{n} \left(\frac{x_j - c_j}{\sigma_j} \right)^2 \right]$$

where n is the number of input data and $s_1, s_2, \ldots, s_n, j = [1, n]$ determine the scalar dispersion in each direction.

To increase the functionality of the function f, we propose to use the Mahalanobis distance in the Gaussian function. This type function is also known as the radial basis function (RBF), and it is defined as follows:

$$F(X - C) = \frac{1}{(2\pi)^{\pi/2} |K|^{1/2}} \exp\left[-\frac{1}{2}(X - C)^T K^{-1}(X - C) \right]$$

where K^{-1} is the inverse of the X covariance matrix, associated with the node of the hidden C layer.

Given n vectors (input data) of p samples, representing p classes, the network may be initiated with the knowledge of the centers (i.e., locations of the samples). If the j-th vector sample is represented, then the weight matrix C can be defined as: $C = [c_1, c_2, \cdots, c_3]^T$ so that the weights in the hidden layer of j-th node are composed of the "center" vector. The output layer is a pondered sum of the outputs of the hidden layer. When presenting an input vector for the network, the network implements Y as follows:

$$Y = W \cdot f(\|X - C\|)$$

where f represents the functional output vector of the hidden layer, and C represents the corresponding center vector. After supplying some data with the desired results, the weights matrix W can be determined using the least mean square (LMS) training algorithm [25] interactively and noninteractively using the descendant and pseudo inverse gradient techniques, respectively. The learning in the intermediate (hidden) layer is executed using the nonsupervised method, such as a cluster or heuristic cluster algorithm or supervised method to find the centers, i.e., the C nodes that represent the connections between the input layer and the intermediate layer, in the hidden layer. The Lloyd (or K-means) algorithm is the most common technique employed to determine these centers [25].

To determine s_2, the variation parameter for the Gaussian function, one could choose to (i) approximate them to the average distance among all training data, (ii) calculate the distances among the centers in each dimension and use some percentage of this distance for the scale factor to approximate s_2, or (iii) use the p-nearest neighbor algorithm [25]. In our design, we choose the latter, i.e., p-nearest technique, to perform the classification. Our main motivation behind using a neural network algorithm (NNA) for mobile users classification are: (1) NNA has the intrinsic capacity of learning input data and generalizing; (2) the network is nonparametric and makes more assumptions regarding the distribution of the input data than the static traditional methods (Bayesian); and (3) NNA is capable of creating decision boundaries that are highly nonlinear in the space of characteristics.

A neural network algorithm was used to find good (suboptimal) classes. The K-means and p-nearest neighbor algorithms were used to obtain the centers and radiuses of each cluster and variance between the centers. The Gauss function was used to obtain the output of a hidden layer (i.e., centers data, input standards, and radii). In order to implement these functions, we employed Matlab and Toolbox software [8].

This algorithm executes the classification of users through the Gauss, K-means, and p-nearest neighbor algorithms. Note that the data obtained by RBF algorithm constitute the baseline file. It represents the database used by CORBA implementation of our system, where every call is compared with this database in order to identify a possible fraud, i.e., a call that does not match with the pattern of the client.

14.8.2 Experimental Results

This author and colleagues [4, 26], used data in which users were classified into seven types:

1. Local users (FLC) class, representing users that make few local calls
2. Local users (MLC) class, representing users that make many local calls
3. Users (FLDC) class, representing users that make few long-distance calls
4. Users (MLDC) class, representing users that make many long-distance calls

5. Users (SLIC) class, representing users that make a few short international calls
6. Users (FLIC) class, representing users that make a few long international calls
7. Users (MLIC) class, representing users that make many long international calls.

Note that class 2 leads to class 1, and class 3 leads to classes 1 and 2, and so forth.

All data were stored in four files, which we refer to as Copenhagen data, (A1.data, A2.data, B1.data, and B2.data), where A1.data and B1.data contain 4061 and 4050 calls, respectively. Each call is identified by the following three parameters: (1) the user phone number, (2) the number called, and (3) the duration of the call. Similarly, A2.data and B2.data contain 4061 and 4050 observations, where each observation contains the type of user, i.e., the class the user belongs to. Note that the Copenhagen data are widely used by many researchers. Input patterns can be seen as points in a multidimensional space defined by the measure of the input characteristics. The main goal of a "pattern classifier" is to split the multidimensional space into decision regions, and identify which one of the classes the input belongs to. The classifier efficiency is strongly dependent to the characteristics that represent the input object.

During our experimentation, we varied the number of neurons from 50 to 150. The results obtained are summarized in Table 14.1. As can be seen, using 110 neurons, for instance, we obtained a good (suboptimal) classification with an error rate of 4.2027. Our experiments also indicated that our system can help to reduce significantly the losses to 0.084% with an error rate of 4.2%, using 110 neurons. Thus, if the profit of a carrier telecom represents $175 million, and the losses due to the frauds and the impostors using cloned mobile phones, consume 2% of the gain, then the telecom company is loosing $35 million.

14.9 CONCLUSION

Due to the rapidly changing telecommunication industry and the increasing popularity of wireless networks, there has been a great deal of concern about security in wireless and mobile telecommunication systems.

TABLE 14.1 Number of neurons in the hidden layer and respective error rate

Number of neurons (hidden layer)	Error rate
50	5.0185
107	4.3758
100	4.4252
110	4.2027
111	4.2027
127	4.3511

Of the five areas of network management—configuration, failures, performance, accounting, and security—the last area has not received its fair share of attention. With the increasing popularity of mobile and wireless networks, it is time to acknowledge the security concerns of potential mobile users and deal with them in a straightforward manner. In this chapter, we focused on the network intrusion detection problem and the fraud of cloned mobile phones. We identified the major problems in network security, and described the major intrusion detection techniques for wireless and mobile systems, including ad hoc networks. We have also presented our security management system, which can used to identify frauds and impostors using cloned mobile phones. Neural network techniques have been used to classify (mobile) phone users into groups according to their (past/current) profiles. Using this classification, it is easy to determine if a call was made by the user or an impostor/intruder. The system might also be used to identify future impostors as well. Consequently, this antifraud system will prevent the cloning of mobile phones, and it will significantly reduce the profit losses of the telecom carriers and the damage that might be done to their clients.

REFERENCES

1. D. S. Alexander, W. A. Arbaugh, A. D. Keromytis, and J. M. Smith, Safety and security of programmable networks infrastructures, *IEEE Communications Magazine, 36,* 10, 84–92.

2. A. Aziz and W. Diffie, Privacy and authentication for wireless local area networks, *IEEE Pers. Comm., 1,* 1, 25–31, 1994.

3. V. Bharghavan, Secure Wireless LANs, in *Proceedings ACM Conference on Computer and Communications Security*, 1994, pp. 10–17.

4. A. Boukerche and M. S. M. A. Notare, Neural fraud detection in mobile phone operations, *4th IEEE BioSP3, Bio-Inspired Solutions to Parallel Processing*, May 2000, pp. 636–644.

5. A. Boukerche, M. Sechi Moretti, and A. Notare, Applications of neural networks to mobile and wireless networks, In *Biologically Inspired Solutions to Parallel and Distributed Computing*, A. Zomaya (Ed.), New York: Wiley, 2001.

6. E. Brinksma. IS 8807—LOTOS—Language of Temporal Ordering Specifications, 1988.

7. D. Brown, M. Abadi, and R. M. Needham, A logic of authentication, *ACM Transactions on Computer Systems, 8,* 1, 18–36, 1995.

8. H. Demuth and M. Beale, Neural network tollbox—For use with MatLab, *Matlab User's Guide*, Version 3, pp. 7.1 – 7.33, 1998.

9. D. Denning, An intrusion-detection model, *IEEE Transactions on Software Eng., 2*(13), 222–232, 1987.

10. Y. Frankel, A. Herzberg, P. A. Karger, C. A. Kunzinger, and M. Yung, Security issues in a CDPD wireless network, *IEEE Pers. Comm., 2,* 4, 16–27, 1995.

11. H. Garavel, *CADP/Eucalyptus Manual,* INRIA, Grenoble, France, 1996.

12. V. Gupta and G. Montenegro, Secure and mobile networking, *ACM/Baltzer MONET, 3,* 381–390, 1999.

13. N. Habra et al., Asax: Software architecture and rule-based language for universal audit trail analysis, in *Proceedings 2nd European Symposium on Research in Computer Security*, LNCS, vol. 648, 1992.

14. S. Jacob and M. S. Corsen, MANET Authentication architecture, MANET Internet Draft, Feb 1999.

15. J. Liu and L. Harn, Authentication of mobile users in personal communication systems, *IEEE Symposium on Personnel Indoor and Mobile Radio Communication,* 1996, pp. 1239–1242.

16. T. Lunt et al., Knowledge-Based Intrusion Detection, in *Proceedings AI Systems in Government Conference,* 1986.

17. T. Lunt, Automated audit trail analysis and intrusion detection: A survey, in *Proceedings 11th International Computer Security Conference,* 1988, pp. 65–73.

18. S. Mohan, Privacy and authentication protocol for PCS, *IEEE Personnel Communication,* 1996, pp. 34–38.

19. G. McGraw and E. Felten, *Java Security,* New York: Wiley, 1997.

20. R. Molva, D. Samfat, and T. Tsudik, Authentication of mobile users, *IEEE Personnel Communication,* 1994, pp. 26–34.

21. C. S. Park, On certificate-based security protocols for wireless mobile communication systems, *IEEE Network,* 1997, pp. 50–55.

22. S. Patel, Weakness of North American wireless authentication protocol, *IEEE Personnel Communication,* No. 3, 1997, pp. 40–44.

23. C. Pfleeger and D. Cooper, Security and privacy: Promising advances, *IEEE Software,* 1997.

24. C. Perkins, *Ad Hoc Networking,* Reading, MA: Addison Wesley, 2001.

25. B. D. Ripley, *Pattern Recognition and Neural Networks,* Cambridge University Press, 1996.

26. M. S. M. A. Notare, A. Boukerche, F. Cruz, B. Risco, and C. Westphal security management against cloning mobile phones, *IEEE Globecom '99,* pp. 969–973. Dec. 1999.

27. S. P. Shieh, C. T. Lin, and J. T. Hsueh, Secure communication in global systems for mobile telecommunication, in *Proceedings of the First IEEE Workshop on Mobile Computing,* 1994, pp. 136–142.

28. F. Stoll, The need for decentralization and privacy in mobile communication networks, *Computers and Security, 4,* 6, 527–539, 1995.

29. B. R. Smith, S. Murphy, and J. J. Garcia-Luna-Aceves, Securing distance-vector routing protocol, in *Proceedings Symposium Networking and Distribution Systems Security,* 1997, pp. 85–92.

30. Z. J. Tzeng and W. G. Tzeng, Authentication of mobile users in third generation mobile systems, *Wireless Personnel Communication Journal, 16,* 35–50, 2001.

31. Y. Zhang and W. Lee, Intrusion detection in wireless ad hoc networks, *IEEE/ACM MobiCom Proc.,* 2000, pp. 275–283.

32. R. Rivest, The MDS message-digest algorithm, RFC286, Internet Engineering Task Force, Symbolic, Inc., 1982.

33. A. Boukerche and M. S. M. A. Notara, Behavior based intrusion detection in mobile phone systems, *Journal of Parallel and Distributed Computing,* in press.

CHAPTER 15

Mobile Ad Hoc Networks

SILVIA GIORDANO
Institute of Computer Communications and Applications, Swiss Federal Institute of Technology, Lausanne, Switzerland

15.1 INTRODUCTION

Future information technology will be mainly based on wireless technology [49, 50, 56]. Traditional cellular and mobile networks are still, in some sense, limited by their need for infrastructure (i.e., base stations, routers). For mobile ad hoc networks, this final limitation is eliminated.

Ad hoc networks are key to the evolution of wireless networks [48]. Ad hoc networks are typically composed of equal nodes that communicate over wireless links without any central control. Although military tactical communication is still considered the primary application for ad hoc networks, commercial interest in this type of networks continues to grow. Applications such as rescue missions in times of natural disasters, law enforcement operations, commercial and educational use, and sensor networks are just a few possible commercial examples.

Ad hoc wireless networks inherit the traditional problems of wireless and mobile communications, such as bandwidth optimization, power control, and transmission quality enhancement. In addition, the multihop nature and the lack of fixed infrastructure generates new research problems such as configuration advertising, discovery, and maintenance, as well as ad hoc addressing and self-routing (see Figure 15.1).

In mobile ad hoc networks, topology is highly dynamic and random. In addition, the distribution of nodes and, eventually, their capability of self-organizing play an important role. The main characteristics can be summarized as follows:

- The topology is highly dynamic and frequent changes in the topology may be hard to predict.
- Mobile ad hoc networks are based on wireless links, which will continue to have a significantly lower capacity than their wired counterparts.
- Physical security is limited due to the wireless transmission.
- Mobile ad hoc networks are affected by higher loss rates, and can experience higher delays and jitter than fixed networks due to the wireless transmission.
- Mobile ad hoc network nodes rely on batteries or other exhaustible power supplies for their energy. As a consequence, energy savings are an important system design

Handbook of Wireless Networks and Mobile Computing, Edited by Ivan Stojmenović.
ISBN 0-471-41902-8   © 2002 John Wiley & Sons, Inc.

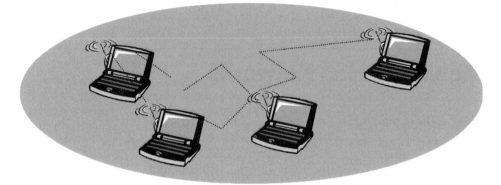

Figure 15.1 A mobile ad hoc network.

criterion. Furthermore, nodes have to be power-aware: the set of functions offered by a node depends on its available power (CPU, memory, etc.).

A well-designed architecture for mobile ad hoc networks involves all networking layers, ranging from the physical to the application layer.

Despite the fact that the management of the physical layer is of fundamental importance, there has been very little research in this area: nodes in mobile ad hoc networks are confronted with a number of problems, which, in existing mobile networks, are solved by the base stations. The solution space ranges from hierarchical cell structures (a self-organized pendant of cellular networks) to completely ad hoc, stochastic allocations. Power management is of paramount importance. General strategies for saving power need to be addressed, as well as adaptation to the specifics of nodes of general channel and source coding methods, radio resource management, and multiple access.

Mobile ad hoc networks do not rely on one single technology; instead, they should be able to capitalize on technology advances. One challenge is to define a set of abstractions that can be used by the upper layers and still not preclude the use of new physical layer methods as they emerge. Primitives of such an abstraction are, for example, the capabilities and covering ranges of multicast and unicast channels.

Information such as node distribution, network density, link failures, etc., must be shared among layers, and the MAC layer and the network layer need to collaborate in order to have a better view of the network topology and to optimize the number of messages in the network.

Mobile ad hoc networks have the unique characteristic of being totally independent from any authority or infrastructure, providing great potential for the users. In fact, roughly speaking, two or more users can become a mobile ad hoc network simply by being close enough to meet the radio constraints, without any external intervention.

Moreover, telecommunication networks are expected to grow with the advent of new (and totally unexpected) applications. Although in the past telecommunication networks were studied and developed as separate building blocks, for users of mobile ad hoc networks the interaction between higher layers and lower layers is essential.

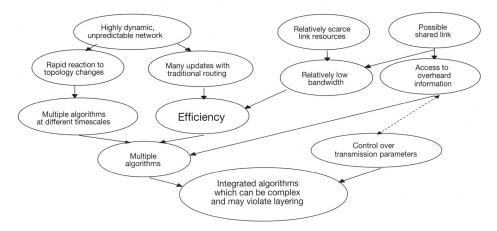

Figure 15.2 Complexity of mobile ad hoc networks. The network can be highly dynamic, implying that (1) traditional routing algorithms will either not stabilize or will generate many routing updates and (2) rapid response to topology change is needed [35].

Resilient and adaptive applications that can continue to perform effectively under degraded conditions can significantly enhance network operations from a user's perspective.
Such applications can also significantly ease the design pressure in complex engineering
areas such as quality of service (QoS) and mobile routing at the network layer [46].

As illustrated in Figure 15.2, communication among layers is the only practical approach
to a demanding environment that raises issues that rarely occur in other networks [35].

This chapter focuses on the state of the art in mobile ad hoc networks and highlights
some of the emerging technologies, protocols, and approaches at different layers for realizing network services for users on the move in areas with possibly no preexisting communication infrastructures.

The remainder of this chapter is organized as follows. In Section 15.2 we present the
layered architecture of mobile ad hoc networks and introduce some relevant concepts and
technologies that will be discussed further. In Section 15.3 we cover some emerging MAC
technologies that can be used for constructing a mobile ad hoc network: IEEE 802.11 and
Bluetooth. In Section 15.4 we provide an overview of the standardization efforts of the Internet Engineering Task Force. Section 15.5 introduces a human-based approach to a particular class of mobile ad hoc networks, referred to as self-organizing networks. In Section
15.6, we present mobile ad hoc networking from the users/applications point of view. Finally, Section 15.7 provides a discussion on the future evolution and applications of mobile ad hoc networks.

15.2 LAYERED ARCHITECTURE OF MOBILE AD HOC NETWORKS

The precursor of ad hoc networking technology was the packet radio network [33, 34].
Packet radio applies packet communications to a radio channel rather than to a wire-based

medium. This technology can be used to create LANs that link devices, as well as to provide gateways to other network systems and databases [11]. The current version, referred to as "distributed packet radio," is completely distributed, permitting flexible and rapid adaptation to changes and to mobility.

Later research focused mainly on cellular systems that are, in principle, single-hop wireless systems. Within the framework of multihop wireless systems, research communities worked on projects that mainly addressed medium access control and routing issues.

Appropriate physical and data link protocols need to be developed for wireless mobile networks in conjunction with the embedded MAC sublayer and the higher-level networking and/or transport layers.

A key aspect of wireless communications is the radio propagation channel, which introduces cochannel and adjacent channel interference among users. Exploiting the physical environment and controlling the location of radio users as much as possible is one way to mitigate interference, but this is not realistic for uncoordinated wireless systems that share the same radio spectrum. For ad hoc networks that share the same spectrum, new methods of cooperation are required to permit coexistence. Such methods are difficult to research without real-world channel models and simulation methodologies; there is still fundamental work to be done in this area [49].

There have been many successful attempts to reduce the power consumption of digital circuits. Today, there are many different techniques known, starting from the circuit level [19] and reaching into architecture and software. Clearly, the energy necessary to execute a given algorithm very much depends on the implementation technology. For current radio software projects, emphasis has been placed on low power consumption, see [66] and [55].

Current research covers lower-layer issues such as modulation and coding, multiple access, wireless/mobile protocols, and location protocols. In the United States, most of the research in this and in the sensor network fields is sponsored by NSF (Advanced Networking Infrastructure and Research Division and Computer–Communications Research Division) and DARPA (Microelectromechanical Systems and Global Mobile Information Systems); see [3, 14, 23, 42, 51]. Similar projects are conducted in Europe in the mobility and personal communications networks domain [2], in ETSI [25], in some universities (e.g., [20]), by industrial consortia (e.g., [8, 60]), and by operators (e.g., [59]).

The MAC layer specified in the IEEE 802.11 standard [29] or its variations, is typically applied in the existing ad hoc network projects. The standard is built on the carrier sense multiple access with collision avoidance (CSMA/CA) scheme that is extended with the capability for short channel allocation and acknowledgment control messages. In 802.11, all the nodes must use the same channel. All nodes can communicate with every other node that is within range. In 802.11 standard can be a good platform to implement a one-level, multihop architecture because of its extreme simplicity. IEEE 802.11 is a digital wireless data transmission standard aimed at providing a wireless LAN (WLAN) between portable computers and between portable computers and a fixed network infrastructure. Although it is easy to foresee that the WLANs will be the solution for home and office automation [5], the existing standard does not support multihop systems, and since only one frequency can be used, the achievable capacity is limited. HomeRF [27] is seen as the main contender to 802.11 for use in home networks. This is based on the shared wireless access protocol (SWAP) that defines a new common interface supporting wireless voice and data networking in the home. Wireless LAN technology is already widely commercially available. The main aim of Bluetooth technology [8, 10] is to guarantee interoperability between different applications on devices in the same area that may run over different protocol stacks, and therefore to provide a solution for wireless personal area networks. Section 15.2 covers the MAC layer in more detail.

The Internet Engineering Task Force (IETF) Working Group on Mobile Ad Hoc NETworks (MANET) is standardizing routing in ad hoc networks. The group studies routing specifications, with the goal of supporting networks scaling up to hundreds of routers [40]. The work of MANET relies on other existing IETF standards such as mobile IP and IP addressing. Most of the currently available solutions are not designed to scale to more than a few hundred nodes. Section 15.3 presents some aspects of the protocols designed to extend Internet services to mobile ad hoc network users.

Designing protocols that scale to very large wireless networks is among the main challenges of research in this field, and there are several factors that distinguish different protocols for realizing wide-area, mobile ad hoc networks, as explained in Section 15.4.

Location management functions make it possible to access a network regardless of the user's location. Not limited only to users, it is easily imagined that entire networks might one day be mobile as well, e.g., networks on aircraft or other vehicles. Location management works at several layers and is, therefore, a complex process [48].

The well-established techniques to locate mobile devices in infrastructure-based networks, even if they contain concepts to deal with nomadic nodes, are not useful as soon as infrastructure is no longer available.

As stated by the Zeroconf Working Group of the IETF [76], the common TCP/IP protocols commonly used for the network configuration, e.g., DHCP, DNS, MADCAP, and LDAP, are not appropriate for mobile ad hoc networks because they must be configured and maintained by an administrative staff.

For all these networks, an administrative staff will not exist, and the users of these networks have neither the time nor inclination to learn network administration skills. Instead, these networks need protocols that require zero user configuration and administration. New approaches are being investigated, as described in Chapter 21 of this book.

Bootstrapping protocols and a basic infrastructure must be available, however. Current schemes on the network layer are incorporated in Bluetooth and related technologies [8], whereas Jini [31] is the most prominent example of a system enabling federations of services and clients on the services layer.

At the service level, for IP networks, the service location protocol (SLP) proposed by the Internet Engineering Task Force [72] is used; other examples are SSDP (simple service discovery protocol) in universal plug and play networks [71] that are XML based, or SDP (service discovery protocol) in Bluetooth [8].

Finally, also at the application level, the location requires the choice of a topology, addressing within the topological space, and location- and distance-dependent operations, as in [30] and [47].

Information transport and its associated infrastructure must demonstrate high assurance capabilities in times of crisis and attack, as well as under normal conditions. Scarce attention has been given to security in mobile ad hoc networks so far. This computing environment is very different from the ordinary computing environment. In many cases, mobile computers will be connected to the network via wireless links. Such links are particularly vulnerable to passive eavesdropping, active replay attacks, and other active attacks [18]. To our knowledge, few works have been published on this topic (see [64], [77], and [18]), and much effort is required in order to overcome the vulnerability (in particular, the privacy vulnerability) of this type of network with an integrated approach that is not limited at the routing layer.

Security in networks (including ad hoc networks) mainly involves confidentiality and integrity of information, as well as legitimate use and availability of services [21]. In military applications, confidentiality is considered to be the most important security objective. In civilian scenarios, the major user requirement is availability [65].

Denial-of-service attacks are typically impossible to prevent. However, they can be made very expensive by exploiting the inherent redundancy of ad hoc networks [77]. For instance, a packet can be sent to its destination via several disjoint routes, which makes its interception considerably more expensive for the attacker.

A fundamental tool to achieve network security objectives is cryptography. The challenge of using cryptography in mobile ad hoc networks is the management of cryptographic keys. Since nodes are mobile, their interactions are spontaneous and unpredictable, which makes public key cryptography more appropriate in this setting than conventional cryptography. The most widely accepted solution for the public key management problem is based on public key certificates that are issued by (online) certification authorities and distributed via (online) key distribution servers.

The design issues associated with the real-time services become particularly important for multimedia delivery, e.g., voice, images and video. The multimedia data will typically be provided with some form of coding and be in the form of multiple data streams each with their own QoS requirements.

New networking technologies engender a radical transformation in high-end applications and the manner in which researchers and educators throughout the globe access and manipulate resources [52]. There are limitless possibilities for mobile applications. Although potential applications exist in commerce, education, medicine, government, public safety, and numerous other areas, market and social forces will determine which are accepted or rejected [48].

Indeed, the telecommunications industry expects exponential growth of subscribers for wireless services (PCS, GSM, and mobile IP). This growth will occur in an environment characterized by rapid development and migration of end-user applications.

A related characteristic is the evolution of new applications, made possible by mobility and ubiquitous access that would normally not be found in fixed networks. Researchers in the field must understand and explore these problems, finding solutions that will integrate efficiently with existing systems and endure over time [48].

In mobile computing, geographic location is critical for distributed applications. Several projects currently address the problem of location-aware applications [30, 39, 47, 70]. Information management in highly distributed and mobile applications recently became the core of a new field called cooperative information systems [17].

Notable applications of ad hoc networks are sensor networks, which can be used for several purposes such as hospital instrumentation or atmospheric instrumentation to predict weather [67], as well as social networks [41, 57].

Information technologies are an integral part of our lives, businesses, and society. The wide acceptance of Internet standards and technologies is helping us build global computer networks capable of connecting everything and reaching everyone [56].

Almost daily, new wired or wireless e-business models emerge: e-shopping, e-procurement, e-auctions, e-malls, third-party marketplaces, virtual communities, value chain service providers, value chain integrators, collaborative platforms, information brokerages and trusts [69]. Mobile ad hoc networks are envisioned to naturally support these applications. However, in order to realize these new technologies, it is necessary to understand related economic, social, and policy issues in much greater depth.

15.3 MAC LAYER

We present here two emerging technologies for wireless media interfaces that can be used for building a mobile ad hoc network: the IEEE 802.11 standard for wireless LANs (WLANs) [1, 29] and the Bluetooth technology [8, 10] which is the de-facto standard for wireless personal area networks (WPAN). A WLAN is a wireless network characterized by a small scope, whereas a WPAN is a network constituted by connected devices placed inside a circle with a radius of 10 meters. The Bluetooth Special Interest Group releases the Bluetooth specifications. In addition, the IEEE 802.15 Working Group for Wireless Personal Area Networks has started a project to publish and approve a standard derived from the Bluetooth specifications.

Bluetooth and IEEE 802.11 technologies also exemplify the two categories in which multiple access networks can be roughly categorized: random access (e.g., CSMA, CSMA/CD) and demand assignment (e.g., Token Ring) [5]. Due to the inherent flexibility of random access systems (e.g., random access allows unconstrained movement of mobile hosts) the IEEE K.11 standard committee decided to adopt a random access, CSMA-based scheme for WLANs. On the other hand, demand assignment access schemes are more suitable for an environment that needs to provide guarantees on the Quality of Service (QoS) perceived by its users. The Bluetooth technology that is designed to support delay-sensitive applications (such as voice traffic) beyond data traffic adopts a (implicit) token-based access method.

15.3.1 IEEE 802.11

IEEE 802.11 is a digital wireless data transmission standard in the 2.4 GHz ISM band aimed at providing wireless LANs between portable computers and between portable computers and a fixed network infrastructure. This standard defines a physical layer and a MAC layer. Three different technologies are used as an air interface physical layer for contention-based and contention-free access control: infrared, frequency hopping, and direct sequence spread spectrum. The most popular technology is the direct sequence spread spectrum, which can offer a bit rate of up to 11 Mbps in the 2.4 GHz band, and, in the future, up to 54 Mbps in the 5 GHz band. The basic access method in the IEEE 802.11 MAC protocol is the distributed coordination function (DCF) which is a carrier sense multiple access with collision avoidance (CSMA/CA) MAC protocol.

802.11 can be used to implement either an infrastructure-based W-LAN architecture or an ad hoc W-LAN architecture (see Figure 15.3). In an infrastructure-based network, there is a centralized controller for each cell, often referred to as an access point. The access point is normally connected to the wired network, thus providing the Internet access to mobile devices. All traffic goes through the access point, even when it is sent to a destination that belongs to the same cell. Neighboring cells can use different frequencies to avoid interference and increase the cell's capacity. All the cells are linked together to form a single broadcast medium at the LLC layer. A so-called distribution system handles the packet forwarding toward destination devices outside the cell across the wired network infrastructure. The distribution medium that forwards packets between the access points is not defined by the standard. It is possible to use a wireless link to connect the different access points, for example an 802.11 ad hoc link in another frequency. Such a feature permits the implementation of a two-level, multihop architecture.

In the ad hoc mode, every 802.11 device in the same cell, or independent basic service set (IBSS), can directly communicate with every other 802.11 device within the cell, without the intervention of a centralized entity or an infrastructure. In an ad hoc cell, identified by an identification number (IBSSID) that is locally managed, all devices must use a predefined frequency. Due to the flexibility of the CSMA/CA algorithm, it is sufficient to synchronize devices to a common clock for them to receive or transmit data correctly. Synchronization acquirement is a scanning procedure used by an 802.11 device for joining an existing IBSS. If the scanning procedure does not result in finding any IBSSs, the station may initialize a new IBSS. Synchronization maintenance is implemented via a distributed algorithm, based on the transmission of beacon frames at a known nominal rate, which is performed by all of the members of the IBSS. Additionally, given the constraints

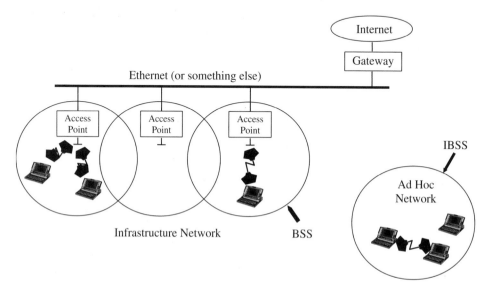

Figure 15.3 Infrastructure and ad hoc networks.

on power consumption in mobile networks, 802.11 offers power saving (PS) policies. The policy adopted within an IBSS should be completely distributed for preserving the self-organizing behavior.

The 802.11 standard is an interesting platform to experiment with multihop networking. This standard cannot do multihop networking as is. The development of a number of protocols is required.

It must be noted that, as illustrated via simulation in [5], depending on the network configuration, the standard protocol can operate very far from the theoretical throughput limit. In particular, it is shown that the distance between the IEEE 802.11 and the analytical bound increases with the number of active networks. In the IEEE 802.11 protocol, due to its backoff algorithm, the average number of stations that transmit in a slot increases with the number of active networks, and this causes an increase in the collision probability. A significant improvement of the IEEE 802.11 performance can thus be obtained by controlling the number of stations that transmit in the same slot.

15.3.2 Bluetooth

Bluetooth is a digital wireless data transmission standard operating in the 2.4 GHz Industrial, Scientific, and Medicine (ISM) band aimed at providing a short-range wireless link between laptops, cellular phones, and other devices. In this band, 79 different radio frequency (RF) channels spaced 1 MHz apart are defined.

The baseband and the Bluetooth radio layers compose the Bluetooth core protocols. Bluetooth radio provides the physical links among Bluetooth devices, whereas the Baseband layer provides a transport service of packets on the physical link.

The physical layer utilizes a frequency hopping spread spectrum (FHSS) as a technique of transmission, where the hopping sequence is a pseudorandom sequence of 79 hop length, and it is unique for each ad hoc network that we establish. Therefore the establishment of a physical channel is associated with the definition of a channel frequency hopping sequence that has a very long period length and that does not show repetitive patterns over short time intervals. Bluetooth is based on a low-cost, short-range radio link integrated into a microchip, enabling protected ad hoc connections for wireless communication of voice and data in stationary and mobile environments. The air interface symbol rate of Bluetooth is 1 Ms/s. If a binary FSK modulation is used, this gives a raw data rate of 1 Mb/s.

From a logical standpoint, Bluetooth belongs to the contention-free, token-based multi-access networks [5]. In a Bluetooth network, one station has the role of master and all other Bluetooth stations are slaves. The master decides which slave is the one to have the access to the channel. More precisely, a slave is authorized to deliver a single packet to the master only if it has received a polling message from the master.

The Bluetooth protocol uses a combination of circuit and packet switching. Slots can be reserved for synchronous packets. Two types of physical links are defined: the synchronous connection-oriented (SCO) link, a point-to-point, symmetric circuit-switched connection between the master and a specific slave used for delivering delay-sensitive traffic, and the asynchronous connectionless (ACL) link, a packet-switched connection between the master and all its slaves that can support the reliable delivery of data.

Two or more devices (units) sharing the same frequency hopping sequence (channel) form a piconet. A unit can belong to more than one piconet, but can be master to only one. Different piconets are not synchronized, and when they overlap they form a scatternet (see Figure 15.4).

A maximum of one ACL link can be opened between a master and a slave. A master can have up to three SCO links with one or several slaves. A slave can support SCO links with different masters at the same time, but only one SCO link with each. A slave may communicate with different piconets only in a time-multiplexing mode. This means that for any time instant it can only transmit on a single piconet. In fact, it has to change its synchronization parameters before listening to different channels.

Therefore, the communication among devices within different piconets can happen only in an asynchronous mode, unless the device acting as router between two piconets has two Bluetooth interfaces. We note here that the multihop networking routing protocols are still to be defined.

Before starting a data transmission, a Bluetooth unit inquires, by continuously sending an inquiry message, about its operating space in order to discover the presence of other units. Another unit listening to the channel used for the inquiry message, on the same frequency, replies to the inquiry by exploiting a random access protocol. The unit that starts paging it is automatically elected the master of the new connection and the paged unit is the slave. A unit can periodically listen to the channel to find a page message by tuning its receiver to the frequencies of the paging hopping sequence. After the paging procedure, the slave has an exact knowledge of the master clock and of the channel access code, so it and the master can enter the connection state. However, the real transmission will begin only after a polling message from the master to the slave. When a connection is established, the active slaves have to maintain the synchronization. A sketch of Bluetooth performance is given in [5].

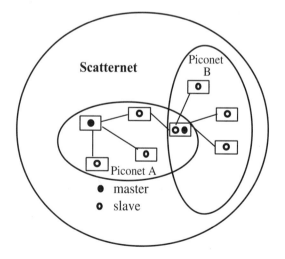

Figure 15.4 Bluetooth scatternet and piconets.

Bluetooth can support one asynchronous data link between two devices, up to three simultaneous synchronous voice links, or a link that simultaneously supports asynchronous data and synchronous voice. Each voice link supports a synchronous data rate of 64 kb/s in each direction. The asynchronous link can support a maximal asymmetric data rate of 723.2 kb/s (and up to 57.6 kb/s in the return direction), or a symmetric data rate of 433.9 kb/s.

The main aim of the Bluetooth specification is to guarantee the interoperability between different applications that may run over different protocol stacks. A number of service profiles define how Bluetooth-enabled devices should use the Bluetooth links and physical layer, and this allows manufacturer interoperability. All profiles define end-to-end services: cordless telephony, intercom, serial port, headset, dial-up, fax, LAN access (with PPP), generic object exchange, object push, file transfer, and synchronization. However, in order to implement a wireless multihop network over Bluetooth, a packet switch layer and/or a circuit switch layer need to be defined on top of the Bluetooth data link layer protocol (L2CAP).

15.4 MOBILE AD HOC NETWORKS AND THE INTERNET

The wide acceptance of Internet standards and technologies was and is one of the key steps for building global computer networks capable of connecting everything and reaching everyone. In the near future, with the advent of inexpensive wireless technologies, a large number of users will be mobile.

Extending IP internetworking for seamless operation over wireless communication technologies challenges present performance requirements of network protocols and applications, especially if wireless technologies evolve to become a significant part of the infrastructure [46].

The Internet Engineering Task Force (IETF) Working Group on Mobile Ad Hoc NETworks (MANET) is standardizing routing in ad hoc networks. The group studies routing specifications, with the goal of supporting networks scaling up to hundreds of routers [40]. The work of MANET relies on other existing IETF standards such as mobile IP and IP addressing.

A mobile ad hoc network that explicitly supports the Internet still presents the major salient characteristics we described above, as described in [16]:

1. Dynamic topologies
2. Bandwidth-constrained and variable capacity links
3. Energy-constrained operation
4. Limited physical security

However, the managing of IP addresses of the nodes in a mobile ad hoc network is not straightforward, as discussed below (see Figure 15.5).

As presented in [46], the approach followed by the protocols produced in the MANET working group, and by similar protocols worked on outside of MANET, is based on the

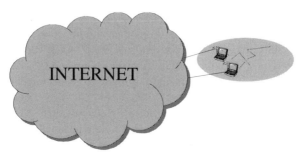

Figure 15.5   A mobile ad hoc IP network.

traditional two-level hierarchy routing architecture. These routing protocols fall into the class of interior gateway protocols, i.e., protocols used to route within a (mobile wireless) network or a set of interconnected (mobile wireless) networks under the same administration authority. Several of these protocols [7, 9, 12, 24, 32, 53, 54, 58] have been implemented in prototypes [44] and, although they are not yet available commercially, some of them are under commercial consideration [21].

In [16], a list of desirable qualitative properties of mobile ad hoc networks routing protocols for the Internet is given. These are:

1. Distributed operation
2. Loop-freedom
3. Demand-based operation
4. Proactive operation
5. Security
6. "Sleep" period operation
7. Unidirectional link support

Also, a list of quantitative metrics is given that can be used to assess the performance of any of these routing protocols:

1. End-to-end data throughput and delay
2. Route acquisition time
3. Percentage out-of-order delivery
4. Efficiency

These protocols are generally categorized according to their method of discovering and maintaining routes between all source–destination pairs:

- Proactive protocols
- Reactive protocols

Proactive protocols (also referred to as table-driven protocols) attempt to maintain routes continuously, so that the route is already available when it is needed for forwarding a packet. In such protocols, routing tables are exchanged among neighboring nodes each time a change occurs in the network topology. In contrast, the basic idea of reactive protocols (also referred to as source-initiated protocols) is to send a control message for discovering a route between a given source–destination pair only when necessary.

Most of the existing protocols for mobile ad hoc networks are not univocally proactive or reactive, as some of the protocols have a hybrid proactive and reactive design or simply present elements of both approaches.

The proactive approach is similar to the connectionless approach of traditional datagram networks, which is based on a constant update of the routing information [62]. Maintaining consistent and up-to-date routes between each source–destination pair requires the propagation of a large amount of routing information, whether needed or not. As a consequence, in proactive protocols, a route between any source–destination pair is always available, but such protocols cannot perform properly when the mobility rate in the network is high or when there are a large number of nodes in the network. In fact, the control overhead, in terms of both traffic and power consumption, is a serious limitation in mobile ad hoc networks, in which the bandwidth and power are scarce resources [62]. The proactive approaches are more similar in design to traditional IP routing protocols; thus, they are more likely to retain the behavior features of presently used routing protocols. Existing transport protocols and applications are more likely to operate as designed using proactive routing approaches than on-demand routing approaches [46].

A reactive protocol creates and maintains routes between a source–destination pair only when necessary, in general when requested by the source (on-demand approach). Therefore, in contrast to the proactive approach, in reactive protocols the control overhead is drastically reduced. However, similar to connection-oriented communications, a route is not initially available and this generates a latency period due to the route discovery procedure. The on-demand design is based (1) on the observation that in a dynamic topology routes expire frequently and (2) on the assumption that not all the routes are used at the same time. Therefore, the overhead expended to establish and/or maintain a route between a given source–destination pair will be wasted if the source does not require the route prior to its invalidation due to topological changes. Note that this assumption may not hold true in all architectures, but it may be suitable for many wireless networks. The validity of this design decision is dependent, in part, on the traffic distribution and topology dynamics of the network [46].

As previously stated, some protocols can combine both proactive and reactive characteristics in order to benefit from the short response time provided by the proactive approach under route request and to limit the control overhead as in reactive protocols. An obvious, advantageous approach is to proactively handle all the routes that are known to be more frequently used and to create on demand all the other routes.

Achieving the right balance between reactive and proactive operation in a hybrid approach may require some a priori knowledge of the networking environment or additional mechanisms to adaptively control the mode of operation [46]. A general comparison of the two protocols categories is presented in both RT99 [62] and [46].

As we anticipated above, one critical aspect of Internet-based mobile ad hoc networks is the addressing. In fact, the addressing approach used in wired networks, as well as its adaptation for mobile IP [45], do not work properly. Approaches based on fixed addressing cannot reflect the topological network for mobile networks. The approach used in mobile IP networks is based on home use, and it is not suitable for ad hoc networks in which there is no fixed infrastructure. Therefore, a new addressing approach for such networks is required. Moreover, given that, in the foreseen topology of the addressing approach, the interaction among different routing protocols could easily happen, a common addressing approach is necessary.

This issue is still a matter of ongoing research. The IETF document describing Internet mobile ad hoc networks states that [16]:

> The development of such an approach is underway, which permits routing through a multi-technology fabric, permits multiple hosts per router and ensures long-term interoperability through adherence to the IP addressing architecture. Supporting these features appears only to require identifying host and router interfaces with IP addresses, identifying a router with a separate Router ID, and permitting routers to have multiple wired and wireless interfaces.

Geographical location of nodes, i.e., node coordinates in two- or three-dimensional space, has been suggested, among other purposes, for simplifying the addressing issue in combination with the Internet addressing scheme. The existing location-based routing protocols (see Chapter 21 in this book for details) propose to use location information for reducing the propagation of control messages, thus reducing the intermediate system functions or for making packet-forwarding decisions.

Geographical routing allows nodes in the network to be nearly stateless; the only information that nodes in the network have to maintain is about their one-hop neighbors. A detailed review of geographical routing and related issues is given in Chapter 21.

There are also solutions that do not rely on Internet addresses. A solution wherein each node has a permanent, unique end system identifier and a temporary, location-dependent address is proposed in [26]. The location-dependent addresses management, which is based on the association of each end-system identifier to an area of geographical coordinates that acts as a distributed location database, allows a node to obtain a probable location of any other node with a known end system identifier [43, 74].

The work proposed in the context of Internet mobile routing considers networks traditionally classified as small networks. However, even in networks of one hundred nodes, scalability is an important performance. One approach for achieving scalability in mobile ad hoc networks is clustering. With this approach, the network is partitioned into subsets (clusters). Within a cluster, a traditional MANET algorithm is assumed, and the communication between clusters is done by means of clusterheads and border nodes. The clusterheads form a dominant set that works as backbone for the network. In cluster-based algorithms, one of the main issues is the determination of the clusters and, consequently, of the clusterheads in such a way that the reconfigurations of the network topology are minimized. However, choosing clusterheads optimally is an NP-hard problem [4].

Other strategies for dominating sets for ad hoc networks, which are able to build better performing dominating sets than clustering, are described in [78].

Finally, multicast routing is a strategy that could allow optimization of resource usage;

this is seen to be as an important feature for energy- and bandwidth-constrained networks as mobile ad hoc networks are. Additionally, the underlying layer has a broadcast nature that can be exploited by an integrated design, as done, for example, in [75]. Several multicast routing algorithms have been proposed and evaluated [37]. Although there is the conviction that multicast mobile routing technology is a relatively immature technology area and much of what is developed for unicast mobile routing—if proven effective—can be extended to develop multicast mobile routing variants [46], some work has assessed the definition of network protocols with an integrated approach, thereby permitting improved energy efficiency [75]. However, shortest-path-based multicast algorithms require too much power (quadratic at network size), because they require that each node maintain a global view of the network. Real power savings can be obtained only with localized algorithms in which nodes only know their neighbors' information and make decisions based only on that [63].

Mobile ad hoc networks do not provide QoS by design. Although there has been controversial discussion about whether or not QoS mechanisms are needed in the wired Internet, it is indisputable that some applications can be supported by wireless networks only under QoS provisioning.

Architecture for supporting QoS in mobile ad hoc networks should have two primary attributes [13]:

- Flexibility. Necessary for the heterogeneity of the physical and MAC layers, as well as multiple routing protocols.
- Efficiency. Necessary for the limited processing power and storage capabilities of nodes, as well as the scarce bandwidth available.

In the literature, several approaches have been adopted for assessing the issue of QoS in mobile ad hoc networks, such as the QoS routing protocol [15, 28, 61] and signaling systems for resource reservation [36]. Although some work has been done to date, more studies need to be conducted to further explore the problem of QoS provisioning for mobile ad hoc networks.

15.5 ROUTING IN SELF-ORGANIZED NETWORKS

As stated above, ad hoc networks can be considered small networks (up to hundreds of routers [40]) in which the nodes are typically IP routers with a large computing capacity. However, large mobile ad hoc networks are the natural solution for applications based on models similar to the business models of citizen band, amateur radio, and walkie-talkie systems, in which multihop wireless communications allow voice and data messaging among all users. These networks are likely to be very large and not Internet-based, both because they will be more dedicated to human communications and because they would be unacceptably complex.

The step toward such a network (larger than a thousand nodes, and/or constituting a wide or geographical network) consisting of nodes with limited resources is not simple. It is clear that existing solutions are not designed for such an environment. They (1) do not easily adapt to a large number of mobile nodes, and (2) they do not exploit certain key characteristics of these networks (e.g., cooperation among nodes). Moreover, other relevant issues like the distribution of nodes or the ability of nodes to self-organize are not usually addressed in current ad hoc networks research, which focuses mainly on pure communication aspects.

We refer to these networks as self-organized networks (Figure 15.6) in order to distinguish them from traditional mobile ad hoc networks and to emphasize their self-organization peculiarities:

- Self-organized networks are nonauthority-based networks, i.e., they can act independently of any provider or common denominator, such as the Internet. However, similar to amateur radio networks, they require regulation (self-organization) [34].
- Self-organized networks are potentially very large and not regularly distributed. In principle, one single network can cover the entire world. There can be small areas with high density, as well as large areas with very low density.
- Self-organized networks are highly cooperative. The tasks at any layer are distributed over the nodes and any operation is the result of the collaboration of a group of them.

The "small world" design has been proposed for self-organized networks [6]. Small world graphs are very large graphs that tend to be sparse, clustered, and have a small diameter. The small world phenomenon was inaugurated as an area of experimental study in the social sciences through the work of Stanley Milgram in the 1960s. Experiments have shown that the acquaintanceship graph connecting the entire human population has a diameter of six or less edges. Thus, the small world phenomenon allows one to speak of "six degrees of separation."

Self-organized networks can be structured as a small world graph, emphasizing the fact

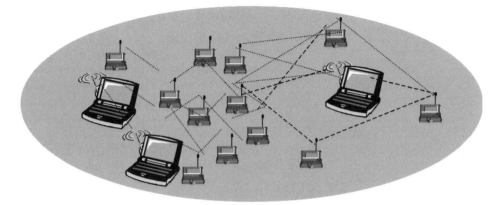

Figure 15.6 A self-organized network.

that nodes can collaborate in a "human way" to find a route between each source–destination pair when needed [6]. In this case, the routing solution is designed with three requirements in mind: (1) to scale well in a very large network; (2) to cope with dynamically changing network connectivity owing to mobility; and (3) to be based on high collaboration among nodes that are assumed not to use complex algorithms or protocols. For the first requirement, the solution is designed such that a node relies only on itself and a small number of other nodes for packet forwarding. The uncertainty in the network due to the nodes' mobility is addressed by considering multipath routing as a rule. The third requirement is assessed by design.

The solution proposed in [6] combines two routing protocols: (1) a mechanism that allows reaching destinations in the vicinity of a node and does not use location information for making packet forwarding decisions; and (2) a mechanism that is used to send data to remote destinations and uses geographic information. The latter is the small world graph element that is introduced for achieving scalability and reduced dependence on intermediate systems.

The small world graph approach is mainly used for route discovery. For a potentially large network, both traditional proactive and reactive approaches are not feasible, due to the large amount of information that must be maintained and the high latency, respectively. With the small world graph approach, a source discovers a (possible) route to the destination with the collaboration of some other nodes within the network. This is done on-demand, thus avoiding large routing tables, but inquires only a small set of nodes, thus avoiding flooding of a large number of nodes. The returned route is not a list of nodes but a rough shape of the geographical path from the source to the destination, a set of points (anchors) described by geographical coordinates. This geographical information, rather than a traditional list of nodes' addresses, permits coping with the network dynamism (which increases with distance between the source–destination pair). Between anchors, geodesic packet forwarding is performed; this is a greedy method that follows successively closer geographic hops to the next point or the final destination [79]. If no closer neighbor exists, routing is based on planar graph construction and routing, guaranteeing delivery, as described in [80].

A comparison between this approach and the Internet-based one presented in the previous section does not hold, as the target is completely different. It is straightforward that a wireless subnet connected to the Internet will work better with a solution designed with the characteristics described in the previous section. The solution presented here is more appropriate for "users' networks," in which a (potentially large) number of users (with potentially small devices) combine in a network, eventually connected to the Internet.

15.6 PEOPLE-BASED NETWORKS

In people-based networking, instead of sharing and routing information via a physical network, the information is transmitted by people with personal devices of some type [such as a personal digital assistant (PDA)] to other people close by with similar devices, and so on. Such a network is, evidently, a mobile ad hoc network with no central administration, each part of it being based on a person who is free to constantly move about. These networks may be, because their behavior is so self-organizing, fairly robust; there are no wires to break, and if one "router" fails, there are many others around—as many as there are people carrying them.

The users have, simultaneously, their traditional role and the "network" role. The way the network is built depends mainly on the way the users interact and the type of application(s) run.

With this user/application-oriented approach, the architecture is dictated by the configuration requirements posed by the application. In [22] some challenges posed by this approach are presented, as well as some possible techniques that can be used to address them. Together with traditional aspects of mobile ad hoc networking—network boundaries are poorly defined, the network is not planned, hosts are not preconfigured, there are no central servers—this work points out that users are not experts, and therefore, it is important to minimize the inexpert user's exposure to the administrative infrastructure and make necessary activities as intuitive as possible.

The area of people-based networking ranges from issues of networking, such as the best way to send messages to a particular device through a network, to those of the kinds of applications and activities that such a technology may support, ranging over everything from low-level technical issues, to those relating to users and collaboration.

Applications of people-based networking are multiple, mainly devoted to studying and enhancing the social interaction among people, and facilitating their daily life. For example, augmenting everyday face-to-face interaction between various types of technological support, using a variety of devices such as "thinking tags" (which could be used in various ways to indicate how alike people were in relation to a number of common topics), or "MEME tags," which could be programmed with "ideas" that people might then talk about and also might want to keep [41].

Another example is PDAs that carry information, which "attaches" to the devices as pollen does to bees. This information is then transmitted across nodes where the PDAs dock. Every time the PDA docks, it collects packets of "pollen" as well as the information for which it has docked.

The pollen network makes it possible for information to be shared and distributed where needed simply by the everyday actions of groups of people. People need not be aware of how the distribution is taking place nor of the details of their participation in the process. As a side effect, information (such as hints, tips, and other comments) can be associated with physical objects in the user environment. Through the cumulative actions of many people interacting with devices and other people, messages are transferred node-by-node across the network [57].

15.7 CONCLUSION

Ad hoc networks are seen as key in the evolution of wireless networks. They have several potentialities that are not available with traditional wireless networks and can be used in different environments. The research in mobile ad hoc networking covers all the networking layers, ranging from the physical to the application layer, including social and economic aspects. We presented an overview of some MAC layer technologies that can be used for ad hoc networks, as well as the Internet-based and human-based approaches to routing. Finally we illustrated a user/application approach, highlighting some applications and social aspects of mobile ad hoc networks.

Although there are several applications for mobile ad hoc networks that will require being part of the Internet, mobile ad hoc networks are also envisioned for different application models. For example, applications devoted to studying and enhancing the social interaction among people and facilitating their daily lives, as well as applications based on models similar to the business models of citizen band, amateur radio, and walkie-talkie systems, in which multihop wireless communications allow voice and data messaging among all users.

ACKNOWLEDGMENTS

Many thanks to Ljubica Blazevic, Marco Conti, Piergiorgio Cremonese, and Ivan Stojmenovic for very useful comments and suggestions.

REFERENCES

1. IEEE P802.11/D10, Draft Standard, Wireless LAN medium access control and physical layer specifications, 14 January, 1999.
2. Advanced Communications Technologies and Services (ACTS) in Europe, Domain4—Mobility and Personal Communications Networks, projects list, http://www.infowin.org/ACTS/RUS/PROJECTS/DOMAINS/d4.htm.
3. NSF Advanced Networking Infrastructure and Research (ANIR) Division, http://www.cise.nsf.gov/anir/index.html.
4. S. Basagni, I. Chlamtac, and A. Farago, A generalized clustering algorithm for peer-to-peer networks, *Workshop on Algorithmic Aspects of Communication,* Bologna, Italy, July, 1997.
5. R. Bruno, M. Conti, and E. Gregori, Bluetooth: Architecture, protocols and scheduling algorithms, in *Proceedings of Hicss34,* Maui, Hawaii, 2001.
6. Lj. Blazevic, L. Bittyan, S. Capkun, S. Giordano, J.-P. Hubaux, and J.-Y. Le Boudec, Self-organization in mobile ad hoc netwrks: The approach of terminals, *IEEE Communication Magazine,* June, 2001.
7. J. Broch, D. Johnson, and D. Maltz, The dynamic source routing protocol for mobile ad hoc networks, IETF Internet-Draft draft-ietf-manet-dsr-03.txt, October, 1999.
8. Bluetooth home page: http://www.bluetooth.com/.
9. B. Bellur, R. Ogier, and F. Templin, Topology broadcast based on reverse-path forwarding (TBRPF), IETF Internet-Draft draft-ietf-manet-tbrpf-00.txt, August, 2000.
10. Specification of the Bluetooth System—Core. Version 1.0B. December 1st 1999. http://www.bluetooth.net/download/core_10_b.pdf.
11. G. Cleveland, *Packet Radio: Applications for Libraries in Developing Countries,* UDT Series on Data Communication Technologies and Standards for Libraries, Ottawa: IFLA, 1993
12. S. B. Lee, G. S Ahn, and A. T. Campbell, Improving UDP and TCP performance in mobile ad hoc networks, *IEEE Communication Magazine,* June, 2001.

13. M. S. Corson and A. T. Campbell, Towards supporting quality of service in mobile ad-hoc networks, in *First Conference on Open Architecture and Network Programming,* San Francisco, April 1998.

14. NSF Division of Computer-Communications Research (C-CR), http://www.cise.nsf.gov/ccr/index.html.

15. T. W. Chen, M. Gerla, and T. C. Tsai, QoS routing performance in multihop Wireless networks, in *Proceedings of IEEE ICUPC97,* San Diego, 1997.

16. S. Corson and J. Macker, Mobile ad hoc networking (MANET), IETF RFC 2501, January, 1999.

17. *Proceedings of the Fourth IFCIS International Conference on Cooperative Information Systems,* Edinburgh, Scotland, September 2–4, 1999.

18. S. Corson, et al., An internet MANET encapsulation protocol (IMEP) Specification, IETF internet draft, August, 1999.

19. A. P. Chandrakasan, S. Sheng, and R. W. Brodersen, Low-power CMSO digital design, *IEEE Journal of Solid State Circuits, 27*(4), pp. 473–484, 1992.

20. Digital Inter Relay Communication (DIRC), http://www.dirc.net/home/index.html.

21. W. Ford, *Computer Communications Security, Principles, Standard Protocols and Techniques,* Upper Saddle River, NJ: Prentice Hall, 1994.

22. L. M. Feeney, B. Ahlgren, and A. Westerlund, spontaneous networking: An application-oriented approach to ad hoc networking, *IEEE Communication Magazine,* June 2001.

23. DARPA—Global Mobile Information Systems (GLOMO), list of GLOMO projects, February 2000, http://www.darpa.mil/ito/research/glomo/projlist.html.

24. J. Garcia-Luna and M. Spohn, Source tree adaptive routing (STAR) protocol, IETF Internet-Draft draft-ietf-manet-star-00.txt, October, 1999.

25. HIPERLAN (High Performance Radio Local Area Network) page, Project HIPERCOM (ETSI), November, 1999, http://donald2.inria.fr/hiperlan/hiperlan.html.

26. J-P. Hubaux, J-Y. Le Boudec, S. Giordano, and M. Hamdi, The nodes project: Towards mobile ad-hoc WANs, *Proceedings International Conference on Mobile Multimedia Communication (MOMUC99),* November, 1999.

27. HomeRF™ Working Group Web Site, http://www.homerf.org/.

28. Y. C. Hsu, T. C. Tsai, and Y. D. Lin, QoS Routing in multihop packet radio environment, in *Proceedings of IEEE ISCC'98,* 1998.

29. ISO/IEC 8802-11:1999(E) ANSI/IEEE Std 802.11, Part 11: Wireless LAN Medium Access Control (MAC) and Physical Layer (PHY) specifications, 1999.

30. T. Imielinski and S. Goel, DataSpace—Querying and monitoring deeply networked collections in physical space, in *Proceedings of MobiDE 1999,* Seattle, WA, August 20, 1999, pp. 44–51.

31. Arnold, K., Wollrath, A., O'Sullivan, B., Scheifler, R., and Waldo, J., *The Jini Specification,* Reading, MA: Addison-Wesley, 1999.

32. P. Jacquet, P. Muhlethaler, A. Qayyum, et al., Optimized link state routing protocol, IETF Internet-Draft draft-ietf-manet-olsr-02.txt, July, 2000.

33. J. Jubin and J. D. Tornow, The DARPA packet radio network protocols, *Proceedings of the IEEE, 75,* 1, 21–32, 1987.

34. P. Karn, H. Price, and R. Diersing, Packet radio in amateur service, *IEEE JSAC, SAC-3,* 3, May, 1985.

35. G. S. Lauer, *Routing in Communication Networks,* Englewood Cliffs, NJ: Prentice Hall, 1995.

36. S. B. Lee, G. S. Ahn, and A. T. Campbell, Improving UDP and TCP performance in mobile ad-hoc networks, *Communication Magazine,* June, 2001.

37. S. J. Lee, W. Su, J. Hsu, M. Gerla, and R. Bagrodia, A performance comparison Study of ad hoc wireless multicast protocols, *Proceedings of IEEE Infocom 2000,* March, 2000.

38. C.-H. R. Lin and M. Gerla, A Distributed control scheme in multi-hop packet radio networks for voice/data traffic support, *IEEE GLOBECOM,* 1995.

39. DeepMap project, http://www.villa-bosch.de/eml/english/research/deepmap/deepmap.html.

40. The Internet Engineering Task Force Mobile Ad-Hoc Networking Page (MANET): http://www.ietf.org/html.charters/manet-charter.html.

41. R. Borovoy, Media Laboratory—MIT, Boston, USA, the MEME tags project, http://fredm. www.media.mit.edu/people/fredm/projects/memetag/.

42. DARPA—Microelectromechanical Systems (MEMS), Project Summaries, http://www.arpa. mil/MTO/MEMS/Projects/index.html#PrimaryKey10.

43. J. Li, J. Jannotti, D. De Couto, D. Karger, and R. Morris, Scalable location service for geographic ad hoc routing, *Mobicom00,* Boston, 2000.

44. MANET mailing list, ftp://manet.itd.nrl.navy.mil/pub/manet.archive, discussion on applications for mobile ad-hoc networking with Subject:: MANET application scenarios.

45. C. Perkins (Ed.), IP mobility support, *IETF RFC 2002,* October, 1996.

46. J. P. Macker, V. D. Park, and M. S. Corson, Mobile and wireless internet services: Putting the pieces together, *IEEE Communication Magazine,* June, 2001.

47. The Nexus project, http://www.informatik.unistuttgart.de/ipvr/vs/projekte/nexus/index.html.

48. NFS Wireless and Mobile Communications Workshop, Northern Virginia, March, 1997.

49. *NFS Tetherless T3 and Beyond Workshop,* interim report, November, 1998.

50. NFS Wireless Information Technology and Networks Program Announcement, NSF 99-68, 1999.

51. National Science Fundation, Program Announcements and Information, http://www.nsf.gov/home/programs/recent.htm.

52. Recommendations for an Advanced Research Infrastructure Supporting the Computational Science Community, Report from the Post vBNS Workshop, March, 1999.

53. V. Park and M. S. Corson, Temporally-ordered routing algorithm (TORA) Version 1 Functional Specification, IETF Internet-Draft draft-ietf-manet-tora-spec-02.txt, October, 1999.

54. C. Perkins, *Ad Hoc Networking,* Reading, MA: Addison-Wesley, 2000.

55. J. Rabaey, P. Wright, and B. Brodersen, The Pico radio project: http://www.eecs.berkeley.edu/Research/Pico_Radio.

56. Report to the President, Information Technology: Transforming our Society, *PITAC Report,* February 1999.

57. N. Glance and D. Snowdon, Xerox Research Centre Europe, France, The Pollen Project: http://www.xrce.xerox.com/research/ct/projects/pollen/home.html.

58. C. Perkins, E. Royer, and S. Das, Ad hoc on demand distance vector (AODV) routing, IETF Internet-Draft draft-ietf-manet-aodv-06.txt, July, 2000.

59. France Telecom, RNRT: The PRIMA Project: http://www.telecom.gouv.fr.

60. Rooftop Communications, http://www.rooftop.com/.

61. R. Ramanathan and M. Streenstrup. Hierarchically-organized, multihop mobile wireless networks for quality-of service support, *Mobile Networks and Applications,* January, 1998.

62. E. Royer and C.-K. Toh, A Review of current routing protocols for mobile ad-hoc networks, *IEEE Personal Communications,* April, 1999.

63. I. Stojmenovic, Location updates for efficient routing in ad hoc networks, Chapter 23, this volume.

64. J. Stevens, SURAN network susceptibilities study (U), Report Number SRTN-39, November, 1985.

65. F. Stajano and R. Anderson, The resurrecting duckling: Security issues for ad-hoc wireless networks. In *Proceedings of the 7th International Workshop on Security Protocols,* Cambridge, UK, April, 1999.

66. S. Sheng, L. Lynn, J. Peroulas, K. Stone, I. O'Donnell, and R. Brodersen, A low-power CMOS chipset for spread-spectrum communications, *1996 IEEE International Solid-State Circuits Conference,* p. 39, February, 1996.

67. The SMART DUST Project, Autonomous sensing and communication in a cubic millimeter, Supported by the DARPA/ETO MEMS program, http://robotics.eecs.berkeley.edu/~pister/SmartDust/.

68. J. Macker, Software implementation work related to MANET, Feb. 2000, http://tonnant.itd.nrl.navy.mil/manet/survey/survey.html.

69. P. Timmers, Business models for electronic markets, *Journal of Electronic Markets, 8,* 2, 3–8, 1998.

70. H. Tarumi, K. Morishita, M. Nakao, and Y. Kambayashi, SpaceTag: An overlaid virtual system and its applications, *ICMCS, 1,* 207–212, 1999.

71. Universal Plug and Play Forum: http://www.upnp.org/.

72. J. Veizades, E. Guttman, C. Perkins, and S. Kaplan: Service location protocol (SLP), Internet RFC 2165, June, 1997.

73. www.w3c.org.

74. J.-P. Hubaux, J.-Y. Le Boudec, S. Giordano, M. Hamdi, L. Blazevic, L. Buttyan, and M. Vojnovic, Towards mobile ad-hoc WANs: Terminodes, in *Proceedings of the IEEE Wireless Communications and Networking Conference (WCNC'00),* Chicago, September, 2000.

75. J. E. Wieselthier, G. D. Nguyen, and A. Ephremides, Energy-efficient multicast of session traffic in bandwidth and transceiver-limited wireless, to appear in *Cluster Computing,* 2002.

76. M. Hattig (Ed.), Zeroconf Requirements, IETF Internet draft draft-ietf-zeroconf-reqts-06.txt, November, 2000.

77. L. Zhou and Z. J. Haas, Securing ad-hoc networks, *IEEE Network Magazine, 13,* 6, 1999.

78. J. Wu, M. Gao, and I. Stojmenovic, On calculating power-aware connected dominating sets for efficient routing in ad hoc wireless networks, in *Proceedings of the ICPP '01,* Valencia, Spain, September 3–7, 2000.

79. G. G. Finn, Routing and addressing problems in large metropolitan-scale internetworks, ISI Research Report ISU/RR-87-180, March, 1987.

80. P. Bose, P. Morin, I. Stojmenovic and J. Urrutia, Routing with guaranteed Ddlivery in ad hoc wireless networks, *Third International Workshop on Discrete Algorithms and Methods for Mobile Computing and Communications,* Seattle, August 20, 1999, pp. 48–55.

CHAPTER 16

Broadcast Scheduling for TDMA in Wireless Multihop Networks

ERROL L. LLOYD

Department of Computer Science and Information Sciences, University of Delaware

16.1 INTRODUCTION

Wireless multihop networks, also known as packet radio networks and ad hoc networks, hold great promise for providing easy to use mobile services for many applications, especially military and disaster relief communications. Such networks can provide robust communication, be rapidly deployed, and respond quickly in dynamic environments. However, effectively deploying and utilizing such networks poses many technical challenges. One such challenge is to make effective use of the limited channel bandwidth. In this chapter, we describe one approach to this challenge, namely broadcast scheduling of channel usage by way of TDMA (time division multiple access). Our emphasis is on the fundamental computational and algorithmic issues and results associated with broadcast scheduling.

The chapter is organized as follows. In the next section we provide background and terminology on broadcast scheduling and related topics. Section 16.3 examines the computational complexity of broadcast scheduling. Sections 16.4 and 16.5 study approximation algorithms in centralized and distributed domains. Section 16.6 briefly outlines some related results. Finally, Section 16.7 summarizes the chapter and outlines prominent open problems.

16.2 WHAT IS BROADCAST SCHEDULING?

Background and terminology associated with wireless multihop networks, the modeling of such networks, and related concepts are provided in this section.

16.2.1 Basic Concepts of Wireless Multihop Networks

We define a wireless multihop network as a network of stations that communicate with each other via wireless links using radio signals. All of the stations share a common channel. Each station in the network acts both as a host and as a switching unit. It is required

Handbook of Wireless Networks and Mobile Computing, Edited by Ivan Stojmenović.
ISBN 0-471-41902-8 © 2002 John Wiley & Sons, Inc.

that the transmission of a station be received collision-free by all of its one-hop (i.e., direct) neighbors. This cannot occur if a station transmits and receives simultaneously or if a station simultaneously receives from more than one station. A collision caused by transmitting and receiving at the same time is called a primary conflict. A collision caused by simultaneously receiving from two stations is called a secondary conflict. We note that as a practical matter, some existing multihop networks may violate one or more of the above assumptions.

A wireless multihop network can be modeled by a directed graph $G = (V, A)$, where V is a set of nodes denoting stations in the network and A is a set of directed edges between nodes, such that for any two distinct nodes u and v, edge $(u, v) \in A$ if and only if v can receive u's transmission. As is common throughout the literature, we assume that $(u, v) \in A$ if and only if $(v, u) \in A$. That is, links are bidirectional, in which case it is common to use an undirected graph $G = (V, E)$. Throughout this chapter we use undirected graphs to model wireless multihop networks.

Sharing a common channel introduces the question of how the channel is accessed. Channel access mechanisms for wireless multihop networks fall into two general categories: random access (e.g., ALOHA) and fixed access. Broadcast scheduling, the focus of this chapter, is a fixed access technique that preallocates the common channel by way of TDMA so that collisions do not occur.

16.2.2 Defining Broadcast Scheduling

The task of a broadcast scheduling algorithm is to produce and/or maintain an infinite schedule of TDMA slots such that each station is periodically assigned a slot for transmission and all transmissions are received collision-free. In this framework, most broadcast scheduling algorithms operate by producing a finite length nominal schedule in which each station is assigned exactly one slot for transmission, and then indefinitely repeating that nominal schedule. Except where noted otherwise, throughout this chapter the term broadcast schedule refers to a nominal schedule.

16.2.3 Graph Concepts and Terminology

In modeling wireless multihop networks by undirected graphs, many variants are possible in regard to network topology. Among the possibilities, the three most relevant to this chapter are:

1. Arbitrary graphs. Such graphs can model any physical situation, including for example, geographically close neighbors that cannot communicate directly due to interference (e.g., a mountain) on a direct line between the stations.

2. Planar graphs. A graph is planar if and only if it can be drawn in the plane such that no two edges intersect except at common endpoints. Planar graphs are among the most widely studied classes of graphs.

3. Unit disk graphs. Formally introduced in [9] for use in network modeling, and studied in conjunction with broadcast scheduling in [28], unit disk graphs [9, 3] model

the situation in which all stations utilize a uniform transmission range R, and there is no interference. Thus, the transmission of a station v will be received by all stations within a Euclidean distance R of v. In these graphs, there is an edge between nodes u and v if and only if the Euclidean distance between stations u and v does not exceed R. An example of a unit disk graph model of a wireless multihop network and a nominal schedule are shown in Figure 16.1. In that figure, there is a link between a pair of stations if and only if the circles of radius $R/2$ centered at the pair of stations intersect, including being tangent. The slots assigned to the stations are the numbers inside the brackets.

Regardless of the graph model utilized, if there is an edge between nodes u and v, then u is a one-hop neighbor/neighbor of v and likewise v is a neighbor of u. The degree of a node is the number of neighbors. The degree ρ of a network is the maximum degree of the nodes in the network. The distance-2 neighbors of a node include all of its one-hop neighbors and the one-hop neighbors of its one-hop neighbors. The two-hop neighbors of a node are those nodes that are distance-2 neighbors, but are not one-hop neighbors. The unit subset of node u consists of u and its distance-2 neighbors. The distance-2 degree $D(u)$ of u is the number of distance-2 neighbors of u, and the distance-2 degree D of a network, is the maximum distance-2 degree of the nodes in the network.

Relevant to broadcast scheduling is distance-2 coloring [22, 13] of a graph $G = (V, E)$, where the problem is to produce an assignment of colors $C : V \rightarrow 1, 2, \ldots$ such that no two nodes are assigned the same color if they are distance-2 neighbors. An optimal coloring is a coloring utilizing a minimum number of colors. A distance-2 coloring algorithm is said to color nodes in a greedy fashion (i.e., greedily) if when coloring a node, the color

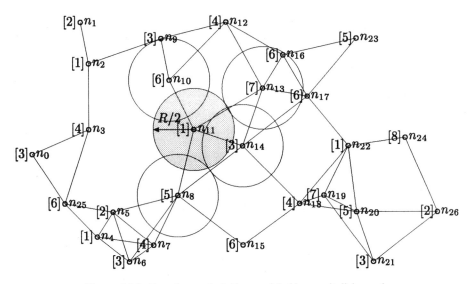

Figure 16.1 Broadcast scheduling modeled by a unit disk graph.

assigned is the smallest number color that can be assigned without resulting in conflicts. Here, the constraint number of a node is the number of different colors assigned to the node's distance-2 neighbors.

In the context of broadcast scheduling, determining a nominal schedule is directly abstracted to distance-2 coloring, whereby slots that are assigned to stations are translated into colors that are assigned to nodes. In this chapter, we will interchangeably use the terms network and graph, station and node, and slot and color.

16.2.4 Varieties of Broadcast Scheduling Algorithms

There are two main varieties of broadcast scheduling algorithms—centralized and distributed.

Centralized Algorithms

Centralized algorithms are executed at a central site and the results are then transmitted to the other stations in the network. This requires that the central site have complete information about the network. This is a strong assumption that is not easy to justify for wireless multihop networks with mobile stations. The study of centralized algorithms, however, provides an excellent starting point for both the theory of broadcast scheduling and the development of more practical algorithms. Further, for some stationary wireless networks, it is reasonable to run a centralized algorithm at the net management center and then distribute schedules to stations.

In the centralized algorithm context, there are two types of algorithms corresponding to how the input is provided:

1. *Off-line algorithms.* The network topology is provided to the central site in its entirety. The algorithm computes the schedule for the entire network once and for all.

2. *Adaptive algorithms*: With off-line algorithms, if the network topology changes, then the algorithm is rerun for the entire network. However, as wireless networks are evolving towards thousands of stations spread over a broad geographical area and operating in an unpredictable dynamic environment, the use of off-line scheduling algorithms is not realistic. In practice, it is absolutely unaffordable to halt communication whenever there is a change in the network, so as to produce a new schedule "from scratch." In such circumstances, adaptive algorithms are required That is, given a broadcast schedule for the network, if the network changes (by the joining or leaving of a station), then the schedule should be appropriately updated to correspond to the modified network. Thus, an adaptive algorithm for broadcast scheduling is one that, given a wireless multihop network, a broadcast schedule for that network, and a change in the network (i.e., either a station joining or leaving the network), produces a broadcast schedule for the new network. The twin objectives of adaptive algorithms are much faster execution (than an off-line algorithm that computes a completely new schedule) and the production of a provably high-quality schedule. We note that many other network changes can be modeled by joining or leaving or a combination of the two (e.g., the moving of a station from one location to another).

Distributed Algorithms

Although centralized algorithms provide an excellent foundation, algorithms in which the computation is distributed among the nodes of the network are essential for use in practice. In these distributed algorithms, network nodes have only local information and participate in the computation by exchanging messages. Distributed algorithms are important in order to respond quickly to changes in network topology. Further, the decentralization results in decreased vulnerability to node failures. We distinguish between two kinds of distributed algorithms:

1. *Token passing algorithms.* A token is passed around the network. When a station holds the token, it computes its portion of the algorithm [26, 2]. There is no central site, although a limited amount of global information about the network may be passed with the token. Token passing algorithms, while distributing the computation, execute the algorithm in an essentially sequential fashion.

2. *Fully distributed algorithms.* No global information is required (other than the global slot synchronization associated with TDMA), either in individual or central sites. Rather, a station executes the algorithm itself after collecting information from stations in its local vicinity. Multiple stations can simultaneously run the algorithm, as long as they are not geographically too close, and stations in nonlocal portions of the network can transmit normally even while other stations are joining or leaving the network. Fully distributed algorithms are essentially parallel, and are typically able to scale as the network expands.

16.3 THE COMPLEXITY OF BROADCAST SCHEDULING

In this section the computational complexity of broadcast scheduling is studied.

16.3.1 Computing Optimal Schedules

As noted in the previous section, determining a minimum nominal schedule in a wireless multihop network is equivalent to finding a distance-2 graph coloring that uses a minimum number of colors. The NP-completeness of distance-2 graph coloring is well established [22, 6, 26, 5]. The strongest of these [6] shows that distance-2 graph coloring remains NP-complete even if the question is whether or not four colors will suffice. They utilize a reduction from standard graph coloring. Thus:

Theorem 1 Given an arbitrary graph and an integer $k \geq 4$, determining if there exists a broadcast schedule of length not exceeding k, is NP-complete.

By way of contrast, in [25] it is shown that when k is three, the problem can be solved in polynomial time. Given the NP-completeness of the basic problem, we are left with the possible approaches of utilizing approximation algorithms to determine approximately minimal solutions, or considering the complexity on restricted classes of graphs. Most of the remainder of this chapter is devoted to the former. In regard to the latter, we note:

Theorem 2   [25] Given a planar graph, determining if there exists a broadcast schedule of length not exceeding seven, is NP-complete.

16.3.2   What About Approximations?

From the NP-completeness results cited above, finding minimum length broadcast schedules is generally not possible. Thus, it is necessarily the case that we focus on algorithms that produce schedules that are approximately minimal. For such an approximation algorithm, its approximation ratio α [8, 10], is the worst case ratio of the length of a nominal schedule produced by the algorithm to the length of an optimal nominal schedule. Such an algorithm is said to produce α-approximate solutions. In the context of adaptive algorithms, the analagous concept is that of a competitive ratio. Here, the ratio is the length of the current nominal schedule produced by the algorithm to an optimal off-line nominal schedule. Additional information on such ratios and alternatives may be found in [8, 10].

What quality of approximation ratio might be possible for broadcast scheduling? Most often, the goal in designing approximation algorithms is to seek an approximation ratio that does not exceed a fixed constant (i.e., a constant ratio approximation algorithm). One would hope, as in bin packing and geometric traveling salesperson [10], that approximation ratios of two or less might be possible. Unfortunately, this is not the case, not only for any fixed constant, but also for much larger ratios:

Theorem 3   [1] Unless $NP = ZPP$, broadcast scheduling of arbitrary graphs cannot be approximated to within $O(n^{1/2-\epsilon})$ for any $\epsilon > 0$.

This result is tight since there is an algorithm (see the next section) having an approximation ratio that is $O(n^{1/2})$.

16.4   CENTRALIZED ALGORITHMS

Since broadcast scheduling is NP-complete, in this section (and the next) we investigate approximation algorithms that are alternatives to producing optimal schedules. These algorithms are evaluated on the basis of their running times and approximation ratios.

16.4.1   A Classification of Approximation Algorithms for Broadcast Scheduling

An overview of approximation algorithms for broadcast scheduling is given in this section. Only a few particular algorithms are specifically described, and the reader is referred to [11, 25] for a more comprehensive treatment.

In developing approximation methods for broadcast scheduling, the classic algorithm *P_Greedy* takes a purely greedy approach. That algorithm is an iterative method in which a node is arbitrarily chosen from the as yet uncolored nodes and is greedily colored. The running time of *P_Greedy* is $O(n\rho^2)$ on arbitrary graphs and $O(n\rho)$ on unit disk graphs.

The approximation ratio of *P_Greedy* is min(ρ, $n^{1/2}$) [26, 22] on arbitrary graphs, and 13 on unit disk graphs [18].

Aside from *P_Greedy*, a variety of centralized approximation algorithms have been proposed for broadcast scheduling. These algorithms can be placed into three general categories, using a classification adapted from [11]:

1. *Traditional algorithms* that preorder the nodes according to a specified criterion, and then color the nodes in a greedy fashion according to that ordering. A representative of such methods is *Static_min_deg_last* [11]. In this method, the nodes are placed into descending order according to their degrees. The nodes are then greedily colored according to that ordering. The running time is $O(n \min(n, \rho^2))$ on arbitrary graphs and $O(n \log n + n\rho)$ on unit disk graphs. The algorithm is ρ-approximate on arbitrary graphs, and 13-approximate on unit disk graphs [18].

2. *Geometric algorithms* that involve projections of the network onto simpler geometric objects, such as the line. A representative of such methods is *Linear_Projection* [11], in which the positions of the nodes are projected onto a line, and then an optimal distance-2 coloring is computed for those projected points. One effect of projecting nodes onto a line is that the projections of nodes may now be within distance-2, whereas the original nodes were not within distance-2. The algorithm selects a line for projection that minimizes the number of such "false" distance-2 neighbors. *Linear_Projection* runs in time $O(n^2)$ on arbitrary graphs. There are no results on the approximation ratio.

3. *Dynamic greedy methods* that also color nodes in a greedy fashion, but in which the order of the coloring is determined dynamically as the coloring proceeds. A representative of such methods is *max_cont_color* [16]. This algorithm initially colors an arbitrary node and then all of the one-hop neighbors of that node. At each subsequent step, the algorithm chooses for coloring a node that is now most constrained by its distance-2 neighbors. Results [16, 18] show that this algorithm has the best simulation performance among all existing broadcast scheduling algorithms. A careful implementation [18] yields a running time of $O(nD)$ on arbitrary graphs and $O(n\rho)$ on unit disk graphs. The algorithm is ρ-approximate on arbitrary graphs, and 13-approximate on unit disk graphs [18].

16.4.2 A Better Approximation Ratio

The best approximation ratio for arbitrary graphs of the methods cited above is $min(n^{1/2}, \rho)$, which is also the ratio of the simplest of these algorithms, *P_Greedy*. Below, an algorithm of the "traditional greedy" variety is described that has an arguably stronger ratio for most graphs. The algorithm is similar to *Static_min_deg_last* but the nodes are ordered in a "dynamic," rather than static, fashion. The term progressive is taken from [23].

Algorithm progressive_min_deg_last(*G*)
    Labeler(*G*, *n*);
    for j ← 1 to *n do*

let u be such that $L(u) = j$;
greedily color node u;

The function **Labeler**, which assigns a label between 1 and n to each node, is defined as follows:

Labeler(G, ℓ)
  if G is not empty
    let u be a vertex of G of minimum degree;
    $L(u) \leftarrow \ell$;
    Labeler$(G - u, \ell - 1)$;

Here, *G-u* is the graph obtained from G by removing u and all incident edges. It is straightforward to see that *progressive_min_deg_last* produces a legal coloring, since the coloring is performed in a greedy fashion. This will be true for all of the algorithms described in this chapter, and we will make no further reference to algorithm correctness.

Theorem 4 For a planar graph, *progressive_min_deg_last* is 9-approximate.

Proof: Consider the neighbors of an arbitrary node u, and suppose that k of those nodes have labels smaller than $L(u)$. Hence, there are up to $\rho - k$ neighbors of u with labels larger than $L(u)$.

It follows from the properties of planar graphs, and the specification of Labeler, that $k \leq 5$. Each node with a label smaller than $L(u)$ may have at most $\rho - 1$ neighbors (not including u) and hence those k nodes and their neighbors utilize at most $k(\rho - 1) + k = k\rho$ colors that may not be assigned to u.

Now consider the up to $\rho - k$ nodes with labels larger than $L(u)$. When u is colored, none of these nodes are colored (recall that coloring is done in increasing order of labels). However, the neighbors of these nodes may have lower labels than $L(u)$ and the already assigned colors of these nodes may not be assigned to u. Since the minimum node degree in a planar graph is always five or less, it follows from the specification of Labeler that there can be at most $4 \cdot (\rho - k)$ 2-hop neighbors of u that are already colored (i.e., four for each uncolored $1 -$ hop neighbor of u, not counting u itself).

Thus, u can be colored using no more than $k\rho + 4 \cdot (\rho - k) + 1$ colors, and with $k \leq 5$, this is at most $9\rho - 19$. Since the minimum coloring uses at least $\rho + 1$ colors, the approximation ratio is bounded above by nine. $\qquad\square$

For arbitrary graphs, the approximation ratio of *progressive_min_deg_last* depends on the thickness of the graph. That is, the minimum number of planar graphs into which the graph may be partitioned. Note that the algorithm does not compute the thickness (indeed, computing the thickness is NP-complete [21]), but rather only the bound depends on that value. Further, experimental results [25] establish that the thickness is generally much less than ρ.

Corollary 1 For an arbitrary graph of thickness θ, *progressive_min_deg_last* has an approximation ratio that is $O(\theta)$.

The corollary follows from the prior proof by noting that in a graph of thickness θ, there is at least one node of degree not exceeding $6\theta - 1$ [25].

The analysis in [14] establishes:

Theorem 5   For q-inductive graphs, *progressive_min_deg_last* has an approximation ratio of $2q - 1$.

Several classes of graphs, including graphs of bounded genus, are q-inductive. See [12] for additional information on q-inductive graphs.

In regard to running times, it is shown in [24]:

Theorem 6   For planar graphs, *progressive_min_deg_last* has a running time of $O(n\rho)$. For arbitrary graphs of thickness θ, *progressive_min_deg_last* has a running time of $O(n\theta\rho)$.

16.4.3   A Better Ratio for Unit Disk Graphs

Among the methods cited above, several are 13-approximate when applied to unit disk graphs. These ratios follow from a general result of [18] on the performance of "greedy" algorithms. The best approximation ratio relative to unit disk graphs belongs to the following algorithm (of the traditional greedy variety):

Algorithm Continuous_color(G):
    Let u be an arbitrary node of G;
    $L \leftarrow$ a list of the nodes of G sorted in increasing order of Euclidean distance to u;
    while $L \neq \emptyset$ do
        Let v be the first node of L;
        Greedily color v and remove v from L;

Theorem 7   For unit disk graphs, *Continuous_color* has an approximation ratio of seven.

Key to the proof of this theorem is the following result that establishes that certain nodes in geographical proximity to one another must be distance-2 neighbors.

Lemma 1   Given a node p, let b_1 and b_2 be two points on the boundary of p's interference region (i.e., the circle of radius $2R$ centered at p). If $|b_1 b_2| \leq R$, then any two nodes that are both:

- in the unit subset of p, and
- within the area bounded by the line segments from p to b_1 and b_2 and by the boundary of the interference region of p that runs between b_1 and b_2 (we refer to this area as section pb_1b_2 and show it as the shaded area in Figure 16.2)

are distance-2 neighbors.

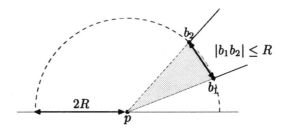

Figure 16.2   The locations of b_1 and b_2.

The proof of Lemma 1 involves the extensive use of trigonometric functions to establish the proximity of points, and may be found in [18].

Proof: From *Continuous_color*, when a node v is to be colored, the already colored distance-2 neighbors of v lie on at most half of v's interference region. The perimeter of that half of an interference region can be partitioned into seven sections such that the distance between the extreme perimeter points in each section does not exceed R. Within each of these sections, from Lemma 1, all of the nodes are distance-2 neighbors, hence each of the nodes must receive a distinct color. Let x be the largest number of nodes in any one of these sections. Then $x + 1$ is a lower bound on the number of different colors assigned to v and its already colored neighbors. Likewise, $7x + 1$ is an upper bound on the number of different colors used by *Continuous_color*. The theorem follows from the ratio of the upper to lower bound.   □

In regard to running time, it is easy to see that the running time of *Continuous_color* is $O(n \log n + nD)$ when applied to arbitrary graphs. Since D may be as large as ρ^2, we have:

Lemma 2   For arbitrary graphs, the running time of *Continuous_color* is $O(n \log n + n\rho^2)$.

For unit disk graphs the running time is less. Key to that result is the following, which establishes that D and ρ are linearly related:

Lemma 3   In unit disk graphs, $D \le 25\rho$.

Proof: Consider the interference region of an arbitrary node s in a unit disk graph. Clearly, all distance-2 neighbors of s lie within the interference region of s. Now, define an S-cycle to be a circle of radius $R/2$ (it could be centered anywhere) and note that all nodes lying within any given S-cycle are one-hop neighbors. Thus, at most ρ nodes lie within any given S-cycle. The lemma follows since the interference region of any node can be covered with 25 S-cycles as shown in Figure 16.3 (in that figure, S-cycles are shown both shaded and unshaded to make them easier to visualize).   □

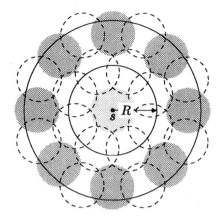

Figure 16.3 $D \leq 25\rho$.

Corollary 2 For unit disk graphs, the running time of *Continuous_color* is $O(n \log n + n\rho)$.

16.4.4 An Adaptive Algorithm

An adaptive algorithm for broadcast scheduling is described in this section.

16.4.4.1 The Effects of the Joining and Leaving of Nodes

In designing adaptive algorithms, it is important to understand how the schedule might be affected by the joining or leaving of a node (the algorithm presented in this section focuses on these basic functionalities):

- The joining of a node may introduce conflicts among the node's one-hop neighbors, thus turning a previously conflict-free schedule into a conflicting schedule. An adaptive broadcast scheduling algorithm must modify the existing schedule to remove these conflicts.

- The leaving of a node never introduces conflicts into the schedule, though the schedule may now be longer than necessary (though that is not easy to determine!). Further, if A is the deleted node, that deletion may result in a neighbor of A with a color larger than its number of distance-2 neighbors. The use of such a color is never required.

Algorithm_IR (Iteratively Remove) handles the joining of a node A as follows:

Algorithm IR_Station_Join(A)
 increase the degree of the neighbors of A by 1;
 update $D(u)$ for each distance-2 neighbor u of A;
 $RECOLOR\_LIST \leftarrow min\_conflict\_set(A)$;

    uncolor the nodes (if any) in *RECOLOR_LIST*;
    add *A* to *RECOLOR_LIST*;
    while RECOLOR_LIST ≠ ∅ *do*
        $v \leftarrow$ a node in *RECOLOR_LIST* with largest constraint number;
        greedily color node v;
        delete v from *RECOLOR_LIST*;

Within *IR_Station_Join*, function *min_conflict_set*(A) returns the minimum conflict set of node A, determined as follows: Let U be the set consisting of all one-hop neighbors of A that now conflict on a given color c (this occurs because the presence of A makes these nodes into 2-hop neighbors). Among the nodes in U, let u_i be a node with largest conflict number. Then $U - u_i$ is a c-conflict clique of A. A minimum conflict set of A is the union of its c-conflict cliques (one per color).

    Algorithm_IR handles the leaving of a node as follows:

    Algorithm *IR_Station_Leave*(A)
        decrease the degree of the neighbors of A by 1;
        update $D(u)$ for each distance-2 neighbor u of A;
        for each distance-2 neighbor u of A *do*
            if COLOR(u) > $D(u)$ + 1
                greedily recolor u;

We note that *Algorithm_IR* as given in [19, 18] contains a third procedure, *maintenance*. That procedure, which attempts a recoloring around a node of maximum color after each joining and leaving, is essential for the excellent performance of *Algorithm_IR* as measured by simulations. That additional procedure does not however affect (positively or negatively) the approximation ratio, hence its omission from this chapter.

16.4.4.2 Approximation Ratio
To determine the approximation ratio of *Algorithm_IR*, we begin with the following lower bound on the length of an optimal schedule:

Lemma 4   For unit disk graphs, an optimal schedule uses at least $1 + D/13$ colors.

Proof: Recall that D is the distance-2 degree of the graph. Given a node v in a unit disk graph, all of its distance-2 neighbors lie within the interference region of v. Partition the interference region of v into 13 sections of equal angle around v. As in the proof of Theorem 7, each section satisfies the conditions of Lemma 1, hence all of the distance-2 neighbors of v within a given section are within distance-2 of one another. It follows that each of the nodes in a given section must be assigned different colors. Thus, any coloring must use at least $1 + D(v)/13$ colors in coloring v and its distance-2 neighbors. Hence, an optimal schedule for the graph uses at least $1 + D/13$ colors.   □

Theorem 8   For unit disk graphs, *Algorithm_IR* has an approximation ratio of 13.

Proof: For any unit disk graph consider the coloring produced by *Algorithm_IR* via a sequence of joinings and leavings of nodes. A careful consideration of *IR_Station_Join* and *IR_Station_Leave* establishes the invariant that for each node v, $COLOR(v) \leq 1 + D(v)$. It follows that the algorithm uses at most $1 + D$ colors. Since by the prior lemma an optimal schedule utilizes at least $1 + D/13$ colors, the approximation ratio follows.   □

An alternative algorithm with a 13-approximation ratio that handles the on-line joining of stations appears in [27].

16.4.4.3 Running Time
An examination of the two procedures associated with *Algorithm_IR* shows that the running time for the joining or leaving of a node is bounded by $O(\rho^2 + \rho D + D^2)$. How are ρ and D related? Lemma 3 establishes that D is $O(\rho)$ in unit disk graphs, hence:

Theorem 9   For unit disk graphs, the worst case running time for the joining or leaving of a node is $O(\rho^2)$. The time for an arbitrary graph is $O(\rho^4)$.

How good is this running time? For coloring a unit disk graph of n nodes the running times of *P_greedy* and *max_cont_color* are both $O(n\rho)$, whereas the running time for *Continuous_color* is $O(n \log n + n\rho)$. When applied in sequence to n nodes, *Algorithm_IR* runs in time $O(n\rho^2)$, which is a loss of $O(\rho)$ in comparison with the centralized algorithms. But that comparison is to a single execution of *P_greedy* or *max_cont_color*. In the absence of an adaptive algorithm, the only alternative when the graph changes is to recompute the entire schedule, which requires time per change of $O(n\rho)$ using *P_greedy* or *max_cont_color*. Since typically $\rho \ll n$, the $O(\rho^2)$ time required by *Algorithm_IR* is much superior for unit disk graphs.

16.5 DISTRIBUTED ALGORITHMS

Two distinctly different distributed algorithms are described in this section. The first utilizes token passing to distribute the computation, and has a strong approximation ratio when applied to arbitrary graphs. The second is a fully distributed algorithm based on moving away from simply computing a nominal schedule, and has a constant approximation ratio when applied to unit disk graphs.

16.5.1 A Token Passing Algorithm

We begin by describing an efficient token passing algorithm for broadcast scheduling. A first attempt would be to implement the *progressive_min_deg_last* algorithm using token passing. However, the labeling phase of that algorithm requires that nodes be labeled in a precise order, and it may be that consecutively numbered nodes are quite far apart in the network. Reconciling this in a token-passing approach seems to be problematic.

In the algorithm described here, nodes are partitioned into classes based on the degrees of the nodes. Coloring is then done in inverse order, starting with the last class. The nodes of a class are colored in a single pass over the network.

16.5.1.1 The Algorithm DBS

For clarity, a centralized version of the algorithm is presented first. A discussion of a distributed implementation follows the algorithm.

The algorithm is parameterized, taking as input a parameter τ. Typically this parameter would be fixed for a given network. There is a trade-off between τ and the number of passes the algorithm makes over a network. This trade-off and explanations of the algorithm will become apparent in the analyses of running time and approximation ratio that follow the algorithm specification.

Algorithm DBS(G, τ)
    classcnt $\leftarrow$ 0;
    neededratio $\leftarrow (\tau - 6)/\tau$;
    incrementratio $\leftarrow \tau/6$;
    thickness $\leftarrow$ 1;
    currsize $\leftarrow n$;
The Assign Classes Phase:
    while there exists a node v not yet assigned to a class *do*
        classcnt++;
        found $\leftarrow$ 0;
        for each node v not yet assigned to a class *do*
            deglocal $\leftarrow$ the number of 1-hop neighbors of v who were not yet in a class at the
                       start of this iteration of the while loop;
        if deglocal $\leq \tau$*thickness*
           assign v to class *classcnt*;
           found++;
        if found < *currsize*neededratio*
           thickness $\leftarrow$ *incrementratio*thickness*;
        currsize $\leftarrow$ *currsize* – *found*;
The Coloring Phase:
    for i $\leftarrow$ *classcnt* downto 1 *do*
        for each node v in class i *do*
           greedily color v;

16.5.1.2 The Running Time of DBS

A critical issue in limiting the running time of DBS, and the number of passes that it makes over the network, is the number of classes into which the nodes are partitioned. The following lemma [17] is helpful in that regard:

Lemma 5   Given an arbitrary graph G of thickness θ, and a parameter $\tau > 6$, there are at least $(\tau - 6)n/\tau$ nodes of degree not exceeding $\tau\theta$.

It follows from this lemma that if graph G is of thickness θ and τ is 12, then at least one-half of the nodes in G are of degree not exceeding 12θ. Thus, in the execution of DBS, the first class will contain at least one half of the nodes in G, and the second class will contain at least one quarter of the nodes in G, and so on. All together there will be no more than $\log_2 n$ classes. More generally, it follows from Lemma 5 that:

Given an arbitrary graph G of thickness θ, and $\tau > 6$, then the number of classes does not exceed $\log_{\tau/6} n$.

Thus, it would seem that there is a range of suitable values for τ. Unfortunately, the above results are based on knowing the thickness of the network and, as mentioned previously, it is NP-complete to determine the thickness of an arbitrary network. Thus, we need a way of estimating the thickness. Fortunately, a natural approach is suggested by Lemma 5. Namely, given an estimate for the thickness, say θ_e, construct a class consisting of all of the nodes of degree not exceeding $\tau\theta_e$. If the number of nodes in the class is at least $(\tau - 6)n/\tau$, then all is well. If, on the other hand, the number of nodes is less than $(\tau - 6)n/\tau$, then the current value of θ_e is less than the actual thickness, and the value of θ_e is increased before forming the next class. The process continues in this fashion with: classes being formed; the size of the class compared to the known bound; and, if the class is too small, then the estimate of the thickness increased. The only care that needs to be taken is to not increase the estimate too quickly (it would make classes very large and not spread nodes among classes) or too slowly (there will be too many classes, hence too many passes over the network will have been made). Fortunately, it is possible to increase the estimate of θ at an intermediate pace that is satisfactory from both points of view. These ideas form the basis of the proof given in [17] that establishes:

Lemma 6   *DBS* makes $O(\log n)$ passes over the graph.

This lemma and a careful examination of *DBS* provides:

Lemma 7   For arbitrary graphs, the running time of *DBS* is $O(n\rho \log n + n\rho^2)$.

16.5.1.3   An Approximation Ratio for DBS

Theorem 10   For a graph of thickness θ, *DBS* has an approximation ratio of $O(\theta)$.

Recall from our earlier discussion that most previous broadcast scheduling algorithms have an $O(\rho)$ bound on their performance. Since θ is generally much less than ρ, the performance of *DBS* may be markedly superior to that of earlier algorithms (depending on the constants involved).

The proof of the theorem may be found in [17]. Here we consider only a key lemma:

Lemma 8   Let θ_f be the final value of thickness utilized by *DBS*, and let θ_a be the actual thickness of the network G. Then, $\theta_f \leq (\tau/6)\theta_a$.

Proof: To establish the lemma, we show that in *DBS*, once the value of the variable *thickness* is at least θ_a, the value of *thickness* will never again be modified. To see that is so, consider any iteration of the while-loop after *thickness* has attained a value that is at least that of θ_a. At that point in the algorithm, the only nodes that are of relevance are those that have not yet been placed into some class. Thus, consider the graph restricted to those nodes and the edges between them. Let θ' be the thickness of this reduced graph and note that $\theta' \leq \theta_a$. It follows from results in [17] that there are at least *currsize · neededratio* nodes of degree not exceeding $\tau\theta'$. But, since $\theta' \leq \theta_a \leq \theta_f$, there are at least *currsize · neededratio* nodes of degree not exceeding $\tau\theta_a$. Thus, the value of *found* will be at least *currsize · neededratio*, hence *thickness* will not be modified. □

16.5.1.4 A Token Passing Implementation

To implement *DBS* using token passing is straightforward. Recall that a token is passed around the network and only the node holding the token can execute the algorithm. The path taken by the token is a depth first search of the network. Then:

1. Each iteration of the while loop corresponds to a pass through the network.
2. The only pieces of global information required by a processor are: 1) an indication of the phase that the algorithm is in (Assign Classes or Coloring), along with the class number in that phase; 2) the current value of the variable thickness; and 3) a count of the number of nodes that have been visited on this pass. These several pieces of information can be passed along with the token itself.
3. Within each pass in the Assign Classes phase, when a node receives the token, if that node has already been assigned to a class, it simply passes the token on. If the node is not yet assigned to a class, then it is easy for that node to check on the number of its neighbors also not yet assigned to a class (as of the start of this iteration of the *while* loop), and if appropriate, to assign itself to the current class.
4. Within each pass of the Coloring phase, a node colors itself by querying its distance-2 neighbors so as to determine their colors (if any).

16.5.2 A Fully Distributed Algorithm

A fully distributed algorithm for broadcast scheduling is presented in this section. The algorithm is distinguished in the following ways:

- It is assumed that stations have the capacity of global slot synchronization (i.e., standard TDMA).
- No global information is required, either in central or individual sites. Rather, a station schedules itself after collecting information from its one-hop and two-hop neighbors.
- The method is fully distributed. Thus, multiple stations can simultaneously run the scheduler portion of the protocol, and stations in nonlocal portions of the network can transmit normally even while other stations are joining or leaving the network.
- The method has a constant competitive ratio (though admittedly large: 26).

This algorithm is termed Power of Two Scheduling (POTS) (named FDAS in [20]). There are three aspects to the algorithm: the basic scheduling method, the adaptive implementation, and the distributed implementation. In the next three sections these are addressed in turn.

16.5.2.1 Power of Two Scheduling

Diverging from the "nominal schedule" approach taken in earlier sections, we consider a scheduling framework that focuses on determining two essential components for each station: its transmission slot and its transmission cycle. A station transmits for the first time in its transmission slot, and then every transmission cycle number of slots thereafter. Thus, the transmission cycle is a fixed number of slots between two consecutive transmissions.

Interestingly, nominal schedules can also be framed in this context. In nominal schedules, the transmission cycle is the same for each station, hence each station needs to know not only which slot it is assigned, but also the maximum slot in the entire nominal schedule.

The approach taken in POTS is that a priori there is no reason why each station must utilize the same transmission cycle as every other. For correctness,* all that is required is that transmissions be received collision-free and that each station have a periodic opportunity to transmit. Thus, POTS utilizes nonuniform transmission cycles. By so doing, each station produces its transmission slot and transmission cycle locally, without the need for global information.

Since the transmission slot specifies the first time that a station transmits, the assignment of a transmission slot to a station is identical to the problem faced in algorithms using the nominal schedule approach. Specifically, a transmission slot must be assigned to a station so as not to conflict with the transmission slots of the station's distance-2 neighbors. This is identical to distance-2 coloring, and the coloring terminology is utilized in specifying the algorithm.

> **Algorithm** *POTS_Slot_Assign(A)*
> *RECOLOR_LIST* ← *min_conflict_set(A)*;
> uncolor the nodes in *RECOLOR_LIST*;
> add *A* to *RECOLOR_LIST*;
> *while RECOLOR_LIST* ≠ ∅ *do*
> > *v* ← a node in *RECOLOR_LIST* with largest constraint number;
> > *T_SLOT(v)* ← least color not used by *v*'s distance-2 neighbors;
> > delete *v* from *RECOLOR_LIST*;

Here, *min_conflict_set(A)* is as specified in Section 16.4.

Now, suppose that all stations have been assigned transmission slots. Consider a station u, and let C_u denote the maximum transmission slot of any station in the unit subset of u. Then, the transmission cycle for u is set to the least power of two that is greater than or equal to C_u. Figure 16.4 provides an example of a schedule derived from transmission slots and cycles.

---

*On the issue of fairness (since some stations transmit more frequently than others), note that experimental results [18] show that relatively little is lost in overall schedule length when compared with nominal schedules.

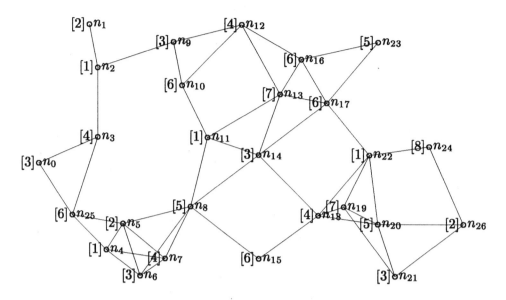

The number in the bracket on the left side of a node indicates it's transmission slot. Nodes n_0, n_1, n_2, n_3, n_4, n_5, n_6, n_8, n_9, n_{12}, n_{20}, n_{24} and n_{26} have transmission cycles of 8, while all other transmission cycles are 16. An initial segment of the schedule induced by these transmission slots and cycles follows.

1	2	3	4	5	6	7	8
n_1	n_6	n_9	n_2	n_3	n_0	n_7	n_{21}
n_4	n_8	n_{14}	n_{10}	n_{13}	n_{16}	n_{15}	
n_5	n_{17}	n_{22}	n_{12}	n_{26}		n_{19}	
n_{11}		n_{23}	n_{20}				
n_{18}		n_{24}					

9	10	11	12	13	14	15	16	1	
n_{25}								n_1	...
								n_4	...
n_1	n_6	n_9	n_2	n_3	n_0			n_5	...
n_4	n_8	n_{24}	n_{12}	n_{26}				n_{11}	...
n_5			n_{20}					n_{18}	...

Figure 16.4   Schedule derived using *POTS*.

In utilizing the transmission slot and cycle approach, the critical element is that there are never any conflicts in the resulting schedule. The following theorem establishes that this is indeed the case:

Theorem 11   For any two stations A and B that are distance-2 neighbors, if A and B are assigned transmission slots and cycles as specified above, then A and B never transmit in the same slot.

The proof follows in a straightforward fashion from a specification of the transmission slots and cycles for A and B. The details appear in [20, 18].

16.5.2.2   Making the Method Adaptive

In this section, we describe how to extend the algorithm given above from the off-line to the adaptive case.

The joining of stations is easy since an existing schedule can be updated to include the joining station simply by running *POTS_Slot_Assign* (which may modify the transmission slots of one-hop neighbors of the joining station) and then recomputing the transmission cycle for each station in the unit subset of any station whose slot was modified. The only additional issue is that some coordination is required to ensure that all stations, old and new, are operating under an identical point of reference relative to the start of the schedule. The details of this coordination are described in [18].

Since the leaving of a station from the network cannot introduce conflicts into the schedule, the only scheduling effect produced by the leaving of a station is that the transmission cycles of some of the stations may now be longer than necessary. Thus, when a station leaves the network, some adjustments of the schedule may be appropriate. These adjustments concern the transmission slot assignment of nodes in the unit subset of the leaving station. The details are provided below.

Algorithm POTS_Deletion(A)
>*for* each one-hop and two-hop neighbor u of A *do*
>>update the degree of u and/or $D(u)$ as appropriate;
>>*if* $T\_SLOT(u) > D(u) + 1$
>>>greedily recolor u;
>>*for* each node that had a member of its unit subset change color *do*
>>>update the transmission cycle of that node;

16.5.2.3   The Approximation Ratio and Running Time

In the context of broadcast scheduling based on transmission slots and cycles, we define the approximation ratio of an algorithm to be the ratio of the maximum transmission cycle produced by the algorithm to the optimal maximum transmission cycle. In that context:

Theorem 12   For unit disk graphs, *POTS* has a competitive ratio of 26.

Proof: Using Lemma 1, it can be shown that the ratio of the maximum transmission slot to the optimal maximum transmission cycle is bounded above by 13. Since the maximum transmission cycle is less than twice the maximum transmission slot, the competitive ratio of 26 follows. ☐

Finally, in regard to the running time of *POTS*:

Theorem 13 The running times of *POTS_Slot_Assign* and *POTS_Deletion* are $O(\rho^2)$ for unit disk graphs [18], and $O(\rho^4)$ for arbitrary graphs.

Note that these match the running times of the adaptive *Algorithm_IR* of the previous section.

16.5.2.4 *Making the Method Fully Distributed*

The key to producing a distributed implementation of POTS is to note that the scheduling of a station requires NO global information. Rather, information is required only from the one and two-hop neighbors of the station. In this respect, implementing the algorithm in a distributed fashion is straightforward: from the perspective of an individual station, its actions in regard to scheduling precisely follow the method outlined above. The only complications arise in the communication aspects, including: station registration when joining the network, coordination of geographically close stations attempting to run the algorithm in an overlapping fashion, and coordination of station actions when a neighboring station leaves the network. Discussion of such an implementation is beyond the scope of this chapter. The reader is referred to [18] for implementation details. An alternative fully distributed broadcast scheduling algorithm is given in [31].

16.6 RELATED RESULTS

This section provides an overview of some results related to broadcast scheduling.

16.6.1 Experimental Results

Almost all papers dealing with broadcast scheduling have included some experimental results. Most often these experiments have been conducted on networks that can be modeled by unit disk graphs, although the networks are not often identified as such. The most comprehensive treatments to date are given in [11, 28], although the more recent algorithms of [19, 20] are obviously not included there. In overall simulation performance, the algorithm *max_cont_color* generally outperforms all others by at least a minimal amount. In comparison [16] with *P_Greedy*, *max_cont_color* produces schedules (for unit disk graphs) that are roughly 10% longer than optimal, while the schedules of *P_Greedy* averaged nearly 30% longer than optimal. The algorithms *Algorithm_IR* and *POTS* likewise outperform *P_Greedy* by a significant amount, although they are not as strong as *max_cont_color* [18]. Due to its sometimes longer transmission cycles (due to being a power of two), *POTS* is slightly weaker than *Algorithm_IR*. Finally, experimental results detailing a *gradual neural network* broadcast scheduling algorithm are given in [7]. The reader is referred to individual papers for specifics on experimental results for these and many other algorithms.

16.6.2 Other Classes of Graphs

Aside from the results cited earlier in this chapter, only limited results are known for other classes of graphs. Most notable among these are:

- A proof that broadcast scheduling is NP-complete for intersection graphs of circles is given in [28]. For these graphs, a 13-approximation algorithm is given in [27]. Unit disk graphs are a special type of intersection graph in which each circle has the same radius.
- A 2-approximation algorithm is given in [14] for (r, s)-civilized graphs [29]. Note that (r, s)-civilized graphs include intersection (hence, unit disk) graphs provided that there is a fixed minimum distance between the nodes. For these special types of intersection and unit disk graphs, the 3-approximation of [14] is much superior to the general bounds of 14 and 7, respectively.
- For planar graphs, there is a 2-approximation algorithm [1].
- For graphs whose treewidth is bounded by a constant k, optimal broadcast schedules can be computed in polynomial time [30].

16.6.3 Link Scheduling

In the context of a wireless multihop network, link scheduling is an alternative to broadcast scheduling. In link scheduling, the links between the stations are scheduled such that it is guaranteed that there will be no collision at the endpoints of the scheduled link, although there may be collisions at nodes not scheduled to receive or transmit in that time slot.

Analogous results to many of the broadcast scheduling results described in this chapter have appeared for link scheduling. These include a pure greedy method, an algorithm with an $O(\theta)$ approximation ratio for arbitrary graphs and an $O(1)$ ratio for planar graphs, and both token passing and fully distributed algorithms. Although the results are analogous to those for broadcast scheduling, the methods, particularly those producing the $O(\theta)$ approximation ratios, are considerably more involved. The reader is referred to [25, 15, 4, 17, 24] for the details. A distributed link scheduling algorithm under somewhat different assumptions is given in [4].

16.6.4 Unifying TDMA/CDMA/FDMA Scheduling

Frequency division multiplexing (FDMA) and code division multiplexing (CDMA) serve as alternates to TDMA as channel access methods, although scheduling has been somewhat less studied in those contexts. In [23], an algorithm is given for scheduling regardless of the channel access mechanism. That general algorithm is based on the *progressive_min_deg_last* method described earlier.* The algorithm takes as input not only a graph, but a general constraint set that specifies when nodes or links must receive

---

*In [23], the method is named progressive min degree first, with the "first" referring to the order in which nodes are labeled.

different colors. It is shown in [23] that the algorithm has an approximation ratio of $O(\theta)$ for any of some 128 problem variations.

16.7 SUMMARY AND OPEN PROBLEMS

This chapter studied the problem of broadcast scheduling in wireless multihop networks. The focus was on complexity and algorithmic issues associated with such scheduling. Since the basic problem is NP-complete, research has concentrated on the development of approximation methods. In this chapter's treatment of approximation algorithms, we have attempted both to provide a flavor of the research issues and directions, and to enumerate the strongest known results. Specifically:

- For arbitrary graphs, there are centralized and token passing algorithms having $O(\theta)$ approximation ratios. This is in comparison with the typical ρ-approximations associated with most other broadcast scheduling methods.
- In unit disk graphs, the best centralized algorithm has an approximation ratio of seven, while there is a fully distributed algorithm with a ratio of 26. The latter produces schedules that allow stations to have different transmission cycles, thereby moving away from the nominal schedule approach taken in other works.

In regard to open problems, we list only two general problems, and refer the reader to individual research papers for more comprehensive lists.

- From a theoretical perspective, there is tremendous room for improvement in all of the approximation ratios. We do not believe that any of the cited ratios are tight.
- From a practical perspective, the development and/or study of other graph models appears important. None of the models studied to date appears to capture the situations that most often arise in practice. There, some concept of "almost" unit disk graphs seems most appropriate in accounting for interference that eliminates some links from the network.

ACKNOWLEDGMENTS

I would like to thank S.S. Ravi, Ram Ramanathan, and Xiaopeng Ma for providing comments and suggestions on a draft version of this chapter.

REFERENCES

1. G. Agnarsson and M., Halldorsson. Coloring powers of planar graphs, *Proceedings of the 11th Annual Symposium on Discrete Mathematics (SODA)*, pp. 654–662, January 2000.

2. I. Chlamtac and S. Kutten, Tree-based broadcasting in multi-hop radio networks, *IEEE Transactions on Computers, 36:* 1209–1223, 1987.

3. B. N. Clark, C. J. Colbourn, and D. S. Johnson, Unit disk graphs, *Discrete Mathematics, 86:* 165–167, 1990.

4. J. Flynn D. Baker, A., Ephremedes. The design and simulation of a mobile radio network with distributed control, *IEEE Journal on Selected Areas in Communications, SAC-2:* 226–237, 1999.

5. A. Ephremedis and T. Truong, A distributed algorithm for efficient and interference free broadcasting in radio networks, In *Proceedings IEEE INFOCOM*, 1988.

6. S. Even, O. Goldreich, S. Moran, and P. Tong, On the NP-completeness of certain network testing problems, *Networks, 14:* 1–24, 1984.

7. N. Funabiki and J. Kitamichi, A gradual neural network algorithm for broadcast scheduling problems in packet radio networks, *IEICE Trans. Fundamentals, E82-A:* 815–825, 1999.

8. M. R. Garey and D. S. Johnson, *Computers and Intractability—A Guide to the Theory of NP-Completeness*, W. H. Freeman, San Francisco, 1979.

9. W. Hale, Frequency assignment: theory and applications, *Proceedings of the IEEE, 68:* 1497–1514, 1980.

10. D. S. Hochbaum, *Approximation Algorithms for NP-hard problems*, PWS, Boston, 1997.

11. M. L. Huson and A. Sen, Broadcast scheduling algorithms for radio networks, *IEEE MILCOM,* pp. 647–651, 1995.

12. S. Irani, Coloring inductive graphs on-line, *Algorithmica, 11:* 53–72, 1994.

13. D. S. Johnson, The NP-completeness column, *Journal of Algorithms, 3:* 184, June 1982.

14. S. O. Krumke, M. V. Marathe, and S. S. Ravi, Models and approximation algorithms for channel assignment in radio networks, *Wireless Networks, 7,* 6, 567–574, 2001.

15. R. Liu and E. L. Lloyd, A distributed protocol for adaptive link scheduling in ad-hoc networks, in *Proceedings of the IASTED International Conference on Wireless and Optical Communications,* June 2001, pp. 43–48.

16. E. L. Lloyd and X. Ma, Experimental results on broadcast scheduling in radio networks, *Proceedings of Advanced Telecommunications/Information Distribution Research Program (ATIRP) Conference*, pp. 325–329, 1997.

17. E. L. Lloyd and S. Ramanathan, Efficient distributed algorithms for channel assignment in multi-hop radio networks, *Journal of High Speed Networks, 2:* 405–423, 1993.

18. X. Ma, *Broadcast Scheduling in Multi-hop Packet Radio Networks.* 2000. PhD Dissertation, University of Delaware.

19. X. Ma and E. Lloyd, An incremental algorithm for broadcast scheduling in packet radio networks, in *Proceedings IEEE MILCOM '98*, 1998.

20. X. Ma and E. L. Lloyd, A distributed protocol for adaptive broadcast scheduling in packet radio networks, in *Workshop Record of the 2nd International Workshop on Discrete Algorithms and Methods for Mobile Computing and Communications (DIAL M for Mobility)*, October 1998.

21. A. Mansfield, Determining the thickness of graphs is NP-hard, *Math. Proc. Cambridge Philos. Society, 93:* 9–23, 1983.

22. S. T. McCormick, Optimal approximation of sparse Hessians and its equivalence to a graph coloring problem, *Mathematics Programming, 26*(2): 153–171, 1983.

23. S. Ramanathan, A unified framework and algorithm for channel assignment in wireless networks, *Wireless Networks*, 5: 81–94, 1999.

24. S. Ramanathan and E. L. Lloyd, Scheduling algorithms for multi-hop radio networks, *IEEE/ACM Transactions on Networking, 1:* 166–177, 1993.

25. S. Ramanathan, *Scheduling Algorithms for Multi-hop Radio Networks*, 1992. PhD Dissertation, University of Delaware.

26. R. Ramaswami and K. K. Parhi, Distributed scheduling of broadcasts in a radio network, in *Proceedings IEEE INFOCOM*, 1989.

27. A. Sen and E. Malesinska, On approximation algorithms for radio network scheduling, in *Proceedings of the 35th Annual Allerton Conference on Communications, Control and Computing*, pp. 573–582, 1997.

28. A. Sen and M. L. Huson, A new model for scheduling packet radio networks, *Wireless Networks, 3:* 71–82, 1997.

29. S. H. Teng, *Points, Spheres and Separators, A Unified Geometric Approach to Graph Separators*, PhD Dissertation, Carnegie Mellon University, 1991.

30. X. Zhou, Y. Kanari and T. Nishizeki, Generalized vertex colorings of partial k-trees, *IEICE Transaction Fundamentals, E-A4:* 1–8, 2000.

31. C. Zhu and M. S. Corson, A five-phase reservation protocol (FPRP) for mobile ad hoc networks, in *Proceedings IEEE INFOCOM*, pp. 322–331, 1998.

CHAPTER 17

Mobile Ad Hoc Networks and Routing Protocols

YU-CHEE TSENG

Department of Computer Science and Information Engineering, National Chiao-Tung University, Hsin-Chu, Taiwan

WEN-HUA LIAO

Department of Computer Science and Information Engineering, National Central University, Tao-Yuan, Taiwan

SHIH-LIN WU

Department of Electrical Engineering, Chang Gung University, Tao-Yuan, Taiwan

17.1 INTRODUCTION

The maturity of wireless transmissions and the popularity of portable computing devices have made the dream of "communication anytime and anywhere" possible. Users can move around, while at the same time still remaining connected with the rest of the world. We call this mobile computing or nomadic computing, which has received intensive attention recently [2, 11, 24, 33]. Generally, most of the nomadic computing applications today require single hop connectivity to the wired network. This is the typical cellular network model that supports the needs of wireless communications by installing base stations or access points. In such networks, communications between two mobile hosts completely rely on the wired backbone and the fixed base stations.

Nevertheless, the wired backbone infrastructure may be unavailable for use by mobile hosts for many reasons, such as unexpected natural disasters and radio shadows. Also, it might be infeasible to construct sufficient fixed access points due to cost and performance considerations; for instance, having fixed network infrastructure in wilderness areas, festival grounds, or outdoor assemblies, outdoor activities is sometimes prohibitive. In emergency search-and-rescue or military maneuvers, a temporary communication network also needs to be deployed immediately.

In the above situations, a mobile ad hoc network (MANET) [16] can be a better choice. A MANET consists of a set of mobile hosts operating without the aid of the established infrastructure of centralized administration (e.g., base stations or access points). Communication is done through wireless links among mobile hosts through their antennas. Due to concerns such as radio power limitation and channel utilization, a mobile host may not be able to communicate directly with other hosts in a single hop fashion. In this case, a multihop scenario occurs, in which the packets sent by the source host must be relayed by sev-

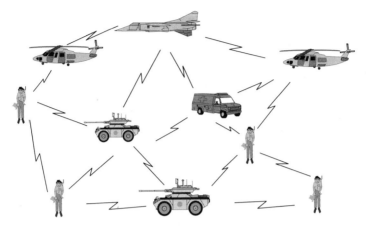

Figure 17.1   An example of a mobile ad hoc network.

eral intermediate hosts before reaching the destination host. Thus, each mobile host in a MANET must serve as a router. A scenario of MANET in a military action is illustrated in Figure 17.1. The two helicopters must communicate indirectly by at least two hops.

Extensive efforts have been devoted to MANET-related research, such as medium access control, broadcast, routing, distributed algorithms, and QoS transmission issues. In this chapter, we will focus on the routing problem, which is one of the most important issues in MANET. In Section 17.2, we review some existing routing protocols for MANET. Broadcasting-related issues and protocols for MANET are addressed in Section 17.3. Section 17.4 reviews multicast protocols for MANET. Routing protocols which guarantee quality of service are discussed in Section 17.5. How to extend base stations in cellular networks with ad hoc links are discussed in Section 17.6. Conclusions are drawn in Section 17.7.

17.2   UNICAST ROUTING PROTOCOLS FOR MANET

Routing protocols for a MANET can be classified as proactive (table-driven) and reactive (on-demand), depending on how they react to topology changes [10, 28]. A host running a proactive protocol will propagate routing-related information to its neighbors whenever a change in its link state is detected. The information may trigger other mobile hosts to recompute their routing tables and further propagate more routing-related information. The amount of information propagated each time is typically proportional to the scale of the MANET. Examples of proactive protocols include wireless routing protocol (WRP) [17] and destination sequenced distance vector (DSDV) [22].

Observing that a proactive protocol may pay costs to construct routes even if mobile hosts do not have such need, thus wasting the limited wireless bandwidth, many researchers have proposed using reactive-style protocols, in which routes are only constructed on-demand. Many reactive protocols have been proposed based on such on-demand philosophy, such as dynamic source routing (DSR) [4], signal stability-based adaptive routing (SSA) [9], ad hoc on-demand distance vector routing (AODV) [23], and temporally ordered routing algorithm (TORA) [21]. Recently, a hybrid of proactive and reactive approaches, called the zone routing protocol (ZRP) [10], has also been proposed. Route maintenance, route optimization, and error recovery are discussed in [35].

17.2.1 Proactive Protocols

One representative proactive protocol is the destination-sequenced distance vector routing (DSDV) protocol. It is based on the traditional distance vector routing mechanism, also called the Bellman–Ford routing algorithm [26], with some modifications to avoid routing loops. The main operations of the distance vector scheme are as follows. Every router collects the routing information from all its neighbors, and then computes the shortest paths to all nodes in the network. After generating a new routing table, the router broadcasts this table to all its neighbors. This may trigger other neighbors to recompute their routing tables, until routing information is stable.

DSDV is enhanced with freedom from loops and differentiation of stale routes from new ones by sequence numbers. Each mobile host maintains a sequence number by monotonically increasing it each time the host sends an update message to its neighbors. A route will be replaced only when the destination sequence number is less than the new one, or two routes have the same sequence number but one has a lower metric.

17.2.2 On-Demand Routing Protocols

An on-demand routing protocol only tries to discover/maintain routes when necessary. Generally speaking, a routing protocol for MANET needs to address three issues: route discovery, data forwarding, and route maintenance. When a source node wants to deliver data to a destination node, it has to find a route first. Then data packets can be delivered. The topology of the MANET may change. This may deteriorate or even disconnect an existing route while data packets are being transmitted. Better routes may also be formed. This is referred to as route maintenance. In the following, we review several protocols according to these issues.

17.2.2.1 Route Discovery
Route Discovery of DSR. Dynamic source routing (DSR) [4] is derived from the concept of source routing. If a source node needs a route to a destination node, it broadcasts a route request (ROUTE_REQ) packet to its neighbors. On a node receiving this request, two things may happen. If the node does not know a route to the destination, it appends its own address to the packet and propagates the ROUTE_REQ packet to its neighbors. Thus, paths leading to the destination can be tracked by ROUTE_REQ packets. Loops can also be avoided by looking at the packet content. When the destination receives a ROUTE_REQ, it returns to the source node a route reply (ROUTE_REPLY) packet containing the route indicated in the ROUTE_REQ. The ROUTE_REPLY then travels, through unicast, in the reverse direction of the discovered route or on a path already known by the destination, to the source. The source node, on receiving the ROUTE_REPLY, will place the route in its route cache. An example is shown in Figure 17.2.

In the second case, an intermediate node is also allowed to return a ROUTE_REPLY if

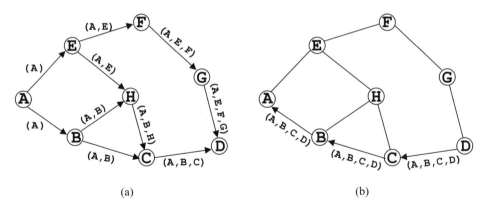

Figure 17.2   An example of route discovery in DSR, with *A* as the source and *D* as the destination. (a) The propagation of ROUTE_REQ packets. An arrow represents the transmission direction from the corresponding sender to receiver. The sequence of letters associated with each arrow indicates the traversed hosts that are recorded in the packet header. (b) The transmission of the ROUTE_REPLY packet from the destination.

it already knows a route fresh enough in its route cache. If so, it simply concatenates the route in ROUTE_REQ and that in its route cache, and supplies this new route to the source. Also note that an intermediate node should register the ROUTE_REQ it has received to discard duplicate ROUTE_REQs.

Route Discovery of SSA. The signal stability adaptive protocol (SSA) [9] tries to discover longer-lived routes based on signal strength and location stability. Each link is differentiated as strong or weak according to the average signal strength at which packets are heard. Beacons are sent periodically by each host for its neighbors to measure its stability. The protocol tends to choose a path that has existed for a longer period of time. Each host maintains a signal stability table, as shown in Figure 17.3.

Like DSR, the SSA protocol also broadcasts ROUTE_REQ packets to discover routes. The source can also specify the quality of the route it desires. Possible route qualities are:

Host	Signal Strength	Last	Clicks	Set
c	S	10:33	7	SC
G	W	10:26	5	WC

Figure 17.3   The signal stability table of SSA. Each row is for one link. The signal strength and the last fields indicate the signal strength and the time, respectively, of the last beacon received. The clicks field registers the number of beacons that have recently been continuously received. Each link is classified as SC (strongly connected) or WC (weakly connected) in the set field, according to the last few clicks received.

STRONG_LINK_ONLY, STRONG_PREFERRED, and NO_PREFERENCE. It is suggested that the STRONG_LINK_ONLY option be used in the first attempt. A receiving node should help propagating the request if (1) the ROUTE_REQ is received over a strong link, and (2) the request has not been forwarded previously. The path traversed by ROUTE_REQ is also appended at the packet. The propagation stops when the destination is reached or a node having a nonstale route to the destination is reached, on which event a ROUTE_REPLY packet is sent.

The ROUTE_REPLY packet should travel in the reverse direction of the ROUTE_REQ. On its way back, each intermediate node can set up the next hop leading to the destination in its routing table. This is because SSA takes the next-hop routing approach. Besides, there are some "gratuitous" routes that can be added to the routing table during the transmission of the ROUTE_REPLY packet. Specifically, if the discovered route is $a \to \cdots \to b \to \cdots \to d$, host b can learn a route to each downstream node.

If multiple ROUTE_REPLYs are received by the source, it can choose the one with the best quality to use. If the source fails to receive a ROUTE_REPLY packet after a time-out period, it can broadcast another ROUTE_REQ with other quality options (such as STRONG_PREFERRED and NO_PREFERENCE) to find a weaker route.

Route Discovery of AODV. The AODV routing protocol [23] is based on the DSDV protocol described in Section 17.2.1. AODV improves DSDV by using an on-demand philosophy to reduce the route maintenance costs, so hosts that are not on an active path do not have to maintain or exchange any control information. Each host maintains its own destination sequence like DSDV to prevent looping and compare the freshness between routes.

A host broadcasts a ROUTE_REQ packet to its neighbors when it determines that it needs a route to a destination but does not have one available. If a neighbor is an intermediate host and doesn't have any route to the destination, it rebroadcasts the ROUTE_REQ packet. Also, if a neighbor has a route to the destination but the corresponding sequence number is less than the sequence number registered in the ROUTE_REQ packet, the neighbor rebroadcasts the ROUTE_REQ. If a neighbor is the destination host or an intermediate host with a route of a destination sequence number no less than that in the ROUTE_REQ packet, the neighbor can reply to the request of the source host by using a ROUTE_REPLY packet containing its own destination sequence number, following the reverse link leading to the source. On the ROUTE_REPLY's way back to the source, the next-hop routing entry can be created in each intermediate host's routing table (this is similar to the procedure described in the SSA protocol).

Route Discovery of TORA. The temporally ordered routing algorithm (TORA) is characterized by a multipath routing capability [21]. Each mobile host is associated with a height metric. A wireless link is then assigned a direction by going from the host with a higher metric to the one with a lower metric. By doing so, the network can be regarded as a DAG (directed acyclic graph) with the destination host as the sink. In graph theory, a sink is a node in a directed graph with no outgoing links. For example, Figure 17.4 (a) is a DAG with host D as the sink. No other hosts except the destination host can be a sink.

The formation of a DAG is done by broadcasting a query from the source host toward the destination host, similar to the earlier protocols. To send a data packet, a host simply forwards the packet to any neighboring host with a lower metric. Any host receiving the data packet will do the same thing. Since the network is maintained as a DAG, the data packet will eventually reach the destination. With such multipath property, one may balance/distribute traffic by a randomization technique. Also, some level of fault tolerance to route breakage can be provided.

Note that for simplicity, the above discussion only covers one DAG. In TORA, one DAG should be maintained with respect to each destination. So, intuitively, there are totally n DAGs overlapping with each other in a network with n hosts.

17.2.2.2   Data Forwarding

The data forwarding part specifies how data packets are forwarded. Two ways are possible: source routing and next-hop routing. In source routing, the whole path to be traversed by a data packet is specified in each packet header, and an intermediate node simply follows the path to deliver the packet, so there is no need to check the routing tables of intermediate hosts during the packet's transmission. The DSR protocol falls in this category. On the contrary, in next-hop routing, only the destination host is specified in the data packets. Each intermediate host must keep a routing table to determine to which host to forward the packet. The AODV, TORA, and SSA protocols fall into this category.

The advantage of source routing is that intermediate hosts are free from keeping any routing information; all the related burdens are put on the source host. The disadvantages are a longer data packet, which must carry complete routing information, and the overhead, which will increase proportionally with respect to the path length.

In next-hop routing, routing information is set up in intermediate hosts. Since routing tables may change dynamically, data packets belonging to the same session do not necessarily follow the same path. This allows some level of fault tolerance. So this approach is more resilient to host mobility because we are allowed to fix some broken links or change to other routes locally without this being noticed by the source host, whereas in source routing, whenever an intermediate host roams away, we must go back to the source host to discover a new route.

17.2.2.3   Route Maintenance

There are several ways to detect a broken link. In DSR, which uses source routing, when an intermediate node forwards a data packet to the next node, the former node can snoop at the latter's traffic for some predefined time. If the former hears no transmission from the latter, it assumes that the link to the next node is broken, in which case it will send an error packet to the source node. For those protocols using the next-hop routing, route entries can be maintained even when no data packets are sent. A host can maintain a list of all neighbors. Route entries with a nonexistent neighbor can be removed.

In most protocols, on knowing that a route is broken, an intermediate host with undelivered data packets at hand can issue an ERROR packet to the source host. On such notification, the source host can invoke another route discovery to construct a new route. Also, on its way back to the source, the ERROR packet can be used to invalidate those stale route entries in other intermediate hosts.

On finding that a route is broken, it is not necessary to construct a completely new route by issuing another route discovery process. This could be too costly. In most cases, a route may become broken simply because one intermediate host in the route roams away. The other part of the route may remain unchanged. There are three protocols employing this idea to improve performance.

1. Query localization techniques are proposed in [5] to use the previous route to restrict the flooding areas on which we propagate the ROUTE_REQ packets to reconstruct the route. These ROUTE_REQ packets will be sent with limited hop counts. In other words, the query packets will be limited within the neighborhood of the previous route only, hence eliminating the possibility of global flooding of the query packets.

2. A simple local route recovery is proposed in [35]. This means that we only fix a broken link using a partial route local to where the broken link is. When a host finds that its next host in a route is missing, a local route discovery with a limited hop count (typically not exceeding 4) will be issued so as to avoid a global flooding. ROUTE_REQ packets with a limited time-to-live will be issued from the host that finds the broken link. It is expected that some ROUTE_REQ packets will reach a host that has an active connection to the destination host. ROUTE_REPLY packets will be returned to that host too. If this succeeds, the route is remedied locally and no global flooding of ROUTE_REQ is necessary. However, this mechanism is only used once because the host that finds the broken link may have a higher probability of recovering the broken route locally. If this fails, error messages will be delivered to the source host to trigger a global ROUTE_REQ.

3. A more complicated local route recovery mechanism is proposed in [32]. It is proposed to send a partial route discovery to the destination host from the host in which a broken link is found. Suppose that a host x finds that its connection to the next host is broken. It can broadcast a ROUTE_REQ packet with a hop limit equal to the remaining number of hops it was supposed to traverse to the destination host before the route was broken. If this succeeds, the route is remedied and no route error will be reported. Otherwise, a route error will be reported to the host preceding x in the route, which will in turn repeat the above local route recovery routine (with a hop limit of one more than the previous host). This is recursively repeated until the broken route is fixed.

Another approach to reduce the potential cost in the event of route breakage is to keep backup routes [8, 18]. When a global route discovery is issued, we usually can collect a lot of routes to the destination. These routes can be kept and used for backup purposes. When the active (and usually the shortest) one becomes broken, we may replace it by another backup route. A backup route may be a complete path leading to the destination or a partial route connecting two points in the active route. Of course, backup routes may also become stale due to host mobility and need some maintenance.

The TORA protocol has an interesting route maintenance process. In TORA, when any host other than the destination finds that it has become a sink, a partial reversal mechanism will be performed to revert to some link leading to itself. Figure 17.4 illustrates how this works. Let us assume that the link between hosts G and D is broken. Then host G will find that it has no outgoing link, as shown in (a). G will reverse all its incoming links, which will result in hosts F and H becoming sinks, as illustrated in (b). In turn, F and H will reverse all their incoming links except those just reverted to by G, resulting in the scenario in (c). Similarly, E will find itself to be a sink and do a partial reversal, resulting in the final DAG in (d). Note that the reversal of links is actually done by changing hosts' height metrics.

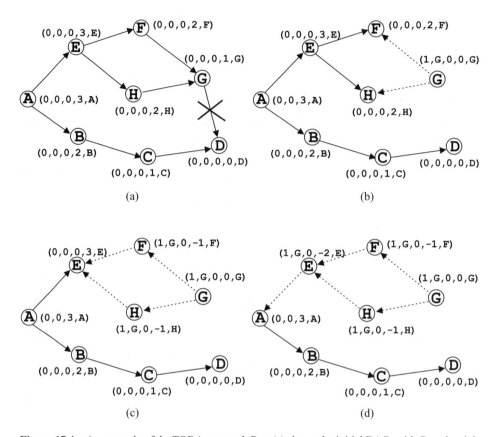

Figure 17.4 An example of the TORA protocol. Part (a) shows the initial DAG, with D as the sink. Supposing the link from G to D becomes broken, parts (b), (c), and (d) show how to repair the DAG. In TORA, each host maintains an order quintuple $H_i = (\tau_i, oid_i, \gamma_i, \delta_i, i)$. The quintuple is further divided into two parts. The first part contains the first three tuples and represents the reference time that a link failure is detected downstream from a host in the DAG. The first tuple, τ_i, is the time tag, which is set to the "time" of the link failure. The second tuple, oid_i, is the originator ID of an event such as link failure. The third tuple, γ_i, is for avoiding looping in the link reversal (not shown in this example). The second part contains the last two tuples. The first tuple, δ_i, is used to order hosts in a common reference level. The last tuple, i, is the unique ID of a host.

17.2.3 Hybrid Routing Protocols

The zone routing protocol (ZRP) [10] is a hybrid of proactive and reactive approaches. With respect to each node, the set of nodes within r hops is called a zone, where r is a predefined value. For each host, routing information inside its zone is constantly collected in a proactive fashion. To do so, whenever a node's link state is changed, a notice will be sent as far as r hops away based on DSDV [22]. Hence, a node always knows how to reach a node inside its zone. This also limits the number of updates triggered by a link state change to a local range.

On the other hand, interzone routing is done in a reactive fashion. It is suggested to use a modified DSR protocol as follows. When a node needs a route to a node outside its zone, it performs a border casting by sending a ROUTE_REQ to each node on the "border" of its zone. On receiving such a packet at a border node, it first checks its intrazone routing table for existence of a route to the requested destination node. If found, a ROUTE_REPLY can be sent; otherwise, it performs another border casting in its zone. This is repeated until a route is found.

A modified source routing style is used for interzone routing. A routing path only contains the border nodes that have to be traversed. This is alright because we always have up-to-date routing information from a host to its border hosts. Thus, some level of fault tolerance (i.e., link change) is provided inside a zone for a path. Once a data packet reaches a border node whose zone contains the destination, its intrazone routing table will be used to forward the packet.

17.2.4   Route Bandwidth in a MANET

To investigate the delay and bandwidth of a route in MANET, an implementation result is reported in [35], based on a next-hop routing protocol on top of the Linux operating system. The platform used in [35] consisted of a number of notebooks of a variety of speeds (Pentium 200MMX, Pentium 233MMX, Pentium II 350, etc.), each equipped with a Lucent WaveLAN wireless card conformed to the IEEE 802.11 MAC protocol operating at the 2.4 GHz band. The transmission rate of these network cards is claimed to be 2 Mbit/sec.

With this platform, the authors observed the effect of hop count on the delay to discover a route. The mobile hosts were placed in a linear manner such that each host could hear only one or two of its neighbors. The first experiment used the ping command at a certain host to contact another host, observe the delay, and discover a new route. This experiment was done in an environment in which all mobile hosts had no up-to-date entries in their route caches. The result is shown in Figure 17.5. As can be seen, the delay is quite small.

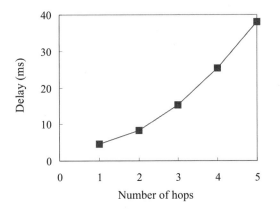

Figure 17.5   The delay to discover a new route versus route length in a MANET by a ping command.

The time needed to find a route will increase linearly with respect to the hop count, which is reasonable.

The second experiment reported in [35] used the ftp command (under binary mode) to determine the communication bandwidth at different hop counts. The result is shown in Figure 17.6. Mobile hosts were again placed in a line. In the "simplex" curve, one ftp request was initiated from a source host to a destination host separated by a certain number of hops. In the "duplex" curve, two ftp requests were initiated between two hosts in both directions. One interesting observation is that the bandwidth degrades to 1/2 when the hop count changes from 1 to 2. The bandwidth further degrades to 1/3 when the hop count changes from 1 to 3. After three hops, the bandwidth still keeps on degrading, but at a slower speed. This shows that optimizing the route length is very critical in a MANET as it improves the end-to-end bandwidth. Of course, the level of contention on the medium can also be reduced if routes are shorter. How to optimize routes on-the-fly for several routing protocols is discussed in [35].

It is also worth commenting on the "Upper Bound" curve in Figure 17.6. Obviously, given a sender–receiver pair that are next to each other, the theoretical bound on bandwidth is 2 Mbit/sec. Given a sender–receiver pair that are two hops away, the theoretical bound will suddenly reduce to 1 Mbit/sec. The reason is that none of the hosts in the (two-hop) route can transmit at the same time. Following the same line of reasoning, given a sender–receiver pair that are three hops away, the theoretical bound will reduce to 2/3 Mbit/sec. This results from the effect of signal interference and the hidden terminal problem [31]. However, after three hops, these factors will disappear and a pipelining effect may appear. Specifically, two hosts separated by three or more hops may be able to send at the same time. For instance, in Figure 17.7, we show 10 mobile hosts arranged in a linear array. Hosts 1, 4, and 7 can send simultaneously; hosts 2, 5, and 8 can send simultaneously; and hosts 3, 6, and 9 can send simultaneously. This can in fact be formulated by the well-known graph-coloring problem. Thus, if the "perfect" pipeline can be formed, then the theoretical upper bound on bandwidth will be 2/3 Mbit/sec.

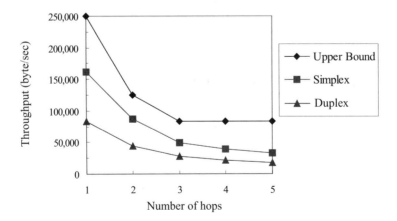

Figure 17.6   The bandwidth of a route versus route length in a MANET by a ftp command.

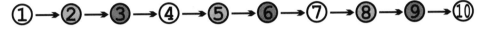

Figure 17.7   An illustration of the pipelining effect used to derive the theoretical upper bound of bandwidth in a multihop path. Hosts of the same color can transmit at the same time.

17.3   BROADCASTING PROTOCOLS FOR MANET

Broadcasting is a common operation in a network, used to resolve many issues. In a MANET in particular, due to host mobility, such operations are expected to be executed more frequently. For example, all the above protocols have to do some sort of broadcasting in route discovery. Important messages/signals may also be disseminated by broadcasting.

A straightforward approach to perform a broadcast is to use flooding. A host, on receiving a broadcast message for the first time, has the obligation to rebroadcast the message. Clearly, this costs n transmissions in a MANET with n hosts. In a CSMA/CA network, because radio signals are likely to overlap with others in a geographical area, straightforward broadcasting by flooding is usually very costly and will result in serious redundancy, contention, and collision, which we refer to as the broadcast storm problem. This problem was first identified in [19].

By redundancy, we mean that when a mobile host decides to rebroadcast a broadcast message to its neighbors, all its neighbors may already have the message. In a MANET environment, redundancy could be very serious. Let us use two examples to demonstrate how much redundancy could be generated. In Figure 17.8(a), it only takes two transmissions for the white node to broadcast a message, whereas four transmissions will be carried out if flooding is used. Figure 17.8(b) shows an even more serious scenario: only two transmissions are sufficient to complete a broadcast from the white node, as opposed to seven transmissions caused by flooding.

The main reason for such redundancy is that radio signals from different antennas are very likely to overlap with each other. Assuming that the area that can be covered by an antenna forms a circle, we show in Figure 17.9 the signal overlapping problem corre-

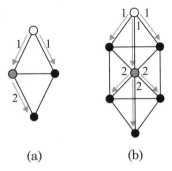

(a)   (b)

Figure 17.8   Two optimal broadcasting schedules in MANETs. Connectivity between hosts is represented by links. White nodes are source hosts, and gray nodes are relay hosts.

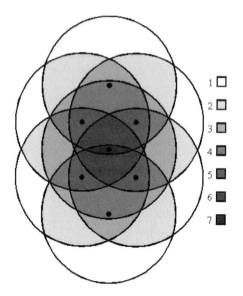

Figure 17.9   The signal overlapping problem corresponding to the scenario in Figure 17.8(b).

sponding to the scenario in Figure 17.8(b). The gray levels in the figure indicate the levels of signal overlapping. As can be seen, many areas are covered by the same broadcast packet more than once. In the worst case, an area can be covered by the packet seven times.

In [19], it is shown, surprisingly, that a rebroadcast can provide at most 61% additional coverage over the area already covered by the previous transmission. Through calculus, it is further shown that on average a rebroadcast can cover only an additional 41% of the area. The calculation is illustrated in Figure 17.10.

Now consider the scenario in which a host X has received the same broadcast packet k times. We would like to know the benefit of X rebroadcasting the packet. Let us denote the additional area that can be covered by X's rebroadcast by $EAC(k)$ (expected additional coverage). Figure 17.11 shows the simulation result. As can be seen, when $k \geq 4$, the EAC is quite low (below 5%).

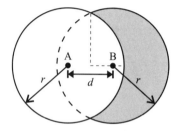

Figure 17.10   Analysis of the extra area that can benefit from a rebroadcast: A sends a broadcast packet and B decides to rebroadcasts the packet.

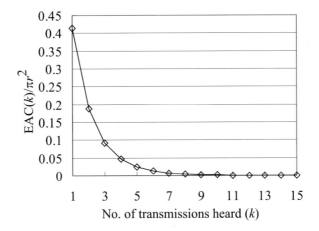

Figure 17.11 Analysis of redundancy: the expected additional coverage $EAC(k)$ (divided by πr^2) after a host has heard a broadcast message k times.

In [19], several threshold-based schemes are proposed to relieve the broadcast storm problem. These protocols are for unreliable broadcast. Reliable broadcasting protocols are proposed in [1, 20].

17.4 MULTICASTING PROTOCOLS FOR MANET

Previous sections have discussed unicast routing and broadcasting protocols. This section will introduce multicasting protocols. The multicasting protocols can be classified into two categories based on how multicast trees are constructed: source-based and core-based (or group-shared) [29, 34]. The source-based protocol tries to maintain a per-source multicast tree from each source host to every member in the multicast group. Thus, there may exist multiple multicast trees in the network. The core-based protocol, on the other hand, uses only one multicast tree rooted at a core host. The tree then spans from the core host to every member of the multicast group. Although multicasting can be achieved by using multiple unicast routing, the traffic might be too high and choke the network. Hence, many multicast protocols have been developed with applications adopting multicasting technologies. Video conferencing is one important example.

Multicasting in MANET is much more complex than in wired networks because of host mobility, interference of wireless signals, and the broadcast nature of wireless communication. In the following, we review two such protocols.

17.4.1 ODMRP

In the on-demand multicast routing protocol (ODMRP) [3, 14], the multicast tree is established by the source host's periodical JOIN packets. Consider the example in Figure 17.12(a). The source node S, desiring to send data packets to multicast members, will

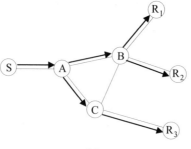

(a)

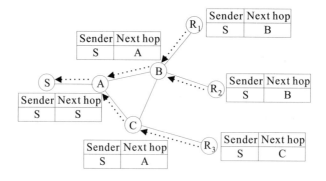

(b)

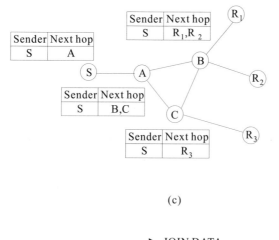

(c)

$\longrightarrow$ JOIN DATA

$\cdots\cdots\blacktriangleright$ JOIN TABLE

Figure 17.12 An example of ODMRP. (a) Propagation of JOIN_DATA packets. (b) Propagation of JOIN_TABLE packets. (c) The final multicast tables.

flood a JOIN_DATA to the whole network. When a host receives a JOIN_DATA for the first time, it will rebroadcast the packet and establish a reverse path to the previous host. Then each host that is a multicast receiver and has received the JOIN_DATA will reply a JOIN_TABLE packet to its upstream host on the reverse path. Each host that receives the JOIN_TABLE for the first time will repeat the process until the source host S is reached. Figure 17.12(b) shows how these packets are forwarded to S.

On receiving JOIN_TABLEs, a host also has to build its multicast table for forwarding future multicast packets. For example, when B receives R_1's JOIN_TABLE, it will add R_1 as its next hop. When B receives R_2's JOIN_TABLE, it will also add R_2 as its next hop. However, this time, no JOIN_TABLE will be sent to A. The final multicast table for each host is shown in Figure 17.12(c).

17.4.2 Multicast AODV

The multicast operation of the ad-hoc on-demand distance vector routing protocol (multicast AODV) [27] is extended from the unicast AODV protocol [23]. When a host joins a multicast group, it has to be added to the corresponding multicast tree. A route request (RREQ) packet can be broadcast for this purpose. Figure 17.13(a) illustrates the propagation of RREQ from a host S. If a host receives a RREQ for a multicast group of which it is not a member or to which it does not have a route, it will rebroadcast the RREQ to its neighbors.

When a multicast group member receives the RREQ, it will unicast Route Reply (RREP) packet to the sending host S [shown in Figure 17.13(b)]. As hosts along the path to the sending host S receive the RREP, they will add entries to their multicast routing tables for the hosts from which they received the RREP. This process will create the forward path. Eventually, one or more than one RREP will reach the sending host S. S can pick the host to which the RREP is returned with the minimum hop count as its next hop leading to the multicast tree. Then S will unicast a multicast activation (MACT) packet to its next hop. The next hop, on receiving the MACT packet, will likewise enable for the source host the route entry with the minimum hop count leading to the multicast tree and send the MACT. This will be repeated until a member of the multicast tree is reached. Figure 17.13(c) illustrates the final multicast tree that is created.

17.5 QoS ROUTING

The specification and management of quality of service (QoS) is important to support multimedia applications (such as video and audio transmissions). QoS defines nonfunctional characteristics of a system that affect the perceived quality of the result. In multimedia, this might include picture quality, image quality, delay, and speed of response. From a technological point of view, QoS characteristics may include timeliness (e.g., delay or response time), bandwidth (e.g., bandwidth required or available), and reliability (e.g., normal operation time between failures or down time from failure to restarting normal operation) [6].

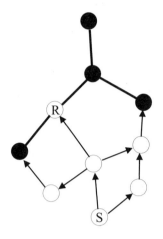

(a)

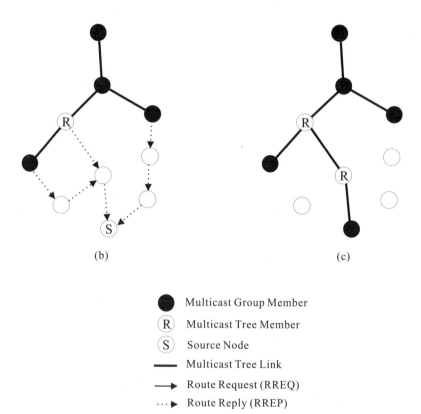

(b)   (c)

Figure 17.13   An example of branch addition in the multicast AODV protocol. (a) The propagation of RREQ packets. (b) The propagation of RREP packets. (c) The final multicast tree.

It is difficult to provide QoS in a MANET due to its broadcast and dynamic nature. First, unlike wired networks, a wireless link's bandwidth may be affected by the transmission activity of its adjacent links. Second, unlike cellular networks, which only need to guarantee quality for one hop, in MANET we must guarantee the quality for multiple hops in a path. Third, mobile hosts may join, leave, and rejoin at any time and at any location; existing links may disappear and new links may be formed as mobile hosts move.

Recently, the QoS transmission problem in a MANET was addressed in several works [7, 12, 13, 15, 30]. We review some of these works from several aspects in the following subsections.

17.5.1 QoS at the MAC Layer

Reference [30] considers the medium access control (MAC) layer to support QoS in an ad hoc wireless network. With their mechanism, real-time hosts contend for access of the common radio channel based on their priorities. A host's transmission priority is determined based on how long it has been waiting for the channel to become idle. It gives priority access to real-time traffic and ensures collision-free transmission of real-time packets.

17.5.2 Bandwidth Calculation

In [15], a mechanism is proposed for QoS transmission in a multihop path. A TDMA-over-CDMA model is assumed. Neighboring hosts are assigned to different transmission codes to avoid collision. Each code is time-framed. Each frame consists of N time slots, indexed from 1 to N. Two hosts that are neighbors of a common host cannot send to that host in the same time slot using the same code or collision will occur. However, if their transmission codes are separated, their transmission will be fine. Another constraint is that a host cannot send and receive in the same time slot. For example, Figure 17.14 shows a contention-free assignment in a path from A to E.

Under such constraints, [15] addresses the bandwidth calculation problem on a multihop path. The set of the common free time slots between two adjacent hosts is defined as their link bandwidth. Taking Figure 17.15(a) as an example, the link bandwidth between B and C is $BW(B, C) = \{4, 5, 6, 7, 8, 9, 10\}$, and the link bandwidth between B and A is

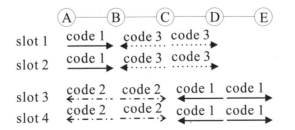

Figure 17.14 Contention-free assignment under the TDMA-over-CDMA model.

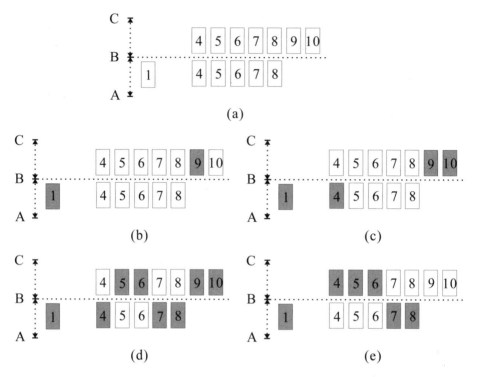

Figure 17.15   Bandwidth calculation in a two-hop path for QoS transmission.

$BW(A, B) = \{1, 4, 5, 6, 7, 8\}$. We need to calculate the end-to-end bandwidth from C to A. First, let us take a set subtraction:

$$BW(B, C) - BW(A, B) = \{9, 10\}$$

These time slots can be used exclusively by C since they are not in the set $BW(A, B)$. Similarly, we can take another subtraction to find the exclusive slots for B

$$BW(A, B) - BW(B, C) = \{1\}$$

This means that we can arbitrarily assign slot 9 or 10 to C and assign slot 1 to B to obtain a bandwidth of one time slot from C to A. The result of choosing slot 9 for C is shown in Figure 17.15(b). After updating $BW(A, B)$ and $BW(B, C)$, we have $BW(B, C) - BW(A, B) = \{10\}$ and $BW(A, B) - BW(B, C) = 0/$. To match C's slot 10, we have to pick one slot, say 4, for B. This results in the assignment in Figure 17.15(c). Finally, because $BW(A, B) \subset BW(B, C)$, we pick half of free slots of $BW(A, B)$ for B, say $\{7, 8\}$, and arbitrarily pick two slots for C, say $\{5, 6\}$. The final result is shown in Figure 17.15(d), which gives an end-to-end bandwidth of 4 slots from C to A.

In Figure 17.15(e), we show a naive solution of assigning slots 4, 5, and 6 to C and slots 1, 7, and 8 to B. The end-to-end bandwidth is only 3.

17.5.3 Ticket-Based QoS Routing

In [7], a ticket-based protocol is proposed to support QoS routing. This protocol maintains the end-to-end state information at every node for every possible destination. This information is updated periodically by a distance-vector-like protocol (namely DSDV [22]).

A source node S, on requiring a QoS route, can issue a number of probing packets each carrying a ticket. Each probe is in charge of searching for one path, if possible. The basic idea of using tickets is to confine the number of route-searching packets to avoid blind flooding (flooding in a MANET is unwise according to [19]). One guideline is: the tighter the QoS requirements are, the more tickets we should issue. Each probe, on reaching any intermediate host, should choose one outgoing path that satisfies the QoS requirements. If a probe enters a node that has no outgoing link satisfying the QoS requirements, the intermediate node sends an invalidated ticket to the destination node. To save the number of probing packets, several tickets may be carried by one packet and, if so, the probe can be split in the middle into multiple probes, each carrying some of the tickets and being responsible for searching a different downstream subpath. Thus, the maximum number of probes at any time is bounded by the total number of tickets.

For example, Figure 17.16 shows a MANET in which the number associated with each link is its corresponding bandwidth. The arrows show the progress of two tickets issued from S to D. It is assumed that a path of bandwidth 3 is required, so the probe going through C fails but that through B and E succeeds.

17.6 EXTENDING CELLULAR SYSTEMS WITH AD HOC LINKS

Personal communication services (PCS) is one of the fastest growing industries. Such systems are typically based on a cellular structure. Capacity and channel limitations are im-

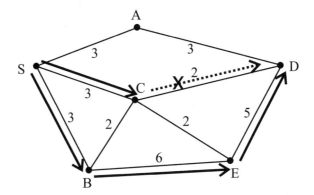

Figure 17.16 A route search example in the ticket-based QoS routing protocol.

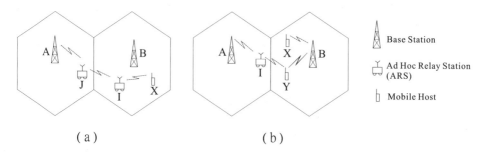

Figure 17.17   Call relays by ad hoc links in the iCAR system: (a) primary relay and (b) secondary relay.

portant concerns. In [25], an architecture called iCAR is proposed to extend the base stations (BS) with some ad hoc relay links. This will have potential benefits in balancing traffic load between cells, increasing a system's capacity, and providing services for shadow areas.

The hardware components of iCAR are illustrated in Figure 17.17. In addition to base stations and mobile hosts, an ad hoc relay system (ARS) is proposed. An ARS is a wireless communication device that can be deployed by a network operator. It has two radio interfaces: a C interface for communication with a base station and an R interface for communication with mobile hosts or other ARS's. The C interface uses traditional licensed bands such as 850 MHz or 2 GHz, and the R interface uses an unlicensed band of 2.4 GHz. The R interface is similar to that used in wireless LAN or ad hoc networks.

Each mobile host has, in addition to a C interface in the PCS handset, an R interface for communication with an ARS. Before communicating with a base station, a mobile host or an ARS must acquire a unique data channel (DCH). Such a system will have potential benefits in balancing/distributing traffic load between base stations. We show two examples here. The first example is called a primary relay, as shown in Figure 17.17(a). Suppose that mobile host X needs to make a call but there is no free DCH in cell B. Typically, X's call will be blocked. In iCAR, X can go through the ad hoc links from ARS I to ARS J and then to a noncongested base station A. So X's call will not be blocked.

The second example is called secondary relay, as depicted in Figure 17.17(b). Assume that mobile host X needs to make a call in a congested cell B, but there is no nearby ARS around X. Suppose that there is a mobile host Y currently occupying a DCH connecting to B. If Y can be connected to ARS I, which can be connected to the noncongested base station A, we can relocate the Y's call to A so as to vacate a DCH in B. Then X's new call can be satisfied. These examples show how ad hoc links can be used in cellular networks to reduce the blocking probability. How to place ARS's is also addressed in [25].

17.7   CONCLUSIONS

In this chapter, we have introduced mobile ad hoc networks. Such wireless network architectures can be used when the construction of base stations is too costly or infeasible. We have discussed unicast, broadcast, multicast, and QoS transmission on a MANET.

ACKNOWLEDGMENTS

The authors would like to thank Prof. C.-H. Lin (National Sun Yat-Sen University) and Prof. S. Das (University of Cincinnati) for reviewing the contents of this chapter. The authors' work is supported by the Ministry of Education, ROC, under grant 89-H-FA07-1-4 (Learning Technology) and the National Science Council, ROC, under grants NSC89-2218-E-008-003, NSC 89-2218-E-008-012, and 89-2218-E-008-013.

REFERENCES

1. S. Alagar and S. Venkatesan, Reliable broadcast in mobile wireless network, *MILCOM '95,* 1995, pp. 236–240.

2. A. Archarys and B. R. Badrinath, A framework for delivering multicast messages in networks with mobile hosts, *ACM/Baltzer J. of Mobile Networks and Applications, 1,* 2, 199–219, 1996.

3. S. H. Bae, S.-J. Lee, W. Su, and M. Gerla, The design, implementation, and performance evaluation of the on-demand multicast routing protocol in multihop wireless networks, *IEEE Network,* Jan./Feb., 70–77, 2000.

4. J. Broch, D. B. Johnson, and D. A. Maltz, The dynamic source routing protocol for mobile ad hoc networks, Internet draft, Dec. 1998.

5. R. Castaneda and S. R. Das, Query Localization techniques for on-demand routing protocols in ad hoc networks, in *Proceedings of MOBICOM '99,* Aug. 1999, pp. 186–194.

6. D. Chalmers and M. Sloman, A survey of quality of service in mobile computing environments, *IEEE Communications Surveys,* Second Quarter, 2–10, 1999.

7. S. Chen and K. Nahrstedt, Distributed Quality-of-Service Routing in ad hoc networks, *IEEE Journal on Selected Areas in Communications, 17,* 8, 1488–1505, 1999.

8. Y.-S. Chen and K.-C. Lai, MESH: Multi-eye spiral-hopping routing protocol in a wireless ad hoc network, in *Proceedings of ICCCN 2000,* Oct. 2000.

9. R. Dube, C.D. Rais, K. Wang, and S. K. Tripathi, Signal stability-based adaptive routing (SSA) for ad-hoc mobile networks, *IEEE Personal Communications,* Feb. 1997.

10. Z. J. Haas and M. R. Pearlman, The zone routing protocol (ZRP) for ad-hoc networks, Internet draft, Aug. 1998.

11. A. Harter and A. Hopper, A Distributed location system for the active office, *IEEE Network, 8,* 1, 1994.

12. Y.-K. Ho and R.-S. Liu, On-demand QoS-based routing protocol for ad hoc mobile wireless networks, in *IEEE Symposium on Computers and Communications ISCC '00,* 2000.

13. G. D. Kondylis, S. V. Krishnamurthy, S. K. Dao, and G. J. Pottie, Multicasting sustained CBR and VBR traffic in wireless ad-hoc networks, in *IEEE ICC '00,* 2000.

14. S.-J. Lee, M. Gerla, and C.-C. Chiang, On-demand multicast routing protocol (ODMRP) for ad hoc networks, Internet draft, draft-ietf-manet-odmrp-01.txt, Jun. 1999, work in progress.

15. C. R. Lin and J.-S. Liu, QoS routing in ad hoc wireless networks, *IEEE Journal on Selected Areas in Communications, 17,* 8, 1426–1438, 1999.

16. IETF MANET Working Group, http://www.ietf.org/html.charters/manet-charter.html.

17. S. Murthy and J. J. Garcia-Luna-Aceves, An efficient routing protocol for wireless networks, *ACM Mobile Networks and Application,* Oct. 183–197, 1996.

18. A. Nasipuri and S. R. Das, On-demand multipath routing for mobile ad hoc networks, in *Proceedings of ICCCN '99,* Oct. 1999.

19. S.-Y. Ni, Y.-C. Tseng, Y.-S. Chen, and J.-P. Sheu, The broadcast storm problem in a mobile ad hoc network, in *Proceedings of MOBICOM '99,* Aug. 1999, pp. 151–162.

20. E. Pagani and G. P. Rossi, Providing reliable and fault tolerant broadcast delivery in mobile ad-hoc networks, *Mobile Networks and Applications, 4,* 175–192, 1999.

21. V. D. Park and M. S. Corson, A Highly Adaptive distributed routing algorithm for mobile wireless networks, in *Proceedings of INFOCOM '97,* April 1997.

22. C. Perkins and P. Bhagwat, Highly dynamic destination-sequenced distance-vector (DSDV) routing for mobile computers, in *ACM SIGCOMM Symposium on Communications, Architectures and Protocols,* September 1994, pp. 234–244.

23. C. Perkins and E. M. Royer, ad hoc On demand distance vector (AODV) routing (Internet draft), August 1998.

24. R. Prakash and M. Singhal, Low-cost checkpointing and failure recovery in mobile computing systems, *IEEE Trans. on Parallel and Distributed Systems, 7,* 10, 1035–1048, 1996.

25. C. Qiao, H. Wu, and O. Tonguz, iCAR: An integrated cellular and ad-hoc relay system, in *IEEE International Conference on Computer Communications and Networks,* 2000.

26. G. Malkin, RIP Version 2 carrying additional information, *RFC, 1723,* 1994.

27. E. M. Royer and C. E. Perkins, Multicast operation of the ad-hoc on-demand distance vector routing protocol, in *Proceedings ACM/IEEE MOBICOM '99,* Seattle, WA, Aug. 1999, pp. 207–218.

28. E. M. Royer and C.-K. Toh, A Review of current routing protocols for ad hoc mobile wireless networks, *IEEE Personal Communications,* Apr., 46–55, 1999.

29. L. H. Sahasrabuddhe and B. Mukherjee, Multicast routing algorithms and protocols: A tutorial, *IEEE Network,* Jan./Feb., 90–102, 2000.

30. J. L. Sobrinho and A. S. Krishnakumar, Quality-of-Service in ad hoc carrier sense multiple access wireless networks, *IEEE Journal on Selected Areas in Communications, 17,* 8, 1353–1368, 1999.

31. A. S. Tanenbaum, *Computer Networks,* Prentice Hall, Englewood Cliffs, NJ, 1996.

32. C.-K. Toh, A Novel Distributed routing protocol to support ad-hoc mobile computing, in *Proceedings 1996 IEEE 15th Annual International Phoenix Conference Computing and Communications,* 1996, pp. 480–486.

33. R. Want, A. Hopper, V. Falcao, and J. Gibbons, The Active Badge Location System, *ACM Trans. on Information Systems, 10,* 1, 91–102, 1992.

34. B. Wang and J. C. Hou, Multicast routing and Its QoS extension: Problem, algorithms, and protocols, *IEEE Network,* Jan./Feb., 22–35, 2000.

35. S.-L. Wu, S.-Y. Ni, Y.-C. Tseng, and J.-P. Sheu, Route maintenance in a wireless mobile ad hoc network, *Telecommunication Systems, 18,* 1/3, 61–84, 2001.

CHAPTER 18

Routing with Guaranteed Delivery in Geometric and Wireless Networks

JORGE URRUTIA

Instituto de Matematicas, Universidad Nacional Autonoma de Mexico

18.1 INTRODUCTION

The vertices of a geometric network are points on the plane, and its edges straight line segments joining them. A geometric network is called planar if it contains no two edges that intersect other than perhaps at a common endpoint. In the remainder of this paper we will assume that all our graphs, unless otherwise stated, are planar geometric networks.

Our main goal here is that of studying routing algorithms that take advantage of the location of the nodes of geometric networks. Early papers on routing ignored information regarding the physical location of the nodes of the networks. With the advent of new technologies such as global positioning systems (GPS), the user's location is becoming common information that can be retrieved from GPS, and then used to develop better routing algorithms.

For other applications, we can use the location of a node as part of its label. This can in turn can be used to obtain efficient routing algorithms. In many applications, such as wireless cellular networks, Internet service providers, and others, many nodes have fixed locations. Networks such as cellular communication networks consist of a backbone subnetwork and a collection of mobile users that move around freely and connect through fixed switches. In many of these networks, the use of global positioning systems allow users to obtain the physical location or geographical information regarding users and switches of a network [18].

Information regarding the position of the nodes of a network can and indeed has been used to obtain new routing schemes that take advantage of this information. A number of papers proposing various types of routing algorithms using geographical data have been written [3, 5, 7, 12, 14, 15, 22, 27].

In this paper we will focus on on-line or local routing algorithms for connected planar geometric graphs that take advantage of the physical location of the nodes of the networks. We are mainly interested in on-line routing algorithms that use geographic information on the nodes and links of a network, and that in addition guarantee that messages arrive at their destination. Our approach differs from similar algorithms studied in the lit-

Handbook of Wireless Networks and Mobile Computing, Edited by Ivan Stojmenović.
ISBN 0-471-41902-8   © 2002 John Wiley & Sons, Inc.

erature, particularly in the context of wireless networks in which numerous routing schemes have been developed and mostly tested experimentally.

Some earlier work such as [11] and [7] proposed location-based algorithms based on various notions of progress. Most of those routing protocols do not necessarily guarantee message delivery. Indeed, some of the routing schemes proposed recently [2, 15] can also lead to the same problem [27]. In many schemes, e.g., flooding routing algorithms [10], multiple redundant copies of the messages are sent in the hope that one of them will eventually reach its destination. Sending multiple copies of messages creates other problems such as network congestion. We believe that the usage of algorithms such as those presented here will become paramount as the number of users of communication networks increases. In [14] another method called compass routing is proposed that is shown to work for some specific types of networks. Briefly if a message is located at a node v, and wants to reach node t, compass routing will send it to the neighbor u of v such that the slope of the line segment joining u to v is the closest to the slope of the segment joining v to t. While compass routing may occasionally fall into infinite loops failing to reach t, it works for some important classes of networks. In particular, it is shown in [14] that compass routing works correctly for Delaunay triangulations, a result that will be useful in developing routing algorithms for wireless communication networks. We will also study variations of compass routing that will enable it to work for planar geometric networks.

In [20], similar problems are studied. Shortest-path problems are studied in which a map is not known in advance. They seek dynamic decision rules that optimize the worst-case ratio of the distance covered to the length of the shortest paths.

We will show how our results can be used to solve some routing problems in wireless communication networks that are not necessarily planar. To this end, we will develop fully distributed techniques to calculate planar subnetworks of wireless communication networks. This will be achieved by using some standard tools in computational geometry. The resulting algorithms are also guaranteed to deliver messages to their destination. Some future lines of research are pointed out at the end of the chapter.

It has been proposed that the algorithms presented here can be considered as a safeguard method to be used when heuristic techniques such as those proposed in [13, 11, 19, and 28] fail. We argue that algorithms of the type presented here should become standard, as they not only guarantee that a message gets to its destination, but also tend to create little overhead, which in turn solves other problems arising from broadcasting multiple copies of data messages.

18.1.1 Local Position-Aided Routing Algorithms

In this section, we present some of the basic ideas used in the development of our location-aided or geometric on-line routing algorithms on planar geometric networks. Some of these algorithms have been refined and improved, yet the basic ideas remain. By a location-aided or geometric on-line routing algorithms we mean an algorithm that works under the following restrictions:

1. A typical message contains the location of its starting point s, the location of its destination t, the contents of the message, e.g., the text of an e-mail, and perhaps a con-

stant amount of extra storage in which a constant amount of information regarding some data concerning the route that a message has traveled is recorded.

2. At each node of the network, a processor has some geographical local information concerning only the location of its neighbors.

3. Based only on the local information stored at the nodes of the network, the locations of s and t, and the information stored in the extra memory the message itself carries, a decision is taken regarding on where to send the message next.

It is not straightforward to develop a routing algorithm that satisfies the above restriction and yet guarantees that a message arrives at its destination. In fact, some earlier papers on the subject [5] seemed to assume that their algorithms guaranteed message delivery! Our objective in this section is to develop such an algorithm.

18.1.2 Compass Routing

Suppose that we want to travel from an initial vertex s to a destination vertex t of a planar geometric network. Assume that all the information available to us at any point in time is:

1. The coordinates of our starting and destination points

2. Our current position

3. The directions of the edges incident with the vertex where we are located

With this information available, we define the following rule to route in geometric networks:

Compass Routing: Starting at s, we will in a recursive way choose and traverse the edge of the geometric graph incident to our current position and with the slope closest to that of the line segment connecting the vertex we are standing at to t. Ties are broken randomly.

Unfortunately, compass routing (Figures 18.1 and 18.2) does not guarantee arrival to the destination. This is evident if we use it in geometric graphs with low connectivity or graphs with nonconvex faces. What is somewhat unexpected is that compass routing fails even in geometric graphs in which all of its faces are triangles and the external face is bounded by a convex polygon The geometric graph shown in Figure 18.2 has these properties, and yet when we try to use compass routing to go from $s = u_0$ to t we get stuck around the cycle with vertex set $\{v_0, w_i; i = 0, \ldots, 3\}$. The graph consists of two concentric squares, one of which is rotated slightly. The line segment $t - v_i$ is orthogonal to the edge joining v_i to w_i, and w_i lies on $t - v_i$, $i = 0, \ldots, 3$. It is now easy to see that under these conditions, if we are at point v_i (resp. w_i), compass routing will choose next the edge connecting v_i to w_i (resp. w_i to v_{i+1}, addition taken mod 4). Similar constructions exist in which instead of using a square to start the construction, we use a regular polygon with n vertices, $n \geq 4$.

At this point, we would like to mention that our initial motivation to study on-line location-aided routing algorithms arose from an interesting routing scheme called interval

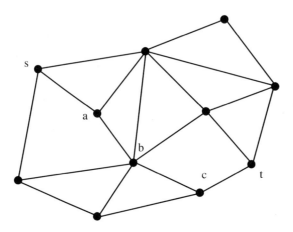

Figure 18.1   Traveling from s to t using compass routing will follow the path s, a, b, c, t.

routing introduced by Santoro and Khatib [23]. The goal in interval routing is that of finding, whenever possible, a labeling of the vertices of a graph with the integers $1, \ldots, n$ such that for every vertex i of the graph, we can assign to each edge e_i incident to i a disjoint interval $[a_i, b_i]$ with the property that if $j \in [a_i, b_i]$, then there is a shortest path from i to j containing e_i. Each edge is assigned two intervals, one at each of its endpoints; see Figure 18.3. One of the motivations for interval routing was that of having a fast and efficient method to forward information received at a node whose final destination was not

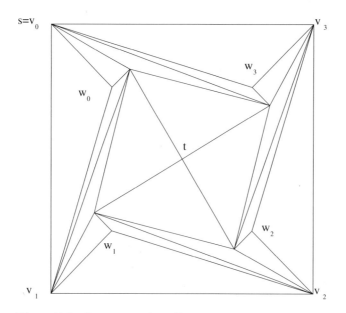

Figure 18.2   Compass routing will not reach t from u_i, $i = 0, \ldots, 3$.

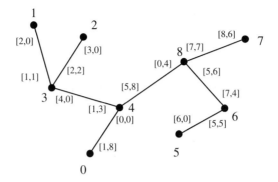

Figure 18.3   An interval routing scheme for a tree with 9 vertices. The intervals are taken mod 9. For example, interval [7, 4] consists of the elements {7, 8, 0, 1, 2, 3, 4}.

the node itself. Interval routing reduces the forwarding problem to that of performing a simple search on the set of intervals assigned to the edges incident to a vertex of a graph. Observe that compass routing also reduces the forwarding problem to a search problem. It is easy to see that as is the case with compass routing, most graphs have no labeling scheme that supports interval routing. However when interval and compass routing work, they give efficient, fast, and reliable routing protocols.

We say that a geometric graph G supports compass routing if for every pair of its vertices s and t, compass routing (starting at s) produces a path from s to t.

The Delaunay triangulation $\mathcal{D}(P_n)$ of a set P_n of n points on the plane, is the partitioning of the convex hull of P_n into a set of triangles with disjoint interiors such that

- The vertices of these triangles are points in P_n
- For each triangle in the triangulation, the circle passing through its vertices contains no other point of P_n in its interior

It is well known that when the elements of P_n are in general circular position, i.e., no four of them are cocircular, then $\mathcal{D}(P_n)$ is well defined. For the rest of this section we will assume that P_n is in general circular position. The next result was proved in [14]:

Theorem 1.1.1   Let P_n be a set of n points on the plane; then $\mathcal{D}(P_n)$ supports compass routing.

The proof relies on the fact that each time we move along an edge, the Euclidean distance to t always decreases. This can be easily seen from Figure 18.4. Indeed suppose that s and t are not adjacent, and that the line connecting s to t intersects the triangle with vertices $\{s, x, y\}$ of $\mathcal{D}(P_n)$. By definition, t does not belong to the circle passing through s, x, and y, and the segment $s - t$ intersects the segment $x - y$. It is easy to see now that if compass routing chooses to move from s to say x, then the distance from x to t is strictly smaller than the distance from s to t. Experimental results by Morin [17] show that the average

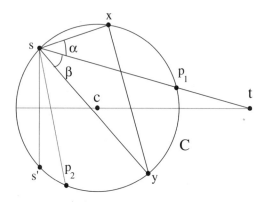

Figure 18.4 Routing on Delaunay triangulations.

link and distance dilation of compass routing on Delaunay triangulations of randomly generated point sets in the unit square with up to 500 points are less than 1.4 and 1.1, respectively.

18.1.3 Compass Routing on Convex Subdivisions

A geometric graph is called a convex subdivision if all its bounded faces are convex and the external face is the complement of a convex polygon. By randomizing compass routing Morin [17] was able to guarantee message delivery not only in triangulations but in convex subdivisions.

Morin's modification is indeed simple. Suppose that we want to reach vertex t, and that a message is currently located at vertex v. Let $cw(v)$ and $ccw(v)$ be the two vertices defined as follows: $cw(v)$ is the vertex adjacent to v that minimizes the clockwise angle $\angle^{cw} t, v, u$, and $ccw(v)$ the vertex adjacent to v that minimizes the counterclockwise angle $\angle^{ccw} t, v, u$; see Figure 18.5. Random Compass sends the message with equal probability to $ccw(v)$ or to $cw(v)$.

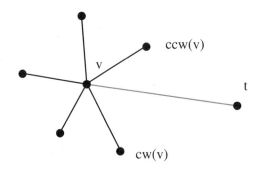

Figure 18.5 Defining $ccw(v)$ and $cw(v)$.

Morin proved:

Theorem 1.1.2 Random compass guarantees message delivery in any convex subdivision.

In theory, it could take an arbitrarily large amount of time before a message arrives at its destination. However experimental results also presented in [17] show that random compass performs well on the average. Its dilation is better than 1.7 for Delaunay triangulations with up to 500 vertices. No experimental results are reported for convex subdivisions.

Although compass routing fails for triangulations, we now show how a slight modification of it will enable it to work in convex subdivisions.

Compass Routing on Convex Subdivisions [14]
The following procedure stops upon reaching t.

1. Starting at s determine the face F incident to s intersected by the line segment $s - t$. Pick any of the two edges of F incident to s, and start traversing the edges of F until we find the second edge of F intersected by $s - t$.
2. Update F to be the second face of the geometric graph containing $u - v$ on its boundary.
3. Traverse the edges of our new F until we find a second edge $x - y$ intersected by $s - t$. At this point we update F again as in the previous point. We iterate our current step until we reach t

To prove that a message always gets to its destination, we proceed as follows: Let us label the faces intersected by the line segment joining s to t by $\{F_1, \ldots, F_m\}$ according to the order in which they are intersected. Initially $F = F_1$. Observe that each time we update F we move from F_i to F_{i+1} for some i. Thus, eventually we reach the face F_m containing t, and thus t. See Figure 18.6. Observe that our algorithm traverses each edge of our graph at most once. It is easy to see that if the faces of a geometric graph are not convex, the previous algorithm may fall into a loop. In the next section we show how to modify compass routing so that it will also work for arbitrary geometric graphs. The price we pay is that, in general, the paths we have to traverse might increase substantially in length. This is a consideration to have in mind when using the results in the next subsection for particular applications.

18.1.4   Compass Routing on Geometric Graphs

Observe first that the vertices and edges of any geometric graph G induce a partitioning of the plane into a set of connected regions with disjoint interiors, not necessarily convex, called the faces of G. The boundary $\mathcal{B}_i$ of each of these faces is a closed polygonal in which we admit some edge of G to appear twice. For example in the graph shown in Figure 18.7, in the polygonal bounding the external face, the edge $u - v$ appears twice.

Suppose now that we want to travel from a vertex s to a vertex t of G. As before, calcu-

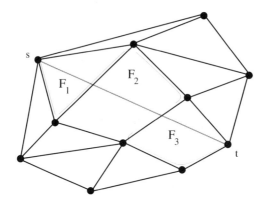

Figure 18.6 Routing using compass routing on convex subdivisions.

late the line segment joining s to t, and determine the face $F = F_0$ incident to s intersected by $s - t$. We now traverse the polygonal determined by F_0. Each time we intersect $s - t$ at a point p, while traversing the boundary of $F(0)$, we calculate the distance from p to s. Upon returning to s (unless we reach t, in which case we stop), all we need to recall is the point p_0 at which the polygonal bounding F_0 intersects $s - t$, which maximizes its distance to s. We now traverse the boundary of F_0 again until we reach p_0, at which point we update F to be the second face whose boundary contains p_0. We repeat our procedure using p_0 and our new F instead of s and $F(0)$. It is straightforward to see that we eventually reach t. Notice that each edge of our graph is contained in at most two faces. Observe that if the edges of

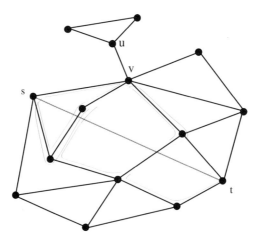

Figure 18.7 Routing using compass routing on nonconvex subdivisions. Observe that the length of the path traversed from s to t is considerably longer than the one we obtained for convex subdivisions.

a face are traversed, they are traversed at most twice. It follows that each edge is traversed at most four times. A slight modification can be used so that each edge is traversed at most three times [3].

Thus we have proved:

Theorem 1.1.3 [14] There exists a local information routing algorithm on geometric graphs that guarantees that we reach our destination. Moreover, our algorithm is such that we traverse a linear number of edges.

It should be pointed out that the main objective of the algorithms presented in this section is that of finding on-line local routing algorithms that guarantee message delivery. This implicitly implies that the routes generated by our algorithms will be in general not the shortest paths connecting s to t. In fact, it is straightforward to see that for every k we can construct examples in which the lengths of the paths found by our algorithms are k times longer than that of the shortest paths connecting s to t. This can be achieved if the length of a path is measured either in terms of the sum of the lengths of its edges or the number of edges used in the path. In practice, however, this does not happen often. For details see [3, 17].

We stress this point here, as there are numerous papers in which many ad hoc routing techniques are proposed and tested for numerous types of communications such as ad hoc and wireless networks. A common parameter measure in most of these methods is the success rate, i.e., the percentage of messages that arrive at their destination. In addition, many of these algorithms broadcast multiple copies of a message in hope that at least one of them will reach its destination. Observe that this creates a large overload in terms of the amount of traffic generated. In time, this will become an important factor to be avoided. In contrast, our algorithms have a 100% success rate and send only one copy of each message. In the next section, we will show how the results presented in this section are used to obtain routing algorithms in wireless communication networks such as cellular telephone networks. Our algorithms guarantee message delivery.

18.2 APPLICATIONS TO AD HOC WIRELESS COMMUNICATION NETWORKS

A wireless communication network can be modeled as a set of radio stations located on a set of points $P_n = \{p_1, \ldots, p_n\}$, each of which has associated with it a real number r_i, its transmission power, such that two points p_i, p_j are connected if their distance is smaller than the minimum of $\{r_i, r_j\}$. We now address the problem of developing an on-line local routing algorithm for wireless cellular communication networks.

Cellular telephone communication networks consist of a set of fixed, low-powered radio stations located on $P_n = \{p_1, \ldots, p_n\}$, all with the same transmission power $r(i) = 1$, and a set of mobile users that move freely. The mobile users connect to the network through the closest fixed radio station. The set of fixed radio stations defines a unit wireless communication network $UW(P_n)$ on P_n, in which two elements $p, q \in P_n$ are connected if their distance is at most 1.

We proceed now to develop an on-line local routing algorithm for unit wireless communication networks. Observe first that $UW(P_n)$ is not necessarily planar. For instance if P_n consists of 12 points contained within a circle of radius 1, $UW(P_n)$ is not planar.

In order to use the results presented in the previous section, we should be able to extract a planar subnetwork from any $UW(P_n)$. Two requirements must be satisfied by the method we use to extract the planar subgraph to fully ensure its functionality for real-life applications:

1. If a cellular communication network is connected, the resulting planar subgraph must be connected.
2. We must have a local protocol so that each node of the network can decide in a consistent manner which neighbor connections to keep, and ensure that, collectively, and without the need to communicate, the set of edges chosen individually by the nodes of the network form a planar graph.

The necessity for the second condition follows from our desire to have fully distributed protocols that avoid the use of any kind of centralized protocols.

The problem of extracting or even deciding if a graph contains a planar connected subgraph is a well-known *NP-complete* problem [16]. Fortunately, $UW(P_n)$ networks always have such a subgraph and, in fact, finding it is relatively straightforward.

The key to our result arises from the use of Gabriel graphs [1]. Given two points p and q on the plane, let $C(p, q)$ be the circle passing through them such that the line segment joining p to q is a diameter of $C(p, q)$. Given a set of n points $P_n = \{p_1, \ldots, p_n\}$ on the plane, the Gabriel graph of P_n is the graph whose set of vertices is P_n, in which two points u and v of P_n are adjacent iff the $C(p, q)$ contains no other points of P_n. Let $G'(P_n)$ be the graph with vertex set P_n such that two vertices p and q are adjacent in $G'(P_n)$ iff $C(p, q)$ contains no other points of P_n and p and q are adjacent in $UW(P_n)$, that is $G'(P_n)$ is the intersection of the Gabriel graph of P_n with $UW(P_n)$. The following result was proved in [3]:

Theorem 1.2.1   If $UW(P_n)$ is connected then $G'(P_n)$ is also connected.

The easiest proof of this result proceeds as follows. Let p and q be such that they are adjacent in $UW(P_n)$ and there is no path connecting them in $G'(P_n)$. Suppose further that their distance is the smallest possible among all such pairs of points in P_n. Since p and q are not connected in $G'(P_n)$, $C(p, q)$ contains at least a third point $r \in P_n$. Observe that the distances from r to p and q are smaller than the distance from p to q, and thus there is a path P' in $G'(P_n)$ connecting r to p and a path P'' connecting r to q. The concatenation of these paths produces a path from p to q in $G'(P_n)$. Our result follows.

It is obvious that each node p in $UW(P_n)$ can decide locally which of its neighbors in $UW(P_n)$ should be its neighbors in $G'(P_n)$. It simply collects the locations from all its neighbors (i.e., the elements of P_n at distance at most 1 from p, and tests for each q of them if the circle $C(p, q)$ is empty. This can be done using standard algorithms in computational geometry in $O(k \ln k)$, where k is the number of neighbors of p in $UW(P_n)$ [21].

We now have the general tools to obtain an on-line local routing algorithm on unit wireless communication networks. First find $G'(P_n)$, and then use the routing algorithm in Theorem 1.1.3 to send messages. The calculation of $G'(P_n)$ can be done only once, or periodically in cases where node failures can happen.

Thus we have proved:

Theorem 1.2.2 There exists an on-line routing algorithm for unit wireless communication networks that guarantees delivery. Any message takes at most a linear number of steps to reach its destination.

Some fine-tuning of the algorithm resulting from the previous theorem was done in [3, 17]. These papers make some modifications to compass routing for arbitrary planar geometric networks that improve the worst-case scenario regarding the number of edges traversed. The reader interested in the details can consult [3, 17]. In the same papers, experimental results that show that, in practice, our algorithms perform well are available. Details of simulations and variations of our algorithms are also included in those papers.

Another routing algorithm using ideas similar ours was presented in [3]. The main idea of their algorithm is as follows. Start routing using a greedy-type algorithm such as compass routing until a problem arises, e.g., none of the possible candidates to visit next is strictly closer to our destination than our current position. At this point, we switch to a routing algorithm that guarantees delivery, e.g., use geometric routing on arbitrary geometric graphs, until a node strictly closer to our destination than our current position is reached. At this point we switch back to compass routing.

Another modification to our algorithms was presented in [5]; they use some of the edges in $UW(P_n)$ that are not present in the Gabriel graph of P_n as shortcuts. Further, they also use and refine techniques presented in [29] that make use of independent sets of vertices of graphs to obtain an algorithm that in practice performs very well.

Stojmenovic and Lin [27] also studied a hybrid single path/flooding algorithm that guarantees delivery of a message.

18.3 DELAUNAY TRIANGULATIONS

A common approach in serial network design is that of finding good architectures that guarantee good performance, e.g., hypercubes, and then building networks that satisfy those architectures. In many applications of wireless communication networks, the cost of the actual radio stations is relatively cheap. In those applications, the best way to tackle routing problems is suggested by Theorem 1.1.1. If a wireless network, not necessarily a unit wireless communication network, does not contain the Delaunay triangulation as a subgraph, make it do so. This can be achieved in two different ways. In the first, we can deploy extra stations until our objective is reached. The second method to achieve this would be to increase, if the conditions of our application allow us to do so, the transmission power of our stations until the Delaunay triangulation is contained in our wireless communication network. In some instances, e.g., when all nodes of a wireless communication network can communicate with each other, the Delaunay triangulation $\mathcal{D}(P_n)$ can be calculated locally [25]. This follows from that fact that once we have calculated the Voronoi diagram of P_n, we also have the Delaunay triangulation [1]. Once the Delaunay trinagulation is calculated, for each vertex we can define for each element of P_n the parameter $Del(p_i)$ to be the distance from p_i to its furthest neighbor in $\mathcal{D}(P_n)$. This value can then be used to determine the minimum transmission power required by p_i so that its furthest neighbor in $\mathcal{D}(P_n)$ can be reached. This, in turn, will help save energy, which is essential in several wireless communication networks [4, 26, 8]. In case direct communication is not possible, it is still possible to run a distributed setup procedure to calculate $Del(p_i)$ by forwarding the position of all the nodes of our network to each vertex. The value of $Del(p_i)$ can then be used to adjust the transmission power of p_i.

18.4 CONCLUSIONS

In this chapter we reviewed on-line routing algorithms on geometric networks and wireless communication networks that guarantee that a message arrives to its destination. In practice, our algorithms are also competitive, and have the advantage of sending only one copy of a message, in contrast to many of the algorithms developed to date. The algorithms presented here thus eliminate the overhead created by many existing algorithms that send multiple copies of a message that, in turn, may lead to traffic problems. A more ample review of routing algorithms in ad hoc networks appears in Chapter 23 of this book.

ACKNOWLEDGMENTS

Supported by a grant from CONACyT-REDII, Universidad Nacional Autónoma de México.

REFERENCES

1. F. Aurenhammer and R. Klein, Voronoi diagrams, in *Handbook of Computational Geometry,* J. R. Sack and J. Urrutia eds. Amsterdam: Elsevier Science Publishers, 2000, pp. 201–290.

2. S. Basagni, I. Chlamtac, V. R. Syrotiuk, and B. A. Woodward, A distance routing effect algorithm for mobility (DREAM), in *Proceedings MOBICOM, 1998,* pp. 76–84.

3. P. Bose, P. Morin, I. Stojmenovic, and J. Urrutia, Routing with guaranteed delivery in ad hoc wireless networks, in *Proceedings of 3rd International Workshop on Discrete Algorithms and Methods for Mobile Computing and Communications,* Seattle, August 20, 1999, pp. 48–55; *ACM/Kluwer Wireless Networks, 7,* 6, 609–616, 2001.

4. J. H. Chang and L. Tassiulas, Routing for maximum system lifetime in wireless ad hoc networks, in *Proceedings 37th Annual Alerton Conference on Communication, Control and Computing,* Monticello, IL, Sept., 1999.

5. S. Datta, I. Stojmenovic, and J. Wo, Internal node and shortcut based routing with guaranteed delivery in wireless networks, in *Proceedings IEEE International Conference on Distributed*

Computing and Systems (Wireless Networks and Mobile Computing Workshop), Phoenix, AZ, April 16–19, 2001, to appear in *Cluster Computing.*

6. Dijkstra, E. W., A note on two problems in connexion with graphs, *Numer. Math., 1,* 269–271, 1959.

7. G. G. Finn, Routing and addressing problems in large metropolitan-scale network, ISR research report ISU/RR87-180, March, 1987.

8. P. Gupta and P. R. Khumar, Critical power for asymtotic connectivity in wireless networks, in *Stochastic Analysis, Control, Optimization and Applications: A volume in honor of W. H. Fleming,* W. M. McEneaney, G. Yin, and Q. Zhang (eds.) Birkhauser, Boston, 1998.

9. S. M. Hedetniemi, S. T. Hedetniemi, and A. L. Liestman, A survey of gossiping and broadcasting in communication networks, *Networks, 18,* 319–349, 1988.

10. C. Ho, K. Obraczka, G. Tsudik, and K. Viswanath,Flooding for reliable multicast in multiple-hop ad hoc networks, in *Proceedings MOBICOM,* pp. 243–254, August, 1999.

11. T. C. Hu, and V. O. K. Li, Transmition range control in multihop packet radio networks, *IEEE Transactions on Communications, 34,* 1, 1986, 38–44.

12. T. Imielinski and J. C. Navas,GPS-based addressing and routing, in *IETF RFC 2009,* Rutgers University Computer Science, November, 1996.

13. Y-B. Ko and N. H. Vaidya, Using location information in wireless ad hoc networks, in *IEEE Vehicular Technology Conference (VTC'99),* May, 1999.

14. E. Kranakis, H. Singh, and J. Urrutia, Compass routing on geometric networks, in *Proceedings 11th Canadian Conference on Computational Geometry,* pp. 51–54, Vancouver, Aug. 15–18, 1999.

15. Ko, Y. B. and N. H. Vaidya, Location-aided routing in mobile ad hoc networks, in *Proceedings MOBICOM,* 1998, pp. 66–75.

16. P. C. Liu and Geldmacher, R. C., On the deletion of nonplanar edges of a graph, in *Proceedings of the Tenth Southeastern Conference on Combinatorics, Graph Theory and Computing,* Florida Atlantic University, Boca Raton, FL, 1979, pp. 727–738.

17. P. R. Morin, *On line Routing in Geometric Graphs,* Ph.D. Thesis, School of Computer Science, Carleton University, 2000.

18. J. C. Navas and T. Imielinski, Geocast-Geographic addressing and routing.

19. R. Nelson, and L. Kleinrock, The spatial capacity of a slotted ALOHA multihop packet radio network with capture, *IEEE Transations on Communications, 32,* 6, 684–694, 1984.

20. C. H. Papadimitriou, and M. Yannakakis, Shortest paths without a map. *Theoret. Comput. Sci., 84,* 1, 127–150, 1991.

21. F. P. Preparata and M. I. Shamos, *Computational Geometry, an Introduction,* New York: Springer-Verlag, 1985.

22. S. Ramanathan and M. Steenstrup, A survey of routing techniques for mobile communications networks, *ACM/Baltzer Mobile Networks and Applications, 1,* 2, 89–104, 1996.

23. N. Santoro and R. Khatib, Labeling and implicit routing in networks, *The Computer Journal, 28,* 1, 5–8, 1985.

24. I. Stojmenovic, Location updates for efficient routing in ad hoc networks, Chapter 23, this volume.

25. I. Stojmenovic, Voronoi diagram and convex hull based geocasting and routing in wireless networks, Tchnical report TR-99-11, December 1999, SITE, University of Ottawa.

26. I. Stojmenovic and X. Lin,Power aware localized routing in wireless networks, in *IEEE Interna-*

tional Parallel and Distributed Processing Symposium, Cancun, Mexico, May 1–5, 2000, pp. 371–376.

27. I. Stojmenovic, and X. Lin, GEDIR: loop-free hybrid single-path flooding/routing algorithms with guaranteed delivery for wireless networks, *IEEE Transactions on Parallel and Distributed Systems, 12,* 10, 1023–1032, 2001.

28. H. Takagi and L. Kleinrock, Optimal transmission rates for randomly distributed packet radio terminals, *IEEE Transactions on Communications, 32,* 3, 246–257, 1984.

29. J. Wu and H. Li, On calculating connected dominating sets for efficient routing in ad hoc wireless networks, *Proceedings DIALM,* Seattle, WA, Aug. 1999, pp. 7–14.

CHAPTER 19

Power Optimization in Routing Protocols for Wireless and Mobile Networks

STEPHANIE LINDSEY and KRISHNA M. SIVALINGAM
School of Electrical Engineering and Computer Science, Washington State University

CAULIGI S. RAGHAVENDRA
Department of Electrical Engineering, University of Southern California

19.1 INTRODUCTION

Wireless data networks are increasingly becoming an important part of the next-generation network infrastructure. This is made possible by the availability of inexpensive wireless network devices such as Bluetooth [1] and wireless LANs [20]. The objective of these networks is to provide users with "anytime, anywhere" data access. The end-user devices range from small handheld PDAs to larger laptops. The computing and storage capabilities of these devices cover a wide spectrum.

One of the chief limitations of these wireless networks is the limited battery power of the network nodes. Therefore, power management is one of the challenging problems in wireless communication, and recent research has addressed this problem. Examples include a collection of papers available in [26] and a recent conference tutorial [21], both devoted to energy-efficient design of wireless networks. A summary of research done on energy-efficient network protocols is available in [11].

Wireless networks are typically classified as: (i) infrastructure networks, in which all end node communication is through a more powerful entity called the base station, which is connected to a wired network infrastructure; and (ii) ad hoc networks, in which end nodes establish a network among themselves and communicate with each other in a multi-hop manner. Newer types of networks such as the personal area networks (PANs) [9] and wireless sensor networks [16, 6] are becoming prevalent. These networks tend to be characterized as infrastructure, ad hoc, or hybrid.

This chapter specifically considers ad hoc networks and packet routing in these networks. Routing is a significant consumer of battery power since a packet is routed through many intermediate nodes before reaching its destination. Energy costs related to communication can be high in mobile nodes but this chapter only considers the costs related to routing. The design of energy-efficient routing protocols has attracted the attention of researchers in the past few years [4, 7, 22, 25]. This chapter presents a summary of some of this research ac-

Handbook of Wireless Networks and Mobile Computing, Edited by Ivan Stojmenović.
ISBN 0-471-41902-8   © 2002 John Wiley & Sons, Inc.

tivity. The objective is to outline the key concepts of the several proposed solutions in order to stimulate the design and implementation of more solutions to the problem.

19.2   BACKGROUND

This section provides a brief background on the different types of wireless networks and the basics of energy consumption issues.

19.2.1   Wireless Network Types

Wireless networks may be classified into these two different general categories:

1. *Infrastructure-based networks.* Wireless networks often extend, rather than replace, wired networks, and are referred to as infrastructure networks. A hierarchy of wide area and local area wired networks is used as the backbone network. The wired backbone connects to special switching nodes called base stations. They are responsible for coordinating access to one or more transmission channel(s) for mobiles located within their coverage area. The end-user nodes communicate via the base station using their respective wireless interfaces. Wireless LANs and WANs are a good example of this type of network.

2. *Ad hoc networks.* Ad hoc networks consist of radio-equipped nodes such as laptops and personal digital assistants (PDAs), which communicate with each other without a central authority. Ad hoc networks are characterized by dynamic, random, multihop topologies with typically no infrastructure support. The end users are assumed to be mobile, resulting in constant changes in network topology. Thus, mobility has a significant effect on protocol design and system performance. All nodes cooperate to maintain connectivity and packets are routed through the network in a multihop manner.

Mobile ad hoc networks have attracted considerable attention, as evidenced by the IETF working group MANET (mobile ad hoc networks). This has produced various Internet drafts, RFCs, and other publications [13, 14]. Also, a recent conference tutorial presents a good introduction to ad hoc networks [23]. Ad hoc networks have largely been studied for military applications, but they are expected to be used commercially in the near future.

Newer wireless network types, such as sensor networks and personal area networks, are beginning to emerge. Sensor networks consist of inexpensive sensor nodes that are deployed for data collection from the field [2, 5, 12]. A personal area network (PAN) is defined as a wireless network consisting of devices within 10 meters of an individual. Standardization efforts for PANs are in progress [9].

19.2.2   Sources of Power Consumption

The sources of power consumption, with regard to network operations, can be classified into two types: communication-related and computation-related.

Communication involves usage of the transceiver at the source, intermediate (in the case of ad hoc networks), and destination nodes. The transmitter is used for sending control, route request, and response messages, as well as data packets originating at or routed through the transmitting node. The receiver is used to receive data and control packets, some of which are destined for the receiving node and some of which are forwarded.

Understanding the power characteristics of the mobile radio used in wireless devices is important for the efficient design of communication protocols. A typical mobile radio may exist in three modes: transmit, receive, and standby. Maximum power is consumed in the transmit mode, and the least in the standby mode. Thus, the goal of protocol development for environments with limited power resources is to optimize the transceiver usage for a given communication task. Computation costs, involving packet processing and the CPU, are not considered in this chapter.

19.2.3 Routing Protocols

Routing protocols for mobile ad hoc networks can be categorized as on-demand and proactive. With on-demand protocols, the route selection process is initiated by the sender only when it has a packet to transmit. With proactive protocols, mobiles periodically exchange routing control packets (like OSPF or RIP in the Internet) and update their routing tables. The former approach results in fewer control packets and is more adaptive to topology changes, but leads to longer route setup delay before a packet may be sent. The AODV protocol (ad hoc on-demand distance vector) [15] is a good example. The latter approach requires more control packets but does not incur the additional route setup delay. However, it is possible that the precomputed route is incorrect, leading to potential lost packets. A survey of routing protocols for ad hoc networks is available in [19].

Since routing is an important and significant energy-consuming activity in ad hoc networks, research attention has been devoted to designing energy-efficient routing protocols. The rest of this chapter describes the various research efforts done in the area of power-aware routing protocols.

Section 19.3 describes work done on analysis of the energy consumption of the AODV and DSR routing protocols considered in the IETF MANET working group [7, 14]. Section 19.4 presents work described in [22, 25] on power-aware link metrics that enable selection of appropriate routes. Section 19.5 presents research reported in [4] that studies routing techniques based on balancing nodes' battery reserves to maximize network lifetime. Section 19.6 describes research done in design of energy efficient broadcast and unicast trees reported in [24]. Section 19.7 discusses work reported in [17] on the use of topology control to maximize the lifetime of the network.

19.3 ENERGY ANALYSIS OF AODV AND DSR ROUTING PROTOCOLS

This section reports work presented in [7] that evaluates the energy consumption behavior of two ad hoc network routing protocols: AODV (ad hoc on-demand distance vector) and DSR (dynamic source routing) [10, 15].

AODV and DSR have been well studied for their routing capabilities, but their energy characteristics had not been studied until now. Both protocols are deemed on-demand protocols since they discover and maintain routes only when needed. All network nodes participate equally in the routing process. These two protocols differ in that AODV is destination-oriented, based on the Bellman–Ford algorithm, and uses distance vector routing information. DSR is a topology-oriented source routing protocol that uses aggressive caching of network-wide topology information. More details on how these protocols work can be found in the respective references listed earlier.

Energy Cost Equations

Feeney [7] presents the energy calculations for various routing operations. In general, there is a fixed channel-acquisition cost and an incremental cost proportional to the size of the packet:

$$cost = m \cdot size + b$$

where m denotes the packet size multiplicative factor and b the fixed channel acquisition cost. The fixed cost relates to acquiring the channel, for example, as part of the medium access control procedure. The variable cost depends on the packet size, distance, receiver sensitivity, and so on. The total cost is the sum of all the costs incurred by the source and destination nodes.

Traffic is classified as broadcast traffic and point-to-point. For broadcast traffic, the sender listens briefly to the channel and sends data if the channel is clear. If the channel is not clear, the sender waits and retries later. Fixed channel-access costs and incremental payload costs combined in the previous equation result in a new cost equation:

$$cost = m_{send} \cdot size + b_{send} + \sum_{n \in S} (m_{recv} \cdot size + b_{recv})$$

where m_{send} is the unit cost for sending a byte, m_{recv} is the cost for receiving a byte, and S denotes the set of nodes that are in radio range of sender's transmitter.

For point-to-point traffic, the fixed cost includes channel access and the MAC negotiation. The incremental costs associated with the payload are the same as in broadcast traffic. Nodes which discard traffic also consume energy whose amount is dependent on the MAC implementation. Small control messages are assumed to have the same fixed cost for the sake of simplicity. The costs at the source are:

$$cost = b_{sendctl} + b_{recvctl} + m_{send} \cdot size + b_{send} + b_{recvctl}$$

and the costs for the destination are:

$$cost = b_{recvctl} + b_{sendctl} + m_{recv} \cdot size + b_{recv} + b_{sendctl}$$

The first two costs above are for the RTS/CTS message pair, the next two are for sending (receiving) the packet, and the final are for the ACK message. Since messages may be lost due to collision, the equations also factor in the total number of transmission attempts.

The nondestination nodes in the range of the sender overhear the RTS messages and data, whereas the nodes in the range of the destination overhear the CTS and ACK messages. The analysis considers nondestination nodes operating in promiscuous mode and otherwise. The cost for nodes not operating in promiscuous mode is:

$$cost = \sum_{n \in S} b_{\text{discardctl}} + \sum_{n \in D} b_{\text{discardctl}} + \sum_{n \in S} (m_{\text{discard}} \cdot size + b_{\text{discard}}) + \sum_{n \in D} b_{\text{discardctl}} \quad (19.1)$$

where $b_{\text{discardctl}}$ denotes the cost for discarding a control packet; b_{discard} denotes the cost for discarding a data packet, including the cost associated with entering a reduced energy state during data transmission; S denotes the set of nodes in the sender's transmit range; and D denotes the set of nodes in destination's transmit range. Feeney [7] also presents cost equations for promiscuous nodes, but those are not repeated here.

In the worst case, nodes receive packets and then ignore them if they were not destined for them. A more efficient strategy is for nondestination nodes to enter a reduced energy consumption state while the media carries uninteresting traffic. The Lucent WaveLAN IEEE 802.11 PC card uses the following strategy: based on the information size in the control message, nondestination nodes in the range of the sender and receiver enter a reduced energy consumption mode when data is being transmitted.

Some concerns of protocol designers were addressed in [7]. First, receiving a message incurs a high cost. If a broadcast message is received by approximately four neighbors, then the total cost of receiving the message is more than the cost of sending it. Second, the fixed cost of sending or receiving a packet is large compared to the incremental cost. For small packets, the fixed cost is greater than the incremental cost of sending or receiving. Source router headers are quite inexpensive in terms of energy consumption. Third, discarding a packet usually consumes much less energy than receiving it. Finally, although the cost of broadcast traffic is higher for receiving, point-to-point traffic has higher send/receive costs but allows nondestination nodes to discard traffic. If discarding costs are high, then the advantages of point-to-point traffic are collision avoidance and data acknowledgment. However, there are some substantial energy savings if discarding costs are low.

Simulation Results

A modified version of the CMU Monarch Project's mobility-enhanced ns-2 simulator was used along with the model to analyze the energy consumption of the routing protocols [7]. For the simulations, transmit and receive characteristics were based on specifications for the Lucent WaveLAN 2.4 GHz DSSS IEEE 802.11 PC card. The transmission range is 400 meters, and 50 mobile nodes were used for a 2400 m × 480 m network for 900 seconds of simulation time. The node density used was 10.9 nodes per 400 m radius. Each node waits a certain interval of time and then moves to a random destination at a constant velocity in the range of 0 m/s to 32 m/s, then the node waits again. The networks were either stationary or mobile with varying degrees of mobility. Twenty source–destination pairs were chosen and four 64-byte IP packets were sent to the destination each second.

DSR-np, a variant of DSR that does not include eavesdropping, was also studied in the analysis.

In summary, the results shows that although DSR is usually the most efficient in terms of bandwidth utilization, it is less energy efficient than AODV and DSR-np due to eavesdropping. The details follow.

Figure 19.1 shows the total estimated energy consumption with respect to traffic sent, received, dropped due to collisions, discarded, or received in promiscuous mode. Broadcast traffic is used in all three protocols for on-demand route discovery. DSR and DSR-np use this less often and more efficiently than AODV. For DSR and DSR-np, most routing traffic is sent point-to-point. The proportion of broadcast traffic is large enough to contribute to the energy costs. The amount of traffic received is so much larger than the amount of traffic sent that it accounts for 40–70% of the energy consumption.

Figure 19.2 shows the routing overhead energy consumption, which includes routing packets, source routing headers, and all traffic received in promiscuous mode (for DSR). DSR does not require the use of promiscuous mode. In DSR-np, only the forwarding nodes extract topology information from source routing headers. Therefore, nodes must initiate the route discovery process more frequently, resulting in higher energy costs for broadcast and point-to-point traffic. However, since overheard traffic can be discarded, energy savings outweigh the additional costs incurred. DSR-np reduces the cost of the route discovery process because rebroadcast messages are jittered in time to reduce the

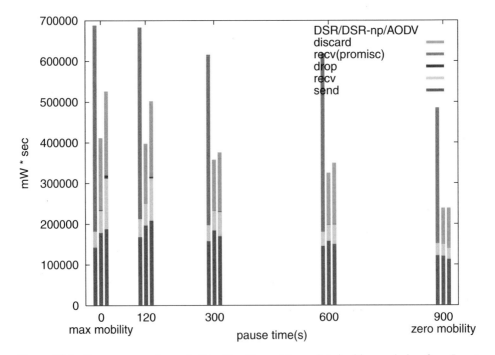

Figure 19.1   Energy comparison of all traffic. (From [7], reprinted with permission from Laura Feeney.)

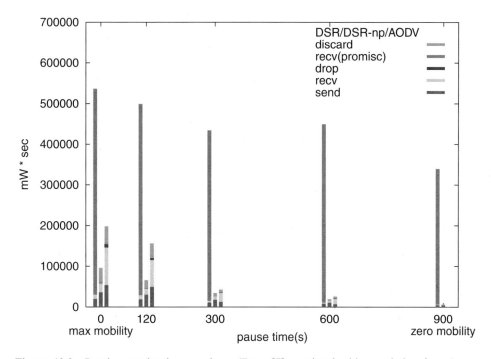

Figure 19.2   Routing overhead comparison. (From [7], reprinted with permission from Laura Feeney.)

risk of collisions. An expanding ring search, in which a sequence of hop-count-limited route discoveries limits the route request messages dispersed, is also used.

The results also show that operating in ad hoc mode of the network interface incurs a significant cost. Allowing the use of the low-power sleep mode will be important to the practical development of ad hoc networks. It will also be necessary for energy-aware protocol design in the future. Variable transmit power could be used in an ad hoc routing protocol that could also be used as a QoS metric for network-wide resource management and load balancing.

19.4 POWER-AWARE ROUTING METRICS

Typical metrics used to evaluate ad hoc routing protocols are shortest hop, shortest delay, and locality stability [25]. However, these metrics may have a negative effect in wireless networks because they result in the overuse of energy resources of a small set of mobiles, decreasing mobile and network life.

The research in power-aware routing protocols has considered two types of traffic: unicast and broadcast. Unicast traffic is defined as traffic in which packets are destined for a single receiver. Broadcast traffic is intended for all network nodes.

19.4.1   Global Information-Based Algorithms

In [25], routing of unicast traffic is addressed with respect to battery power consumption. The authors' research focuses on designing protocols to reduce energy consumption, increase the life of each mobile, and increase network life. To achieve this, five different metrics were defined: (i) energy consumed per packet; (ii) time to network partition, where the network is partitioned because of node death; (iii) variance in power levels across mobiles; (iv) cost per packet; and (v) maximum mobile cost.

In order to conserve energy, the goal is to minimize all the metrics except for the second, which should be maximized. As a result, a shortest-hop routing protocol may no longer be applicable; rather, a shortest-cost routing protocol with respect to the five energy efficiency metrics would be pertinent. For example, a cost function may be adapted to accurately reflect a battery's remaining lifetime. The premise behind this approach is that although packets may be routed through longer paths, the paths contain mobiles that have greater amounts of energy reserves. Also, energy can be conserved by routing traffic through lightly loaded mobiles because the energy expended in contention and retransmission is minimized.

The properties of power-aware metrics and the effect of the metrics on end-to-end delay are studied in [25] using simulation. A comparison of shortest-hop routing and the power-aware, shortest-cost routing schemes was conducted. The performance measures were delay, average cost per packet, and average maximum node cost. Results show that usage of power-aware metrics result in no extra delay over the traditional shortest-hop metric. This is true because congested paths are often avoided. However, there was significant improvement in average cost per packet and average maximum mobile cost, in which the cost is in terms of the energy efficient metrics defined above. The improvements were substantial for large networks and heavily loaded networks. Therefore, a more energy-efficient routing scheme may be obtained by adjusting routing parameters.

19.4.2   Local Information-Based Algorithms

Most of the routing protocols may be considered global algorithms that incorporate global topology and other information. Stojmenovic and Lin [22] consider the concept of localized routing algorithms in which routing decisions are made based on the location of a source node's neighbors and the destination. Their paper assumes that the nodes have global positioning system (GPS) receivers to provide location information to nodes, which allows the nodes to use the least transmission power needed for reception. The research considers networks that may be static, quasistatic, or mobile.

Stojmenovic and Lin define a new power cost metric based on the combination of a node's lifetime and distance-based power metrics. Power, cost, and power cost, GPS-based localized routing algorithms are also proposed. The goal of the power-aware algorithm is to minimize the total power needed to route a message from source to destination. The goal of the cost-aware algorithm is to extend a node's worst-case lifetime. The goal of the combined power cost algorithm is to minimize the total power needed and to avoid nodes with short battery lifetimes. Stojmenovic and Lin also show that the algorithms are loop-free—an important characteristic.

Stojmenovic and Lin generalize the model of Rodoplu and Meng [18] and assume that the power needed for transmission and reception of a signal is $u(d) = ad^\alpha + bd + c$ in order to include models that attenuate signal power of various exponents. The coefficient a depends upon the physical environment, unit of length considered, unit size of a signal, and so on. The distance between two nodes is denoted as d. The factor α represents signal attenuation and is adjusted depending on the model used. Typically, $\alpha = 2$ and $\alpha = 4$ are used for free-space and urban environments. The factor c represents energy consumption for activities such as computer processing and encoding/decoding.

General Concepts of Localized Algorithms

A localized algorithm defines each node as being capable of making forwarding decisions based on its own location, the locations of its neighboring nodes and the destination, and a constant amount of additional information.

It is assumed that every node stores the geographic location information of all other nodes in the network in its routing table. This includes the time when the location of the node is established. The location update is done as follows. The sender attaches its latest location to an outgoing message. Intermediate nodes may use their most recent location information, replace the location information in the header, and also update their own. Path adjustments can be made as the message travels closer to the destination. The routing table is only used to provide approximate location information of the destination node and accurate information about the location of neighboring nodes.

If nodes have information about the position and activity of all other nodes in the network, then Dijkstra's single source, shortest weighted path algorithm can be applied as the optimal power saving algorithm. For this algorithm, each edge has a weight of $u(d) = ad^\alpha + bd + c$, as described earlier. This paper [22] describes a corresponding localized routing algorithm. A source node or intermediate node, S, selects one of its neighbors, A, to forward a packet towards its destination node so that the power required to transmit from S to A is minimized. If we assume a triangle with vertices A, B, and D, where $r = |AB|$, $d = |BD|$, and $s = |AD|$, then the power needed for transmission from B to A is $u(r) = ar^\alpha + br + c$. It is assumed that the power consumption for the rest of the routing algorithm is optimal. This means the power needed for transmission from A to D is approximately $v(s) = bs + sc[a(\alpha - 1)/c]^{1/\alpha} + sa[a(\alpha - 1)/c]^{(1-\alpha)/\alpha}$. When α is equal to 2, $v(s) = 2s(ac)^{1/2} + bs$.

Power-Aware Algorithms

In the localized power-efficient routing algorithm, each node B selects one of its neighbors A that will minimize $p(B, A) = u(r) + v(s)$. If the destination node, D, is a neighbor of B, then the packet is sent directly to D if it reduces energy. D can be treated as any other neighbor, and the algorithm proceeds until the destination is reached, if possible. If looping is detected, then the algorithm stops. The algorithm attempts to minimize $p(B, A) = u(r) + tv(s)$, where t is a network parameter. In the experiments reported in this paper [22], t is set to one.

Another metric measuring a node's lifetime is studied in [25]. The cost of each node is represented as $f(A) = 1/g(A)$, where $g(A)$ stands for the remaining lifetime. This paper describes a localized version of this algorithm, and constant power for each transmission is assumed. The cost, $c(a)$, of a route from B to D using a neighboring node A is the sum of the cost $f(A) = 1/g(A)$ and the estimated cost of the route from A to D. Node B has knowledge of the cost $f(A)$ of each of its neighbors. It is assumed that the cost of the remaining nodes on the path between A and D is proportional to the number of hops between A and D. The number of hops is proportional to the distance between A and D and is inversely proportional to radius R. Thus, the cost can be represented as ts/R, where different values of t have been investigated. The cost definitions, $c(A) = f(A)ts/R$ and $c(A) = f(A) + ts/R$ are suggested for investigation, since it is not clear which will give the best results.

Then, power and cost factors are merged into a single routing algorithm. Merging based on the product or sum of the two metrics is proposed. In the first case, the power cost of sending a message from B to a neighbor A is represented as *power cost*$(B, A) = f(A)u(r)$, where r is equal to the distance between A and B. The power cost algorithm can find the optimal power cost by applying the single-source, shortest weighted path Dijkstra's algorithm. In the second case, it may be represented as *power cost*$(A, B) = \alpha u(r) + \beta f(A)$, with suitable values for α and β.

The power-cost-efficient routing algorithm can be described as follows. Let A be the neighbor of B that minimizes $pc(B, A) = $ *power cost*$(B, A) + v(s)f'(A)$, where $s = 0$ for D, if D is a neighbor of B. This algorithm is referred to as power cost 0 when *power cost*$(B, A) = f(A)u(r)$. Power-cost 1 refers to *power cost*$(B, A) = f'(S)u(r) + u(r')f(A)$. The packet is delivered to neighbor A. The packet does not have to be delivered to D when D is B's neighbor. The algorithm keeps running until the destination node is reached, if possible. The second term can be modified to compensate for different network conditions. A variation, power cost 2, minimizes $pc(B, A) = f(A)[u(r) + v(s)]$, and power cost P switches selection criteria from power cost to the power metric when destination D is a neighbor of current node A. Stojmenovic and Lin [22] provide proofs to show that these three routing algorithms are loop-free.

Simulation Results

Experiments are conducted using random 100-node unit graphs, as reported in [22]. The average node degree, $k = 10$, is controlled. Disconnected graphs are ignored. The distributed power efficient routing algorithm was seen to outperform the GPS-based algorithms for all network sizes. The results assume greater significance for a larger network. Also, the power-efficient algorithm produced paths close to the optimal ones (obtained by SP).

For the evaluation of cost and power-cost-efficient routing algorithms, it is assumed that nodes have different remaining powers. An iteration is defined as a routing task specified by a random choice of source and destination nodes. Experiments are run to determine the number of iterations until the first node dies. The simulations are run for 20 graphs for different network sizes and for HCB models [8].

Both cost functions and the different power-cost methods give similar simulation results. The performance of the proposed localized cost and power cost methods and the corresponding nonlocalized shortest path cost and power cost algorithms are found to be comparable. The cost and power cost algorithms last significantly longer in terms of iterations than the power algorithm. The average remaining power at each node after the network dies for the most competitive methods were analyzed. It was seen that the cost methods have more remaining power only when $m = 10$ (smallest network). Two better power cost methods leave about 15% more power at nodes than the cost method for larger values of m. Therefore, since networks will continue to operate after the first node dies, the power cost method may outperform cost methods.

The experiments do not give a complete answer to the selection of the approach that would maximize the life of each node in the network. The routing algorithms can be improved by multiplying the power cost for the remaining transmissions by a factor that depends on network conditions. Neighbor selection and power-efficient broadcasting can also be studied further. Finally, Dijkstra's algorithm runs in $O(n^2)$, and can be improved to run in $O[n \log(n)]$ using more complicated data structures. This may possibly result in higher time complexity for smaller networks.

19.5 ROUTING BASED ON BALANCED ENERGY CONSUMPTION OF NODES

Chang and Tassiulas [4] studied the problem of data gathering in static wireless networks, in which information is generated in certain nodes and is routed to a set of designated nodes. An example network is a wireless sensor network, where sensor nodes gather different types of data, such as acoustic, magnetic, and seismic data, and transmit it to a gateway node. This gateway node can have greater processing power for further processing of the information or have a larger transmission range to transmit to a larger network.

The study assumes that each node can adjust its transmitting power, which determines the set of possible one-hop neighbors. Multihop paths are used where one-hop communication is not possible. In [4], the authors studied the problem of routing from a single source to a single destination. They showed the problem of maximizing network lifetime to be a linear programming problem, solvable in polynomial time. They extended the study to the multicommodity case, in which each commodity is sent to a set of destinations. The paper focuses on trying to balance the energy consumption among nodes. It proposes algorithms that select routes based on remaining battery power levels and shortest cost paths instead of just selecting a minimum cost path. The algorithms are applicable to static networks or networks in which the change in topology is slow enough that there is enough time for optimally balancing the traffic between changes.

Each node is assumed to generate a set of commodities and each commodity is targeted to a set of destinations. The objective of the algorithm is to determine the flow partitioning of these commodities among the network links that will maximize the network partition time. A class of flow augmentation algorithms that use the shortest-cost path is presented. For determining the shortest path, each link between nodes i and j is associated with a cost, denoted by:

$$c_{ij} = e_{ij}^{x_1} \underline{E}_i^{-x_2} E_i^{x_3}$$

where the e_{ij} denotes the transmit power from node i to j, E_i and $\underline{E}_i$ respectively denote the initial energy and remaining battery power of node i, and x_1, x_2, x_3 are nonnegative weighting factors.

The link cost function is developed so that when nodes have a lot of battery power, the shortest-cost path is emphasized, but after the nodes' batteries have drained, the remaining battery power levels are emphasized. If $\{x_1, x_2, x_3\} = \{0, 0, 0\}$ then the shortest-cost path is the minimum-hop path. If it is $\{1, 0, 0\}$, then the shortest-cost path is the path with minimum transmitted energy. If $x_2 = x_3$, the normalized remaining battery power is used, and if $x_3 = 0$, the absolute remaining battery power is used. The notation $FA(x_1, x_2, x_3)$ is used to denote the algorithm with weight factors of (x_1, x_2, x_3).

Performance Evaluation

A total of 200 random graphs were generated to evaluate the performance of the proposed algorithms [4]. The performance of FA(1, 1, 1) and FA(1, 50, 50) were compared to the minimum transmitted energy (MTE) routing algorithm and the maximum residual energy path (MREP) routing algorithm proposed in [3]. The MREP algorithm uses a link cost function, $c_{ij} = (E_i - e_{ij}\lambda)^{-1}$, where λ is the augmentation step size. The metric measured is the ratio, R_X, of the maximum lifetime obtained using a given algorithm to the maximum lifetime using the optimal algorithm (described in [4]).

The results shows that $R_{FA(1,50,50)}$ is always over 0.99 of the optimal performance. FA(1, 1, 1)'s performance is comparable to MREP's performance. The system lifetimes of FR, MREP, and FA(1, x, x) where $x \geq 1$, are greater than 0.95 of the optimal, whereas MTE is only three-fourths of optimal. R_{FR} and R_{MREP} are over 0.9 about 90% of the time, whereas MTE is over 0.9 only 33% of the time. The algorithm gained a system lifetime of 49% to 55% compared to MTE. A similar study was conducted for the multicommodity case, in which the average gain in system lifetime obtained by the algorithms was between 40% and 62% compared to MTE.

19.6   BROADCAST AND MULTICAST TREE CONSTRUCTION

Wieselthier et al. [24] presents an algorithm for the construction of energy efficient broadcast and multicast trees for all-wireless applications. The multicast-based nature of wireless networks is exploited to construct the trees. The paper considers static wireless networks in which the locations of the nodes are fixed. The nodes are assumed to be distributed randomly over a region and capable of supporting several multicast sessions simultaneously. The power level of each node cannot exceed a maximum value p_{max}.

The power required to transmit from a node i to a node j is given by $P_{ij} = r^\alpha$, where r is the distance between the nodes i and j, and α is a constant between 2 and 4 that depends on the communication medium. The power required by node i in order to reach two nodes j and k is $P_{i,(j,k)} = \max(P_{ij}, P_{ik})$. This implies that all nodes within the communication range of the transmitting node can receive the transmission and the power required is the power required to transmit to the farthest node. This is referred to as the wireless multicast advantage.

To construct the minimum energy broadcast tree, two broadcasting methods are considered: (i) use a series of links, in which a node forwards to another, thus reaching all the nodes; (ii) broadcast with high power in a single transmission, reaching all the nodes. It is possible that the first method consumes less energy than the second. However, as the number of nodes increases, the complexity of the first approach increases.

Wieselthier et al. introduce the broadcast incremental power (BIP) algorithm, which uses the wireless multicast advantage to construct the minimum power broadcast tree, rooted at the source. The algorithm is as follows:

1. For all nodes i in the tree and all nodes j not in the tree, evaluate $P'_{ij} = P_{ij} - P(i)$, where P_{ij} is defined earlier, $P(i)$ denotes the transmit power level at of node i, and P'_{ij} denotes the incremental cost associated with adding j to the tree.
2. The pair $\{i, j\}$ that results in a minimum value of P'_{ij} is chosen, and j added to the tree.

This procedure is continued until all nodes are included in the tree.

The total power to maintain the tree is the sum of transmission powers at each of the transmitting nodes. The complexity of the algorithm is $O(N^3)$. The performance of the BIP algorithm is compared to two other link-based broadcast algorithms—the broadcast least unicast cost (BLU) and broadcast link-based MST (BLiMST) algorithms. Although the complexity of these two algorithms is $O(N^2)$, the BIP algorithm results in lower power expenditure. The authors also suggest a "sweep" procedure in the above algorithms to remove unnecessary transmissions.

For multicast traffic, the algorithms presented—multicast incremental power (MIP) algorithm, multicast least unicast cost (MLU) algorithm, and multicast link-based MST (MLiMST) algorithm—are analogous to the broadcast algorithms mentioned above.

Performance results of these multicast algorithms (broadcast is considered to be a special case of multicast) are reported for several randomly generated networks, assuming the maximum transmitter power (p_{max}) of each node to be infinity. The metric used is the total power of the multicast tree. Results have been presented for 100 network instances of 10-node and 100-node networks with $\alpha = 2$ and $\alpha = 4$. The results indicate that the MIP algorithm performs better than the MLiMST and MLU algorithms for network sizes of 10 or more. For smaller networks, the MIP algorithm performs better than MLiMST but not better than MLU.

19.7 TOPOLOGY CONTROL USING TRANSMIT POWER ADJUSTMENT

The previous sections focussed on routing techniques to minimize energy consumption, but Ramanathan and Hain [17] approach the problem by controlling the topology of the network. The premise of this work is that using transmit power control, the nodes' transmission reach can be varied to help create a topology with the desired energy consumption characteristics. (This is different from transmit power control techniques used for controlling the signal-to-noise ratio of two neighboring sources.) A network with a "wrong" topology can considerably reduce the capacity, increase the end-to-end packet delay, and decrease the robustness to node failures. A network that is sparse can cause frequent network partitioning and high end-to-end delays. Dense networks, on the other hand, can cause limited spatial reuse, thereby reducing network capacity.

The conventional representation of ad hoc networks contain edges between nodes that can communicate with one another. In this paper [17], the geographical locations, propagation characteristics, and node transmission parameters are kept separate. The input to the topology determination algorithm is the wireless network denoted by $M = (N, L)$, where N is the number of nodes and L the set of node coordinates, and a least-power function λ. The objective of the algorithms is to determine the appropriate topology and output the transmit power levels of the network nodes.

Topology Generation

Ramanathan and Hain [17] propose two centralized algorithms for static networks: one results in a connected network and the other a biconnected network. The paper considers a biconnected network for which the loss of a single node will not partition the network. This network also provides multiple-path redundancy between every pair of nodes enabling fault tolerance, load balancing, or both. The goal of the algorithm is to minimize the maximum transmit power rather than the total power over all nodes. This is because battery life is a local reserve and so collective minimization may not have much practical value. The two algorithms are shown to be optimal and to execute in $O(n^2 \log n)$ time.

In a mobile ad hoc network, the topology is presumed to be changing often. Therefore, the transmit powers of nodes must continually readjust to maintain the desired topology. Two distributed heuristics for topology control are presented: local information no topology (LINT) and local information link-state topology (LILT). These protocols differ in the nature of the feedback information used and the network property needed to be maintained. LINT uses locally available neighbor information collected by some routing protocol and attempts to place a bound on the number of neighbors. LILT also uses locally available neighbor information, but also makes use of global topology information that is available with some routing protocols. These protocols do not use any special control messages to operate.

Adjusting the transmit power can cause links to go up or down. In many routing protocols, this causes routing updates. With a large number of updates, the network bandwidth consumed will increase and the effective throughput will decrease as a result. To minimize this problem, LINT and LILT are incremental, meaning they calculate the new transmit powers based on the current values.

Performance Evaluation

The performance of the algorithms was studied by implementation in a wireless prototype testbed at BBN Technologies [17]. A psuedorandom mobility model was used. The system parameter varied was the node density (nodes per square mile). The performance metrics studied were throughput, maximum transmit power, and average delay.

In the first study, CONNECT and BICONNECT algorithms were compared to a system with no topology control. With no topology employed, the throughput was acceptable for a small range of density values. For a more sparse network, the network was poorly connected, and for a more dense network, interference reduced spatial reuse and hence capacity. Algorithm BICONN performed the best in terms of throughput and adapted well to changing densities. It improved the throughput by about 227% for densities above one node/sq mile. Algorithm BICONNECT used more power than CONNECT at lower densities. Also, only a few nodes's transmit powers were close to the maximum power. The paper concludes that even for a simple algorithm implementing topology control, the effect on throughput is significant. It is also concluded that at high densities, it is better to use BICONNECT instead of CONNECT. However, at low densities, the choice of algorithm depends on whether battery power conservation or higher throughput is more important.

The paper also compares the performance of LILT and LINT schemes. For density greater than 1 node per square mile, increasing density resulted in a decrease in throughput in all cases. For these cases, LILT and LINT cause the nodes to decrease their powers in order to reduce interference and increase throughput. The observed throughput gain with the two schemes (over a system with no adaptive algorithm) is about 53% for a density of two. LINT also performed better than LILT. The study also considered the dependence on delay but concluded that there was no significant difference between the LILT, LINT, and basic schemes.

19.8 SUMMARY

This chapter discussed recent research done on the design and analysis of energy-efficient routing protocols for wireless networks. The work presented included the analysis of energy consumption in ad hoc routing protocols, power-aware metrics, broadcast and multicast tree construction, topology generation, and power-balancing routing protocols. Much more work is required in this area, particularly in prototype and experimental research that demonstrates which of these techniques are feasible and understanding the performance gains.

ACKNOWLEDGMENTS

The first author is presently with Microsoft Corporation, Redmond, WA. The second author is currently on leave at Jasmine Networks, San Jose, CA. Part of the research was supported by Air Force Office of Scientific Research grants F-49620-97-1-0471 and F-49620-99-1-0125; Laboratory for Telecommunications Sciences, Adelphi, Maryland; and Intel Corporation. The authors thank Ms. Harini Krishnamurthy for her invaluable help in preparing this document.

REFERENCES

1. Bluetooth Initiative, http://www.bluetooth.com, 2001.
2. The WINS Project, http://www.janet.ucla.edu/WINS, 2001.
3. Chang, J. and Tassiulas, L., Routing for maximum system lifetime in wireless ad-hoc networks, in *Proceedings of 37th Annual Allerton Conference on Communcation, Control, and Computing*, Monticello, IL, September, 1999.

4. Chang, J.-H. and Tassiulas, L., Energy conserving routing in wireless ad-hoc networks, in *Proceedings IEEE INFOCOM*, pp. 22–31, Tel-Aviv, Israel, March 2000.

5. Estrin, D., Govindan, R., Heidemann, J., and Kumar, S., Next century challenges: Scalable coordination in sensor networks, in *Proceedings ACM MobiCom*, Seattle, WA, August 1999, pp. 263–270.

6. Estrin, D., Govindan, R., and Heidemann, J. (Guest Editors), Special issue: Embedding the Internet. *Communications of the ACM, 43*(5), 2000.

7. Feeney, L. M., An Energy-consumption model for performance analysis of routing protcols for mobile ad hoc networks. *ACM/Baltzer Mobile Networks and Applications*, in press.

8. Heinzelman, W., Chandrakasan, A., and Balakrishnan, H., Energy-efficient communication Protocol for wireless microsensor networks, in *Proceedings of Hawaii Conference on System Sciences*, January 2000.

9. IEEE, IEEE 802.15 Working Group for Wireless Personal Area Networks (WPANs). http://grouper.ieee.org/groups/802/15/, 2001.

10. Johnson, D. B., Maltz, D. A., Hu, Y.-C., and Jetcheva, J. G., The dynamic source routing protocol for mobile ad hoc networks. IETF Draft, MANET Working Group, 2000.

11. Jones, C. E., Sivalingam, K. M., Agrawal, P., and Chen, J.-C., A survey of energy efficient network protocols for wireless networks. *ACM/Baltzer Wireless Networks, 7,* 4, 343–358, 2001.

12. Heinzelman, W., Kulik, J., and Balakrishnan, H., Adaptive protocols for information dissemination in wireless sensor networks, in *Proceedings of ACM Mobicom 1999*, Seattle, WA, August 1999, pp. 174–185.

13. Macker, J. and Corson, M., Mobile ad-hoc networking and the IETF. *ACM Mobile Computing and Communications Review, 2*(1). (1998.

14. Macker, J. and Corson, M., IETF Working Group: Mobile ad-hoc networks (MANET). http://www.ietf.org/html.charters/manet-charter.html, 2000.

15. Perkins, C. E., Royer, E. M., and Das, S. R., Ad hoc on-demand distance vector (AODV) Routing. IETF Draft, MANET Working Group, 2000.

16. Pottie, G. and Kaiser, W., Wireless integrated network sensors. *Communications of the ACM, 43*(5), 51–58, 2000.

17. Ramanathan, R. and Hain, R., Topology control of multihop wireless networks using transmit power adjustment, in *Proceedings of Infocom '00*, Tel-Aviv, Israel, March 2000, pp. 404–413.

18. Rodoplu, V. and Meng, T., Minimum energy mobile wireless networks, in *IEEE Journal on Selected Areas in Communications, 17, 8*, 1334–1344, 1999.

19. Royer, E. and Toh, C. K., A Review of Current routing protocols for ad-hoc mobile wireless networks. *IEEE Personal Communications, 6*:46–55. (1999.

20. Salkintzis, A. and Mathiopoulos, P. T. (Guest Editors), The evolution of mobile data networking. *IEEE Personal Communications, 3*(2), 2000.

21. Srivastava, M., Tutorial: Energy efficiency in mobile computing and networking, in *ACM MobiCom Tutorials*, Boston, MA: ACM, 2000.

22. Stojmenovic, I. and Lin, X., Power-aware localized routing in wireless networks, in *Proceedings of the IEEE International Parallel and Distributed Processing Symposium*, Cancun, Mexico, May 2000, pp. 371–376.

23. Vaidya, N., Tutorial: Mobile ad hoc networks: Routing, MAC and transport issues, in *ACM MobiCom Tutorials*, Boston, MA: ACM, 2000.

24. Wieselthier, J. E., Nguyen, G. D., and Ephremides, A., On the aonstruction and energy-efficient

broadcast and multicast trees in wireless networks, in *Proceedings IEEE INFOCOM*, Tel-Aviv, Israel, March 2000, pp. 586–594.

25. Woo, M., Singh, S., and Raghavendra, C. S., Power aware routing in mobile ad hoc networks, in *Proceedings ACM MobiCom*, pp. 181–190, Dallas, TX. (1998.

26. Zorzi, M. (Guest Editor), Energy management in personal communications and mobile computing. *IEEE Personal Communications, 5*(3). (1998.

CHAPTER 20

Dominating-Set-Based Routing in Ad Hoc Wireless Networks

JIE WU

Department of Computer Science and Engineering, Florida Atlantic University

20.1 INTRODUCTION

An ad hoc wireless network is a special type of wireless network in which a collection of mobile hosts with appropriate interfaces may form a temporary network, without the aid of any established infrastructure or centralized administration. Communication in an ad hoc wireless network is based on multiple hops. Packets are relayed by intermediate hosts between the source and the destination; that is, routes between two hosts may consist of hops through other hosts in the network. Mobility of hosts can cause unpredictable topology changes. Therefore, the task of finding and maintaining routes in an ad hoc wireless network is nontrivial.

We can use a simple graph $G = (V, E)$ to represent an ad hoc wireless network, where V represents a set of wireless mobile hosts and E represents a set of edges. An edge between host pairs (v, u) indicates that both hosts v and u are within their wireless transmitter ranges. Unless otherwise specified, we assume that all mobile hosts are homogeneous, i.e., their wireless transmitter ranges are the same. In other words, if there is an edge $e = (v, u)$ in E, it indicates that u is within v's range and v is within u's range. Thus, the corresponding graph is an undirected graph called a unit graph, in which connections of hosts are determined by their geographical distances.

Routing in ad hoc wireless networks poses special challenges. In general, the main characteristics of mobile computing are low bandwidth, mobility, and low power. Wireless networks deliver lower bandwidth than wired networks and, hence, information collection (during the formation of a routing table) is expensive. Mobility of hosts, which causes topological changes of the underlying network, also increases the volatility of network information. In addition, the limitation of power leads users to disconnect mobile hosts frequently in order to save power consumption. This feature may also introduce more failures into mobile networks.

Traditional routing protocols in wired networks, which generally use either link state [21, 23] or distance vectors [15, 22], are not suitable for ad hoc wireless networks. In an environment with mobile hosts as routers, convergence to new, stable routes after dynamic changes in network topology may be slow; this process could be expensive due to low

Handbook of Wireless Networks and Mobile Computing, Edited by Ivan Stojmenović.
ISBN 0-471-41902-8   © 2002 John Wiley & Sons, Inc.

bandwidth. Routing information has to be localized to adapt quickly to changes such as host movement. Cluster-based routing [19] is a convenient method for routing in ad hoc wireless networks. In an ad hoc wireless network, hosts in a vicinity (i.e., physically close to each other) form a cluster or clique, which is a complete subgraph. Each cluster has one or more gateway hosts to connect to other clusters in the network. Gateway hosts (from different clusters) are usually connected. In Figure 20.1, hosts u, v, and y form one cluster and hosts w and x form another; v and w are gateway hosts which are connected. Backbone-based routing [6] and spine-based routing [7] use a similar approach. The backbone (spine) consists of hosts similar to gateway hosts.

Note that gateway hosts form a dominating set [14] of the corresponding wireless network. A subset of the vertices of a graph is a dominating set if every vertex not in the subset is adjacent to at least one vertex in the subset. Moreover, this dominating set should be connected for ease of routing within the induced graph consisting of dominating nodes only. We refer to all routing approaches that use gateway hosts to form a dominating set as dominating-set-based routing. The main advantage of dominating-set-based routing is that it simplifies the routing process to one in a smaller subnetwork generated from the connected dominating set. This means that only gateway hosts need to keep routing information. As long as changes in network topology do not affect this subnetwork, there is no need to recalculate routing tables.

Clearly, the efficiency of this approach depends largely on the process of finding and maintaining a connected dominating set and the size of the corresponding subnetwork. Unfortunately, finding a minimum connected dominating set is NP-complete for most graphs. In this chapter, we consider a simple and efficient distributed algorithm that can quickly determine a connected dominating set in ad hoc wireless networks. This algorithm is a localized algorithm [11], hosts interact with others in a restricted vicinity. Each host performs exceedingly simple tasks such as maintaining and propagating information markers. Collectively, these hosts achieve a desired global objective, i.e., find-

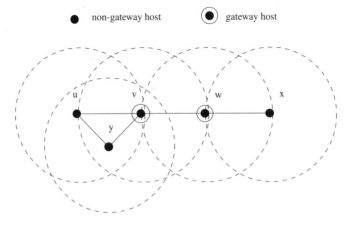

Figure 20.1   A sample ad hoc wireless network.

ing a small connected dominating set. It has been shown in [36] that this approach out-performs several classical approaches in terms of finding a small dominating set and does so quickly.

This chapter is organized as follows. Section 20.2 overviews the dominating set con-cept, dominating-set-based routing, and related work. Section 20.3 discusses the decen-tralized formation of a connected dominating set. Section 20.4 considers several exten-sions, including networks with unidirectional links, hierarchical dominating sets, power-aware routing, and multicasting and broadcasting. In Section 20.5 we summarize the results and discuss future research in this area. Throughout the chapter, the terms hosts, nodes, and vertices are used interchangeably.

20.2 PRELIMINARIES

20.2.1 Dominating Set

In the past quarter century, graph theory has experienced explosive growth concurrent with the growth of computer science. One of the fastest-growing areas within graph theo-ry is the study of domination and its related problems. Basically, a subset of the vertex set in a graph is called a dominating set if every vertex in the graph is in the subset or is adja-cent to an element of the subset.

The origin of the dominating set concept can trace back to the 1850's, when the follow-ing problem was considered among chess enthusiasts in Europe: Determine the minimum number of queens that can be placed on a chessboard so that all squares are either attacked by a queen or are occupied by a queen. It was found that five is the minimum number of queens that can dominate all of the squares of an 8 × 8 chessboard. The five queen prob-lem is about the placement of these five queens.

A real-life example of the dominating set concept is defining a school bus route within a school district (see Figure 20.2). In this figure, black nodes are dominating nodes (also called gateway nodes), and white nodes are dominated nodes (also called nongateway

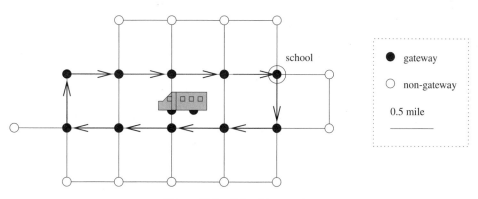

Figure 20.2 School bus route.

nodes). A bus route is defined based on certain rules. One such rule is that no student shall have to walk farther than, say, half a mile to a bus pickup point. In addition, the route is (strongly) connected. It is desirable that the length of the route be as short as possible. Other applications of dominating sets include radio stations, social network theory, and land surveying [14].

The domination number γ for a given graph is the size of the minimum dominating set. Finding the domination number for a given graph is an NP-complete problem. Therefore, most research in the graph theory community focuses on bounds on the domination number. Another area of focus is to determine special classes of graphs for which the domination problem can be solved in polynomial time.

20.2.2   Dominating-Set-Based Routing

Assume that a connected dominated set has been determined for a given ad hoc wireless network. The routing process in dominating-set-based routing is usually divided into three steps:

1. If the source is not a gateway host, it forwards the packets to a source gateway, which is one of the adjacent gateway hosts.

2. This source gateway acts as a new source to route the packets in the induced graph generated from the connected dominating set.

3. Eventually, the packets reach a destination gateway, which is either the destination host itself or a gateway of the destination host. In the latter case, the destination gateway forwards the packets directly to the destination host.

There are in general two ways to perform routing within the induced graph: proactive routing and reactive routing. In proactive routing, routes to all destinations are computed a priori and are maintained in the background via a periodic update process. In reactive routing, a route to a specific destination is computed "on demand," i.e., only when needed. In the following, we use the destination-sequenced distance vector routing protocol (DSDV) [26] as a sample proactive routing to illustrate the idea. It is critical to note that routing within the induced graph is not limited to proactive routing, which usually uses routing tables; reactive routing can also be applied. DSDV is based on the distributed Bellman–Ford (DBF) routing mechanism to construct routing tables. DBF is augmented with sequence numbers so that mobile hosts can distinguish stale routes from new ones, thereby avoiding the formation of routing loops.

Each nongateway host keeps an adjacent gateway list, whereas each gateway host keeps the gateway domain member list and gateway routing table. The gateway domain member list is a list of nongateway hosts that are adjacent to gateway hosts. The gateway routing table includes one entry for each gateway host, together with its domain member list. For example, given an ad hoc wireless network as shown in Figure 20.3 (a), the corresponding routing information at host 8 is shown in Figure 20.3 (b), which shows that host 8 has three members—3, 10, and 11—in its gateway domain member list. Figure 20.3 (c) shows the gateway routing table at host 8, which consists of a set of entries for each gateway and

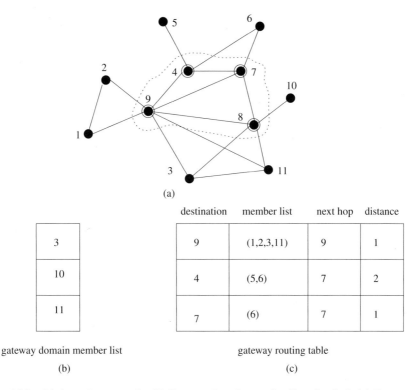

(a)

destination	member list	next hop	distance
9	(1,2,3,11)	9	1
4	(5,6)	7	2
7	(6)	7	1

3
10
11

gateway domain member list   gateway routing table

(b)   (c)

Figure 20.3   (a) A routing example. (b) Gateway domain member list of node 8. (c) Gateway routing table of node 8.

its member list. The third column of this table shows the next-hop information of a shortest path (here defined as a path with a minimum hop count) and the fourth column the distance (in hop count) to each destination.

20.2.3 Related Work

Routing protocols for wired networks can be classified into link state and distance vector schemes. The link state approach [21] runs the centralized version of a shortest path algorithm such as Dijkstra's algorithm. The distance vector approach uses the distributed Bellman–Ford (DBF) algorithm [18]. Both approaches are not suitable for dynamic networks, especially for quick-changing wireless networks such as ad hoc wireless networks. The main problems are computational burden, bandwidth overhead, and slow convergence of routing information. As indicated in [16, 26], these problems are especially pronounced in ad hoc wireless networks that have low power, limited bandwidth, and unrestricted mobility.

Various design choices are available for designing routing protocols for ad hoc wireless networks, they are:

1. Proactive versus reactive
2. Flat versus hierarchical
3. GPS-based versus non-GPS-based

Other classifications of routing protocols can be found in [29]. In a flat routing scheme, all hosts are treated equally and, therefore, any host can be used to forward packets between arbitrary sources and destinations. In general, a set of homogeneous processes is applied at each host. These processes include information collection, mobility management, and routing. To permit scaling, hierarchical techniques are usually applied. The major advantage of hierarchical routing is the reduction of routing table storage and processing (including searching) overhead [31, 33]. In non-GPS-based routing, the routing process is based solely on the connections of hosts in the network. In GPS-based routing, each host knows its physical location through geolocation techniques such as GPS. Routing is governed by physical location of the destination, that is, the packets are forwarded toward the destination based on the physical location of the destination.

Among hierarchical routing schemes, the cluster-based algorithm [19] divides a given graph into a number of nonredundant clusters that may overlap with each other. This approach can be considered as a restricted version of the dominating-set-based approach. Each cluster is a clique that is a complete subgraph. A cluster is nonredundant if it cannot be covered by a set of other clusters. One or more representative nodes, called boundary nodes, is selected from each cluster to form a connected subnetwork in which the routing process proceeds and this subnetwork forms a connected dominating set. Each boundary node has a complete view of the subnetwork captured by an associated routing table. In this way, the routing process reduces the whole network to a small connected subnetwork. The routing protocol is completed in two phases: cluster formation and cluster maintenance. Note that the initial cluster formation algorithm is fully sequential, causing a high computational complexity. The resultant cluster structure also depends on the order in which mobile hosts are examined in calculation. Lin and Gerla [20] proposed an efficient distributed algorithm for clustering. However, it is rather complex to maintain the cluster structure during host movement.

Das et al. [6, 7, 30] proposed a series of hierarchical routing algorithms for ad hoc wireless networks. Similar to cluster-based routing, the idea is to identify a subnetwork that forms a minimum connected dominating set (MCDS). Again, each node in the subnetwork maintains a routing table that captures the topological structure of the whole network. Each node in the subnetwork is called a spine node or backbone node (or gateway host in the dominating-set-based approach). The formation of MCDS is based on Guha and Khuller's approximation algorithm [13]. This MCDS calculation algorithm has several advantages over to the cluster-based approach [19]. The main drawback of this algorithm is that it still needs a nonconstant number of rounds to determine a connected dominating set. Other hierarchical routing protocols [4] exist that do not require cluster heads (dominating nodes) to be connected. However, a different mobility management method is used.

Johnson's [17] dynamic source routing (DSR) is a reactive approach without constructing the routing tables usually used in a proactive approach such as DSDV. Normally, the resultant routing path is not the shortest. However, this protocol adapts quickly to route changes when host movement is frequent, yet requires little or no overhead during periods in which hosts move less frequently. The approach consists of route discovery and route maintenance. Route discovery allows any host to dynamically discover a route to a destination host. Each host also maintains a route cache in which it caches source routes that it has learned. Unlike regular routing-table-based approaches that have to perform periodic route updates, route maintenance only monitors the routing process and informs the sender of any routing errors. One can easily apply Johnson's approach to dominating-set-based routing, in which route discovery is restricted to the subnetwork containing the connected dominating set.

Zone-based routing [25] is a compromise approach between proactive and reactive approaches. Each routing table keeps information for destinations within a certain distance (the corresponding area is called a zone). Information for destinations outside the zone area is obtained on an on-demand basis, i.e., through a route recovery phase as in DSR. Also, zone-based routing limits topology update propagation to the neighborhood of the change.

20.3 FORMATION OF A CONNECTED DOMINATING SET

As mentioned earlier, we focus on the decentralized formation of a dominating set. Some desirable features for such a process are listed below:

- The formation process should be distributed and simple. Ideally, it requires only local information and a constant number of iterative rounds of message exchanges among neighboring hosts.
- The resultant dominating set should be connected and close to minimum.
- The resultant dominating set should include all intermediate nodes of any shortest path. In this case, an all-pair shortest paths algorithm only needs to be applied to the subnetwork generated from the dominating set.

20.3.1 Marking Process

The marking process is a localized algorithm [11] in which hosts only interact with others in a restricted vicinity. Each host performs exceedingly simple tasks such as maintaining and propagating information markers. Collectively, these hosts achieve a desired global objective, i.e., finding a small connected dominating set. The marking process marks every vertex in a given connected and simple graph $G = (V, E)$. $m(v)$ is a marker for vertex $v \in V$, which is either T (marked) or F (unmarked). We will show later that marked vertices form a connected dominating set. We assume that all vertices are unmarked initially. $N(v) = \{u | (v, u) \in E\}$ represents the open neighbor set of vertex v. Initially, each vertex v has its open neighbor set $N(v)$.

The Marking Process

1. Initially, assign marker F to each v in V.
2. Each v exchanges its open neighbor set $N(v)$ with all its neighbors'.
3. Each v assigns its marker $m(v)$ to T if there exist two unconnected neighbors.

In the example of Figure 20.1, $N(u) = \{v, y\}$, $N(v) = \{u, w, y\}$, $N(w) = \{v, x\}$, $N(y) = \{u, v\}$, and $N(x) = \{w\}$. After Step 2 of the marking process, vertex u has $N(v)$ and $N(y)$, B has $N(u)$, $N(w)$, and $N(y)$, w has $N(v)$ and $N(x)$, y has $N(u)$ and $N(v)$, and x has $N(w)$. Based on Step 3, only vertices v and w are marked T.

Clearly, each vertex knows distance-2 neighborhood information after Step 2 of the marking process, i.e., neighbor information of its neighbors. The cost of checking the connectivity of two neighbors is upper bounded by $\Delta^2 (G)$ or simply Δ^2, where Δ is the degree of graph G, i.e., $\Delta(G) = \max\{|N(v)||v \in V\}$. There are $|N(v)|(|N(v)| - 1)/2$ possible pairs of neighbors of vertex v, which is upper bounded by Δ^2. Therefore, the cost of the marking process at each vertex is $O(\Delta^2)$. The amount of message exchange at each vertex is also $O(\Delta)$, which corresponds to the number of neighbors.

20.3.2   Properties

Assume that V' is the set of vertices that are marked T in V, i.e., $V' = \{v|v \in V, m(v) = T\}$. The induced graph G' is the subgraph of G induced by V', i.e., $G' = G[V']$. The following two theorems show that G' is a connected dominating set of G.

Theorem 1   Given a graph $G = (V, E)$ that is connected but not completely connected, the vertex subset V', derived from the marking process, forms a dominating set of G.

Proof: Randomly select a vertex v in G. We show that v is either in V' (a set of vertices in V that are marked T) or adjacent to a vertex in V'. Assume that v is marked F. If there is at least one neighbor marked T, the theorem is proved. If all its neighbors are marked F, we consider the following two cases.

  Case 1: All the other vertices in G are neighbors of v. Based on the marking process and the fact that $m(v) = F$, all these neighbors must be pairwise connected, i.e., G is completely connected. This contradicts the assumption that G is not completely connected.

  Case 2: There is at least one vertex u in G that is not adjacent to vertex v. Construct a shortest path path, $(v, v_1, v_2, \ldots, u)$, connecting vertices v and u. Such a path always exists since G is a connected graph. Note that v_2 is u when v and u are distance-2 apart in G, i.e., $d_G(v, u) = 2$. Also, v and v_2 are disconnected; otherwise, $(v, v_2, \ldots, u)$ is a shorter path connecting v and u. Based on the marking process, vertex v_1, with both v and v_2 as its neighbors, must be marked T. Again this contradicts the assumption that neighbors of v are all marked F.   □

When the given graph G is completely connected, all vertices are marked F. This is desirable, because if all vertices are directly connected, there is no need for gateway ·hosts.

Theorem 2   The induced graph $G' = G[V']$ is a connected graph.

Proof: We prove this theorem by contradiction. Assume that G' is disconnected and v and u are two disconnected vertices in G'. Assume $dis_G(v, u) = k + 1 > 1$ and $(v, v_1, v_2, \ldots, v_k, u)$ is a shortest path between vertices v and u in G. Clearly, all $v_1, v_2, \ldots, v_k$ are distinct; and among them there is at least one v_i such that $m(v_i) = F$ (otherwise, v and u are connected in G'). On the other hand, the two adjacent vertices of v_i, v_{i-1} and v_{i+1}, are not connected in G; otherwise, $(v, v_1, v_2, \ldots, v_k, u)$ is not a shortest path. Therefore, $m(v_i) = T$ based on the marking process. This brings a contradiction. □

The next theorem shows that, except for source and destination vertices, all intermediate vertices in a shortest path are contained in the dominating set derived from the marking process.

Theorem 3   The shortest path between any two nodes does not include any nongateway node as an intermediate node.

Proof: We prove this theorem also by contradiction. Assume that a shortest path between two vertices v and u includes a nongateway node v_i as an intermediate node; in other words, this path can be represented as $(v, \ldots, v_{i-1}, v_i, v_{i+1}, \ldots, u)$. We label the vertex that precedes v_i on the path as v_{i-1}; similarly, the vertex that follows v_i on the path is labeled as v_{i+1}. Because vertex v_i is a nongateway node, i.e., $m(v_i) = F$, there must be a connection between v_{i-1} and v_{i+1}. Therefore, a shorter path between v and u can be found as $(v, \ldots, v_{i-1}, v_{i+1}, \ldots, u)$. This contradicts the original assumption. □

Since the problem of determining a minimum connected dominating set of a given connected graph is NP-complete, the connected dominating set derived from the marking process is normally nonminimum. In some cases, the resultant dominating set is trivial, i.e., $V' = V$ or $V' = \{\ \}$. For example, any vertex-symmetric graph will generate a trivial dominating set using the proposed marking process. However, the marking process is efficient for an ad hoc wireless network where the corresponding graph tends to form a set of localized clusters (or cliques). The simulation results shown in [36] confirm this observation. When the transmission radius of a mobile host is not too large, the proposed algorithm generates a small connected dominating set.

20.3.3 Dominating Set Reduction

In the following, we propose two rules to reduce the size of a connected dominating set generated from the marking process. We first assign a distinct ID, $id(v)$, to each vertex v in G'. $N[v] = N(v) \cup \{v\}$ is the closed neighbor set of v, as opposed to the open one, $N(v)$.

Rule 1: Consider two vertices v and u in G'. If $N[v] \subseteq N[u]$ in G and $id(v) < id(u)$, change the marker of v to F if node v is marked, i.e., G' is changed to $G' - \{v\}$.

The above rule indicates that the closed neighbor set of v is covered by that of u and vertex v can be removed from G' if the ID of v is smaller than that of u. Note that if v is marked and its closed neighbor set is covered by the one of u, it implies vertex u is also marked. When v and u have the same closed neighbor set, the vertex with the smaller ID is removed. It is easy to prove that $G' - \{v\}$ is still a connected dominating set of G. The condition $N[v] \subseteq N[u]$ implies that v and u are connected in G'.

In Figure 20.4 (a), since $N[v] < N[u]$, vertex v is removed from G' if $id(v) < id(u)$ and vertex u is the only dominating node in the graph. In Figure 20.4 (b), since $N[v] = N[u]$, either v or u can be removed from G'. To ensure one and only one is removed, we pick the one with the smaller ID.

Rule 2: Assume that u and w are two marked neighbors of marked vertex v in G'. If $N(v) \subseteq N(u) \cup N(w)$ in G and $id(v) = \min\{id(v), id(u), id(w)\}$, then change the marker of v to F.

The above rule indicates that when the open neighbor set of v is covered by the open neighbor sets of two of its marked neighbors, u and w, if v has the smallest ID of the three, it can be removed from G'. The condition $N(v) \subseteq N(u) \cup N(w)$ in Rule 2 implies that u and w are connected. The subtle difference between Rule 1 and Rule 2 is the use of open and closed neighbor sets. Again, it is easy to prove that $G' - \{v\}$ is still a connected dominating set. Both u and w are marked, because the facts that v is marked and $N(v) \subseteq N(u) \cup N(w)$ in G usually do not imply that u and w are marked. Therefore, if one set of u and w is not marked, v cannot be unmarked (change the marker to F). To apply Rule 2, an additional step last step needs to be included in the marking process: If v is marked $[m(v) = T]$, send its status to all its neighbors.

Consider the example in Figure 20.4 (c). Clearly, $N(v) \subseteq N(u) \cup N(w)$. If $id(v) = \min\{id(v), id(u), id(w)\}$, vertex v can be removed from G' based on Rule 2. If $id(u) = \min\{id(v), id(u), id(w)\}$, then vertex u can be removed based on Rule 1, since $N[u] \subseteq N[v]$. If $id(w) = \min\{id(v), id(u), id(w)\}$, no vertex can be removed. Therefore, the ID assignment also decides the final outcome of the dominating set. Note that Rule 2 can be easily extended to a more general case where the open neighbor set of vertex v is covered by the union of open neighbor sets of more than two neighbors of v in G'. However, the connectivity requirement for these neighbors is more difficult to specify at vertex v.

The role of ID is very important for avoiding "illegal simultaneous" removal of vertices

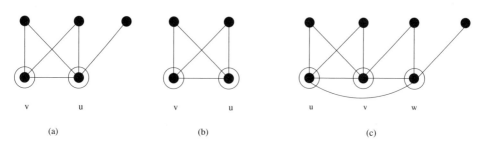

Figure 20.4   Three examples of dominating set reduction.

in G'. In general, vertex v cannot be removed even if $N[v] < N[u]$, unless $id(v) < id(u)$. Consider the example of Figure 20.4 (c) with $id(v) = \min\{id(v), id(u), id(w)\}$. If the above rule were not followed, vertex u would be unmarked to F (because $N[u] \subset N[v]$ even though $id(v) < id(u)$); and based on Rule 2, vertex v would be unmarked to F. Clearly, the only vertex w in V' does not form a dominating set any more.

20.3.4 Example

Figure 20.5 shows an example of using the proposed marking process and its extensions to identify a set of connected dominating nodes. Each node keeps a list of its neighbors and sends the list to all its neighbors. By doing so, each node has distance-2 neighborhood information, i.e., information about its neighbors and the neighbors of all its neighbors.

Node 1 does not mark itself as a gateway node because its only neighbors, 2 and 3, are connected. Node 3 marks itself as a gateway node because there is no connection between neighbors 1 and 4 (2 and 4). After node 3 marks itself, it sends its status to its neighbors 1,

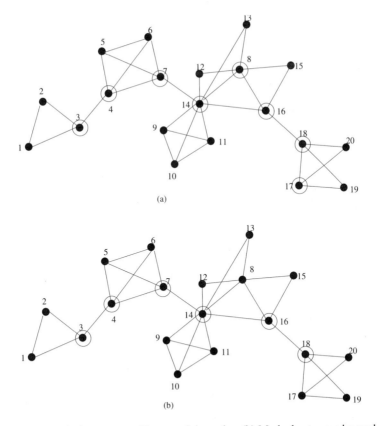

Figure 20.5 (a) Marked gateways without applying rules. (b) Marked gateways by applying Rules 1 and 2.

2, and 4. This gateway status is used to apply Rule 2 to unmark some gateway nodes to nongateway nodes. Figure 20.5 (a) shows the gateway nodes (nodes with double cycles) derived by the marking process without applying two rules.

After applying Rule 1, node 17 is unmarked to the nongateway status. The closed neighbor set of node 17 is $N[17] = \{17, 18, 19, 20\}$, and the closed neighbor set of node 18 is $N[18] = \{16, 17, 18, 19, 20\}$. Apparently, $N[17] \subseteq N[18]$. Also the ID of node 17 is less than the ID of node 18, thus node 17 can unmark itself by applying Rule 1.

After applying Rule 2, node 8 is unmarked to nongateway status, as shown in Figure 20.5 (b). Node 8 knows that its two neighbors 14 and 16 are all marked. This invokes node 8 to apply Rule 2 to check whether condition $N(8) \subseteq N(14) \cup N(16)$ holds or not. The neighbor set of node 14 is $N(14) = \{7, 8, 9, 10, 11, 12, 13, 16\}$, the neighbor set of node 8 is $N(8) = \{12, 13, 14, 15, 16\}$, the neighbor set of node 16 is $N(16) = \{8, 14, 15, 18\}$, and therefore, $N(14) \cup N(16) = \{7, 8, 9, 10, 11, 12, 13, 14, 15, 16, 18$. Apparently, $N(8) \subseteq N(14) \cup N(16)$. The ID of node 8 is the smallest among nodes 8, 14, and 16. Thus node 8 can unmark itself by applying Rule 2.

20.3.5 Mobility Management

In an ad hoc wireless network, each host can move around without speed and distance limitations. Also, in order to reduce power consumption, mobile hosts may switch off at any time and then switch on later. We can categorize topological changes of an ad hoc wireless network into three different types: mobile host switching on, mobile host switching off, and mobile host movement.

The challenge here is to find when and how each vertex should update/recalculate gateway information. The gateway update means that only individual mobile hosts update their gateway/nongateway status. The gateway recalculation means that the entire network recalculates gateway/nongateway status. If many mobile hosts in the network are in movement, gateway recalculation may be a better approach, i.e., the connected dominating set is recalculated from scratch. On the other hand, if only a few mobile hosts are in movement, then gateway information can be updated locally. It is still an open problem as to when to update gateways and when to recalculate gateways from scratch.

In the following, we will focus only on the gateway update for the three types of topology changes mentioned above. Without lost of generality, we assume that the underlying graph of an ad hoc wireless network always remains connected. We show that for both switching on and switching off operations, the update of node status (gateway/nongateway) can be limited to neighbors of the node that switches on or off.

When a mobile host v switches on, only its nongateway neighbors, along with host v, need to update their status, because any gateway neighbor will still remain as gateway after a new vertex v is added. For example, in Figure 20.6 (a), when host v switches on, the status of gateway neighbor host u is not affected, because at least two of u's three neighbors, u_1, u_2, and u_3, are not connected originally and these connections will not be affected by host v's switching on. On the other hand, in Figure 20.6 (b), host v's switching on may lead to non-gateway neighbor w to mark itself as gateway, depending on the connection between host w's neighbors w_1, w_2, and w_3. The corresponding update process can be as follows:

new link

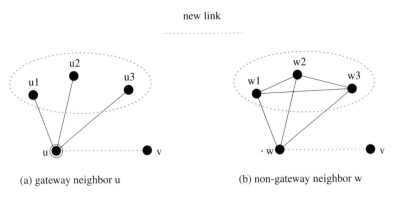

(a) gateway neighbor u   (b) non-gateway neighbor w

Figure 20.6 Mobile host v switching on.

Switching On

1. Mobile host v broadcasts to its neighbors about its switching on.
2. Each host $w \in v \cup N(v)$ exchanges its open neighbor set $N(w)$ with its neighbors.
3. Host v assigns its marker $m(v)$ to T if there are two unconnected neighbors.
4. Each nongateway host $w \in N(v)$ assigns its marker $m(w)$ to T if it has two unconnected neighbors.
5. Whenever there is a newly marked gateway, host v and all its gateway neighbors apply Rule 1 and Rule 2 to reduce the number of gateway hosts.

When a mobile host v switches off, only gateway neighbors of that host need to update their status, because any nongateway neighbor will still remain as nongateway after vertex v is deleted. The corresponding update process can be as follows.

Switching Off

1. Mobile host v broadcasts to its neighbors about its switching off.
2. Each gateway neighbor $w \in N(v)$ exchanges its open neighbor set $N(w)$ with its neighbors.
3. Each gateway neighbor w changes its marker $m(w)$ to F if all neighbors are pairwise connected.

Note that since the underlying graph is connected, we can easily prove by contradiction that the resultant dominating set (derived from the above marking process) is still connected when a host (gateway or nongateway) switches off.

A mobile host v's movement can be viewed as several simultaneous or nonsimultaneous link connections and disconnections. For example, when a mobile host moves, it may lead to several link disconnections from its neighbor hosts and, at the same time, it may have new link connections to the hosts within its wireless transmission range. These new links may be disconnected again depending on the way host v moves. Other details of mobility management can be found in [38].

20.4 EXTENSIONS

20.4.1 Networks with Unidirectional Links

In this subsection, we extend the dominating-set-based routing to ad hoc wireless networks with unidirectional links. In an ad hoc wireless network, some links may be unidirectional due to different transmission ranges of hosts or the hidden terminal problem [34], in which several packets intended for the same host collide and, as a result, they are lost. With few exceptions, such as the dynamic source routing protocol (DSR) [3], most existing protocols assume bidirectional links. Prakash [27] studied the impact of unidirectional links on some of the existing distance vector routing protocols such as destination-sequenced distance vector (DSDV) [26], and found that unidirectional links prove costly. It is shown that hosts need to exchange $O(|V|^2)$ amount of information with each other, where $|V|$ is the number of hosts in the network.

In a network with directed links, the domination concept has to be redefined. Specifically, an ad hoc wireless network is represented as a directed graph $D = (V, A)$ consisting of a finite set V of vertices and a set A of directed edges, where $A \subset V \times V$. D is a simple graph without self-loop and multiple edges. A directed (also called unidirectional) edge from u to v is denoted by an ordered pair uv. If uv is an edge in D, we say that u dominates v and v is an absorbant of u. A set $V' \subset V$ is a dominating set of D if every vertex $v \in V - V'$ is dominated by at least one vertex $u \in V'$. Also, a set $V' \subset V$ is called an absorbant set if for each vertex $u \in V - V'$, there exists a vertex $v \in V'$ which is an absorbant of u. The dominating neighbor set of vertex u is defined as $\{w|wu \in A\}$. The absorbant neighbor set of vertex u is defined as $\{v|uv \in A\}$. A directed graph D is strongly connected if for any two vertices u and v, a uv path (i.e., a path connecting u to v) exists. It is assumed that D is strongly connected. If it is not strongly connected, the network management subsystem will partition the network into a set of independent subnetworks, each of which is strongly connected. Other concepts related to graph theory and, in particular, directed graphs can be found in [2]. The objective here is to quickly find a small set that is both dominating and absorbant in a given directed graph. Note that the absorbant subset may overlap with the dominating subset. In an undirected graph, these two concepts are the same and, hence, a dominating set is an absorbant set.

To determine a set that is both dominating and absorbant, we propose an extended marking process. $m(u)$ is a marker for vertex $u \in V$, which is either T (marked) or F (unmarked). We will show later that the marked set is both dominating and absorbant.

Extended Marking Process

1. Initially assign F to each $u \in V$.
2. u changes its marker $m(u)$ to T if there exist vertices v and w such that $wu \in A$ and $uv \in A$, but $wv \notin A$.

Figure 20.7 (a) shows four gateway hosts, 4, 7, 8, and 9, derived from the extended marking process. Figure 20.7 (b) and (c) show gateway domain number at host 8 and gateway routing table at host 8, respectively. Node ids appended with subscripts a and d correspond to absorbant neighbors and dominating neighbors, respectively. A bidirectional edge (v, u) can be considered as two unidirectional edges vu and uv. Arrow dashed lines correspond to unidirectional edges and solid lines represent bidirectional edges. Note that the above extended marking process requires each vertex u to know only its absorbant neighbor set. Figure 20.8 shows three assignments of u, with one dominating neighbor w and one absorbant neighbor v. The only case in Figure 20.8 with $m(u) = F$ is when $wv \in A$, for each dominating neighbor w and each absorbant neighbor v of u. The fourth case, where v and w are bidirectionally connected [a combination of Figures 20.8 (a) and (b)], is not shown. Assume that V' is the set of vertices that are marked T in V, i.e., $V' = \{u|u \in V, m(u) = T\}$. The induced graph D' is the subgraph of D induced by V', i.e., $D' = D[V']$. Most of results for undirected graphs (Theorems 1 to 4) also hold for directed graphs, as shown in the following propositions. The proofs of these results can be found in [37].

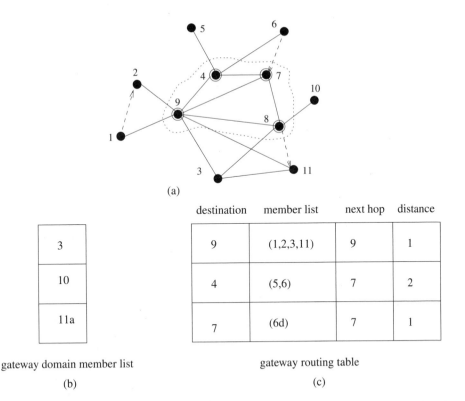

(a)

destination	member list	next hop	distance
9	(1,2,3,11)	9	1
4	(5,6)	7	2
7	(6d)	7	1

3
10
11a

gateway domain member list

(b)

gateway routing table

(c)

Figure 20.7 (a) A sample ad hoc wireless network with unidirectional links. (b) Gateway domain member list at host 8. (c) Gateway routing table at host 8.

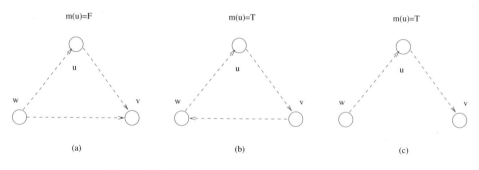

Figure 20.8 Marker of u for three different situations.

Proposition 1: Given a $D = (V, A)$ that is strongly connected, the vertex subset V', derived from the extended marking process, has the following properties:

- V' is empty if and only if D is completely connected, i.e., for every pair of vertices u and v, there are two edges uv and vu.
- If D is not completely connected, V' forms a dominating and absorbant set.

When the given D is completely connected, all vertices are marked F. This make sense, because if all vertices are directly connected, there is no need to use a dominating and absorbant set to reduce D.

Proposition 2: V' includes all the intermediate vertices of any shortest path.

Proposition 3: The induced graph $D' = D[V']$ is a strongly connected graph.

Propositions 1, 2, and 3 serve as bases of the dominating-set-based routing. The dominating and absorbant set derived from the extended marking process has the desirable properties of routing optimality (Proposition 2) and connectivity (Proposition 3). However, in general, the derived dominating and absorbant set is not minimum.

In the following, we propose two rules to reduce the size of a connected dominating and absorbant set generated from the extended marking process. We first randomly assign a distinct label, $id(v)$, to each vertex v in V. In a directed graph, $N_d(u)[N_a(u)]$ represents the dominating (absorbant) neighbor set of vertex u. In general, the neighbor set is the union of the corresponding dominating neighbor and absorbant neighbor sets, i.e., $N(u) = N_a(u) \cup N_d(u)$. Vertex u is called neighbor of vertex v if u is a dominating, absorbant, or dominating and absorbant neighbor of v.

Rule 1a: Consider two vertices u and v in induced graph D'. Unmark u, i.e., D' is changed to $D'_u = D' - \{u\}$, if the following conditions hold.

1. $N_d(u) - \{v \subseteq N_d(v)$ and $N_a(u) - \{v \subseteq N_a(v)$ in D.
2. $id(u) < id(v)$.

The above rule indicates that when the dominating (absorbant) neighbor set of u (excluding v) is covered by the dominating (absorbant) of v, vertex u can be removed from D' if the ID of u is smaller than that of v. Note that u and v may or may not be connected (they are bidirectional or unidirectional). The role of ID is very important in avoiding "illegal simultaneous" removal of vertices in V' when Rule 1a is applied "simultaneously" to each vertex. In general, vertex u cannot be removed even if $N_d(u) - \{v\} \subseteq N_d(v)$ and $N_a(u) - \{v\} \subseteq N_a(v)$ in D, unless $id(u) < id(v)$. Consider a graph of four vertices, u, v, s, and t, with four undirected edges (u, s), (s, v), (v, t), and (t, u). All four vertices will be marked using the extended marking process. Also, $N_d(u) = N_d(v) = N_a(u) = N_a(v) = (s, t)[N_d(s) = N_d(t) = N_a(s) = N_a(t) = (u, v)]$. Without using ID, both u and v (also s and t) will be unmarked, leaving no marked vertex. With ID, one of u and v (also s and t) will be unmarked, leaving two marked vertices.

Rule 2a: Assume that v and w are two marked vertices in D'. Unmark u if the following conditions hold.

1. $N_d(u) - \{v, w\} \subseteq N_d(v) \cup N_d(w)$ and $N_a(u) - \{v, w\} \subseteq N_a(v) \cup N_a(w)$ in D.
2. $id(u) = \min\{id(u), id(v), id(w)\}$.
3. v and w are bidirectionally connected.

The above rule indicates that when u's dominating (absorbant) neighbor set (excluding v and w) is covered by the union of dominating (absorbant) sets of v and w, vertex u can be removed from D' if the ID of u is smaller than those of v and w. Again, u and $v(w)$ may or may not be connected.

Figure 20.9 shows an example of using the extended marking process and its extensions (two rules) to identify a set of connected dominating and absorbant nodes. Figure 20.9 (a) shows the gateway nodes (nodes with double cycles) derived by the extended marking process without applying two rules. Figure 20.9 (b) shows the remaining gateway nodes after applying two rules.

Assume that V'_* is the resultant dominating and absorbant set when Rule 1a and Rule 2a are simultaneously applied to all vertices in V'. The following result shows that V'_* (its induced graph is D'_*) is still a connected dominating and absorbant set of V. The shortest path property of Proposition 3 still holds in D'_* for Rule 1a, but not for Rule 2a.

Proposition 4: If V' is a strongly connected dominating and absorbant set of D derived by using the extended marking process, then V'_* derived by using Rule 1a and Rule 2a on all vertices in V' is still a strongly connected dominating and absorbant set of V. In addition, if V'_* is derived by applying Rule 1 alone, then V'_* still includes all intermediate vertices of at least one shortest path for any pair of vertices in V.

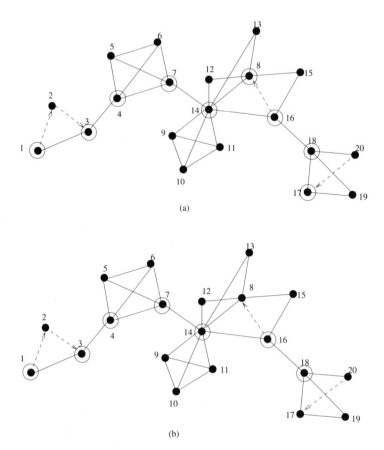

Figure 20.9 (a) Marked gateways using the extended marking process. (b) Marked gateways obtained by applying Rules 1a and 2a.

Actually, for each application of Rule 2a, the length of a shortest path (that includes u as an intermediate node) increases by at most one.

20.4.2 Hierarchical Dominating Sets

Hierarchical routing aggregates hosts into clusters, clusters into superclusters, and so on. If addresses of the destination host and the host that is forwarding the packet belong to different superclusters, then forwarding will be done via an intersupercluster route; if they belong to the same supercluster but to different clusters, forwarding will be done via intercluster routes; if they belong to the same cluster, forwarding will be done via intracluster routes.

The extended marking process can be applied to the induced graph to generate a dominating set of a given dominating set (here interpreted as dominating and absorbant set).

The resultant graph forms a supercluster. In this way, we can define a hierarchy of networks, with the original network being at level 1, the induced graph derived from the dominating set being at level 2, and so on. To evaluate the effectiveness of the extended marking process in obtaining a dominating set from a given unit graph, we introduce a concept called dominating ratio (DR), which is the ratio of the size of the resultant dominating set and the size of the original network. Clearly, $0 < DR \leq 1$. A small DR corresponds to a small dominating set. Unfortunately, the minimum dominating ratio is not known a priori. There are several lower bounds [14] of dominating ratio for graphs of different properties and these bounds can be used as references of comparison. In Figure 20.3, the DR at level 1 is 4/11 (four dominating nodes out of a total of eleven hosts in the network) and the DR at level 2 is 2/4, since nodes 7 and 9 form the dominating set at level 2 in the induced graph from nodes 4, 7, 8, and 9.

One critical issue in the design of a hierarchical structure is to decide on an appropriate level of hierarchy. The extended marking process is said to be ineffective for a given network if the corresponding dominating ratio is close to 1 or above a given threshold. A threshold can be defined in such a way that the benefit from the reduction of the network overweighs the cost of maintaining an extra level of hierarchy. If the extended marking process is applied repeatedly on the resultant graph (induced from the dominating set) until it is no longer effective, the corresponding level is called the maximum hierarchical level. Implementing hierarchical routing in a highly dynamic network requires sound solutions of several issues. Other than the dynamic formation of hierarchy, routing protocols must adapt to changes in hierarchical connectivity as well as changes in their connections to other mobile hosts.

20.4.3 Power-Aware Routing

In ad hoc wireless networks, the limitation of power of each host poses a unique challenge for power-aware design [28]. There has been an increasing focus on low-cost and induced-node power consumption in ad hoc wireless networks. Even in standard networks such as IEEE 802.11, requirements are included to sacrifice performance in favor of reduced power consumption [12]. In order to prolong the life span of each node and, hence, the network, power consumption should be minimized and balanced among nodes. Unfortunately, nodes in the dominating set generally consume more energy in handling various bypass traffic than nodes outside the set. Therefore, a static selection of dominating nodes will result in a shorter life span for certain nodes, which in turn will result in a shorter life span of the whole network. In this subsection, we propose a method for calculating power-aware connected dominating sets based on a dynamic selection process. Specifically, in the selection process of a gateway node, we give preference to a node with a higher energy level. The simulation results in [35] show that the proposed selection process outperforms several existing ones in terms of longer life span of the network.

Wu, Gao, and Stojmenovic [35] proposed two rules based on energy level (EL) to prolong the average life span of a node and, at the same time, to reduce the size of a connected dominating set generated from the marking process. We first assign a distinct ID, $id(v)$, and an initial EL, $el(v)$, to each vertex v in G'. In a dynamic system such as an ad hoc wireless network, network topology changes over time. Therefore, the connected dominating set also needs to change. Subsection 20.3.5 on mobility management shows that the connected dominating set only needs to be updated in a localized manner, i.e., only neighbors of changing nodes need to update their gateway/nongateway status. An update interval is the time between two adjacent updates in the network. Assume that d and d' are energy consumption in a given interval for a gateway node and a nongateway node, respectively. That is, each time after applying both Rule 1b and Rule 2b (discussed below), the EL of each gateway node will be decreased by d and the EL of each nongateway node will be decreased by d'. When the energy level of u, $el(u)$, reaches zero, it is assumed that node u ceases to function. In general, d and d' are variables that depend on the length of update interval and bypass traffic. Given an initial energy level of each host and values for d and d', the energy level associated with each host has multiple discrete levels.

Rule 1b: Consider two vertices v and u in G'. The marker of v is changed to F if one of the following conditions holds:

1. $N[v] \subseteq N[u]$ in G and $el(v) < el(u)$.
2. $N[v] \subseteq N[u]$ in G and $id(v) < id(u)$ when $el(v) = el(u)$.

The above rule indicates when the closed neighbor set of v is covered by the one of u, vertex v can be removed from G' if the EL of v is smaller than that of u. ID is used to break a tie when $el(v) = el(u)$.

In Figure 20.4 (a), since $N[v] < N[u]$, node v is removed from G' if $el(v) < el(u)$ and node u is the only dominating node in the graph. In Figure 20.4 (b), since $N[v] = N[u]$, either v or u can be removed from G'. To ensure that one and only one node is removed, we pick the one with a smaller EL.

Rule 2b: Assume that u and w are two marked neighbors of marked vertex v in G'. The marker of v is changed to F if one of the following conditions holds:

1. $N(v) \subseteq N(u) \cup N(w)$, but $N(u) \not\subseteq N(v) \cup N(w)$ and $N(w) \not\subseteq N(u) \cup N(v)$ in G.
2. $N(v) \subseteq N(u) \cup N(w)$ and $N(u) \subseteq N(v) \cup N(w)$, but $N(w) \not\subseteq N(u) \cup N(v)$ in G; and one of the following conditions holds:
   (a) $el(v) < el(u)$, or
   (b) $el(v) = el(u)$ and $id(v) < id(u)$.
3. $N(v) \subseteq N(u) \cup N(w)$, $N(u) \subseteq N(v) \cup N(w)$ and $N(w) \subseteq N(u) \cup N(v)$ in G; and one of the following conditions holds:
   (a) $el(v) < el(u)$ and $el(v) < el(w)$,
   (b) $el(v) = el(u) < el(w)$ and $id(v) < id(u)$, or
   (c) $el(v) = el(u) = el(w)$ and $id(v) = \min\{id(v), id(u), id(w)\}$.

The above rule indicates that when the open neighbor set of v is covered by the open neighbor sets of two of its marked neighbors, u and w, then in case (1), if the node v has the smallest EL among u, v, and w, it can be removed from G'; in case (2), if node v is covered by its marked neighbors, u and w, neither of u, v, or w has the smallest EL. Only when it satisfies Rule 2b can node v be removed from G'. The condition $N(v) \subseteq N(u) \cup N(w)$ in Rule 2b implies that u and w are connected. Again, it is easy to prove that $G' - \{v\}$ is still a connected dominating set. Both u and w are marked, because the facts that v is marked and $N(v) \subseteq N(u) \cup N(w)$ in G do not imply that u and w are marked. Therefore, if either u or w is not marked, v cannot be unmarked (change the marker to F).

In [35], another version of Rules 1 and 2 is proposed. Unlike Rules 1b and 2b, in which ID is used when there is a tie in EL, the version in [35] uses ND (node degree) when there is a tie in EL. ID is used only when there is a tie in ND.

20.4.4 Multicasting and Broadcasting

Various multicast schemes have been proposed for ad hoc wireless networks. Basically, two schemes exist in proactive approaches: shortest path multicast tree [10] and core tree [1]. The shortest path multicast tree approach is based on maintaining one multicast tree for each source. The core tree approach uses a shared tree (also called core tree) spanning the members in the multicast group. Packets sent to the shared tree are forwarded to all receiver members.

Here we take a look at another multicast approach based on dominating set; it is a hybrid of flooding and shortest tree multicast. This approach is similar to forwarding group multicast protocol (FGMP) [5]. A multicast group (MG) consists of senders and receivers (a sender can also be a receiver). A multicast initiated from a particular source has a forward group (FG). Any node in the FG is in charge of forwarding (through broadcasting, since the wireless medium is broadcast by nature) multicast packets to the MG, as in flooding. The difference is that although all neighbors can hear it, only neighbors that are in the FG will respond. In implementation, a forwarding table (FT) is a subset of the routing table consisting of destinations within the MG only. After the FT is broadcast by the sender, only neighbors listed in the next-hop list (next-hop neighbors) accept it. Each neighbor in the next hop list creates its FT by extracting the entries in which it is the next-hop neighbor, and so on through the routing table to find the next table. Note that the FTs are not stored like routing tables. They are created and broadcast to neighbors only when new FTs arrive.

Only gateway nodes are eligible to be forward nodes in the FG. If all receiver members of a forward node are itself and/or immediate nongateway neighbors, the node is a "leave" and it stops generating the FT. Depending on whether its member list is in the multicast group or not, the leave node may need to send multicast packets one more time. To form an FT at the source gateway, an entry is extracted from the associated routing table if its destination, one member of its member list, or both is in the multicast group. To distinguish these three cases, two bits are introduced that are associated with each entry of the FT: m_1 (for destination) and m_2 (for member list). $m_1 = 1$ ($m_2 = 1$) represents the fact that the destination (at least one member) is a receiver.

In dominating-set-based multicast, each gateway node keeps the gateway domain member list and gateway routing table. Two fields, m_1 and m_2, are added to each entry. In addition, nongateway nodes that are not in the multicast group are masked. (In this case, the m_2

field becomes optional when the member list mask is used.) Although each nongateway may have several gateway neighbors, it is assumed that each nongateway is tied to only one gateway neighbor.

Dominating-Set-Based Multicast

Given a multicast group MG:

1. If the source is a nongateway, it sends a MG to one of its adjacent gateways called a source gateway; otherwise, the source is the source gateway.
2. At the source gateway, the initial FT is constructed based on the routing table associated with the source gateway and the MG. In addition, m_1 and m_2 are attached. The FT is then broadcast to the neighbors together with multicast packets.
3. When a gateway neighbor u receives multicast packets,

   - u accepts a copy of the packets if u appears in the destination field of an entry and $m_1 = 1$.
   - u creates its FT by extracting the entries of the incoming FT in which it is the next-hop neighbor and constructs the next FT based on the routing table associated with u.
   - The FT (if any) is then broadcast to the neighbors together with the packets.

4. When a nongateway neighbor u receives multicast packets, it accepts the packets if u appears in the member list.

Figure 20.10 shows a sample multicast initiated from node 11, where MG = {4, 5, 6, 9}. Source 11 first sends multicast packets to the source gateway 8, where the initial FT is generated [see Figure 20.10 (b)]. Members in the member list that are not in the MG are masked. Note that node 6 appears in the member list of both nodes 4 and 7. It is assumed that node 6 is assigned to node 7 and, hence, it is masked in the member list of node 4. When node 4 receives the incoming FT [see Figure 20.10 (c)], it finds out that in the entry in which the next hop is 4, its destination is also 4; that is, node 4 is a leave. Because m_2 is set (i.e., at least one nongateway neighbor of node 4 is in the multicast set), node 4 needs to broadcast the packets once more to its nongateway neighbors.

Broadcast can be considered as a special case of multicast, so the above two approaches can also be used to carry out a broadcast. However, since broadcast covers all nodes in the network, the flooding approach is more efficient. In flooding, whenever a node receives packets, it will forward them to all its neighbors (except the one along the incoming channel) if the packets are not duplicates. However, straightforward broadcasting by flooding is normally very costly and will result in serious redundancy, contention, and collision. These problems are summarized in [24] and are called the broadcast storm problem. Stojmenovic, Seddigh, and Zunic [33] proposed significantly reducing or eliminating the communication overhead of a broadcast by using the dominating set concept. Specifically, retransmissions by gateway nodes is sufficient. In addition, Rules 1 and 2 are modified by using node degrees instead of node IDs as primary keys in gateway node decisions.

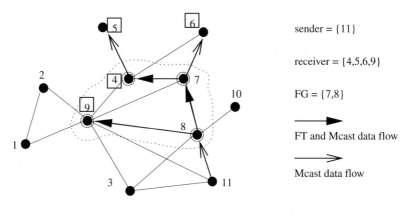

sender = {11}

receiver = {4,5,6,9}

FG = {7,8}

FT and Mcast data flow

Mcast data flow

(a)

destination	member list	next hop	distance	m1	m2
9	()	9	1	1	0
4	(5)	7	2	1	1
7	(6)	7	1	0	1

(b)

destination	member list	next hop	distance	m1	m2
4	(5)	4	1	1	1
7	(6)	7	1	0	1

(c)

Figure 20.10 (a) A sample multicast in an ad hoc wireless network. (b) The FT of node 8. (c) The FT of node 7.

20.5 CONCLUSIONS AND FUTURE DIRECTIONS

In this chapter, we have proposed a simple and efficient distributed algorithm for calculating the connected dominating set in an ad hoc wireless network. When the transmission radius of a mobile host is not too large, the proposed algorithm generates a small connected dominating set. Our proposed algorithm calculates connected dominating sets in $O(\Delta^2)$ time with distance-2 neighborhood information, where Δ is the maximum node degree in the graph. In addition, the proposed algorithm uses constant (1 or 2) rounds of message exchange, compared with $O(\gamma)$ rounds of message exchange in many existing approaches, where γ is the domination number. The search space for a routing process can be reduced to an induced graph generated from the connected dominating set.

One future direction of dominating-set-based routing is to integrate it with existing approaches. For example, the dominating set concept can be used together with location information obtained via geolocation techniques such as GPS. Some preliminary results have been reported in [9] and [32].

ACKNOWLEDGMENTS

This work was supported in part by NSF grants CCR 9900646 and ANI 0073736. The author wishes to thank Hailan Li, who participated in the early stage of this project. The author can be reached at jie@cse.fau.edu.

REFERENCES

1. T. Ballardie, P. Francis, and J. Crowcroft, Core based trees (CBT): An architecture for scalable inter-domain multicast routing, *Proceedings of ACM SIGCOMM'93,* p. 85, 1993.

2. J. A. Bondy and U. S. R. Murty, *Graph Theory with Applications,* Amsterdam: North-Holland, 1976.

3. J. Broch, D. B. Johnson, and D. A. Maltz, *The Dynamic Source Routing Protocol for Mobile Ad Hoc Networks,* IETF, Internet Draft, draft-ietf-manet-dsr-00.txt,, 1998.

4. C.-C. Chiang, Routing in clustered multihop, mobile wireless networks with fading channels, *Proceedings of IEEE SICON'97,* p. 197, 1997.

5. C.-C. Chiang, M. Gerla, and L. Zhang, Forwarding group multicast protocol (FGMP) for multihop, mobile wireless networks, *Cluster Computing, 1,* 2, 187, 1998.

6. B. Das, E. Sivakumar, and V. Bhargavan, Routing in ad hoc networks using a virtual backbone, *Proceedings of the 6th International Conference on Computer Communications and Networks (IC3N'97),* 1997.

7. B. Das, E. Sivakumar, and V. Bhargavan, Routing in ad hoc networks using a spine, *IEEE International Conference on Computers and Communications Networks (ICC'97),* 1997.

8. B. Das and V. Bhargavan, Routing in ad hoc networks using minimum connected dominating sets, *IEEE International Conference on Communications (ICC'97),* 1997.

9. S. Datta, I. Stojmenovic, and J. Wu, Internal nodes and shortcut cased routing with guaranteed delivery in wireless networks, in *Proceedings of the International Workshop on Wireless Networks and Mobile Computing* (in conjunction with ICDCS 2001), p. 461, 2001.

10. S. E. Deering and D. R. Cheriton, Multicast routing in datagram internetworks and extended LANs, *ACM Transactions on Computer Systems, 8,* 85, 1990.

11. D. Estrin, R. Govindan, J. Heidemann, and S. Kumar, Next century challenges: Scalable coordination in sensor networks, *Proceedings of ACM MOBICOM'99,* p. 263, 1999.

12. IEEE Standards Departments, *IEEE Draft Standard—Wireless LAN,* New York: IEEE Press, 1996.

13. S. Guha and S. Khuller, Approximation algorithms for connected dominating sets, *Algorithmica, 20*, 4, 374, 1998.

14. T. W. Haynes, S. T. Hedetniemi, and P. J. Slater, *Fundamentals of Domination in Graphs,* New York: Marcel Dekker,, 1998.

15. C. Hedrick, Routing Information protocol, *Internet Request For Comments RFC 1058*, 1998.

16. D. B. Johnson, Routing in ad hoc networks of mobile hosts, *Proceedings of the IEEE Workshop on Mobile Computing Systems and Applications*, p. 158, 1994.

17. D. B. Johnson and D. A. Maltz, Dynamic source routing in ad hoc wireless networks, in *Mobile Computing,* T. Imielinski and H. F. Korth (Eds.), Norwood, MA: Kluwer Academic Publishers, p. 153, 1996.

18. J. Jubin and J. D. Tornow, The DARPA packet radio network protocols, *Proceedings of the IEEE, 75*, 1, 21, 1987.

19. P. Krishna, M. Chatterjee, N. H. Vaidya, and D. K. Pradhan, A cluster-based approach for routing in ad hoc networks, *Proceedings of the 2nd USENIX Symposium on Mobile and Location-Independent Computing,* p. 1, 1995.

20. C. R. Lin and M. Gerla, Adaptive clustering for mobile wireless networks, *IEEE Journal on Selected Areas in Communications, 15,* 7, 1265, 1997.

21. J. M. McQuillan, I. Richer, and E. C. Rosen, The new routing algorithm for ARPANET, *IEEE Transactions on Communications, 28*, 5, 171, 1980.

22. J. M. McQuillan and D. C. Walden, The ARPA network design decisions, *Computer Networks, 1*, 5, 243, 1977.

23. J. Moy, OSPF Version 2, *Internet Request For Comments RFC 1247*, 1991.

24. S. Y. Ni, Y. C. Tseng, Y. S. Chen, and J. P. Sheu, The broadcast storm problem in a mobile ad hoc network, *Proceedings of ACM MOBICOM'99,* p. 151, 1999.

25. M. R. Pearlman and Z. J. Hass, Determining the optimal configuration for the zone routing protocol, *IEEE Journal on Selected Areas in Communications, 17*, 8, 1395, 1999.

26. C. E. Perkins and E. M. Royer, Highly Dynamic destination-sequenced distance-vector routing (DSDV) for mobile computers, *Proceedings of ACM SIGCOMM'94,* p. 234, 1994.

27. R. Prakash, Unidirectional links prove costly in wireless ad hoc networks, *Proceedings of the 3rd International Workshop on Discrete Algorithms and Methods for Mobile Computing and Communications,* p. 15, 1999.

28. C. Rohl, H. Woesner, and A. Wolisz, A short look on power saving mechanisms in the wireless LAN Standard Draft IEEE 802.11, *Proceedings of the 6th WINLAB Workshop on Third Generation Wireless Systems,* 1997.

29. E. M. Royer and C. -K. Toh, A review of current routing protocols for ad hoc mobile wireless networks, *IEEE Personal Communications,6,* 2, 46, 1999.

30. R. Sivakumar, B. Das, and V. Bhargavan, An improved spine-based infrastructure for routing in ad hoc networks, *Proceedings of the International Symposium on Computers and Communications (ISCC'98),* 1998.

31. M. Steenstrup, *Routing in Communications Networks*, Upper Saddle River, NJ: Prentice Hall,, 1995.

32. I. Stojmenovic and X. Lin, GEDIR: Loop-free location based routing in wireless networks, *IASETED International Conference on Parallel and Distributed Computing and Systems,* p. 1025, 1999.

33. I. Stojmenovic, M. Seddigh, and J. Zunic, Internal node based broadcasting algorithms in wireless networks *Proceedings of the 34th Annual IEEE Hawaii International. Conference on System Sciences*, 2001.

34. A. Tanenbaum, *Computer Networks*, Upper Saddle River, NJ: Prentice Hall,, 1996.

35. J. Wu, M. Gao, and I. Stojmenovic, On calculating power-aware connected dominating sets for efficient routing in ad hoc wireless networks, Technical Report, FAU-CSE-01 – 03, Florida Atlantic University, Feb., 2001.

36. J. Wu and H. Li, On calculating connected dominating set for efficient routing in ad hoc wireless networks, *Proceedings of the 3rd International Workshop on Discrete Algorithms and Methods for Mobile Computing and Communications,* p. 7, 1999.

37. J. Wu and H. Li, Domination and its applications in ad hoc wireless networks with unidirectional links, *Proceedings of the 2000 International Conference on Parallel Processing,* p. 189, 2000.

38. J. Wu and H. Li, A Dominating set based routing scheme in ad hoc wireless networks, *Telecommunication Systems Journal,* Special issue on wireless networks, *18,* 1–3, 13, 2001.

CHAPTER 21

Location Updates for Efficient Routing in Ad Hoc Networks

IVAN STOJMENOVIĆ

DISCA, IIMAS, UNAM, Universidad Nacional Autonoma de Mexico

21.1 INTRODUCTION

Mobile ad hoc networks consist of wireless hosts that communicate with each other in the absence of a fixed infrastructure. Some examples of the possible uses of ad hoc networking include soldiers on the battlefield, emergency disaster relief personnel, and networks of laptops. Sensor networks are a similar kind of network that have recently been investigated. Nodes in a sensor network are lighter, computationally less powerful, and more likely to be static compared to nodes in an ad hoc network. Hundreds or thousands of such nodes may be placed to monitor and control a physical environment from possibly remote locations. These nodes frequently switch their activity status to preserve battery power, which poses additional challenges for the design of efficient data collection algorithms. Ad hoc and sensor networks are self-organized and collaborative. Zero configuration networking is also required for environments in which administration is impractical or impossible, such as home or small offices or embedded systems "plugged together" (as in an automobile), or for allowing impromptu networks between the devices of strangers on a train [50].

In this chapter, we consider the routing task in which a message is to be sent from a source node to a destination node. Due to propagation path loss, the transmission radii are limited. Thus, routes between two hosts in a network may consist of hops through other hosts in the network. The task of finding and maintaining routes in the network is nontrivial since host mobility causes frequent unpredictable topological changes. "Sleep period operation" (when some nodes become temporarily inactive) poses additional challenges for routing protocols.

Macker and Corson [35] listed qualitative and quantitative independent metrics for judging the performance of routing protocols. Desirable qualitative properties include: distributed operation, loop-freedom (to avoid the worst-case scenario of a small fraction of packets spinning around in the network), demand-based operation, and "sleep period operation." Some quantitative metrics that are appropriate for assessing the performance of any routing protocol include [35] end-to-end data delay and average number of data bits (or control bits) transmitted per data bits delivered. Our review (with primary interest in location-based techniques) indicates that most proposed routing algorithms (more precisely, their performance evaluations) ignore one or more of these important metrics.

Ad hoc networks are best modeled by minpower graphs constructed in the following way. Each node A has its transmission range $t(A)$. Two nodes A and B in the network are neighbors (and thus joined by an edge) if the Euclidean distance between their coordinates in the network is less than the minimum between their transmission radii (i.e., $d(A, B) <$ min $\{t(A), t(B)\}$. If all transmission ranges are equal, the corresponding graph is known as the unit graph. In the unit graph model, forwarded messages simultaneously provide acknowledgments for received messages. The minpower and unit graphs are valid models when there are no obstacles in the signal path (e.g., a building). Ad hoc networks with obstacles can be modeled by subgraphs of minpower or unit graphs. Most papers use unit graphs for the performance evaluation of proposed routing protocols.

In the next section, we classify existing routing algorithms according to a number of criteria. This section will also review a number of routing protocols. In Section 21.3, location updates between neighboring nodes are discussed. Sections 21.4 through 21.7 describe several existing location update methods. Priority is given to newer algorithms with novel approaches. Performance evaluation issues are discussed in Section 21.8. The reference section gives an extensive list of relevant articles.

21.2 CLASSIFICATION OF ROUTING ALGORITHMS

We shall now review the main characteristics of proposed routing algorithms in light of desired qualitative and quantitative properties [35] and a few additional characteristics.

21.2.1 Demand-Based Operation

Routing algorithms can be classified as proactive or reactive. Proactive protocols maintain routing tables when nodes move, independently of traffic demand, and thus may have unacceptable overhead when data traffic is considerably lower than mobility rate. For instance, shortest- (weighted) path-based-solutions [3, 43, 45] are too sensitive to small changes in local topology and activity status (the later even does not involve node movement). The communication overhead involved in maintaining global information about the networks is not acceptable for networks whose bandwidth and battery power are severely limited. They are not elaborated on further in this chapter.

Routes in reactive algorithms are established when they are needed, in order to minimize the communication overhead. They are adaptive to "sleep period" operation, since inactive nodes simply do not participate at the time the route is established. One of well-known reactive algorithms is the source-initiated, on-demand routing strategy [5, 22, 41, 44, 45]. In this strategy, the source or intermediate node S issues destination search request if the route to destination D is not available. The destination search is performed by flooding a "short" search message, so that each node in the network is reached. Flooding algorithms that reduce the number of retransmissions are surveyed and discussed in [50]. The path to destination is memorized in the process [5, 22, 41, 44, 45]. A variant of this strategy is proposed in [53]. Several search "tickets" (each ticket is a "short" message containing the sender's ID and location, the destination's ID and best-known location and time when that location was reported, and a constant amount of additional information) that will look for the exact position of the destination node are issued by source S. When the first ticket arrives at the destination node D, D will report back to the source with a brief message containing its exact location, and possibly create a route for the source (the second phase). In the third phase, the source node then sends a full data message ("long" message) toward the exact location of destination. The efficiency of destination search depends on the corresponding location update scheme. A quorum-based, home-agent-based, and depth-first-search-based destination search and corresponding location update schemes are being developed [49, 53, 54]. Other location update and destination search schemes may be used, including an occasional flooding. If the routing problem is divided as described, the mobility issue can be algorithmically separated from the routing issue, allowing the application of routing algorithms with known destination in the second and third phases of the protocol. The choice is justified whenever the destination does not move significantly between its detection and message delivery, and information about neighboring nodes is regularly maintained. In the described approach, the communication overhead of routing algorithm is divided into the following components: location updates, destination searches (performed in accordance to location update scheme), and path creation (or reporting from destination back to source).

An interesting compromise between proactive and reactive methods is proposed in [7]. The algorithm is destination-initiated: a destination initiates a global path computation to itself using dynamic link metrics, which include a measure of "hotness" of the particular destination and congestion in the vicinity of the destination. The updated routes are shortest cost path routes, where queue length at each link (which is proportional to delay) is taken as the cost measure.

21.2.2 Distributed Operation

We shall divide all distributed routing algorithms into localized and nonlocalized. Localized algorithms [12] are distributed algorithms that resemble greedy algorithms in which simple local behavior achieves a desired global objective. In a localized routing algorithm [4, 6, 14, 28, 29, 47–49, 55], each node makes the decision of which neighbor to forward the message based solely on the location of itself, its neighboring nodes, and the destination. Although neighboring nodes may update each other's location whenever an edge is broken or created, the accuracy of destination location is a serious problem. In some cases such as monitoring the environment by sensor networks, the destination is a fixed node known to all nodes (i.e., monitoring center). Localized algorithms are directly applicable in such environments. Otherwise, they may use destination search as the first step, routing short messages from destination to source as the second, and, finally, routing full message from source to destination. Localized routing algorithms that guarantee delivery [6, 11] (assuming that the destination location is accurate and message transmissions by nodes on the route do not collide with other traffic) show that localized algorithms can nearly match the performance of shortest path algorithms. All nonlocalized routing algorithms proposed in the literature are variations of shortest weighted path algorithm [3, 5, 9, 22, 32, 41, 43]. Zone-based approaches combining shortest paths within a zone and interzonal destination searches or routing tables are elaborated in [23, 33]. In zone-based routing algorithms [23], nodes are divided into nonoverlapping zones. Each node only knows node connectivity within its own zone, and routing within the zone is performed directly. If the destination is outside the zone, one location request is sent to every zone to find the destination. This seems to add significant overhead, indicating that combined requests in this planar interzonal graph should be designed instead. Additional problems may arise when nodes within the same zone are disconnected and neighboring zones are not reachable from all nodes within a zone. Thus, this promising protocol needs further development. A zone-based protocol that does not use location information of nodes is described in [21]. GRID protocol [33] selects one node in each grid or zone, and these nodes serve as the backbone for routing tasks.

21.2.3   Location Information

Most proposed routing algorithms do not use the location of nodes, that is, their coordinates in two- or three-dimensional space, in routing decisions [5, 23, 44, 45]. The distance between neighboring nodes can be estimated on the basis of incoming signal strengths (if some control messages are sent using fixed power). Relative coordinates of neighboring nodes can be obtained by exchanging such information between neighbors. Alternatively, the location of nodes may be available directly by communicating with a satellite through GPS (Global Positioning System) if nodes are equipped with a small low-power GPS receiver. We believe that the advantages of using location information outweigh the cost of additional hardware, if any. The distance information, for instance, allows nodes to adjust their transmission powers and reduce transmission power accordingly. This enables using power, cost, and power cost metrics [10, 43, 48] and corresponding routing algorithms [48] in order to minimize energy required per routing task and to maximize the number of routing tasks that a network can perform. Routing tables that are updated by mobile software agents modeled on ants are used in [8]. Ants collect and disseminate location information about nodes.

21.2.4   Single-Path versus Multipath Strategies

There exist several multipath, full-message strategies in which each node on the path sends a full message to several neighbors that are best choices for all possible destination positions [4]. There is significant communication overhead, and lack of guaranteed delivery can make this approach inferior to even a simple flooding algorithm. Clever flooding algorithms may use about half of the nodes only for retransmissions [50], which often matches the number of nodes participating in routing in this method. In addition, flooding guarantees delivery and requires no prior location updates for improved efficiency. In [20], it was argued that flooding is the best routing method for very high mobility rates. Multipath methods [4, 29, 52] may be regarded as flooding that is restricted to the request zone and, as such, can be used for geocasting (in which a message is to be delivered to all nodes located within a region). A multipath algorithm that consists of several single paths is proposed in [47]. A single nonoptimal path, full-message strategy is proposed in [1]. A short message, multipath destination search, full-message, optimal singlepath method was discussed above. The localized algorithms in this category will be briefly described below.

Several GPS-based methods were proposed in 1984–1986 using the notion of progress. Define progress as the distance between the transmitting node and receiving node projected onto a line drawn from the transmitter toward the final destination. A neighbor is in the forward direction if the progress is positive; otherwise it is said to be in the backward direction. In the random progress method [38], packets destined toward D are routed with equal probability toward one neighboring node that has positive progress. In the *NFP* method [17], a packet is sent to the nearest neighboring node with forward progress. Takagi and Kleinrock [35] proposed the MFR (most forward within radius) routing algorithm, in which a packet is sent to the neighbor with the greatest progress. The method is modified in [17] by proposing to adjust the transmission power to the distance between the two nodes. Finn [14] proposed a Cartesian routing method that allows choosing any successor node that makes progress toward the packet's destination. The best choice depends on the complete topological knowledge. Finn [14] adopted the greedy principle in his simulation: choose the successor node that is closest to the destination. When no node is closer to the destination than the current node, the algorithm performs a sophisticated procedure that does not guaranty delivery. Recently, three articles [4, 28, 29] independently reported variations of routing protocols based on direction of destination. In the compass routing (or DIR) method proposed by Kranakis, Singh, and Urrutia [28], the source or intermediate node A uses the location information for the destination D to calculate its direction. The location of one-hop neighbors of A is used to determine for which of them, say C, the direction AC is closest to the direction of AD. The message m is forwarded to C. The process repeats until the destination is, hopefully, reached. The GEDIR routing algorithm [47] is a variant of greedy routing algorithm [14] with a "delayed" failure criterion. GEDIR, MFR, and compass routing algorithms fail to deliver messages if the best choice for a node currently holding a message is to return it to the previous node [47]. A GFG routing algorithm that guarantees delivery by finding a simple path between source and destination is described in [6]. It is based on constructing a planar subgraph (e.g., Gabriel graph) and providing routing in the planar subgraph that guarantees delivery. This procedure is called on whenever the greedy algorithm fails, and is recalled whenever a closer node (than the previously failing node) is encountered. The GFG algorithm [6] was implemented in [26] by including MAC layer considerations and location updates for experiments with moving nodes. The performance of the GFG algorithm was improved in [11] by adding a shortcut procedure and applying the internal node concept of Wu and Lee [57]. The hop count is very close to the hop count of the shortest path algorithm for dense graphs (below 20% excess hop count for graphs with average degrees ≥ 6) and about twice as long for sparse graphs. Corresponding power- and cost-aware routing algorithms with guaranteed delivery are developed in [46].

21.2.5 Loop Freedom

Interestingly, loop freedom, a basic criterion of Macker and Corson [35] was neglected in many papers. GEDIR and MFR algorithms are inherently loop-free [47]. The proofs of this are based on the observation that distances (or dot products) of nodes toward the destination are decreasing. A counterexample showing that undetected loops can be created in directional-based methods [4, 28, 29] is given in [47]. The method is therefore not loop-free. The algorithms in [6, 11, 14, 35] and shortest-weighted-path-based routing schemes are loop-free.

21.2.6   Memorization of Past Traffic

Most reported algorithms require some or all nodes to memorize past traffic as part of current the routing protocol or to memorize the previous best paths for providing future path to the same destination. Solutions that require nodes to memorize routes or particular information about past traffic are sensitive to node queue size and changes in node activity and node mobility while routing is ongoing. One form of such memorization is provided by routing tables, which memorize the last successful path to each destination. Reduction in the size of routing tables (and, consequently, in the communication overhead to maintain them) was proposed in [25, 57] by defining backbone structures. Each node in the network is either in the virtual backbone or at most r hops away from a virtual backbone node. Clustering has frequently been used to provide such a backbone [25], where the r-cluster is defined as the set of all the nodes within distance at most r hops from a given node, referred to as the clusterhead of the r-cluster. Border nodes are nodes that belong to two or more clusters. Clusterheads are backbone nodes, and two "neighboring" backbone nodes may be up to $2r + 1$ hops away. Thus, communication between two backbone nodes may go through both backbone and nonbackbone nodes. A distributed scheme for initiating is based on selecting, repeatedly, a node with a maximal number of unassigned r hop neighbors as the backbone node, and assigning all its r hop neighbors to that node. Such a backbone is also used in the routing algorithm [30]. The maintenance of cluster structure is known to require significant communication overhead (for instance, local changes may cause global updates by the chain effect) [57]. A significantly better backbone structure, one that does not require any communication overhead and provides connectivity between nodes, is described in [57] and is based on several definitions of dominating sets.

Localized routing algorithms discussed above [6, 14, 28, 46–48, 55] do not memorize past traffic at any node. The algorithms [4, 29, 52] require nodes to memorize past traffic to avoid infinite mutual flooding between neighboring nodes. Memorization of escape loops is needed in directional-based methods (alternatively, messages need to carry time-out stamps). In flooding GEDIR and MFR algorithms [47], messages are flooded at nodes in which basic algorithms fail, and these nodes refuse further copies of the same message. These algorithms guaranty delivery. Routing algorithms that use depth-first search (DFS) in the search for destination are discussed in [24, 49]. Memorization here is imposed by the DFS process. The algorithm guarantees delivery but the efficiency depends on the accuracy of the destination information. Memorization is needed in sensor networks for data fusion [12] to avoid multiple reports of the same information. Quality of service routing, in which the path needs to satisfy delay, bandwidth, and connection time criteria [49], requires that nodes memorize the QoS path; thus, using DFS for its construction does not impose any memorization overhead.

21.3 LOCATION UPDATES BETWEEN NEIGHBORING NODES

One of most important ingredients in all location update schemes is the update between neighboring nodes. The question is when does a node decide to send a message to all its neighbors announcing its new location. We shall review the methods used in literature. As a basic (or "bonus") update, nodes may update their location information with each exchange of routing messages between them.

Karumanchi, Muralidharan, and Prakash [27] discussed the question when to update location, and argued that distance-based updates (based on absolute distance traveled since the last update) and movement-based updates (based on the velocities of nodes) may have limited usefulness in ad hoc networks (such location updates are used in [4, 29]). For instance, nodes may move within a small circle, causing unnecessary location updates. They concluded experimentally that the best strategy is to update when a certain prespecified number of links incident on a node have been established or broken since the last update [27].

The basic update procedure is performed by each moving node whenever it observes that, due to its movement, an existing edge will be broken (that is, the distance between two nodes becomes $>R$). In order to minimize the number of location update messages, the message could be sent by only the node endpoint (of the broken edge) with greater speed. Similarly, the same action may be taken when a new neighbor is detected. New neighbor X may be detected after X transmitted its location update following an edge breakup with another node. Thus, new neighbors that receive such messages may then react by informing X about their presence. Alternatively, the creation of a new link can be detected if two-hop information is available to nodes.

To decide whether an edge is made or broken, a node may use last available information about its direct neighbors and other nodes in the network. However, when all nodes are moving in the same direction (as in military or rescue missions), such a procedure may result in unnecessary updates. To reduce overhead in such scenarios, connection time is introduced as follows. The availability of GPS enables nodes to estimate the connection time with other nodes, as proposed in [49, 51]. The connection time is defined as the estimated duration of a connection between two neighboring nodes. Neighboring nodes frequently update their location to each other, and this information may be used to estimate the direction and speed of their movements. In turn, this suffices to estimate the connection time. Let A and B be the two neighboring nodes that move at speeds a and b, respectively. Here, A and B are position vectors and a and b are directional vectors. At time t, they move to new positions $A' = A + at$ and $B' = B + bt$. They will loose their connection when the distance between them becomes $>R$, where R is the radius of the corresponding unit graph (or the smaller of their transmission radii in case of minpower graphs). The time t at which the connection will be lost can be estimated by solving the quadratic equation $|A'B'| = |B - A + (b - a)t| = R$ [49, 51]. When the time expires, the edge is assumed to broken and a location update is sent to all neighbors. Similar criteria can be used to estimate the time a connection will be made, and act accordingly.

The variants of this basic update may include adjusting transmission radius to tR for some value of t, to reach more or fewer neighbors. Location updates are short messages, and nodes may spend more energy for short messages, as suggested by Lin and Liu [32]. They discussed this difference and even proposed an extreme difference in radii for short and long messages. They found that nodes are able to send their new location to all other nodes in a network with a single broadcast (single-hop network for location updates). However, when sending exact data, the network is treated as a multihop one. Note that the single-hop location update broadcast may fail to reach a number of nodes due to obstacles in the field or presence of other transmissions. Another possible solution is to keep the transmission radius at R, but retransmit from each of the neighbors that are a few hops away. However, these retransmissions also require power (from neighboring nodes), and may cause the broadcast storm problem [NTCS]; therefore, their efficiency is doubtful.

Note that a node that receives a location update aimed at known neighboring nodes, and discovers that it is now a neighbor of transmitting node that is not aware of it, will treat this event as the creation of a new edge and react by sending its own location update in response.

This basic location update procedure may be used as a counter for "deeper" location updates. For instance, Basagni et al. [4] used parameter p (the distance traveled from the last update) as such a counter. Two-hop, four-hop, and flooding messages are sent on every first, second, and third counter, respectively.

21.4 REQUEST ZONE ROUTING

A distance routing effect algorithm for mobility (DREAM) is described in [4]. The source or any intermediate node A calculates the direction of destination D and, based on the mobility information about D, chooses an angular range. The message m is forwarded to all neighbors whose direction belongs to the selected range. The range is determined by the tangents from A to the circle centered at D, with radius equal to a maximal possible movement of D since the last location update. The area containing the circle and two tangents is referred as the request zone [29]. Ko and Vaidya [29] described, independently, an almost identical algorithm, called the LAR Scheme 1, and a few modifications of it. The modifications include sending route requests before the message itself [22]. Note that a route request may be considered as a routing of short messages, as discussed above. Recovery procedures, based on partial or full flooding, to start flooding if the given algorithm fails to find the route within a timeout interval, are proposed in both papers [4, 29]. Ko and Vaidya [29] also proposed the LAR Scheme 2. In this scheme, the source or each intermediate node A will forward the message to all nodes that are closer to the destination than A is. Wu and Harms [56] proposed to improve the location update part of the LAR algorithm. In [56], any two neighboring nodes periodically exchange full routing table (information about all nodes in the network).

The definition of the request zone [4, 29] was modified in [52] in order to provide a uniform framework with the corresponding notions in GEDIR and MFR methods. Stojmenovic [52] discusses the V-GEDIR, CH-MFR, and R-DIR methods, in which m is forwarded to exactly those neighbors that may be the best choices for a possible position of destination (using the appropriate criterion). The request zone in the R-DIR method [52] may include one or two neighbors that are outside of angular range, because they can have the closest direction for the tangents to the circle. In the V-GEDIR method, these neigh-

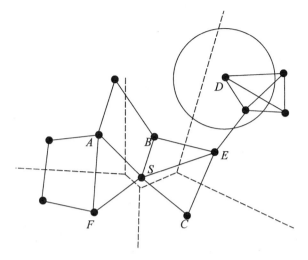

Figure 21.1 Voronoi diagram and the request zone.

bors are determined by intersecting the Voronoi diagram of neighbors with the circle (or rectangle) of possible positions of destination; the portion of the convex hull of neighboring nodes is analogously used in the CH-MFR method.

The Voronoi diagram of n distinct points in the plane is a partition of the plane into n Voronoi regions, each one associated with each point. The Voronoi region associated with node A consists of all the points in the plane that are closer to A than to any other node. It can be shown that each region is a convex polygon (possibly unbounded) determined by bisectors of A and other nodes (more precisely, each region is the intersection of all such bisectors). It is well known that the Voronoi diagram for n points in the plane can be constructed in $O(n \log n)$ time [40] and consists of $O(n)$ line segments.

Node S, currently holding a message for destination D, computes the Voronoi diagram of all its n neighbors. For example, in Figure 21.1, the Voronoi diagram of five neighbors A, B, C, E, and F is shown in dashed lines. Consider the circle (or other region) where destination D can be located. Different locations of D inside the circle correspond to different choices of closest nodes among A, B, C, E, and F. For each position of D, the closest node is the one whose Voronoi region contains the position. Thus, the nodes that are closest to some positions of destination are exactly those nodes whose Voronoi regions intersect the circle of possible destination positions (e.g., B and E in Figure 21.1).

21.5 DOUBLING CIRCLES ROUTING

Amouris, Papavassiliou, and Lu [1] presented a position-based, multizone routing protocol for wide area mobile ad hoc networks. Their algorithm is based on position updates within circles of increasing radii. Each node updates its location to all nodes located within a circle of radii P, $2P$, $4P$, $8P$, . . . (each subsequent circle has a twice larger radius than

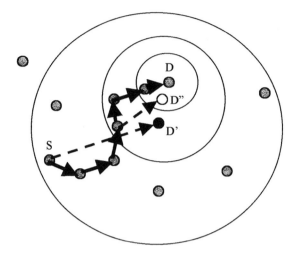

Figure 21.2 Routing from S toward D', D'', and D.

the previous one). Whenever a given node A moves outside one of these circles of radius $2^t P$ for some t, node A broadcasts its location update to all nodes located inside a circle centered at the current node position and with radius $2^{t+1}P$. The routing toward destination then follows these circles of last updates. Source nodes send messages toward the last reported position of destination (using the DIR method) that has moved within the circle of some radius since the last report. As routing the message moves closer to the destination, the information about position of destination becomes more precise, and nodes are able to send messages toward the centers of circles with twice smaller radii than previously, until the node is eventually reached. This process is illustrated in Figure 21.2. The source S sends a message toward D', the last known position of destination D. The routing is later redirected toward newer position D' and finally to exact position D. This method is very interesting and certainly competitive. We observe that the radii of larger circles may encompass almost all nodes of the network, and that the routing paths discovered by the algorithm do not have near-optimal hop counts (which may be important in quality of service applications). However, if the path quality is important, one can consider this algorithm only as the destination search step in the three-phase routing algorithm described above. A similar algorithm, using squares instead of circles and additional sophisticated techniques, is proposed in [31].

The location update techniques discussed so far include occasional flooding of location information to all or a large portion of nodes in the network. In the next two sections, methods that never use such flooding are discussed.

21.6 QUORUM-BASED STRATEGIES

Quorum-based approaches for information dissemination are based on replicating information at multiple nodes acting as repositories. The choice of repositories and the query search must be mutually compatible. Such query and update strategies have been previously employed for location management in cellular networks. Given a set S of n servers, a quorum system is a set of mutually disjoint subsets of S whose union is S. When one of servers requires information from the other, it suffices to query one server from each quorum. In fixed networks, the set of queried servers is bound to contain at least one server that belonged to the quorum that received the latest update. Hence, each query returns the latest value of the queried data. It is possible to form quorums of size approximately $n^{1/2}$ [34]. For example, 25 servers can be organized into 5 rows and 5 columns. Each column serves as a quorum. Thus each node (i, j) (located in i-th row and j-th column) replicates its data to all servers (i', j) in its column. To extract the information from server (i, j), server (i', j') may inquire within its i'-th row, and the server (i', j) will provide the requested information. Modifications of quorum-based strategies for use in dynamic or partitionable servers have been considered in [13, 16, 18, 19, 27, 30]. The main idea in [13, 16, 27] is that each server (or node) selects one of the quorums at random to increase the chance of obtaining relatively up-to-date information in several "columns."

Karumanchi, Muralidharan, and Prakash [27] discussed information dissemination in partitionable mobile ad hoc networks. They studied the problem of getting the location of some other node in the network and the surroundings of that node (e.g., firefighter) without the need to route any message to that node. Their performance evaluation is limited in measuring the accuracy of the obtained information (i.e., the distance between the found and exact location of the other node). In [27], n nodes are divided into $n^{1/2}$ groups with $n^{1/2}$ nodes in each, in two ways, and such quorums are preserved while moving.

Haas and Liang [18, 19, 30] proposed another variant of the quorum-based distributed mobility management scheme. First, a virtual backbone [25, 30] is initiated and maintained. Nodes in the virtual backbone are database servers for location information. They define a quorum system, that is, a set of subsets such that any two subsets intersect in a small number (preferably constant number t) of databases. Each subset then has the same size k. In [18] the choice of subsets is uniform and is performed by applying a centralized, balanced, incomplete block design algorithm. The random selection of these subsets was discussed in [19]. When a node moves, it updates its location, with one subset containing the nearest backbone node. Each source node then queries the subset containing its nearest backbone for the location of the destination, and uses that location to route the message. The routing algorithm is not discussed in [18, 19, 30]. It can be easily observed that location updates and destination searches are not local, and that they involve routing between backbone nodes. Thus, backbone nodes must exchange their location information in order to perform their duties. It is not clear, taking all the overhead into account, whether the whole algorithm will perform better than a simple flooding algorithm with redundant retransmissions eliminated [50]. The flooding algorithm does not require any location updates, and does not require communication overhead for its own backbone structure, which is the dominating set, as defined in [57]. In particular, the same backbone structure can be used for efficient flooding [50] and efficient routing [57].

The main problem with the described quorum-based strategies is that quorums are themselves fixed, and movement of nodes can make nodes in the same quorum far apart from each other, with no clear way of visiting them all in order to find destination information that may be no more difficult to find than the other nodes in the same quorum. A different quorum-based strategy, which deals with network dynamics, is proposed in [53].

In [53], nodes in an ad hoc network do not stay in the same "column," and the distributed information may easily disperse due to node movement. Moreover, it is not clear what the "column" is, and how all the nodes in a column, once defined, will receive the latest updates. Nevertheless, we believe that this idea is worth pursuing.

The main location update method is to forward the new location information (and the node's identifier) within a "column" in the network, in the following way. Each node uses a counter to count the number of previously made changes in edge existence (the number of created or broken edges). When the counter reaches a fixed threshold value e, location information is forwarded along the "column" and e is reset to 0. The "column" may have arbitrary "thickness," but we shall assume, for clarity, thickness 1 here, which means that the created column is a single path in the north–south direction, including neighbors of nodes in that path. A initiates two routing messages, in the directions north and south, whereas other nodes follow only one of the directions. Each follows variation of the MFR algorithm [55], with destination always to the north (or south) of the current node, as follows. Current node B transmits update information to all its neighbors, and indicates, in the same message, which of them is its northernmost (or southernmost) neighbor. That node will, in turn, do the same until a node is reached that does not have such a neighbor.

The frequent problem with the scheme is that the northernmost node, as determined by the northward update, may only be locally northernmost. A "horizontal" destination search can miss such a node, which can remain "below" it. To overcome this problem, each locally northernmost node may switch to FACE mode [6] until another, more northern, node is found on a face. It then converts back to regular upward movement. This switching can be repeated a few times. The FACE algorithm can be improved by applying a shortcut scheme [11]. The final result will be that all nodes at the outer face of the network will receive a location update. This method guarantees that "horizontal" destination search and "vertical" location update will intersect at one of the nodes on the outer face. The drawback is that nodes on the outer boundary will have more traffic demands.

The search for destination is performed similarly, using a horizontal east–west direction instead. The search message includes time of last available information, and other nodes are requested to provide more up-to-date information, if they have it. Nodes that are not on the horizontal path but receive the search message and have more up-to-date information about destination will respond in the process with their information. Thus, data link layer protocols should be efficient in such cases by avoiding collisions. When easternmost and westernmost nodes are reached (or the outer boundary is traversed if the FACE algorithm is also incorporated), the search strategy changes. The message search is then oriented toward the destination, using the latest available information for each search message. There are three searches initiated. The first one originates at sender node S, using the best locally available information. This search does not need to wait for the result of searches in the east and west directions. The easternmost and westernmost nodes in a given "row" may initiate two other searches. Each of three search tasks follows a path toward the destination, using the greedy/GEDIR strategy [14, 47] or GFG algorithm [6]. That is, at each step, the neighbor closest to the destination is selected to forward the message. Nodes that hear messages between two neighbors may react should they have better information about the destination's location.

Figure 21.3 illustrates location update and destination search schemes. Destination

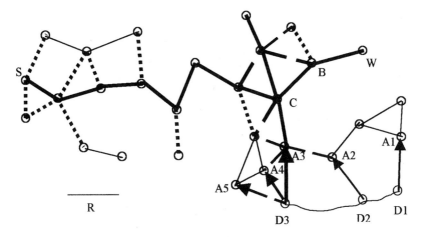

Figure 21.3 Location update from $D3$ and destination search from S.

node D moves (other nodes in Figure 21.3 are assumed to be static) from positions $D1$ to $D2$ and finally to $D3$, and causes creation or breaking of some edges (indicated by arrows, with nodes $A1$, $A2$, $A3$, and $A4$). At position $D3$, it decides to send a location update in its current "column" by sending its position in the northern direction (it does so in the southern direction as well, but there is no neighbor in that direction in Figure 21.3). The main update path is indicated in bold lines, and bold, long dashed lines indicate some other nodes that hear the update message. Source node S initiates a destination search in the east–west direction (in Figure 21.3 it only has neighbors in western direction). The search path is indicated by bold lines, whereas some other nodes, which observe the search, are connected by short bold dashed lines. The location update column and destination search row intersect in Figure 21.3 in seven nodes. The easternmost and westernmost points in the row and node S then turn the search toward learned position of D. In Figure 21.3, point W learned the up-to-date information and may find the destination by applying any localized routing algorithm for static nodes (in Figure 21.3, GEDIR algorithm would produce path W–B–C–$A3$–$D3$).

21.7 HOME-AGENT-BASED STRATEGY

The location update idea proposed in [2, 54] for mobile ad hoc or sensor networks is similar to the one used in cellular phone networks and mobile IP. When a phone user moves away from his home server (agent) to a new location, the visitor's location periodically sends messages to the home agent, giving its current coordinates. When a phone call is made to that user, the call is first sent toward the user's home agent. The home agent then directs the call toward the visitor's position.

The main location update procedure is performed by each node as follows [54]. At the beginning, each node informs every other node about its initial position, which will be its home agent. More precisely, the home agent will consist of all nodes that are currently located inside a circle with radius pR, where p is network parameter, centered at the initial position of the node. In [2], the fixed center of the home region is known by means of some predefined hash function made aware of universally. The size of the home region in [2] adapts to the density of the area, in order to maintain an approximately constant number of nodes inside the region. Each node A uses a counter to count the number of previously made changes in edge existence (the number of created or broken edges). When the counter reaches a fixed threshold value e, node A sends a location update message to its home agent using greedy/GEDIR [14, 47] or GFG [2] algorithm. Nodes on the path and their neighbors also update information about A. If current node B is inside the home agent base, the algorithm changes to flooding inside the home. Note that the update may fail if home agent is disconnected from the current node location. Such failure may be reported back to the node, which will then choose a new home.

Now suppose that source S wants to route a message to a destination D. Destination search messages will be issued, looking for D. S sends exactly two such messages. One is sent toward D using the location information about D currently available to S, applying greedy or GFG algorithms. More up-to-date location information will be taken on the way to the destination (if any is available). The second message is sent toward the center C of the home agent circle of D, which may be at a different region than the current position of D. The search message will stop in the same way as the location update message, at node B, hopefully inside D's home. Node B will then act on the basis of the best information available, and redirect the message toward the location of the destination.

The location update and destination search schemes are illustrated in Figure 21.4. It shows an ad hoc network with radius R, as indicated. Destination D is the only node that moves (for clarity). $D1$, $D2$, and $D3$ are its positions during the move. Upon every link

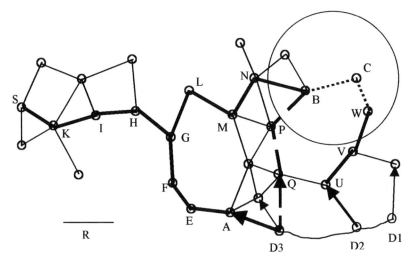

Figure 21.4 Location update from $D2$ and destination search from S.

change (making or breaking), *D* informs its neighbors (indicated by an arrow). At position *D*2, it decides to inform its home agent, drawn as a circle, about its current position. The location update message follows the path *D*2–*U*–*V*–*W* (indicated by a bold line), and is broadcast from *W* to other nodes inside home agent circle (e.g., to nodes *B* and *C*, indicated by dotted lines). Now suppose that source *S* initiates a destination search when the destination is at position *D*3. The destination search message is forwarded toward the center of home agent circle and follows path *S*–*K*–*I*–*H*–*G*–*L*–*M*–*N*–*B*. Node *B* then forwards the search message toward position *D*2, for which node *P* is the best neighbor (following a GEDIR-like method). On the path *B*–*P*–*Q*–*D*3 (indicated by bold and long dashed lines), node *Q* has the up-to-date location of *D* and the destination is found. The destination *D* then initiates the path creation phase following the GFG algorithm [6] and finds the source *S* using the path *D*3–*A*–*E*–*F*–*G*–*H*–*I*–*K*–*S* (indicated by bold lines). Source *S* may then send the data toward *D*.

21.8 PERFORMANCE EVALUATION ISSUES

We shall now discuss the issues arising from performance evaluation of routing algorithms. These will include quantitative metrics used, selection of parameters, comparison with existing methods, mobility patterns, and selection of simulators.

21.8.1 Delivery Rate

The delivery rate is defined as the ratio of numbers of messages received by the destination and sent by senders. The best routing methods employing this metric are those that guarantee delivery, such as [6], in which message delivery is guaranteed assuming "reasonably" accurate destination and neighbor location and no message collisions.

21.8.2 End-to-End Data Delay

This is also referred to as latency, and is the time needed to deliver the message. Data delay can be divided into queuing delay and propagation delay. If queuing delay is ignored, propagation delay can be replaced by hop count, because of proportionality. Retransmissions can be included if the MAC (medium access control) layer is used in experiments. Several papers suggested that it is more important to minimize the power needed per message or the number of routing tasks a network can perform before partitioning [10, 43, 48].

21.8.3 Communication Overhead

Communication overhead can be defined as the average number of control and data bits transmitted per data bits delivered [35]. Control bits include the cost of location updates in the preparation step and destination searches and retransmission during the routing process. However, this metric is rarely used in the literature. In fact, most of the papers avoid measuring it altogether. The portion of ignored overhead may often be more significant than the measured one.

21.8.4 Performance on Static Networks

Although the algorithm is designed with moving nodes in mind, static nodes are important special cases to be verified. Some networks, such as sensor networks, are static most of time, and sometimes destination and neighbor information is accurate. How can one claim that a routing algorithm that performs "well" on moving nodes (with carefully selected moving patterns and network parameters) is a "winning" algorithm if it performs badly on static networks? Experiments with static networks allow significant reduction of the number of parameters and simplification of experiments, thus "fine tuning" the algorithm before real experiments.

21.8.5 MAC Layer Considerations

Initial experiments may ignore the data link layer, but for similar reasons (in the absence of message collisions, routing algorithms should have superb performance, e.g., guaranteeing delivery), further experiments, even on static networks, should consider it. A study on whether the choice of MAC protocol affects the relative performance of the routing protocols was done in [42]. Table-driven protocols are not affected significantly by the choice of MAC protocol. Protocols with hello messaging, when run over IEEE 802.11, have considerably less control traffic than when they run over CSMA (carrier sense multiple access) or MACA (multiple access with collision avoidance). Therefore, IEEE 802.11 can be considered as a standard for MAC specifications in wireless networks.

21.8.6 Comparison with the Shortest Path Algorithm

There is a notable tendency in the literature to compare the performance of proposed routing algorithms with the worst possible solution—flooding—but such comparisons are not properly done, since improper flooding algorithms are used. Algorithms that are able to flood with reduced numbers of retransmissions (roughly half) are surveyed in [50]. If flooding is used for comparison, then the proper version of it should be used. Although some existing algorithms can also be used for comparison, especially if they belong to the same class with the same classification criteria, the ideal shortest path (SP) algorithm is certainly the ultimate goal, and one should verify how far from that goal the proposed algorithm is. If the cost of location updates for both proposed and SP algorithms is ignored, the flooding rate [47] (the ratio of the number of message transmissions and the shortest possible hop count between two nodes) can be used for fair comparison, especially for multipath methods. Each transmission in multiple routes is counted, and messages can be sent to all neighbors with one transmission.

21.8.7 Generating Sparse and Dense Graphs

For experiments with static networks, random unit graphs should be generated. Each of n nodes should select at random x and y coordinates in the interval $[0 \ldots m]$. Subgraphs can be used if obstacles are taken into account. The connectivity depends on the selected transmission radius R. Since transmission radius R for a given piece of equipment is normally fixed (or should be selected from a few discrete values), most papers use a fixed value of R and change m to evaluate graphs of different density (or, in many cases, fix m as well, without discussing impact of graph density). Ignoring the graph density issue in performance evaluations is the single most misleading point in the experimental design and interpretation of results. Routing algorithms perform differently on sparse and dense graphs; thus, it is the graph density that is a primary independent variable to be considered. The best measure of graph density is the average number d of neighbors for each node. There is a relation between R, m, and d, and one should choose d as independent variable. If R is fixed, then change m accordingly. If m is fixed, then R can be found as follows [47]. Sort (in increasing order) all $n(n-1)/2$ possible edges in the graph and choose R to be equal to the length of the $nd/2$-th edge in the sorted list. If R is to have a fixed value for some reason, adjust m linearly with R, to keep the same underlying graph. Generated graphs that are disconnected may or may not be eliminated (it is difficult to control full connectivity with moving nodes; initial connectivity does not secure connectivity during node movements).

21.8.8 Node Mobility

Some papers use random movements at each simulation step in four or eight possible directions. Random walks tend to keep all nodes close to their initial positions, and thus analysis using this model is largely misleading. We also believe that this is not a natural kind of movement, and suggest using movement patterns as in [9, 22, 36]. One possible analogous design is as follows. Each node generates a random number, *wait*, in interval [0 . . . *maxwait*]. The node does not move for wait seconds. This is called the station time. When this time expires, the node chooses to move with a probability p. It generates a new *wait* period if it decides not to move. Otherwise, it generates a random number, *travel*, in interval [0, *maxtravel*], and a new random position within the same square in the second case. The node then moves from its old position to a new position along the line segment joining them, at equal speed for the duration of *travel* seconds. Upon arriving at the new location, the node again chooses its waiting period, etc. The mobility rate is given by the formula *mobrate* = $p*maxtravel/(maxtravel + maxwait)$ and is one of the main mobility parameters. Note that this movement pattern does not cover the case of nodes moving more or less in the same direction, which may often be the case in military and rescue operations. Thus, an additional component should be added in experiments—moving with the same speed and in the same direction by all nodes.

21.8.9 Simulators

There exist several wireless network simulators that are used in the literature. The two most widely used are Glomosym [15] and ns-2 [37]. Although it is desirable to have some kind of benchmark testing facility, the problem with these simulators is a painful learning curve. Several researchers who have used it confirmed that it takes about one month of full-time work to learn how to use these simulators. Thus, they may be a good choice for long-term projects (and long-term grant holders), but not for researchers with limited human resources. The other drawback of using these simulators is that experiments with static nodes and important parameters (e.g., graph density) are easily ignored. Preliminary experiments with static nodes and even moving nodes can be obtained by a simplified design using any programming language (e.g., C or Java), and valuable conclusions can be made. This should be done even if a simulator is used afterward. We agree, of course, that real simulations are necessary for a complete performance evaluation, if resources for doing so are available.

21.9 CONCLUSION

Our discussion indicates that the problem of routing in mobile wireless networks is far from being solved, whereas the special cases of static networks, fixed destination, or known location of destination seems to have been solved satisfactorily. We therefore expect that the research on location updates for efficient routing in wireless network will continue, and hope that this chapter will provide a valuable source of information and directions for future work and experimental designs.

REFERENCES

1. K. N. Amouris, S. Papavassiliou, and M. Li, A position based multi-zone routing protocol for wide area mobile ad-hoc networks, *Proceedings 49th IEEE Vehicular Technology Conference*, 1999, pp. 1365–1369.

2. L. Blazevic, L. Buttyan, S. Capkun, S. Giordano, J.-P. Hubaux, and J.-Y. Le Boudec, Self-organization in mobile ad hoc networks: the approach of terminodes, *IEEE Communication Magazine*, June 2001.

3. S. Basagni, I. Chlamtac, and V. R. Syrotiuk, Dynamic source routing for ad hoc networks using the global positioning system, *Proceedings IEEE Wireless Communications and Networking Conference*, New Orleans, Sept., 1999.

4. S. Basagni, I. Chlamtac, V. R. Syrotiuk, B. A. Woodward, A distance routing effect algorithm for mobility (DREAM), *Proceedings MOBICOM*, 1998, pp. 76–84.

5. J. Broch, D. A. Maltz, D. B. Johnson, Y. C. Hu, and J. Jetcheva, A performance comparison of multihop wireless ad hoc network routing protocols, *Proceedings MOBICOM*, 1998, pp. 85–97.

6. P. Bose, P. Morin, I. Stojmenovic, and J. Urrutia, Routing with guaranteed delivery in ad hoc wireless networks, *3rd International Workshop on Discrete Algorithms and Methods for Mobile Computing and Communications,* Seattle, August 20, 1999, pp. 48–55.

7. J. Chen, P. Druschel, and D. Subramanian, A new approach to routing with dynamic metrics, *Proceedings IEEE INFOCOM*, 1999.

8. D. Camara and A. F. Loureiro, A novel routing algorithm for ad hoc networks, *Telecommunication Systems*, to appear.

9. S. Chen and K. Nahrstedt, Distributed quality-of-service routing in ad hoc networks, *IEEE Journal Selected Areas in Communications, 17,* 8, 1999, 1488–1505.

10. J. H. Chang and L. Tassiulas, Energy conserving routing in wireless ad-hoc networks, *Proceedings IEEE INFOCOM*, March, 2000.

11. S. Datta, I. Stojmenovic, and J. Wu, Internal node and shortcut based routing with guaranteed delivery in wireless networks, Cluster Computing, to appear.

12. D. Estrin, R. Govindan, J. Heidemann, and S. Kumar, Next century challenges: Scalable coordination in sensor networks, *Proceedings MOBICOM*, 1999, Seattle, pp. 263–270.

13. A. El Abbadi, D. Skeen, and F. Cristian, An efficient fault-tolerant algorithm for replicated data management, *Proceedings 5th ACM SIGACT-SIGMOD Symposium on Principles of Database Systems,* 1985, pp. 215–229.

14. G. G. Finn, Routing and addressing problems in large metropolitan-scale internetworks, ISI Research Report ISU/RR-87-180, March 1987.

15. http://pcl.cs.ucla.edu/projects/domains/glomosim.html.

16. M. Herlihy, Dynamic quorum adjustment for partitioned data, *ACM Transactions on Database Systems, 12,* 2, 170–194, 1987.

17. T. C. Hou and V. O. K. Li, Transmission range control in multihop packet radio networks, *IEEE Transactions on Communications, 34,* 1, 38–44, 1986.

18. Z. J. Haas and B. Liang, Ad hoc mobility management with uniform quorum systems, *ACM/IEEE Transactions on Networks, 7,* 2, 228–240, 1999.

19. Z. J. Haas and B. Liang, Ad-hoc mobility management with randomized database groups, *Proceedings of IEEE ICC,* Vancouver, June, 1999.

20. C. Ho, K. Obraczka, G. Tsudik, and K. Viswanath, Flooding for reliable multicast in multi-hop ad hoc networks, *Proceedings MOBICOM*, 1999, pp. 64–71.

21. Z. J. Haas and M. R. Peerlman, The performance of query control schemes for the zone routing protocol, *Proceedings DIAL M,* 1999, pp. 23–29.

22. D. Johnson and D. Maltz, Dynamic source routing in ad hoc wireless networks, in *Mobile Computing* (T. Imielinski and H. Korth, eds.), Norwell, MA: Kluwer, 1996.

23. M. Joa-Ng and I. T. Lu, A peer-to-peer zone-based two-level link state routing for mobile ad hoc networks, *IEEE J. Selected Areas in Communications, 17,* 8, 1415–1425, 1999.

24. R. Jain, A. Puri, and R. Sengupta, Geographical routing using partial information for wireless ad hoc networks, TR-EECS, University of California, Berkeley, December 1999.

25. P. Krishna, N. N. Vaidya, M. Chatterjee, and D. K. Pradhan, A cluster-based approach for routing in dynamic networks, *ACM SIGCOMM Computer Communication Review, 49,* 49–64, 1997.

26. B. Karp and H. T. Kung, GPSR: Greedy perimeter stateless routing for wireless networks, *Proceedings MOBICOM*, August, 2000, pp. 243–254.

27. G. Karumanchi, S. Muralidharan, and R. Prakash, Information dissemination in partitionable mobile ad hoc networks, *Proceedings IEEE Symposium on Reliable Distributed Systems,* Lausanne, Oct., 1999.

28. E. Kranakis, H. Singh, and J. Urrutia, Compass routing on geometric networks, *Proceedings 11th Canadian Conference on Computational Geometry,* Vancouver, August, 1999.

29. Y. B. Ko and N. H. Vaidya, Location-aided routing (LAR) in mobile ad hoc networks, *Proceedings MOBICOM*, 1998, pp. 66–75.

30. B. Liang and Z. J. Haas, Virtual backbone generation and maintenance in ad hoc network mobility management, *Proceedings INFOCOM,* Israel, 2000.

31. J. Li, J. Jannotti, D. S. J. De Couto, D. R. Karger, and R. Morris, A scalable location service for geographic ad hoc routing, *Proceedings MOBICOM,* 2000, 120–130.

32. C. R. Lin and J. S. Liu, QoS routing in ad hoc wireless networks, *IEEE Journal Selected Areas in Communications, 17,* 8, 1426–1438, 1999.

33. W. H. Liao, Y. C. Tseng, and J. P. Sheu, GRID: A fully location-aware routing protocol for mobile ad hoc networks, *Telecommunication Systems,* to appear.

34. M. Maekawa, A $n^{1/2}$ algorithm for mutual exclusion in decentralized systems, *ACM Transactions on Computer Systems, 14,* 159, 1985.

35. J. P. Macker and M. S. Corson, Mobile ad hoc networking and the IETF, *Mobile Computing and Communications Review, 2,* 1, 9–14, 1998.

36. A. B. McDonald and T. F. Znati, A mobility-based framework for adaptive clustering in wireless ad hoc networks, *IEEE Journal Selected Areas in Communications, 17,* 8, 1466–1487, 1999.

37. http://mash.cs.berkeley.edu/ns.

38. R. Nelson and L. Kleinrock, The spatial capacity of a slotted ALOHA multihop packet radio network with capture, *IEEE Transactions on Communications, 32,* 6, 684–694, 1984.

39. S. Y. Ni, Y. C. Tseng, Y. S. Chen, and J. P. Sheu, The broadcast storm problem in a mobile ad hoc network, *Proceedings MOBICOM,* Seattle, Aug., 1999, pp. 151–162.

40. A. Okabe, B. Boots, and K. Sugihara, *Spatial Tessellations: Concepts and Applications of Voronoi Diagrams,* New York: John Wiley, 1992.

41. C. Perkins, Ad hoc on demand distance vector (AODV) routing, internet draft, draft-ietf-manet-aodv-00. txt, November, 1997.

42. E. M. Royer, The effects of MAC protocols on ad hoc network communication, *Proceedings IEEE Wireless Communications and Networking Conference,* Chicago, IL, September, 2000.

43. V. Rodoplu and T. H. Meng, Minimum energy mobile wireless networks, *IEEE Journal on Selected Areas in Communications, 17,* 8, 1333–1344, 1999.

44. S. Ramanathan and M. Steenstrup, A survey of routing techniques for mobile communication networks, *Mobile Networks and Applications, 1,* 2, 89–104, 1996.

45. E. M. Royer and C. K. Toh, A review of current protocols for ad hoc mobile wireless networks, *IEEE Personal Comunications,* April, 46–55, 1999.

46. I. Stojmenovic and S. Datta, Power aware routing with guaranteed delivery in wireless networks, unpublished manuscript, 2001.

47. I. Stojmenovic and X. Lin, GEDIR: Loop-free location based routing in wireless networks, *IASTED International Conference on Parallel and Distributed Computing and Systems,* Nov. 3–6, 1999, Boston, MA, pp. 1025–1028.

48. Ivan Stojmenovic and Xu Lin, Power aware localized routing in wireless networks, *IEEE International Parallel and Distributed Processing Symposium,* Cancun, Mexico, May 1–5, 2000, pp. 371–376.

49. I. Stojmenovic, M. Russell, and B. Vukojevic, Depth first search and location based localized routing and QoS routing in wireless networks, *IEEE International Conference on Parallel Processing,* August 21–24, 2000, Toronto, pp. 173–180.

50. I. Stojmenovic, M. Seddigh, and J. Zunic, Internal node based broadcasting in wireless networks, *Proceedings IEEE Hawaii International Conference on System Sciences,* January 2001.

51. W. Su, S. J. Lee, M. Gerla, Mobility prediction in wireless networks, *Proceedings IEEE MILCOM,* October, 2000.

52. I. Stojmenovic, Voronoi diagram and convex hull based geocasting and routing in ad hoc wireless networks, Computer Science, SITE, University of Ottawa, TR–99–11, December, 1999.

53. I. Stojmenovic, A routing strategy and quorum based location update scheme for ad hoc wireless networks, Computer Science, SITE, University of Ottawa, TR–99-09, September, 1999.

54. I. Stojmenovic, Home agent based location update and destination search schemes in ad hoc wireless networks, Computer Science, SITE, University of Ottawa, TR-99-10, September, 1999.

55. H. Takagi and L. Kleinrock, Optimal transmission ranges for randomly distributed packet radio terminals, *IEEE Trans. on Communications, 32,* 3, 246–257, 1984.

56. K. Wu and J. Harms, Location trace aided routing in mobile ad hoc networks, *Proceedings IEEE ICCCN,* Las Vegas, Oct., 2000.

57. J. Wu and H. Li, On calculating connected dominating set for efficient routing in ad hoc wireless networks, *Proceedings DIAL M,* Seattle, Aug., 1999, pp. 7–14.

58. O. Wolfson, A. P. Sistla, S. Chamberlain, and Y. Yesha, Updating and querying databases that track mobile units, *Distributed and Parallel Databases Journal, 7,* 3, 1–31, 1999.

59. Zero Configuration Networking (zeroconf) Working Group, IETF, www.ietf.org/html.charters/zeroconf-charter.html.

CHAPTER 22

Topological Design, Routing, and Handover in Satellite Networks

AFONSO FERREIRA, JÉRÔME GALTIER, and PAOLO PENNA

Mascotte Team, INRIA/CNRS/UNSA, Sophia Antipolis, France

22.1 INTRODUCTION

A low earth orbit (LEO) satellite constellation consists of a set of satellites orbiting the Earth with high constant speed at a relatively low altitude (a few thousand kilometers) [1]. Each satellite is equipped with a fixed number of antennas that allow it to communicate with ground transmitters/receivers and with other satellites. One of the major advantages of LEO satellites (as opposed to geostationary—GEO—satellites) is that they are closer to the Earth's surface. This reduces the communication delay and the energy required to directly connect a user with a satellite. On the other hand, two major issues arise due to their low altitude. First, because a single satellite can only cover a small geographical area (called footprint) at the Earth's surface, many satellites are required to provide global coverage. Second, the footprint of each satellite moves continuously, implying a high mobility of the whole network, in contrast with other cellular systems.

In the following, we will see how the topology of LEO constellations is limited by physical constraints. Then we will review how these factors have been taken into account in the design of routing and handover policies.

22.2 TOPOLOGIES

During the systems design phase, several parameters come into play, such as satellites' altitude, number of satellites, number of orbits and satellites per orbit, how to deploy the orbits, and how to interconnect the satellites. All such factors determine the topology of the network, as shown in this section.

22.2.1 Orbits

A closer look at the feasible types of orbits shows that unless the orbits have the same altitude and inclination, their relative positions change so often that intersatellite links

(ISLs) can hardly connect them for a sufficient amount of time (for more details on orbit mechanics with respect to telecommunication services see [1, 39]). Under such constraints, different kinds of constellations can be obtained according to how the orbits are deployed.

The so-called π-constellations form the structure of the Iridium system [20, 22] and were the basis of the original plans for the Teledesic system [21, 30]. The basic structure of a π-constellation consists of a set of orbits that are deployed along a semicircle when viewed from a pole, as shown in Figure 22.1(a). The satellites are placed along the orbits so as to obtain maximum coverage of the Earth's surface. In Figure 22.1(c) the deployment of satellites along with their footprints is shown. We can see that in a π-constellation there are two extreme orbits that are adjacent, but whose satellites move in opposite directions. As a result, a seam appears that divides the network into two parts: those satellites moving from south to north and those moving from north to south [see Figure 22.1(a)–(b)].

From a communication network viewpoint, the seam is the main drawback of π-constellations, as will be seen later. Also, π-constellations suffer from excessive polar coverage. Finally, their unique coverage in many areas and, therefore, sensitivity to many obstacles, like trees and buildings, does not always ensure sufficient radio signal quality.

In order to avoid these kinds of problems, 2π-constellations have been proposed. A 2π-constellation is constructed by spacing the orbits along a complete circle as shown in Figure 22.2. The 2π-constellation is used in the Globalstar constellation [9], and has also been planned for the future Skybridge project and the now abandoned Celestri.

Another important aspect concerns the use of "inclined" orbits, that is, orbits whose inclination is between the equatorial inclination (0 degrees) and the polar one (90 degrees). Usually, π-constellations use polar orbits (informally, orbits that "roughly" cross the polar axis) for coverage reasons (see Section 22.2.5), and therefore are called "polar" constellations. On the other hand, inclined orbits allow a better optimization of 2π-constellations,

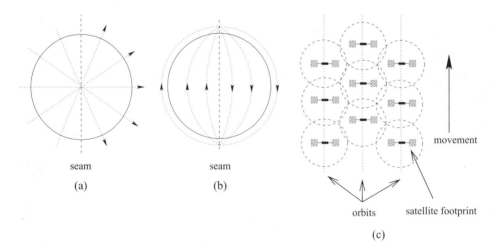

Figure 22.1   The structure of π-constellations. (a) View from the north pole. (b) View from the equatorial plane. (c) The position of satellites on adjacent orbits and the resulting coverage.

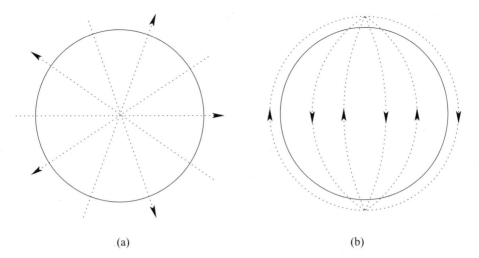

(a)   (b)

Figure 22.2 2π-constellations. (a) View from the north pole. (b) View from the equatorial plane.

hence the name "inclined" constellations. The use of inclined orbits allows for an increase in the number of simultaneously visible satellites on more populated or wealthier areas.

It is worth observing that there is no technical reason to forbid the use of polar orbits on 2π-constellations, and vice versa. Moreover, the use of inclined orbits does not affect the network topology [for instance, π-constellations that use inclined orbits still result in the mesh-like topology shown in Figure 22.4(b)].

22.2.2 Intersatellite Links

The next step is to interconnect the satellites through the ISLs. In particular, we distinguish between intraorbital and interorbital links. The former connect consecutive satellites on the same orbits, and the latter connect two satellites that are on different orbits. In Figure 22.3 we show three possible patterns that can be obtained by using interorbital links between adjacent orbits: the "W" pattern and the "inclined" pattern in Figures 22.3(a)–(b) use four ISLs per satellite, whereas the pattern in Figure 22.3(c) uses only three ISLs.

Consider now the "W" pattern in Figure 22.3(a). In order to obtain the network topology, we have to take into account the seam and the relative position of satellites crossing the poles, as follows.

For π-constellations, one has to consider the problem of connecting two satellites moving in opposite directions, which is too expensive or even infeasible with the existing technology (see Section 22.2.5). Hence, it is commonly assumed that two such satellites cannot be directly connected over the seam, even though they are "physically" close one to each other. Therefore, long user-to-user delay can occur even when the two parties are geographically close to each other but the covering satellites are separated by the seam. Also notice that two adjacent satellites swap their relative position whenever crossing the poles [see Figure 22.4(a)]. Hence, the network topology can be represented

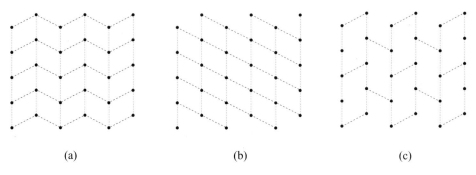

(a)   (b)   (c)

Figure 22.3 Some intersatellite link patterns.

as a two-dimensional mesh in which columns are wrapped around, but rows are not [see Figure 22.4(b)].

In [15] the impact of the ISLs architecture (for instance, the use of antennas that support higher angular velocity) has been studied, and further patterns to connect the satellites of a π-constellation have been proposed. Such patterns use interorbital links that connect satellites in nonadjacent orbits, typically the neighboring orbit of the neighboring

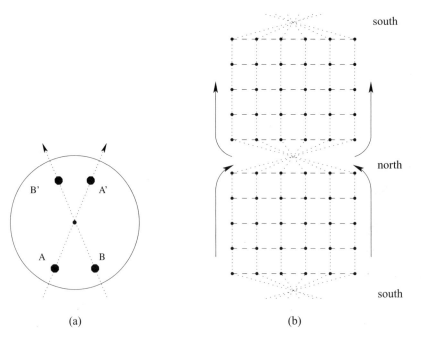

(a)   (b)

Figure 22.4 The relative position of two adjacent satellites crossing the pole and the resulting topology of π-constellations.

orbit. This reduces the user-to-user delay when the communication takes place between two positions that are quite far apart (or when the communications have to go across the seam). Assuming use of ISLs that support high angular velocity, the delay effects of ISLs that cross the seam have also been investigated in [15].

With respect to intersatellite links for 2π-constellations, neither Globalstar nor Skybridge have implemented ISLs in their design, although it seems that they had been considered in the early phases of these projects, as was the case in Celestri. At that point in time, many designers thought those projects were too innovative accelerate the introduction of this additional new feature. Nevertheless, there is a strong belief that future designs of 2π-constellations will introduce such links.

From the topology point of view, it is worth observing that the regular torus turns into a skewed torus if an inclined ISL pattern such as the one of Figure 22.3(b) is adopted [17]. Notice that 2π-constellations do not present any seam. Thus, their coverage has smoother properties. On the other hand, a unique position may be covered by two satellites quite far one from another in the network topology (e.g., two satellites that move in opposite directions), especially when the user is close to the equator.

22.2.3 ISLs versus Terrestrial Gateways

The use of ISLs is intended to implement communications that do not use any terrestrial infrastructure. However, the use of terrestrial gateways still present some advantages such as a reduced number of computing devices on board the satellites. For instance, gateways can be used to compute the routing tables that are used by the satellites.

A more extensive use of the gateways has been adopted in the Globalstar system, in which the satellites operate in a "bent pipe" mode. Their main function is to redirect user signals to ground gateways, and vice versa. As a result, the operator has to build many gateways, one for each area in which the service is opened. Additionally, part of the radio spectrum is used to support the communications between the satellites and the gateways. Unfortunately, radio resources are becoming a scarce resource. Currently, several systems share the same spectrum of frequencies (Globalstar, ICO, and probably Ellipso), which is the source of several interference problems.

We note that the use of ISLs presents significant advantages, like reducing the communications between the satellites and the gateways, reducing the number of gateways, balancing the load between the gateways, and preventing gateway faults.

22.2.4 Multiple Coverage

Another important issue for satellite constellations with ISLs is multicoverage goals. From the radio and signal propagation points of view, a single satellite may not suffice to ensure the real-time connection, especially if some obstacles exist between the user and the satellite. Systems like Globalstar [9] answer this problem using multipath techniques. Instead of being received by one satellite, the signal is received by two to four satellites and merged to recover a clear signal. When a new satellite is visible to the user, its signal contribution is introduced progressively into the global merging of the signals.

We remark that routing with multipath techniques in a satellite constellation is very challenging. A single user may be directly connected to two (or more) satellites that are very far one from another in the network topology, mainly in inclined constellations. From the algorithmic point of view, this characteristic essentially turns a basic network routing problem into a multicasting problem.

22.2.5 Physical and Technological Constraints

In this section we discuss some of the main physical and technological factors that impact on many of the above design choices.

22.2.5.1 ISLs Geometry

The main technological constraints to take into account in ISL design are the relative angular velocity of the endpoints and their visibility [17]. This is because antennas cannot tolerate excessive angular speed and the atmosphere is also a source of fading of the signal.

22.2.5.2 Mobility of ISLs

As a satellite moves along its orbit, the set of satellites visible from it changes continuously. This happens for those satellites that are not in adjacent orbits and, in polar constellations, whenever the satellite approaches the poles. This is due to the small distance between adjacent satellites approaching the pole, which results in a higher angular velocity [1, 15]. Additionally, ISLs between adjacent orbits must be turned off when crossing the poles because of the satellites' relative position switching (see Figure 22.4). As observed in [15], ISLs that support higher angular velocity allow maintainence of intraorbital links at higher latitudes. An unexpected side effect of the angular velocity is that the tracking system may affect the stability of the satellite within its orbit and therefore result in an additional consumption of fuel, which in turn impacts the satellite's weight and time in service.

22.2.5.3 Shortest (Delay) Path

It is worth observing that the distance between two adjacent polar orbits decreases as they get closer to the poles. Hence, for π-constellations using the "W" ISLs pattern, for instance, the minimum delay path is the one that uses a minimal number of ISLs and interorbital links whose latitude is the maximum latitude between the two satellites to be connected.

Notice that routing algorithms on mesh-like topologies may return suboptimal time/delay paths, since such models do not consider that the orbit distance varies with the latitude. In [10] a model that takes this issue into account has been investigated.

22.3 NETWORK MOBILITY AND TRAFFIC MODELING

There are two main factors that should be taken into account when designing routing algorithms for LEO satellite constellations:

1. *Users' distribution:* the fact that the position of the users and the duration of the communications are not known in advance.

2. *Network mobility:* the fact that satellites move, constantly changing the network topology.

Although the first aspect has been extensively studied for classical cellular networks, such networks use wired connections in order to connect two base stations. Hence, the main issue in these "terrestrial networks" is to provide enough resources for the user's connection to last. There is a lot of flexibility in the size of the cells, but the users may move from one to another, and at different speeds. Conversely, LEO cells are big enough to consider the users immobile. However, routing problems occur, since on-board resources, in particular the maximum number of connections using ISLs—are scarce.

The second aspect, namely the network mobility, is a distinguishing factor of LEO constellations. Indeed, even if we assume a static set of communications (i.e., pairs of users that want to communicate one with each other), the problem of maintaining active connections over time is not a trivial task—the satellite's movement triggers both handovers and connections updates (rerouting) when a topology change occurs.

In both cases, mobility is the main cause of call blocking, call dropping, and unbounded delay in communications. However, there is a fundamental difference between the users' mobility and the network's mobility: The users' behavior is not deterministic, whereas changes to the network topology are predictable. Hence, two different approaches are generally adopted:

1. The network's behavior is deterministic and can be "predicted" quite accurately (see Section 22.3.1).
2. The users' behavior is usually modeled by means of a probability distribution (see Section 22.3.2).

It is worth observing that if we consider the relative movement between a user and the satellites, then the major part of such movement is due to the satellites' speed. Hence, the probability distributions used to model users' mobility mainly focus on the issue of managing requests whose position and duration are not known prior to their arrival.

22.3.1   Satellite Mobility

One of the main differences between "classical" cellular networks and LEO constellations is the high mobility of the system. Complicating factors such as the satellite movement and the Earth's self-rotation make the problem of connecting "immobile" users nontrivial. In the following, we describe the interplay between these two factors and the previously mentioned aspects, and also how network mobility can be modeled.

22.3.1.1   Satellites Movement

Satellite movement is the main cause of handovers. Two types of handover may occur:

1. A satellite handover is the transfer of a user from one satellite to another during a communication.

2. A cell handover is the transfer of a user from one spot beam to another within the same satellite. A satellite antenna directed to terminals is composed of a series of beams. Such a decomposition of the satellite footprint allows reuse of the radio frequencies several times in its coverage area. These handovers have no impact on intersatellite routing, but seriously impact on-board computations.

If a user is just on the border of the coverage area of a satellite, his/her connection time to an individual satellite can be extremely small. Hence, in general, constellations are designed in such a way that the footprints overlap and extremely small connection times to an individual satellite never happen. Nevertheless, the maximum connection time is still limited. A user's trajectory, viewed from the satellite, will resemble a straight line crossing the center of the coverage area. The apparent (or relative) speed of the user is then the speed of the satellite. This causes the following undesirable phenomena: visibility changes, varying topologies (ISLs changes), footprint handover, and need for rerouting.

22.3.1.2   Earth's Self-Rotation

The Earth's self-rotation introduces some more complication in the system. In Figure 22.5, we plot the maximum time between two satellite handovers against the altitude h and the elevation angle ε of a constellation, in two cases:

1. The Earth's self-rotation is not taken into consideration and the satellite's inclination can be arbitrary.
2. The Earth's self-rotation is taken into account and the orbit of the satellite is equatorial.

22.3.1.3   Modeling the Network Mobility

Notice that the maximum handover time, shown in Figure 22.5, can vary from some minutes up to several hours. Also, inclined orbits can be used to exploit the Earth's self-rotation to increase the visibility period. Hence, the mobility of the network can also vary a lot. Roughly speaking, one can distinguish between low and high mobility, depending on the maximum handover time.

Low Mobility (periodic). In [5], the mobility of a satellite constellation is described in terms of finite state automation (FSA) by a series of states described along the time period in round robin fashion. The main advantage of this model is that we have to consider only a finite set of configurations of the satellite constellation (in which the satellites are assumed to be immobile), and provide efficient routing solutions for each of them, inspired by classical telecommunication problems.

Low Mobility (aperiodic). It is worth observing that the "periodicity" assumption of the FSA model may be, in some cases, too strong. This is essentially due to the combination of "physical" factors, such as the Earth's self-rotation, the satellite's speed, and the use of inclined orbits. They make the system aperiodic for all practical purposes, i.e., a satellite will find again the same position only after such a long time that too many intermediate states would be necessary. In this case, a possible approach consists in taking a series of

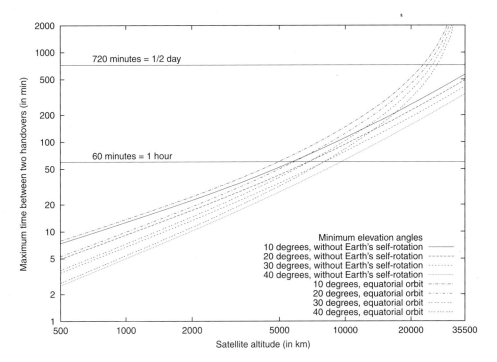

Figure 22.5   Maximum time between two satellite handovers.

snapshots or fixed constellation topologies, a method sometimes referred to as discretiza-tion [11, 37, 38]. Then the routing problem is solved with respect to that fixed "constella-tion."

High Mobility. The above two models are interesting when the mobility of the satellite network is negligible with respect to the mobility of the users' requests, e.g., if most of the requests have very low duration, let us say a few minutes, while the handover time would be one hour or more. In that case, before the network configuration changes (significant-ly) several (many) requests will have been satisfied.

Moreover, these models do not take into account the dependence between consecutive states of the network. Thus, between two states, the complete routing scheme of the con-stellation should be changed. Clearly, in the case of highly dynamic constellations and/or long call durations, almost all requests may pass through several states and thus may be rerouted several times.

22.3.2 User Distribution: Common Traffic Assumptions

Depending on the application, three major scenarios can be identified for satellite mar-kets. The first and most natural one states that satellites will serve countries where the telecommunication infrastructure is insufficient or nonexistent. The second one, which appears to be more and more probable, is that the satellites will provide additional capaci-

TABLE 22.1 Characteristics of foreseeable usages of satellite constellations

Type	Developing	Overload	International
Location	Poor countries/oceans	Rich countries	International
Time distribution	Poisson-like	Bursty	Nearly deterministic
User concentration	Sparse	Huge	Irregular
Call duration	Short	Exponential	Long
Call distance	Average	Short	Long

ties to countries that already have good telecommunication infrastructures, but which suffer from overload of their resources. A third market concerns people who require a seamless connection in their international activities. Of course, depending on the scenario, the traffic may have different characteristics, as summarized in Table 22.1.

Little is known about the two first classes of applications. The last one has been investigated in [35], where an analysis of the international activities led to a map of different zones, worldwide. In this model, the planisphere is divided into 288 cells, with 24 bands along the longitude and 12 along the latitude. The intensity levels from 0 to 8 shown in Figure 22.6 correspond to traffic expectations for the year 2005 of 0, 1.6, 6.4, 16, 32, 95, 191, 239, and 318 millions of addressable minutes/year. In [15] the traffic requirement matrix is obtained from trading statistics, namely the imports/exports between any two regions. Further market studies on satellites can be found in [23].

In the following, we describe how the users mobility can be modeled by means of some traffic assumptions. In particular, we group traffic assumptions into three categories:

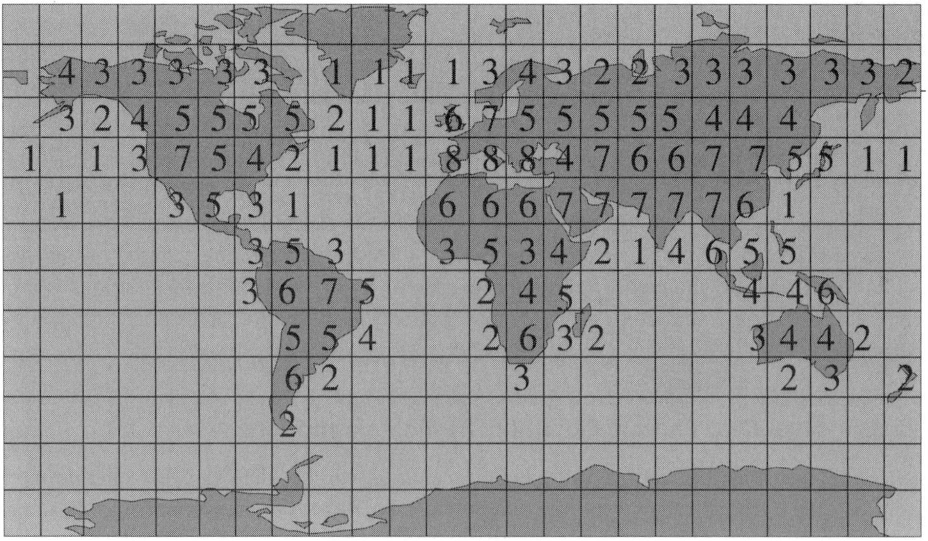

Figure 22.6 Intensity levels on the planisphere for the distribution of users.

1. Geographical distribution: On which satellite the user requests are expected to arrive.
2. Time distribution: How long they are expected to be active.
3. Rate distribution: How much resources they will require.

22.3.2.1 Geographical Distribution

Statistical models have been developed to represent the load all over the Earth. A structure that appears promising is the notion of point process over the two-dimensional Euclidean space [8, 3, 16, 18]. A point process is a family $X = \{X(B), B \in \mathcal{B}\}$ of nonnegative integer-valued variables, where $X(B)$ denotes the random number of points that lie in the set B. A *homogeneous Poisson process* with parameter $\lambda > 0$ is a point process X as follows.

- The number of points $X(B)$ is Poisson distributed with parameter $\lambda\mu(B)$ for each bounded Borel set B.
- The random variables $X(B_1), \ldots, X(B_n)$ are independent for each sequence $B_1, \ldots, B_n$ of disjoint Borel sets.

In fact, the homogeneous Poisson process reflects quite well the traffic load within a country with uniform development. More generally, when trying to map a point process to the entire world, it would be interesting to either choose a measure μ that reflects the economic development of each region (i.e., for instance, the map of Figure 22.6), or try a model with different properties, such as MMPP or multifractal models [2] (for more details, we refer the reader to the survey in [13]).

22.3.2.2 Time Distribution

The traditional way to model the distribution of the call durations consists in using a Poisson law. In fact, the behavior of the traffic is then very close to that obtained on phone systems. However, new broadband applications, made possible by the Internet, generate other types of traffic. In [24] a comparative study between self-similar and Poisson traffics is done in the satellite constellation context.

22.3.2.3 Rate Distribution

It is quite natural to relate the rate distribution to the locations of the different parties of a communication. In [36], the load of intercontinental traffic is evaluated. It is estimated that between 81% and 85% of the traffic is within continents, the remaining traffic being shared with the closest and/or most populated areas. Another method of generating traffic is suggested in [6]: once a pair (u, v) of locations is selected (u and v are viewed here as points on the unit sphere), associated with potential requirement densities w_u and w_v, the traffic requirement between the two nodes is given by

$$T(u, v) = \frac{(w_u w_v)^\alpha}{d(u, v)^\beta}$$

where α and β are two parameters set by the user. In [6], it is assumed that $\alpha = 0.6$ and $\beta = 0.5$.

22.4   ROUTING AND HANDOVER

A good routing strategy should mainly prevent (1) the congestion of ISLs due to too many routes passing trough them; (2) routing requests along paths containing many links, since this results in poor resources utilization and a higher delay in the communication; (3) dropping an ongoing call or blocking a new one.

22.4.1   Problems and Optimization Criteria

Here we describe more in detail the main goals concerning the design of efficient routing algorithms for LEO constellations.

22.4.1.1   Maximum Throughput and ISL Usage

Maximizing the throughput under limited ISL capacity is one of the main objectives of constellation designers. Clearly, because of the limited ISL capacity, a good routing strategy should minimize the maximum link usage (e.g., the load due to the overall traffic passing through such a link) among all the ISLs.

22.4.1.2   Shortest/Bounded Delay and Jitter

One of the main motivations for using LEO systems is the reduction of the communication delay. Indeed, the minimum delay to open a connection through a geostationary satellite is around 240 ms, whereas a LEO could connect two users in around 20 ms. However, although the connection is roughly independent of the parties' location in a GEO system, the delay significantly increases for LEO systems when the parties get further from one another. However, although the ISLs offer straight free-space propagation, the delay between the satellites is governed by the speed of light.

The multipath techniques and in-the-air merging of the signal (see Section 22.2.4) should create a new delay problem. Indeed, merging two signals that are far apart in the network topology takes time comparable to that required to reach a geostationary satellite. The same problem occurs in π-constellations when the communications have to go across the seam. In each case, the communication delay could take, in the worst case, an additional 100 ms to be completed (the time to reach the furthest satellite in the constellation).

The jitter (in other words, the delay variation) is relatively important in LEO constellations, since the distance between the user and the satellite (and also between the satellite and the gateway, and even between two satellites of different orbits) changes continuously during the lifetime of a communication. This behavior cannot be avoided and can lead to storage optimization issues in the satellite (in case the terminal is not able to handle it).

22.4.1.3   Guaranteed Handover

The next optimization problem concerns the quality of service and more precisely the guarantee that is given to the users that a communication will not be dropped because of a handover. This can be done either by fixing an acceptable rate of call dropping or by forcing the system to avoid call dropping at any price.

22.4.1.4   *Call Admission and Routing*

The guaranteed handover feature greatly impacts the call admission procedure and can lead to additional call blocking. Blocked calls may also be a consequence of scarce link resource availability. This may happen either because a user cannot be connected to the visible satellite(s) or no route between the two satellites used in the communication can be found without overloading the ISLs' capacity.

22.4.2   Algorithmic Solutions

22.4.2.1   *Call Admission for Handovers*

The call admission procedure decides whether an incoming communication request will be handled or not. A user will be refused entry into the system when there is not enough available capacity to take the request into consideration. A user may be also rejected because the system is not able to guarantee the duration of the service to sufficiently meet the quality of service goals. For instance, a user could be immediately served, but after one minute the communication will have to be dropped because it interferes with other, more privileged users or those who were already in the system before the latter user's arrival.

Two main schemes can be used to control the resources of the LEO satellite system:

1. *Earth-fixed* cells can be drawn directly on the ground. One cell has a fixed capacity, and is served by the same (set of) satellite(s). Therefore, the handovers occur simultaneously for all users of the cell. This scheme reduces the amount of usable capacity of the satellite, but simplifies the management of the users on board the satellites. This idea has been used for the plans of the Teledesic constellation. The Earth's surface was divided into 160 km stripes parallel to the equator from the south to the north, each stripe being redivided along the longitude into squares of approximatively 160 km by 160 km, for a total of around 20,000 cells. Those "super-cells" were then further subdivided into elementary cells of 53.3 km by 53.3 km [21]. It is then to the responsibility of the constellation's designer to make sure that at each instant of time each cell will be served by at least one satellite.

2. *Satellite-fixed* cells, the most common scheme, have been used, in particular, for Iridium. The users are handled individually by the satellite and several satellites may serve a user at the same time.

As mentioned in Section 22.3, the satellite speed is responsible for the greatest part of the system mobility, followed by the Earth's self-rotation, and then the terminal's mobility.

The admission control and resource allocation work has mainly been focused on satellite-fixed cells. Usually, system designers try to include an overlapping area between any two satellite-fixed cells. Therefore, some researchers have proposed that, when a terminal comes into the overlapping area and no channel is available in its new covering cell, it issues a handover request in a queue (the handover queue—HQ) that has priority over incoming calls [28]. Although this idea may enhance the quality of service, the final result depends on many factors, such as the size of the overlapping area and the distribution of the length of the calls. Although this procedure certainly enhances the system, there is no means to reach a target quality of service.

Another idea consists in systematically reserving some channels for the handover requests [19]. In this handover guard (HG) system, if the number of busy channels exceeds a given threshold, then no incoming call is accepted and only handover requests are handled. This system becomes more efficient when the threshold goes down. However, if the threshold is too low, the system will be underloaded in many cases, as incoming calls that could have been accepted are rejected, hence the need of a tradeoff between quality of service and system capacity. In [7], additional concepts of geographical position are integrated into this concept, so that the authors can evaluate a call blocking probability depending on the remaining time the user has in his/her cell, and the expected duration of a call. A new user is accepted into the system if his/her handover call blocking probability will meet QoS requirements, and his/her inclusion does not degrade the existing calls under the QoS target. This results in a more accurate acceptance/rejection of users.

In [29], the authors consider, for each terminal, the servicing time of a satellite cell. In particular, they analyze its movement and deduce the instants t_i and t_e when the terminal enters the cell and when it leaves it, as shown in Figure 22.7. As a result, when a terminal is introduced into the system, not only the present covering cell is reserved, but also a sufficient number of future cells, associated with future utilization, so that the service duration meets the quality of service requirements (this algorithm is called guaranteed handover—GH). If the communication continues, then additional reservations are done in real time. In the worst case, when these lifetime reservations fail, the terminal can be notified that the connection will end within a certain amount of time.

22.4.2.2 ISL Dimensioning

In [4, 15], the impact of the ISL's design phase on the overall performances of the network have been pointed out (see Section 22.2.2). It is worth observing that in these works a unique pattern is chosen once and for all during the design phase.

A different approach has been adopted in [37, 38], in which the authors consider differ-

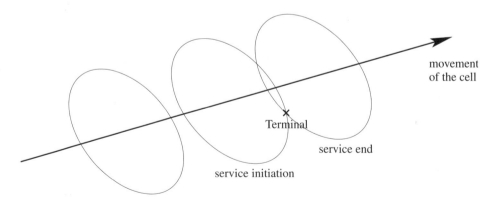

Figure 22.7 Instants of service initiation and service end for a satellite-fixed cell.

ent discrete time steps (each time step corresponds to a "snapshot" of the constellation, that is, the relative positions of the satellites). For each time step, an ISL's dimensioning problem is solved so as to minimize the maximum ISL load, which, in turn, yields the sufficient ISL capacity to route the requests.

22.4.2.3 *Precomputed Routes and Snapshot/FSA Techniques: Deterministic Routing*

In this section, we survey how the deterministic behavior of the network can be exploited to enhance the overall performance of the network. In particular, the following three aspects will be considered: (1) design choices: how satellites are interconnected through ISLs; (2) reservation strategies: how to guarantee that a communication will not be dropped; and (3) "ad hoc" routing algorithms: algorithms that depend on the current state of the network.

Consider a discrete model in which each state of the network corresponds to a visibility state representing the set of satellites that are visible to each other (i.e., those pairs of satellites that, potentially, can be directly connected to each other). Then, two opposite policies (off-line or on-line design) can be adopted: either provide a unique strategy that does not depend on the visibility state (i.e., does not vary over time), or provide a different strategy for every visibility state.

Below we first describe some basic routing heuristics that do not exploit the knowledge of the visibility states. Then we will see how these solutions can benefit from the deterministic behaviour of the network.

Basic Routing Strategies. In [31] different routing and reservation strategies for mesh-like topologies (a 6×11 mesh model is adopted) have been compared. As for the routing strategies, each link is associated with a cost function and the routing algorithm chooses a path with minimum cost. According to different definitions of the cost function, the following four strategies have been compared:

1. Min Hops. the cost of each ISL is 1, hence the connection is always established by choosing any path that minimizes the number of ISLs in it (i.e., the minimum number of hops).

2. Min Load. Each link is associated with a cost given by $1/vacancy$, where *vacancy* is the number of free channels in the link; the chosen path minimizes the sum of the cost of the ISLs in such a path.

3. Min Hops Min Load. Among the set of paths with minimal number of hops, consider the one with lowest maximum link usage. Then, the call is accepted if and only if such route contains no link that is overloaded.

4. Revised Min Hops Min Load. This is defined similarly to (3), with the only difference being that if a request cannot be routed along a min-hops route, then a suboptimal delay path is chosen.

(In [31] such strategies are named minimum hops algorithm, minimum cost algorithm, mesh algorithm, and revised mesh algorithm, respectively.) Notice that the first strategy arbitrarily chooses any min-hop (delay) path, whereas the other strategies aim to keep the link usage as small as possible. Interestingly, the experimental comparison in [31] shows that, at least for some probability distribution, it is fundamental to avoid the use of highly loaded links and the use of paths with sub-optimal length. Indeed, the worse strategy turns out to be the min hops one, and the min hop min load strategy performs better than the revised one.

From On-line to Off-line: Precomputed Routes. In [6], the deterministic behavior of the network has been also exploited to enhance the performance (in terms of call blocking probability) of the routing strategies. In particular, the authors compare a min-cost strategy (similar to those mentioned above) to a static routing, in which the routes are computed off-line in advance. The network is modeled as a FSA (see Section 22.3.1.3) and, for each state (i.e., network topology), a set of routes is precomputed. Clearly, this reduces the communication overhead due to the periodic broadcast operations required to update the link state (i.e., the load) information. Somewhat surprisingly, this approach also has a better call blocking probability. This is mainly due to the fact that, after a network change, the solution provided by the min-cost algorithm is rather "unstable," so several calls are rerouted.

This idea of moving the complexity of routing from an on-line problem to an off-line one is also the basis of [38, 37]. There, for each possible demand pair (i.e., for each possible communication), k different shortest paths are computed. Those paths are then used during the on-line phase, in which the routing algorithm chooses a route between such k candidates. Based on this idea, an upper bound on the ISL's capacity is given by the number of such paths containing a link. Informally speaking, it is assumed that there is a request for each possible pair of satellites and the goal is to compute the minimum l such that, if every ISL capacity is l, then every request can choose between k different paths of minimal length. This problem is formulated by means of a linear programming system. In [37] the authors also consider the problem of relating subsequent states of the network, so that rerouting is performed only when necessary. More precisely, a routing state will be computed and optimized while keeping some remaining routes of the previous states.

22.4.2.4 *Predicting Link Handovers*

Another approach consists in taking advantage of link handovers to manage the mobility of the network.

The Probabilistic Routing Protocol. Upon a call arrival, a first route through the satellites has to be assigned to the call. Such a route can be chosen based on any criterion, such as minimum number of hops, least congestion, minimum cost, etc. The deterministic movement of the satellites allow the prediction of the time frame in which a link handover is to occur. Hence, the probabilistic routing protocol (PRP) proposed in [33] tries to establish an arriving communication through a route that has minimum probability to be cut by a link handover. For this, it supposes the existence of a probability distribution function (PDF) of the call time duration over a route.

The protocol applies Dijkstra's algorithm to find the routes. The cost of each ISL is set to one, implying that the route will be minimum hop. The PDF is used to remove from consideration of Dijkstra's algorithm those ISLs that are likely to hand over during the communication.

It is easy to see that the PRP works for very short calls, since a direct consequence of its implementation is that the route just set will not be cut (with a given target probability) during the call. For instance, a target probability of 0.99 reduces link rerouting operations by 80% when compared to the "pure" Dijkstra's algorithm. Unfortunately, the probability of blocking new calls increases due to the prohibition of many ISLs, amounting to almost 15% of 3-minute calls for the same target probability, or over 1600 calls.

The Footprint Handover Rerouting Protocol. A rerouting strategy, called footprint hand-over rerouting (FHR) was proposed in [32, 34]. It uses information about the network predictability to replace a current route by a new one, based on the successor satellites in the original route, as follows.

Let $R = S_1, S_2, \ldots, S_k$ be a route connecting satellite S_1 to satellite S_k. If both route ends undergo a link handover, then a footprint rerouting can take place and R is rerouted through $R' = S_1', S_2', \ldots, S_k'$, where S_i' denotes the successor of satellite S_i in the same orbit. If only the route end S_1 (or, S_k) has to hand over the communication, but S_k' (respectively, S_1') is not yet visible to the ground user, then the original route R is simply augmented to $R' = S_1', S_1, S_2, \ldots, S_k$ (or $R' = S_1, S_2, \ldots, S_k, S_k'$), until S_k' (or S_1') becomes visible to the ground user. When the second route end undergoes its link handover, a footprint rerouting is used and the new route will be $R' = S_1', S_2', \ldots, S_k'$.

Evidently, if R is a minimum-hop route, then FHR implements a rerouting in which R' is also a minimum-hop route. Further, in the case where the link cost is a function of traffic load, and the latter is time-homogeneous, then R being a minimum-cost route implies that R' is also a minimum-cost route.

The performance of FHR has been evaluated through simulation, particularly against a pure augmentation approach, where a call is dropped if an augmented link cannot be found between the handover satellite and the current route. New call first routes are found through the implementation of the Dijkstra algorithm. Two cost functions are studied, namely minimum hops and congestion. In the case of homogeneous traffic with high call arrival rate, FHR blocks more new calls than pure augmentation, but drops much fewer calls because of handovers, than pure augmentation. This shows the value of taking the deterministic network topology into account.

22.4.2.5 Constellations Viewed as Dynamic Networks

Another idea consists in managing more specifically the mobility of the constellation. The more natural strategy consists in using shortest-path algorithms, which minimize the resources taken by an individual route using a cost based on the links. Each link receives a cost (proportional to its expected load), and the route minimizes the sum of the costs of the links it uses.

An elementary model is inspired by ad hoc networks [26]. The two main strategies are:

1. *Proactive:* all the living nodes are immediately notified of any change of topology.
2. *Reactive:* a request is likely to initiate a flood that will discover the actual state of the network.

The choice between the two methods depends on the dominant activity of the network. Proactive protocols perform better when the traffic throughput is high and the topology changes seldomly, whereas the reactive protocols perform well when the network topology changes often and the traffic is low. An example of a proactive protocol is the extended Bellman–Ford (EXBF), proposed for satellite constellations in [25], in which routing tables are dynamically updated using a shortest paths policy. A reactive protocol, named Darting, was also proposed in [25]. The algorithm broadcasts network information only if it becomes absolutely necessary. In the meantime, the algorithm takes advantage of data packets to update the network topology. Experiments have shown that the Darting algorithm required as much as 72% percent more overhead when compared to the EXBF algorithm in an Iridium-like, lightly loaded network [27].

An immediate simplification occurs when one considers that the weights of the links are uniform and the topology is regular. In the mesh or the torus/mesh cases, one shortest path in terms of number of hops is obtained by XY routing (that is, a route consisting first of a series of interorbital links and then a series of intraorbital links). When one considers the minimum delay instead of the minimum number of hops, it is clear that the cost of interorbital links are smaller when they are closer to the poles (whereas the intraorbital link cost remains constant). Some geodesic considerations may give the advantage to routes that take more polar, interorbital links, as explained in [10].

22.4.2.6 *Reservation Strategies*

A second step toward reducing the call blocking probability is the choice of the link reservation strategy. Indeed, all these algorithms attempt only to minimize the load of the links, without implementing congestion control mechanisms, which would give some guarantee that a communication will not be dropped when one of the links it uses experiences a handover.

Notice that most of the handover techniques we described, such as the HQ, HG, GCAC, and GH, could be applied to enhance the routing. A basic reservation strategy was proposed in [31]. It essentially consists of accepting a call if and only if it is possible to reserve ISLs in such a way that the communication can be maintained after any one link handover event (this can be seen as an extension of the GH concept). Here the deterministic behavior of the network plays a key role: It is assumed that we can determine the next handover and the overall network topology, for each link, so if during the call only one of the links in the path has a handover, it is guaranteed that such call will not be dropped.

Another related strategy is the slack reservation policy, which consists in always accepting the new call and, if possible, also reserving the links for a "next handover" event. Intuitively, we are relaxing the basic reservation strategy, since those calls whose duration is sufficiently short will terminate before the link handover event occurs. However, the experimental results in [31] show that the slack reservation strategy performs worse than the basic one. This is mainly due to the fact that, in the slack reservation, a certain number of calls are accepted with no reserved route. Clearly, such calls are vulnerable to link handovers. On the other hand, calls with reserved routes "consume" more resources than they would without reservation. Hence, with less system resources available, the "vulnerable" calls are more likely to be dropped.

Going a step ahead, an algorithm is presented in [12] that forwards the reservation once it is used. It is shown that the reservation permanently guarantees the communication provided that only southward handovers occur. All kinds of handovers are taken into account in [14], in which the call admission control problem for regular satellite networks is turned into a problem of maximum load of a family of rectangles in a two/three-dimensional space. Communication requests are represented as a series of rectangles. Required capacity is then equivalent to the maximum number of rectangles that intersect on a given point. Therefore, capacity control for call admission policies can be done through geometric algorithms.

22.5 CONCLUSIONS

In this chapter, we reviewed the literature concerning routing and handover techniques for LEO constellations. We showed that they are particularly complex in such a context because of both physical constraints and the movement of the satellites. Notwithstanding this, several interesting results exist. At the time of this writing, the two extant satellite constellations are operational (Iridium and Globalstar). These facts certainly argue for more research to be undertaken in the near future.

ACKNOWLEDGMENTS

This work was partly supported by a fellowship from the European RTN ARACNE project (to P. Penna), the INRIA/CNPq, and the RNRT/Constellation projects.

REFERENCES

1. E. Altman, A. Ferreira, and J. Galtier, *Les réseaux satellitaires de télécommunication,* Paris: Dunod, 1999.
2. S. Appleby, Multifractal characterization of the distribution pattern of the human population. *Geographic Analysis, 28*(2): 147–160, 1996.
3. F. Baccelli, M. Klein, M. Lebourges, and S. Zuyev, Géométrie aléatoire et architecture de réseaux. *Ann. Télécommun., 51:* 158–179, 1996.
4. P. Bergé, A. Ferreira, J. Galtier, and J.-N. Petit, A probabilistic study of inter-satellite links load in polar orbit satellite constellations. *Telecommunication Systems, 18:* 123–135, 2001.
5. H. S. Chang, B. W. Kim, C. G. Lee, Y. Choi, H. S. Yang, and C. S. Kim, Topological design and routing for low-earth orbit satellite networks. In *Proceedings if IEEE Global Telecommunications Conference (GLOBECOM),* pp. 529–535, 1995.
6. H. S. Chang, B. W. Kim, C. G. Lee, S. L. Min, Y. C., H. S. Yang, D. N. Kim, and C. S. Kim, Performance comparison of optimal routing and dynamic routing in low-earth orbit satellite networks. In *Proceedings of IEEE Vehicular Technology Conference (VTC),* pp. 1240–1243, 1996.
7. S. Cho, I. F. Akyildiz, M. D. Bender, and H. Uzunalioğlu, A New Connection Admission Control for Spotbeam Handover in LEO Satellite Networks. In *Proceedings of IEEE Global Telecommunications Conference (GLOBECOM),* San Francisco, pp. 1156–1160, 2000.
8. D. R. Cox and V. Isham, *Point Processes.* London: Chapman and Hall, 1980.
9. F. J. Dietrich, The globalstar satellite cellular communication system design and status. In *Pro-*

ceedings of the 5th International Mobile Satellite Conference. pp. 139–144, Pasadena, CA, June, 1997.

10. E. Ekici, I. F. Akyildiz, and M. Bender, Datagram Routing Algorithm for LEO Satellite Networks. In *Proceedings of IEEE INFOCOM,* pp. 500–508, 2000.

11. A. Ferreira, J. Galtier, P. Mahey, G. Mateus and A. Oliveira, An optimization model for routing in low earth orbit satellite constellations. In *Proceedings of ISPAN,* Dallas, December 2000, New York: IEEE CS Press.

12. A. Ferreira, J. Galtier, J.-N. Petit and H. Rivano, Re-routing algorithms in a meshed satellite constellation. *Annales des Télécommunications, 56:* 169–174, 2001.

13. A. Frey and V. Schmidt, Marked point processes in the plane I—A survey with applications to spatial modeling of communication networks. *Advances in Performance Analysis, 1*(1): 65–110, 1998.

14. J. Galtier, Geographical reservation for guaranteed handover and routing in low earth orbit constellations. *Telecommunication Systems, 18:* 101–121, 2001.

15. B. Gavish and J. Kalvenes, The impact of intersatellite communication links on LEOS performance. *Telecommunication Systems, 8:* 159–190, 1997.

16. N. Gerlich, On the spatial multiplexing gain of SDMA for wireless local loop access. Technical Report 161, Universität Würzburg, January, 1997.

17. P. Gvozdjak, *Modeling communications in Low-Earth-Orbit satellite networks.* PhD thesis, School of Computing Science, Simon Fraser University, 2000.

18. M. Hellebrandt and R. Mathar, Cumulated interference power and bit-error-rates in mobile packet radio. *Wireless Networks, 3:* 169–172, 1997.

19. D. Hong and S. Rappaport, Traffic model and performance analysis for cellular mobile radio telephone systems with prioritized and nonprioritized handoff procedures. *IEEE Transactions on Vehicular Technology, 36*(3): 77–92, 1986.

20. Y. C. Hubbel and L. M. Sanders, A comparison of the IRIDIUM and AMPS systems. *IEEE Network, 12*(2): 52–59, 1997.

21. D. M. Kohn, Providing global broadband internet access using low-earth-orbit satellites. *Computer networks and ISDN systems, 29:* 1763–1768, 1997.

22. R. J. Leopold, Low-earth orbit global cellular communications network. In *Proceedings of IEEE International Conference on Communications (ICC),* pp. 1108–1111, 1991.

23. J. A. Musey, W. Kidd, and P. Fuhrmann, The satellite report. http://www.unterberg.com.

24. E. Papapetrou, I. Gragopoulos, and F.-N. Pavlidou, Performance evaluation of LEO satellite constellations with intersatellite links under self-similar and Poisson traffic. *International Journal of Satellite Communications, 17:* 51–64, 1999.

25. S. R. Pratt, C. E. Fossa Jr., R. A. Raines, and M. A. Temple, An operational and performance overview of the IRIDIUM Low Earth Orbit satellite system. *IEEE Communications Surveys,* pp. 2–10, second quarter 1999.

26. A. Qayyum, *Analysis and evaluation of channel access schemes and routing protocols in wireless LANs.* PhD thesis, University of Paris-Sud, November 2000.

27. R. Raines et al., Simulation of routing protocols operating in a low earth orbit satellite communication network environment. In *1997 IEEE Military Communications Conference,* volume 1, pp. 429–433, Monterey, CA, November 1997.

28. E. D. Re, R. Fantacci, and G. Giambene, Efficient dynamic allocation techniques with handover queuing for mobile satellite networks. *IEEE Journal on Selected Areas in Communications, 13*(2): 397–405, 1995.

29. J. Restrepo and G. Maral, Guaranteed Handover (GH) service in a non-Geo constellation with "satellite-fixed cell" (SFC) systems. In *Proceedings 5th International Mobile Satellite Conference (IMSC),* pp. 19–24, Pasadena, CA, June 1997.

30. M. A. Sturza, Architecture of the Teledesic satellite system. In *Proceedings of the International Mobile Satellite Conference (IMSC),* pp. 214–218, 1995.

31. P. T. S. Tam, J. C. S. Lui, H. W. Chan, Cliff C. N. Sze, and C. N. Sze, An optimized routing scheme and a channel reservation strategy for a low earth orbit satellite system. In *Proc. of IEEE Vehicular Technology Conference (VTC 1999–Fall). IEEE VTS 50th, Volume 5,* pp. 2870–2874, 1999.

32. H. Uzunalioğlu, I. F. Akyildiz, Y. Yesha, and W. Yen, Footprint handover rerouting protocol for low Earth orbit satellite networks. *ACM Journal on Wireless Networks, 5*(5): 327–337, 1999.

33. H. Uzunalioğlu, M. D. Bender, and I. F. Akyildiz, A routing algorithm for low earth orbit (LEO) satellite networks with dynamic connectivity, *ACM-Baltzer Journal of Wireless Networks (WINET), 6*(3): 181–190, 2000.

34. H. Uzunalioğlu, W. Yen, and I. F. Akyildiz, A connection handover protocol for LEO satellite ATM networks. In *Proceedings of the 3rd ACM/IEEE International Conference on Mobile Computing and Networking (MOBICOM),* pp. 204–214, Budapest, Hungary, September 1997.

35. M. D. Violet, The development and application of a cost per minute metric for the evaluation of mobile satellite systems in a limited-growth voice communication market. Massachusetts Institute of Technology, Cambridge, MA, 1995.

36. M. Werner and G. Maral, Traffic flows and dynamic routing in LEO intersatellite link networks. In *Proceedings of the 5th International Mobile Satellite Conference (IMSC),* pp. 283–288, 1997.

37. M. Werner and P. Révillon, Optimization issues in capacity dimensioning of LEO intersatellite links networks. In *Proceedings of ECSC 5,* November 1999

38. M. Werner, F. Wauquiez, J. Frings, and G. Maral, Capacity dimensioning of ISL networks in broadband LEO satellite systems. In *Proceedings of the 6th International Mobile Satellite Conference (IMSC),* pp. 334–341, Ottawa, 1999.

39. W. W. Wu, E. F. Miller, W. L. Pritchard, and R. L. Pickholtz, Mobile satellite communications. *Proceedings of the IEEE, 82*(9): 1431–1448, 1994.

CHAPTER 23

Multicasting: From Fixed Networks to Ad Hoc Networks

THOMAS KUNZ

Systems and Computer Engineering, Carleton University, Ottawa, Canada

23.1 INTRODUCTION

Multicasting can efficiently support a variety of applications that are characterized by the close degree of collaboration typical of many ad hoc applications currently envisioned. Within the wired network, well-established routing protocols exist to offer efficient multicasting service. As nodes become increasingly mobile, these protocols need to evolve to provide similarly efficient service in the new environment. This survey will briefly describe the basic approaches to multicasting in wired networks. It then gradually relaxes the requirement that all nodes be stationary, discussing multicast protocols for cellular networks (which are characterized by a fixed infrastructure with mobile end nodes) and ad hoc networks (completely infrastructureless mobile networks).

23.2 MOTIVATION

Multicasting is the transmission of datagrams to a group of zero or more hosts identified by a single destination address. A multicast datagram is typically delivered to all members of its destination host group with the same reliability as regular unicast datagrams. In the case of IP, for example, the datagram is not guaranteed to arrive intact at all members of the destination group or in the same order relative to other datagrams [1].

Multicasting is intended for group-oriented computing. There are more and more applications in which one-to-many dissemination is necessary. The multicast service is critical in applications characterized by the close collaboration of teams (e.g., rescue patrols, military battalions, scientists, etc.) with requirements for audio and video conferencing and sharing of text and images. In the Internet (IPv4), multicasting facilities were introduced via the multicast backbone (MBone), a virtual overlay network on top of the Internet. This overlay network consists of multicast-capable islands connected by tunnels. Each island contains one or more special routers called multicast routers, which are logically connected by these tunnels. These routers manage group membership and cooperate to route data to all hosts wishing to participate in a multicast group. IP multicast groups are identified by special IP addresses.

Handbook of Wireless Networks and Mobile Computing, Edited by Ivan Stojmenović.
ISBN 0-471-41902-8 © 2002 John Wiley & Sons, Inc.

Typically, the membership of a host group is dynamic; that is, hosts may join and leave groups any time. There is no restriction on the location or number of members in a host group. A host may be a member of more than one group at a time. A host does not have to be a member of a group to send datagrams to it.

A host group may be permanent or transient. A permanent group has a well-known, administratively assigned address. It is the address not the membership of the group that is permanent; at any time, a permanent group may have any number of members, even zero. Those IP multicast addresses that are not reserved for permanent groups are available for dynamic assignment to transient groups, which exist only as long as they have members.

The use of multicasting within a network has many benefits. Multicasting reduces the communication costs for applications that send the same data to multiple recipients. Instead of sending via multiple unicasts, multicasting minimizes the link bandwidth consumption, sender and router processing, and delivery delay [2]. In addition, multicasting provides a simple yet robust communication mechanism whereby a receiver's individual address is unknown or changeable transparently to the source.

Maintaining group membership information and building optimal multicast trees is challenging even in wired networks. However, nodes are increasingly mobile. One particularly challenging environment for multicast is a mobile ad hoc network (MANET). A MANET consists of a dynamic collection of nodes with sometimes rapidly changing multihop topologies that are composed of relatively low-bandwidth wireless links. There is no assumption of an underlying fixed infrastructure. Nodes are free to move arbitrarily. Since each node has a limited transmission range, not all messages may reach all the intended hosts. To provide communication through the whole network, a source-to-destination path could pass through several intermediate neighbor nodes. Unlike typical wireline routing protocols, ad hoc routing protocols must address a diverse range of issues [3]. The network topology can change randomly and rapidly, at unpredictable times. Since wireless links generally have lower capacity, congestion is typically the norm rather than the exception. The majority of nodes will rely on batteries, thus routing protocols must limit the amount of control information that is passed between nodes.

The goal of MANETs is to extend mobility into the realm of autonomous, mobile, wireless domains, where a set of nodes form the network routing infrastructure in an ad hoc fashion. The majority of applications for the MANET technology are in areas where rapid deployment and dynamic reconfiguration are necessary and the wireline network is not available [3]. These include military battlefields, emergency search and rescue sites, classrooms, and conventions where participants share information dynamically using their mobile devices. These applications lend themselves well to multicast operation. In addition, within a wireless medium, it is even more crucial to reduce the transmission overhead and power consumption. Multicasting can improve the efficiency of the wireless link when sending multiple copies of messages by exploiting the inherent broadcast property of wireless transmission. However, besides the issues for any ad hoc routing protocol listed above, wireless mobile multicasting faces several key challenges [4]. Multicast group members move, thus precluding the use of a fixed multicast topology. Transient loops may form during tree reconfiguration, so tree reconfiguration schemes should be simple to keep channel overhead low.

This chapter briefly describes the basic approaches to multicasting in wired networks.

It then gradually relaxes the requirement that all nodes be stationary. In a first step, multicast members are allowed to be mobile, connecting to a fixed infrastructure. In this cellular architecture, multicast protocols are based on extensions/modifications of the basic mobile IP [5,6] protocol used to provide unicast services to mobile end nodes. These mobile-IP-based protocols, however, cannot be applied to MANETs, which inherently lack infrastructure. We will look at proposed extensions to traditional multicast protocols, as well as multicast proposals developed specifically for MANETs.

23.3 MULTICASTING IN FIXED/WIRED NETWORKS

On the Internet, there are two popular wired network multicast schemes, namely, per-source shortest tree and shared tree. The per-source tree scheme consists of broadcasting the packet from the source to all destinations along the source tree in a manner that avoids loops. This is accomplished by using "reverse path forwarding" or RPF. In RPF, a router forwards a broadcast packet on its remaining interfaces if and only if the packet is received on an interface that is on the shortest path from the router to the source. Thus, only those packets are forwarded that arrive on the reverse shortest path from the router to the sender. Examples of per-source tree protocols commonly used in the Internet are DVMRP and PIM dense mode [7]. In the wireline environment, per-source tree multicasting has many attractive properties. For example, the shortest tree from each source to all destinations is inherent in the routing protocol. Furthermore, source tree multicast distributes the traffic evenly in the network (assuming that the source and receivers are evenly distributed), and it does not rely on a control point (rendezvous point).

In the shared tree multicast scheme, each multicast group has a single tree rooted at a special router called the rendezvous point (RP). Each multicast group has its own RP, and "grows" its own shared tree. The intermediate routers in the tree are responsible for forwarding the multicast data to members. In this manner, all receivers join the multicast group by explicitly sending a JOIN message toward the RP. Senders send data to the RP, and the RP uses a single unidirectional shared tree to distribute the data to the receivers. Examples of shared-tree approaches are core based tree (CBT) [8] and PIM sparse mode. The shared tree is beneficial if multiple senders transmit data to the same host group, since only one tree needs to be built and maintained. However, it also has some drawbacks with respect to the per-source scheme. Traffic is concentrated on the backbone, rather than evenly distributed across the network, and paths are often suboptimal.

23.4 MULTICASTING IN FIXED INFRASTRUCTURE CELLULAR NETWORKS

Mobile networks with fixed infrastructure, or cellular networks, consist of stationary base stations and mobile endpoints. Each base station is assigned a geographic area, or cell, and is responsible for connecting mobile endpoints to the wired portion of the network. Mobile users communicate via a single-hop wireless channel with a base station, which is in turn connected to a wired backbone.

Mobile IP [5, 6] is the basic mechanism currently used to manage mobility to these end hosts. In mobile IP, a mobile node may change its location without changing its IP address. The way this is achieved is through the use of a home agent and a foreign agent. While the mobile node is visiting a foreign network, it is assigned a care-of address that represents the mobile node's current point of attachment. This care-of address is then registered with the home agent to allow the home agent to know where to tunnel datagrams to the mobile node. A home agent represents a router (typically) or other computer on the mobile node's home network that is responsible for encapsulating datagrams for delivery to the mobile node when it is away from home. A foreign agent represents a router or other computer on a mobile node's visited network that provides routing services to the mobile node while it is registered. The foreign agent decapsulates and delivers to the mobile node datagrams that were encapsulated by the mobile node's home agent. In the reverse direction, for datagrams sent by the mobile node, standard IP routing is used to deliver the datagrams to their respective destinations; it is not necessary to pass them through the home agent.

Achieving multicast service for mobile nodes becomes a challenging problem. A node that wishes to receive group multicast datagrams should join the group repeatedly as it changes location. The branches and leaves of a multicast tree may change along with the node's mobility. Mobile nodes have to choose a location (IP subnet) to describe their membership. The structure and charactistics of the dynamic tree depend on where a mobile node chooses to declare its multicast membership. Possible choices are the home network, the currently visited network, or several combined networks. Different approaches will result in different multicast trees and tree maintenance overheads over time.

There are currently two ways to extend mobile IP to support multicast services to mobile hosts in a fixed-infrastructure cellular network: foreign-agent-based multicast and home-agent-based multicast. In the foreign-agent-based multicast proposal, each mobile node has to obtain a "colocated" care-of address (i.e., a care-of address exclusively used by the mobile node) when roaming into a foreign network. The mobile node will subscribe to the multicast group at the foreign network. The multicast router in the foreign network propagates this information for the mobile node. Processing this in the same way as dynamic group membership changes, the multicast tree will extend to the foreign network. This scheme has the advantage of offering an optimal routing path (within the limits of IP routing) and avoids delivering duplicate copies of datagrams. However, when a mobile host is highly mobile, its multicast service may be very expensive because of the difficulty in managing the multicast tree. Furthermore, the extra delay incurred when rebuilding a multicast tree can create the possibility of a disruption in multicast data delivery. Therefore, if the host is likely to be stationary for an extended period of time, this option is preferred. As expressed in [9]: "Remote subscription does provide the most efficient delivery of multicast packets, but this service may come at a high price for the networks involved and the multicast routers that must manage the multicast tree. For hosts that want guaranteed two-way communication with the multicast group and are unable to acquire a colocated address, or hosts that are highly mobile, a different method is needed that will not overload the multicast routers."

In the home-agent-based multicast proposal, when a mobile node is roaming in a foreign network, multicast packets will be encapsulated by the home agent and delivered to the mobile node as unicast packets. The mobile node only subscribes to the multicast group in its home network. Its multicast group membership is transparent to any foreign network. There are a number of problems with this approach, however. If the mobile node is far from its home network and in the same network with the source of the multicast tree, the extended branch will be extremely long: the multicast packet will travel to the home network and then travel back to the source network again. If the number of mobile nodes is large, many branches are extended from the home network. This will increase the network traffic significantly. Consider the following scenario: the mobile node roams into a foreign network, which is a member of the multicast group. But the mobile node's membership is transparent to the foreign network; it still receives the multicast packets from its home network via a unicast tunnel. If two or more mobile nodes belong to the same home agent and subscribe to the same multicast group, the home agent will duplicate packets from the same multicast packet, and send them separately to the same foreign agent. So the main disadvantages of this approach are suboptimal packet routing and unnecessary packet duplication.

To address these problems of home-agent-based multicast, the MoM (mobile multicast) proposal [9, 10] suggested a number of modifications to this protocol. First, a home agent only forwards a single copy of multicast packets to a foreign network even if two or more mobile nodes belonging to this home agent roam in the same foreign network. The foreign network uses link-layer multicast to distribute the packets to separate mobile nodes. In this way, packet duplication will decrease. However, multiple tunnels from different home agents can still terminate at one foreign agent. When multiple home agents have mobile nodes visiting the same foreign network, one copy of every multicast packet is forwarded to the same foreign agent by each home agent. The foreign agent suffers from the convergence of tunnels set up by each home agent. So the second new concept introduced by MoM is the designated multicast service provider (DMSP). DMSP is one home agent selected by a foreign agent, forwarding only a single copy of a multicast datagram to a foreign network. The management of the DMSP adds overhead. If a mobile node whose home agent works as a DMSP moves out of the foreign network, the foreign agent must select another DMSP.

Mobile multicast agent (MMA) is an attempt to improve the optimality of the multicast tree [11]. The MMA approach uses a multicast agent (MA) that provides multicast services to mobile nodes. A mobile node receives multicast traffic from the tunneling of a certain MA or directly from the multicast router at the current network. Each MA has to support a group service with one multicast forwarder (MF) per group. A MF is one of the MAs that are in charge of forwarding multicast data to other MAs. For each network, both the MA and the mobile node, which resides in the same network, use the same MF. Initially, if a mobile node wants to join a group in any foreign network, subscriptions are done through the MA on the foreign network, which must be a multicast router. This MA becomes a MF itself, and in this network mobile hosts receive multicast service directly from the multicast router. Then, when the mobile node moves to another network, it notifies the MA in the new network of its group ID and its MF during registration. This MF information is used by the MA in the new network as the previous MF of the visiting mobile node. If the MA in the new network does not have a group member, then it configures its own MF value with the previous MF of the mobile node. Otherwise, if the new network has group members and an MF, the MA executes the MF selection algorithm and selects either the current MF of the MA or the MF of the visiting mobile node. Both the MA and the mobile node replace their MF value with the newly selected MF. From the point of the multicast tree, a MA extends the tree from an MF among adjacent networks that belong to the multicast delivery tree for the group. Because the mobility of mobile nodes is expected to show locality characteristics, this MF is one of the more adjacent multicast tree nodes from the current network.

Comparing these proposals, the multicast tree in the foreign-agent based proposal is the most optimal one. But frequent movement requires frequent reconfigurations of the multicast tree. This puts a high load on the multicast routers. The MMA proposal has the second-best tree, and not every movement will cause the multicast tree to change. It therefore provides good multicast support for mobile nodes. However, every foreign network has to deploy MAs. All these schemes assume that the mobile host is just one wireless hop away from the fixed infrastructure, which is characteristic of cellular networks. They are therefore not able to handle truly ad hoc networks, in which intermediate nodes are mobile as well.

23.5   MULTICASTING IN MOBILE AD HOC NETWORKS: ADOPTING WIRELESS PROTOCOLS

In mobile ad hoc networks, there are three basic categories of multicast algorithms. A first, naive, approach is to simply flood the network. Every node receiving a message floods it to a list of neighbors. Flooding a network acts like a chain reaction that can result in exponential growth. The proactive approach precomputes paths to all possible destinations and stores this information in routing tables. To maintain an up-to-date database, routing information is periodically distributed throughout the network. These protocols are discussed in the next few paragraphs. The final approach is to create paths to other hosts on demand. The idea is based on a query-response mechanism or reactive multicast. In the query phase, a node explores the environment. Once the query reaches the destination, the response phase is entered and establishes the path. This category of protocols is the subject of the next section.

In MANETs, traditional per-source tree approaches for multicasting present a problem. Suppose a source moves faster than the routing tables can track it. In this case, some of the nodes will have obsolete routing tables pointing in the "wrong direction." Following the "reverse path forwarding" principle, multicast packets are discarded at such nodes, and may never reach some of the receivers. One way to alleviate this problem is to increase the routing update rate with mobility. However, the periodic full broadcast in implementations like DVMRP introduces costly control overhead on the low-bandwidth wireless channel and is not suitable for sparse distributed membership and scaling the network size. Chiang et al. [12] propose wireless extensions to DVMRP, whereby each sender selectively "floods" multicast packets to all nodes within a specified range using RPF. However, this approach suffers from the periodic data flooding overhead incurred by the source in order to reestablish any new or lost connections. This periodic flooding causes considerable transmission overhead for the low-bandwidth wireless channel. Also, with the RPF mechanism, if the shortest path changes and no multicast packets arrive on the new shortest path, the node becomes disconnected from the tree. Finally, scalability to a large number of senders becomes problematic since each internal tree node stores the list of sources and associated timers. Storage and processing overheads grow linearly with the number of sources. The shared tree eliminates this problem.

In general, shared trees are potentially less sensitive to source mobility and can in part overcome the fast-moving source problem. Basically, a fast source will send its packet to the RP in unicast mode. Packets are correctly delivered to the RP on shortest paths, irrespective of the speed of the source. The RP will then multicast the packet on the shared tree to the intended destinations. This works as long as the shared tree is stable and the RP itself is not moving fast. If all the nodes are moving fast (relative to the routing table updates), the shared tree solution also fails. Also, as the entire network moves and the membership changes dynamically, the RP may not be in the center, aggravating the nonoptimality of the paths. Chiang et al. [13] propose a shared tree wireless network multicast (ST-WIM) algorithm based on adapting PIM-SM to MANET. Several simulations were performed using the ST-WIM protocol measuring metrics like join latency, control packet overhead, throughput when varying multicast group size, and node mobility. ST-WIM's results show that the performance of both hard- and soft-state multicast tree maintenance mechanisms degrades rapidly with increased mobility (beyond 10 m/s) and an increased number of mobile nodes.

Chiang and Gerla [14] introduce a modified version of the CBT multicast algorithm. Each multicast group has a unique multicast identifier. Each multicast address identifies a host group, the group of hosts that should receive a packet sent to that address. Each multicast group is initialized and maintained by a multicast server that becomes the core of the CBT for this multicast group. Initially, the multicast server broadcasts the multicast identifier and its own node identifier using a flooding algorithm. When a node receives this information, it will use it when it needs to join or quit the multicast group. Simulations were performed to evaluate performance based on several criteria like control packet overhead, robustness to mobility, scaling properties with respect to multicast group membership, and response time to joining a group. Their simulation results show a rapid decrease in throughput and an increase in control-packet overhead with increased mobility of the nodes.

Chiang et al. [15] discuss an adaptive shared tree multicast that attempts to reduce path costs and distribute traffic more evenly in the network, by allowing a receiver to request, under certain circumstances, that a source deliver the multicast messages to it on the shortest path rather than on the shared tree path. Although this approach offers an improvement over ST-WIM [13], there is still a significant decrease in throughput as node mobility increases. As speed increases, throughput decreases, due to the inability of the routing and multicast protocols to keep up with node movements.

Results on the two approaches (per source and shared tree) show that these schemes scale well to large network size and can survive moderate speeds. In comparison with the per-source-tree solution, the shared tree scheme exhibits lower throughput at heavy load, as expected, due to higher traffic concentration on the common tree. It shows, however, much less control overhead than the per-source tree, since the latter must constantly refresh separate trees rooted at different sources. It also offers better scalability to large net-work size. As node mobility increases, both schemes perform rather poorly, indicating the need to explore alternative multicast strategies.

23.6   MULTICASTING IN MOBILE AD HOC NETWORKS: MANET-INSPIRED MULTICAST PROTOCOLS

The development of specific MANET routing protocols is an open and active research area. The following paragraphs briefly describe two distinct on-demand multicast proto-cols currently proposed for standardization to the IETF before results of performance studies are discussed.

23.6.1   Multicast Ad Hoc On-Demand Distance Vector

The MAODV (multicast ad hoc on-demand distance vector) routing protocol [16] discov-ers multicast routes on demand using a broadcast route-discovery mechanism. A mobile node originates a route request (RREQ) message when it wishes to join a multicast group, or when it has data to send to a multicast group but does not have a route to that group. Only a member of the desired multicast group may respond to a join RREQ. If the RREQ is not a join request, any node with a fresh enough route (based on group sequence num-ber) to the multicast group may respond. If an intermediate node receives a join RREQ for a multicast group of which it is not a member, or if it receives a RREQ and it does not have a route to that group, it rebroadcasts the RREQ to its neighbors.

As the RREQ is broadcast across the network, nodes set up pointers to establish the re-verse route in their route tables. A node receiving a RREQ first updates its route table to record the sequence number and the next-hop information for the source node. This reverse route entry may later be used to relay a response back to the source. For join RREQs, an additional entry is added to the multicast route table. This entry is not acti-vated unless the route is selected to be part of the multicast tree.

If a node receives a join RREQ for a multicast group, it may reply if it is a member of the multicast group's tree and its recorded sequence number for the multicast group is at least as great as that contained in the RREQ. The responding node updates its route and multicast route tables by placing the requesting node's next-hop information in the tables, and then unicasts a request response (RREP) back to the source node. As nodes along the path to the source node receive the RREP, they add both a route table and a multicast route table entry for the node from which they received the RREP, thereby creating the forward path.

When a source node broadcasts a RREQ for a multicast group, it often receives more than one reply. The source node keeps the received route with the greatest sequence num-ber and shortest hop count to the nearest member of the multicast tree for a specified peri-od of time, and disregards other routes. At the end of this period, it enables the selected next hop in its multicast route table, and unicasts an activation message to this selected next hop. The next hop, on receiving this message, enables the entry for the source node in its multicast route table. If this node is a member of the multicast tree, it does not propagate the message any further. However, if this node is not a member of the multicast tree, it will have received one or more RREPs from its neighbors. It keeps the best next hop for its route to the multicast group, unicasts an activation message to that next hop, and enables the corresponding entry in its multicast route table. This process continues until the node that originated the RREP (member of tree) is reached. The activation message ensures that the multicast tree does not have multiple paths to any tree node. Nodes only forward data packets along activated routes in their multicast route tables.

The first member of the multicast group becomes the leader for that group. The multicast group leader is responsible for maintaining the multicast group sequence number and broadcasting this number to the multicast group. This is done through a group hello message. The group hello contains extensions that indicate the multicast group IP address and sequence numbers (incremented every group hello) of all multicast groups for which the node is the group leader. Nodes use the group hello information to update their request table.

Since AODV maintains hard state in its routing table, the protocol has to actively track and react to changes in this tree. If a member terminates its membership with the group, the multicast tree requires pruning. Links in the tree are monitored to detect link breakages. When a link breakage is detected, the node that is further from the multicast group leader (downstream of the break) is responsible for repairing the broken link. If the tree cannot be reconnected, a new leader for the disconnected downstream node is chosen as follows. If the node that initiated the route rebuilding is a multicast group member, it becomes the new multicast group leader. On the other had, if it was not a group member and has only one next hop for the tree, it prunes itself from the tree by sending its next hop a prune message. This continues until a group member is reached. Once these two partitions reconnect, a node eventually receives a group hello for the multicast group that contains group leader information that differs from the information it already has. If this node is a member of the multicast group, and if it is a member of the partition whose group leader has the lower IP address, it can initiate reconnection of the multicast tree.

23.6.2   On-Demand Multicast Routing Protocol

ODMRP (on-demand multicast routing protocol) [17] is mesh-based, and uses a forwarding group concept (only a subset of nodes forwards the multicast packets). A soft-state approach is taken in ODMRP to maintain multicast group members. No explicit control message is required to leave the group.

In ODMRP, group membership and multicast routes are established and updated by the source on demand. When a multicast source has packets to send, but no route to the multicast group, it broadcasts a join-query control packet to the entire network. This join-query packet is periodically broadcast to refresh the membership information and update routes.

When an intermediate node receives the join-query packet, it stores the source ID and the sequence number in its message cache to detect any potential duplicates. The routing table is updated with the appropriate node ID (i.e., backward learning) from which the message was received for the reverse path back to the source node. If the message is not a duplicate and the time-to-live (TTL) is greater than zero, it is rebroadcast.

When the join-query packet reaches a multicast receiver, it creates and broadcasts a "join reply" to its neighbors. When a node receives a join reply, it checks to see if the next hop node ID of one of the entries matches its own ID. If it does, the node realizes that it is on the path to the source and thus is part of the forwarding group, and sets the FG_FLAG (forwarding group flag). It then broadcasts its own join table built on matched entries. The next hop node ID field is filled by extracting information from its routing table. In this way, each forward group member propagates the join reply until it reaches the multicast source via the selected path (shortest). This whole process constructs (or updates) the routes from sources to receivers and builds a mesh of nodes called the forwarding group.

After the forwarding group establishment and route construction process, sources can multicast packets to receivers via selected routes and forwarding groups. While it has data to send, the source periodically sends join-query packets to refresh the forwarding group and routes. When receiving the multicast data packet, a node forwards it only when it is not a duplicate and the setting of the FG_FLAG for the multicast group has not expired. This procedure minimizes the traffic overhead and prevents sending packets through stale routes.

In ODMRP, no explicit control packets need to be sent to join or leave the group. If a multicast source wants to leave the group, it simply stops sending join-query packets since it does not have any multicast data to send to the group. If a receiver no longer wants to receive from a particular multicast group, it does not send the join reply for that group. Nodes in the forwarding group are demoted to nonforwarding nodes if not refreshed (no join tables received) before they time out.

23.6.3   Comparing MAODV and ODMRP

The two on-demand protocols share certain salient characteristics. In particular, they both discover multicast routes only in the presence of data packets to be delivered to a multicast destination. Route discovery in either protocol is based on request and reply cycles in which multicast route information is stored in all intermediate nodes on the multicast path. However, there are several important differences in the dynamics of the two protocols, which may give rise to significant performance differences.

First, MAODV uses a shared multicast tree for forwarding data packets, whereas ODMRP maintains a mesh topology rooted from each source. MAODV uses a multicast group leader to maintain up-to-date multicast tree information, whereas ODMRP source nodes periodically send request messages in order to refresh the multicast mesh.

Second, ODMRP broadcasts the reply back to the source, whereas MAODV unicasts the reply back to the source. By using a broadcast mechanism, ODMRP allows for multiple possible paths from the multicast source back to the receiver. Since MAODV unicasts the reply back to the source, if an intermediate node on the path moves away, then the reply is lost and the route is lost.

Third, MAODV does not activate a multicast route immediately, whereas ODMRP does. In MAODV, a potential multicast source must wait for a specified time, allowing for multiple replies to be received before sending an activation message along the multicast route that it selects. Again, when an intermediate node on the chosen path moves away before a route activation is sent, the path is lost.

Fourth, MAODV sends control messages to repair broken links and to manage network partitions. Since there are no redundant links, MAODV needs to recover from breaks in links. If two network partitions come together, MAODV requires explicit action to merge two network partitions. ODMRP uses a soft-state approach, and lets broken links time out. Routes from multicast sources to receivers in ODMRP are periodically refreshed by the source.

23.6.4 Performance Comparisons

Bagrodia et al. [18] simulated several multicast routing protocols developed specifically for MANET: ad hoc multicast routing (AMRoute) [19], ODMRP [17], ad hoc multicast routing protocol utilizing increasing id numbers (AMRIS) [20], and core-assisted mesh protocol (CAMP) [21]. These protocols were evaluated under diverse network scenarios using the GloMoSim library [22]. AMRoute is a tree-based protocol. It creates a bidirectional shared multicast tree using unicast tunnels to provide connections between multicast group members. Each group has at least one logical core that is responsible for member and tree maintenance. AMRIS establishes a shared tree for multicast data forwarding. Each node in the network is assigned a multicast session ID number. The ranking order of ID numbers is used to direct the flow of multicast data. CAMP supports multicasting by creating a shared mesh structure. All nodes in the network maintain a set of tables with membership and routing information.

To explore the effect of mobility on the protocol performance, the speed of the network hosts was varied. The number of data packets sent by senders was varied to emulate a variety of multicast applications. Different multicast group member sizes were simulated to investigate the impact on performance. Various traffic loads were also applied to study how traffic patterns influence multicast performance. Metrics were used to show the "efficiency" and "effectiveness" of the protocols. The reported results show that mesh protocols performed significantly better than the tree protocols in mobile scenarios. Similarly, [23] compared MAODV and ODMRP and found that ODMRP performs significantly better than MAODV under very adverse conditions (high traffic and node mobility). However, the per-source-based mesh and the periodic refresh messages to update the soft state also resulted in significantly higher protocol overheads, and limited the scalability of ODMRP with respect to number of senders in a multicast group and multicast group size.

Lim and Kim [24] evaluated multicast tree construction and proposed two new flooding methods that can improve the performance of the classic flooding method. Their paper proposes the use of self-pruning and dominant pruning to reduce the flooding cost by utilizing neighborhood information. Self-pruning uses direct neighbor information only, whereas dominant pruning uses neighborhood information up to two hops away. Based on extended neighborhood information, each node computes a reduced forward list for the next transmissions on the broadcast tree. The performance gain from dominant pruning is greater than that from self-pruning. However, dominant pruning has larger overheads than self-pruning and the overheads increase with host mobility. Thus, the self-pruning method could be more appropriate when the mobility of the host is high and the network is small. In contrast, the dominant pruning method could be the method of choice when the mobility is moderate and the network is large.

23.7 CONCLUSIONS

Multicasting can efficiently support a wide variety of applications that are characterized by a close degree of collaboration, typical of many MANET applications currently envisioned. Within the wired network, well-established routing protocols exist to offer efficient multicasting service. As nodes become increasingly mobile, these protocols need to evolve to provide similarly efficient service in the new environment. For cellular architectures, multicast protocols are typically based on extensions to mobile IP, with trade-offs between tree optimality and protocol overhead due to mobility. Adding infrastructure elements can help in reducing protocol overhead while reducing the size of the multicast tree. Adopting wired multicast protocols to MANETs, which are completely lacking in infrastructure, appears less promising. These protocols, having been designed for fixed networks, may fail to keep up with node movements and frequent topology changes due to host mobility, and substantially increase the protocol overheads. New protocols that operate in an on-demand manner are being proposed and investigated. Existing studies show that tree-based on-demand protocols are not necessarily the best choice. In a harsh environment, where the network topology changes very frequently, mesh-based protocols seem to outperform tree-based protocols, due to the availability of alternative paths, which allow multicast datagrams to be delivered to all or most multicast receivers even if links fail. Much still has to be done to improve protocol performance (as measured by the packet delivery ratio) while reducing the associated overhead.

ACKNOWLEDGMENTS

The author would like to thank Prof. James P. Black and Prof. Carey Williamson for their detailed review of an earlier draft of this chapter and their suggestions for improvement.

REFERENCES

1. S. Deering, Host extensions for IP multicasting, RFC 1112, August 1989, available at http://www.ietf.org/rfc/rfc1112.txt.

2. S. Paul, *Multicasting on the Internet and Its Applications,* Norwell, MA: Kluwer Academic Publishers, 1998.

3. S. Corson and J. Macker, Mobile ad hoc networking (MANET): Routing protocol performance issues and evaluation considerations, RFC 2501, January 1999, available at http://www.ietf.org/rfc/rfc2501.txt.

4. C.-C. Chiang, *Wireless Network Multicasting,* PhD dissertation, University of California, Los Angeles, Department of Computing Science, 1998.

5. C. E. Perkins, *Mobile IP Design Principles and Practices,* Reading, MA: Addison Wesley, 1997.

6. C. E. Perkins, IP mobility support, RFC 2002, October 1996, available at http://www.ietf.org/rfc/rfc2002.txt.

7. S. Deering, D. Estrin, D. Farinacci, V. Jacobson, C.-G. Liu, and L. Wei, The PIM architecture for wide-area multicast routing, *IEEE/ACM Transactions on Networking 4,* 153–162, 1996.

8. T. Ballardie, P. Francis, and J. Crowcroft, Core based trees (CBT), in *Proceedings of the*

SIGCOMM Symposium on Communications Architectures and Protocols, San Francisco, September 1993, pp. 85–95.

9. V. Chikarmane, C. Williamson, R. Bunt, and W. Mackrell, Multicast support for mobile hosts using Mobile IP: Design issues and proposed approach, *ACM/Baltzer Journal on Mobile Networks and Applications (MONET), 3,* No.4, pages 365–379, 1998.

10. C. L. Williamson, T. G. Harrison, W. L. Mackrell, and R. B. Bunt, Performance evaluation of the MoM mobile multicast protocol, *ACM/Baltzer Journal on Mobile Networks and Applications (MONET), 3,* 2, 189–201, 1998.

11. H.-S. Shin, Y.-J. Suh, and D.-H. Kwon, Multicast routing protocol by multicast agent in mobile networks, in *Proceedings of the 2000 International Conference on Parallel Processing,* Toronto, August 2000, pp. 271–278.

12. C.-C. Chiang, M. Gerla, and L. Zhang, Tree multicast strategies in mobile, multihop wireless networks, *ACM/Baltzer Journal on Mobile Networks and Applications (MONET), 4,* 3, 193–207, 1999.

13. C.-C. Chiang, M. Gerla, and L. Zhang, Shared tree wireless network multicast, in *Proceedings of the Sixth International Conference on Computer Communications and Networks,* 1997, pp. 28–33.

14. C.-C. Chiang and M. Gerla, Routing and multicast in multihop, mobile wireless networks, in *Proceedings of the IEEE International Conference on Universal Personal Communications (ICUPC'97),* 1997, pp. 28–33.

15. C.-C. Chiang, M. Gerla, and L. Zhang, Adaptive shared tree multicast in mobile wireless networks, *Proceedings of Globecom '98,* Sydney, Australia, November 1998, pp. 193–207.

16. E. Royer and C. E. Perkins, Multicast operation of the ad-hoc on-demand distance vector routing protocol, in *Proceedings of the 5th Annual ACM/IEEE Annual Conference on Mobile Computing and Networking,* Seattle, August 1999, pp. 207–218.

17. S. H. Bae, S.-J. Lee, W. Su, and M. Gerla, The design, implementation, and performance evaluation of on-demand multicast routing protocol in multihop wireless networks, *IEEE Network, 14,* 1, 70–77, 2000.

18. R. Bagrodia, M. Gerla, J. Hsu, W. Su, and S.-J. Lee, A performance comparison study of ad hoc wireless multicast protocols, in *Proceedings of the Nineteenth Annual Joint Conference of the IEEE Computer and Communications Societies (INFOCOM),* March 2000, vol. 2, pp. 565–574.

19. R. Talpade, T. McAuley, J. Xie, and M. Liu, AMRoute: Ad hoc multicast routing protocol, to appear in *Mobile Networks and Applications,* special issue on multipoint communication in wireless mobile networks.

20. C. W. Wu and Y. C. Tay, AMRIS: A multicast protocol for ad hoc wireless networks, in *Military Communications Conference Proceedings, 1999 (MILCOM 1999),* vol. 1, pp. 25–29. New York: IEEE, 1999.

21. J. J. Garcia-Luna-Aceves and E.vL. Madruga, The core-assisted mesh protocol, *IEEE Journal on Selected Areas in Communications, 17,* 8, pp. 1380–1394, 1999.

22. UCLA Computer Science Department Parallel Computing Laboratory and Wireless Adaptive Mobility Laboratory, GloMoSim: A scalable simulation environment for wireless and wired network systems, available at http://pcl.cs.ucla.edu/projects/domans/glomosim.html.

23. E. Cheng, On-demand multicast routing in mobile ad hoc networks, M. Eng. thesis, Carleton University, Ottawa, Canada, Department of Systems and Computer Engineering, 2001.

24. H. Lim and C. Kim, Multicast tree construction and flooding in wireless ad hoc networks, in *Proceedings of the 3rd ACM International Workshop on Modeling, Analysis and Simulation of Wireless and Mobile Systems,* Boston, August 2000, pp. 61–68.

CHAPTER 24

Broadcasting in Radio Networks

ANDRZEJ PELC

Département d'Informatique, Université du Québec à Hull, Hull, Québec, Canada

24.1 INTRODUCTION

Broadcasting is one of the fundamental tasks in network communication. Its goal is to transmit a message from one node of the network, called the source, to all other nodes. Remote nodes get the source message via intermediate nodes, along paths in the network. In this chapter we consider broadcasting in radio networks. (Broadcasting in other types of networks, in particular point-to-point networks, has been extensively studied and is surveyed in [22, 26, 27].) A radio network is a collection of transmitter–receiver devices (referred to as nodes). Every node can reach a given subset of other nodes, depending on the power of its transmitter and on the topographic characteristics of the surrounding region.

Two types of models of radio networks prevail in the literature. The first one is a graph model. Nodes of the graph represent nodes of the network and the existence of a directed edge (uv) means that node v can be reached from u. In this case, u is called a neighbor of v. If the power of all transmitters is the same, any node u can reach v, if and only if it can be reached by v, i.e., the graph is symmetric. The second type of model has a more geometric flavor. Each node of the radio network is represented by a point in the plane, and each of those points has a region associated with it, often a circle of given radius centered at this point. It is assumed that any node v of the network represented by a point within the region associated to a given node u can be reached by the transmitter of u. Again u is called a neighbor of v in this case.

It is clear that the first type of model is more general than the second. Given the geometric setting described above, it is easy to construct a graph on the set of points, in which a directed edge from u to v exists if v is within the circle associated with u. On the other hand, it is not difficult to construct graphs that cannot be obtained in this way. As for the applicability, each of the representations is appropriate in a different physical situation. If the region in which the transmitter–receiver devices are situated is approximately flat and free of large obstacles, every transmitter reaches to the same distance in every direction, and consequently the geometric model with circular regions is appropriate, the radius of each circle depending on the power of the transmitter. If, on the other hand, the topography of the region is complicated by obstacles, either natural, such as mountains, or man-made, such as buildings, then more complicated reachability graphs may be needed to model the network because obstacles obstruct radio waves in some directions.

We assume that communication in a radio network proceeds in synchronous rounds. In every round every node acts either as a transmitter or as a receiver. A node w acting as a transmitter in a given round sends a message to all nodes within its reach. (This means a message is sent to all nodes to which there is an edge from w in the graph model, and all nodes within the region associated with w in the geometric model.) A node u acting as a receiver in a given round gets a message if and only if exactly one of its neighbors transmits in this round. If at least two neighbors v and v' of u transmit simultaneously in a given round, none of the messages is received by u in this round. In this, case we say that a collision occurred at u.

One of the most important performance parameters of a broadcasting scheme is the total time, i.e., the number of rounds used to inform all the nodes of the network. In this chapter, we focus attention on this efficiency measure and show how to design fast broadcasting algorithms under various settings. We also show lower bounds on time, which are intrinsic performance limitations of any broadcasting scheme.

The previously mentioned characteristics of radio communication (multidirectional transmitting and inability to receive in the case of a collision) indicate the main difficulty in designing a time-efficient broadcasting algorithm. Although the fact that a node simultaneously transmits a message to all nodes within its reach seems to speed up the broadcasting process, it is also the most important cause of slow-downs in many situations. If two nodes, u and v, have a common node w within their reach, they need to decide which of them informs w; the other cannot transmit in this round. This is a potential reason for communication delay, as the waiting node may be the only one capable of transmitting the source message to some part of the network. For this reason, scheduling a fast broadcast turns out to be a difficult task in many radio networks.

This chapter is organized as follows. In Section 24.2, we discuss several communication scenarios most often studied in the literature. In Sections 24.3 and 24.4, we present broadcasting algorithms and describe results concerning their running time, for the graph model and the geometric model, respectively. In Section 24.5, we briefly mention some other variations of the problem: communication tasks related to but different from broadcasting and/or other communication models for radio networks. Section 24.6 contains conclusions and open problems.

24.2 COMMUNICATION SCENARIOS

In this section, we present various assumptions concerning the communication process in radio networks. Their numerous combinations result in many communication scenarios used in the literature and significantly affecting the design of broadcasting algorithms and their efficiency.

The first choice concerns the use of randomness in the communication process. Randomized algorithms accomplish the broadcasting task with high probability but not always. On the other hand, we will see that they usually run much faster than deterministic algorithms, require very little knowledge of the network, and are easy to implement in a distributed way, without any central monitor.

The issue of centralized versus distributed control is crucial in all network communication. A centralized algorithm assumes the existence of a monitor having full knowledge of network topology and scheduling transmissions for all nodes. If nodes have access to a global clock, such a centralized algorithm can be implemented in a distributed way, provided that each node has global knowledge of network topology: in every round each node simply acts in the way it would be ordered to do so by the central monitor. The situation becomes more complicated when each node has only limited knowledge of the network; for example, it knows only its close vicinity—the part of the network at a small distance from it, or, in the extreme case, only its own label. With such limited information, centralized algorithms requiring full knowledge of the network cannot be applied, and it becomes necessary to design distributed broadcasting schemes relying only on local knowledge available to nodes.

The next feature that may significantly affect the communication process is that of adaptivity. Nonadaptive algorithms have all transmissions scheduled ahead of time, prior to the begining of broadcasting, whereas in adaptive algorithms, a node may schedule future transmissions on-line, depending on its previous history. In a centralized algorithm with a known source of broadcasting, all transmissions can be scheduled off-line, before broadcasting begins. In this case, adaptivity does not help, as nodes cannot learn any information during broadcasting that could affect scheduling of future transmissions. If the source is not known, adaptivity can help even when nodes have full knowledge of network topology. The label of the source can be appended to the source message. Upon receiving it, a node can decide how to schedule retransmissions of the source message depending on its origin. Adaptivity can help even more significantly in distributed broadcasting when nodes have only limited knowledge of network topology. In this case, a node can receive, together with the source message, some precious information concerning the topology of remote parts of the network, which can help it to schedule retransmissions in a way that accelerates the rest of the broadcasting process.

As mentioned above, a node can gain knowledge about the network from previously obtained messages. There is, however, another potential way of learning useful information. The availability of this method depends on what exactly happens during a collision, i.e., when u acts as a receiver and two or more neighbors of u transmit simultaneously. As previously mentioned, u does not get any of the messages in this case. However, two scenarios are possible. Node u may either hear nothing (except for the background noise), or it may receive interference noise different from any message received properly but also different from background noise. These two scenarios are often referred to as the absence (or availability) of collision detection (cf., e.g., [5]). Which of the two scenarios occurs in a particular situation may depend on technological characteristics of the transmitter/receiver devices used by the nodes. A discussion justifying both scenarios can be found in [5, 24]. We will see that efficiency and even feasibility of a particular communication task are significantly influenced by the choice between these scenarios.

Another issue concerning network communication in general, and broadcasting in radio networks in particular, is that of fault tolerance. Most algorithms are designed assuming that the communication environment is fault-free. However, this is not a realistic assumption, as the growing size and complexity of communication networks make them increasingly vulnerable to component failures. A fault-tolerant broadcasting algorithm should guarantee that all fault-free nodes will be informed, under some assumptions on the number of faults (usually upper bounds on their number or the probability of their occuring), without knowing their location. Faults can be of various types: omission (when a faulty node does not transmit messages) or Byzantine (when faulty nodes can corrupt messages arbitrarily), transient or permanent, and situated randomly or according to a worst-case distribution. It is not surprising that there exist trade-offs between the degree of fault tolerance of a broadcasting algorithm (e.g., in terms of the maximum number of faults under which it still works correctly) and its speed. The difficulty in designing good fault-tolerant broadcasting schemes consists in getting maximum efficiency while preserving a given degree of robustness with respect to faults.

The assumptions about communication presented above can be applied to both models of radio networks mentioned in the Section 24.1: to the graph model and to the geometric model. In the rest of this chapter, we study algorithms and results concerning broadcasting in both models, under communication scenarios resulting from various combinations of these assumptions.

24.3   THE GRAPH MODEL

In this section, we discuss broadcasting in radio networks modeled by directed graphs with a distinguished node s called the source. We assume that there exists a directed path from s to all other nodes, otherwise broadcasting from s is impossible. There are no other restrictions on the topology of the graph. Many authors, e.g. [2, 5, 23, 30], use the model of undirected connected graphs instead, which is a more restrictive assumption corresponding to the situation when the reachability graph is symmetric. Hence, we will use the more general setting of directed graphs, pointing out cases when a given algorithm uses symmetry of the graph.

Important parameters that influence the performance of broadcasting in radio networks are:

- The number n of nodes in the graph
- The maximum in-degree Δ, i.e., the maximum number of neighbors of a node
- The eccentricity D of the source in the graph, i.e., the largest distance from the source to any other node.

The eccentricity D is a trivial lower bound on the time of any broadcasting algorithm.

24.3.1   Deterministic Algorithms

Early work on broadcasting in radio networks concentrated on deterministic algorithms. One of the most natural questions is the following optimization problem in the context of centralized broadcasting. Given a graph and a designated source, find a broadcasting schedule using the shortest possible time. It is shown in [8] that this problem is NP-hard. In the same paper, the authors propose a centralized broadcasting algorithm working in time $O(D\Delta)$.

The first (centralized and deterministic) broadcasting algorithm whose running time is slower than the lower bound D only by a factor polylogarithmic in the number of nodes is given in [10]. Below, we present the main idea of this algorithm, which uses time $O(D\log^2 n)$. The authors call their approach "wave expansion," as the progress of broadcasting is viewed as a wave front carrying the message: it starts at the source and advances farther away until all nodes are informed.

At each round of the algorithm execution, we denote by X a subset of the set of informed nodes and by Y a subset of the set of uninformed nodes. The front in this round is the set F of pairs (x, y), such that $x \in X$, $y \in Y$, and x is a neighbor of y. The covered front $X_F = \{x \in X : (x, y) \in F$, for some $y \in Y\}$ (or the uncovered front $Y_F = \{y \in Y : (x, y) \in F$, for some $x \in X\}$) is the set of informed (or uninformed) nodes that belong to a couple in the front F. We define the spokesmen set $S \subseteq X_F$ as the set of those informed nodes in the front that act as transmitters in the next round. For any spokesmen set S, $R_S \subseteq Y_F$ denotes the set of nodes that receive the message correctly when exactly nodes from S transmit. Hence R_S consists of those nodes in Y_F that have exactly one neighbor in S. The main difficulty of the algorithm is to choose S at each round in such a way that R_S is as large as possible and so that the choosing process is polynomial. Clearly, inspection of all possible candidate sets is out of the question. In [10], the following spokesmen election algorithm (SEA) is described.

Algorithm SEA

Phase 1. Finding the size of the spokesmen set S.

For every $1 \leq i \leq n$, let S_i be the family of all i-element subsets of X_F. Let w_i be the average size of sets R_S over all $S \in S_i$. Let k be the index i for which this average is maximized. This will be the size of the chosen set S.

Phase 2. Finding the elements of the spokesmen set S.

Elements of S are found one by one, in k iterations. In the beginning $S = \emptyset$, $N = X_F$. The mth iteration, for $1 \leq m \leq k$, starts with S containing $m - 1$ nodes and $N = X_F \setminus S$. For each $x \in N$, we define $F_{S,x}$ as the family of all sets of the form $S \cup \{x\} \cup P$, where P is any $(k - m)$-element subset of $N \setminus \{x\}$. For any $x \in N$, let $u_{S,x}$ denote the average of $|R_T|$ over all sets T in the family $F_{S,x}$. The element $x \in N$ for which $u_{S,x}$ is the largest is transfered from N to S, i.e., $S := S \cup \{x\}$ and $N := N \setminus \{x\}$. The algorithm ends after k iterations, with the set S of size k. $\qquad\square$

It is shown in [10] that the averages w_i in Phase 1 and $u_{S,x}$ in Phase 2 can be computed in polynomial time, hence Algorithm SEA runs in polynomial time. Moreover, the spokesmen set S obtained by this algorithm satisfies the property $|R_S| > |Y_F|/\ln|X_F|$. This means that the choice of S guarantees that at least a fraction $1/\ln|X_F|$ of nodes that can potentially receive the source message for the first time are actually informed in a given round.

Algorithm SEA is used as a subroutine in the main algorithm called wave expansion broadcast (WEB). This algorithm is structured according to layers in the graph, where the ith layer L_i is defined as the set of those nodes whose distance from the source is i. Clearly, the number of layers is $D + 1$, where D is the eccentricity of the source.

Algorithm WEB

The algorithm works in D phases called superwaves. During the ith superwave, the front is formed from layers L_{i-1} and L_i. The ith superwave consists of a certain number of rounds called *waves*. In the beginning of this superwave, $X_F = L_{i-1}$ and $Y_F = L_i$. In consecutive waves, the Algorithm SEA is applied to the current front, yielding the spokesmen set S. Then all (newly informed) elements of the set R_S are removed from Y_F, and X_F remains unchanged. In the next wave, Algorithm SEA is applied to this new front. Waves of the ith superwave are executed until Y_F is exhausted. This terminates the ith superwave. The algorithm stops at the end of the Dth superwave.   □

The above-mentioned property of SEA guaranteeing that $|R_S| > |Y_F|/\ln|X_F|$ permits us to prove the following bound on the number t_i of rounds (waves) in the ith superwave: $t_i < \ln|L_{i-1}|\ln|L_i|$. The first superwave clearly lasts one round. Hence, the total running time of Algorithm WEB is bounded by $1 + t_2 + \cdots + t_D < 1 + \Sigma_{i=2}^{D}\ln|L_{i-1}|\ln|L_i|$. This number is maximized when all layers are of equal size, thus giving running time $O(D \log^2 n)$ of Algorithm WEB on an arbitrary graph.

The order of magnitude $O(D \log^2 n)$ of the time of broadcasting cannot be improved in general. Indeed, in [2] the existence of a family of networks with $D = 2$ is proved, for which any broadcast schedule requires time $\Omega(\log^2 n)$. Hence, for these networks Algorithm WEB from [10] is asymptotically optimal. However, for networks whose source has large eccentricity, this is not always the case. In [23] the authors show a centralized deterministic algorithm that performs broadcasting in time $O(D + \log^5 n)$, and is thus asymptotically optimal for networks with source eccentricity $\Omega(\log^5 n)$. The order of magnitude of optimal broadcasting time for radio networks with D nonconstant but below $\Theta(\log^5 n)$ remains an open problem.

We now turn our attention to distributed broadcasting in the situation when nodes have only limited knowledge of the topology of the radio network. We start with the most extreme scenario, when the knowledge of each node is restricted to its own label, and labels are distinct integers between 1 and n. (Note that all results remain valid when labels are distinct integers between 1 and $M \in O(n)$.) Thus, the initial situation is that of complete ignorance concerning the network: nodes do not know even their immediate neighborhood and are unaware of global parameters such as the size n of the network or the eccentricity D of the source. On the other hand, the assumption about the existence of distinct labels is necessary. If the radio network is anonymous, it is clear that deterministic broadcasting cannot be done even in the 4-cycle. The importance of designing efficient broadcasting algorithms that do not assume any knowledge that nodes may have about the rest of the network comes, e.g., from applications in mobile networks whose topology and size may change over time.

The lack of knowledge concerning the network raises the problem of precise definition of the task of broadcasting and of its execution time. In a centralized algorithm, time of broadcasting can be known in advance, and thus all nodes can be aware of the termination of broadcasting as soon as it is completed. A different situation occurs in the distributed setting with restricted knowledge. Since even the size of the network is unknown, broadcast can well be finished but no node need be aware of this fact. Consequently, the following two communication tasks are distinguished in [12]. In radio broadcasting (RB) the goal is simply to communicate the source message to all nodes. In acknowledged radio broadcasting (ARB) the goal is to achieve RB and inform the source about it. This may be essential, e.g., when the source has several messages to disseminate, and none of the nodes are supposed to learn the next message until all nodes get the previous one.

It is assumed that the algorithm starts in round 1 and the current round number is indicated by the global clock. An algorithm accomplishes RB in t rounds if all nodes know the source message after round t and no messages are sent after round t. An algorithm accomplishes ARB in t rounds, if it accomplishes RB in t rounds and if, after round t, the source knows that all nodes know the source message.

Distributed broadcasting in radio networks with unknown topology was first investigated in [5]. Under this scenario, adaptivity of algorithms may be important, and hence it should be made precise if collision detection (as discussed previously) is or is not available. We first present results assuming the latter scenario. This is the assumption made in [5]. One of the main results of that paper is the lower bound $\Omega(n)$ on deterministic broadcasting time, even for the restricted class of symmetric networks, and even when each node knows its immediate neighborhood. The authors construct a class of symmetric networks of bounded diameter, for which every deterministic broadcasting algorithm uses time $\Omega(n)$. (Later it was shown in [28] that deterministic broadcasting time for this class of networks is the same as for the class of arbitrary symmetric networks and is in fact equal to $n - 1$.) A matching upper bound is established in [12]: the authors construct an algorithm accomplishing radio broadcasting in time $O(n)$, for arbitrary symmetric networks, under the most restrictive assumption that each node knows only its own label. A subtle point should be mentioned here. The algorithm from [12] makes heavy use of *spontaneous* transmissions: the ability of nodes that have not yet gotten the source message to transmit some control messages. (The lower bound from [5] remains valid under this assumption.) If this is precluded, linear time broadcasting is not possible any more: in [7] a class of symmetric networks of diameter D is constructed for which any broadcasting requires time $\Omega(D \log n)$ if spontaneous transmissions are forbidden. In particular, for D linear in n, this gives the lower bound of $\Omega(n \log n)$ on broadcasting time.

On the other hand, in [12] the authors prove the surprising result that acknowledged radio broadcasting is impossible even in symmetric networks if collision detection is not available. The idea of the proof is as follows. Suppose that there exists an ARB-protocol $\mathcal{P}$. This protocol works in some time t for the graph that consists only of the source. In [12] the authors construct a (large) symmetric graph G such that the protocol $\mathcal{P}$, when run on G, causes the source to obtain no messages in the first t rounds and does not inform some nodes during these rounds. Since during these first t rounds the source has the same input as when $\mathcal{P}$ is run on the graph consisting only of the source, the protocol induces the source to falsely conclude that ARB is accomplished on G after t rounds.

As opposed to the case of symmetric radio networks, for which an asymptotically optimal algorithm has been constructed, for arbitrary directed networks the problem is not completely solved. We start by presenting lower bounds on broadcasting time in this general case. In [12], a family of directed graphs with source of eccentricity D is constructed, for which any broadcasting algorithm requires time $\Omega(D \log n)$. This family is similar to the one from [7], except that it is not symmetric and the lower bound holds even when spontaneous broadcasting is permitted. In [15] this lower bound is sharpened to $\Omega(n \log D)$. Although, in terms of the size of the network only, both results give the same bound $\Omega(n \log n)$, the result from [15] shows that linear time broadcasting is impossible even for some networks with quite small eccentricity of the source.

On the upper bound side, a series of recent papers establish broadcasting algorithms of increasing efficiency. This series was initiated by Chlebus et al. [12] who proposed the following simple algorithm working in time $O(n^2)$. First suppose that all nodes know n. Then broadcasting can be accomplished by the following procedure.

Procedure Round-Robin (n)
The procedure works in n identical phases. In each phase, all nodes that have the source message act as transmitters in turn: the node with label i is in the ith round of the phase. □

If n is unknown, the above procedure should be applied many times using the following doubling technique.

Algorithm Simple-Sequencing
The algorithm works in phases numbered by positive integers. In phase k, Procedure Round-Robin (2^k) is executed by all nodes with labels 1 to 2^k, with the following modification: a node that obtained the source message and transmitted it in some round remains silent in all subsequent rounds. □

In every round, at most one node acts as a transmitter, hence collisions are avoided. It is easy to see that after phase $\lceil \log n \rceil$ all nodes get the source message, and the first $\lceil \log n \rceil$ phases use a total of $O(n^2)$ rounds.

In the same paper, a more sophisticated broadcasting algorithm is constructed, working in time $O(n^{11/6})$. This algorithm is based on the notion of a selective family of sets. A family $\mathcal{F}$ of subsets of U is said to be k-selective for the set U iff for any $X \subseteq U, |X| \leq k$, there is a set $Y \in \mathcal{F}$ satisfying $|X \cap Y| = 1$. The existence of a small sufficiently strongly selective family has to be proved, and this family is then used to construct appropriate sets of transmitters that avoid collisions.

Subsequently, a series of faster broadcasting algorithms have been proposed, including one constructive algorithm with execution time $O(n^{3/2})$ [13], and three nonconstructive algorithms based on probabilistic methods, with execution times $O(n^{5/3}\log^{1/3}n)$ [16], $O(n^{3/2}\sqrt{\log n})$ [34], and $O(n \log^2 n)$ [14]. All these algorithms, apart from the one in [13] which uses finite geometries, are based on (a variation of) the concept of selective families. It should be stressed that the nonconstructive algorithms are, in fact, deterministic. Probability is used only to establish the existence of an appropriate selective family of sets, and given this family (which may, e.g., be found by all nodes off-line) the rest of the scheme is entirely deterministic. Recall that broadcasting time is defined as the number of communication rounds, and hence the time of local computations of nodes (used, e.g., to find an appropriate family of sets) is ignored.

Below, we describe the idea of the fastest of these algorithms (and, in fact, the fastest currently known distributed deterministic broadcasting algorithm working for arbitrary radio networks with unknown topology): the $O(n \log^2 n)$ algorithm from [14]. As before, we assume that n is known. This assumption can be removed by modifying the algorithm using the doubling technique described in the context of Procedure Round-Robin.

The following variation of the concept of a selective family is used in [14]. An m-element family $S = \{S_0, S_1, \ldots, S_{m-1}\}$ of subsets of $\{1, \ldots, n\}$ is called a w-selector, if it satisfies the following property:

- For any two disjoint sets X, Y with $w/2 \leq |X| \leq w$ and $|Y| \leq w$, there exists i for which $|S_i \cap X| = 1$ and $S_i \cap Y = \emptyset$

It is proved in [14] that for each n and each $w \leq n/\log n$ there exists an m-element w-selector $S = \{S_0, S_1, \ldots, S_{m-1}\}$ with $m \in O(w \log n)$.

The broadcasting algorithm is now defined as a sequence of transmission sets specifying that nodes act as transmitters in a given round: if S is the transmission set corresponding to round t, nodes acting as transmitters in round t are those that got the source message and whose labels are in S.

Let $l = \log (n/\log n)$, $w_j = 2^j$, for each $j = 1, \ldots, l$, and $S_0 = [\{1\}, \{2\}, \ldots, \{n\}]$. For $j > 0$, let S_j be a w_j-selector of size $m_j \in O(w_j \log n)$.

Algorithm DoBroadcast
The algorithm consists of stages, each of which consists of $l + 1 \in O(\log n)$ rounds. The transmission set in the jth round of stage s is defined as the set from S_j with index s mod m_j. □

It is proved in [14] that Algorithm DoBroadcast informs all nodes in time $O(n \log^2 n)$.

The above algorithm, as well as the previously mentionned broadcasting schemes preceeding it, were designed to perform efficiently in arbitrary networks. However, a few broadcasting algorithms have been also designed to work particularly fast for sparse networks, i.e., those with small maximum degree Δ. In [13] two such algorithms were proposed: one working in time $O\left(n \cdot \left(\frac{\log n}{\lceil \log \Delta \rceil}\right) \cdot \Delta \log n\right)$, and the other in time $O[n\Delta^2 \log^3 n/\log(\Delta \log n)]$. However, they are both superlinear in n regardless of other parameters of the network. This has been further improved in [15]: the authors propose a broadcasting algorithm working in time $O(D\Delta \log^3 n)$, and hence sublinear in n for sparse networks with small eccentricity of the source. In particular, for D and Δ polylogarithmic in n, this gives polylogarithmic broadcasting time, unlike any of the previous algorithms.

The above results do not use the assumption about availability of collision detection. Under the scenario with collision detection, broadcasting may be done faster in some cases. For the class of strongly connected graphs, a radio broadcasting algorithm working in time $O(nD)$ is described in [12]. This algorithm is thus faster than the other ones for small eccentricity D and large maximum degree Δ. It is also observed how the collision detection capability can be used to code messages. Using noise and silence essentially as bits of the transmitted message, the authors show a simple scheme that broadcasts a message of size l in time $O(lD)$, hence they get an asymptotically optimal algorithm to broadcast messages of size $O(1)$, in arbitrary graphs.

The impact of collision detection is even more significant for the task of acknowledged radio broadcasting. This problem is also investigated in [12]. Although ARB is impossible to achieve without this capability, availability of it permits us to perform this task rather fast. For symmetric graphs, the authors show an algorithm for ARB working in time $O(n)$ for n-node graphs, and thus asymptotically optimal. If the graph is nonsymmetric, in order to make ARB possible, it must be at least strongly connected. For such graphs, an algorithm for acknowledged radio broadcasting working in time $O(nD)$ is proposed in [12].

24.3.2 Randomized Algorithms

Randomized algorithms usually have the advantage of being simple and not relying on much knowledge available to nodes. The first randomized broadcasting algorithm for arbitrary radio networks was proposed in [5]. Not only does it not assume any knowledge about the topology of the network and does not use collision detection, but (unlike for deterministic broadcasting) nodes do not need to have distinct identities, and thus the algorithm works for anonymous networks as well. The only knowledge available to nodes is the error bound ε and the size n of the network. (The result still holds if any polynomial upper bound on n is known instead of n itself.) The algorithm achieves broadcasting with probability $1 - \varepsilon$ and works in time $O((D + \log (n/\varepsilon))\log n)$. (If the maximum degree Δ is additionally known to nodes, time can be improved to $O((D + \log (n/\varepsilon))\log \Delta)$.)This performance closely matches known lower bounds: the previously mentioned lower bound $\Omega(\log^2 n)$ from [2] (the family of networks constructed in this paper does not admit any faster broadcasting scheme, even randomized), and the lower bound $\Omega(D \log(n/D))$ from [30] on randomized broadcasting time in any network. Hence the algorithm from [5] is asymptotically optimal for all D not very close to linear in n, e.g., for $D \in O(n^\alpha)$, for $\alpha < 1$. For D linear in n, or, e.g., $D \in \Theta(n/\log n)$, a small gap remains between the performance of the algorithm and the lower bounds.

Below, we sketch the algorithm from [5]. The algorithm is based on the following procedure. A set of nodes that already have the source message compete for a round in which exactly one of them transmits. This can be achieved with positive probability in relatively few trials based on randomly decreasing the number of competitors. At a call of the procedure, each node knows if it competes or not.

Procedure Decay (k)
The procedure is executed in k rounds. In each round, all competing nodes act as transmitters and transmit the source message. At the end of each round each competing node sets its variable coin randomly to 0 or 1 with probability 1/2. Those nodes with value 0 of coin stop competing. □

It is proved in [5] that if the number of competing nodes at the call of Procedure Decay (k) is d then, for $k \geq 2\lceil \log d \rceil$, the probability that there exists a round in the execution of the procedure in which exactly one of the originally competing nodes transmits exceeds 1/2. Hence, if the initially competing nodes are the d informed neighbors of some node x, and k is as above, node x becomes informed with probability greater than 1/2 upon completion of Procedure Decay (k).

The broadcasting algorithm consists of several applications of the above procedure. Since k must be at least $2\lceil \log d \rceil$, where d is the number of informed neighbors of a node, we set k to $2\lceil \log \Delta \rceil$, and if Δ is unknown, to $2\lceil \log n \rceil$. Since all competing nodes must start Procedure Decay(k) in the same round, the procedure is called only in rounds that are multiples of k. We formulate the algorithm as executed by each processor.

Algorithm Broadcast

$k := 2\lceil \log \Delta \rceil$, $t := \lceil \log (n/\varepsilon) \rceil$. Wait until receiving the source message. Repeat t times: in the earliest round with number divisible by k start competing and execute Decay (k). $\square$

The execution of the algorithm in the network consists of the transmission by the source in the first round and of the execution of Algorithm Broadcast by each node. It is proved in [5] that, with probability at least $1 - \varepsilon$, all nodes get the source message and stop transmitting after $O((D + t)k)$ rounds. This gives time $O((D + \log(n/\varepsilon))\log \Delta)$ (according to the algorithm formulation), and time $O((D + \log(n/\varepsilon))\log n)$, if Δ is unknown.

The above algorithm works for networks of arbitrary unknown topology. Clearly, if the underlying graph is complete (such networks are called single-hop), the broadcasting problem, as defined in this chapter, is trivial. However, for such networks the problem of k-broadcasting has been extensively studied, and several—mostly randomized—solutions have been proposed. See Section 24.5.1. for the definition of the problem and pointers to relevant literature.

24.4 THE GEOMETRIC MODEL

As mentioned in the Section 24.1, the geometric model is less general than the graph model but rather faithfully represents reality when the region in which nodes of the radio network are situated is approximately flat and free from large obstacles. Nodes of the network are represented by points of the k-dimensional Euclidean space, and with each node we associate the set of points at some distance r from it. These points can be reached by the transmitter of the node. The most interesting and natural case is $k = 2$, when nodes are situated in the plane and regions are circles centered at respective nodes. Another case considered in the literature is $k = 1$, i.e., when nodes are on a line and regions correspond to segments centered at nodes. Although all positive results proved for the graph model clearly hold in the geometric model as well, some negative results and lower bounds are not true any more. In fact, those results are due to the existence of some "pathological" graphs that do not correspond to geometric situations.

Following [18], we define a geometric radio network (GRN) as a directed graph obtained from a set of points in the plane with assigned circles centered at these points, in the following way. Nodes of the graph are these points, and a directed edge from u to v exists if v is inside the circle assigned to u. Hence the problem of broadcasting in radio networks using the geometric model is equivalent to the problem in the graph model but restricted to GRNs. We define a linear GRN analogously, when points are on the line. The radius of the associated circle (or the half-length of the segment for a linear GRN) is called the range of the node.

Distributed deterministic broadcasting in linear GRNs was first investigated in [36]. The authors consider n nodes randomly and uniformly distributed on a line of length L_n. The range of each node is 1, and a node knows positions of all nodes at distance at most 1 from it. The authors propose a (deterministic) broadcasting algorithm working (with high probability) in time L_n if L_n is of order n^α, for $0 < \alpha < 1$, and in time αL_n if L_n is of order αn, for $\alpha > 0$.

Broadcasting in linear GRNs was also investigated in [20], under different assumptions. The authors consider two scenarios. Nodes are situated at integer points on a line, and each node has very limited knowledge: in the first scenario it knows only its own position and the maximum R over all ranges (but does not even know its own range) and in the second scenario every node additionally knows its own range. In both scenarios, collision detection is available. Under the first (extreme) scenario a sharp lower bound is proved in [20]. The authors show a family of networks with source eccentricity 2, which require time $\Omega(R)$ for broadcasting. Under the second, more realistic scenario, they prove the lower bound $\Omega(D + (\log^2 R)/(\log \log R))$ on broadcasting time in any network, and construct a deterministic broadcasting algorithm working in time $O(D(\log^2 R)/(\log \log R))$, and thus asymptotically optimal when source eccentricity D is constant. They also announce another deterministic broadcasting algorithm working in time $O(D + \log^2 R)$ under the same assumptions, and thus asymptotically optimal for $D \in \Omega(\log^2 R)$.

Arbitrary geometric radio networks were first investigated in [39]. The authors study the problem of optimal centralized broadcasting in GRNs. They prove that finding a shortest time broadcasting scheme, given a GRN and a source, is NP-hard. This is a strengthening of a result from [8] where this is proved for general graphs. On the other hand, the authors of [39] show an algorithm working in time $O(n \log n)$ and producing a shortest time broadcasting scheme given a linear GRN and a source.

Broadcasting in general GRNs was extensively studied in [18]. The focus of this paper is the trade-off between the amount of knowledge about the network that is available to nodes and the time of broadcasting. It is assumed that each node knows the part of the network within knowledge radius s from it, i.e., it knows the positions, labels, and ranges of all nodes at distance at most s. The authors establish results about time of broadcasting in an n-node GRN with source eccentricity D, depending on the value of knowledge radius. It is assumed that the set of possible ranges is bounded and known to all nodes. Both models with and without collision detection are investigated.

We first summarize the results assuming no collision detection. For s exceeding the largest range, or s exceeding the largest distance between any two nodes, the authors design an (optimal) broadcasting algorithm working in time $O(D)$ [18]. In particular, this yields a centralized $O(D)$ broadcasting algorithm when global knowledge of the GRN is available. This should be contrasted with the lower bound $\Omega(\log^2 n)$ from [2] valid for some graphs with constant D: the graphs constructed in [2] are "pathological," in particular they are not GRNs.

For $s = 0$, i.e., when the knowledge of each node is limited to itself, asymptotically tight bounds on broadcasting time are established in [18]. The authors show a broadcasting algorithm working in time $O(n)$, and they show a family of (symmetric) GRNs of constant diameter that require time $\Omega(n)$ for broadcasting. It should be stressed that the linear time algorithm works for arbitrary GRNs, not only symmetric GRN, unlike the algorithm from [12] designed for arbitrary symmetric graphs. The linear time algorithm from [18] should be contrasted with the lower bound from [12] showing that some graphs require broadcasting time $\Omega(n \log n)$. Indeed, the graphs witnessing to this lower bound are not GRNs. More surprisingly, it is shown in [18] that this sharper lower bound does not require very unusual graphs. Although the authors observe that counterexamples from [12] are not GRN, it turns out that the reason for a longer broadcasting time is really not the topology of the graph but the difference in knowledge available to nodes. Indeed, in GRNs with knowledge radius 0, it is assumed that each node knows its own position (apart from its label and range): the upper bound $O(n)$ uses this geometric information extensively. If nodes do not have this knowledge (but only know their own label and range), it is shown in [18] that even some GRNs require time $\Omega(n \log n)$ for broadcasting.

Under the scenario with collision detection, much faster broadcasting algorithms are designed in [18]. For a symmetric GRN with knowledge radius $s = 0$ (every node knows only its own label, position, and range), the authors show an $O(D + \log n)$ broadcasting algorithm and prove the lower bound $\Omega(\log n)$ for a family of symmetric bounded-diameter GRN. This, together with the obvious lower bound $\Omega(D)$, shows that their algorithm is asymptotically optimal under the collision detection scenario. It also shows the power of collision detection when contrasted with the $\Omega(n)$ lower bound for symmetric GRNs without this capability.

The results from [18] show sharp contrasts between the efficiency of broadcasting in geometric radio networks as compared with broadcasting in arbitrary graphs. Hence, in situations where the geometric model is appropriate, broadcasting schemes designed for GRNs are often more advantageous than algorithms designed for arbitrary graphs. The results from [18] also show quantitatively the impact of various types of knowledge available to nodes on broadcasting time in GRNs. Information influencing efficiency of broadcasting includes knowledge radius, knowledge of individual positions when knowledge radius is zero, and awareness of collisions.

24.5   OTHER VARIANTS OF THE PROBLEM

In the two previous sections, we discussed information dissemination in radio networks in its simplest form, i.e., when one node has to broadcast one message. We also restricted our attention to a few scenarios most common in the literature on the subject, such as the graph versus the geometric representation of the network, centralized versus distributed broadcasting, or the availability of collision detection versus lack of it. In this section, we overview other variations of the problem: on the one hand, we look at other, usually more complex communication tasks, and, on the other hand, we discuss different assumptions concerning communication, referring to more specific features of the radio network.

24.5.1 Other Communication Tasks

Among communication tasks other than broadcasting, one of the most important is "gossiping," also called all-to-all broadcasting [26]. Every node of the network has a message, and the goal is to get all messages to all nodes. Gossiping has been extensively studied in the context of radio networks as well. Note that for gossiping to be possible, the network must be a strongly connected graph.

Distributed deterministic gossiping under the assumption that nodes know only their label is studied in [14, 15]. In [14], a gossiping algorithm is shown that works in time $O(n^{3/2} \log^2 n)$ for n-node networks. In [15], a different algorithm is designed. It is faster than the above for sparse networks of small diameter D. Indeed, it works in time $O(D\Delta^2 \log^3 n)$, where D is the diameter of the network and Δ its maximum, in degree.

Gossiping in linear geometric radio networks is studied in [37]. The authors use the same model as in [36] and design an asymptotically optimal algorithm for gossiping. These results are further extended in [38] by considering radio networks in which nodes are randomly situated on a ring.

A related task is that of communication among neighbors only: every node has to communicate its message to all neighbors. In [35], this task is considered for symmetric networks under the additional constraint that all collisions should be avoided. The authors prove that the problem of finding a shortest time schedule for this problem is NP-hard, and give a heuristic method to find a suboptimal schedule. In [4], a more general problem of communicating many messages to all neighbors is considered. Again, any collisions are forbidden. The authors show a heuristic algorithm working for arbitrary networks, and show an optimal algorithm designed specifically for trees.

Communication among neighbors is also studied in [19]. The authors restrict attention to networks with the ring topology. Unlike in [4, 35], collisions are permitted and the results hold both with and without collision detection. The focus of the paper is the impact of the amount of knowledge available to nodes on the efficiency of accomplishing communication among neighbors. This knowledge is measured by knowledge radius r, defined similarly as in [18]: knowledge radius r means that every node knows labels of nodes at distance up to r from it, where distance is meant in the graph sense (on the ring). For $r = 0$ matching upper and lower bounds $\Theta(\log n)$ on time are shown, and a logarithmic time algorithm for the task is provided. For $2 \leq r \leq c \log * n$, where $c < 1/2$, the authors prove the lower bound $\Omega(\log * n)$ on the time of communication among neighbors, and give an algorithm accomplishing this task in time $O(\log^{(2^{\lceil r/2 \rceil})} n)$. Finally, for $r \geq \log * n$, they show an algorithm completing communication among neighbors in constant time.

In [6], the following communication tasks are studied. A k-point-to-point transmission is the task of transmitting a message from u_i to v_i, for some pairs of nodes (u_i, v_i), for all $1 \leq i \leq k$. A k-broadcast is the task consisting of broadcasting messages from k different sources. (Thus gossiping is an n-broadcast). In [6], randomized algorithms for these tasks are studied in symmetric radio networks in which every node knows its neighbors (all nodes have distinct labels), and knows the size n of the network and its maximum degree Δ. The size of all messages is logarithmic in n. Algorithms designed in [6] for both these tasks require a setup phase during which a BFS tree is constructed. This phase takes time $O((n + D \log n)\log \Delta)$. In the second phase messages are pipelined along edges of this tree. After setup, a k-point-to-point transmission takes time $O((k + D)\log \Delta)$ on average, and a k-broadcast takes time $O((k + D)\log \Delta \log n)$ on average.

k-broadcast, especially in the situation when each of the broadcasting nodes has many messages to transmit, is an important problem even for the single-hop networks, i.e., networks whose underlying graph is complete. In this case, broadcasting nodes compete for the use of a multiple access channel. Many communication algorithms, most of them randomized, have been developed for this problem. An extensive survey of these and related issues can be found in [11].

24.5.2 Other Communication Scenarios

Here we briefly survey some work on communication in radio networks that adopts assumptions different from the most common models discussed previously. One of these hypotheses concerns the important issue of fault tolerance. Although most papers assume that all nodes of a radio network are functional, it is well known that, on the contrary, the growing size of radio networks increases their vulnerability to failures. One of the first papers addressing this issue was [33], in which a broadcasting protocol tolerating transient node failures is proposed.

Broadcasting in radio networks with permanent node failures was first studied in [29]. The authors restrict attention to special types of geometric radio networks, in which nodes are situated either at integer points of a line or in the plane at grid points of a square or hexagonal mesh. In the latter case, regions of reachability of each node are squares or hexagons. The model with collision detection is used. It is assumed that at most t nodes are faulty, and the location of faults is worst-case and unknown. A faulty node does not send or receive any messages, and the goal is to transmit the source message to all fault-free nodes or, in the case when faulty nodes disconnect the network, to all nodes in the fault-free component containing the source. The authors distinguish between nonadaptive and adaptive algorithms. For the first class, they show that optimal broadcasting time is $\Theta(D + t)$, and for the second class it is $\Theta(D + \log(\min(R, t)))$, where R is the range of each node and D is the diameter of the fault-free component of the network containing the source. In each case, asymptotically optimal, fault-tolerant broadcasting algorithms are provided.

In [31] the authors are interested in computing threshold functions, such as AND, OR, or MAJORITY, in noisy radio networks. They restrict attention to complete graphs and assume that each node has a bit, and all nodes must compute a threshold function on these bits, with high probability of correctness. Whenever a node transmits, all other nodes obtain its bit with some random noise, i.e., altered with probability $p < 1/2$. The main result of the paper is a protocol accomplishing the above task and using only $O(n)$ transmissions. In fact, the protocol works in three rounds.

Other computation tasks in mobile radio networks represented by complete graphs are studied in [32]. The authors adopt a radio model with many possible transmission frequencies. Nodes using different frequencies do not interfere. Three tasks are studied: (1) permutation routing, in which every node stores the same number of messages, each with a unique destination, and all messages must reach their destinations; (2) ranking, in which nodes hold elements of a totally ordered set and each node must learn the rank of elements it holds; and (3) sorting, which consists of permutation routing according to ranks. The main contribution of the paper are efficient algorithms for these problems under the assumption that the number of available frequencies is small, more precisely, when it does not exceed the square root of the number of nodes.

Although time is the main efficiency measure of broadcasting algorithms considered in the literature on radio networks, other parameters of broadcasting schemes are also considered. In [9], a new measure called bandwidth consumption of a broadcasting scheme is introduced. This measure, for a given node v, is the number of rounds during which v cannot correctly receive messages other than the broadcasted one. Small average bandwidth consumption of a broadcasting scheme, where the average is taken over all nodes of the network, allows many nonbroadcast-related transmissions to be performed concurrently with broadcasting. This permits more efficient spatial reuse between various communication protocols. In [9], it is shown that minimizing the average bandwidth consumption is an NP-hard problem, and a fast broadcasting algorithm with average bandwidth consumption bounded by $\Delta + 1$ is described.

In [17], another parameter is also analyzed: the cost of broadcasting, measured by the number of transmissions. (Cost was previously the focus of research on broadcasting in models other than radio communication, e.g., in [3].) The authors concentrate their study on execution time of deterministic broadcasting algorithms that have cost close to minimum and work in networks of unknown topology. They show that the minimum cost of broadcasting in an n-node network with source eccentricity D is either n or $n - 1$, depending on whether nodes know or do not know at least one of the parameters D or n. The main contribution of the paper are lower bounds on time of low-cost broadcasting. It is shown that if nodes know neither n nor D, then any broadcasting algorithm whose cost exceeds the minimum by $O(n^\beta)$, for any constant $\beta < 1$, must have execution time $\Omega(Dn \log n)$ for some network. The authors also show a minimum-cost algorithm that does not assume knowledge of these parameters, and always works in time $O(Dn \log n)$. (A similar algorithm is independently given in [34].) On the other hand, assuming that nodes know either n or D, it is shown how to broadcast in time $O(Dn)$. This time cannot be improved by any low-cost algorithm knowing even both n and D. Indeed, a lower bound is proved showing that any algorithm whose cost exceeds the minimum by at most αn, for any constant $\alpha < 1$, requires time $\Omega(Dn)$. In addition, it turns out that very fast broadcasting algorithms must have high cost. It is proved that every broadcasting algorithm that works in time $O(nt(n)))$, where $t(n)$ is polylogarithmic in n, requires cost $\Omega(n \log n/\log \log n)$. Since the fastest known broadcasting algorithm works in time $O(n \log^2 n)$ [14], its cost (as well as the cost of any faster broadcasting algorithm, if it exists) must be higher than linear.

The classic model of radio networks assumes that all powers of transmitters are fixed (although they can be different for different nodes of the network). This assumption is removed in [1], where the authors consider power-controlled networks in which nodes have the ability to change their transmission power. These networks are abstractly modeled by complete undirected graphs with weights on all edges. Weight $\tau(\{u, v\})$ on edge $\{u, v\}$ represents the lowest transmission power that allows u to send a message to v and vice versa. A node that intends to send a packet decides which transmission power it wants to use in this round. A constant $\alpha > 1$ is fixed. If a node v attempts to send a packet with transmission power t, then all nodes that require less than αt power to receive a message from v

are blocked by v in this round. Nodes blocked by v cannot receive any information from nodes other than v in the given round. Thus, the classic radio model is the special case of the above, where $\tau(\{u, v\})$ is 1 for edges of the graph and ∞ for all other pairs of nodes, and the only possible transmission power for any node is 1. In [1] the authors consider the problem of permutation routing in the power-controlled model.

In [25] the authors investigate a different issue concerning communication in radio networks: the synchronization of the system. In most papers in this area, it is assumed that transmissions occur in synchronized rounds controlled by a global clock. Nodes of the network have access to this clock, and, in particular, they are aware of the current round number, common for all processors. This round number can be used as an input in a distributed broadcasting algorithm run by processors. This scenario is called global synchronization in [25]. The authors distinguish it from local synchronization, in which some nodes wake up spontaneously, and in this round their local clock starts ticking, with ticks synchronized for all woken nodes. However, no common global round number is available. In [25] the fundamental problem of waking up all processors of a completely connected system is considered. Some nodes wake up spontaneously, whereas others have to be woken up. Only awake nodes can send messages; a sleeping node is woken up upon hearing a message. Nodes hear a message in a given round if and only if exactly one node sends a message in that round. Hence, the communication model is that of a radio network without collision detection, represented by a complete graph. The goal is to wake up all processors as fast as possible in the worst case, assuming that an adversary controls which processors wake up and when. The problem is analyzed in both the globally synchronous and locally synchronous models, with or without the assumption that the size n of the network is known to the nodes. The authors propose randomized and deterministic algorithms for the problem, as well as lower bounds in some of the cases. These bounds establish a gap between the globally synchronous and locally synchronous models, showing the power of the assumption of availability of a global clock.

24.6 CONCLUSION AND OPEN PROBLEMS

We presented a survey of results on broadcasting in radio networks, under various models of such networks and under different communication scenarios. Our focus was on broadcasting algorithms and their efficiency, usually measured by the number of rounds (time) to accomplish broadcasting. The design of algorithms and their performance significantly depend on the adopted assumptions about communication. The choice of those should be motivated by the technical characteristics of the radio network and by the topography of the region in which it operates. The right formulation of the model may in fact be crucial for the best choice of a broadcasting algorithm, and for its applicability in a concrete situation. A too general model may preclude some algorithms that would not work, or work poorly only in some pathological situations that we are unlikely to encounter in our setting. A too restrictive model, on the other hand, may induce us to use an algorithm that will fail because its assumptions are often violated in our case.

The above study also shows how significantly the performance of broadcasting algorithms depends on the knowledge that nodes have about the network. This knowledge may vary a lot in real situations. In mobile wireless networks that operate over extensive periods of time, the characteristics of the network are likely to change, and hence it is advisable to use communication algorithms that do not require knowledge of network topology, or even of its size. On the other hand, in more stable situations it may be better to use the most efficient centralized algorithms.

In our presentation, we focused attention on the design of algorithms and on mathematical analysis of their performance. A more experimental approach to broadcasting in wireless networks can be found, e.g., in [40] and in the literature therein.

We conclude this chapter by proposing a short list of open problems. This list is by no means complete, and the choice of problems reflects personal interests of this author. The order of problems corresponds to the order of the relevant material in this chapter, and some of them were already mentioned in the respective parts of the exposition. We refer the reader to the appropriate sections for information on the related results known to date.

1. Find a centralized deterministic broadcasting algorithm working in asymptotically optimal time for arbitrary radio networks, assuming that the central monitor has complete knowledge of the graph.

2. Find a distributed deterministic broadcasting algorithm working in asymptotically optimal time for arbitrary radio networks of unknown topology.

3. Find a distributed deterministic broadcasting algorithm working in asymptotically optimal time under the assumption that every node knows the part of the radio network at (graph) distance at most r from it.

4. Find a distributed randomized broadcasting algorithm working in asymptotically optimal time for arbitrary radio networks of unknown topology.

5. Establish the exact trade-off between time and cost (number of transmissions) of deterministic broadcasting for arbitrary radio networks of unknown topology.

ACKNOWLEDGMENTS

Supported in part by NSERC grant OGP 0008136.

REFERENCES

1. M. Adler and C. Scheideler, Efficient communication strategies for ad-hoc wireless networks, *Proceedings 10th ACM Symposium on Parallel Algorithms and Architectures,* Puerto Vallarta, Mexico, pp. 259–268, 1998.

2. N. Alon, A. Bar-Noy, N. Linial, and D. Peleg, A lower bound for radio broadcast, *Journal of Computer and System Sciences 43,* 290—298, 1991.

3. B. Awerbuch, O. Goldreich, D. Peleg, and R. Vainish, A Tradeoff between Information and Communication in Broadcast Protocols, *Journal of the ACM, 37,* 238–256, 1990.

4. A. Bagchi and S. L. Hakimi, Data transfers in broadcast networks, *IEEE Trans. on Computers 41,* 842–847, 1992.

5. R. Bar-Yehuda, O. Goldreich, and A. Itai, On the time complexity of broadcast in multi-hop radio networks: An exponential gap between determinism and randomization, *Journal of Computer and System Sciences 45,* 104–126, 1992.

6. R. Bar-Yehuda, A. Israeli, and A. Itai, Multiple communication in multihop radio networks, *SIAM Journal on Computing, 22,* 875–887, 1993.

7. D. Bruschi and M. Del Pinto, Lower bounds for the broadcast problem in mobile radio networks, *Distr. Comp., 10,* 129–135, 1997.

8. I. Chlamtac and S. Kutten, On broadcasting in radio networks—problem analysis and protocol design, *IEEE Transactions on Communications, 33,* 1240–1246, 1985.

9. I. Chlamtac and S. Kutten, Tree based broadcasting in multihop radio networks, *IEEE Trans. on Computers, 36,* 1209—1223, 1987.

10. I. Chlamtac and O. Weinstein, The Wave Expansion Approach to Broadcasting in Multihop Radio Networks, *Proceedings INFOCOM,* 1987.

11. B. S. Chlebus, Randomized communication in radio networks, in *Handbook on Randomized Computing,* vol. I, pp. 401–456, P. M. Pardalos, S. Rajasekaran, J. Reif, and J. D. P. Rolim (Eds.), Norwell, MA: Kluwer Academic Publishers, 2001.

12. B. S. Chlebus, L. Gąsieniec, A. Gibbons, A. Pelc, and W. Rytter, Deterministic broadcasting in unknown radio networks, *Proceedings 11th Annual ACM-SIAM Symposium on Discrete Algorithms* (SODA'2000), pp. 861–870, 2000.

13. B. S. Chlebus, L. Gąsieniec, A. Östlin, and J. M. Robson, Deterministic radio broadcasting, *Proceedings 27th International Colloquium on Automata, Languages and Programming* (ICALP'2000), July 2000, Geneva, Switzerland, LNCS 1853, pp. 717–728.

14. M. Chrobak, L. Gąsieniec, and W. Rytter, Fast broadcasting and gossiping in radio networks, *Proceedings 41st Symposium on Foundations of Computer Science* (FOCS 2000), Redondo Beach, California, pp. 575–581, 2000.

15. A. E. F. Clementi, A. Monti, and R. Silvestri, Selective families, superimposed codes, and broadcasting on unknown radio networks, *Proceedings 12th Annual ACM-SIAM Symposium on Discrete Algorithms* (SODA'2001), pp. 709–718, 2000.

16. G. De Marco and A. Pelc, Faster broadcasting in unknown radio networks, *Information Processing Letters, 79,* 53–56, 2001.

17. A. Dessmark and A. Pelc, Deterministic radio broadcasting at low cost, *Proceedings 18th Annual Symposium on Theoretical Aspects of Computer Science* (STACS 2001), LNCS 2010, pp. 158–169, Dresden, Germany, February 2001.

18. A. Dessmark and A. Pelc, Tradeoffs between knowledge and time of communication in geometric radio networks, in *Proceedings of the 13th Annual ACM Symposium on Parallel Algorithms and Architectures* (SPAA 2001), pp. 59–66, Crete, Greece, July 2001.

19. A. Dessmark and A. Pelc, Distributed coloring and communication in rings with local knowledge, *Proceedings International Parallel and Distributed Processing Symposium* (IPDPS 2001), San Francisco, April 2001.

20. K. Diks, E. Kranakis, D. Krizanc, and A. Pelc, The impact of knowledge on broadcasting time in radio networks, *Proceedings 7th Annual European Symposium on Algorithms,* ESA'99, Prague, Czech Republic, July 1999, LNCS 1643, pp. 41–52.

21. K. Diks, E. Kranakis, A. Malinowski, and A. Pelc, Anonymous wireless rings, *Theoretical Computer Science 145,* 95–109, 1995.

22. P. Fraigniaud and E. Lazard, Methods and problems of communication in usual networks, *Disc. Appl. Math., 53,* 79–133, 1994.

23. I. Gaber and Y. Mansour, Broadcast in radio networks, *Proceedings 6th Annual ACM-SIAM Symposium on Discrete Algorithms,* SODA'95, pp. 577–585, 1995.

24. R. Gallager, A Perspective on multiaccess channels, *IEEE Trans. on Information Theory, 31,* 124–142, 1985.

25. L. Gąsieniec, A. Pelc and D. Peleg, The wakeup problem in synchronous broadcast systems, *in Proceedings 19th Annual ACM Symposium on Principles of Distributed Computing* (PODC'2000), Portland, Oregon, July 2000, pp. 113–122.

26. S. M. Hedetniemi, S. T. Hedetniemi, and A. L. Liestman, A survey of gossiping and broadcasting in communication networks, *Networks, 18,* 319–349, 1988.

27. J. Hromkovič, R. Klasing, B. Monien, and R. Peine, Dissemination of information in interconnection networks (broadcasting and gossiping), in Ding-Zhu Du and D. Frank Hsu (Eds.), *Combinatorial Network Theory*, Norwell, MA: Kluwer Academic Publishers, pp. 125–212, 1995.

28. F. K. Hwang, The time complexity of deterministic broadcast radio networks, *Discrete Applied Mathematics, 60,* 219–222, 1995.

29. E. Kranakis, D. Krizanc, and A. Pelc, Fault-tolerant broadcasting in radio networks, *Proceedings 6th Annual European Symposium on Algorithms,* ESA'98, Venice, Italy, August 1998, LNCS 1461, pp. 283–294.

30. E. Kushilevitz and Y. Mansour, An $\Omega(D \log (N/D))$lLower bound for broadcast in radio networks, *SIAM Journal on Computing, 27,* 702–712, 1998.

31. E. Kushilevitz and Y. Mansour, Computation in noisy radio networks, in *Proceedings 9th Annual ACM-SIAM Symposium on Discrete Algorithms* (SODA'98), San Francisco, January 1998, pp. 236–243, 1998.

32. K. Nakano, S. Olariu, and J. L. Schwing, Broadcast-efficient protocols for mobile radio networks, *IEEE Trans. on Parallel and Distributed Systems, 10,* 1276–1289, 1999.

33. E. Pagani and G. P. Rossi, Reliable broadcast in mobile multihop radio networks, in *Proceedings 3rd Annual ACM/IEEE International Conference on Mobile Computing and Networking* (MOBICOM'97), pp. 34–42, 1997.

34. D. Peleg, Deterministic radio broadcast with no topological knowledge, unpublished manuscript (2000.

35. R. Ramaswami and K. K. Parhi, Distributed scheduling of broadcasts in a radio network, in *Proceedings IEEE INFOCOM,* vol. 3, pp. 497–504, 1989.

36. K. Ravishankar and S. Singh, Broadcasting on [0, *L*], *Discrete Applied Mathematics, 53,* 299–319, 1994.

37. K. Ravishankar and S. Singh, Asymptotically optimal gossiping in radio networks, *Discrete Applied Mathematics, 61,* 61–82, 1995.

38. K. Ravishankar and S. Singh, Gossiping on a ring with radios, *Parallel Processing Letters, 6,* 115–126, 1996.

39. A. Sen and M. L. Huson, A new model for scheduling packet radio networks, in *Proceedings 15th Annual Joint Conference of the IEEE Computer and Communication Societies* (IEEE INFOCOM'96) pp. 1116–1124, 1996.

40. I. Stojmevovic and M. Seddigh, Internal nodes based broadcasting algorithms in wireless networks, in *Proceedings International Conference on Advances in Infrastructure for Electronic Business, Science and Education on the Internet,* SSGRR, L'Aquila, Italy, July 2000.

CHAPTER 25

Mobile IP Protocols

CHRISTOS DOULIGERIS and THANOS VASILAKOS
Institute of Computer Science, FORTH, Heraklion, Crete, Greece

25.1 INTRODUCTION

The Internet currently offers access to a variety of information worldwide in an efficient and, through the use of web technologies, user-friendly manner. It is based on the Transport Control/Internet Protocol (TCP/IP) protocol stack [6] which has been developed with data communications and fixed access location points in mind. The wide use of wireless technologies for voice communications and the proliferation of handheld and other devices that can provide access to the Internet call for a new paradigm for connecting mobile users to the Internet. Such an endeavor needs to take into account the existing Internet protocols, compatibility issues, and the requirements of mobile users.

Mobile IP, as proposed by the Internet Engineering Task Force (IETF) in RFC 2002 [1] and subsequent RFCs [2], provides an efficient, scalable mechanism for node mobility within the Internet. Nodes may move and change their point of attachment to the Internet without changing their IP address. This allows them to maintain transport and higher-layer connections while moving. Node mobility is realized without the need to propagate host-specific routes throughout the Internet routing fabric. The mobile node uses two IP addresses: a fixed home address and a care-of address that changes at each new point of attachment.

Mobile IP is intended to solve node mobility issues over the IP layer. It is just as suitable for mobility across homogeneous media as it is for mobility across heterogeneous media. Mobile IP facilitates node movement from one Ethernet segment to another as well as handling node movement from an Ethernet segment to a wireless local area network (LAN).

One can think of mobile IP as solving the "macro" mobility management problem. It is less well suited for more "micro" mobility management applications, for example, handoff amongst wireless transceivers, each of which covers only a very small geographic area. In this situation, link layer mechanisms for link maintenance (i.e., link layer handoff) might offer faster convergence and fewer overheads than mobile IP.

Finally, it is noted that mobile nodes are assigned (home) IP addresses largely the same way in which stationary hosts are assigned long-term IP addresses; namely, by the authority that owns them. Properly applied, mobile IP allows mobile nodes to communicate using only their home address, regardless of their current location. Mobile IP, therefore,

Handbook of Wireless Networks and Mobile Computing, Edited by Ivan Stojmenović.
ISBN 0-471-41902-8   © 2002 John Wiley & Sons, Inc.

makes no attempt to solve the problems related to local or global addressing (IP address, renumbering etc).

In brief, mobile IP routing works as follows. Packets destined to a mobile node are routed first to their home network—a network identified by the network prefix of the mobile node's (permanent) home address. At the home network, the mobile node's home agent intercepts such packets and tunnels them to the mobile node's most recently reported care-of address. At the endpoint of the tunnel, the inner packets are decapsulated and delivered to the mobile node. In the reverse direction, packets sourced by mobile nodes are routed to their destination using standard IP routing mechanisms.

The mobile IP protocol defines the following:

- An authenticated registration procedure by which a mobile node informs its home agent(s) of its care-of address(es).
- An extension to Internet Control Message Protocol (ICMP) Router Discovery [9], which allows mobile nodes to discover prospective home agents and foreign agents.
- The rules for routing packets to and from mobile nodes, including the specification of one mandatory tunneling mechanism [4] and several optional tunneling mechanisms [7, 2].

This chapter will present the mobile IP standard as well as current efforts within the IETF to provide connectivity in the future wireless world. In the next section, an introduction to the requirements and constraints imposed by IP in a mobile environment are presented, as well as necessary functions a mobile protocol should perform and principles it should adhere to. Section 25.3 presents in detail the mobile IP protocol as defined in RFC2002 and its revisions. The following sections present issues that the mobile IP community faces regarding route optimization, transferring to an Ipv6 environment, organization of databases, and security.

25.2 MOBILITY REQUIREMENTS AND CONSTRAINTS IN AN IP ENVIRONMENT

IP Version 4, which is the current, most implemented version of IP, assumes that a node's IP address uniquely identifies the node's point of attachment to the Internet. A node must be located on the network indicated by its IP address in order to receive datagrams destined for it; otherwise, datagrams destined to the node would be undeliverable. If a node changes its point of attachment, in order not to lose its ability to communicate, one of the two following mechanisms must typically be employed:

1. The node must change its IP address whenever it changes its point of attachment.
2. Host-specific routes must be propagated throughout much of the Internet.

The first alternative makes it impossible for a node to maintain transport and higher-layer connections when the node changes location. The second does not scale very well.

A mobile node must be able to communicate with other nodes after changing its link layer point of attachment to the Internet, yet without changing its IP address. A mobile node must be able to communicate with other nodes that do not implement these mobility functions. No protocol enhancements are required in hosts or architectural entities. All messages used to update another node as to the location of a mobile node must be authenticated in order to protect against remote redirection attacks.

Wireless links have substantially lower bandwidth and higher error rates than traditional wired networks. Minimizing power consumption is important for battery powered mobile nodes. Therefore, signaling and processing should be minimized. Integration of mobility with IP should also place no additional constraints on the assignment of IP addresses. The companies or organizations that own the mobile nodes should assign IP addresses.

25.3 MOBILE IP PROTOCOL OVERVIEW

25.3.1 Mobile IP New Architectural Entities

Mobile IP introduces three new functional entities:

1. *Mobile Node.* A host or router that changes its point of attachment from one network or subnetwork to another. A mobile node may change its location without changing its IP address; it may continue to communicate with other Internet nodes at any location using its (constant) IP address, assuming link layer connectivity to a point of attachment is available.
2. *Home Agent.* A router on a mobile node's home network that tunnels datagrams for delivery to the mobile node when it is away from home, and maintains current location information for the mobile node.
3. *Foreign Agent.* A router on a mobile node's visited network that provides routing services to the mobile node while registered. The foreign agent detunnels and delivers datagrams to the mobile node that were tunneled by the mobile node's home agent. For datagrams sent by a mobile node, the foreign agent may serve as a default router for registered mobile nodes.

A mobile node is given a long-term IP address on a home network. This home address is administered in the same way that a "permanent" IP address is provided to a stationary host. When away from its home network, a "care-of address" is associated with the mobile node that reflects the mobile node's current point of attachment. The mobile node uses its home address as the source address of all IP datagrams that it sends and for datagrams sent for certain mobility management functions.

The following terminology is used in the mobile IP documents.

Agent Advertisement. An advertisement message constructed by attaching a special Extension to a router advertisement message.

Care-of Address. The termination point of a tunnel toward a mobile node, for datagrams forwarded to the mobile node while it is away from home. The protocol can use two different types of care-of addresses: a "foreign agent care-of address" is an address of a foreign agent with which the mobile node is registered, and a "colocated care-of address" is an externally obtained local address that the mobile node has associated with one of its own network interfaces.

Correspondent Node. A peer with which a mobile node is communicating. A correspondent node may be either mobile or stationary.

Foreign Network. Any network other than the mobile node's home network.

Home Address. An IP address that is assigned for an extended period of time to a mobile node. It remains unchanged regardless of where the node is attached to the Internet.

Home Network. A network, possibly virtual, having a network prefix matching that of a mobile node's home address. Note that standard IP routing mechanisms will deliver datagrams destined to a mobile node's home address to the mobile node's home network.

Link Layer Address. The address used to identify an endpoint of some communication over a physical link. A facility or medium over which nodes can communicate at the link layer.

Link. Typically, the link layer address is an interface's media access control (MAC) address.

Mobility Agent. Either a home agent or a foreign agent.

Mobility Binding. The association of a home address with a care-of address, along with the remaining lifetime of that association.

Mobility Security Association. A collection of security contexts between a pair of nodes that may be applied to mobile IP protocol messages exchanged between them. Each context indicates an authentication algorithm and mode, a secret (a shared key or appropriate public/private key pair), and the style of replay protection in use.

Node. A host or a router.

Nonce. A randomly chosen value, different from previous choices, inserted in a message to protect against replays.

Security Parameter Index (SPI). An index identifying a security context between a pair of nodes among the contexts available in the Mobility Security Association. SPI values 0 through 255 are reserved and must not be used in any Mobility Security Association function.

Tunnel. The path followed by a datagram while it is encapsulated. It is routed to a knowledgeable decapsulating agent, which decapsulates the datagram and then correctly delivers it to its ultimate destination.

Virtual Network. A network with no physical instantiation beyond a router (with a physical network interface on another network). The router (e.g., a home agent) generally advertises reachability to the virtual network using conventional routing protocols.

Visited Network. A network other than a mobile node's home network, to which the mobile node is currently connected.

Visitor List. The list of mobile nodes visiting a foreign agent.

25.3.2 Operation of Mobile IP

Mobile IP provides two basic functions: agent discovery and registration. During agent discovery, home agents and foreign agents may advertise their availability on each link for which they provide service. A newly arrived mobile node can send a solicitation on the link to learn if any prospective agents are present. When the mobile node is away from home, it registers its care-of address with its home agent during the registration phase. Depending on its method of attachment, the mobile node will register either directly with its home agent, or through a foreign agent that forwards the registration to the home agent.

The following steps provide a rough outline of operation of the mobile IP protocol [1]:

- Mobility agents (i.e., foreign agents and home agents) advertise their presence via agent advertisement messages. A mobile node may optionally solicit an agent advertisement message from any locally attached mobility agents through an agent solicitation message.
- A mobile node receives these agent advertisements and determines whether it is on its home network or a foreign network.
- When the mobile node detects that it is located on its home network, it operates without mobility services. If returning to its home network from being registered elsewhere, the mobile node deregisters with its home agent through exchange of a registration request and registration reply message with it.
- When a mobile node detects that it has moved to a foreign network, it obtains a care-of address on the foreign network.The care-of address can either be determined from a foreign agent's advertisements (a foreign agent care-of address), or by some external assignment mechanism such as the dynamic configuration protocol (DHCP) [6] (a colocated care-of address).
- The mobile node operating away from home then registers its new care-of address with its home agent through exchange of a registration request and registration reply message with it, possibly via a foreign agent.
- Datagrams sent to the mobile node's home address are intercepted by its home agent, tunneled by the home agent to the mobile node's care-of address, received at the tunnel endpoint (either at a foreign agent or at the mobile node itself), and finally delivered to the mobile node.
- In the reverse direction, datagrams sent by the mobile node are generally routing mechanisms, not necessarily passing through the home agent.

When away from home, mobile IP uses protocol tunneling to hide a mobile node's home address from intervening routers between its home network and its current location.

The tunnel terminates at the mobile node's care-of address. The care-of address must be an address to which datagrams can be delivered via conventional IP routing. At the care-of address, the original datagram is removed from the tunnel and delivered to the mobile node.

Mobile IP provides two alternative modes for the acquisition of a care-of address:

- A "foreign agent care-of address" is a care-of address provided by a foreign agent through its agent advertisement messages. In this case, the care-of address is an IP address of the foreign agent.
- A "colocated care-of address" is a care-of address acquired by the mobile node as a local IP address through some external network interfaces.

The mode of using a colocated care-of address has the advantage that it allows a mobile node to function without a foreign agent, for example, in networks that have not yet deployed a foreign agent. It does, however, place additional burden on the IPv4 address space because it requires a pool of addresses within the foreign network to be made available to visiting mobile nodes. It is difficult to efficiently maintain pools of addresses for each subnet that may permit mobile nodes to visit.

Figure 25.1 illustrates the routing of datagrams to be registered with the home agent. In the figure, the mobile node is using a foreign agent care-of address. In Step 1, a datagram to a mobile node arrives on the home network via standard IP routing. In Step 2, the datagram is intercepted by home agent and is tunneled to the care-of address. In Step 3, the datagram is detunneled and delivered to the mobile node. In Step 4, for datagrams sent by the mobile node, standard IP routing delivers each of them to its destination. Note that the foreign agent is the mobile node's default router.

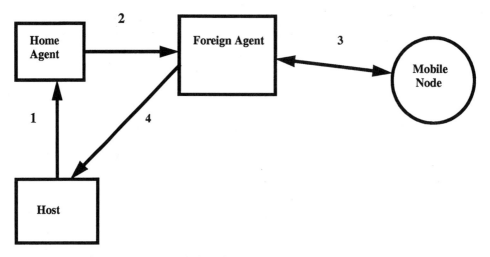

Figure 25.1   Transmission of messages in a mobile IP environment.

25.3.3 Message Formats

Mobile IP defines a set of new control messages, sent with the user datagram protocol (UDP) [17]. Currently, the following two message types are defined:

1. Registration request
2. Registration reply

In addition, for agent discovery, mobile IP makes use of the existing router advertisement and router solicitation messages defined for ICMP router discovery [4].

Mobile IP defines a general extension mechanism to allow optional information to be carried by mobile IP control messages or by ICMP router discovery messages. Extensions allow variable amounts of information to be carried within each datagram. Each of these extensions (with one exception) is encoded in the following type–length–value format:

0 1 2 3 4 5 6 7 8 9 10 11 12 13 14 15 16 17 18 19 20 21 22

Type	Length	Data

Type indicates the particular type of extension.

Length indicates the length (in bytes) of the data field within this extension. The length does not include the type and length bytes.

Data indicates the particular data associated with this extension. This field may be zero or more bytes in length. The type and length fields determine the format and length of the data field.

The total length of the IP datagram indicates the end of the list of extensions.

Two separately maintained sets of numbering spaces, from which extension type values are allocated, are used in mobile IP:

The first set consists of those extensions that may appear only in mobile IP control messages. Currently, the following types are defined for extensions appearing in mobile IP control messages:

32	Mobile Home Authentication
33	Mobile Foreign Authentication
34	Foreign Home Authentication

The second set consists of those extensions that may appear only in ICMP router discovery messages [4]. Currently, mobile IP defines the following types for extensions appearing in ICMP router discovery messages:

0	One-byte Padding (encoded with no length nor data field)
16	Mobility Agent Advertisement
19	Prefix Lengths

25.3.4   Agent Discovery

Agent discovery is the method by which a mobile node determines whether it is currently connected to its home network or to a foreign network, and by which a mobile node can detect when it has moved from one network to another. When connected to a foreign network, the methods specified in this section also allow the mobile node to determine the foreign agent care-of address being offered by each foreign agent on that network.

Mobile IP extends ICMP router discovery [4] as its primary mechanism for agent discovery. Including a mobility agent advertisement extension in an ICMP router advertisement message forms an agent advertisement. An agent solicitation message is identical to an ICMP router solicitation [with IP time-to-live (TTL) set to 1]. Agent advertisement and agent solicitation may not be necessary for link layers that already provide this functionality

25.3.4.1   Agent Advertisement

To advertise its services on a link, a mobility agent transmits agent advertisements. Mobile nodes use these advertisements to determine their current point of attachment to the Internet. An agent advertisement is an ICMP router advertisement that has been extended to also carry a mobility agent and, optionally, a prefix length extension, one-byte padding extension, or other extensions that might be defined in the future.

Within an agent advertisement message, ICMP router advertisement fields of the message are required to conform to the following additional specifications:

Link Layer Fields

Destination Address. The link layer destination address of a unicast agent advertisement must be the same as the source link layer address of the agent solicitation that prompted the advertisement.

IP Fields

TTL. The TTL for all agent advertisements must be set to 1.

Destination Address. As specified for ICMP router discovery [4], the IP destination address of an agent advertisement must be either the "all systems on this link" multicast address (224.0.0.1) [5] or the "limited broadcast" address (255.255.255.255). The subnet-directed broadcast address of the form <prefix>.<-1> cannot be used since mobile nodes will not generally know the prefix of the foreign network.

ICMP Fields

Code. The Code field of the agent advertisement is interpreted as follows:

0 = The mobility agent handles common traffic, that is, it acts as a router for IP datagrams not necessarily related to mobile nodes.

16 = The mobility agent does not route common traffic. However, all foreign agents must (minimally) forward to a default router any datagrams received from a registered mobile node.

Lifetime. The maximum length of time that the advertisement is considered valid in the absence of further advertisements.

Router Address(es). Addresses that may appear in this portion of the agent advertisement.

Num Addrs. The number of router addresses advertised in this message. Note that in an agent advertisement message, the number of router addresses specified in the ICMP router advertisement portion of the message may be set to 0.

The protocol also specifies the periodicity of the transmission of these messages. A home agent must always be prepared to serve the mobile nodes for which it is the home agent. When a foreign agent wishes to require registration even from those mobile nodes that have acquired a colocated care-of address, it sets a special bit, the "R" bit, to one. An agent solicitation is identical to an ICMP router solicitation (with the IP TTL field set to 1).

Foreign Agent and Home Agent Considerations
Any mobility agent that cannot be discovered by a link layer protocol must send agent advertisements. An agent, which can be discovered by a link layer protocol, should also implement agent advertisements. However, the advertisements need not be sent, except when the site policy requires registration with the agent, or as a response to a specific agent solicitation. All mobility agents should respond to agent solicitations. If the home network is not a virtual network, then the home agent for any mobile node should be located on the link identified by the mobile node's home address, and agent advertisement messages sent by the home agent on this link must have the "H" bit set. In this way, mobile nodes on their own home network will be able to determine that they are indeed at home.

If the home network is a virtual network, mobile nodes are always treated as being away from home.

Mobile Node Considerations
Every mobile node must implement agent solicitation. Solicitations should only be sent in the absence of agent advertisements and when a care-of address has not been determined through a link-layer protocol or other means. The mobile node uses the same procedures, defaults, and constants for agent solicitation as specified for ICMP router solicitation messages [4], except that the mobile node may solicit more often than once every three seconds, and a mobile node that is currently not connected to any foreign agent may solicit more times than a specified maximum number. The mobile node must limit the rate at which a mobile node sends solicitations.

A mobile node can detect that it has returned to its home network when it receives an agent advertisement from its own home agent. If so, it should deregister with its home agent.

25.3.5 Registration

Mobile IP registration provides a flexible mechanism for mobile nodes to communicate their current reachability information to their home agent. It is the method by which mobile nodes request forwarding services when visiting a foreign network, inform their home agent of their current care-of address, renew a registration that is due to expire, and/or deregister when they return home.

Registration messages exchange information between a mobile node (optionally), a foreign agent, and the home agent. Registration creates or modifies a mobility binding at the home agent, associating the mobile node's home address with its care-of address for the specified lifetime.

Several other (optional) capabilities are available through the registration procedure; these enable a mobile node to: maintain multiple simultaneous registrations, deregister specific care-of addresses while retaining other mobility bindings, and discover the address of a home agent if the mobile node is not configured with this information.

25.3.5.1 Registration Overview

Mobile IP defines two different registration procedures, one via a foreign agent that relays the registration to the mobile node's home agent, and one directly with the mobile node's home agent. The following rules determine which of these two registration procedures to use in any particular circumstance.

- If a mobile node is registering a foreign agent care-of address, the mobile node must register via that foreign agent.
- If a mobile node is using a colocated care-of address, and receives an agent advertisement from a foreign agent on the link on which it is using this care-of address, the mobile node should register via that foreign agent (or via another foreign agent on this link) if the "R" bit is set in the received agent advertisement message.
- If a mobile node is otherwise using a colocated care-of address, the mobile node must register directly with its home agent.
- If a mobile node has returned to its home network and is (de)registering with its home agent, the mobile node must register directly with its home agent.

Both registration procedures involve the exchange of registration request and registration reply messages. When registering via a foreign agent, the registration procedure requires the following four messages:

- The mobile node sends a registration request to the prospective foreign agent to begin the registration process.
- The foreign agent processes the registration request and then relays it to the home agent.
- The home agent sends a registration reply to the foreign agent to grant or deny the request.
- The foreign agent processes the registration reply and then relays it to the mobile node.

When the mobile node instead registers directly with its home agent, the registration procedure requires only the following two messages:

- The mobile node sends a registration request to the home agent.
- The home agent sends a registration reply to the mobile node, granting or denying the request.

25.3.5.2 *Authentication*

Each mobile node, foreign agent, and home agent must be able to support a mobility security association for mobile entities, indexed by their SPI and IP address. Registration messages between a mobile node and its home agent must be authenticated with the mobile home authentication extension. This extension immediately follows all nonauthentication extensions, except those foreign agent-specific extensions that may be added to the message after the mobile node computes the authentication.

25.3.5.3 *Registration Request*

A mobile node registers with its home agent using a registration request message so that its home agent can create or modify a mobility binding for that mobile node (e.g., with a new lifetime). The request may be relayed to the home agent by the foreign agent through which the mobile node is registering, or it may be sent directly to the home agent in the case in which the mobile node is registering a colocated care-of address.

25.3.5.4 *Registration Reply*

A mobility agent returns a registration reply message to a mobile node that has sent a registration request message. If the mobile node is requesting a service from a foreign agent, that foreign agent will receive the reply from the home agent and subsequently relay it to the mobile node. The reply message contains the necessary codes to inform the mobile node about the status of its request, along with the lifetime granted by the home agent, which may be smaller than the original request.

25.3.5.5 *Mobile Node Considerations*

A mobile node must be configured with its home address, a netmask, and a mobility security association for each home agent. In addition, a mobile node may be configured with the IP address of one or more of its home agents; otherwise, the mobile node may discover a home agent using specific procedures.

For each pending registration, the mobile node maintains the following information:

- The link layer address of the foreign agent to which the registration request was sent, if applicable
- The IP destination address of the registration request
- The care-of address used in the registration
- The identification value sent in the registration
- The originally requested lifetime
- The remaining lifetime of the pending registration

25.3.5.6   Foreign Agent Considerations

The foreign agent plays a mostly passive role in mobile IP registration. It relays registration requests between mobile nodes and home agents, and, when it provides the care-of address, decapsulates datagrams for delivery to the mobile node. It should also send periodic agent advertisement messages to advertise its presence, if not detectable by link layer means.

A foreign agent must not transmit a registration request except when relaying a registration request received from a mobile node to the mobile node's home agent. A foreign agent must not transmit a registration reply except when relaying a registration reply received from a mobile node's home agent, or when replying to a registration request received from a mobile node in the case in which the foreign agent is denying service to the mobile node. In particular, a foreign agent must not generate a registration request or reply because a mobile node's registration lifetime has expired. A foreign agent also must not originate a registration request message that asks for deregistration of a mobile node; however, it must relay valid (de)registration requests originated by a mobile node.

Each foreign agent must be configured with a care-of address. In addition, for each pending or current registration, the foreign agent must maintain a visitor list entry containing the following information obtained from the mobile node's registration request:

- The link layer source address of the mobile node
- The IP source address (the mobile node's home address)
- The IP destination address
- The UDP source port
- The home agent address
- The identification field
- The requested registration lifetime
- The remaining lifetime of the pending or current registration

25.3.5.7   Home Agent Considerations

Home agents play a reactive role in the registration process. The home agent receives registration requests from the mobile node (perhaps relayed by a foreign agent), updates its record of the mobility bindings for this mobile node, and issues a suitable registration reply in response to each.

A home agent must not transmit a registration reply except when replying to a registration request received from a mobile node. In particular, the home agent must not generate a registration reply to indicate that the lifetime has expired.

25.3.6   Routing Considerations

This section describes how mobile nodes, home agents, and (possibly) foreign agents cooperate to route datagrams to/from mobile nodes that are connected to a foreign network. The mobile node informs its home agent of its current location using the registration procedure described in the previous sections. Home agents and foreign agents must support tunneling datagrams using IP in IP encapsulation [14]. Any mobile node that uses a colocated care-of address must support receiving datagrams tunneled using IP in IP encapsulation. Minimal encapsulation [15] and GRE encapsulation [8] are alternate encapsulation methods that may optionally be supported by mobility agents and mobile nodes.

The protocol specifies unicast, broadcast, and multicast datagram routing. In this chapter, we focus on the procedures for unicast datagram routing.

25.3.6.1 Unicast Datagram Routing

Mobile Node Considerations

When connected to its home network, a mobile node operates without the support of mobility services. That is, it operates in the same way as any other (fixed) host or router. The method by which a mobile node selects a default router when connected to its home network, or when away from home and using a colocated care-of address, is outside the scope of this document. ICMP router advertisement [4] is one such method.

When registered on a foreign network, the mobile node chooses a default router by the following rules.

1. If the mobile node is registered using a foreign agent care-of address, then the mobile node must choose its default router from among the router addresses advertised in the ICMP router advertisement portion of that agent advertisement message. The mobile node may also consider the IP source address of the agent advertisement as another possible choice for the IP address of a default router, along with the (possibly empty) list of router addresses from the ICMP router advertisement portion of the message. In such cases, the IP source address must be considered to be the worst choice (lowest preference) for a default router.

2. If the mobile node is registered directly with its home agent using a colocated care-of address, then the mobile node should choose its default router from among those advertised in any ICMP router advertisement message that it receives for which its externally obtained care-of address and the router address match under the network prefix. If the mobile node's externally obtained care-of address matches the IP source address of the agent advertisement under the network prefix, the mobile node may also consider that IP source address as another possible choice for the IP address of a default router, along with the (possibly empty) list of router addresses from the ICMP router advertisement portion of the message. If so, the IP source address must be considered to be the worst choice (lowest preference) for a default router. The network prefix may be obtained from the prefix lengths extension in the router advertisement, if present. The prefix may also be obtained through other mechanisms beyond the scope of this document.

Foreign Agent Considerations

Upon receipt of an encapsulated datagram sent to its advertised care-of address, a foreign agent must compare the inner destination address to those entries in its visitor list. When the destination does not match the address of any mobile node currently in the visitor list, the foreign agent must not forward the datagram without modifications to the original IP header, because otherwise a routing loop is likely to result. The datagram should be silently discarded. ICMP destination unreachable must not be sent when a foreign agent is unable to forward an incoming tunneled datagram. Otherwise, the foreign agent forwards the decapsulated datagram to the mobile node.

The foreign agent must not advertise to other routers in its routing domain, nor to any other mobile node, the presence of a mobile router.

The foreign agent must route datagrams it receives from registered mobile nodes. At a minimum, this means that the foreign agent must verify the IP header checksum, decrement the IP time to live, recompute the IP header checksum, and forward such datagrams to a default router. In addition, the foreign agent should send an appropriate ICMP redirect message to the mobile node.

Home Agent Considerations
The home agent must be able to intercept any datagrams on the home network addressed to the mobile node while the mobile node is registered away from home. Proxy and gratuitous ARP may be used in enabling this interception.

The home agent must examine the IP destination address of all arriving datagrams to see if it is equal to the home address of any of its mobile nodes registered away from home. If so, the home agent tunnels the datagram to the mobile node's currently registered care-of address capability of multiple simultaneous mobility bindings, it tunnels a copy to each care-of address in the mobile node's mobility binding list. If the mobile node has no current mobility bindings, the home agent must not attempt to intercept datagrams destined for the mobile node, and thus will not in general receive such datagrams. However, if the home agent is also a router handling common IP traffic, it is possible that it will receive such datagrams for forwarding onto the home network. In this case, the home agent must assume that the mobile node is at home and simply forward the datagram directly onto the home network.

If the lifetime for a given mobility binding expires before the home agent has received another valid registration request for that mobile node, then that binding is deleted from the mobility binding list. The home agent must not send any registration reply message simply because the mobile node's binding has expired. The entry in the visitor list of the mobile node's current foreign agent will expire naturally, probably at the same time as the binding expired at the home agent. When a mobility binding's lifetime expires, the home agent must delete the binding, but it must retain any other (non-expired) simultaneous mobility bindings that it holds for the mobile node.

When a home agent receives a datagram, intercepted for one of its mobile nodes registered away from home, the home agent must examine the datagram to check if it is already encapsulated. If so, the following special rules apply in the forwarding of that datagram to the mobile node. If the inner (encapsulated) destination address is the same as the outer destination address (the mobile node), then the home agent must also examine the outer source address of the encapsulated datagram (the source address of the tunnel). If current care-of address is the same as the mobile node's, the home agent must silently discard that datagram in order to prevent a likely routing loop. If, instead, the outer source address is not the same as the mobile node's current care-of address, then the home agent should forward the datagram to the mobile node. In order to forward the datagram in this case, the home agent may simply alter the outer destination address to the care-of address, rather than reencapsulating the datagram. Otherwise (the inner destination address is not the same as the outer destination address), the home agent should encapsulate the datagram again (nested encapsulation), with the new outer destination address set equal to the mobile node's care-of address.

25.3.7 Security Considerations

The mobile computing environment is potentially very different from the ordinary computing environment. In many cases, mobile computers will be connected to the network via wireless links. Such links are particularly vulnerable to passive eavesdropping, active replay attacks, and other active attacks.

25.3.7.1 Message Authentication Codes
Home agents and mobile nodes must be able to perform authentication. The default algorithm is keyed MD5 [21], with a key size of 128 bits. The default mode of operation is to both precede and follow by the 128-bit key the data to be hashed; that is, MD5 is to be used in "prefix + suffix" mode. The foreign agent must also support authentication using keyed MD5 and key sizes of 128 bits or greater, with manual key distribution. More authentication algorithms, algorithm modes, key distribution methods, and key sizes may also be supported.

25.3.7.2 Areas of Security Concern in this Protocol
The registration protocol described in RFC 2002 will result in a mobile node's traffic being tunneled to its care-of address. This tunneling feature could be a significant vulnerability if the registration were not authenticated. Such remote unauthenticated redirection, for instance, as performed by the mobile registration protocol, is widely understood to be a security problem in the current Internet [2]. The use of "gratuitous ARP" brings with it all of the risks associated with the use of ARP. Since it is not authenticated, it can potentially be used to steal another host's traffic.

25.3.7.3 Key Management
This specification requires a strong authentication mechanism (keyed MD5) which precludes many potential attacks based on the mobile IP registration protocol. However, because key distribution is difficult in the absence of a network key management protocol, messages with the foreign agent are not all required to be authenticated. In a commercial environment, it might be important to authenticate all messages between the foreign agent and the home agent, so that billing is possible, and service providers do not provide service to users that are not legitimate customers of that service provider.

25.3.7.4 Replay Protection for Registration Requests
The identification field is used to let the home agent verify that the mobile node, not replayed by an attacker from some previous registration, has freshly generated a registration message. Two methods are described in this section: time stamps (mandatory) and

"nonces" (optional). All mobile nodes and home agents must implement time-stamp-based replay protection. These nodes may also implement nonce-based replay protection.

The style of replay protection in effect between a mobile node and its home agent is part of the mobile security association. A mobile node and its home agent must agree on which method of replay protection will be used. The interpretation of the identification field depends on the method of replay protection as described in the subsequent subsections.

Whatever method is used, the low-order 32 bits of the identification must be copied unchanged from the registration request to the reply. The foreign agent uses those bits (and the mobile node's home address) to match registration requests with corresponding replies. The mobile node must verify that the low-order 32 bits of any registration reply are identical to the bits it sent in the registration request.

The identification in a new registration request must not be the same as that in an immediately preceding request, and should not repeat while the same security context is being used between the mobile node and the home agent.

25.4 ROUTE OPTIMIZATION

The base mobile IP protocol [12], allows any mobile node to move about, changing its point of attachment to the Internet, while continuing to be identified by its home IP address. Correspondent nodes send IP datagrams to a mobile node at its home address in the same way as with any other destination. This scheme allows transparent interoperation between mobile nodes and their correspondent nodes, but forces all datagrams for a mobile node to be routed through its home agent, usually through very long and inefficient routes, placing a heavy burden on the network.

Route optimization extensions to the mobile IP protocol [16] provide a means for nodes to cache the binding of a mobile node and to then tunnel their own datagrams directly to the mobile node's home agent. Extensions are also provided to allow datagrams in flight when a mobile node moves, and datagrams sent based on an out-of-date cached binding, to be forwarded directly to the mobile node's new binding.

All operations of route optimization change the routing of IP datagrams to the type of mechanisms defined in the base mobile IP protocol. This authentication generally relies on a mobility security association established in advance between the sender and receiver of such messages. The association can be created using ISAKMP [7], or any of the registration key establishment methods specified in [11].

25.4.1 Route Optimization Overview

Route optimization can be seen to have two different parts:

1. Updating binding caches (a cache of mobility bindings of mobile nodes, maintained by a node for use in tunneling datagrams to those mobile nodes)
2. Managing smooth handoffs between foreign agents

25.4.1.1 Binding Caches

Route optimization provides a means for any node to maintain a binding cache containing the care-of address of one or more mobile nodes. When sending an IP datagram to a mobile node, if the sender has a binding cache entry for the destination mobile node, it may tunnel the datagram directly to the care-of address indicated in the cached mobility binding.

In the absence of any binding cache entry, datagrams destined for a mobile node will be routed to the mobile node's home network in the same way as any other IP datagram, and then tunneled to the mobile node's current care-of address by the mobile node's home agent. This is the only routing mechanism supported by the base mobile IP protocol. With route optimization, as a side effect of this indirect routing of a datagram to a mobile node, the original sender of the datagram may be informed of the mobile node's current mobility binding, giving the sender an opportunity to cache the binding.

Any node may maintain a binding cache to optimize its own communication with mobile nodes. A node may create or update a binding cache entry for a mobile node only when it has received and authenticated the mobile node's mobility binding. As before, each binding in the binding cache also has an associated lifetime, specified in the binding update message in which the node obtained the binding. After the expiration of this time period, the binding is deleted from the cache. In addition, a node cache may use any reasonable strategy for managing the space within the binding cache. When a new entry needs to be added to the binding cache, the node may choose to drop any entry already in the cache, if needed, to make space for the new entry. For example, a least recently used (LRU) strategy for cache entry replacement is likely to work well.

When sending an IP datagram, if the sending node has a binding cache entry for the destination node, it should tunnel the datagram to the mobile node's care-of address using the encapsulation techniques used by home agents, described in [9, 10, 4].

25.4.1.2 Foreign Agent Smooth Handoff

When a mobile node moves and registers with a new foreign agent, the base mobile IP protocol does not notify the mobile node's previous foreign agent. IP datagrams intercepted by the home agent after the new registration are tunneled to the mobile node's new care-of address, but datagrams in flight that had already been intercepted by the home agent and tunneled to the old care-of address when the mobile node moved are likely to be lost and are assumed to be retransmitted by higher-level protocols if needed. The old foreign agent eventually deletes its visitor list entry for the mobile node after the expiration of the registration lifetime.

Route optimization provides a means for the mobile node's previous foreign agent to be reliably notified of the mobile node's new mobility binding, allowing datagrams in flight to the mobile node's previous foreign agent to be forwarded to its new care-of address. This notification also allows any datagrams tunneled to the mobile node's previous foreign agent, from correspondent nodes with out-of-date binding cache entries for the mobile node, to be forwarded to its new care-of address. Finally, this notification allows any resources consumed by the mobile node at the previous foreign agent (such as radio channel reservations) to be released immediately, rather than waiting for its registration lifetime to expire.

25.5 MOBILITY SUPPORT FOR IPv6

IPv6 includes many features for streamlining mobility support that are missing in IP Version 4 (current version), including stateless address autoconfiguration [14] and neighbor discovery [15]. IPv6 [5] also attempts to drastically simplify the process of renumbering, which could be critical to the future routability of the Internet.

The design of mobile IP support in IPv6 (Mobile IPv6) represents a natural combination of the experiences gained from the development of mobile IP support in IPv4 (Mobile IPv4) [19, 18, 20], together with the opportunities provided by the design and deployment of a new version of IP itself (IPv6) and the new protocol features offered by IPv6. Mobile IPv6 thus shares many features with Mobile IPv4, but the protocol is now fully integrated into IP and provides many improvements over Mobile IPv4. This section summarizes the major differences between Mobile IPv4 and Mobile IPv6 [3]:

- Support for what is known in Mobile IPv4 as "route optimization" [21] is now built in as a fundamental part of the protocol, rather than being added on as an optional set of extensions that may not be supported by all nodes as in Mobile IPv4.

- Support is also integrated into Mobile Ipv—and into IPv6 itself—for allowing mobile nodes and mobile IP to coexist efficiently with routers that perform "ingress filtering" [7]. A mobile node now uses its care-of address as the source address in the IP header of packets it sends, allowing the packets to pass normally through ingress filtering routers. The ability to correctly process a home address option in a received packet is required in all IPv6 nodes, whether mobile or stationary, host or router.

- The use of the care-of address as the source address in each packet's IP header also simplifies routing of multicast packets sent by a mobile node. With Mobile IPv4, the mobile node had to tunnel multicast packets to its home agent in order to transparently use its home address as the source of the multicast packets. With Mobile IPv6, the use of the home address option allows the home address to be used but still be compatible with multicast routing that is based in part on the packet's source address.

- There is no longer any need to deploy special routers as "foreign agents," as in Mobile IPv4. In Mobile IPv6, mobile nodes make use of IPv6 features, such as neighbor discovery [17] and address autoconfiguration [27], to operate in any location away from home without any special support required from its local router.

- Unlike Mobile IPv4, Mobile IPv6 utilizes IP Security (IPsec) [11, 12, 13] for all security requirements (sender authentication, data integrity protection, and replay protection) for binding updates (which serve the role of both registration and route optimization in Mobile IPv4). Mobile IPv4 relies on its own security mechanisms for these functions, based on statically configured "mobility security associations."

- The movement detection mechanism in Mobile IPv6 provides bidirectional confirmation of a mobile node's ability to communicate with its default router in its current location (packets that the router sends are reaching the mobile node, and packets that the mobile node sends are reaching the router).

- Most packets sent to a mobile node while away from home in Mobile IPv6 are sent using an IPv6 routing header rather than IP encapsulation, whereas Mobile IPv4 must use encapsulation for all packets.

- While a mobile node is away from home, its home agent intercepts any packets for the mobile node that arrive at the home network, using IPv6 neighbor discovery [17] rather than ARP [23], as in Mobile IPv4. The use of neighbor discovery improves the robustness of the protocol.

- The dynamic home agent address discovery mechanism in Mobile IPv6 uses IPv6 anycast [10] and returns a single reply to the mobile node, rather than the corresponding Mobile IPv4 mechanism that used IPv4 directed broadcast and returned a separate reply from each home agent on the mobile node's home link. The Mobile IPv6 mechanism is more efficient and more reliable, since only one packet need be sent back to the mobile node. The mobile node is less likely to lose one of the replies because no "implosion" of replies is required by the protocol.

- Mobile IPv6 defines an advertisement interval option on router advertisements (equivalent to agent advertisements in Mobile IPv4), allowing a mobile node to decide for itself how many router advertisements (agent advertisements) it is willing to miss before declaring its current router unreachable.

- The use of IPv6 destination options allows all Mobile IPv6 control traffic to be piggybacked on any existing IPv6 packets, whereas in Mobile IPv4 and its route optimization extensions, separate UDP packets were required for each control message.

25.6 CONNECTIVITY WITH 3G NETWORKS

Mobile IP requires link layer connectivity between the mobile node and the foreign agent. If another wireless network is used, then [30] proposes a protocol for achieving this. In particular, this protocol applies to CDMA2000 networks in which the physical layer terminates at a radio network node (RNN) and the FA resides inside a separate packet data serving node (PDSN). The PDSN is responsible for establishing, maintaining, and terminating the link layer to the mobile node. A RNN is responsible for relaying the link layer protocol between a mobile node and its corresponding PDSN.

The interface between the RNN and the PDSN is called the RP interface. This interface requires mobility management for handling handoff from one RNN to another without interrupting end-to-end communication. It also requires the support of the link layer protocol encapsulation.

The messages used for mobility management across the RP interface include registration request, registration reply, registration update, and registration acknowledge. Both registration request and registration update messages must be sent with UDP using the well-known port number 699.

The high-level architecture of a third generation CDMA2000 network RP interface is shown in Figure 25.2. In the figure, the PDSN will be responsible for establishing, maintaining, and terminating the link layer to the mobile node. It initiates the authentication, authorization, and accounting for the mobile node and optionally, securely tunnels to the home agent.

The RNN is responsible for mapping the mobile node identifier reference to a unique link layer identifier used to communicate with the PDSN. RNN validates the mobile station for access service and manages the physical layer connection to the mobile node.

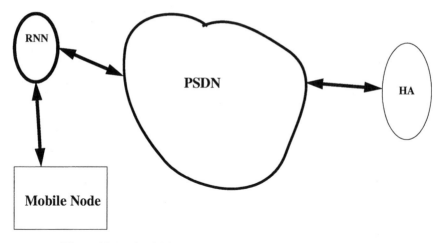

Figure 25.2 The third generation cdma200 network RP interface.

The extensions to mobile IP include enabling general routing encapsulation (GRE) and reverse tunneling during registration. A new extension called session-specific extension is defined and is mandatory in the registration acknowledge messages. The home address field must be set to zero in the registration request, registration reply, and registration update, and registration acknowledge messages.

Two new messages (registration update and registration acknowledge) are defined to support the RP session disconnection in order to speed up resource reclamation.

25.6.1 GRE Encapsulation

GRE encapsulation, as described in [8], is supported during user data transmission. A new protocol type might be required to support the link layer protocol defined for the third generation CDMA2000 network. The key field is required, and its value is the same as the one from the session-specific extension as described above. The sequence number may be required, depending on the requirement of the protocol encapsulated within the GRE frame.

During traffic tunneling, the sender inserts the key value from the registration request message into the key field of the GRE header. The receiver uses the key value from the GRE header to decide where to forward the user data.

25.6.2 Security Considerations

The protocol presented in [30] is designed for use over a protected, private network between RNN and PDSN. Prearranged security associations in the style of Mobile IPv4 are assumed to exist among every (RNN, PDSN) pair that will form an RP connection. Also, it is assumed that the session-specific information is authenticated by means outside the scope of this draft.

Several potential vulnerabilities exist if these assumptions are not met. First, if the network connecting the RNN and PDSN is accessible to an attacker, user traffic may be intercepted and/or spoofed if there are no other end-to-end security mechanisms in place. Second, the mobile IP control messages must be authenticated to prevent tunnel set-up and tear-down by unauthorized parties. Mobile IP authentication extensions are used to provide this additional protection for control messages. Finally, if session-specific information is not authenticated, a denial-of-service attack is possible if a RNN unknowingly sends a registration request to the PDSN with a spoofed session-specific extension. The PDSN would then send an explicit tunnel tear-down to the previous RNN, causing user traffic to be misdirected to the new RNN. This would cause a loss of service and possibly interception of traffic, depending on what other security measures are in place.

25.7 MANAGEMENT OF INFORMATION BASES

The required objects for the management information base (MIB) for use with network management protocols in TCP/IP-based internets is proposed in RFC 2006 [25]. In particular, it describes managed objects used for managing the mobile node, foreign agent, and home agent of the mobile IP protocol.

The Internet standard network management framework (SNMP) presently consists of three major components. The SMI, described in RFC 1902 [26], presents the mechanisms used for describing and naming objects for the purpose of management. The MIB-II, STD 17, RFC 1213 [28] gives the core set of managed objects for the Internet suite of protocols. The protocols RFC 1157 [22] and/or RFC 1905 [24], describe the way to access managed objects. The framework permits new objects to be defined for the purpose of experimentation and evaluation.

25.7.1 Objects

Managed objects are accessed via a virtual information store, termed the management information base or MIB. Objects in the MIB are defined using the subset of Abstract Syntax Notation One (ASN.1) defined in the SMI. In particular, an object identifier, an administratively assigned name, names each object type. The object type together with an object instance serves to uniquely identify a specific instantiation of the object. For human convenience, we often use a textual string, termed the descriptor, to refer to the object type.

To be consistent with the Internet Advisory Board (IAB) directives and good engineering practice, some criteria have been applied to select managed objects for the mobile IP protocol:

- Partition management functionality among the mobile node, home agent, and foreign agent according to the partitioning seen in the mobile IP protocol.
- Require that objects be essential for either fault or configuration management.
- Exclude objects that are simply derivable from others in this or other MIBs.

RFC 2006 [25] specifies the objects used in managing these entities, namely, the mobile node, the home agent, and the foreign agent.

Objects in this MIB are arranged into groups. Each group is organized as a set of related objects. The overall structure and the relationship between groups and the mobile IP entities are shown below:

Groups	Mobile node	Foreign agent	Home agent
mipSystemGroup	X	X	X
mipSecAssociationGroup	X	X	X
mipSecViolationGroup	X	X	X
mnSystemGroup	X		
mnDiscoveryGroup	X		
mnRegistrationGroup	X		
maAdvertisementGroup		X	X
faSystemGroup		X	
faAdvertisementGroup		X	
faRegistrationGroup		X	
haRegistrationGroup			X
haRegNodeCountersGroup			X

25.8   CONCLUSIONS

Wireless communications and Internet technologies are combined in an efficient manner in the mobile IP framework. The mobile IP specification establishes the mechanisms that enable a mobile host to maintain and use the same IP address as it changes its point of attachment to the network. Standardization efforts in the IETF are addressing a variety of issues in order to provide for a lightweight, efficient, and effective protocol that will be compatible with other technologies and will allow users a secure, fast access to a network wherever they are.

Current efforts address optimization of the routing functions, integration with modern high-speed wireless networks, and providing access through firewalls [16].

Mobility implies higher security risks than with static operation, because the traffic may at times take unforeseen network paths with unknown or unpredictable security characteristics. The mobile IP specification makes no provisions for securing data traffic. Current effort suggest mechanisms (see RFC 2356 [29]) that allow a mobile node out on a public sector of the Internet to negotiate access past a firewall and construct a secure channel into its home network. In addition to securing traffic, these mechanisms allow a mobile node to roam into regions that impose ingress filtering and use a different address space.

Connection and interoperability with existing and future broadband wireless networks are topics that are increasingly receiving attention in the mobile IP community.

REFERENCES

1. C. Perkins (Ed.), IP mobility support, IETF RFC 2002, Oct. 1996 and revised in September 2000.

2. C. Perkins, *Mobile IP: Design Principles and Practice,* Addison-Wesley Longman, Reading, MA, 1998.

3. D. Johnson and C. Perkins, Mobility support for IPv6, IETF Internet Draft, Nov. 2000.

4. S. Deering and R. Hinden, Internet Protocol, Version 6 (IPv6) Specification, IETF RFC 1883, Dec. 1995.

5. R. Hinden and S. Deering, IP Version 6 addressing architecture, IETF RFC 1884, Dec. 1995.

6. J. B. Postel (Ed.), Internet Protocol, IETF RFC 791, Sept. 1981.

7. CDPD Consortium, Cellular digital packet data specification, PO Box 809320, Chicago, Ill., July 1993, http://www.cdpd.org/public/specification/index.html.

8. Hanks, S., Generic routing encapsulation (GRE), RFC 1701, Oct. 1994.

9. S. E. Deering (Ed.), ICMP Router discovery messages, IETF RFC 1256, Sept. 1991.

10. C. Perkins, IP Encapsulation within IP, IETF RFC 2003, May 1996.

11. C. Perkins, Minimal Encapsulation within IP, IETF RFC 2004, May 1996.

12. V. L. Voydock and S. T. Kent, Security mechanisms in high-level networks, *ACM Computer Surveys, 15,* 2, pp. 135–171, 1983.

13. R. L. Rivest, The MD5 message-digest algorithm, IETF RFC 1321, Apr. 1992.

14. S. Thomson and T. Narten, IPv6 stateless address autoconfiguration, IETF RFC 1971, Aug. 1996.

15. T. Narten, E. Nordmark, and W. Simpson, Neighbor discovery for IP Version 6 (IPv6), IETF RFC 1970, Aug. 1996.

16. C. Perkins, Route optimization in mobile IP, IETF Internet Draft, Nov. 2000.

17. S. Bradner and A. Mankin, The recommendation for the IP next generation protocol, IETF RFC 1752, Jan. 1995.

18. D. Johnson and C. Perkins, Mobility support in IPv6, *ACM Mobicom 96,* ACM, Nov. 1996, pp. 27–37.

19. A. Conta and S. Deering, Generic packet tunneling in IPv6, ftp://ftp.ietf.org/internet-drafts/draft-ietf-ipngwg-ipv6-tunnel-07.txt, July 1996.

20. M. Khalil (Ed.), Mobile IP Extensions rationalization (MIER), IETF Internet Draft, May 2000.

21. S. Kent and R. Atkinson, IP authentication header, ftp://ftp.ietf.org/internet-drafts/draft-ietf-ipsec-auth-header-03.txt, Nov. 1997 (work in progress).

22. Case, J., Fedor, M., Schoffstall, M., and J. Davin, Simple network management Protocol, RFC 1157, May 1990.

23. C. Perkins and P. Bhagwat, A Mobile Networking system based on Internet protocol (IP), in *Proceedings USENIX Symposium on Mobile and Location-Independent Computing,* Aug. 1993, USENIX Assoc., pp. 69–82.

24. J., McCloghrie, K., Rose, M., and S. Waldbusser, Protocol operations for version 2 of the simple Network Management Protocol (SNMPv2), RFC 1905, Jan. 1996.

25. D. Cong and M. Hamlen C. Perkins, The definitions of managed objects for IP mobility support, Using SMIv2, IETF RFC 2006, October 1996.

26. J. Case, K. McCloghrie, M. Rose, and S. Waldbusser, Structure of management information for Version 2 of the simple network management protocol (SNMPv2), RFC 1902, Jan. 1996.

27. W. R. Cheswick and S. Bellovin, *Firewalls and Internet Security,* Addison-Wesley, Reading, MA, 1994.

28. McCloghrie, K., and M. Rose (Eds.), Management information base for network management of TCP/IP-based internets: MIB-II, STD 17, RFC 1213, March 1991.

29. G. Montenegro and V. Gupta, Sun's SKIP firewall traversal for mobile IP, IETF RFC 2356, June 1998.

30. Y. Xu (Ed.), Mobile IP based micro mobility management protocol in the third generation wireless network, IETF Internet Draft, Nov. 2000.

CHAPTER 26

Data Management in Wireless Mobile Environments

SANDEEP K. S. GUPTA

Department of Computer Science and Engineering, Arizona State University, Tempe

PRADIP K. SRIMANI

Department of Computer Science, Clemson University, Clemson, South Carolina

26.1 INTRODUCTION

The need for "information anywhere anytime" has been a driving force for the increasing growth in Web and Internet technology, wireless communication, and portable computing devices. The field of mobile computing is the result of the merger of these advances in computing and communication with the aim of providing a seamless and ubiquitous computing environment for mobile users. In such mobile environments, database applications are enhanced with useful features of wireless technology. For example, users are allowed to establish a mobile office from which they can communicate with other users, access information, and manage their work while staying mobile. This feature is important for supporting ubiquitous services such as weather and forecasting services, financial market reporting, yellow pages, road maps and directions, telematics, point-of-sale applications, in-field work dispatch, and law enforcement and military support to mobile users. By nature, mobile computing environments have severe resource constraints and unstable operating conditions, which add a new dimension to the technical challenges for data processing and computing.

Many software problems associated with data management, transaction management, and data recovery have their origin in distributed database systems. In mobile computing, however, these problems become more difficult to solve, mainly because of the narrow bandwidth of the wireless communication channels, the relatively short active life of the power supply in mobile devices, and the changing locations of required information (sometimes in cache, sometimes in air, sometimes at the server) and users. Further, in many mobile database applications, data changes very rapidly (or even constantly). Users need to receive timely information in order to make critical decisions (e.g., stock market information and trading).

Traditionally, data management is concerned with the modeling, efficient storage, retrieval, and manipulation of information. From a data management standpoint, mobility of the clients/nodes provides an interesting variation on distributed computing. The mobile computing environment considered in this chapter is shown in Figure 26.1. In this envi-

Handbook of Wireless Networks and Mobile Computing, Edited by Ivan Stojmenović.   **553**
ISBN 0-471-41902-8   © 2002 John Wiley & Sons, Inc.

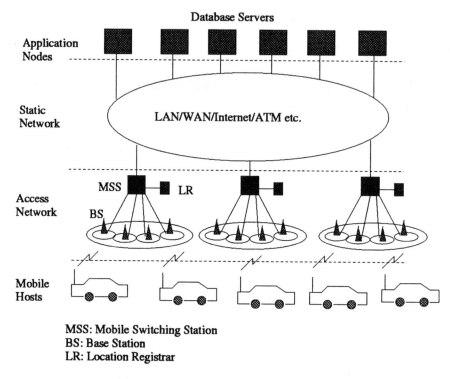

Figure 26.1 Mobile computing environment.

ronment, the mobile hosts (MHs) query the database servers that are connected to a static network. The mobile hosts communicate with the servers via wireless cellular networks consisting of mobile switching stations (MSS) and base stations. In this environment, mobile databases can be distributed within the spectrum of the following two extreme configurations:

1. The entire database can be distributed among the wired components, possibly with full or partial replication. A base station, with a DBMS-like functionality, has full control of its own database.
2. the database is distributed among wired and wireless components. Data management responsibility is shared among base stations and mobile devices.

Thus, these different ways of managing data in mobile environments entail additional considerations and variation with regard to distributed database management.

Moreover, location-based services are gaining a lot of momentum. In addition to the FCC regulation that requires mobile service carriers to implement E911 in the near future, mobile users are interested in services that find locations of nearest emergency centers or that notify of parking availability at an airport. With integration of positioning technologies (e.g., GPS) in mobile devices and networks, location-based services will be available soon. This also leads to a need for extending traditional database functions in mobile database systems.

Finally, personal information management has gradually become an important part of our daily lives. While PDAs and mobile phones have to store and manage some information such as contacts and calendars internally, they usually have to synchronize with some unified information repository to make the intended applications effective. Thus, an interesting issue is the architecture modeling of these device-driven mobile applications. Moreover, this model can be extended to enterprise applications. In this environment, business logic is embedded in enterprise infrastructure and the mobile devices are the terminals. How the mobile devices and network infrastructure combine to serve the users is an interesting research issue and needs further development in mobile database systems.

26.2 DATA MANAGEMENT ISSUES IN MOBILE ENVIRONMENTS

Mobile computing can possibly be viewed as a variation of traditional distributed computing from the data management point of view. In general, there are two possible scenarios: the entire database is distributed only among the wired components, e.g., the mobile switching stations (MSS), each base station managing its own share of the database with the additional capability of locating the components of the databases that are not locally available. The other approach is also similar: the entire database is distributed over both the wired and wireless components of the system. There are several issues that generally complicate the various functionalities of a database management system, including:

- *Design of database.* Mobility of the hosts (clients) and frequent disconnection between clients and servers in an unpredictable manner compounds the problem of global name resolution; also, the dynamic nature of the constantly changing location information to be stored further complicates the design.
- *Replication of data.* Since the data is partially replicated in many places and the availability of the duplicates changes rapidly with time (the expected scenario in mobile computing), the version control and consistency management are more challenging. In addition, providing correct execution of transactions, which are executed at multiple base stations and multiple data sets, needs special attention due to mobility and frequent disconnection of the mobile units.

Most of these and other problems are handled, in some form or other, via caching data in the mobile units and periodically validating these data using different techniques. The protocols and frequency of validation of the data have a profound influence on the performance of the data management in mobile environments.

26.3 CACHING OF DATA

Caching relevant data at the hosts is an effective tool for improving performance (query response time and throughput) in any distributed system. Important issues in designing an effective caching scheme include (1) what to cache (and when and for how long), (2) when and how to invalidate the cached items and at what granularity level, (3) data consistency provided to the user and at what cost. Most of these concerns, especially the consistency management of cached data, are exacerbated in mobile computing environments. Mobile computing environments are characterized by slow wireless links (low bandwidth radio links) that are susceptible to frequent disconnections from the base station (server) and low battery power at the mobile clients (hosts), which necessitates the clients to minimize up-link queries as well as to voluntarily disconnect from the network to conserve battery power. This unique feature of frequent disconnection adds a new dimension to the task of maintaining consistent cache at the mobile client, since the underlying cache maintenance protocol should make optimal use of the limited bandwidth. In addition to being tolerant of disconnections, these protocols should be energy-efficient and adaptive to varying quality-of-service provided by the wireless network. Various models have been suggested in the literature to estimate the usefulness of caching in mobile environments under different cost models [1–5] with encouraging results. Our purpose in this chapter is to consider the problem of management of cache consistency in a mobile wireless environment, once the question of what to cache has been answered. Frequent voluntary and involuntary disconnection of clients from servers makes this a very challenging problem [6].

Efficient caching schemes for mobile environments should ideally take into account the following factors: data access pattern and update rates, communication/access costs, mobility pattern of the client, connectivity characteristics (disconnection pattern, available bandwidth, etc.), and location dependence of the data. Validation checks that are normally used in an wired environment are not at all suitable for mobile environments since they waste precious wireless bandwidth. Almost all the cache coherency schemes proposed for mobile environment are based on a call-back (invalidation report) mechanism. A client may miss invalidation reports from the server if it is disconnected during the broadcast. In an attempt to solve this problem, Barbara and Imielinski [7] have developed a periodic broadcast invalidation report scheme.

In this chapter, we describe a caching scheme, called AS [21], for wireless networks that uses asynchronous invalidation reports (call-backs) to maintain cache consistency, i.e., reports are broadcast by the server only when some data changes, and not periodically. Each mobile client (host) (MH) maintains its own home location cache (HLC) to deal with the problem of disconnections. The HLC of an MH is maintained at a designated home mobile switching station (MSS). It has an entry for each data item cached by the MH and needs to maintain only the time stamp at which that data item was last invalidated. The HLC model fits perfectly into existing architectures to support mobility in wireless networks (e.g., Mobile IP [8]) which also uses the concept of a home agent for each MH. At the cost of this extra memory overhead of maintaining an HLC, an MH can continue to use its cache even after prolonged periods of disconnection from the network. We show through a mathematical model and simulation studies that the hit rate and access latency of this scheme is better than its synchronous counterparts and very close to an optimal strategy that incurs no overhead of maintaining cache consistency.

A mobile host can be in two modes: awake or sleep. When a mobile host is awake (connected to the server) it can receive messages. Hence, this state includes both active and dozing CPU modes. A MH can be disconnected from the network either voluntarily or involuntarily. From the perspective of the mobile host's cache, it is irrelevant whether the invalidation were delayed due to voluntary disconnection (e.g., switching off the laptop) or involuntary disconnection (e.g., wireless link failure, hand-off delay). Hence, for our purposes, a disconnected client is in sleep mode; we use the term "wakeup" to indicate reconnection.

We consider the following computing scenario. The application program runs on the mobile host as a client process and communicates with the database server through messages, i.e., the client sends an up-link request (query) for the data it needs to the database server and the server responds by sending the requested data on the down-link. In order to minimize the number of up-link requests, the client caches a portion of the database in its local memory. The client-cached data is also referred to as active data [9]. Caching data at clients necessitates a protocol between the client and the database server to ensure that the client cache remains consistent with the shared database. We next describe a cache invalidation scheme for mobile environments. The objective of this scheme is to minimize the overhead for the MHs to validate their cache upon reconnection, to allow stateless servers, and to minimize the bandwidth requirement. The general approach is to buffer the invalidation messages at home location cache (HLC), which is a static trusted host on the static network and acts on behalf of a mobile host.

26.4 AN INFORMAL OVERVIEW

In accordance with the mobility management scheme used in Mobile IP, each mobile host has a home address and a care-of-address. The home address is the IP address on the home network of the mobile host. The care-of-address is the address indicating the current location of the mobile host. Two architectural entities—home agent and foreign agent—are used in Mobile IP to deliver datagrams to mobile clients. A home agent tunnels (encapsulates in another datagram packet) any datagrams sent to the mobile client at its home address to its current care-of-address(es). A foreign agent (in the case in which the mobile uses a foreign care-of-address) on the current network of the mobile client decapsulates the packet and delivers it to the mobile client to which the datagram is addressed (see Figure 26.2). We assume that the mobility agents (home or foreign agent) (MAs) are located at the MSSs.

The AS caching scheme for the mobile environment is based on the following assumptions:

- Whenever any data item is updated anywhere in the network, an invalidation message is sent out to all MSS via the wired network; thus, when a mobile host MH is roaming, it gets the invalidation message if it is not disconnected (we assume no message is lost due to communication failure or otherwise in the wired network).
- An MH can detect whether or not it is connected to the network.
- An MH informs its HLC before it stores (or updates) any data item in its local cache.

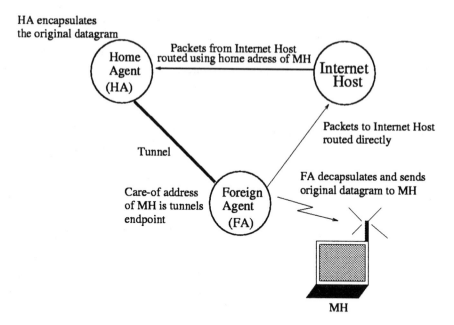

Figure 26.2 Delivering message to a MH in Mobile IP.

• The mobility agent that is nearest to the MH and maintains the HLC of the MH forwards to the MH any invalidation it receives from the server.

The caching architecture is shown in Figure 26.3. The home agent A preassigned static
host of any mobile host (MH) maintains its home location cache (HLC). If a mobile host
is roaming, its HLC is duplicated at the MSS of its foreign agent. current cell. Thus, an
MSS always maintains a HLC for each MH in its coverage area at any given time. Consider an MSS with N mobile hosts (MH_i, $1 \leq i \leq N$) at any given time. For any i, HLC_i for
MH_i, as maintained in the MSS, keeps track of what data has been locally cached at MH_i
(state information of the MH). In general, HLC_i is a list of records (x, T, $invalid\_flag$) for
each data item x locally cached at MH_i, where x is the identifier of a data item and T is the
time stamp of the last invalidation of x. The key feature of the AS scheme is that the invalidation reports are transmitted asynchronously and those reports are buffered at the MSS
(in the HLCs of the mobile hosts) until an explicit acknowledgment is received from the
specific MH. The $invalid\_flag$ (in the HLC record for the specific data item) is set to
TRUE for data items for which an invalidation has been sent to the MH but no acknowledgment has been received. Note that the time stamp is the same as that provided by the
server in its invalidation message.

Each MH maintains a local cache of data items that it frequently accesses. Before answering any queries from the application, it checks to see if the requested data is in a consistent state. We use call-backs from a MSS to achieve this goal. When a MSS receives an
invalidation from a server, the MSS determines the set of MHs that are using the data by

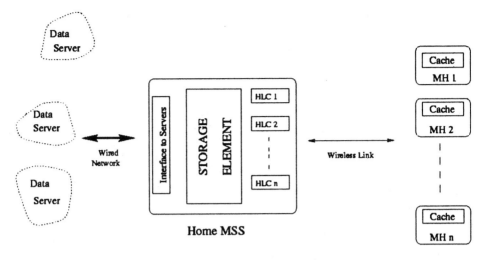

Figure 26.3 System architecture.

consulting the HLCs and sends an invalidation report to each of them. When a MH receives that invalidation message, it marks the particular data item in its local cache as invalid. When an MH receives (from the application layer) a query for a data item, it checks the validity of the item in its local cache; if the item is valid, it satisfies the query from its local cache and saves on latency, bandwidth, and battery power; otherwise, an up-link request to the MSS for the data item is required. The MSS makes a request to the server for the data item on behalf of the MH. When the data item is received, the MSS adds an entry to the HLC for the requested data item and forwards the data item to the MH. Note that the data item may or may not be cached at the MSS.

A mobile host alternates between active mode and sleep mode. In sleep mode, a mobile client is unable to receive any invalidation messages sent to it by its HLC. We use the following time-stamp-based scheme by which the MA can decide which invalidations it needs to retransmit to the mobile host. Each client maintains a time stamp for its cache called the cache time stamp. The cache time stamp of a cache is the time stamp of the last message received by the MH from its MA. The client includes the cache time stamp in all its communications with the MA. The MA uses the cache time stamp for two purposes:

1. To discard invalidations it no longer needs to keep
2. To decide the invalidations it needs to resend to the client

Upon receiving a message with time stamp t, the MA discards any invalidation messages with time stamp less than or equal to t from the MH's HLC. Further, it sends an invalidation report consisting of all the invalidation messages with time stamp greater than t in MH's HLC to the MH. When a MH wakes up after a sleep, it sends a probe message to its HLC with its cache time stamp. In response to this probe message, the HLC sends it an invalidation report. In this way, a MH can determine which data items changed while it was disconnected. A MH defers all queries that it receives after waking up until it has received the invalidation report from its HLC. In this scheme, we do not need to know the time at which the MH got disconnected, and just by using the cache time stamp we can handle both wireless link failures and voluntary disconnections. Even if the MH wakes up and then immediately goes back to sleep before receiving the invalidation report, consistency of the cache is not compromised, as it would use the same value of the cache time stamp in its probe message after waking up and hence get the correct information in the invalidation report. Thus, arbitrary sleep patterns of the MH can be easily handled.

As an example, consider the scenario shown in Figure 26.4. Initially, the cache time stamp of the MH is $t0$ and MH's cache has two data items with ids x and z. When MSS receives an invalidation message notifying it that x has changed at the server at time $t1$, it adds the invalidation message to MH's HLC and also forwards the invalidation message to the MH with (data item id and time stamp), i.e., $(x, t1)$. On receiving the invalidation message from the MSS, the MH updates its cache time stamp to $t1$ and deletes data item x from its cache. Later, when MH wants to access y, it sends a data request with $(y, t1)$ to the MSS. In response to the data request, the MSS fetches and forwards the data item associated with y to the MH and adds $(y, t2)$ to the MH's HLC, where $t2$ is the last updated time stamp provided by the data server. The MH updates its time stamp to $t2$ and adds y to its cache. Now suppose MH gets disconnected from the network and the invalidation message for y is lost due to this disconnection. When MH wakes up, it ignores any invalidation messages it receives (until the first query), since later, upon the first query after waking up, it sends a probe message (invalidation check message) to the MSS. The MSS uses the time stamp in this probe message to determine the invalidations missed by the MH and

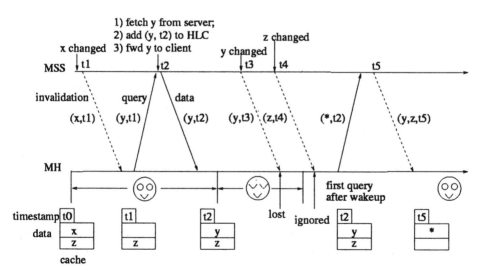

Figure 26.4   An example scenario.

sends an invalidation report with all the missed invalidations by the MH. In this case, the MSS determines from MH's cache time stamp $t2$ that MH has missed invalidation for y and z, so it resends them to the MH.

26.4.1 Comparison of Different Schemes

Existing schemes [7, 10, 11] for maintaining cache consistency in the event of disconnections in a mobile environment are all based on the call-back mechanism. The basic problem is that the call-back break (invalidation) messages get lost when the client is disconnected. As noted above, Barbara and Imilienski [7] have developed a periodic broadcasting invalidation report scheme to address the problem. In this scheme, every L time units a server broadcasts invalidation reports that carry information about all data items that changed during the past $w = kL$ time units. A client still has to discard its entire cache if it is disconnected from the network and misses k consecutive reports, and user queries generated during the past L time units are answered only after receiving an invalidation report. Several other schemes have been proposed that extend the broadcasting invalidation report scheme with respect to optimizing the size of the invalidation [11] report, adjusting the periodicity of invalidation reports in accordance to the query rate and client disconnection time [12], and restricting broadcast to the vicinity of the mobile client [10]. Wu et al. [13] have proposed an enhancement in which the mobile host sends back to the server the ids of all cached data items, along with their time stamps, after a long disconnection. The server identifies the changed data items and returns a validity report. This results in wastage of bandwidth and unnecessary up-link requests and still does not solve the problem of arbitrarily long sleeps, since the local cache has to be discarded after a disconnection time greater than W. Jing et al. [11] have proposed a bit sequence scheme in which each data item in the database is represented by binary bits. The bit sequence structure contains more update history information than the window w, but results in larger invalidation reports when only a few things have changed. The cache still has to be discarded if more than half of the items in the database have changed. Hu and Lee [12] have suggested an adaptive algorithm that predominantly uses the TS and bit sequence approaches but provides better tuning of the system according to the current invalidation and query rates.

The schemes based on synchronous broadcasting invalidation reports have the following characteristics:

1. They assume a stateless server and do not address the issue of mobility (except the work by Liu and Maguire [10]).
2. The entire cache is invalid if the client is disconnected for a period longer than the period of the broadcast (or some multiple of it).
3. scalability for large database systems is not adequately addressed.

The Coda file system [14, 15, 16] provides an alternate mechanism to providing support for disconnected operations on shared files in UNIX-like environments. Coda also uses two mechanisms for cache coherency. When the client is reachable from at least one server, the call-back mechanism is used. When the disconnection occurs, access to possibly stale data is permitted at a client for the sake of improving availability. Upon reconnection, only those modifications at the client that do not cause any conflict are committed. Balance between speed of validating cache (after a disconnection) and accuracy of invalidations is achieved by maintaining version time stamps on volumes (a subtree in the file system hierarchy). However, validating the entire cache upon every reconnection may put an unnecessary burden on the client. Further, since Coda is a distributed file system, it assumes a stateful server that may not be appropriate for other applications such as web caching. Also, the server has to keep the cache state of each client and the client has to perform volume-by-volume validation checks after each reconnection.

26.4.2 Comparison with the AS Scheme

As has already been noted, all of the existing schemes are based on synchronous or periodic broadcast of invalidation reports. None of the cited works investigate the effect of using these schemes on an actual wireless network. All of the schemes are based on aggregating queries for a fixed period of time and then answering them after receiving an invalidation report. This provides very poor network utilization, as there is no traffic for long periods of time followed by a very heavy burst. This also results in higher queuing delay for answering a query.

Unlike these strategies, all of which use synchronous invalidation reports and are based on the basic scheme of [7], the AS scheme is asynchronous and stateful, hence the name AS. In order to compare the AS scheme with the sleepers and workaholics scheme of [7], we note the salient features of that scheme as follows:

- Every L time units, a server broadcasts invalidation reports that carry information about all data items that changed during the past $w = kL$ time units. Two variations of this basic scheme are suggested: (1) TS, where invalidation reports carry information about changes in data items over a larger window ($k > 1$), and (2) AT, for which $k = 1$ (See Fig. 26.5).

- Clients maintain local caches and use the information in invalidation reports to update their caches.

- If a client is disconnected from the network and misses k consecutive reports, it discards its local cache.

- Queries generated during the past L time units are answered only after receiving an invalidation report.

We also consider an "ideal scheme" to compare with the AS scheme. The ideal scheme has the following characteristics: (1) whenever any data is changed at the MSS, the invalidation information is available to the clients instantaneously at no cost; (2) the above holds even when the MH is disconnected from the MSS, i.e., there is no overhead due to disconnections. Clearly, the ideal strategy is infeasible for any practical system; nevertheless, it provides useful reference points on the achievable hit rate and delay. Table 26.1 gives a

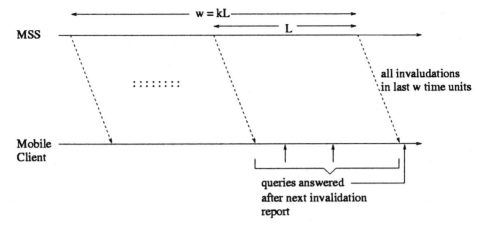

Figure 26.5 Barbara and Imilienski's TS/AT scheme (L = broadcast latency; w = window size; $k > 1$ for the TS scheme and $k = 1$ for the AT scheme).

comparison of the salient features of the proposed scheme with those of the TS and AT schemes. Quantitative bounds are shown in Table 26.2 for a system with N mobile hosts, each of which are caching M data items. The improvement in performance is achieved at the cost of maintaining additional buffer space at the MSS. Since memory is cheap, especially at the stationary MSS, performance benefits outweigh this relatively minor cost.

TABLE 26.1 Comparison of salient features of TS/AT and AS schemes

TS/AT [17]	AS
Server is stateless (no information about client cache is maintained)	Server is stateful (HLC maintained)
Invalidation reports sent regardless of whether clients have any data in cache	Invalidation report broadcast only if any client has valid data in cache
Invalidation reports sent periodically at rate L (synchronous)	Invalidation reports sent as and when data changes (asynchronous)
Average cache access latency is $L/2$ plus network queuing delay	Latency is governed only by the queuing delay on the network
Traffic on the network is bursty as queries are aggregated for a period of time L	Queries are answered as they are generated
Cache restored for sleep limited to a maximum duration of w (TS) or L (AT)	Arbitrary sleep patterns can be supported
Mobility is supported by assuming a replication of data across all stationary nodes (not scalable)	Mobility can be transparently supported by using a mobility-aware network layer, e.g., Mobile IP

TABLE 26.2 Comparison of cache invalidation strategies

Parameter	TS [17]	Ideal	AS
Maximum sleep time supported	w	∞	∞
Up-link overhead on wake up	0	0	0 or 1
Cache access latency	0 to L	0	0
Buffer space required at MSS	$O(N)$	—	$O(MN)$

26.5 FORMAL DESCRIPTION OF THE SCHEME

26.5.1 Data Structures

Every data object has a unique identifier. The letters x, y, and z will be used to denote data identifiers. We will use the notation $Data_x$ to denote the data associated with a data item with identifier x.

The following data structures are maintained at each MH:

- t_s: Time stamp of the last invalidation report or data received by the MH from its home MSS.
- *Cache*: Data cache. An item in the data cache is of the form $(x, Data_x, Valid\_flag)$. The data $Data_x$ can be considered valid only when the *Valid_flag* is TRUE.
- *First_Request*: A flag set to TRUE when an MH wakes up and has yet to make its first query after awakening. The flag is set to FALSE once the the first request after waking up is made.
- *First_Waiting*: A flag set to TRUE when an MH has made its first query after getting reconnected to the network but the data for it has not been received.

The following data structures are maintained at each MSS:

- $HLC[1, .., N]$: an array of lists. $HLC[i]$ is a list of records of the type $(x, T, in-valid\_flag)$, one for each data item x cached by MH_i. N is the total number of MHs that are in the cell of the MSS. T is the time stamp of the last invalidation of x. The *invalid_flag* is set to TRUE for data items for which an invalidation report has been sent but no implicit acknowledgment has been received.

26.5.2 Messages

- INVALIDATION_REPORT (*item_list, T, first_flag*): Sent to an MH by its home MSS to report invalidation of data items in *item_list*. T is the time stamp associated with this report. *first_flag* is set if this invalidation report is in response to the first query of the MH on waking up.
- DATA_REQUEST (*i, x, t, first_request*): Sent by MH_i to its MSS to request data

item *x* when *x* is not found in its local cache. *t* is set to the time stamp t_s maintained by the MH. The flag *first_request* is set if this is the first data request after the MH regains connectivity to the network.

- DATA (*x*, *Data*$_x$, *T*): Broadcast by an *MSS* to send data to all MHs caching *x*. *T* is a time stamp set to the current time at the MSS.

26.5.3 Pseudocode

An MSS continuously executes a procedure called MSS_Main. This procedure handles the following events:

1. MSS receives a request for data from an MH (DATA_REQUEST). With each request, an MH sends the time stamp of the last message it had received from the MSS. The MSS deletes all the entries in the HLC for the MH that had been invalidated before the time stamp carried in the message. Since the messages are assumed to be received in order, this ensures that the MH was awake at the time each of the invalidations was received and the MSS no longer needs to buffer the invalidation. If the data request is the first after a sleep, all the items cached by the MH, marked invalid since the last message received by the MH, are repeated through an invalidation report. The invalidation report carries a time stamp with it. Finally the requested data item is sent to the MH and added to its HLC.

2. Data item(s) updated at MSS. The MSS sends an invalidation report to all the MHs that are caching the changed data item and to whom a previous invalidation has not been sent for the same data. It also updates the data time stamp in the HLC for these MHs and marks those items as invalid.

Each MH continuously executes a procedure called MH_Main. The following events are handled:

1. MH generates a request for a data item. If the MH has woken up after a sleep and this is the first request, it sends a data request for the item and sets a flag (*Flag_Waiting*) to indicate that the buffered invalidations during the sleep period have not yet been received. On receiving those invalidations, it answers successive queries from the cache. If the query is not the first after a wake up, the cache is checked for that data item. If the item is not in the cache, a data request is sent to the MSS and the query is answered once the data arrives from the MSS.

2. MH receives an INVALIDATION_REPORT from the MSS. The MH sets its cache time stamp to the time stamp in the current message and invalidates in its cache all the data items mentioned in the report. All invalidations received between the time an MH awakens and receives the first query are ignored.

3. MH receives DATA from the MSS. It updates its cache with the current information and also updates its cache time stamp.

4. MH wakes up after a disconnection. It sets the *First_Request* flag to TRUE.

26.6 PERFORMANCE ANALYSIS

We develop a simple model to analyze the performance of the proposed cache management scheme. Specifically, we want to estimate the miss probability and mean query delay for the proposed scheme. For the purposes of analysis, we consider the performance in a single cell (as mobility is assumed to be transparently handled) with one MSS and N mobile hosts. We make the following assumptions:

- Total number of data items is M, each of size b_a bits.
- The queries generated by a sleeping MH (i.e., when the MH is disconnected from the MSS) are lost.
- A single wireless channel of bandwidth W is assumed for all transmissions taking place in the cell. All messages are queued to access the wireless channel and serviced according to the FCFS (first come first served) scheduling policy.
- Queries are of size b_q bits and invalidations are of size b_i bits.
- Software overheads are ignored.
- Modeling Query-Update Pattern. The time between updates to any data item is assumed to follow an exponential distribution with mean $1/\mu$. Each MH generates a query according to a Poisson distribution with mean rate of λ. These queries are uniformly distributed over all data items in the database. The query-update model is shown in Figure 26.6.

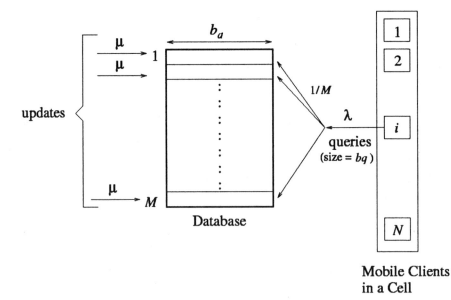

Figure 26.6 Modeling query–update pattern.

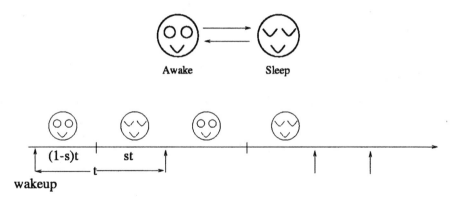

Figure 26.7   Modeling sleep behavior of an MH.

- Modeling Sleep Pattern for an MH. An MH alternates between sleep and awake modes. The sleep/wake up pattern of an MH is modeled by using two parameters (see Figure 26.7): (1) the fraction s, $0 \leq s, \leq 1$, of the total time spent by an MH in the sleep mode; (2) the frequency ω at which it changes state (sleeping or awake). We consider an exponentially distributed interval of time t with mean $1/\omega$. The MH is in the sleep mode for time st, and in the awake mode for time $(1 - s)t$. By varying the value of ω, different frequencies of change of state can be obtained for the same total sleep time.

We want to estimate the average hit ratio at the local cache of an MH, i.e., the percentage of queries, generated at an MH, that would be satisfied by the local cache and the average delay experienced in answering a query.

26.6.1   Estimation of Hit Ratio

Since the queries generated by a sleeping MH are lost, the effective rate of query generation, λ_e, by an MH can be approximated as

$$\lambda_e = (1 - s)\lambda$$

Since queries are uniformly distributed, the rate at which queries are generated for a given data item x, λ_x, is given by

$$\lambda_x = \frac{\lambda_e}{M} = \frac{(1 - s)\lambda}{M}$$

A query made for a specific data item x by an MH would be a miss in the local cache (and would require an up-link request) in the case of either of the following two events (consider the time interval t between the current query for x and the immediately preceding query for x by the MH):

1. Event 1. During this interval t, the data item x has been invalidated at least once [see Figure 26.8(a)].
2. Event 2. Data item x has not been invalidated during the interval t; the MH has gone to sleep at least once during the interval t, it woke up the last time at time $t - t_1$, and the current query is the very first one after waking up from its last sleep [Figure 26.8(b)]. Note that the first query generated by a sleeping MH after waking up needs an up-link request to the MSS regardless of whether the required data item is in the local cache.

We compute the probabilities of Event 1 and Event 2 as follows.

- Probability of miss due to absence of valid data item in cache:

$$P(\text{Event 1}) = \int_0^\infty (\lambda_x e^{-\lambda_x t})(1 - e^{-\mu t})dt = \frac{\mu}{\lambda_x + \mu} = \frac{M\mu}{(1-s)\lambda + M\mu}$$

- Probability of miss due to disconnection:

$$P(\text{Event 2}) = \int_0^\infty P \text{ (no invalidation and query for } x \text{ during time } t)$$

$$\times P \text{ [the query (for } x\text{) is first after wake up]}dt$$

$$= \int_0^\infty \lambda_x e^{-\lambda_x t} e^{-\mu t} \alpha dt = \frac{\omega \lambda_x}{\lambda_e(\omega + \lambda_e)} \left(\frac{\lambda_e}{\mu + \lambda_x} - \frac{\omega + \lambda_e}{\mu + \lambda_x + \omega} + \frac{\omega}{\mu + \lambda_x + \lambda_x + \omega} \right)$$

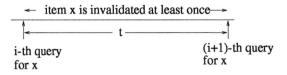

item x is invalidated at least once

i-th query
for x

(i+1)-th query
for x

(a) Miss due to absence of valid data item in cache

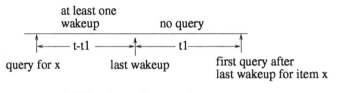

at least one
wakeup

no query

t-t1

t1

query for x

last wakeup

first query after
last wakeup for item x

(b) Miss due to diconnections.

Figure 26.8   Two mutually exclusive events when up-link request messages are needed.

The probability, P_{miss}, of a query requiring an up-link request is the sum of the probabilities for Event 1 and Event 2 and is given by

$$P_{miss} = P(\text{Event 1}) + P(\text{Event 2})$$

and the probability of a hit is

$$P_{hit} = 1 - P_{miss}$$

26.6.2 Estimation of Mean Query Delay

We now estimate the mean query delay T_{delay}. Note that a single wireless channel of bandwidth C is assumed for all transmissions taking place in the cell and all messages are queued to access the wireless channel and serviced according to the FCFS scheduling policy; also, queries are of size b_q bits and invalidations are of size b_i bits.

In order to determine T_{delay} we do the following:

- Model the servicing of up-link queries as a M/D/1 queue under the assumption that there is a dedicated up-link channel of bandwidth C. The query arrival rate λ_q is estimated to be $NP_{miss}\lambda_e$ since there are N MHs in a cell and for each MH in the cell the up-link query generation rate is $P_{miss}\lambda_e$. The query service rate μ_q is then estimated to be $C/(b_q + b_a)$.
- Model the servicing of invalidation on down-link channel as an M/D/1 queue under the assumption that there is a dedicated down-link channel of bandwidth C. The average invalidation arrival rate λ_i is estimated to be $M\mu$ and the invalidation service rate μ_i is then estimated to be C/b_i.
- In order to model a single wireless channel of bandwidth C for both up-link and down-link traffic and estimate the mean query service rate T_q on this shared channel, we combine both the up-link and down-link M/D/1 models. Since we are interested in only the query service rate, the invalidations on the channel merely add to the delay in servicing the queries. Thus, we assume the service rate of the channel for both types of traffic to be μ_q (the service rate for queries) and adjust the arrival rate of invalidations in proportion to the service rate of queries. Thus the effective arrival rate of invalidations is taken as $\tilde{\lambda}_i = (\mu_i/\mu_q)\lambda_i$. The combined M/D/1 queue is shown in Figure 26.9. Using the standard queuing theory result for an M/D/1 queue, the average delay experienced by a query going up-link is given as

$$T_q = \frac{2\mu_q - (\lambda_q + \tilde{\lambda}_i)}{2\mu_q[\mu_q - (\lambda_q + \tilde{\lambda}_i)]}$$

- All queries that are cache hits do not experience any delay. Thus, the average delay experienced by any query in the system is given by $T_{delay} = P_{miss}T_q$.

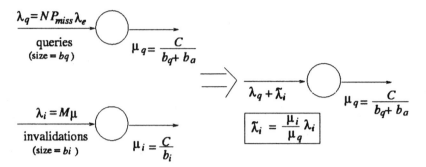

Figure 26.9   Combining the up-link and down-link M/D/1 queues.

26.7 PERFORMANCE COMPARISON

26.7.1 Experimental Setup

In this section, we present the simulated performance result of the AS scheme of cache invalidation. The simulation results are for a single cell with a base station and a varying number of mobile hosts. The purpose of these experiments were twofold: (1) to investigate how closely the experimental results coincide with the values for performance metrics (delay, up-link requests) predicted by the simple model; (2) to investigate how efficiently the AS scheme manages disconnection in a mobile environment; for this purpose the AS scheme was experimentally compared with the Ideal Scheme. The default parameters used for each scenario are as shown in Table 26.3. Delay is defined to be the time it takes to answer a query. The delay is assumed to be zero when there is a local cache hit.

TABLE 26.3   Default parameters for AS and AT/TS

Parameter	Value
N	25
M	100
λ	1/120 query/s
μ	10^{-4} updates/s (low),
	1/1800 updates/s (high)
b_a	1200 bytes
b_q	64 bytes
b_i	64 bytes
C	10000 bits/sec
s	20%
ω	1800 sec
L	10 sec
w (TS)	$100L$

26.7.2   Experimental Results

26.7.2.1   Comparison at Low Data Invalidation Rate

The first scenario studies the performance of the TS and AS schemes when the data changes infrequently. The value of μ used is 10^{-4} updates/sec. Delay and number of up-links per query were studied by varying s. The TS scheme performs better than the AT scheme at low invalidation rates.

Delay. Figure 26.10(a) shows the variation in average delay with the sleep characteristics of the mobile hosts. For the TS scheme, delay has two components: query's waiting time to be serviced by the MSS and the time it must wait for the next invalidation report to be broadcast (to ensure that the data item has not been invalidated since the last update was received). Only the network delay component is shown. If the time to wait for the next invalidation report is added, an additional $L/2$ delay is seen for AT/TS. A significant improvement in total delay is seen when the AS strategy is used. The network delays are higher for TS, as queries tend to go up-link in bursts, causing congestion in the network. This is a consequence of waiting for the next invalidation report to arrive to answer the query. The delay for the TS scheme increases with s, as the cache has to be discarded more often, reducing the hit rate and generating more up-link queries. However, the total query rate is reduced as the sleep rate increases. At very high sleep rates, this effect dominates and the delay decreases.

Up-links. Figure 26.10(b) shows the variation in the number of up-links per query with the sleep characteristics of mobile hosts. AS requires an up-link for the first query after every sleep interval. If the item queried is already in the cache and not invalidated, then this up-link is additional to the ideal scheme. Thus, AS has a marginally higher number of up-links per query as opposed to the ideal scheme, in which they increase as the sleep rate increases. The shape of the TS curve can be explained based on the fact that it has to discard its cache after an extended sleep. This results in low hit rates and more up-link queries. The effect is not so dominant when the sleep rate is low, but increases as the average sleep percentage increases.

26.7.2.2   Comparison at High Data Invalidation Rate

In this section, we present results for a scenario in which the data in the network changes frequently. The data change rate μ is assumed to be $1/1800$ updates/sec. All other parameters are as in Table 26.3. The AS scheme is compared only to the AT scheme, since the AT scheme performs better than the TS scheme at high invalidation rates. This is because the AT scheme wastes less bandwidth than the TS scheme by not repeating the same invalidation report multiple times.

Delay. Figure 26.11(a) shows a plot of average delay against s. The network delays are slightly higher as compared to Figure 26.10. This is due to additional invalidation reports being sent in the AS scheme and the increase in size of each report for the AT scheme. The decrease at a very high sleep rate is due to the number of queries decreasing as most hosts are sleeping. There is an almost seven to eight times improvement in overall delay (network delay + wait for next report) when the AS strategy is compared to an AT similar to that in Figure 26.10.

Up-links. Figure 26.11(b) shows the variation of the number of up-links per query with

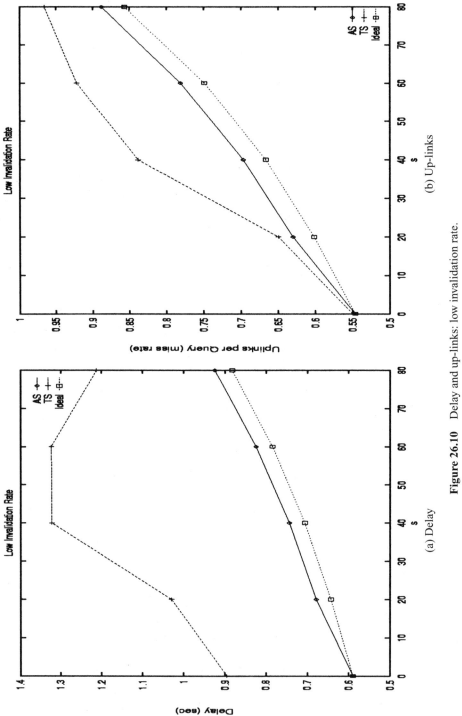

Figure 26.10 Delay and up-links: low invalidation rate.

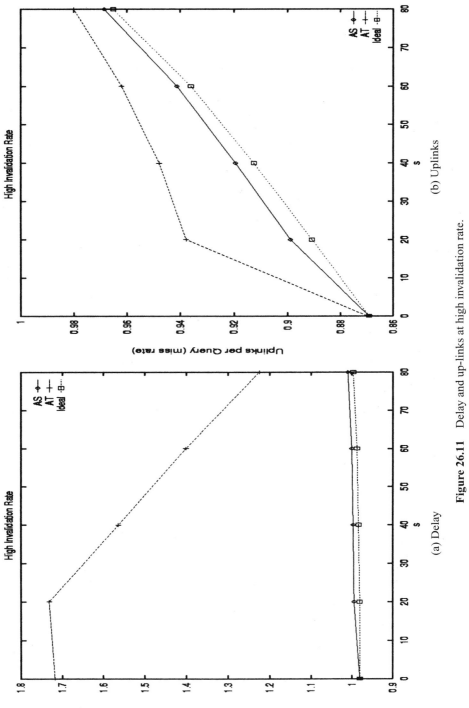

Figure 26.11 Delay and up-links at high invalidation rate.

573

the sleep rate. As the invalidation rate is high, the cache is less effective and more queries result in up-links as compared to the scenario of Section 26.7.2.1. In the AT/TS strategy, the MH must wait for the next invalidation to come before it can answer a query. Since the time window for answering a query is greater, there is a greater probability that the item would be invalidated by that time. The hit rate of the cache is therefore poorer. This combined with the drop in hit rate due to discarding the cache contributes to the number of up-links for AT. AS performs marginally worse than the ideal scheme as in the case of low invalidation rate.

26.7.2.3 *Comparison with Ideal Scheme*
Figures 26.12(a) and (b) show the delay and up-links per query, respectively, at different query rates for the ideal and AS schemes. As the number of queries per second increases, both the number of up-links per query and the average delay to answer a query increase. This is a consequence of the decrease in hit rate. As there is a greater delay between queries, the probability of an invalidation occurring between queries increases. This results in more up-links and higher delay. As the sleep rate increases, the probability of an invalidation between successive queries increases even further. In all cases, the plots for AS closely follow that of the ideal scheme, with the gap increasing as the sleep rate increases.

26.7.2.4 *Model Validation*
Figure 26.13 shows the comparison between the miss rate for the proposed scheme AS obtained through simulation and that predicted by the mathematical model (MM). Figure 26.14 shows the comparison between the delay for the proposed scheme AS obtained through simulation (denoted as Sim in the plots) and that predicted by the mathematical model. The model captures the behavior very well and the results are closer at low invalidation rates. This is because of the heuristic used in the modeling for estimating the equivalent arrival rate of invalidation messages.

26.8 SUMMARY

Cache maintenance is one of the most important issues in providing data to mobile applications. We have described a cache maintenance (invalidation) strategy called AS for a distributed system that is predisposed to frequent disconnections. Such disconnections happen in a mobile wireless environment for various reasons. The proposed algorithm minimizes the overhead, preserving bandwidth and reducing the number of up-link requests and average latency. State information about the local cache at an MH with respect to data items is maintained at the home MSS; by sending asynchronous call-backs and buffering them until implicit acknowledgments are received, the cache continues to be valid even after the MH is temporarily disconnected from the network. The performance analysis and simulation results show the benefits in terms of bandwidth savings (reduction in uplink queries) and data access latency compared to other caching schemes that provide data currency guarantees similar to the AS scheme.

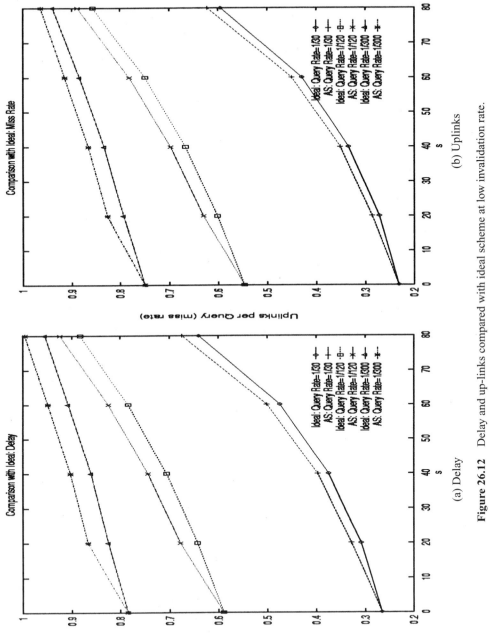

Figure 26.12 Delay and up-links compared with ideal scheme at low invalidation rate.

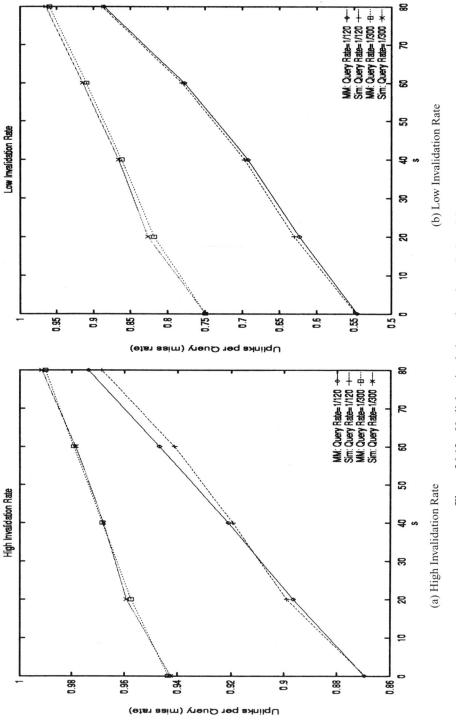

(a) High Invalidation Rate

(b) Low Invalidation Rate

Figure 26.13 Up-links: simulation and mathematical model.

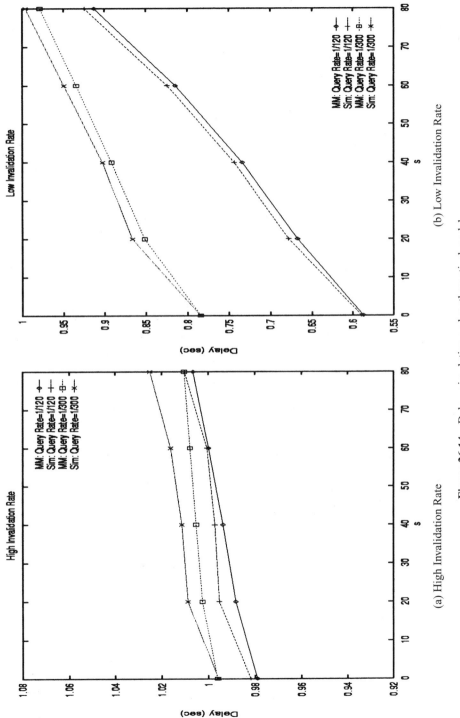

(a) High Invalidation Rate

(b) Low Invalidation Rate

Figure 26.14 Delay: simulation and mathematical model.

Emergence of pervasive or ubiquitous computing environments will bring new challenges to data management. Such pervasive computing environments encompass sensor-based wireless networks. These sensors, for example, can be embedded in household appliances. Efficient gathering, representation, distribution, and processing of data in such low-powered and ad hoc environments need new data management techniques. Such technqiues will most probably exploit application semantics to minimize the overhead of data management. There are several protocols such as Jini by Sun and UPnP by Microsoft that have been developed to enable service discovery in such ad hoc environments. Widespread deployment of such protocols will enable interactions with heterogeneous mobile devices such as PDAs and 3G telephones. In such interaction-rich environments, there will be a need for device-independent, context-sensitive (location-dependent) data exchange and distributed data management techniques that are scalable and secure.

ACKNOWLEDGMENTS

Research of Prof. Gupta and Prof. Srimani is supported in part by NSF Grants ANI-0196156.

REFERENCES

1. A. P. Sistla, O. Wolfson, and Y. Huang, Minimization of communication cost through caching in mobile environments, *IEEE Transactions on Parallel and Distributed Systems, 9*(4): 378–389, 1998.

2. O. Wolfson and Y. Hang, Competitive analysis of caching in distributed databases, *IEEE Transactions on Parallel and Distributed Systems, 9*(4): 391–409, 1998.

3. Y. Huang and O. Wolfson, Dynamic allocation in distributed systems and mobile computers, in *IEEE Proceedings of 10th International Conference on Data Engineering*, pp. 20–29, 1994.

4. J. Cai and K. L. Tan, Energy-efficient selective cache invalidation, *Wireless Networks, 5*(6): 489–502, 1999.

5. J. Dilley, The effect of consistency on cache response time, *IEEE Network, 14*(3): 24–28, 2000.

6. R. Alonso, D. Barbara, and H. Garcia-Molina, Data caching issues in an information retrieval system, *ACM Transactions on Database Systems, 15*: 359–384, September 1990.

7. D. Barbara and T. Imielinski, Sleepers and workaholics: Caching strategies in mobile environments (extended version), *MOBIDATA: An Interactive Journal of Mobile Computing, 1*(1), November 1994.

8. C. Perkins, IP Mobility Support. RFC 2002, October 1996.

9. K. Wilkinson and M.-A. Neimat, Maintaining consistency of client-cached data, in *Proceedings 16th International Conference on Very Large Data Bases (VLDB'90)*, pp. 122–133, Brisbane, Australia, August 1990.

10. G. Y. Liu and G. Q. McGuire Jr., A mobility-aware dynamic database caching scheme for wireless mobile computing and communications, *Distributed and Parallel Databases, 4*: 271–288, 1996.

11. J. Jing, A. Elmagarmid, A. Helal, and R. Alonso, Bit-sequences: an adaptive cache invalidation

method in mobile client/server environments, *Mobile Networks and Applications, 2*: 115–127, 1997.

12. Q. Hu and D. K. Lee, Cache algorithms based on adaptive invalidation reports for mobile environments, *Cluster Computing, 1*: 39–50, 1998.

13. K. L. Wu, P. S. Yu, and M. S. Chen, Energy-efficient caching for wireless mobile computing, in *20th International Conference on Data Engineering,* pp. 336–345, March 1996.

14. M. Satyanarayanan et al., Coda: A highly available file system for a distributed workstation environment, *IEEE Trans. Computers, 39*(4): 447–459, April 1990.

15. L. B. Mummert and M. Satyanarayanan, Variable granularity cache coherence, *Operating Systems Review, 28*(1): 55–60, January 1994.

16. L. B. Mummert and M. Satyanarayanan, Large granularity cache coherence for intermittent connectivity, in *Proceedings of the 1994 Summer USENIX Conference,* June 1994.

17. D. Barbara and T. Imielinski, Sleepers and workaholics: Caching strategies in mobile environments, *Very Large Databases Journal,* December 1995.

18. S. L. Tong and V. Bharghavan, Alleviating the latency and bandwidth problems in WWW browsing, *USENIX Symposium on Internet Technologies and Systems,* 1997.

19. M. Crovella and P. Barford, The network effects of prefetching, in *Proceedings of INFOCOM '98,* 1998.

20. G. H. Kuenning and G. J. Popek, Automated hoarding for mobile computers, in *16th ACM Symposium on Operating System Principles,* 1997.

21. A. Kahol, S. Khurana, S. K. S. Gupta, and P. K. Srimani, An efficient cache management scheme for mobile environment, in *Proceedings of 20th International Conference on Distributed Computing Systems (ICDCS'00),* April 2000.

CHAPTER 27

Mobile, Distributed, and Pervasive Computing

MICHEL BARBEAU

School of Computer Science, Carleton University, Ottawa, Canada

27.1 INTRODUCTION

Pervasive computing aims at availability and invisibility. On the one hand, pervasive computing can be defined as availability of software applications and information anywhere and anytime. On the other hand, pervasive computing also means that computers are hidden in numerous so-called information appliances that we use in our day-to-day lives [4, 29, 30]. Personal digital assistants (PDAs) and cell phones are the first widely available and used pervasive computing devices. Next-generation devices are being designed. Several of them will be portable and even wearable, such as glass embedded displays, watch PDAs, and ring mouses.

Several pervasive computing devices and users are wireless and mobile. Devices and applications are continuously running and always available. From an architectural point of view, applications are nonmonolithic, but rather made of collaborating parts spread over the network nodes. These parts are hereafter called distributed components. As devices and users move from one location to another, applications must adapt themselves to new environments. Applications must be able to discover services offered by distributed components in new environments and dynamically reconfigure themselves to use these new service providers. From a more general point of view, pervasive computing applications are often interaction-transparent, context-aware, and experience capture and reuse capable. Interaction transparency means that the human user is not aware that there is a computer embedded in the tool or device that he or she is using. Context awareness means that the application knows, for instance, its current geographical location. An experience capture and reuse capable application can remember when, where, and why something was done and can use that information as input to solve new tasks.

Pervasive computing is characterized by a high degree of heterogeneity: devices and distributed components are from different vendors and sources. Support of mobility and distribution in such a context requires open distributed computing architectures and open protocols. Openness means that specifications of architectures and protocols are public documents developed by neutral organizations. Key specifications are required to handle mobility, service discovery, and distributed computing.

Handbook of Wireless Networks and Mobile Computing, Edited by Ivan Stojmenović.
ISBN 0-471-41902-8   © 2002 John Wiley & Sons, Inc.

In this chapter, we review the main characteristics of applications of pervasive comput-ing in Section 27.2, discuss the architecture of pervasive computing software in Section 27.3, and review key open protocols in Section 27.4.

27.2 PERVASIVE COMPUTING APPLICATIONS

Characteristics of pervasive computing applications have been identified as interaction transparency, context awareness, and automated capture of experiences [2].

Pervasive computing aims at nonintrusiveness. It contrasts with the actual nontrans-parency of current interactions with computers. Neither input–output devices nor user ma-nipulations are natural. Input–output devices such as mouses, keyboards, and monitors are pure artifacts of computing. So are manipulations such as launching a browser, selecting elements in a Web page, setting up an audio or video encoding mechanism, and entering authentication information (e.g., a log-in and a password).

Biometrics security is a field aimed at making authentication of users natural. It re-moves the log-in and password intermediate between the user and the computer. To identi-fy an individual, it exploits the difference between human bodies. Authentication is based on physical measurements. To be usable, however, the measurements must be noninvasive and fast. DNA analysis does not meet that criteria, but fingerprint identification does. Other alternatives include facial characteristics, voice printing, and retinal and typing rhythm recognition. Input biometric information hardware and software are being market-ed. It is interesting to note that practical evaluations have reported that biometric input is often not recognized and needs to be accompanied by a conventional authentication proce-dure (log-in and password) in case the biometric authentication fails [12].

Another example of interaction transparency is the electronic white-board project called Classroom 2000 [12]. An electronic white-board has been designed that looks and feels like a white-board rather than a computer. With ideal transparency of interaction, the writer would just pick up a marker and start writing with no plug-in, no log-in, and no configuration.

To achieve transparency of interaction, advanced hardware and software tools are need-ed such as handwriting recognition, gesture recognition, speech recognition, free-form pen interaction, and tangible user interfaces (i.e., electronic information is manipulated using common physical objects).

Context awareness translates to adaptation of the behavior of an application as a func-tion of its current environment. This environment can be characterized as a physical loca-tion, an orientation, or a user profile. A context-aware application can sense the environ-ment and interpret the events that occur within it. In a mobile and wireless computing environment, changes of location and orientation are frequent. With pervasive computing, a physical device can be a personal belonging, identified and long-term personalized to its user (such as a cell phone or a PDA) or shared among several users and personalized sole-ly for the duration of a session (such as an electronic white-board).

The project Cyberguide [12] is a pervasive computing application that exploits aware-ness of the current physical location. It mimics on a PDA the services provided by a hu-man tour guide when visiting a new location.

Context-aware components can sense who you are, where you are, and what you are doing and use that information to adapt their services to your needs. Mobility and services on demand are greatly impacted by the location of the devices and the requested services. Examples range from relatively rudimentary device following services such as phone call forwarding to the location of the device, to more complex issues of detecting locations of available services and selecting the optimal location for obtaining the services, such as printing services.

The complexity of the problem increases when both the service users and the service devices are mobile. These problems require dynamic and on-the-fly system configuration. The dynamics of such systems are complex because not only system reconfiguration and low level configuration, e.g., multiple communication and security protocols, are required, but also service detection and monitoring in order to provide the best available services.

Capture and storage of past experiences can be used to solve new problems in the future. Experiences are made of events and computers have the ability to record them automatically. Human users only have to recall that information from the computer when it is needed. For example, a context-aware electronic wallet could capture and store locations, times, and descriptions of payments made by a traveler. Back home, the traveler could use the recorded events to generate an expense report.

27.3 ARCHITECTURE OF PERVASIVE COMPUTING SOFTWARE

The engineering of pervasive computing software is discussed in [1, 2]. The software of pervasive computing applications is subject to the support of everyday use and continuous execution. Robustness, reliability, and availability are therefore required. In what follows, we focus on issues of software engineering for pervasive computing that have to do with mobility and distribution.

An important issue that has been addressed is the architecture of mobile user-interfaces [11]. Mobility, which most of the time implies wireless communication, brings additional issues, namely, narrow-bandwidth communications, limited processing power, and restricted input/output devices (e.g., stylus-based input, small screens).

With pervasive computing, information pursues the user rather than the user pursuing the information as with traditional desktop computing. This has been addressed by a research system called Personal Information Everywhere (PIE) that has been developed by Carmeli, Cohen, and Wecker [7] to provide information to mobile people within an organization. The architecture of this system consists of consumers of information, PDAs running a PIE-specific small kernel, and a supplier of information, a central database server (written in XML). The consumer-to-supplier communication is wireless.

An interesting aspect of this project is the partitioning of the processing between a server and a PDA in order to cope with the light processing capabilities of the latter. The model is called Mobile Application Partitioning. The kernel on the PDA handles interaction with the user. A proxy runs on the server and handles the graphic rendering and user event handling. There is one proxy per PDA. The main logic loop is as follows. The proxy gets data from the database and prepares the layout of the screen. The proxy sends messages to the PDA to render the layout of the screen. Whenever a user-generated event occurs, a signal is sent from the PDA to the proxy. The signal contains the identity of the event and the identity of the object in which the event occurred. The handler of the event is the proxy. The result translates to updates of the screen layout prepared in the proxy and rendered on the PDA.

27.4 OPEN PROTOCOLS

Open protocols are required by pervasive computing for establishing communication and collaboration between distributed components in a global infrastructure-based manner as well as in an ad hoc manner. Mobility, service discovery, and distributed computing are issues that need to be addressed.

The problem of mobility of devices, from network to network, is not solved by plain IP. It is, however, addressed by the mobile Internet protocols (IPs). Mobile IPs are discussed in more detail in Chapter 25 of this book. In the context of the current chapter, it is worth mentioning that IPv6 is a better candidate than IPv4 for pervasive computing [23]. Indeed, pervasive computing puts enormous pressure on the demand for IP addresses. The number of devices will be high and they will be continuously running, hence there is little possibility of temporal sharing of IP addresses as in DHCP. The 128-bit addresses of IPv6 can support considerably more devices than the 32-bit addresses of IPv4. There is a movement in the wireless industry toward IPv6. For instance, the Third-Generation Partnership Project (3GPP) [25] has adopted IPv6 for their next generation of wireless network specifications.

In the subsequent subsections, we focus on application support protocols. Service discovery and distributed computing are discussed in more detail.

27.4.1 Service Discovery

Service discovery protocols are a key technology of pervasive computing. They give to distributed components the capability to advertise and discover each other's services on a network. For instance, a PDA equipped with a service discovery protocol, once attached to a network, can automatically discover a laptop advertising an agenda synchronization service.

There are leading service discovery technologies: Service Discovery Protocol (SDP) of Bluetooth [6], Jini [22], Salutation [9], Service Location Protocol (SLP) [14], and UpnP [10].

In this subsection, we review access to services on an IP network and the highlights of SLP and Jini. We also explore two related issues, namely, service selection facilitation and security.

27.4.1.1 Access to Services on an IP Network

To establish an association with a server process from machine to machine on the Internet, the client requires the IP address of the machine on which the server is running and the port number of the socket on which the server is listening. In addition, the client needs to learn and to run a protocol understood by the server. Services are often registered under human readable names. Service names need to be mapped to machine names and port numbers on which the services are offered. Often, the name of the protocol understood by the server is implicit in the name of the server (e.g., WWW implies http).

A practice in IP networks for mapping service names to machine names on which services are offered consists of naming conventions for machines offering services (e.g., mailhost.scs.carleton.ca, ftp.scs.carleton.ca, www.scs.carleton.ca) and registered associations with a DNS of standard machine name and real machine address or name (e.g., www.scs.carleton.ca is mapped to fusion.scs.carleton.ca). A drawback of this approach is that only one machine per DNS can offer a service under a standardized name. A solution to this problem has been proposed [16]. It is called DNS SRV Resource Records. It allows the mapping of a service name (as defined in file/etc/services, e.g., FTP) to names of machines offering the service.

Machine names then have to be mapped to IP addresses. This translation relies both on a local name server (DNS) and a local file listing associations of machine name and IP address (file/etc/hosts on Unix).

For mapping service names to port numbers on which services are offered, port numbers are standardized. Associations of service name to port number and transport protocol name are stored in a local file (e.g., /etc/services on Unix).

This practice has an advantage. There are no requirements for special infrastructure for service location. That is, in-place naming services support service location. This approach has, however, several disadvantages. It is not possible to advertise several service providers of the same service name (unless DNS SRV Resource Records are used). Clients must be aware of naming conventions. Search by values of attributes is not supported. Machine names and port numbers are discovered using different mechanisms. Updates need to be performed at two different places. The introduction of new types of services requires standardization of new names. Information may not be up-to-date. In other words, this solution lacks the generality and dynamism required by the heterogeneous hardware and distributed components of a pervasive computing environment. Service discovery protocols have been devised to facilitate association of clients to servers in a heterogeneous and dynamic environment.

27.4.1.2 Service Location Protocol

A service may either be of a hardware nature (e.g., a network access point) or a software nature (e.g., a CORBA server). SLP is a general protocol for the advertisement and discovery of network services at the scale of an enterprise network. The service discovery process is of the "yellow pages" type, that is, services can be discovered by type name and by characteristics.

Characteristics of services are described by values given to named attributes. For instance, a network access point would be described by the name of the protocol it supports (e.g., IEEE 802.11), its speed (e.g., 11 Mbps), and encryption algorithm (e.g., WEP). A service type is a collection of services having a common nature (e.g., all the access points) and sharing the same kinds of attributes (e.g., protocol, speed, and encryption algorithm). In SLP, the information required by a client to establish an association with a server is called a service access point (SAP). A SAP typically contains at least a protocol name and a machine name. It could also contain a port number and the path to an executable file. A service advertisement is a structure of information describing a service. It contains the service type name, values of attributes, and SAP.

SLP is a mechanism for facilitating the association of entities that have services to offer or need for services. In the SLP model, there are three kinds of entities: user agent (UA), service agent (SA), and directory agent (DA). A UA represents a consumer of services, an SA represents a provider of services, and a DA represents a database of service advertisements.

SLP proposes two alternative architectures. The first involves only SAs and UAs communicating directly with each other. With the aim of reducing network traffic, a second architecture involves SAs, UAs, and DAs acting as central sources of service advertisements in which SAs register services and UAs enquire about services.

A SAP is represented by a special type of URL, called URLs of scheme "service:" [13] or generic URLs [5]. The scheme service: is discussed in more detail hereafter.

An URL of scheme service: is made of a service type (a name) and access information:

```
"service:" service-type ":" service-access-info
```

SLP has a notion of type of service with a two-level hierarchy and a notion of instance of service. SLP concepts of type of service, hierarchy, and instance are analogous to object-oriented concepts of class, inheritance, and object.

A two-level hierarchy consists of an abstract-type service at the top and one or several concrete-type services at the bottom. An abstract-type service groups several concrete-type services that provide the same function but through different protocols. For instance, a banking service provided by distributed components is a function that can be achieved by several different concrete remote method invocation protocols such as IIOP and RMI. In this case, the abstract-type service is banking and the associated concrete-type services are IIOP and RMI. A concrete-type name provides the name of a protocol to be used by a client to call a method on a distributed component.

Names of services are subject to standardization in order to achieve uniformity from one system to another. An organization that standardizes service types and names is called a naming authority. The authority from which a service name is drawn can be explicitly specified. When it is unspecified, the default naming authority is the Internet Assigned Numbers Authority (IANA). It that case, the specified service type must have been standardized by IANA, e.g., http, ftp, and telnet. A naming authority can have the scope of an enterprise. The naming authority is identified by the name of a company. Other conventions also apply. For example, authority name "test" is for nonstandardized services under test.

The formal syntax of the naming part (service-type) of an URL of scheme service: encompassing the notions of abstract type, concrete type, and naming authority is as follows:

```
abstract-type [ "." naming-authority ] ":" concrete-type
```

Here is an example of two concrete types of service grouped under the same abstract type of service:

```
service:banking.demo:iiop
service:banking.demo:rmi
```

banking is the abstract-type name and banking.demo:iiop and banking.
demo:rmi are concrete-type names. demo (stands for demonstration) is the naming authority. A UA could issue a request for the abstract type of service banking and would
receive replies with the aforementioned two names. Both services perform the same function but through different protocols, i.e. either Internet Inter-ORB Protocol (IIOP) or Remote Method Invocation (RMI). It is also possible to request by full name, both abstract
type and concrete type.

Organization of services in a two-level hierarchy is interesting because it makes possible the grouping of services that are of the same kind, but accessible through different protocols. If this flexibility is not required, a flat organization is possible as well. In that case,
types of services are said to be simple. The name (service-type) of a simple-type of
service is structured as follows:

```
simple-type [ "." naming-authority]
```

Often, the part simple-type corresponds to the name of a protocol, e.g. http. Here is
another example where simple-type is not a protocol name:

```
service:banking.demo
```

In that case, the name of the protocol that should be used to communicate with the service
must by inferred by some means, e.g., using preset conventions.

A URL of scheme service: also contains information required by the UA to communicate with the SA, in addition to the protocol name. Access information essentially consists
of an address of a machine where the service is offered, an optional path to a file (e.g., an
executable program), and an optional list of attributes representing additional information
required to be able to contact the SA. The formal syntax of a URL of scheme service: with
access information is as follows:

```
"/" address-family "/" address-spec
    [ "/" [ url-path ] [ ";" attribute-list ] ]
```

The part address-family indicates the network protocol to be used. A double
slash "//", i.e. the field is empty, is for IP, *at* for Appletalk, and *ipx* for IPX.

The part address-spec contains a host name or an IP address and, optionally, a port
number.

The part url-path is specific to the protocol. For example, if the protocol is http, the
url path is the name of a file containing an HTML page. Here is an example:

```
service:http://fusion.scs.carleton.ca/index.html
```

It is the SAP for a simple-type service named http. The address family is IP and the address is fusion.scs.carleton.ca. The url path is index.html. The attribute list

is empty. It is important to stress that with this naming scheme it is possible to advertise a second Web server in the domain `scs.carleton.ca` provided by a different SA, for instance:

```
service:www.test:http://apex.scs.carleton.ca/index.html
```

UAs request access to Web servers by the service-type name `http`. Two SAPs will be returned. This contrasts with a conventional Internet naming scheme where, by convention, the Web server in domain `scs.carleton.ca` is advertised under the name `www.scs.carleton.ca` and is mapped to a unique machine address.

The attribute list provides additional information required to access a service. The attribute list is made of pairs of attribute id and value according to the following syntax:

```
attribute-id "=" value
```

`attribute-id` is common to all SAs offering the same kind of service. `Value` is specific to every SA. For example, access to a secure banking service may require the client to have a knowledge of a security parameter index (SPI) that determines an authentication key and algorithm to be used by the UA to contact the SA. This can be represented as follows:

```
service:banking.demo:iiop://some.where.net;SPI=19
```

The attribute SPI tells the UA to use an authentication key and algorithm associated with the number 19 (which is arbitrary for this example).

The information represented in service advertisements needs to be described precisely. SLP defines a structure of service location information [13]. It is a model of data for the precise specification of elements of service advertisements (i.e., a type of service, attributes, and a SAP). Besides, it is extensible. That is, the introduction of new types of services is possible.

A service type is described by a structure called a service type template. The concept of template is analogous to the concept of structure in the C programming language. Each service type is described by a template written according to formal syntax rules. Each instance of the service is specified by assigning effective values to each attribute defined in the template and defining the SAP, which may have a service-type specific syntax defined in the template.

The model of a service-type template is pictured in Figure 27.1 using UML notation. A service type template has a name, a version, and a description. It contains zero or more attributes and, optionally, a URL syntax definition.

The purpose of the version field is to capture the evolution of a template. A template that is under development should have a number below 1.0, whereas standardized templates should be numbered from 1.0 and above. The description field is free format text for the purpose of documentation.

Each attribute has a name, a data type, default value(s), a descriptive text, and allowed values. Valid data types are Boolean, integer, string, opaque, and keyword. A value of the

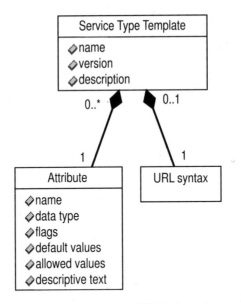

Figure 27.1   Structure of SLP information.

opaque type is an array of bytes. An attribute of the keyword type has no value and is like a constant.

Valid flags are O, M, L, and X. Flag O means that the attribute is optional. Flag M means that the attribute is multivalued. Flag L means that the attribute is a literal and its name cannot be translated into another language. Flag X means that a value for this attribute must be provided by a UA when a service request is formulated for that type of service.

An SA can omit providing values for attributes when registering a service with a DA. In that case, default values apply. The range of values that can be assigned to an attribute can be restricted by specifying allowed values. The syntax of the URL is of scheme service: and is described using augmented BNF. Here is a sample template:

```
template-type = printing
template-version = 0.1
template-description =
A template example for a printing service.
template-url-syntax =
color = BOOLEAN
FALSE
speed = INTEGER 0
page-queue = INTEGER 0
```

It is the template of a printing service called `printing`. It has no specific URL syntax, i.e., scheme service: applies. The template has three attributes. Attribute `color`, modeling support of color printing, is mandatory and has default value false. Attribute speed specifies the speed of the printer, in pages per minute, and is optional. Attribute page-queue is also optional and indicates the current number of pages in the queue of the printer.

Interactions between DAs, SAs, and UAs are based on the following basic messages: Acknowledgment (SrvAck), Service Reply (SrvRply), Service Request (SrvRqst), and Service Registration (SrvReg).

There are two models of interaction: a model involving DAs and a model not involving DAs. Without DAs, UAs send using UDP multicast or broadcast message SrvRqst to SAs. SAs are listening and, when they find a match between a requested service and a service they offer, they reply to the UAs using unicast.

The model involving DAs is pictured in Figure 27.2. Message SrvReg is sent by an SA to a DA, using TCP or UDP unicast. The purpose of this message is registration of a new service. It contains a URL, a type of service name, and descriptive attributes. Message Sr-vAck is sent by a DA to an SA, using TCP or UDP unicast. Message SrvRqst is sent by a UA to a DA using UDP unicast or TCP unicast. TCP is selected when the reply cannot stand in one UDP datagram. The purpose of this message is to look up services. It contains a type of service name and a predicate that is a query evaluated over the attributes of registrations in a DA. Message SrvRply is sent by a DA to a UA using UDP unicast or TCP unicast to respond to SrvRqst. It contains URLs of SAs matching the query.

There are four different ways SAs and UAs can obtain the SAP of their DA: through a configuration file, a DHCP server, active discovery (multicast of requests by SAs and UAs), and passive discovery (multicast of advertisements by DAs).

Figure 27.3 pictures the operation of SLP in a DA-less architecture. A UA sends, using UDP above IP multicast or broadcast, a SrvRqst to SAs. The characteristics of the required service are specified in the SrvRqst as a service type name and a predicate over service descriptive attributes. When a listening SA finds a match between a requested service and a service it offers, it replies to the UA by sending a SrvRply using unicast. The SrvRply contains a SAP.

For ad hoc networks, the DA-less model may be more desirable. By definition, an ad hoc network does not rely on infrastructure.

During the process of discovery of SAs by UAs, when should the transmission of the SrvRqst, using multicast or broadcast, stop? How can the system provide, with reasonable probability, a complete set of available services while not waiting too long for SAs to respond?

Figure 27.2   Interaction among a DA, an SA, and a UA.

SrvRqst(Name, Predicate)

SrvRply(SAP)

Figure 27.3 UA and SA interaction.

To address this issue, SLP defines a multicast convergence algorithm. A SrvRqst is transmitted by a UA up to four times over a period of 15 seconds. Message SrvRqst contains a field called previous responder list. The list contains the IP addresses of the SAs that have returned SrvRplys so far in the execution of the multicast convergence algorithm. An SA listening and receiving a SrvRqst with its own IP address within the previous responder list of the message ignores the request and remains silent.

An important issue that must be addressed by a service discovery system is scalability. For instance, if the number of SAs matching a given request is high, the number of replies and amount of traffic will be high as well. To address scalability, SLP has a notion of scope. A scope is a group of UAs and SAs. DAs support scopes. UAs send SrvRqsts only to SAs and DAs supporting their scope. SAs send SrvRegs only to all the DAs supporting their scope. The concept of scope provides scalability limiting the network coverage of a request and the number of replies. Each scope is named. UAs and SAs can be members of several scopes. They can learn their scope name(s) by, for example, reading a configuration file.

27.4.1.3 Jini

The architecture of a Jini system consists of clients, lookup services, and service providers, which are analogous to the concepts of UAs, DAs, and SAs of SLP. As in SLP, Jini proposes two alternative architectures. The first architecture, with a mode of operation called peer lookup, consists of service providers and clients with direct communication. The second architecture consists of service providers, clients, and lookup services acting as central sources of information.

In Jini, a discovery protocol is used by a service provider or a client to discover a lookup service. Thereafter, a service provider may register with the lookup service with a protocol called Join. A service may be located on the lookup service by a client using a protocol called Lookup.

The discovery protocol proceeds as follows. A service provider or a client sends a discovery request on the local network using multicast. Listening lookup services reply to the service provider or client using unicast. Each lookup service returns a proxy object whose methods are used by the service provider or client to contact the lookup service.

Following the discovery, protocol Join is used. The service provider calls method register () to load a service object (also called a proxy) into the lookup service (see Figure 27.4). The service object consists of a Java interface to the service (i.e., signature of methods and descriptive attributes). The lookup service returns a service registration object that will be used by the service provider to maintain its offer of service.

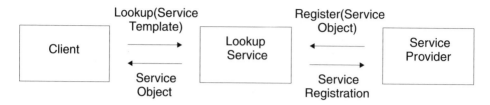

Figure 27.4   Interaction among a client, a lookup service, and a service provider.

Protocol Lookup is used by a client to enquire for service providers with a lookup service. Location is by type of Java interface or by values of attributes of the service. The requirements of the client are specified with a service template.

When a service provider is located, the corresponding service object is taken from the lookup service and loaded into the client. Afterward, the client communicates through the service object (which acts as a proxy) with the service provider. The communication protocol used between the service object and service provider is not in the scope of Jini and is said to be private. RMI can be used for that purpose.

As in SLP, presence of a lookup service is not mandatory. For location of a service when there are no lookup services, a client can apply a technique called peer lookup.

The client sends a message called identification to request registration messages from service providers (the identification message is normally sent by a lookup service). The client then receives registration messages from service providers from which one can be selected (Figure 27.5).

In addition to components client, lookup service, and service provider, Jini requires some elements of infrastructure. When a proxy or a service object is downloaded, only the data members are obtained. The implementation class must be downloaded separately. A Web server is required for downloading the code.

Jini is based on remote method invocation (RMI) [21]. A RMI activation demon is required to start a Java server object on demand, such as the Jini lookup service.

In contrast to SLP, Jini needs a Java virtual machine at the client as well as the service provider nodes. The Java virtual machine, for Jini as well as technologies such as RMI and object serialization on which it depends, may not fit in a small memory-pervasive comput-

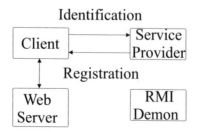

Figure 27.5   Peer lookup.

Figure 27.6   The JiniLite model.

ing device such as a PDA or cell phone. It has also been demonstrated that Jini is substantially more chatty than SLP (for equivalent functions) [3], which is something undesirable for wirelessly connected devices. Jini is better in terms of facilitation of communication because service discovery and service usage can take place in the same environment, the Java RMI environment. To reconcile the physical constraints of small devices with communication capabilities, a lightweight version of Jini called JiniLite has been created by Chen [8].

With JiniLite, the client is made lighter. First, the remote method invocation (RMI) API is simplified (Figure 27.6). Simplification is obtained at the expense of limitations on methods parameters (e.g., only parameters of simple predefined types) and communication model (clients cannot be called back). Second, service objects are not loaded dynamically in the client. Clients are preloaded with service object stubs to provide services for which usage is foreseen. Third, service objects themselves are run on a gateway (a proxy server). Service object stubs in light clients communicate with service objects in gateways through RMILite. Clients are configured with the address of their gateway. In the gateway, service objects are stored in a service registry on which clients can invoke a lookup method. When a service is provided to a client, a copy of the service object is taken from the registry and run within the gateway.

27.4.1.4 Service Selection Facilitation

When a UA requests instances of a type of resource, the selection of any instance of that resource type will often not satisfy the needs. For example, given the need to fax a document, several fax machines can be discovered. There is, however, most probably one of them that is more appropriate than all the others because of physical proximity. For instance, two faxes may be discovered but, for a user located on the first floor, the one situated on the first floor is more attractive then the one situated on the twentieth floor. An issue is how can the selection of the most appropriate service to fulfill a certain need be facilitated? Service selection can be facilitated with the help of tools. Some approaches are discussed below.

Selection of a service can be facilitated by using a service browser. Such a browser is presented in [17]. It provides to the user a view of the available services on the network. Figure 27.7 illustrates a view in which SAPs are listed (upper area) and descriptive attributes of a service are posted (lower area). Using the browser, a user queries the network for a service and selects one of the found services by visual inspection of the listed SAPs and attributes. The user then manually selects the service to be used.

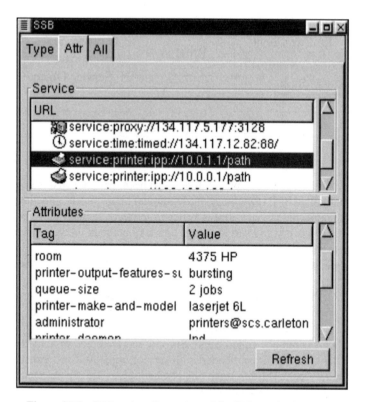

Figure 27.7   SAP and attribute view of the SLP service browser.

Service selection transparency can be achieved. McCormack has developed a mechanism, called service recommendation, that ranks services with respect to one another [18, 20]. An SLP SrvRqst includes a predicate expressing a condition on the values of the attributes of a sought service. Predicates are limited to attribute comparative expressions. Service recommendation extends the predicate syntax with ranking functions. A ranking function takes an expression over the attributes as argument. When the ranking function is evaluated by a DA, a numerical value is returned, thus ranking a service advertisement relative to the other service advertisements registered in the DA that satisfy the predicate in the SrvRqst. The ranking function is formulated by the user or predefined in the application. It is a model of the desirability of a service. Evaluations of the ranking function on all the service advertisements matching a predicate in a SrvRqst are performed simultaneously. The service with the highest/lowest rank is recommended, according to the ranking function. It is called service recommendation because the DA recommends to the UAs a service advertisement that has the highest/lowest rank according to a user-specific ranking scheme. With such a mechanism, it is therefore possible to delegate to a DA the selection, for instance, of a printer with the highest printing speed and shortest queue.

Contextual information about the UAs and SAs can be used to make a service selection decision. Physical location, because of its relevance, is a type of contextual information that can be used to facilitate service selection. Physical location often amounts to physical proximity of the user and service, such as in the same office, same floor, or same building. Location tracking solutions based on networks of sensors or triangulation may not suitable in an ad hoc network environment because of the infrastructure required.

Close proximity can be detected as follows. User and service devices may be equipped with infrared ports and use successful establishment of communication through the infrared ports as a confirmation of proximity.

Figure 27.8 pictures integration of a service discovery protocol with a close-proximity-based selection protocol. There are a UA, a near SA, and a far SA. They are all within RF reach of each other. The UA sends a SrvRqst using broadcast. It is received by both SAs and they both send a SrvRply using unicast. This completes the service discovery phase. To achieve close proximity selection, the UA sends a message called SetIrdLink through the infrared port using multicast. This message is, however, received only by the near SA, which replies with a message called SetIrdLinkConf. This completes the service selection phase.

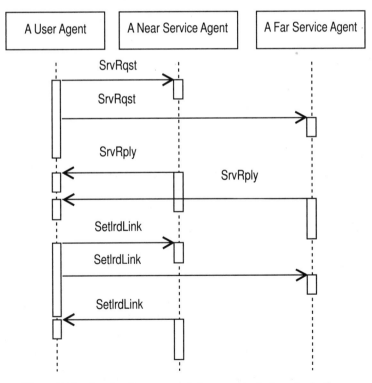

Figure 27.8 Service discovery and close-proximity-based selection.

27.4.1.5 Security

Theft of service is the primary security problem in cellular networks [27]. A similar problem exists with computer network services. Solutions devised for cellular telephony can be applied.

Control of access to services relies on a form of identification. Either a user or a device may be identified. The most desirable form, in the context of service access control, is user identification, because it is independent of the device utilized by the user to access the network.

Identification of a user may be done with an identification number entered by the user before a service is accessed. Further automation can be achieved by using instead a fingerprint captured by a biometrics sensor integrated into the device. However, a number or a fingerprint should not be transmitted unprotected because these identifiers can be copied by malicious listeners. Encryption can be used for that purpose and it is supported by most of the service discovery protocols.

Device identification may be considered equivalent to user identification in cases where the device is a personal belonging of the user. Indeed, in contrast to a desktop, which can be shared by several members of a family, a PDA is a personal assistant. Identification of the palmtop also means identification of its user. Each Bluetooth device has a 48-bit identifier that can be used for that purpose.

Secret key authentication can also be used to identify users or devices. Authentication is supported by most of the service discovery protocols.

RF fingerprinting can be used as well to identify a device (more exactly its air interface). It has been observed that radio transmitters that are built according to the same specifications all exhibit unique signal characteristics. The characteristics are obtained by measuring characteristics of the signal, e.g., the time–frequency relation of the signal at the start of the transmission. Most of the RF fingerprinting technology is proprietary or subject to patents.

27.4.2 Distributed Computing

A distributed system includes resources, resource managers, and clients. A resource may correspond, for instance, to a printer, a window on a software application, or a data element. Telecommunications networks are the infrastructure on which distributed systems rely. Concretely, each resource is located on a network node and can be used remotely from other nodes using telecommunications. A resource manager is a piece of software responsible for the administration of a type of resource. It has a telecommunications interface through which users access and update the resources. A manager also enforces access policies associated with each type of resource.

The concept of component is based on the concept of object. Like an object, a component is a logical entity containing information and capable of executing operations on it. A subset of the operations is accessible to the environment of a component and constitutes its interface. A call to an operation by a client of a component, a process, or another component, is achieved through the transmission of a message intercepted by the interface that dispatches the request to a method associated with the operation. The method eventually returns a response to the caller.

A component deserves a new term because it is more than a normal object. An object is a unit of software reusable, without pain, as long as the hosting software is written in the same language, is on the same platform, and is colocated with the object. A distributed component infrastructure facilitates the reuse of software units, called components, across programming languages, operating systems, and network nodes.

According to the distributed component model, resources, local or remote, are abstracted as components. A uniform syntax is used to call the components, whether or not they are in the same program, process, or network node. This is called access transparency.

In contrast to a client–server model, in which the client talks to a server process, in the distributed component model, the client talks to a remote object that exists within a container process. That container process can embed several objects (see Figure 27.9).

Every component has a unique identity. A component can be mobile, i.e., its host can change, to improve the performance of fault tolerance. When the location of a component changes, its identity is invariant. This is called transparency of migration. Moreover, in contrast to a client–server model, the naming scheme is uniform and doesn't change from one type of resource to another.

The entity responsible for the management of a component is called a component manager. The manager of the component is normally colocated with the component.

Fault transparency can be provided through the notion of service. A collection of components distributed over different nodes can supply the same services. Clients of the services select any supplier.

The common object request broker architecture (CORBA) [15] is a realization of the distributed component model. For communication between clients and distributed components, CORBA has a notion of object request broker (ORB). It transmits client requests, i.e., operations calls, to components. Clients and components can be on different nodes, run on different operating systems, and be programmed in different languages. An ORB has the capability to forward requests over the network, from one operating system to another, and from one programming language to another.

When a caller and a callee are not colocated, there are two acting ORBs: an ORB colocated with the caller that encodes and sends the request on the network and an ORB colo-

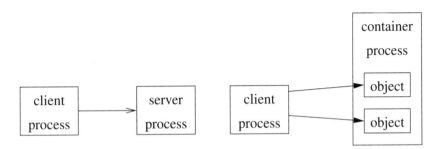

client–server model   distributed component model

Figure 27.9   The client–server model versus the distributed component model.

cated with the callee that receives the request from the network, decodes it, and dispatches it to the component. Inter-ORB communication is done through the Internet Inter-ORB Protocol (IIOP). A request, sent from one location to another, is encapsulated within a packet containing the identity of the target component, an operation name, and parameters. CORBA is a middleware, i.e., a software that goes between parts of distributed applications.

CORBA clearly separates the notion of interface from the notion of implementation of the interface. The implementation is changeable and, behind an interface, can hide several different implementations. This provides flexibility. The interface is specified with a CORBA-specific language called the interface definition language (IDL). Implementations can be programmed, however, is several different languages such as C, C++, and Java.

The development of an implementation is done as follows. The interface is written in the IDL. The IDL specification is processed by a translator that generates a representation in a target implementation language. The programmer writes in that target language methods associated to the operations of the interface. The component is compiled. The code of the component contains the elements required for its registration with an ORB when it is launched.

There is a CORBA implementation for a popular PDA operating system called Palm OS. It is a port of an open source implementation for CORBA called Mico [24]. Mico for CORBA [26] provides an API for creating CORBA clients on Palm OS. Servers cannot run on Palm OS. The capability to run servers on a PDA is a promising development. Indeed, a PDA could abstract its databases, such as address book and agenda, as CORBA objects and make them available to other applications on the PDA. There are no IDL compilers for Palm OS, hence the client stubs have to be written by the programmer. Recently, commercial versions of CORBA for PDAs have been announced [28].

CORBA and Jini CORBA can coexist with a service discovery protocol such as Jini and this issue has been addressed before by Jai et al. [19]. A client-side proxy, associated with a CORBA component, is registered with the lookup service by some entity (see Figure 27.10). Having the same interface as the CORBA component, the proxy, after it has been discovered, is downloaded and colocated with the client. The proxy hides the protocol, i.e., IIOP, for the communication with the the CORBA component.

27.5 SUMMARY

Characteristics of pervasive computing applications have been discussed in Section 27.2. Interaction transparency means that human-to-computer interaction is natural and based on

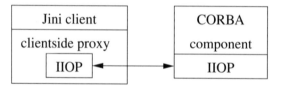

Figure 27.10   The coexistence of CORBA and Jini.

ordinary life objects and operations. Context awareness means that applications can sense and exploit information about the physical environment in which they are running. Automated capture of experiences exploits knowledge about actions performed in the past bound to contextual information to assist and make the resolution of new problems easier and faster.

Issues of architectures of pervasive computing that have to do with mobility and distribution were reviewed in Section 27.3. Pervasive computing platforms may be characterized by relatively narrow bandwidth channels, slow processing power, and limited input/output capabilities. To cope with these issues, some tasks can be delegated by a pervasive computing device to a server. This approach is called application partitioning. The component-based distributed computing model is well suited to the design of such applications.

We raised the need for open protocols to enable interoperability between the elements of pervasive computing. Service discovery protocols and distributed components architectures were addressed in more detail. Service discovery protocols, such as SLP and Jini, provide mechanisms with which distributed components can discover what each has to offer to other in terms of services. With an open distributed computing architecture, components can collaborate together using a common communication language. CORBA is an open distributed components architecture that achieves location transparency, programming language independence, and platform independence of service providers. Other open protocols not discussed in this chapter, such as mobile Internet protocols and ad hoc networking protocols, are also required to support mobile and distributed pervasive computing.

ACKNOWLEDGMENTS

The author would like to thank the following persons for many fruitful discussions about the issues discussed in the chapter: Victor Azondekon, Francis Bordeleau, Bogdan Gheorghe, Javier Govea, Evan Hughes, David McCormack, and Ramiro Liscano.

REFERENCES

1. G. D. Abowd, Software engineering and programming language considerations for ubiquitous computing, *ACM Comput. Surv., 28*(4), December 1996. Article 190.

2. G. D. Abowd, Software engineering issues for ubiquitous computing, in *Proceedings of the 1999 International Conference on Software Engineering,* pp. 5–84, 1999.

3. M. Barbeau, Bandwidth usage analysis of Service Location Protocol, in *Proceedings of Workshop on Pervasive Computing, International Conference on Parallel Processing,* pp. 51–56, Toronto, August 2000. The International Association for Computers and Communications (IACC).

4. J. Birnbaum, Pervasive information systems, *Communications of the ACM, 40*(2): 40–41, February 1997.

5. T. Berners-Lee, R. Fielding, U. C. Irvine, and L. Masinter, Uniform Resource Identifiers (URI): Generic syntax. IETF Request for Comments: 2396, August 1998.

6. Bluetooth, Specification of the Bluetooth system. www.bluetooth.com, December 1999.

7. B. Carmeli, B. Cohen, and A. J. Wecker, Personal information everywhere (PIE), in *Proceedings of the Eleventh ACM on Hypertext and Hypermedia,* pp. 252–253, 2000.

8. M. Chen, JiniLite white paper. www.cs.berkeley.edu/silkworm/jinilite/whitepaper.html. October 2000.

9. Salutation Consortium, Salutation architecture specification. www.salutation.org/specordr.htm, 1999.

10. Microsoft Corporation, Universal plug and play: Background. www.upnp.org/resources/UP-nPbkgnd.htm, 1999.

11. A. Dix, D. Ramduny, T. Rodden, and N. Davies, Places to stay on the move—software architectures for mobile user interfaces, *Personal Technologies, 4*(2), 2000.

12. D. A. Finck (Ed.), Biometrics security—body language, in *Laptop Buyer's Guide and Handbook,* pp. 94, 96, Brentwood, TN: Bedford Communications, 2000.

13. E. Guttman, C. Perkins, and J. Kempf, Service templates and service: schemes, IETF Request for Comments: 2609, June 1999.

14. E. Guttman, C. Perkins, J. Veizades, and M. Day, Service location protocol, version 2, IETF Request for Comments: 2608, June 1999.

15. Object Management Group, The Common Object Request Broker: Architecture and specification. ftp.omg.org, 1999.

16. A. Gulbrandsen and P. Vixie, A DNS RR for specifying the location of services (DNS SRV), IETF Request for Comments: 2052, October 1996.

17. E. Hughes, D. McCormack, M. Barbeau, and F. Bordeleau, An application for discovery, configuration, and installation of SLP services. MICON 2000. Available at www.scs.carleton.ca/barbeau, 2000.

18. E. Hughes, D. McCormack, M. Barbeau, and F. Bordeleau. Service recommendation using SLP, in *IEEE International Conference on Telecommunications 2001,* Bucharest, 2001.

19. B. Jai, M. Ogg, and A. Ricciardi. Effortless Software Interoperability with Jini connection technology. *Bell Technical Journal,* 88–101, April-June 2000.

20. D. McCormack, Service Recommendation in SLP. Report for Honours Project, School of Computer Science, Carleton University. Available at www.scs.carleton.ca/barbeau, 2000.

21. Sun Microsystems, Java remote method invocation specification, December 1999.

22. Sun Microsystems, JINI architecture specification, November 1999.

23. L. D. Paulson, Will wireless be IPv6's killer app? *Communications of the ACM, 34*(1): 28–29, January 2001.

24. A. Puder and K. Romer, *Mico: An Open Source CORBA Implementation.* San Francisco: Morgan Kaufmann, 2000.

25. Third-Generation Partnership Project, 3GPP—a global initiative. http://www.3gpp.org, 2001.

26. A. Puder, Mico for the Palm Pilot. http://diamant-atm.vsb.cs.uni-frankfurt.de/mico/pilot/, 1999.

27. M. J. Riezenma, Cellular security: Better, but foes still lurk, *IEEE Spectrum, 37*(6): 39–42, June 2000.

28. Vertel, Vertel launches next-generation CORBA for Palm OS first-ever wireless CORBA. http://www.vertel.com, April 2000.

29. M. Weiser, The computer of the 21st century, *Scientific American, 265*(3): 66–75, September 1991.

30. M. Weiser, Some computer science issues in ubiquitous computing, *Commun. ACM, 36*(7): 75–84, July 1993.

CHAPTER 28

Indoor Wireless Environments

LAKSHMI RAMACHANDRAN

Trillium Digital Systems (an Intel company), Bangalore, India

28.1 INTRODUCTION

The explosive research in mobile computing in recent years has opened up the field of indoor wireless networks [26]. The rapid expansion in this field is also a result of advances in digital communications, portable devices, semiconductor technology and the availability of license-free frequency bands. Another major factor that presents a real opportunity for data networking in indoor environments is the massive growth and usage of the Internet. Examples include homes, offices, trading floors in stock exchanges, conventions and trade shows, and so on.

Applications for indoor environments typically require ad hoc connectivity, especially in the case of a population of mobile users while they are within range of foreign agents or stations connected to the Internet. These users might need to send data files to each other, run some local applications or use any of the existing internet-based applications available on wired terminals located within their range. Ad hoc networking is a name given to the creation of dynamic and multihop networks that are created by the mobile nodes as needed for their communication purposes [26]. This area has also received a lot of attention from the research community, and represents interesting challenges for networking applications. The IETF Mobile Ad Hoc Network (MANET) group [20] is attempting to establish standards for creation of ad hoc networks.

Several technologies have emerged to support wireless networking in indoor environments. Some of the most popular ones are wireless local area networks (LANs) [4, 10, 17], HomeRF [9, 24], and Bluetooth [33]. Wireless LANs are especially suitable for applications that involve Internet addressable devices. Wireless LAN devices communicate packets "over the air," and their programming models are similar to those of wired LANs. HomeRF, as its name suggests, is chiefly aimed at the home environment. This presents an opportunity to extend the reach of the PC and Internet throughout the home, to legacy applications like telephony, audio/video entertainment, home appliances, and home control systems. Bluetooth is a technology meant for low-cost, low-power, indoor environments, and provides ad hoc connectivity among wireless devices; this is fast gaining popularity in the pervasive computing space as a cable-replacement solution.

The rest of the chapter is organized as follows. We first discuss issues in the design of

Handbook of Wireless Networks and Mobile Computing, Edited by Ivan Stojmenović.
ISBN 0-471-41902-8   © 2002 John Wiley & Sons, Inc.

the physical layer, followed by a detailed description of some media access control protocols proposed specifically for the indoor environment. We then discuss network topologies, with special reference to Bluetooth. Finally, we point to possible characterizations of indoor environments, and the new emerging paradigm of nomadic computing.

28.2 THE PHYSICAL LAYER

At the physical layer, the main objective is to detect signals between the two endpoints of a wireless communication link. Wireless media typically have vague and uncontrollable boundaries for broadcast range, low to medium bandwidth, and possibly asymmetric connectivity. One of the main problems encountered with indoor radio wave propagation is the multipath spread of signals due to reflection off walls and internal objects, resulting in fast (or short-term) fading. Slow (or long-term) fading is also a characteristic of indoor channels; it is due to mobile objects in the range of the transmitter or receiver.

Multipath propagation is the simultaneous arrival at the receiver of signals propagated over different paths, with different path lengths. When the path lengths differ by more than a small fraction of the symbol time, multipath propagation produces intersymbol interference—the presence of energy from a previous symbol at the time of detection of the current symbol. When the path lengths differ by a (a multiple of) half a wavelength, signals arriving over different paths may partially or totally cancel at the receiver. This phenomenon is called Raleigh fading. Multipath effects can be mitigated by spread spectrum techniques and diversity in the receivers [34]. Considerable work has been done on diversity techniques, though this is not the focus of this chapter.

Some of the important issues in designing indoor wireless environments are transmission media like infrared or radio frequency; channel coding schemes like TDMA, CDMA, etc., and spreading techniques like direct spread, frequency hopping, etc. From the point of view of higher-level protocols, the channel encoding scheme and physical medium are orthogonal issues.

28.2.1 Transmission Medium

The choice of transmission media [4], namely infrared or radio frequency, is one of the first issues to be resolved when designing a wireless network. Infrared (IR) frequencies require line-of-sight transmission and reception. There is also severe attenuation by walls, people, etc., which can be used to one's advantage since it makes it difficult to intercept. The transmitters and receivers are also less expensive since it detects the power of optical signals and not their frequency or phase. Another advantage is that it is license-free. However, the need for line-of-sight signaling makes it extremely susceptible to mobility and there is also a strong possibility of collisions going undetected. IR systems share a region of the electromagnetic spectrum dominated by natural sunlight and also used by incandescent lights and fluorescent lights, which limits the environments in which it is used. Although IR signals are impaired by multipath propagation, they are not significantly affected by Raleigh fading because of their extremely short wavelength and hence extremely small spatial extent of a fade.

Radio frequency (RF) transmission has been around for a long time and has therefore placed demands on the frequency spectrum, limiting its availability. This also leads to the interest in the Industrial, Scientific, and Medical (ISM) band, which is license-free. The Federal Communications Commission (FCC) has set forth rules and regulations for use of this band for use in the United States. The ITU-T coordinates these assignments world-wide. Limited availability has also lead to the growth of spread spectrum signaling techniques, which require complex transmitters and receivers. An advantage of RF over IR is that it is not easily attenuated by walls, floors, etc. and hence can be used for building-wide connectivity. However, RF is extremely susceptible to interference from office equipment like copiers, etc. and from microwave ovens, which operate in the same band, in addition to atmospheric and galactic noise. RF signals are also impaired by multipath propagation and Raleigh fading. Since the wavelengths used may be comparable to the dimensions of a portable computer, the probability of occurrence of a Raleigh fade is very high.

28.2.2 Transmission Technology

In radio systems, the choice of transmission technology determines the performance to a large extent, in terms of cost, interference rejection, and the capability to isolate adjacent coverage areas. The most successful signaling techniques in dealing with interference in a noisy medium are the spread spectrum techniques, which spread the signal's energy over the full bandwidth of the channel. Two of these methods have gained popularity—frequency hopping spread spectrum (FHSS) and direct sequence spread spectrum (DSSS). Spread spectrum techniques also have built-in security since pseudorandom sequences are used by the transmitter and receiver for detecting the signals, which mitigates multipath effects.

In FHSS systems, the signal is spread over a wide frequency band, i.e., the bandwidth of any one chip or hop interval is much smaller than the full frequency band. Both transmitter and receiver hop on a pseudorandom sequence of frequencies. Frequency hopping achieves interference suppression by avoidance. The time spent on each channel is called a chip. There are two types of frequency hopping, namely, slow frequency hopping and fast frequency hopping, based on whether the rate at which the frequency is changed (chip rate) is less than or greater than the bit rate, respectively. Fast frequency hopping systems are more robust, but are also costly and consume more power compared to slow frequency hopping systems. FHSS systems are also not scalable to very high bandwidth systems due to physical constraints on the attainable chip rate, as is evident by the choice of DSSS for the next-generation systems.

In DSSS systems, a pseudorandom sequence is used to modulate the transmitted signal. This is typically accomplished by XOR-ing the user data and the sequence. At the receiver, the signal is demodulated and the signal is XOR-ed with the same sequence to get back the original signal. The relative rate between the pseudorandom sequence and the user data (the spreading factor) is typically between 10 and 100 for commercial systems. DSSS systems utilize the averaging method for interference suppression, unlike the FHSS systems.

The IEEE 802.11 wireless LAN draft standard provides for three different types of physical layers: the 2.4 GHz ISM band FHSS radio, the 2.4 GHz ISM band DSSS radio, and the IR light. The specified data rates are 1 Mbps and 2 Mbps for each of the above. However, most of the attention has been on the radio physical layers. The FH systems defined in this standard are slow FH systems, in which the data is transmitted over a sequence of 79 frequencies, with the transmitter "dwelling" on each frequency for a fixed length of time. Adjacent and overlapping cells use different hopping patterns, thus making it unlikely that the same frequency will be used at the same time by two adjacent cells. In the DS physical layer, only one predefined spreading signal is used, with a spreading factor of 11 (10.4 dB), which permits some resilience to narrowband noise.

The HomeRF sees the shared wireless access protocol (SWAP) as one of the options of the main connectivity options. SWAP has native support for TCP/IP networking and internet access, and for voice telephony. The physical layer specification for SWAP was largely adapted from the IEEE 802.11 FH and OpenAir standards with modifications to reduce costs while maintaining performance. Some of the key SWAP physical layer specifications include hopping time of 300 microseconds. In the optional low-power mode, typical range is expected to be 10–20 m, but higher powers could result in a range of about 50 m.

Bluetooth systems operate in the 2.4 GHz ISM band, which allows a maximum data rate of 1 Mbps. These are frequency hopping systems with a 79 or 23 frequency pseudorandom sequence, where the hop rate is 1600 hops per second, which makes the dwell time on each frequency is 625 microseconds. The channel is slotted, each time slot corresponding to one frequency. The basic unit of a Bluetooth network is called a piconet (see Section 28.4 for more details) and has a star topology, with a "master" device at the center of the star. The frequency hopping sequence is determined by the clock of the master device, to which all the "slave" devices connected to it are synchronized. This also makes the hopping sequence unique for a piconet.

A comparison of the essential features of the physical layers of the IEEE 802.11, HomeRF, and Bluetooth standards are shown in Table 28.1.

28.3 MEDIA ACCESS CONTROL

The function of media access control (MAC) is to allow multiple devices to use the same shared medium, the wireless channel in this case, with minimum interference and maximum performance benefits. Existing MAC protocols can be divided into two groups: contention-based and contention-free. A contention-based protocol requires a station to compete for control of the transmission channel each time it sends a packet. In this section, we

TABLE 28.1 Physical layer characteristics

	HomeRF	IEEE 802.11	Bluetooth
Peak data rate	1.6 Mbps	1 Mbps & 2 Mbps	1 Mbps
Transmit power	Up to +24 dBm	100 mW or less	1 mW
Receiver sensitivity	−80 dBm		−70 dBm
Hopping time	300 microseconds	<400 milliseconds	625 microseconds
Range in home	> 50 m	> 50 m	< 10 m

give a brief overview of a well-known contention-based protocol, namely, the CSMA family. We then describe the balanced media access methods, which have been proposed for commercial wireless LANs, followed by the hybrid CDMA/ISMA protocol. Among the contention-free protocols, we discuss the GAMA-PS protocol, which is aimed at indoor environments. We then give a brief description of the MACs of IEEE802.11, HomeRF, and Bluetooth.

28.3.1 Contention-Based Protocols

The simplest type of access method is the ALOHA system [1, 13], in which a station is allowed to broadcast its packets freely and packets are resent after waiting a random amount of time (pure ALOHA). This type of ALOHA has a serious drawback: the maximum throughput is only 1/2e. Slotted ALOHA is an improvement over this; it makes all stations synchronized and also requires all packets to be of the same length. In terms of complexity, ALOHA systems are the simplest since the stations can only be in one of two states: transmitting or idle.

Carrier Sense Multiple Access Protocols

CSMA (carrier sense multiple access) protocols, which belong to the ALOHA family, have been used in several packet radio networks as well as wireline media like Ethernet. These protocols attempt to prevent a station from transmitting simultaneously with other stations in its radio range by asking the station to listen before it transmits. These are also termed random access techniques since there is no predictable or scheduled time for a station to transmit. In a CSMA system, stations can be in three possible states: transmitting, idle, or listening. These are simple to implement. When the propagation delay is small compared to the packet transmission time, the throughput of the CSMA system is significantly better than that of ALOHA. However, the CSMA systems are also unstable under heavy loads. Carrier sensing may also not always be possible in a wireless medium due to the hidden terminal problem. A station that wants to transmit a packet cannot accurately ascertain if it will arrive without collisions at the receiver, since it cannot hear the transmissions from other senders that might arrive at the same intended receiver. The performance of CSMA degrades to that of ALOHA in the presence of hidden terminals. 1-persistent, nonpersistent, and p-persistent CSMA [16] are some of the CSMA protocols that have been proposed; they are rightly called CSMA/CD (CSMA with collision detection). CSMA/CD is very difficult to implement in indoor environments as it may not be possible for sources to actually detect a collision in the presence of severe fading. Another disadvantage is that packet delays are unbounded, which makes it unsuitable for voice traffic.

CSMA with collision avoidance (CSMA/CA) was proposed to alleviate the hidden station problem. CSMA/CA with a four-way handshake is used to combat the problem of indoor fading channels. In this version of CSMA, the channel is reserved by an RTS/CTS (request to send message/clear to send message) exchange, and then transmission is ensured by data/ACK exchange. CSMA/CA is based on multiple access collision avoidance (MACA) protocols [11]. The basic idea is for the sender to transmit an RTS that the receiver acknowledges with a CTS. If this exchange is successful, the sender is allowed to transmit data packets. If not, then the source station backs off for a random time period before trying again. The MACA and MACAW [5] protocols perform poorly since the time periods of RTS contentions can be very long. Several other protocols have been proposed that are based on RTS/CTS exchanges; they differ in the methods used to resolve the collisions of RTSs. FAMA [6] protocols that use carrier sensing perform well in networks with hidden terminals, but carrier sensing is not available in several spread spectrum radios.

Balanced Media Access Methods

Since the wireless medium is a critical shared resource, it is important that the MAC protocol provide fairness and robustness to the wireless network. This is called the fairness problem. There has been some recent work on balanced MACs [26], which are easy to implement in commercial wireless LANs. These are basically p-persistent CSMA-based algorithms in which a fair wireless access for each user is achieved using a precalculated link access probability, p_{ij}, that represents the link access probability from station i to station j. In classical p-persistent protocols, the probability p is constant, and a station sends packets with this probability after the back-off period, or back off again with probability $1 - p$, using the same back-off window size. The balanced MAC methods show how to vary these probabilities dynamically by using a distributed approach. These probabilities are calculated at the source station in two ways: connection-based and time-based. Each active user broadcasts information either on the number of logical connections or the average contention time to the stations within range. This exchange provides a partial understanding of the topology of the network of stations. Based on the mechanism of information exchange (during the link access or periodic), the balanced MAC can be of two types: connection-based and time-based.

In the connection-based balanced MAC, stations calculate link access probabilities for their logical links based on the information of the number of connections of themselves and neighbor stations. A logical link between two stations within wireless range and "visible" to each other represents the physical link between them. An example topology is given in Figure 28.1. Let A_i be the source station and B_j be the group of stations visible to it. Let C_k be the group of stations hidden from A_i. Each C_k is connected to at least one B_j. The rest of the stations are denoted by D_1. Source station A_i attempts to send an RTS packet to station B_j after the back-off period with probability p_{ij}, or backs off again with probability $1 - p_{ij}$, using the same back-off window size. Each station broadcasts information on the number of connections to all stations within its reach. The computation of link access probabilities for station A_i is described below.

- V_i: The set of stations that are visible to the source station A_i. The members of this set correspond to the stations labeled B_j. This is called the visible set.
- S_j: The number of logical connections of station B_j.
- S: The set of all S_j's for each B_j. This is called the connection set.
- S_A: The number of connections of the source station A_i. This is called the connection value, which has the following property: $S_A \leq \Sigma_{j \in V_i} S_j$.
- $S_A^{\max}$: The maximum value of the members in the connection set, known as the maximum connection value and defined as $S_A^{\max} = \max_{j \in V_i} \{S_j\}$.

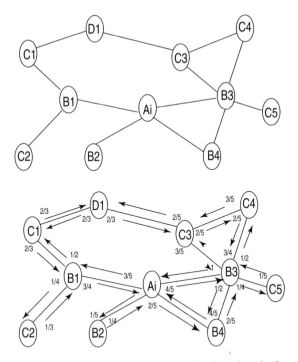

Figure 28.1 Balanced MAC (connection-based method).

The link access probabilities are calculated as follows:

- Case 1: If $S_A \geq \Sigma_{j \in V_i} S_j$, then $p_{ij} = 1 \ \forall \ j \in V_i$. This corresponds to the case where the source station is directly connected to all stations and there is no hidden terminal.
- Case 2: If $S_A < \Sigma_{j \in V_i} S_j$ and $S_j = S_A^{\max}$, then $p_{ij} = \min\{1, (S_A/S_A^{\max})\}$.
- Case 3: If $S_A < \Sigma_{j \in V_i} S_j$ and $S_j \neq S_A^{\max}$, then $p_{ij} = (S_j/ S_A^{\max})$.

The last two cases imply that either connection A_i has hidden terminals or there is at least one connection between at least one pair of B_j stations. Clearly, this method gives higher priority to the station with the maximum connection value, since this station has higher data traffic than other stations in a fully loaded network. The priorities of the other links are in proportion to their maximum connection value. Figure 28.1 shows the link access probabilities calculated according to the above method.

In the time-based balanced MAC, the link access probabilities are calculated according to the average contention period, which is defined as the time interval between the arrival of the packet to the MAC layer and its actual transmission. This period covers collisions, back-off periods, and listening periods, in which another station captures the channel. (A listening period is the time interval for which the intended sender is a nonparticipant station until the channel is idle again.)

In this method, each station periodically broadcasts a packet to all its logical links. This packet contains information on the average contention period of that specific link and a traffic link descriptor, L_{ij}. Stations update link access probabilities every time they receive this packet. The link traffic descriptor is defined as:

$$L_{ij} = \begin{cases} 1, & \text{if station } i \text{ had traffic for station } j \\ 0, & \text{otherwise} \end{cases}$$

The link access probability from station i to station j is defined as

$$p_{ij} = \frac{T_{ij}^{\gamma}}{\dfrac{1}{\Sigma_{k \in V_i\,(k \neq i)}(L_{ki} + L_{ik})} \cdot \Sigma_{k \in V_i\,(k \neq i)}(T_{ki}^{\gamma} L_{ki} + T_{ik}^{\gamma} L_{ik})}$$

where T_{ij} is an average contention period from station i to station j and γ is a weight factor of the average contention period. Thus, the time-based method calculates the link access probability of a link by dividing its average contention period by the mean value of the contention periods of all its neighbor links. If the link is blocked, the average contention period of that specific link increases and, eventually, the contention period of all its neighbor links decreases. In this way, higher priority is given to a link that is blocked and less priority to a link that is dominant over other links. The weight factor, γ, controls the rate of increase of the probability according to the contention period. In this algorithm, the link traffic descriptor carries the information on the traffic demand in the previous period and, hence, a link with no traffic is not taken into consideration.

It should be noted that the connection-based method does not have any overheads as does the periodic broadcast of the time-based method. Moreover, in the latter method, the weight factor needs to be estimated for each scenario. However, the performance of the time-based method is found to be better than the connection-based method when the network load differs from link to link, as seen from the simulation results provided in [25]. The results also show that the connection-based method always achieves a very reasonable fair access.

Hybrid CDMA/ISMA Protocol

It is well known that code division multiple access (CDMA) improves the survival chance of packets in the wireless channel. CDMA is a DSSS method that uses noise-like carrier waves, which makes the effective noise the sum of all other user signals. Multiple users can use each CDMA carrier frequency, as they are allocated different codes by which their signals are modulated. However, in an indoor environment, implementing full CDMA would mean that the number of codes used would equal the number of terminals in the network, which can be quite large. It would also become expensive, since a separate receiver would be needed for each code.

Another MAC protocol that has gained widespread acceptance is the inhibit sense multiple access (ISMA) method. In this method, the current state of the medium is signaled via a busy tone. The base station signals on the downlink (to the terminals), and the terminals do not transmit until the busy tone stops. The base stations signals collisions and successful transmissions via the busy tone and acknowledgements, respectively. ISMA is known to limit contention in the channel, and p-persistent ISMA is the form of ISMA in which a station transmits with probability p at the end of a busy period.

It is natural to expect that the performance of a hybrid CDMA/ISMA network will be quite good—at least better than the performance of the protocols separately. The hybrid protocol proposed in [32] for indoor wireless communications combines CDMA with p-persistent ISMA. This protocol has two key features: it solves the hidden terminal problem by routing all traffic via a central base station; it also allows many users with a relatively short transmission code onto the same network by having the users share the same code function using the ISMA protocol. Thus, for an indoor wireless network, N_t users will be divided into n groups with different codes, where each group will have N_t/n users with the same code.

The network is modeled as a set of receivers star-connected by wire to a central base station. Around each receiver we have a cluster of terminals sharing the same transmission code (see Figure 28.2). The model assumes perfect power control, and does not take the near–far effect into account. It also assumes that the terminal being serviced can determine within the same time slot whether the transmission was errorless or not by listening to the broadcast packet. When a data packet needs to be transmitted by the user, the terminal waits for the beginning of the next time slot and transmits the data to its receiver, which forwards it to the base station. The base station, in turn, broadcasts the packet to all terminals and the destination terminal receives it. In order to control the flow of traffic, the base station broadcasts the busy tone to all the terminals. At the beginning of each time slot, the busy tone is interrupted long enough to allow all terminals to start their transmissions. If more than one terminal forwards a packet to the base station, the base station picks a packet to service at random and broadcasts it to all terminals. All other packets are ignored and must be retransmitted.

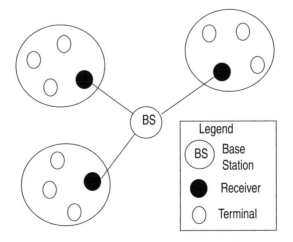

Figure 28.2   CDMA/ISMA network architecture.

Thus, terminals in the network have two states: idle or blocked. Initially, all terminals are idle. Whenever a packet arrives at a terminal, it goes into the blocked state and services the packet according to the algorithm described in Figure 28.3. Each blocked terminal waits for the start of the next time slot before it attempts transmission. It then transmits the packet with probability p.

The performance of this method has also been analyzed using a Markov model [31].

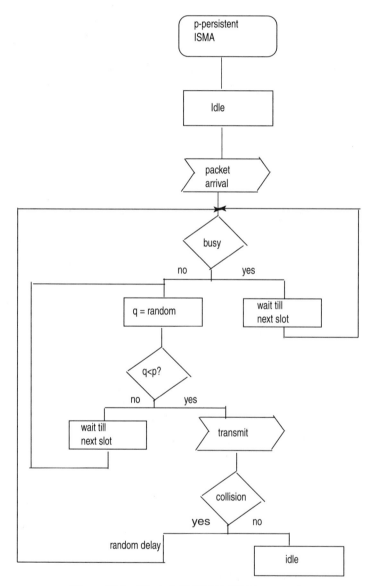

Figure 28.3 The hybrid CDMA/ISMA protocol.

28.3.2 Contention-Free Protocols

Many contention-free protocols have also been proposed, including fixed assignment (in time or frequency), polling, token passing, or dynamic reservations. With completely deterministic access method like the time division multiple access (TDMA), a central entity would be required for assigning the channel to the various stations. Such a method is also not feasible for indoor environments, which have strong fading characteristics. However, it makes the management and control of the network easier and more effective. Portable units using this scheme would be simpler and would use significantly less power. Recent examples of dynamic reservation protocols that build a transmission schedule include the collision avoidance and resolution multiple access (CARMA-NTG) [7] and the group allocation multiple access (GAMA) [22] protocols.

Group Allocation Multiple Access with Packet Sensing (GAMA-PS)

The concept of GAMA protocols was first introduced in [22] to provide performance guarantees in asynchronous MAC protocols. GAMA/CD provides the advantages of both TDMA and CSMA/CD by maintaining a dynamically sized cycle that varies in length depending on the network load; each cycle is composed of a contention period and a group transmission period. During the contention period, a station with one or more packets to send competes for membership in the transmission group. Once a member of the transmission group, a station is able to send data without collision during each cycle; as long as a station has data to send, it maintains its position in the group. This can be viewed as either allowing stations to "share the floor" in an organized manner, or as establishing frames that are not synchronized on a slot basis and vary their length dynamically based on demand.

Wireless LANs using spread spectrum radios cannot provide accurate carrier sensing and time slotting. The GAMA-PS (packet sensing), proposed in [23] is aimed at such environments and provides dynamic reservations of the channel. It can operate in fully connected wireless LANs without base stations and in wireless LANs with hidden terminals by means of base stations. With packet sensing, stations are unable to detect the carrier and must operate on the basis of complete packets they receive; asynchronous access to the channel means that no time slotting is required for the protocol to operate. The complexity of this protocol is comparable to that of CSMA and enables efficient wireless LANs with inexpensive radios.

The GAMA-PS divides the transmission channel into a sequence of cycles; each cycle begins with a contention period and ends with a "group transmission" period. The group transmission period is divided into a set of zero or more individual transmission periods, which are similar to time slots, though the GAMA-PS needs no synchronization. It uses a form of dynamic reservation to improve efficiency and to ensure that there are no collisions involving data packets. To make a "reservation," a station transmits an RTS using the packet sensing strategy, i.e., a station backs off only if it senses an entire packet, and not just the carrier. If the RTS is received, the destination node replies with a CTS; this exchange occurs during a contention period. Once a station has successfully completed an RTS/CTS exchange, it is allocated its own transmission period and the station maintains ownership of this period as long as it has data to transmit (not necessarily to the same station). A station relinquishes its transmission period by announcing its departure from the group.

GAMA-PS maintains a "transmission group," which consists of all the stations that have been allocated transmission periods. Each member of this group listens to the channel and are thus aware of every RTS/CTS exchange and idle periods. The station also knows how many stations are present in the group, and its own position in it. The size of the group transmission period varies based on the number of stations in the transmission group. The method used for building the schedule is described below.

Members of the transmission group take turns transmitting data. Packet sensing is achieved by each station transmitting a small packet (of length ϕ), called the "begin transmission period" (BTP) packet before transmitting data. This packet contains the state of the transmission group (the transmitting station's position within the group and the number of group members, as a minimum). Thus, when a new station enters the network, the maximum length of time, L, that it must wait before it receives a BTP or data packet equals $\delta + 2\tau + \phi$, where τ is the maximum propagation delay, and $\delta \gg \phi$ is the length of a data packet. Figure 28.4 shows a sample transmission group. Since each member station is required to listen to the channel for the duration of its membership, it is aware of the start and end of each transmission period, which are synchronized by the reception of each entire packet within τ seconds or less of one another. In case the station is not ready to send a data packet during its transmission period, it sends a small control packet equivalent to the BTP, which refreshes the state of the network and allows a very short turn for the station.

When a station receives a message to transmit, it listens to the channel for L seconds, and if no packet is received, it transmit an RTS of length γ, where $\gamma > 2\tau$. A group member recognizes that the station assigned to a transmission period has failed if it does not receive any BTP within $2\tau + \phi$ seconds, which is the maximum interval between the reception of a data packet and the recognition of the following BTP. Therefore, the channel will be empty for L seconds only if the transmission group is empty or if there is an idle transmission period. To ensure that an RTS/CTS exchange during this period is not successful, each station transmits a jamming packet of size $2\tau + \phi + \gamma$.

An attractive feature of this protocol is that its collision intervals are bounded. Stations in the group keep track of whether they are the last or not and if so, send another control packet, called the transmit request (TR) packet. Any station waiting to send an RTS sends it immediately on receipt of the TR packet. This packet also shortens the maximum length of the contention period since it forces any station contending for group membership to do so at the start of the contention period. After a station has transmitted an RTS, it waits up to $2\tau + \gamma$ seconds for a CTS. If a CTS is not received within this time, then the station

Channel

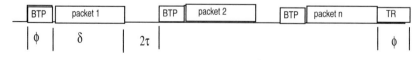

Figure 28.4 GAMA-PS: a sample transmission group.

backs off; otherwise, it is admitted into the transmission group and a new transmission period is added to the end of the cycle. Figure 28.5 shows a successful RTS/CTS exchange.

The impact of hidden terminals in GAMA-PS is that stations may not hear the RTS or a CTS from hidden senders, and collisions of data packets could occur. A modified GAMA-PS, which uses base stations, has been suggested to solve the hidden terminal problem. In this version, the base station is responsible for synchronizing all its group members, and instead of the destination node sending a CTS, the base station sends it. The base station also sends out the BTP packet before each transmission period. This makes GAMA-PS with base station a form of dynamic polling. The approximate throughput and average delay have been analyzed using Markov models, and the reader is referred to [23] for the same.

The IEEE 802.11 WLAN MAC. The important characteristics of the 802.11 MAC protocol, as per the draft standard [10], are its ability to support:

- Access-point-oriented and ad hoc networking topologies
- Both asynchronous and time-critical traffic
- Power management

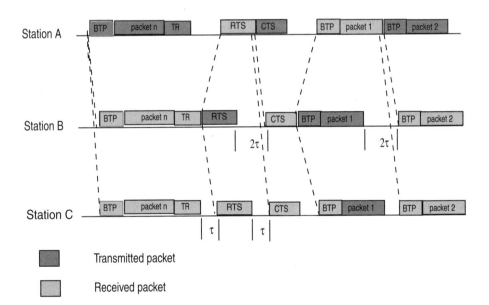

A message to be transmitted arrives at station B during the last transmission period. After receiving the TR packet sent by station A, station B transmits an RTS, which arrives at its destination (station A) in τ seconds. After receiving the RTS, station A responds with a CTS, which arrives at station B τ seconds later. After receiving the CTS, station B is allocated a new transmission period, which is added to the end of the group transmission period.

Figure 28.5   GAMA-PS: a successful RTS/CTS exchange between stations A and B.

The primary access method is drawn from the CSMA/CA family. The random backoff time is uniformly distributed, where the maximum extent of the range is called the contention window (CW). This parameter is doubled each time a frame transmission is unsuccessful, as determined by the absence of an ACK frame. This exponential backoff mechanism helps reduce collisions in response to increasing numbers of contending stations. Priorities for transmission are achieved using the interframe space (IFS), which can take various values. The highest priority frames are transmitted using the short IFS (SIFS), which makes sure that no other station intervenes. The next longest IFS is the point coordination IFS (PIFS), which ensures that time-critical frames are transmitted before asynchronous frames, which use the longest IFS, the distributed coordination function IFS (DIFS).

In order to solve the hidden terminal problem, the protocol includes, as an option, the use of two control frames: an RTS frame that a potential transmitter issues to a receiver, and a CTS frame that a receiver issues in response to an RTS frame. Because of the signaling overhead involved, this feature is not used for short packets, for which the collision likelihood and cost are small anyway.

The HomeRF MAC. The SWAP MAC has been optimized for the home environment and is designed to carry both voice and data traffic and interoperate with the PSTN using a subset of the Digital Enhanced Cordless Telecommunications (DECT) standard, which is a digital cordless standard used in residential applications. The MAC is designed for use with a frequency-hopping radio and includes a TDMA service to support the delivery of isochronous data (e.g., interactive voice), and a CSMA/CA service derived from WLAN standards.

The MAC protocol uses a superframe, which incorporates two contention-free periods (CFPs) and a contention period. The duration of the superframe is fixed and is the same as the dwell or hop period. During each CFP, the mechanism used is TDMA, whereas during the contention period it is CSMA/CA. Each CFP is divided into a number of pairs of fixed length slots, two per voice connection. Each pair is meant for downlink and uplink transmissions. The second CFP at the end of the superframe is used for initial transmission of voice, whereas the first one at the start of the superframe is used for the optional retransmission of any lost data. The two CFPs are separated by a frequency hop, giving frequency and time diversity, which is important for noisy indoor environments.

For data traffic, CSMA/CA is used during the contention period of the superframe. This provides efficient data bandwidth, even with concurrent active voice calls.

The Bluetooth MAC. Bluetooth is a master-driven, time division duplex (TDD) system, where a central master node (or station) is directly connected to several slave nodes, forming a piconet (see next section for more details). The stations in a single piconet share the same frequency hopping channel, and the master controls the traffic to all its slaves. Master transmissions always start at even slots and slave transmissions always start at odd slots. A slave can transmit a packet only after the master has polled it. However, at connection set-up time, the maximum packet size of each connection is negotiated between the master and the slave, and is used by the master while scheduling the slaves. The protocol supports both synchronous connection-oriented (SCO) channels for voice, which are simply periodic slots, and asynchronous connectionless (ACL) channels for data. Bluetooth also defines Quality of Service parameters similar to the leaky bucket scheme. Thus, scheduling with QoS is an interesting problem in Bluetooth [27]. The Bluetooth MAC also provides interesting power-saving features, which we do not describe here for want of space; the reader is referred to [33] for a detailed description of the same.

28.4 NETWORK TOPOLOGY

An important issue in planning an indoor wireless network from the power and cost perspectives is the selection of a network topology. Although cellular topology is most commonly used in wide area networks, other alternatives like ad hoc topologies have also been proposed. From the power consumption point of view, cellular topologies are at an advantage—the base stations serve as access points for mobile devices to the wired network infrastructure. In the access point based approach, complex functionality can be shifted to the access points, which are not power limited. There has been a lot of research on clustering algorithms and network formation [8, 29], for ad hoc networks in particular. As described below, the network topologies for 802.11 WLAN and the HomeRF are fairly straightforward but the Bluetooth topology poses interesting challenges.

28.4.1 The IEEE 802.11 WLAN Topology

With TDMA-based MAC protocols, it is necessary to have a central entity that assigns slots to the various stations. A cell can be defined as the coverage area associated with a single base station. As base stations are normally fixed, the coverage of the area is fully determined and is predictable. The other type of topology that has been proposed is the peer-to-peer ad hoc topology, which does not assume any fixed stations and in which the transmission range is determined by the network diameter. With such networks, it is necessary to install a dedicated access point for the stations to communicate with the wired network. In peer-to-peer networks functions like security, scheduling, prioritizing traffic, etc. have to be distributed between the various remote stations, unlike the TDMA-based topology, in which the base station takes care of all this. 802.11 supports both ad-hoc and base-station-based topologies.

28.4.2 The HomeRF Network Topology

The SWAP architecture combines the features of a managed network for providing isochronous services and ad hoc peer-to-peer networks for traditional data networking. Devices in a SWAP network can be of the following types:

- A connection point (CP), which acts as the gateway between the personal computer, PSTN, and SWAP-compatible devices
- Voice devices (also called I-nodes)
- Asynchronous data devices (also called A-nodes)

The control point is usually connected to the main home PC and may have a connection to the PSTN. This entity manages the network and provides priority access. However, it is peer-to-peer between the data devices. It is designed to support the variety of applications that occur in a residential setting, rather than support hundreds of users doing similar things.

28.4.3   The Bluetooth Network Topology

The basic unit of a Bluetooth network is called a piconet, which has a star topology. A master node is the center of the star and is connected to a number of slave devices. There is a bound on the number of slaves that a master can be connected to (considering only active nodes [33], this limit is seven). A set of connected piconets is called a scatternet. Neighboring piconets in a scatternet have common nodes, called bridges, which are used for routing data across piconets. These bridge nodes belong to more than one piconet on a time division basis. Thus, a slave can be a bridge node by being a slave of two masters (the rate at which it switches between the two piconets is negotiated [33]); this is called a slave–slave bridge. A master becomes a bridge when it is master of one piconet and slave in the other; this is called a master–slave bridge. Clearly, slave–slave bridges are expected to perform better, since a master–slave bridge would disable (deactivate) an entire piconet during the time it is an active slave in the other piconet. Thus, we have a set of connected stars of bounded size, the connection between stars being made through noncenter nodes in an ideal topology. The Bluetooth standard does not provide scatternet formation algorithms, although it specifies device discovery procedures used for devices to discover the presence and identity of neighboring devices, in detail. Another desirable feature is that there should be a bound on the number of piconets to which a slave–slave bridge can belong. Since Bluetooth is a completely ad hoc network, with no facility for a centralized infrastructure that has knowledge of the entire topology, the network formation algorithms need to be completely distributed, and should run on top of the device discovery procedures.

   The feasibility problem of scatternet formation (requiring bridges to be slave–slave) when not all stations are within radio range of each other, has been proved to be NP-complete [3]. The set of Bluetooth nodes is modeled as a graph in which each station is represented by a vertex, with an edge between two vertices if the corresponding stations are within radio range of each other. A greedy centralized algorithm in which a hypothetical central entity knows the complete topology has been proposed, as have approximation bounds derived for a special class of graphs, namely the clique-coverable graphs. In order to be feasible for implementation in real scatternets, the algorithm needs to be distributed. Distributed algorithms have also been proposed in [3] that assume 2-hop neighborhood information. This is achievable in Bluetooth, since the identities of the neighboring nodes are known at the end of the device discovery procedure. The nodes are made to exchange this neighborhood information with each of their neighbors so that they have 2-hop information and a partial view of the underlying topology.

   Clearly, the problem is not hard when the underlying topology is a complete graph, i.e., all nodes are within radio range of each other. However, this problem is also interesting when the Bluetooth communication model is to be used and limited information has to be exchanged during device discovery. In [28], randomized and deterministic algorithms have been proposed to solve this problem using the Bluetooth device discovery communication model. In [32], fast connection establishment procedures have been investigated. A typical scatternet is shown in Figure 28.6. We briefly describe the $O(N)$ deterministic algorithm proposed in [28] below.

The system model and problem statement are as follows. The set of Bluetooth devices is modeled as an undirected graph, and each node has a unique id, known to itself, but not to other nodes. The total number of nodes, N, and the maximum number of slaves that can be attached to a master, S, are known to all nodes. The network is asynchronous and there is no notion of global time, with each node keeping its own local clock. It is assumed that there is no centralized entity that has complete knowledge of the network.

All nodes use a common fixed set of frequencies to communicate. A node trying to discover another node repeatedly broadcasts a message (the inquiry message) on a sequence of frequencies. This sequence is determined by its local clock. The transmitting node listens in between broadcasts for replies. A listening node also listens in on a sequence of frequencies, and a message reaches it only when the frequencies of the transmitting and listening nodes match. When the listening node successfully receives a message, it sends a reply (the inquiry response message), which is also broadcast. The nodes use a random back-off mechanism while replying, so that collisions can be assumed to be absent. The inquiry message does not contain the id of the node transmitting it, and so the replying

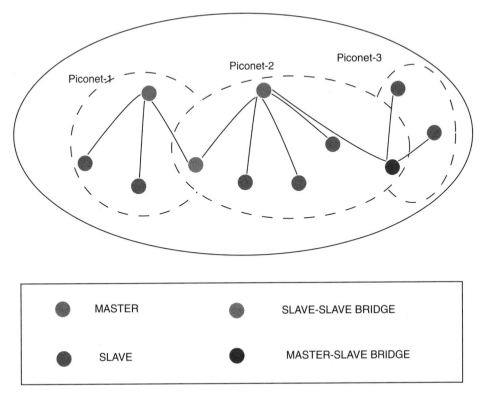

Figure 28.6 A Bluetooth scatternet.

node does not know to whom it is replying. This makes this model different from other models found in literature. Further, a node can be in one of the following states [33]:

- INQUIRY: A device in this state broadcasts inquiry packets.
- INQUIRY_SCAN: A device in this state listens for inquiry packets and broadcasts an inquiry response packet in return. This response contains the sender's unique id and clock, which can be used to determine its broadcast frequency at any future instant. A limited amount of information can be assumed to be piggybacked on this packet.
- PAGE: In this state, a device tries to connect to a node whose id and clock are known to it by sending page packets that contain the destination node id. If the connection is successful, then this node automatically becomes a master.
- PAGE_SCAN: In this state, a device listens for a page packet and acknowledges it on receipt, completing the connection establishment.
- CONNECTED: In this state, a device is part of a piconet after a successful handshake as described above.

A node is in one of these states at any point of time, and since they are not synchronized, the set of nodes in the INQUIRY/INQUIRY_SCAN or PAGE/PAGE_SCAN states is random. Clearly, two nodes should be in complementary states in order to discover each other. The algorithm described below makes the assumption that connection establishment with a node that has been discovered using the inquiry procedures is almost instantaneous. Another assumption is that once any two nodes are connected to each other, any amount of information can be exchanged between them with very little overhead. It also assumes that up to $\log S$ bits of information can be piggybacked on the inquiry response packet, and each device is equally likely to become a master or a slave.

The algorithm aims to organize the nodes into a minimum set of star-shaped clusters of maximum size $S + 1$ with a clusterhead (master) at the center of the star. Each node should be identified as a master or a slave (autonomously). The exchange of master/slave roles is expensive in the Bluetooth context and needs to be avoided. The transfer of nodes from one piconet to another after connection establishment is also undesirable. The algorithm does not attempt to find bridge nodes and instead elects a "supermaster" node that has complete information on the formed piconets. Since all nodes are in radio range, this node can use a suitable algorithm to find the bridge nodes. The algorithm also ensures that there are no orphan nodes.

The basic idea of the algorithm is that nodes discovering each other form a tree of responses, the root of each tree being a master (see Figure 28.7). This parallelizes the formation of each piconet. Each node i maintains a "phase" variable, which is the number of inquiry responses received by it and all the nodes in its subtree. Once a node receives an inquiry response from another node, it increments its phase by the phase of the replying node. A node which has sent an inquiry response goes out of the competition for becoming a master. A node whose phase is $S + 1$ declares itself master and all the nodes that replied to it (directly or indirectly) and contributed to its phase become its slaves. However, the master thus elected has id and clock information only for those nodes that directly

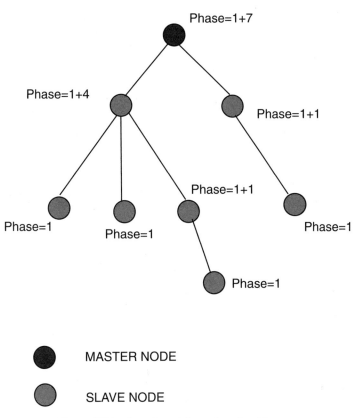

Phase=1+7

Phase=1+4

Phase=1+1

Phase=1+1

Phase=1

Phase=1

Phase=1

Phase=1

Phase=1

MASTER NODE

SLAVE NODE

Figure 28.7 A scatternet formation algorithm.

replied to it. Hence, the master first establishes connections with the nodes that replied directly to it. Once such a connection is established, the slave sends information on the replies it has received to its master. This type of chaining of message exchanges eventually results in the master collecting information about all the nodes in its subtree. At the end of this procedure, the master is directly connected to all its slaves, completing the piconet formation (see Figure 28.7). It should be noted that there is a possibility of the phases of two nodes discovering each other, adding up to more than $S + 1$. In such a situation, the node that has received the response instructs either some of its slaves or the nodes that have replied to the responding node to go back to the INQUIRY state.

The second half of the algorithm involves the election of a supermaster from among the masters. The above procedure can be repeated such that only the masters participate in the second half, and the first node that reaches a phase of $\lceil N/S + 1 \rceil$ becomes the supermaster and conveys this message to all the masters. In order to ensure that no orphan nodes are present, timeout values can be used as described in [28].

Many more interesting problems arise from the scatternet formation. The protocols referred to above could be enhanced to include the cases in which a node enters or leaves the network, such that the reorganization incurred is minimal. The same problem could also be tackled taking into account a mobility model for the nodes. Another variation could be to take the services assigned by each node into account and form a scatternet such that interpiconet communication is minimized. This problem is related to the facility location problem [15] and is expected to be very hard.

28.5 CHARACTERIZATION OF THE ENVIRONMENT

The challenges in the indoor wireless environment may need to be attacked differently based on various application types or usage profiles. In [20], the authors have discussed possible classifications of the indoor environment while proposing resource reservation methods. The classification is oriented more towards the WLAN architecture and makes the assumption that there exists a wired backbone component and that base stations are connected to the wired network and provide networking to portable devices via a single-hop wireless link. However, we feel similar characterizations are justified for an ad hoc network, too. In the following discussion, we use the term "cell" to mean the radio-range neighborhood of a device, e.g., a piconet in the case of Bluetooth.

The cells can be classified based on the predictive behavior of their occupants: office, corridor, or lounge. Cells can be assumed to be small, about the size of room. A typical office is a single cell, a corridor is a row of cells, and larger meeting rooms are clusters of cells. Other specific types of indoor environments like factories have also been discussed [18].

28.5.1 The Office and Corridor Case

An office is a cell with a small set of regular occupants and, hence, will have predictable bandwidth requirements that do not change drastically over time. In a corridor, users typically move in and out of several possible locations and mobility is high.

28.5.2 The Lounge Case

A lounge is a cell which has many nonregular users. It does not distinguish a single user's behavior, but aggregates the behavior of all users in its cell. Based on aggregate behavior, a lounge could be classified into three categories:

1. Cafeteria-type environment with slow time-varying profile
2. Meeting room-type environment characterized by bursts of activity and mobility
3. Default with random time-varying profile

28.5.3 The Factory Case

The factory environment could be different from the conventional environments in terms of traffic characterization, and is expected to have relatively short alarm/sensor type messages. It also becomes easy to deploy a central controller in a factory. Other differences include maximum operation distance and maximum allowable message delay, since factory operations might require real-time messages.

28.5.4 The Trading Floor Case

Typical trading floors would need an enormous number of cells packed close to each other and the users in each cell can be assumed to be connected to a backbone wired network. This makes the interference problem more challenging since other-cell interference has a stronger possibility of occurring in this case.

28.6 CHALLENGES FOR THE FUTURE: NOMADIC COMPUTING

Another point that needs to be kept in mind while designing protocols for indoor environments is that most of the applications and devices that are used will also be used to connect to wide area or wired networks. Nomadic computing is a newly emerging technology that has led to predictions of a paradigm shift in the way computing is performed. Recent research [12] points to the need for transparency with respect to the location, communication device, communication bandwidth, computing platform, and mobility. Some of the key system parameters that must be addressed while designing nomadic computing systems include bandwidth, latency, reliability, error rate, storage, processing power, interference, interoperability, user interface, cost, etc. What makes these parameters of special interest is that their values may change dramatically as a user moves from location to location. Nomadicity also exacerbates the problems of disconnectedness and unpredictable movement, which demand innovative solutions. Some work [12] has been done in defining system architectures and network protocols for such environments, including a nomadicity reference model. Kleinrock [12] also points to need for strong cooperation across disciplines like database systems, file systems, and wireless communications, to name a few.

28.7 SUMMARY

In this chapter, we discussed issues and problems specific to the indoor wireless environment, with special reference to three popular technologies: IEEE 802.11 WLAN, HomeRF, and Bluetooth. We first pointed to design challenges in the physical layer, followed by a more detailed description of some MAC layer protocols proposed specially for such environments. We also described network topology issues, especially the scatternet formation problem in Bluetooth. We then gave a brief overview of possible characterizations of the indoor environment and the new paradigm of nomadic computing.

ACKNOWLEDGMENTS

The author would like to thank Thyagarajan Nandagopal (UIUC), Ivan Stojmenovic (University of Ottawa), and Madhavi Kumari (CMU) for reviewing the chapter and suggesting useful changes.

REFERENCES

1. N. Abramson, The ALOHA system—Another alternative for computer communications, *Proceedings Fall Joint Computer Conference.*

2. M. Alasti and N. Farvardin, D-PRMA: A dynamic packet reservation multiple access protocol for Wireless Communications, *MWSiM,* ACM, 1999.

3. K. Balaji, S. Kapoor, A. A. Nanavati, and L. Ramachandran, Scatternet formation algorithms in the Bluetooth network, Submitted for publication.

4. D. F. Bantz and F. J. Bauchot, Wireless LAN Design Alternatives, *IEEE Network,* 43–53, Mar./Apr., 1994.

5. V. Bhargavan, A. Demers, S. Shenker, and L. Zhang, MACAW: A media access protocol for wireless LANs, *Proceedings ACM SIGCOMM,* 1994.

6. C. L. Fullmer and J. J. Garcia-Luna-Aceves, Solutions to hidden terminal problems in wireless networks, *Proceedings ACM SIGCOMM,* 1997.

7. R. Garces and J. J. Garcia-Luna-Aceves, Collision avoidance and resolution multiple access with transmission groups, *Proceedings IEEE INFOCOM,* 1997.

8. M. Gerla and J. T. C. Tsai, Multicluster, mobile, multimedia radio network, *ACM Baltzer Journal of Wireless Networks, 1,* 3, 255–265, 1995.

9. HomeRF, Technical summary of the SWAP specification, Documentation available at http://www.homerf.org/tech/, Feb. 1999.

10. IEEE802. 11 Standard, Wireless LAN Medium Access Control (MAC) and Physical Layer (PHY) Specifications, 1997.

11. P. Karn, MACA—A new channel access method for packet radio, *ARRL/CRRL Amateur Radio 9th Computer Networking Conference,* 1990.

12. L. Kleinrock, Nomadicity: Anytime, anywhere in a disconnected world, in *Mobile Networks and Applications,* vol. 1, pp. 351–357, Baltzer 1996.

13. L. Kleinrock and F. A. Tobagi, Packet switching in radio channels: Part I—Carrier sense multiple access and their throughput delay characteristics, *IEEE Trans. Commun., 23, 12,* 1975.

14. P. Y. Kong, B. Bensaou and K. C. Chua, Multi-code DSSS MAC protocol for integrated services wireless home networks, *IEEE Globecom,* 1999.

15. M. R. Korupolu, C. G. Plaxton and R. Rajaraman, Analysis of a local search heuristic for facility location problems, *Proceedings 9th Annual ACM-SIAM Symposium on Discrete Algorithms,* pp. 1–10, 1998.

16. J. F. Kurose, M. Schwartz, and Y. Yemini, Multiple-access protocols and time-constrained communication, *ACM Computing Survey, 16,* 1, 43–70, 1984.

17. R. O. LaMaire, A. Krishna, P. Bhagwat and J. Panian, Wireless LANs and mobile networking: Standards and future directions, *IEEE Communications Magazine,* 86–94, Aug., 1996.

18. E. Lo and R. H. S. Hardy, Indoor wireless LAN access methods for factories, IEEE, 1990.

19. S. Lu, R. Srikant, and V. Bhargavan, Adaptive resource reservation for indoor wireless LANs, IEEE, 1996.

20. Mobile Ad Hoc Networks (MANET). http://www.ietf.org/html.charters/manet-chater.html

21. M. P. Moroney and C. J. Burkley, Multiple access protocols for Indoor wireless communications, ICWC, 1992.

22. A. Muir and J. J. Garcia-Luna-Aceves, Supporting real-time multimedia traffic in a wireless LAN, *Proceedings SPIE MMCN,* 1997.

23. A. Muir and J. J. Garcia-Luna-Aceves, An efficient packet sensing MAC protocol for wireless networks, *Mobile Networks and Applications,* Vol. 3, pp. 221–224, Baltzer, 1998.

24. K. J. Negus, A. P. Stephens, and J. Lansford, HomeRF: Wireless networking for the connected home, *IEEE Personal Communications,* Feb., 2000.

25. T. Ozugur, M. Nagshineh, P. Kermani, C. M. Olsen, B. Rezvani, and J. A. Copeland, Balanced media access methods for wireless networks, *Proceedings ACM MobiCom,* 1998.

26. C. E. Perkins, Mobile networking in the Internet, *Mobile Networks and Applications,* Vol. 3, pp. 319–334, Baltzer, 1998.

27. L. Ramachandran and A. Sarkar, Optimal quality of service for polling-based scheduling, IBM IRL Research Report #00A005, March 2000.

28. L. Ramachandran, M. Kapoor, A. Sarkar, and A. Aggarwal, Clustering algorithms for wireless ad hoc networks, *4th International Workshop on Discrete Algorithms and Methods for Mobile Computing, Dial M for Mobility,* held in conjunction with ACM MobiCom, 2000.

29. C. V. Ramamoorthy, J. Srivatsava and W. T. Tsai, Clustering techniques for large distributed systems, *Proceedings IEEE INFOCOM,* 1986.

30. T. S. Rappaport, Indoor Radio communications for factories of the future, *IEEE Communications Magazine, 27,* 5, 15–24, May, 1989.

31. H. Roosmalen, J. Nijhof, and R. Prasad, Performance analysis of a hybrid CDMA/ISMA protocol for indoor wireless computer communications, *4th International Symposium On Personal, Indoor and Mobile Radio Communications (PIMRC 1993),* IEEE, 1993.

32. T. Salonidis, P. Bhagwat, and L. Tassiulas, Proximity awareness and fast connection setup in Bluetooth, *MobiHOC,* 2000.

33. The Bluetooth SIG, documentation available at http://www.bluetooth.com, Feb. 1999.

34. A. Viterbi, wireless digital communication: A view based on three lessons learned, *IEEE Comunications Magazine,* 33–36, Sept., 1991.

Index